South Carolina
Bird Life

FRONTISPIECE: DUCKS IN CYPRESS SWAMP

Oil Painting by Francis Lee Jaques

Extreme left flying duck: Black Duck. Other flying ducks, top to bottom: Mallard (male), Mallard (female), Baldpate (female), and Baldpate (male). Swimming ducks, left to right: Ring-necked Duck (male) and Ring-necked Duck (female).

REVISED EDITION, WITH A SUPPLEMENT
BY E. MILBY BURTON, DIRECTOR OF THE CHARLESTON MUSEUM

South Carolina Bird Life

BY

ALEXANDER SPRUNT, JR.

Staff member, National Audubon Society
Member, American Ornithologists' Union

AND

E. BURNHAM CHAMBERLAIN

Curator of Zoölogy, The Charleston Museum
Member, American Ornithologists' Union

Original Paintings by
FRANCIS LEE JAQUES
ROGER TORY PETERSON
EDWARD VON S. DINGLE
JOHN HENRY DICK

UNIVERSITY OF SOUTH CAROLINA PRESS · COLUMBIA

PUBLISHER'S NOTE ON THE REVISED EDITION

The First Edition of this book, published in 1949, bore the legend "Contributions from the Charleston Museum: XI." The book was originated by the Charleston Museum, and publication was made possible by a generous subsidy that the Charleston Museum made available to the University of South Carolina Press.

In Memory of
ARTHUR TREZEVANT WAYNE
Ornithologist, Teacher, Friend

Acknowledgments

THIS book has been made possible by the efforts of so many people that it is indeed a futile task to attempt to express adequately the gratitude which is felt for the contribution of each. However, some have played such important parts in the development of *South Carolina Bird Life* that the book would be incomplete without brief mention of the debt which is owed to them.

The inclusion of so many original paintings in full color would have been impossible except for the generosity of Mrs. Carll Tucker, William R. Coe, Marshall Field, George Widener, Donald D. Dodge, Duncan H. Read, Bayard W. Read, Orlando S. Brewer, and Mr. and Mrs. Guthrie Shaw. To these public-spirited citizens, together with John T. Jenkins who enlisted the support of several of them, is due the gratitude of all who enjoy the paintings.

Sincere thanks are offered to Drs. John W. Aldrich, Ira N. Gabrielson, Robert Cushman Murphy, James L. Peters, John T. Zimmer, J. Harold Easterby, and Chapman J. Milling for substantial assistance. Likewise of importance was the help of Thomas D. Burleigh, Allen J. Duvall, Charles K. Nichols, Charles E. O'Brien, Allen R. Phillips, Frank Pitelka, Chandler S. Robbins, Herbert L. Stoddard, Emmet R. Blake, James E. Mosimann, Newton A. Seebeck, Jr., James T. Gittman, and Mrs. J. Hubert Noland, Jr.

Thanks must also be extended to Arthur C. Bent for permission to quote from his *Life Histories of North American Birds*; to Richard G. Kuerzi for detailed notes on birds in Horry county; to Ivan R. Tomkins for many data on species in the Beaufort area; to Dr. Eugene E. Murphey for data on the Aiken-Augusta region; to the National Audubon Society and Mrs. Carll Tucker for permission to quote from Arthur H. Howell's *Florida Bird Life*; to Harry T. Davis, director of the North Carolina State Museum, for permission to quote from the *Birds of North Carolina*, and for other favors; to the Clemson College Department of Biology, through Prof. R. E. Ware, for assistance including inspection of specimens; to E. J. DeCamps, of Beaufort, and H. L. Harllee, of Florence, for use of their extensive collections of birds and eggs, as well as for numerous data, and to Dr. James T. Penney, of the University of South Carolina's Department of Biology, for the use of his manuscript check-list of South Carolina birds.

To the artists whose plates are presented in this book—Francis Lee Jaques, Roger Tory Peterson, Edward von S. Dingle, and John Henry Dick—gratitude is due not only for their beautiful paintings but also for the splendid spirit of cooperation in which they approached the making of the book. The assistance of Mr. Jaques in the production of the color plates deserves particular mention.

For the use of their splendid photographs we are indebted to Allan D. Cruickshank (and to the National Audubon Society from whose files most of his pictures came), Samuel A. Grimes, Hugh M. Halliday, Carl Julien, and Russell Maxey. Mrs. J. J. Carroll kindly granted permission for use of photographs by her late talented husband.

The John Simon Guggenheim Foundation made possible the beginning of this work through a grant to Alexander Sprunt, Jr., and the National Audubon Society, through its President, John H. Baker, gave him a year's leave of absence. To both of these agencies is due sincere thanks.

The Charleston Museum made possible the participation of E. Burnham Chamberlain in the writing of the book and threw the entire resources of its staff into the project. Without the support of A. W. Allison, president, and the other members of the Museum's Board of Trustees, the book would have been impossible.

To Arthur St. J. Simons, Robert S. Davis, C. Miles Morrison, and many other members of the staff of The R. L. Bryan Company, and to George T. Bailey of Photogravure and Color Company, we extend heartfelt thanks for assistance far beyond ordinary commercial obligations. P. J. Conkwright of the Princeton University Press contributed valuable suggestions as to format.

Substantial aid was given in this work by Dr. Alexander Wetmore, chairman of the Committee on Nomenclature of the American Ornithologists' Union, and to Dr. Herbert Friedman, curator of the Division of Birds of the United States National Museum.

It is impossible to express adequately our appreciation to George B. Rabb, and Miss Emma B. Richardson of the Museum's staff, for their painstaking attention to details and untiring labor.

No assistance which we have had has been more important than that of Paul R. Weidner, professor of English at the College of Charleston, and Dr. Harry C. Oberholser, of Cleveland, eminent American ornithologist. Mr. Weidner's editorial work is responsible in large measure for the smoothness and unity of the text. To state that Dr. Oberholser's assistance in the preparation of the manuscript has been invaluable is to be guilty of gross understatement.

ALEXANDER SPRUNT, JR.
E. MILBY BURTON
for the Charleston Museum

E. BURNHAM CHAMBERLAIN
FRANK H. WARDLAW
for the Publishers

Foreword

ALMOST forty years have passed since the publication of Arthur T. Wayne's *The Birds of South Carolina.* In its day Wayne's book was standard; it became at once a work of primary importance to the ornithologists of the State; and its usefulness was greatly enhanced by the appearance, in 1931, of *The Supplement to Wayne's Birds of South Carolina,* compiled by Alexander Sprunt, Jr., and E. Burnham Chamberlain. That such a supplement should have been necessary within twenty years of the original work illustrates what is perhaps an obvious fact—that the study of ornithology is not and can not be static. Many new observers have entered the field during the past four decades; many new records and observations have accumulated since Wayne wrote. No matter how complete or how authoritative Wayne's book was at the time of its publication, no matter how high a place it may always occupy in the history of South Carolina ornithology, it can no longer be regarded as the final word. Too many important things have happened in that forty-year period. Such considerations as these explain, in part at least, why the present work was undertaken. Not only is a completely new treatment of the subject called for, it is long past due.

Alexander Sprunt, Jr., and E. Burnham Chamberlain, the authors of the present work, have been students of ornithology from the days of their youth. Their common interest in the subject brought them together when they were boys and made them associates in the Charleston Museum for many years, during which they gathered innumerable records and worked together steadily in the preparation of many of the ornithological exhibits still on display at the Museum. Both of them knew and studied under Wayne. Such unremitting scholarship, over so long a period, eminently qualifies them to be the authors of this book. Sprunt, who is now a member of the staff of the National Audubon Society, has achieved a wide reputation as a lecturer and writer. His work takes him into nearly every state in the Union, either to deliver lectures on birds and wildlife conservation or to conduct Audubon Wildlife Tours. Chamberlain continues as a member of the Charleston Museum staff, where he bears the title of Curator of Vertebrate Zoölogy. His ornithological notes, already voluminous, grow steadily year by year, and he is constantly in correspondence with scientists throughout the nation. Though he is a man of great modesty, his fellow-scientists recognize him as an authority in many fields of natural history. Both men are members of the American Ornithologists' Union.

In *South Carolina Bird Life* the authors have endeavored to write not only for the scientist but for the interested layman. Their purpose has been to give an accurate survey of the natural history of the birds of the State, as complete as available authentic records can make it. The need for preciseness of statement and for the conservation of space has determined the general organization of the book. It has also dictated the use of numbers of technical methods which call for some editorial explanation if the book is to achieve its fullest value for all readers.

Species and subspecies have been limited to those that have been or probably will be accepted by the Committee on Nomenclature of the American Ornithologists' Union. The scientific names, common names, and order follow the 1931 Check-List and its supplements or, in some instances, information furnished by Dr. Alexander Wetmore, chairman of the Committee on Nomenclature. The number given at the left of the bird's name is a somewhat arbitrary one; it is a reference number to indicate the position which the species occupies in this work. The last of these numbers, therefore, gives the total number of species and subspecies included in the book. The number in parenthesis on the right of the name is the number assigned to the bird by the American Ornithologists' Union many years ago. The Union numbers have long been used in marking eggs of the different species, but because of changes in the various Check-Lists they no longer occur in numerical order.

To many people the scientific names of birds, plants, and animals appear very formidable. Such names, however, are often no more difficult to learn than the common English names. In fact, the English names are sometimes identical or virtually identical with the Greek and Latin ones. Such words as *magnolia, geranium, rhinoceros, vireo,* and *junco* provide examples. But the scientific (which is to say, the technical) names are necessary. They form a universal nomenclature; they are intelligible to scientists of all nations. Moreover, they make for precision in identification. The scientific name is composed of either two or three terms. The first of these terms is the generic or family name; the second, the specific name; and the third, if it is added at all, is a designation of the subspecies. In *South Carolina Bird Life* the English meaning or translation of the scientific name is significant, descriptive, or appropriate. These definitions have been checked by Dr. Harry C. Oberholser. English names indicated as local ones are those generally in use in South Carolina. No attempt has been made to supply the local names by which the bird may be known elsewhere.

In their descriptions the authors have deliberately limited themselves to the minimum of detail necessary for a reasonable identification of the bird. The length of the bird is given in inches, for the sake of the general reader; otherwise, all measurements are given in millimeters.

Concerning the status of any bird in South Carolina the authors have tried to present it in terms of the bird's occurrence over the entire State. For instance, a species may be abundant in some localities and only fairly common in others, but throughout the State it may be regarded as common. Terms of abundance are relative. A bird may be said to be *abundant* if it occurs in large numbers either in flocks or otherwise; *common*, if it is of regular or frequent occurrence in substantial numbers; *fairly common*, of rather frequent occurrence in small numbers; *uncommon*, of unusual occurrence in very small numbers; *rare*, of very unusual occurrence; *casual*, of irregular appearance but coming from a regular range not far away; *accidental*, of purely fortuitous occurrence from a distant or unlikely area.

The term *Permanent Resident* applies to any bird that is present in South Carolina throughout the year and usually breeds in the State. It may, however, be applied to a species that is present in every month. The Sandpipers, for example, breed in the Arctic and in the sub-Arctic, but one may see them in South Carolina in every month. A *Summer Resident* is a species that occurs and usually breeds in the State during the summer. A bird which arrives in late March and remains until October is properly spoken of as a summer resident. The term *Transient* is used for birds which pass through the State on their annual fall and spring migrations between their breeding grounds and their winter range. Transients usually appear in the State for only short periods of time, though stragglers may arrive at almost any time. The term *Winter Resident* is given to a bird which spends the winter months within the borders of the State. For such a species South Carolina represents at least a part of its winter range. The term is especially applicable to the duck population of the State. Species which arrive in early October and leave in early April may be classified as winter residents. Finally, a *Visitor* is a bird that is likely to spend only a short time within the borders of South Carolina. Shearwaters are visitors. During the summer months some of the shearwaters seem to feed up and down the entire South Atlantic coast and it is quite possible that the same bird may be seen off one point of the coast at different times during these months. Similarly, certain species that appear from time to time during the winter are to be regarded only as visitors.

The dates given under the heading of Status are extreme; that is, they represent the earliest and latest dates supplied by authentic records. If a bird is not a permanent resident of the State, the History usually indicates when the species may be expected to appear in greatest numbers. The range of each species has been delineated by giving the boundary by counties. For example, the range of the Eastern Kingbird in South Carolina is defined thus: "Recorded north to Greenville and Chester counties; east to Horry County; south to Beaufort County; west to Oconee County." Similarly, the Blue-winged Warbler is "reported north to Chester County; east to Horry County; south to Dewees Island and Summerville; and west to Graniteville (Aiken County)." For each county or place cited there is at least one authentic record of the bird's having been observed there. It is logical to assume that the bird will be found within the area of which the counties named form the corner limits. To continue the example, a glance at the map will thus reveal that the Kingbird ranges through the entire State. Many other birds are to be found in all forty-six counties. Such a method of describing the range avoids the confusion and monotony which would result from giving long alphabetical lists of counties where the species may be found.

For the most part the book includes only species for which actual specimens have been taken. Exceptions to this rule occur when the authors are certain that the sight records from which they are working deal with a species not easily confused with any other and when they know that the observer is a trained student, qualified by experience to recognize the species in its natural environment. The main text of the book makes constant reference to bird specimens taken by Wayne. These specimens, which have been invaluable to the authors, form the greater part of the Wayne collection, purchased by the Charleston Museum shortly after Wayne's death.

One final note. To conserve space the authors have usually omitted the initials or given names of the ornithologists whose records and observations they have repeatedly had occasion to cite. It is not likely that such omissions will cause any difficulty for the reader.

E. MILBY BURTON
Editor

Contents

CONTENTS—*Continued*

Illustrations

PAINTINGS

ILLUSTRATIONS—*Continued*

ILLUSTRATIONS—*Continued*

ILLUSTRATIONS—*Continued*

South Carolina
Bird Life

Ornithology in South Carolina

M ORE species of birds have been made known to science from South Carolina than from any other state. It was this fact which caused Arthur T. Wayne, South Carolina's most eminent ornithologist, to say that his State "thus stands easily first among the States of the Union in ornithological history." On the face of numerical superiority of described species today, this claim might be disputed by California, but the great majority described from that State are subspecies. To quote Wayne again, "of valid species South Carolina has nearly twice as many as California." So then, a great distinction is ours.

The first detailed mention of the birds of the Carolina region was contained in William Hilton's narrative, published in 1664 in London under the title *A Relation of a Discovery Lately Made on the Coast of Florida*. Hilton goes into some detail regarding conditions along the South Carolina coast from what is now the Edisto River to Port Royal. Of birds he says:

> The Country abounds with Grapes, large Figs, and Peaches; the Woods with Deer, Conies, Turkeys, Quails, Curlues, Plovers, Teile, Herons; and as the *Indians* say, in Winter, with Swans, Geese, Cranes, Duck and Mallard, and innumerable of other water-Fowls, whose names we know not, which lie in the Rivers, Marshes, and on the Sands.

He also refers to "great flocks of Parrakeeto's."

Two years after the appearance of Hilton's work, Robert Horne published what he called *A Brief Description of the Province of Carolina* (1666) though he made hardly more than a passing reference to the birdlife.

In 1682 there was published a pamphlet entitled *Carolina, or a Description of the Present State of that Country*, by T. A. Gent, generally supposed to be Thomas Ashe, which went into some interesting detail regarding the birds of the region:

> . . . the red, copped and blew bird, which wantonly imitates the various Notes and sounds of such Birds and Beasts which it hears, wherefore, by

way of Allusion, it's call'd the Mocking Bird; for which pleasing property it's there esteem'd a Rarity. . . .

. . . In Winter huge Flights of wild Turkies, oftentimes weighing from twenty, thiry [sic] to forty pound . . . They have a Bird I believe the least in the whole Creation, named the Humming Bird; in bigness the Wren being much superiour, in magnitude not exceeding the Humble Bee, whose Body in flying much resembles it, did not their long Bills, between two and three Inches, and no bigger than Needles, make the difference. . . . I am informed, that in the more Northern parts of America they sleep the whole Winter; . . .

Samuel Wilson's *Account of the Province of Carolina in America* (1682) contains references to birds, as does *Carolina Described more fully than Heretofore*, which was published anonymously in 1684. In 1700 another gentleman appeared in Carolina and, quite overcome with his observations of the country, the people, and the wildlife, delivered himself of some remarkable statements. This was John Lawson who, though he is usually identified with North Carolina by reason of his *History*, made notes on South Carolina birds during his travels through the province.

Having landed in Charleston in 1700, Lawson set forth from that city on December 28 for the region later to become North Carolina, "being six Englishmen in company, with three Indian men and one woman, wife to our Indian Guide." The account of his journey is replete with references to birds, animals, and insects, in which latter group he includes alligators, snakes, and lizards! It appears that in his day any unknown creature which progressed by crawling was called an insect. Lawson draws comparisons between American and English birds and applies many Old World names to the former. He was, of course, no ornithologist, but his writings, containing as many references to birds as they do, should not be disregarded.

He gives a list of "Birds of Carolina" and comments freely upon them. It is very likely, however, that some of his statements were highly colored by local information. Lawson, like Thomas Ashe, credits great size to the Wild Turkey, but he goes Ashe considerably better than the latter's "twenty, thiry to forty pound." Lawson says of the bird that "There are great Flocks of these in Carolina. I have seen about five hundred of these in a Flock; some of these very large. I have never weighed any myself, but have been informed of one that weighed nearly sixty pound. I have seen half a Turkey feed eight hungry men two meals."

It is interesting to note his remarks on Bull's Island. Of this locality, so famous in the ornithology of the Low-country, he says,

We . . . came Safe into a Creek that is joining to the North End of Bulls Island [Jack's Creek]. . . . On the morrow we went and visited the

Easternmost Side of this Island, it joining to the Ocean, and having very fair and Sandy Beaches, pav'd with innumerable sorts of curious pretty Shells, and very pleasant to the Eye. . . . At our return to our Quarters the Indians had killed two more Deer, two wild Hogs, and three Raccoons, all very lean, except the Raccoons. We had great Store of Oysters, Conks, and Clamps, a Large sort of Cockles. These parts being very well furnished . . . in the Season, [with] good Plenty of Fowl, as Curleus, Gulls, Gannets, and Pellicans, besides Duck and Mallard Geese, Swans, Teal, Widgeon, etc.

One of his typical comments on wildlife is:

Fishermen are like a Duck, but have a narrow Bill, with Sets of Teeth. They live on very small fish which they catch as they go along. They taste fishy. The best way to order them, is upon occasion, to pull out the oil box from the rump, and then bury them five or six hours under ground. Then they become tolerable.

Governor Glen's account of birds, in his *Description of South Carolina* (1761), has been said to be derived from extracts in *A Letter from South Carolina*, which was published in three editions, 1710, 1718, and 1732.

Serious ornithological work in South Carolina began in May, 1722, with the landing at Charleston of Mark Catesby. Southern science owes much to Catesby, and it is to be regretted that more scholars today are not acquainted with his work. Few scientists have left such a substantial contribution, and so little information about themselves, as this modest man.

Mark Catesby was the youngest of several children of John Catesby, Gent., and Elizabeth Jekyll, whose marriage took place in the year Charleston was founded (1670); but the place and date of his birth are not authentically known. It is recorded that he was baptized on March 30, 1682, at Sudbury. He studied in London, apparently always having been interested in natural history.

In 1712 he made a trip to America going to the home of a married sister in Virginia, but he did no painting or collecting there save for a few plants. A journey to Jamaica in 1715 seems to have been equally unproductive. In 1719 he returned to England and for a time considered joining an expedition to Africa. When the plans for the expedition were almost complete, Catesby suddenly declined to go, and, in 1722, he returned to America.

The expenses of this second trip were defrayed by a group of patrons, for whom Catesby was supposed to collect desirable items, an obligation which doubtless irked him at times. He landed at Charleston on May 23, 1722, and spent a year in the coast country. Afterward, he pushed on into the interior with Indian guides to carry some of his necessary equipment.

If his own testimony can be accepted, Catesby was very thorough in his methods and he worked unhurriedly; he says for example, "I believe very few

Birds have escaped my Knowledge, except some Water Fowl and some of those which frequent the Sea." Naturally, the great number of new and strange birds delighted him, but they caused him some difficulty as well, for he knew not what to call them, and in giving some the names he did, he followed the custom then in vogue of applying names of similar Old World species to those in Carolina. As he himself puts it, "Very few of the Birds having Names assigned them in the Country, except some which had *Indian* Names; I have call'd them after *European* Birds of the same Genus, with an additional Epithet to distinguish them."

In addition to the collecting of specimens, Catesby probed into the mystery of migration, and gave some thought as to the introduction of European species in America. Most of his time, however, was taken up with studying the habits of birds and collecting and painting them with appropriate vegetation. He completed a study of some 104 species in this manner.

Catesby's studies in Carolina dealt entirely with the section which is now South Carolina, this being perfectly clear from his own statements. The formal separation of the Province into North and South Carolina did not take place until 1729. The great value of Catesby's work lies not only in its own worth, but also in the fact that Linnaeus based his descriptions of North American birds mainly on Catesby's plates and text. Thus it is that South Carolina has so many species for which it is the type locality.

Catesby's great book *The Natural History of Carolina, Florida and the Bahama Islands,* was first published in London in 1731, and appeared in three editions. The second was edited by George Edwards in 1754, and the third, in English and German, in 1771. The book attracted much scientific attention and was termed at the Royal Society of London, "a curious and magnificent work."

There is a degree of doubt surrounding the circumstances of Catesby's death. That he was unwell in 1749 is attested by a letter written in July, 1749, by one of his friends to another, which stated that "I saw Messrs. Catesby and Edwards who has material for a third volume of Birds, Flies and Animals, but poor Mr. Catesby's legs swell and he looks badly. Drs. Mead and Stack said there was little hopes of him long this side of the grave." One version has it that he died "at his home behind St. Luke's Church in Old Street (London)," and characterized him as "the truly honest and ingenious and modest Mark Catesby." The date is given as December 23, 1749. Another version is that he went to sea late in that year, on the ship Portfield, of the East India Company, and that the log of the vessel contains this entry, "Mark Catesby departed this life 3 a. m. April 20, 1750, having died of a fever and at 8 a. m. amid faint airs and a calm sea, his body was committed to the deep."

A considerable hiatus ensued between the investigations of Catesby and the next important work with Carolina birds. This interim saw a certain scientific activity, but with ornithology somewhat subordinated to botany. Birds were given hardly more than cursory notice by Dr. Alexander Hewat who, in 1779, produced an *Historical Account of the Rise and Progress of the Colonies of South Carolina and Georgia*.

The famous journeys of William Bartram took place from 1773 to 1778, and published accounts of them appeared in 1791. They include a list of some 215 species of birds, covering observations from New England to the Gulf of Mexico, east of the mountains. This list stands as the most comprehensive prior to that of Wilson. Bartram did considerable work in Carolina. His name is perpetuated in ornithology by its occurrence in the scientific name of one of the shore birds, the Upland Plover or Bartramian Sandpiper (*Bartramia longicauda*).

In the early part of the nineteenth century three historians wrote extensively of South Carolina, all of whose works include references to birds. These books were Drayton's *A View of South Carolina* (1802), Ramsay's *History of South Carolina* (1809), and Mill's *Statistics of South Carolina* (1826).

The father of American ornithology, Alexander Wilson, is not adequately recognized even yet. His was a remarkable work, though it has been more or less overshadowed and submerged by that of his contemporary, the versatile and expressive Audubon. Wilson did some of his field work in South Carolina, but he spent little time in this State, concentrating his efforts across the Savannah River in Georgia. Somewhat dour in character, he was a careful, consistent observer and his findings in many cases have proved definitely sound.

The second important era of ornithological work in South Carolina, with which the modern phase of the science may be said to have begun, was initiated by two men. One of them was highly exuberant and, in some ways, flamboyant; the other was methodical, systematic, and conservative. These two divergent characters and firm friends were John James Audubon and Dr. John Bachman, the latter always the steadying check on the former.

Dr. Bachman was for nearly sixty years pastor of St. John's Lutheran Church in Charleston. He was born in 1790, in Rhinebeck, New York. Illness interfered with his college education but he studied theology privately and was licensed to preach in 1813. He began his ministry near his birthplace but ill health forced him to take a cruise to the West Indies; on his return he was notified that he had been called to St. John's in Charleston.

Bachman's interest in nature was greatly stimulated by what turned out to be an important event for himself and his family. In 1831 Audubon came to Charleston. From the first, the families of these two men became firm friends and their association ultimately resulted in the marriage of Audubon's sons to two of Bachman's daughters. While there is no doubt that Audubon's enthusiasm gave great impetus to Bachman's increasing interest in birds, it is equally true that, in later years, Bachman's influence and steadying qualities were of considerable aid to Audubon. Bachman pointed out some mistakes and erroneous conclusions that the American Woodsman, as Audubon liked to call himself, would otherwise have fallen into, and he was of immense assistance in the production of *The Birds of America.* For the later *Quadrupeds* Bachman wrote the entire text, while Audubon did the paintings.

Bachman discovered four birds near Charleston, two of which were named for him by Audubon—Bachman's Warbler and Bachman's Sparrow. His other finds were Swainson's Warbler and Macgillivray's Seaside Sparrow. While working with Bachman, Audubon discovered the King Rail and the Rough-winged Swallow. Migration appeared to interest Bachman greatly and he published notes on this subject. Another problem which commanded his experimental attention, and upon which he also wrote, was whether vultures depend on sight or smell in locating their food. He and Audubon had many discussions on the subject, and his findings and opinions were embodied in a paper which he called *An account of some experiments made on the habits of the Vultures inhabiting Carolina, the Turkey Buzzard, and the Carrion Crow.* This was published in 1834 and is still referred to.

The work of Audubon and Bachman in South Carolina had far-reaching consequences and is still of great value. The two great naturalists were outstanding contributors to the scientific fame of the State.

Subsequent to the Audubon-Bachman era, apparently no systematic work was carried on in South Carolina for some years. Bird lists, however, appeared from time to time in various publications, and some of them deserve mention. Among them was Lewis R. Gibbes' *Catalogue of the Fauna of South Carolina* (1848), which contained a list of 271 species. Prior to its appearance, smaller lists were published in the *Geography of South Carolina,* by Simms, 1843, and in *Carolina Sports by Land and Water,* by Elliott, 1846, this list dealing with those species "which are the objects of sport." Finally, there were *Notes on the Fauna of the Pine Barrens of Upper South Carolina,* by Burnett, 1851, and the *History of the Upper Country of South Carolina,* by Logan, 1859.

There now comes into the history of South Carolina ornithology the name of a scientist widely known among scholars and recognized as one of the really great ornithologists of the century. This was Dr. Elliott Coues. Yet even to those who know his work well it may come as a surprise to learn that Coues worked in South Carolina, for his name is usually associated with other parts of the country. The works which have given him fame are his *Birds of the Northwest* and *The Birds of the Colorado Valley;* when he was working in South Carolina he was far from the eminence he later attained.

Dr. Coues was an army surgeon who found himself stationed early in his career at Columbia, when he was only twenty-six years of age. His medical duties must have been such as to allow him considerable time for field work, and apparently he made good use of it. The results were published in 1868 under the title *A Synopsis of the Birds of South Carolina,* covering 294 species. A word about this publication is necessary.

It must be recalled that, at the time, Coues was a young man; he was in unfamiliar country; and he appears to have leaned rather heavily on hearsay evidence and conjecture. Whatever the cause, the work unfortunately contained many errors,—so many, indeed, that in 1910 Paul M. Rea, when Director of the Charleston Museum and engaged in editing Wayne's *Birds of South Carolina,* wrote that Coues' *Synopsis* "is so unfortunately full of errors that little dependence can be placed upon it." Arthur T. Wayne, finding his own field observations so often at variance with those of Coues, says of the *Synopsis* that it is so full of error that "I have placed many of his species in the hypothetical list, since they are based on purely hypothetical grounds in my opinion, and in the opinion of many of my ornithological friends." Search through the collections of the Boston Society of Natural History and of the United States National Museum, both logical repositories for specimens collected by Coues, failed to reveal several birds which he mentions as occurring in South Carolina, nor did the accession lists show that any of the doubtful ones were ever received. Illustrations of those species about which nothing can be found, other than Coues' unsubstantiated statement that they occurred, are the Tree Sparrow and Warbling Vireo. It must be admitted, regretfully, that Coues' contribution to the State's ornithology is not reliable.

Six years after the appearance of Coues' list, Dr. C. Hart Merriam published in 1874 a list of fifty-four species of birds occurring about Aiken.

From the very beginning, the greater part of work done in the State was limited to the coastal area. That was natural enough in very early days, of course, for there was nothing but wilderness elsewhere. Even much later, however, observers in the interior were rare. Notable exceptions occur both in the late nineteenth century and in recent years. The splendid work done in the Up-country from 1876 to 1892 by Leverett M. Loomis stands as a tremendous contribution to South Carolina ornithology. Coues' work was done in the interior, but that of Loomis was the first systematic accomplishment in the section commonly known as the Piedmont and in the mountains. It stands today as a careful, accurate monument to hard, painstaking field work and study. Loomis published his results largely in the *Auk,* and was a correspondent and collaborator of Arthur T. Wayne, to whom he supplied much information regarding the birds of the Up-country. The annotated list of the Up-country species which appears in Wayne's book is based on Loomis' findings. Twelve species of birds were added to South Carolina by this zealous worker and his removal from the State in 1892 was a distinct loss to science locally.

The year 1883 saw the appearance of *A List of the Vertebrate Animals of South Carolina* by Dr. Frederick W. True, which contained a catalogue of 312 species of birds.

From 1868 to 1901 considerable work in ornithological research was carried on in the southeastern corner of the State, a strategic and very little investigated area, by Walter J. Hoxie. He owned a plantation on St. Helena Island. For some reason, Wayne viewed many of Hoxie's reports with disfavor and questioned some of them outright. That Hoxie, however, possessed much ability has been proved in the light of subsequent events.

Typical of Wayne's attitude toward Hoxie are his expressions regarding Hoxie's records of the American Merganser, and of the Prairie Warbler in winter. Of the former, Hoxie claimed its occurrence in some numbers at irregular intervals. Wayne stated: "As Mr. Hoxie does not appear to have taken any of these ducks . . . this record must be rejected." He added that Hoxie's ducks were "without doubt" specimens of the Red-breasted Merganser. The American Merganser has since been established as a South Carolina bird by actual specimens. In regard to the Prairie Warbler's occurrence in winter, according to Hoxie, Wayne asserted that "these reports are unreliable, and . . . I distrust them because the Prairie Warbler is very susceptible to cold and could not possibly live in South Carolina at the time Mr. Hoxie records it." None the less, he himself later found the Prairie Warbler near his home, much further up the coast than Hoxie's territory, in January, 1922. It has also been seen near Charleston in December. Therefore, Hoxie's records are valid and should stand. Wayne made very positive statements at times which, in the light of subsequent events, he was obliged either to qualify or retract.

The visits of William Brewster, of Cambridge, Massachusetts, to South Carolina in 1883, 1884, and 1885, resulted not only in the addition of new species to the records of the State but in influencing Wayne to give up his business and to adopt ornithology as a life work. Brewster added the European Cormorant and the Acadian Sharp-tailed Sparrow to the State List and recorded for the first time the Bridled Tern, Nelson's Sparrow, and Mountain Solitary Vireo, though the actual specimens of the tern were taken by Hoxie, and those of the sparrow and vireo by Wayne.

In the years 1886-88, Ellison A. Smyth, Jr., did considerable work near Charleston, publishing his records in the *Proceedings of the Elliott Society* and elsewhere.

It is as inevitable to connect Arthur Trezevant Wayne with South Carolina ornithology as it is to connect John James Audubon with the birds of America. There is no doubt that the outstanding aspect of his work was the extremely small territory which it encompassed. Practically all of his field activities, study, and discoveries occurred within 20 miles of his home on Oakland Plantation, near Mt. Pleasant. That accomplishment probably has no parallel in this country. Wayne added a bird to the State list for nearly every year he was in the field.

Wayne, who had always been interested in birds, began his real career in 1883, when, as it has already been said, he withdrew from an unsuccessful business and decided to devote all his time to ornithology.

From 1883 to 1930, Wayne was constantly in the field, except for short periods of illness. He left South Carolina only four times for outside work, all of it being done in Florida, which he visited at the request and instigation of Brewster. These out-of-state excursions took place in 1892-94. In South Carolina itself, he was away from the coast region on but one expedition, in the summer of 1882, when he collected specimens near Greenville. During all other years he lived, moved, and had his being among the birds of Charleston County, his home at Porcher's Bluff being only about 10 miles from the city of Charleston.

Notable among his many remarkable records was the rediscovery of Swainson's Warbler in April, 1884; in that year Wayne took the first known specimen since the bird had been originally secured by Dr. Bachman in 1833 and named by Audubon for the English ornithologist Swainson. Paralleling this accomplishment was his rediscovery in 1901 of Bachman's Warbler in South Carolina after a lapse of sixty-eight years.

It was natural enough that Wayne should, sooner or later, write and publish some account of his work. To this he was urged by his friends and scientific brethren, and at last he consented to do so. Paul M. Rea, then Director of the Charleston Museum, was his constant advisor and assured him from the first that the institution would provide for the publication of the book and handle the details of the undertaking. The plan was carried out, the text was prepared and, in 1910, the Museum published *The Birds of South Carolina*. Considerable interest attaches to it from various points of view, not the least of which is the fact that it was the first state bird book to be produced in the Southeastern States. Having lived and worked in the coast region all his life, Wayne in his book dealt primarily with the birds of that area, but included an annotated list of species of the interior as well, together with a Hypothetical List.

It was the writers' immeasurable privilege to have this remarkable man as their friend and preceptor for many years. Any degree of proficiency to which they may have attained in ornithology is due largely to his influence and teaching. He was ever a keen and devoted teacher, a delightful companion, and wonderful raconteur. Tireless in the field, he could walk all day and skin birds half the night. His knowledge and understanding of them bordered upon the uncanny. He remains the only person the writers have known who could name the sexes of identically plumaged birds. Time and again he did so; for instance, when he had shot an Ipswich Sparrow amid the dunes of a barrier island, and *before he picked up the bird*, he would say "male" or "female." Examination of the organs when the specimen was skinned always confirmed the field identification. Even Wayne himself could not explain how he did it. The amazement of visiting ornithologists at such a performance was often laughable. They invariably admitted that they would not have believed it had they not seen it.

Dr. Witmer Stone, then Editor of the *Auk*, in his obituary note on Wayne stated that ". . . there has been scarcely a volume of the journal in the past forty-five years that did not contain some contribution from his pen on the bird life of his native state. . . . Most eminent of the ornithologists of the South the passing of Arthur Wayne will leave a gap in our ranks that will not soon be filled."

It was Sprunt's sad but highly valued privilege to prepare the memorial account of Wayne's life, the custom for deceased Fellows of the American Ornithologists' Union. It was read at the meeting in Salem, Massachusetts, October 21, 1930, appearing later in the *Auk 48*: 1931, 1-16. The closing paragraph of that account seems particularly appropriate to quote here:

> Arthur Trezevant Wayne has gone but he has left behind, enshrined in many a heart, a living monument and, like the patriarchs of ancient days, "He, being dead, yet speaketh."

Increasing information brought to light through the years made it necessary to bring Wayne's book up to date. This was done in 1931 by the authors of this volume, and was published by the Charleston Museum, under the title of *Second Supplement to Arthur T. Wayne's Birds of South Carolina*. It embodied the additions and changes found since 1910, a period of some twenty-one years. Steady work has gone on since then, and more has been and doubtless will be learned. Eighteen years have elapsed since the appearance of the *Supplement* and this volume now contains the findings on ornithology in the State to the present time.

For many years Wayne worked virtually alone among the birds of South Carolina. Early in this century, however, a few younger men with an interest in ornithology became increasingly active and visiting scientists came and went.

PLATE I: INLAND WATERWAY SCENE
Oil Painting by Francis Lee Jaques

Extreme right flying bird: Double-crested Cormorant. Flying birds at left: Brown Pelicans. Birds in water, left to right: Red-breasted Merganser (male), Red-breasted Merganser (female), Hooded Merganser (female), and Hooded Merganser (male).

More local observers began to go afield and to make notes as interest in birds became more pronounced all over the country. Some of these observers, while not professional ornithologists, have added a great deal to the knowledge of that science and are therefore well deserving of recognition.

Low-country Observers

Herbert Ravenel Sass

Herbert R. Sass began work at the Charleston Museum during his college days. A keen, capable, and careful observer, he has gained nation-wide recognition through his excellent writings on nature, both in article and story form. His powers of description have made the Carolina Low-country live vividly in the minds of thousands who have never seen it, and have brought pleasure to many who have. Sass's greatest contribution, perhaps, has been the recording of birds in his own garden on Legare Street in Charleston. Having lived there all his life, amid varied botanical surroundings, he has accumulated a list of species which now amounts to almost 160. Many of these are far from what are usually considered "city" birds and yet they have come there, been seen, and recorded. It is a remarkable illustration of what one may see without leaving one's premises even in a city, and parallels, in an urban sense, the work of Wayne in a rural area.

Among Sass's observational records of value were his rediscovery of breeding colonies of the Snowy Egret in South Carolina in 1908, and his finding in 1947 of the pair of Eastern Glossy Ibises which later led to the discovery of the nest, the first breeding record for the State.

Francis Marion Weston

Although Francis M. Weston has been a resident of Florida for nearly a generation, he is a Carolina Low-countryman, now and always. Most ornithologists will instantly associate him with the Pensacola region and with reason, for no other worker in the country has placed that area more firmly on the ornithological map. Weston first became interested in birds about Charleston. A colleague of Herbert R. Sass, he shared with him the work of building up the bird records of the Charleston Museum. Both of them knew Wayne, worked with him, and profited much from his tutelage.

For many years Weston was accustomed to spend a month in the Low-country on vacation from his duties at the U. S. Naval Air Station at Pensacola, and roamed the beaches, woods, and marshes of the coast region of his native State. He gathered much interesting information in the field; it is to his observational keenness, for instance, that the occurrence of the Cinnamon Teal was established in South Carolina.

Edward von Siebold Dingle

Edward Dingle, whose interest in birds dates from boyhood, did his first work in Clarendon County, near Summerton. He has concentrated on nesting species and has built up a representative collection, with a knowledge of distribution and dates for various species.

He is one of the few ornithologist-artists. Ten of his bird paintings appear in this volume. Moving to Mt. Pleasant after World War I, during which he served in the Navy, he lived near Wayne and was often in the field with him. Later, upon his marriage, he took up residence at Middleburg Plantation, Cooper River, where he now works with his birds and his paintings.

Much of his work has been with the wildfowl and shore birds, and he has also devoted considerable attention to the wandering tropical species which are blown north by hurricanes. Thorough, conservative, and methodical, his contribution to South Carolina ornithology is extensive and lasting. Dingle has added the following species to the State List: Cory's Shearwater, Eastern Glossy Ibis, Leach's Petrel, European Widgeon, and the Clay-colored Sparrow.

Ellison Adger Williams

Ellison Williams is by profession a banker in Charleston, and by avocation a careful, devoted student of birds. Migration interests him much, and he keeps accurate and valuable records. The colony of Purple Martins in his garden in Charleston is probably watched more carefully than any other in the South, and his years of records on the comings and goings of these birds constitute interesting material. To be certain about everything is his outstanding characteristic, one upon which, after all, the very science of ornithology is founded. He is a disciple beyond reproach. One of his accomplishments was the discovery of the first nest of the Black-necked Stilt in South Carolina.

Harold S. Peters

Harold Peters is the Atlantic Flyway Biologist of the U. S. Fish and Wildlife Service. For many years he made his home in Charleston, from which, however, he was often absent for long periods. He is now stationed in Atlanta, Georgia. His first interest was, for many years, entomology. Ornithology has claimed him now, and in his work, which naturally is largely devoted to wildfowl, he has made observations on many other species which are of high scientific value. He has devoted much time to the study of conditions on the Cape Romain Refuge, which is in the governmental department in which he works. He is an accomplished airplane pilot, and has covered many hundreds of miles of territory in the southeast, searching out the ducks on the annual inventories conducted by the U. S. Fish and Wildlife Service. He cooperates constantly with the Charleston Museum, and his records and advice are always of assistance.

ORNITHOLOGY IN SOUTH CAROLINA

Ivan R. Tomkins

For years Ivan R. Tomkins, Corps of Engineers, United States Army, has done excellent work in the lower Savannah River area. He has made many and very valuable observations and records. Among these is the second record for the State of the Lapland Longspur. Although he is on the dividing line between South Carolina and Georgia many of his findings are actually Carolinian. He is an able photographer and writer, and his articles and pictures in nature magazines are doubtless familiar to many. He is also one of the authors of the *Birds of Georgia* and many of his articles have appeared in scientific journals. In 1939 he was elected a member of the American Ornithologists' Union. He has ever been a firm friend of the Charleston Museum, which has always had access to his carefully kept records.

John Henry Dick

After World War II, John Henry Dick became a resident of the Low-country. He lives at Dixie Plantation, situated about 15 miles below Charleston. A keen and careful observer, he has made copious notes on the migration dates of many species of birds. He is working particularly on the Warblers. Long interested in the painting of birds, which was interrupted by the War, he has now taken it up as a serious work. Four of his paintings appear in this volume.

Edward Milby Burton

E. Milby Burton is the Director of the Charleston Museum. Although his knowledge of icthyology is extensive, birds have long interested him also. For years during school days, he was a companion of Sprunt on many a trip afield for birds' eggs, which fascinated both of them. He has done much work with wildfowl and, in past years, a great deal of work in the banding of ducks, herons, and other colonial nesting water birds of the South Carolina coast.

He has gathered bird specimens assiduously for the building up of the Museum's study skin collection, and he has been instrumental in assembling many additional data, particularly on the water birds. He has added the King Eider to the State list.

Alexander Sprunt, Jr.

Alexander Sprunt, Jr., has been an indefatigable student of ornithology for the past forty years. An early connection with the Charleston Museum and early association with Arthur T. Wayne stimulated his initial interest in the subject and laid the foundations for all his later work. In the years following the first World War he supplemented his field work both as a student in northern museums and as a member of the staff of the Charleston Museum. He worked with E. Burnham Chamberlain in producing the *Second Supplement to Arthur T. Wayne's Birds of South Carolina*, published in 1931; and during the 1930's he devoted much time to writing magazine articles on ornithological and wild life subjects. In 1935 he joined the staff of the National Audubon Society; at present he holds the position of Southern Representative of that organization. His work sends him afield in all the Southern states. In addition, he lectures on wild life conservation and conducts Audubon Tours in Florida, South Carolina, Texas, and elsewhere.

He was elected a member of the American Ornithologists' Union in 1928. He has added to the State List of birds the Atlantic Blue-faced Booby (sight record), Swainson's Hawk, American Rough-legged Hawk (sight record with Wayne), Baird's Sandpiper, Eastern Sooty Tern, Black-throated Gray Warbler (sight record), and Eastern Snow Bunting.

Edward Burnham Chamberlain

The career of E. Burnham Chamberlain in ornithology began, like that of his co-worker, Alexander Sprunt, Jr., almost four decades ago. From boyhood he ranged the fields and beaches of his native South Carolina Low-country, studied birds under the tutelage of Arthur T. Wayne, and perfected himself in the methods of scientific research as a member of the staff of the Charleston Museum since 1924. He is now Curator of Vertebrate Zoology. He has long been recognized as an authority on the ornithology of the State. However, his knowledge is not confined to this field. He is also a recognized mammalogist and herpetologist and has published some of his findings in several scientific journals. He has been interested not only in enlarging the Museum's collection of birds for study and display but also in expanding its files of records for the use of scholars in ornithology everywhere. Although naturally most of his work has been done in the coastal region, he has done considerable observing and collecting in the mountains of Pickens and Greenville counties and has had field experience in most parts of the State. Mention has been made of his collaboration with Sprunt in the compilation of the *Second Supplement* to Wayne's book. The work of the two men has again been joined in the present volume. Chamberlain has added the following birds to the State List: the Lesser Common Loon, Wilson's Phalarope, and Arkansas Kingbird.

OBSERVERS IN THE INTERIOR

In addition to the work of Loomis, already described, much information has been accumulated through the activities of recent field workers in Up-country South Carolina. It is hardly possible, for example, to overestimate the value of the data secured in the northwestern portion of South Carolina by the late Prof. Franklin Sherman, of Clemson College, and his able associate, George E. Hudson, who was a student there in 1926-28. This has long been a region little known ornithologically, except for a few spots in the Mountain Area. The Nashville Warbler was added to the State List by Hudson from Clemson.

Prominent among workers in upper South Carolina is Andrew L. Pickens, of Greenville. A man of diversified interests in the fields of zoology and botany, his ornithological publications have been concerned largely with life zones and the geographic distribution of the birds of the Piedmont. He has published in the *Auk, Condor,* and the *Southern Folklore Quarterly* on the life history and seasonal territorial activities of the Ruby-throated Hummingbird, as well as on such topics as Cherokee Indian bird names.

Gabriel Cannon of Spartanburg and P. M. Jenness of Greenville have long been interested in birds, and furnish important material on occurrence and migration in the Piedmont Region.

Mrs. G. E. Charles, of West Columbia, sends material from that section to the Seasonal Reports in the *Audubon Field Notes,* and contributes important data on nesting and migration. She also writes a newspaper column on birds that has appeared for many years in *The State.*

J. R. and H. T. Nowell worked for many years in the 1890's in the vicinity of Anderson. Many specimens that they collected are now in the Charleston Museum.

F. W. Hahn has done considerable work near Greenwood. He compiled a valuable County List which originally appeared in the Greenwood *Index-Journal* in 1934.

The Rev. John Kershaw, Jr., did excellent work in Aiken, Clarendon, and Oconee counties about 1910. Particularly valuable are his nesting records.

Eugene Edmund Murphey

Although he was born and bred a Georgian and lives in Augusta, Dr. Murphey belongs, as an ornithologist, as much to South Carolina as to his native state. Long an intimate friend of Wayne and a regular visitor to the Bull's Bay region for years, he has made discoveries of great value. Among his activities of special note were those which led to the first record of the Limpkin for this State, and to the second breeding record of Forster's Tern. Despite his busy life as a physician, Dr. Murphey has always found opportunity for bird work. Of late years he has been forced to curtail his medical practice, but his interest in ornithology has never waned; indeed, it has become more intense. His collection of study skins is one of the most comprehensive in the South, of great value to South Carolina as well as to Georgia. Dr. Murphey's life work on birds is well set forth in his *Observations on the Birdlife of the Middle Savannah Valley,* published by the Charleston Museum in 1937. In 1940 he was elected a member of the American Ornithologists' Union. He is also an honorary curator of birds in the Charleston Museum.

OTHER WORKERS

Except for the work of Arthur T. Wayne, most of what may be termed modern ornithological study in South Carolina has occurred within the last three decades. Resident bird students have been and continue to be few in number. Out-of-state students, from all parts of the country, have done a considerable amount of work, but they have limited their observations for the most part to the coastal area for the rather obvious reason that it is better bird country.

The only meetings of the American Ornithologists' Union in the southeastern states were held in Charleston in 1927 and 1937. These brought Fellows, Members, and Associates from all parts of this country and Canada to the Carolina Low-country, and many of them saw their first southern birds on the official field trips.

The National Audubon Society's sanctuary program, which includes South Carolina, has brought workers of the organization into this area. Several members of the then U. S. Biological Survey (now the Fish and Wildlife Service) have done extensive work locally. Owners of several of the large plantations have contributed substantially toward the furtherance of ornithological knowledge not only as observers but as hosts to men whose names are known far and wide as top authorities in ornithology.

Drs. Frank M. Chapman and Robert Cushman Murphy have, on several occasions, been guests of the late Jesse Metcalf, at his plantation Hasty Point, on the Waccamaw River, Georgetown County. Their observations have resulted in additional records of the Limpkin and Sandhill Crane, and of the only winter occurrence of the Mississippi Kite. Dr. Murphy, with E. Milby Burton, also added the Purple Sandpiper to the State List, and has participated in several Christmas Bird Counts.

Mr. and Mrs. Clarence E. Chapman, late owners of The Mulberry, Cooper River, were both ardent bird observers. The careful and valuable notes which they made there for many years have been used by the Museum. It was they who made the first records of the Reddish Egret. Mr. Chapman was an enthusiastic duck hunter and added much valuable informative data on both ducks and geese. Duck-banding was carried on at Mulberry with his able and generous assistance. He recorded the earliest nesting of the Black Vulture in the State and the winter occurrence of the Purple Gallinule.

William R. Coe, owner of Cherokee Plantation, Combahee River, has allowed workers the use of that extensive area and some of the few nesting records of the Woodcock have been made there.

Mr. and Mrs. Francis L. Bartow, former owners of Brewton Plantation, Yemassee, were much interested in birds. It was through the vigilance of Mrs. Bartow that the Great White Heron was first recorded in the State.

Hugh S. Belser of Fairlawn Plantation, Charleston County, has always been of assistance in investigations on that prolific tract. The largest colony of the White Ibis in the State inhabited one of the backwaters of Fairlawn, and it was on this plantation that Wayne and Sprunt, in May, 1922, established the first State record of the breeding of the White Ibis.

The Santee Gun Club, composed of a number of sportsmen from the North, has furthered ornithological work for many years. The great egret rookery on the property is probably the oldest in continued use in the country. It is the spot where Dr. Frank A. Chapman secured the birds and made the background studies for the group of that species in the American Museum of Natural History in New York, and it is the site of the first breeding record of the Eastern Glossy Ibis for the State.

Dr. John C. Phillips, an eminent authority on wildfowl, and one of the great sportsmen of this country, for some years owned Seven Oaks Plantation on John's Island. He was often visited there by Dr. Thomas Barbour, and the two always studied birds, keeping lists and records which have been of material aid.

In his Co-operative Quail Association work, Herbert L. Stoddard often visited the Low-country in the years before World War II. His advice about burning, cover, food, and other matters relating to the Bobwhite was sought after by many large estates and preserves, but he always found time to make investigations of other species. He assisted markedly in the investigation of the Ivory-billed Woodpecker in the Santee Swamp in 1935 and later.

The first southern trip that Roger Tory Peterson took embraced the Carolina Low-country. His visit was an experience the authors of this volume are not likely to forget. He has been back again several times, once on the Audubon Society project concerned with the Ivory-billed Woodpecker. Many bird students in the country know Mr. Peterson as the author of the justly famous *Field Guide* and as a leading ornithological painter. Ten of his paintings are reproduced in this book.

Arthur A. Allen and Paul Kellogg of Cornell University, who have done so much with sound photography have worked in South Carolina on two or three occasions with their complicated equipment for recording bird songs. Allan D. Cruickshank, a well-known nature photographer of the Audubon Society staff, has made several trips to South Carolina for work mainly on Bull's Island. His pictures of ducks and other water birds are widely published, and it was through his photographic evidence that the Black-backed Gull was removed from the Hypothetical List. His observation of Noddy Terns in Charleston Harbor was one of the few for this tropical species.

Eugene Eisenman, George Komorowski, and John Bull, members of the Linnaean Society of New York, added a record to the few existing ones of the

Roseate Spoonbill in the State, and added the Lark Sparrow to the State List in 1943 while working at Bull's Island.

Richard G. Kuerzi conducted an ecological survey of Long Bay Plantation, near Myrtle Beach, from the fall of 1939 to January 1941. He has generously furnished his full notes for use in this book.

John B. May, John H. Baker, and the late Charles Urner visited the Low-country in the spring of 1934, aboard the yacht "Migrant." Sprunt was afield with them for several days when observations were carried on at Bull's, Capers and Dewees islands. Some of the results were the third record of the Stilt Sandpiper since Audubon's time, and the second positive record of the Red Phalarope.

Dr. Harry C. Oberholser has visited the coast country several times, notably during the preliminary surveys connected with the Cape Romain Refuge. His notes have always been made available. Other officials of the then Biological Survey (U. S. Fish and Wildlife Service) who have worked in that area are Ira N. Gabrielson, Dr. Clarence Cottam, Frederick C. Lincoln, Arthur H. Howell, and William P. Baldwin. Andrew H. DuPre, the former Refuge Manager has at all times been of great assistance in furnishing observations and records. One of his contributions was the first specimen of the Western Grebe for South Carolina.

Arthur C. Bent, the author of the monumental *Life Histories of North American Birds,* visited Wayne and also was in attendance at the meetings of the A. O. U. in 1927 and 1937.

E. J. DeCamps, of Beaufort, an enthusiastic oölogist, has an excellent collection of South Carolina species, furnishing many valuable data. He has made them available to the authors freely and gladly, and is often referred to in this volume. Most of his work, extending over a period of many years, has been done in the Beaufort and Greenville regions.

Allan R. Phillips was stationed near Charleston during World War II. He contributed a number of valuable records during his stay there. Among them are the Pomarine Jaeger and the second coastal record for the Tennessee Warbler.

George B. Rabb, James E. Mosimann, Thomas M. Uzzell, Jr., and Newton H. Seebeck, Jr., young men working in cooperation with the Charleston Museum, have made many valuable observations in recent years throughout the State.

Among other workers are W. M. Perrygo, J. S. Webb, and J. S. Y. Hoyt, who did a tremendous amount of collecting throughout the State for the United States National Museum in 1940. Their work is often referred to in this volume. Hoyt was also stationed near Charleston during World War II and sent in

Folly Beach by Moonlight

RUSSELL MAXEY

Front Beach, Pawley's Island

CARL JULIEN

Salt Marsh, Georgetown County   CARL JULIEN

Cypress Stream, Orangeburg County

CARL JULIEN

much valuable data to the Charleston Museum. Of particular interest is his observation of the Audubon's Caracara, the only State record.

Edgar A. Mearns and Joseph H. Riley collected for the United States National Museum during 1911 in the vicinity of Mt. Pleasant.

James L. Peters in 1916 and Thomas D. Burleigh in 1932-35 collected over much of the State for the U. S. Biological Survey.

Collectors for the Cleveland Museum of Natural History, who have worked chiefly in the Beaufort region, are: A. B. Fuller, H. M. Woods, W. H. Corning, N. E. Corning, R. J. Kula, T. H. Sandera, E. P. McCullagh, F. W. Braund, P. M. Moulthrop.

James E. Benedict collected in the vicinity of Beaufort and Georgetown in 1890 and 1891.

BIRD REFUGES IN SOUTH CAROLINA

Efforts have been recently initiated to set up game refuges in the State Forests of South Carolina. The result thus far has been the establishment of a four hundred acre tract in the Harbison State Forest in Richland County. This tract lies in the center of the area and is protected from hunting, which is permitted on the rest of the forest.

On May 10, 1948, the Francis Marion National Forest Wildlife Preserve was established by Presidential proclamation and about sixty thousand acres were set aside for its use. This tract is part of the Francis Marion National Forest, which is situated in Berkeley and Charleston counties and contains about a quarter of a million acres. This area is also a cooperative game management area by agreement with the South Carolina Game and Fish Commission. In addition to many deer, the preserve contains Wild Turkeys of the purest strain. A turkey habitat improvement project is conducted there by the State Game and Fish Commission, cooperating with the United States Fish and Wildlife Service under the Pittman-Robertson Act.

Several cities and towns throughout the State have, through their governing municipal bodies, declared their corporate limits to be bird sanctuaries. The efficacy of such procedure may be questioned but the trend indicated in such movements is gratifying and commendable. The ordinances usually forbid shooting and though they are not always strictly enforced, they carry a considerable amount of moral value and give at least an indirect impetus toward the furtherance of conservation. City limit signs usually give notice to visitors that the community is a bird sanctuary. It is to be hoped that more of these urban refuges will be established.

The comparative absence of State refuges does not, however, mean that bird protection in South Carolina has been neglected. It has, in fact, been sponsored and supported largely by outside organizations, particularly by the United

States Fish and Wildlife Service of the Department of the Interior and the National Audubon Society.

United States Fish and Wildlife Service Refuges

The largest and most important refuges in the State are those owned and administered by this government agency, formerly known as the United States Biological Survey. There are four such refuges—Cape Romain, Savannah, Carolina Sandhills, and Santee.

The Cape Romain National Wildlife Refuge is not only the most important refuge in the State, but one of the most important along the entire Atlantic seaboard. It lies directly on the ocean in Charleston County. It was acquired in 1932 and, with additions since that time, now comprises an area of about sixty thousand acres. The over-all shoreline from the northern to the southern end is about 22 miles. Headquarters are at McClellanville, South Carolina.

Beginning just south of the mouth of the Santee River, the Cape Romain Refuge extends to Price's Inlet, the division between Bull's and Capers islands. Much of the area is a vast expanse of salt marsh, mud flats, and oyster banks, with several islands of varying size. Bull's Bay lies in the center, open to the Atlantic, and has a number of sandy, shelly banks which are sites of sea-bird colonies. The three main islands of the Refuge are Cape Island, Raccoon Key, and Bull's Island. The acquisition of the latter in 1936, through the generosity of its owner, Gayer G. Dominick, tremendously increased the value of the refuge. It is one of the ornithological meccas of the East; the Audubon Wildlife Tours are held there every winter and hundreds of people visit it annually.

Both Cape Island and Raccoon Key are virtually treeless, the latter supporting a dense growth of myrtles and low bushes at its northern end where the abandoned Cape Romain lighthouse stands. Dykes have been constructed on Cape Island and the fresh-water pond thus formed attracts each winter great numbers of ducks and practically all the geese which frequent the South Carolina coast. One of the largest Royal Tern colonies on the Atlantic coast is located on Cape Island, and the northernmost group of Brown Pelicans gathers either on Sandy Point on Raccoon Key, or on a small marshy island in Bull's Bay. Numerous Black Skimmers, Willets, Oyster-catchers, and Wilson's Plover also nest in this area, and the marshes abound with Wayne's Clapper Rails. Herons, Laughing Gulls, and Least Terns breed on the banks in Bull's Bay. Shore birds are present the year round, the winter population attracting most attention because of the great concentration of Oyster-catchers, which is outstanding along the Atlantic coast. Marbled Godwits and Long-billed Curlews winter here, with a host of sandpipers and plovers.

Bull's Island is a heavily wooded, almost jungle-like tract of land. Palmetto, live oak, magnolia, and loblolly pine are the principal trees; cassina, wax myrtle, yellow jessamine, and smilax grow profusely. A wild, gradually sloping beach runs along the 6 mile ocean front. Several fresh-water ponds form a paradise for ducks, some eighteen to twenty species occurring daily throughout the winter. Here also are egrets, other herons, eagles, and shore birds. Wild Turkeys frequent the woods and dunes, and deer, otters, raccoons, and fox squirrels abound. Visitors are welcome at Dominick House, the Island headquarters, the guest book of which reads like the register of a resort hotel. Week after week observers, armed with binoculars and cameras, come to investigate the wildlife which has made this island known the country over among lovers of the out-of-doors.

The Savannah National Wildlife Refuge, also a migratory refuge, lies along the Savannah River above Savannah, partly in South Carolina and partly in Georgia, the river being the State line. Old rice fields form most of the tract, which contains 12,609 acres. Banks and trunks (floodgates) are in good repair and operational use. A program for the control of sawgrass has been instituted on this refuge. In addition to a good breeding population of Wood Ducks, the refuge has many Anhingas, herons, and gallinules during the summer. Song birds are very common in the breeding season; the Red-winged Blackbird is the most numerous species. In winter, many ducks make the refuge their home. The Blue-winged Teal is one of the most abundant species there in the migrations; as many as ten thousand have been recorded at one time.

The Carolina Sandhills National Wildlife Refuge is of the type characterized as a "General Wildlife Refuge." It lies on the fall line, in Chesterfield County, just south of the North Carolina line, the nearest town being Cheraw. Comprising 40,829 acres, it was acquired in 1939. Dr. Ira N. Gabrielson, then Chief of the Service, says:

> The soil is poor and covered with a rather thin growth of scrub-oaks, Virginia pines, and other species of the uplands. The stream bottoms, in contrast, are sometimes dense swamps of gum and other water-loving trees and shrubs. Reintroduction of the wild turkey, long absent from the area, has proved successful, and bob-white are present to near carrying capacity.

Many song and insectivorous birds occur, either as migrants or residents, and some water birds are being attracted by the man-made lakes on the property. The area holds considerable promise.

The Santee National Wildlife Refuge is the most recently acquired national wildlife refuge in South Carolina. It falls into the migratory waterfowl refuge category. It is an attempt to compensate for the loss of some of the finest waterfowl lands in the State, a loss sustained by the construction of the Santee-Cooper Hydro-electric Project which flooded a tremendous stretch of country, mainly in Berkeley County. The project was completed on September 15, 1942. Cut-off dykes have been built across shallow areas and bays of the great lakes, so that water levels can be maintained and aquatic vegetation supported. The refuge area is divided into several separate units up to twenty-two hundred acres. It is already being frequented by numbers of ducks and an increasing number of geese each winter. Herons here find suitable feeding and breeding conditions, and many species of land birds are either resident or migratory. The headquarters are maintained at Manning, South Carolina.

National Audubon Society Sanctuaries

At present this Society maintains but one area, and that on a seasonal basis. It is Buzzard Island, in the marshes of Stono River, Charleston County, a few miles above the mouth of that tidal stream. It is a small island of about two acres, completely surrounded by marsh and accessible only at high water. It was given to the Society in 1913 by the Grimball family of James Island and lies immediately adjacent to their property. Raymond G. Grimball acts as seasonal warden.

Buzzard Island derives its name from the fact that a considerable number of Black Vultures have long used it as a roost. It is very thickly overgrown with Spanish bayonet, live oaks, cassina, and wax myrtle; and it supports a breeding colony of Snowy Egrets, Little Blue Herons, Louisiana Herons, Great Blue Herons, and Black-crowned Night Herons. In recent years, an increasing number of American Egrets have been congregating there. Since the Green Heron breeds there also, this small island supports every species of heron which normally occurs in the State with the exception of the Yellow-crowned Night Heron. The adjacent marshes teem with Wayne's Clapper Rails and Worthington's Marsh Wrens.

In former years almost any nesting colony of Snowy or American Egrets was of such importance that it was guarded by some agency but the increasing number of these beautiful birds somewhat diminishes the need of protection. Typical of the Audubon Society's effort in this regard was the guardianship of the backwater on Fairlawn Plantation, Christ Church Parish, Charleston County, until a few years ago. Here American and Snowy Egrets found protection under the seasonal watchfulness of Arthur T. Wayne during the 1920's.

Following the discovery of the Ivory-billed Woodpecker in the Santee Swamp, Georgetown County, in the spring of 1935, the Society placed and maintained a warden there throughout that year and the next two. This part of the Santee Swamp is on what is known as the Wadmacaun River, an arm of the Santee, inclosing a large area of heavy cypress and gum timber owned by the West Virginia Pulp and Paper Company, through whose cooperation warden service was maintained. After the completion of the Santee-Cooper power project some miles upstream, and the consequent infiltration of salt water into the dwindling volume of the Santee, the birds apparently moved out of the area and it was abandoned as a refuge.

Charleston Museum Sanctuary

After the rediscovery of a breeding colony of the Snowy Egret in South Carolina by Herbert R. Sass in May, 1908 (*Auk, 25*: 1908, 313), the locality where they were found, Heron Island off James Island, was obtained by the Charleston Museum from the Oswald family. A member of that family acted as seasonal warden for many years. The island is another small marsh "hammock" much like Buzzard Island but somewhat larger. The habitat group of herons in the Museum depicts this island in painted background, typical vegetation, and mounted birds. The island continues to be an important colony of nesting herons, and many young birds have been banded there in recent years.

Private Sanctuaries

The virtual refuges which exist on many Low-country plantations under private ownership are extremely important although entirely unofficial. On these great estates, most of them owned by Northerners, wildlife is now infinitely better off than in other days when they could not be maintained and patroled as they deserved. Poaching was common, night-hunting occurred frequently, and there was little, if any, oversight of woods and rice fields. Many of the tracts were abandoned except for a few scattered Negro families.

Many of the new plantation owners are sportsmen who are interested in ducks, Bobwhites, and Wild Turkeys. They have had old houses remodeled, new ones built, and rice-field banks and trunks repaired and put in use again. Fences have been erected, patrols set up, and a new day has dawned for Low-country wildlife. It is true that these places are hunting preserves. Owners and guests gather in the open season, and the boom of guns echoes across the rice fields and through the pinelands. But on the vast majority of the plantations the season's bag of game is only a fraction of the number of birds which find protection from the poacher and the night hunter, as well as abundant food, cover, and water. The plantations have paid heavy dividends in wildlife and one hesitates to think what the state of affairs might be today were it not for them. One of the outstanding properties is that of the Santee Gun Club near McClellanville. On a beautiful backwater there is one of the oldest heron-egret rookeries in continued, recorded use in the country. Rookeries occur on many others.

Indeed, there are dozens of refuges in essence, if not in name, and South Carolinians can be thankful for such areas as Mulberry, Rice Hope, Whitehall, Cherokee, Prospect Hill, Fairlawn, Hasty Point, and Medway. One of the largest and best kept of such refuges is South Island Plantation, Georgetown County, owned by Thomas A. Yawkey. Not only does it support thousands of ducks in winter, but it also harbors numbers of song birds and shore birds. Among the latter are the rare Black-necked Stilt and the Avocet.

Type Locality List

S EVENTY-SEVEN birds have been made known to science for the first time from South Carolina. The list of the species for which South Carolina is the type locality (synonyms not included) follows:

Type Locality

Podilymbus podiceps podiceps (Linnaeus). Pied-billed Grebe........South Carolina
  Colymbus Podiceps Linnaeus, *Syst. Nat., Ed. 10, 1*: 1758, 136 (based on *Prodicipes minor rostro vario,* The Pied-Bill Dopchick, Catesby, *Nat. Hist. Carolina, 1*: 1731, 91).

Pelecanus occidentalis carolinensis Gmelin. Eastern Brown Pelican ....Charleston Harbor
  Pelecanus carolinensis Gmelin, *Syst. Nat., 1,* Pt. 2: 1789, 571.

Florida caerulea caerulea (Linnaeus). Little Blue Heron..........South Carolina
  Ardea caerulea Linnaeus, *Syst. Nat., Ed. 10, 1*: 1758, 143 (based on *Ardea caerulea,* The blew Heron, Catesby, *Nat. Hist. Carolina, 1*: 1731, 76).

Butorides virescens virescens (Linnaeus). Eastern Green Heron......South Carolina
  Ardea virescens Linnaeus, *Syst. Nat., Ed. 10, 1*: 1758, 144 (based on *Ardea stellaris minima,* The small Bittern, Catesby, *Nat. Hist. Carolina, 1*: 1731, 80).

Nyctanassa violacea violacea (Linnaeus). Yellow-crowned Night Heron...South Carolina
  Ardea violacea Linnaeus, *Syst. Nat., Ed. 10, 1*: 1758, 143 (based on *Ardea stellaris cristata Americana,* The crested Bittern, Catesby, *Nat. Hist. Carolina, 1*: 1731, 79).

Guara alba (Linnaeus). White Ibis..........................South Carolina
  (*Scolopax alba* Linnaeus, *Syst. Nat., Ed. 10, 1*: 1758, 145 (based on *Numenius albus,* The White Curlew, Catesby, *Nat. Hist. Carolina, 1*: 1731, 82).

Anas carolinensis Gmelin. Green-winged Teal..................South Carolina
  Anas carolinensis Gmelin, *Syst. Nat., 1,* Pt. 2: 1789, 533.

Type Locality

Anas discors Linnaeus. Blue-winged Teal......................South Carolina
  Anas discors Linnaeus, *Syst. Nat., Ed. 12, 1*: 1766, 205
  (based on *Querquedula Americana variegata*, The White-Face
  Teal, Catesby, *Nat. Hist. Carolina, 1*: 1731, 100).

Aix sponsa (Linnaeus). Wood Duck..........................South Carolina
  Anas Sponsa Linnaeus, *Syst. Nat., Ed. 10, 1*: 1758, 128 (based
  on *Anas Americanus cristatus elegans*, The Summer Duck,
  Catesby, *Nat. Hist. Carolina, 1*: 1731, 97).

Lophodytes cucullatus (Linnaeus). Hooded Merganser...........South Carolina
  Mergus cucullatus Linnaeus, *Syst. Nat., Ed. 10, 1*: 1758, 129
  (based on *Anas cristatus*, The round-crested Duck, Catesby,
  Nat. Hist. Carolina, 1: 1731, 94).

Elanoïdes forficatus forficatus (Linnaeus). Swallow-tailed
  Kite . . . . .South Carolina
  Falco forficatus Linnaeus, *Syst. Nat., Ed. 10, 1*: 1758, 89
  (based on *Accipiter cauda furcata*, The Swallow-Tail Hawk,
  Catesby, *Nat. Hist. Carolina, 1*: 1731, 4).

Buteo jamaicensis borealis (Gmelin). Eastern Red-tailed
  Hawk . . . . .South Carolina
  Falco borealis Gmelin, *Syst. Nat., 1*, Pt. 1: 1788, 266.

Haliaetus leucocephalus leucocephalus (Linnaeus). Southern
  Bald Eagle. . . . . .South Carolina
  Falco leucocephalus Linnaeus, *Syst. Nat., Ed. 12, 1*: 1766, 124
  (based on *Aquila capite albo*, The Bald Eagle, Catesby, *Nat.
  Hist. Carolina, 1*: 1731, 1).

Pandion haliaëtus carolinensis (Gmelin). Osprey...............South Carolina
  Falco Haliaëtos y carolinensis Gmelin, *Syst. Nat., 1*, Pt. 1:
  1788, 263 (based on *Accipiter piscatorius*, The Fishing Hawk,
  Catesby, *Nat. Hist. Carolina, 1*: 1731, 2).

Falco columbarius columbarius Linnaeus. Eastern Pigeon
  Hawk . . . . .South Carolina
  Falco columbarius Linnaeus, *Syst. Nat., Ed. 10, 1*: 1758, 90
  (based on *Accipiter palumbarius*, The Pigeon-Hawk, Catesby,
  Nat. Hist. Carolina, 1: 1731, 3).

Falco sparverius sparverius Linnaeus. Eastern Sparrow Hawk.......South Carolina
  Falco sparverius Linnaeus, *Syst. Nat., Ed. 10, 1*: 1758, 90
  (based on *Accipiter minor*, The Little Hawk, Catesby, *Nat.
  Hist. Carolina, 1*: 1731, 5).

Rallus elegans elegans Audubon. King Rail...................Charleston
  Rallus elegans Audubon, *Birds Amer.* Folio, 3: 1834, pl. 203.

Charadrius vociferus vociferus Linnaeus. Killdeer..............South Carolina
  Charadrius vociferus Linnaeus, *Syst. Nat., Ed. 10, 1*: 1758,
  150 (based on *Pluvialis vociferus*, The chattering Plover,
  Catesby, *Nat. Hist. Carolina, 1*: 1731, 71).

Type Locality

Rynchops nigra nigra Linnaeus. Black Skimmer.......................Coast of
    Rynchops nigra Linnaeus, *Syst. Nat., Ed. 10, 1*: 1758, 138   South Carolina
    (based on *Laurus major rostro inaequali,* The Cut Water,
    Catesby, *Nat. Hist. Carolina, 1*: 1731, 90).

Zenaidura macroura carolinensis (Linnaeus). Eastern Mourn-
    ing Dove...South Carolina
    Columba carolinensis Linnaeus, *Syst. Nat., Ed. 12, 1*: 1766,
    286 (based on *Turtur Carolinensis,* The Turtle of Carolina,
    Catesby, *Nat. Hist. Carolina, 1*: 1731, 24).

Ectopistes migratorius (Linnaeus). Passenger Pigeon..............South Carolina
    Columba migratoria Linnaeus, *Syst. Nat., Ed. 12, 1*: 1766,
    285 (based on *Palumbus migratorius,* The Pigeon of Passage,
    Catesby, *Nat. Hist. Carolina, 1*: 1731, 23).

Columbigallina passerina passerina (Linnaeus). Eastern Ground
    Dove ....South Carolina
    Columba passerina Linnaeus, *Syst. Nat., Ed. 10, 1*: 1758, 165
    (based on *Turtur minimus guttatus,* The Ground-Dove,
    Catesby, *Nat. Hist. Carolina, 1*: 1731, 26).

Conuropsis carolinensis carolinensis (Linnaeus). Carolina
    Paroquet ....South Carolina
    Psittacus carolinensis Linnaeus, *Syst. Nat., Ed. 10, 1*: 1758,
    97 (based on *Psitticus Caroliniensis,* The Parrot of Carolina,
    Catesby, *Nat. Hist. Carolina, 1*: 1731, 11).

Coccyzus americanus americanus (Linnaeus). Yellow-billed
    Cuckoo ....South Carolina
    Cuculus americanus Linnaeus, *Syst. Nat., Ed. 10, 1*: 1758,
    111 (based on *Cuculus Caroliniensis,* The Cuckow of Caro-
    lina, Catesby, *Nat. Hist. Carolina, 1*: 1731, 9).

Otus asio asio (Linnaeus). Southern Screech Owl................South Carolina
    Strix Asio Linnaeus, *Syst. Nat., Ed. 10, 1*: 1758, 92 (based
    on *Noctua aurita minor,* The Little Owl, Catesby, *Nat. Hist.
    Carolina, 1*: 1731, 7).

PLATE II: CYPRESS BACKWATER SCENE

Oil Painting by Francis Lee Jaques

Flying birds, left to right: Little Blue Heron (adult) and Little Blue Heron
(immature). On branch, upper right, left to right: Black-crowned Night Heron
(immature), Black-crowned Night Heron (adult), and Louisiana Heron. Standing
in water, left to right: Yellow-crowned Night Heron (adult) and Yellow-crowned
Night Heron (immature). Swimming, left to right: Wood Duck (male) and Wood
Duck (female).

Type Locality

Caprimulgus carolinensis Gmelin. Chuck-will's-widow . . . . South Carolina
    Caprimulgus carolinensis Gmelin, *Syst. Nat.*, *1*, Pt. 2: 1789,
    1028 (based on *Caprimulgus*, The Goat-Sucker of Carolina,
    Catesby, *Nat. Hist. Carolina*, *1*: 1731, 8).

Chordeiles minor minor (Forster). Eastern Nighthawk . . . . South Carolina
    Caprimulgus minor Forster, *Catal. Anim. N. Amer.*, 1771,
    13 (based on *Caprimulgus minor Americanus*, The Whip-poor-
    Will, Catesby, *Nat. Hist. Carolina*, *2*, Appendix: 1748, 16).

Chaetura pelagica (Linnaeus). Chimney Swift . . . . South Carolina
    Hirundo pelagica Linnaeus, *Syst. Nat.*, *Ed. 10*, *1*: 1758, 192
    (based on *Hirunda cauda aculeata Americana*, The American
    Swallow, Catesby, *Nat. Hist. Carolina*, *2*, Appendix: 1748, 8).

Archilochus colubris (Linnaeus). Ruby-throated Hummingbird . . . . . . South Carolina
    Trochilus Colubris Linnaeus, *Syst. Nat.*, *Ed. 10*, *1*: 1758,
    120 (based on *Mellivora avis Carolinensis*, The Humming-
    Bird, Catesby, *Nat. Hist. Carolina*, *1*: 1731, 65).

Megaceryle alcyon alcyon (Linnaeus). Eastern Belted King-
    fisher . . . . South Carolina
    Alcedo Alcyon Linnaeus, *Syst. Nat.*, *Ed. 10*, *1*: 1758, 115
    (based on *Ispida*, the King-Fisher, Catesby, *Nat. Hist. Caro-
    lina*, *1*: 1731, 69).

Colaptes auratus auratus (Linnaeus). Southern Flicker . . . . South Carolina
    Cuculus auratus Linnaeus, *Syst. Nat.*, *Ed. 10*, *1*: 1758, 112
    (based on *Picus major alis aureis*, The Gold-winged Wood-
    pecker, Catesby, *Nat. Hist. Carolina*, *1*: 1731, 18).

Dryocopus pileatus pileatus (Linnaeus) Southern Pileated
    Woodpecker . . . . South Carolina
    Picus pileatus Linnaeus, *Syst. Nat.*, *Ed. 10*, *1*: 1758, 113
    (based on *Picus niger maximus capite rubro*, The larger red-
    crested Wood-pecker, Catesby, *Nat. Hist. Carolina*, *1*: 1731,
    17).

Centurus carolinus carolinus (Linnaeus). Red-bellied Wood-
    pecker . . . . South Carolina
    Picus carolinus Linnaeus, *Syst. Nat.*, *Ed. 10*, *1*: 1758, 113
    (based on *Picus ventre rubro*, The Red-bellied Wood-pecker,
    Catesby, *Nat. Hist. Carolina*, *1*: 1731, 19).

Melanerpes erythrocephalus erythrocephalus (Linnaeus). Red-
    headed Woodpecker . . . . South Carolina
    Picus eyrthrocephalus Linnaeus, *Syst. Nat.*, *Ed. 10*, *1*: 1758,
    113 (based on *Picus capite toto rubro*, The Red-headed Wood-
    pecker, Catesby, *Nat. Hist. Carolina*, *1*: 1731, 20).

Sphyrapicus varius varius (Linnaeus). Yellow-bellied Sapsucker . . . . . . South Carolina
    Picus varius Linnaeus, *Syst. Nat.*, *Ed. 12*, *1*: 1766, 176
    (based on *Picus varius minor, ventro luteo*, The yellow belly'd
    Wood-pecker, Catesby, *Nat. Hist. Carolina*, *1*: 1731, 21).

Type Locality

Dendrocopos pubescens pubescens (Linnaeus). Southern Downy
Woodpecker . . . . .South Carolina
Picus pubescens Linnaeus, *Syst. Nat., Ed. 12, 1*: 1766, 175
(based on *Picus varius minimus*, The smallest spotted Woodpecker, Catesby, *Nat. Hist. Carolina, 1*: 1731, 21).

Dendrocopos borealis borealis (Vieillot). Red-cockaded Wood-
pecker . . . . .Mt. Pleasant
Picus borealis Vieillot, *Ois. Amer. Sept., 2*: 1808, 66.

Campephilus principalis (Linnaeus). Ivory-billed Woodpecker . . . . . .South Carolina
Picus principalis Linnaeus, *Syst. Nat., Ed. 10, 1*: 1758, 113
(based on *Picus maximus rostro albo*, The largest white-bill
Wood-pecker, Catesby, *Nat. Hist. Carolina, 1*: 1731, 16).

Tyrannus tyrannus (Linnaeus). Eastern Kingbird . . . . .South Carolina
Lanius Tyrannus Linnaeus, *Syst. Nat., Ed. 10, 1*: 1758, 94
(based on *Muscicapa corona rubra*, The Tyrant, Catesby, *Nat.
Hist. Carolina, 1*: 1731, 55).

Myiarchus crinitus crinitus (Linnaeus). Southern Crested Fly-
catcher . . . . .South Carolina
Turdus crinitus Linnaeus, *Syst. Nat., Ed. 10, 1*: 1758, 170
(based on *Muscicapa cristata ventre luteo*, The Crested Fly-
Catcher, Catesby, *Nat. Hist. Carolina, 1*: 1731, 52).

Contopus virens (Linnaeus). Eastern Wood Pewee . . . . .South Carolina
Muscicapa virens Linnaeus, *Syst. Nat., Ed. 12, 1*: 1766, 327
(based on *Muscicapa Carolinensis cinerea, Le Gobemouche
cendré de la Caroline*, Brisson, *Orn., 2*: 1760, 368).

Eremophila alpestris alpestris (Linnaeus). Northern Horned
Lark . . . . .South Carolina
Alauda alpestris Linnaeus, *Syst. Nat., Ed. 10, 1*: 1758, 166
(based on *Alauda gutture flavo*, The Lark, Catesby, *Nat. Hist.
Carolina, 1*: 1731, 32).

Stelgidopteryx ruficollis serripennis (Audubon). Rough-winged
Swallow . . . . .Charleston
Hirundo serripennis Audubon, *Orn. Biog., 4*: 1838, 593.

Cyanocitta cristata cristata (Linnaeus). Florida Blue Jay . . . . .South Carolina
Corvus cristatus Linnaeus, *Syst. Nat., Ed. 10, 1*: 1758, 106
(based on *Pica glandaria caerulea cristata*, The Blew Jay,
Catesby, *Nat. Hist. Carolina, 1*: 1731, 15).

Parus carolinensis carolinensis Audubon. Carolina Chickadee . . . . .Charleston
Parus carolinensis Audubon, *Orn. Biog., 2*: 1834, 341.

Parus bicolor Linnaeus. Tufted Titmouse .South Carolina
Parus bicolor Linnaeus, *Syst. Nat., Ed. 12, 1*: 1766, 340
(based on *Parus cristatus*, The crested Titmouse, Catesby, *Nat.
Hist. Carolina, 1*: 1731, 57).

TYPE LOCALITY LIST

Type Locality

Sitta carolinensis carolinensis Latham. Florida Nuthatch . . . . South Carolina
  Sitta carolinensis Latham, *Index Orn.*, *1*: 1790, 262.

Sitta pusilla pusilla Latham. Brown-headed Nuthatch . . . . South Carolina
  Sitta pusilla Latham, *Index Orn.*, *1*: 1790, 263.

Telmatodytes palustris waynei Dingle and Sprunt. Wayne's
  Marsh Wren . . . . Mt. Pleasant
  Telmatodytes palustris waynei Dingle and Sprunt, *Auk*, *49*:
  1932, 454.

Cistothorus platensis stellaris (Naumann). Short-billed Marsh
  Wren . . . . South Carolina
  Troglodytes stellaris Naumann, *Vögel Deutschl.*, *3*: 1823, table
  to p. 724. ("Carolina"; now restricted to South Carolina).

Toxostoma rufum rufum (Linnaeus). Brown Thrasher . . . . South Carolina
  Turdus rufus Linnaeus, *Syst. Nat.*, *Ed. 10*, *1*: 1758, 169
  (based on *Turdus ruffus*, The Fox coloured Thrush, Catesby,
  Nat. Hist. Carolina, *1*: 1731, 28).

Turdus migratorius migratorius Linnaeus. Eastern Robin . . . . South Carolina
  Turdus migratorius Linnaeus, *Syst. Nat.*, *Ed. 12*, *1*: 1766,
  292 (based on *Turdus pilaris*, *migratorius*, The Fieldfare of
  Carolina, Catesby, *Nat. Hist. Carolina*, *1*: 1731, 29).

Sialia sialis sialis (Linnaeus). Eastern Bluebird . . . . South Carolina
  Motacilla Sialis Linnaeus, *Syst. Nat.*, *Ed. 10*, *1*: 1758, 187
  (based on *Rubicula Americana caerulea*, The Blew Bird,
  Catesby, *Nat. Hist. Carolina*, *1*: 1731, 47).

Vireo olivaceus (Linnaeus). Red-eyed Vireo . . . . South Carolina
  Muscicapa olivacea Linnaeus, *Syst. Nat.*, *Ed. 12*, *1*: 1766, 327
  (based on *Muscicapa oculis rubris*, The red-Ey'd Fly-catcher,
  Catesby, *Nat. Hist. Carolina*, *1*: 1731, 54).

Limnothlypis swainsonii (Audubon). Swainson's Warbler . . . . Edisto River,
  Sylvia Swainsonii Audubon, *Birds Amer.*, Folio, *2*: 1834, pl.   near Charleston
  198.

Vermivora bachmanii (Audubon). Bachman's Warbler . . . . a few miles
  Sylvia Bachmanii Audubon, *Birds Amer.*, Folio, *2*: 1833, pl.   from Charleston
  185.

Parula americana americana (Linnaeus). Southern Parula
  Warbler . . . . South Carolina
  Parus americanus Linnaeus, *Syst. Nat.*, *Ed. 10*, *1*: 1758, 190
  (based on *Parus fringillaris*, The Finch-Creeper, Catesby, *Nat.
  Hist. Carolina*, *1*: 1731, 64).

Dendroica virens waynei Bangs. Wayne's Warbler . . . . near Mt. Pleasant
  Dendroica virens waynei Bangs, *Proc. New England Zoöl.
  Club*, *6*: 1918, 94.

Type Locality

Icteria virens virens (Linnaeus). Yellow-breasted Chat..........South Carolina,
    Turdus virens Linnaeus, *Syst. Nat., Ed. 10, 1:* 1758, 171 200 or 300 miles
    (based on *Oenanthe Americana pectore luteo,* The yellow   from the sea
    brested Chat, Catesby, *Nat. Hist. Carolina, 1:* 1731, 50).

Dolichonyx oryzivorus (Linnaeus). Bobolink...................South Carolina
    Fringilla oryzivora Linnaeus, *Syst. Nat., Ed. 10, 1:* 1758, 179
    (based on *Hortulanus Caroliniensis,* The Rice-Bird, Catesby,
    Nat. Hist. Carolina, 1: 1731, 14).

Sturnella magna magna (Linnaeus). Eastern Meadowlark........South Carolina
    Alauda magna Linnaeus, *Syst. Nat., Ed. 10, 1:* 1758, 167
    (based on *Alauda magna,* The large Lark, Catesby, *Nat. Hist.
    Carolina, 1:* 1731, 33).

Agelaius phoeniceus phoeniceus (Linnaeus). Eastern Red-wing.....South Carolina
    Oriolus phoeniceus Linnaeus, *Syst. Nat., Ed. 12, 1:* 1766, 161
    (based on *Sturnus niger alis superne rubentibus,* The red
    wing'd Starling, Catesby, *Nat. Hist. Carolina, 1:* 1731, 13).

Icterus spurius (Linnaeus). Orchard Oriole.....................South Carolina
    Oriolus spurius Linnaeus, *Syst. Nat., Ed. 12, 1:* 1766, 162
    (based on *Icterus minor,* The Bastard Baltimore, Catesby, *Nat.
    Hist. Carolina, 1:* 1731, 49).

Euphagus carolinus carolinus (Müller). Rusty Blackbird..............Charleston
    Turdus Carolinus Müller, *Natursyst. Suppl.,* 1776, 140
    (based on *Mauvis de la Caroline,* Daubenton, *Pl. Enl.,* pl. 556,
    fig. 2 [female in autumn]).

Quiscalus quiscula quiscula (Linnaeus). Florida Grackle..........South Carolina
    Gracula Quiscula Linnaeus, *Syst. Nat., Ed. 10, 1:* 1758, 109
    (based on *Monedula purpurea,* The Purple Jack-Daw, Catesby,
    Nat. Hist. Carolina, 1: 1731, 12).

Molothrus ater ater (Boddaert). Eastern Cowbird...............South Carolina
    Oriolus ater Boddaert, *Tabl. Pl. Enl.,* 1783, 37 (based on
    Troupiale, de la Caroline, Daubenton, *Pl. Enl.,* pl. 606, fig. 1).

Piranga rubra rubra (Linnaeus). Summer Tanager..............South Carolina
    Fringilla rubra Linnaeus, *Syst. Nat., Ed. 10, 1:* 1758, 181
    (based on *Muscicapa rubra,* The Summer Red-Bird, Catesby,
    Nat. Hist. Carolina, 1: 1731, 56).

Richmondena cardinalis cardinalis (L i n n a e u s). Eastern
    Cardinal ....South Carolina
    Loxia Cardinalis Linnaeus, *Syst. Nat., Ed. 10, 1:* 1758, 172
    (based on *Coccothraustes ruber,* The red Bird, Catesby, *Nat.
    Hist. Carolina, 1:* 1731, 38).

Guiraca caerulea caerulea (Linnaeus). Eastern Blue Grosbeak......South Carolina
    Loxia caerulea Linnaeus, *Syst. Nat., Ed. 10, 1:* 1758, 175
    (based on *Coccothraustes caerulea,* The blew Gross-beak,
    Catesby, *Nat. Hist. Carolina, 1:* 1731, 39).

TYPE LOCALITY LIST

Passerina cyanea (Linnaeus). Indigo Bunting.................South Carolina
　　Tanagra cyanea Linnaeus, *Syst. Nat.*, Ed. 12, 1: 1766, 315,
　　(based on *Linaria caerulea*, The blew Linnet, Catesby, *Nat.*
　　Hist. Carolina, 1: 1731, 45).

Passerina ciris ciris (Linnaeus). Painted Bunting..............South Carolina
　　Emberiza Ciris Linnaeus, *Syst. Nat.*, Ed. 10, 1: 1758, 179
　　(based on *Fringilla tricolor*, The Painted Finch, Catesby, *Nat.*
　　Hist. Carolina, 1: 1731, 44).

Carpodacus purpureus purpureus (Gmelin). Eastern Purple
　　Finch ....Charleston
　　Fringilla purpurea Gmelin, *Syst. Nat.*, 1, Pt. 2: 1789, 923
　　(based on *Pyrrhula carolinensis violacea*, Brisson, *Orn.*, 3:
　　1760, 324, No. 8; *Fringilla purpurea*, The Purple Finch,
　　Catesby, *Nat. Hist. Carolina*, 1: 1731, 41).

Spinus tristis tristis (Linnaeus). Eastern Goldfinch..............South Carolina
　　Fringilla tristis Linnaeus, *Syst. Nat.*, Ed. 10, 1: 1758, 181
　　(based on *Carduelis Americanus*, The American Goldfinch,
　　Catesby, *Nat. Hist. Carolina*, 1: 1731, 43).

Pipilo erythrophthalmus erythrophthalmus (Linnaeus). Red-
　　eyed Towhee...South Carolina
　　Fringilla erythrophthalma Linnaeus, *Syst. Nat.*, Ed. 10, 1:
　　1758, 180 (based on *Passer niger, oculis rubris*, The Towhe-
　　bird, Catesby, *Nat. Hist. Carolina*, 1: 1731, 34).

Ammospiza maritima macgillivraii (Audubon). Macgillivray's
　　Seaside Sparrow...Charleston
　　Fringilla Macgillivraii Audubon, *Orn. Biog.*, 2: 1834, 285.

Aimophila aestivalis bachmani (Audubon). Bachman's Sparrow......Parker's Ferry,
　　Fringilla Bachmani Audubon, *Birds Amer.*, 2: 1833, pl. 165.　　Edisto River

Junco hyemalis hyemalis (Linnaeus). Slate-colored Junco........South Carolina
　　Fringilla hyemalis Linnaeus, *Syst. Nat.*, Ed. 10, 1: 1758, 183
　　(based on *Passer nivalis*, The Snow-bird, Catesby, *Nat. Hist.*
　　Carolina, 1: 1731, 36).

The Region

WHILE birds enjoy a relatively wide adaptation to environment, it will nevertheless be helpful to offer a brief description of the area covered by this treatise, the State of South Carolina.

South Carolina is one of the smaller states, being thirty-ninth in size among the forty-eight. It is fairly representative of the South as a whole in both flora and fauna. Roughly triangular in shape, it lies between 32°, 2′ and 35°, 7′ north latitude and 70°, 30′ and 83°, 20′ west longitude and contains slightly over thirty thousand square miles. The climate is mild and fairly uniform, due in part to the proximity of the Gulf Stream and in part to the wide coastal plain. Temperature varies slightly between Charleston on the Atlantic coast and Greenville at the foot of the mountains. This mean variation, however, is seldom more than four or five degrees, temperature for the whole State averaging about 50° F. in January and 80° F. in midsummer. Extremes of 100° in summer and 20° in winter are experienced perhaps two or three times a year. Rainfall averages close to 50 inches annually, being a little more on the coast and a little less toward the mountains. The climate is thus seen to be considerably milder than that of Virginia but not as truly sub-tropical as Florida. The Camellia japonica, the Azalea, and other exotic plants thrive everywhere except in the narrow mountain region.

The State embraces three distinct topographic areas, the Coastal Plain, or Low-country as it has been called since colonial times, the Up-country or Piedmont, and the Blue Ridge Mountains in the northwestern corner.

The Low-country extends from the coast to the fall line, a ridge of sand hills and shoals which bisects the State from Cheraw to Augusta.

THE COASTAL PLAIN

The Coastal Plain is much the largest natural division and contains an abundance of vegetable and animal life. It is a part of the great Atlantic Coastal

Plain, wide, low, and level, and is commonly referred to as the Low-country. Several rivers cross it, running southeasterly, among them the Pee Dee, Lynch's, Black, Santee, Edisto, and Salkehatchie, the famous "rice rivers" of other days. The largest river system is that of the Santee, which virtually splits the State in the center, being formed by the confluence of the Congaree and Wateree below the fall line.

FIGURE ONE: SOUTH CAROLINA

The coast line of South Carolina extends for 281 miles, being indented by several bays, harbors, and sounds, some of large size, notably Winyah and Bull's Bays, Charleston Harbor, and St. Helena and Port Royal Sounds.

Because of the frequency with which the Coast Region figures in this book, and its great importance in bird life, it seems advisable further to break it down into subdivisions which differ from each other to a considerable degree. Working inland from the ocean, the subdivisions are as follows: Island Area; Salt Marshes; Swamp Area; Ricefield Area; Mainland.

The Island Area is further divided into Barrier Beaches and Sea Islands.

Barrier Beaches

Barrier beaches are long, narrow strips which actually front the ocean itself. Many of them are bordered by dense vegetation, of almost jungle proportions. The beaches themselves are wide and gently sloping, being divided from each other by deep, narrow inlets. The Barriers begin just south of the mouth of the Santee River, about midway of the coastline, and continue practically to the Savannah River. Typical of them are Bull's Island, Isle of Palms, Kiawah, and Big Bay Islands (Edisto Beach).

Parallel ridges of sand dunes appear at high-water mark, behind which the jungle begins, covering the strip until it meets the salt marsh on the inside edge, or back beach. Characteristic of vegetation are sea oats, beach croton, and marsh pennywort, these being predominantly dune growth. The woods are replete with palmettoes, live oaks, magnolias, and loblolly pines, together with a profusion of such vines as smilax, holly, yellow jessamine, and wild grape.

Undergrowth of shrubby plants occurs in the woods, as well as in the open area between these and the beach dunes, and along the back beach. Thoroughly characteristic are the wax myrtle, cassina, and sea myrtle or high-tide bush. Some of the islands have fresh water ponds which support native growth such as cat-tails, bullrushes, wild rice, and pond-weed.

Sea Islands

The sea islands are large, irregularly shaped and, despite their name, do not front the ocean. They lie directly behind the barrier islands, separated therefrom by the salt marshes and winding creeks and rivers. These islands have been under cultivation for generations and are the site of many of the finest Low-country plantations, past and present. They are the home of "sea-island cotton," the famous long staple, now wiped out by the boll weevil. Large areas have been cleared but patches of woodland are still common, the loblolly pine being a characteristic growth, together with the live oak and the sweet gum. The sea islands appear just south of Charleston Harbor and continue southward. Typical of them are James, John's, Wadmalaw, Edisto, and St. Helena Islands. The total Island Area embraces some 800 square miles.

Salt Marshes

The salt marshes are vast stretches of open mud-flats, oyster-banks, creeks, rivers, and estuaries, dotted occasionally with small "hammocks" or slight rises, supporting yuccas, myrtle, cassina, and sometimes small oaks and palmettoes. Much of the area is uniformly and densely grown with the typical marsh grass. Some open sand-mud flat areas support considerable glasswort and sea myrtle.

The salt marshes occur mainly south of the Santee River and embrace an area of 600 square miles. North of the Santee the area of salt marsh narrows considerably and all but disappears back of the Horry strand. From Myrtle Beach to Little River there is only a narrow strip of marsh, chiefly along the Inland Waterway. The beautiful strand is almost unbroken for miles, with a tidal creek or "swash" cutting inland at long intervals.

Swamp Area

The fresh-water swamps of the Low-country are great reservoirs of wildlife. Their situation, vegetation, and abundant natural food produce conditions ideally suited to the needs of a variety of species. They are located on the edge of and beyond the influence of the tides, and not only line the borders of the rivers but occur as heavily forested bottomlands between the numerous streams.

Outstanding trees of the river swamps are the bald cypress and tupelo gum. Mixtures of other growth are quite common but not so thoroughly characteristic. Along some of the river banks is found the unusual Walter's or spruce pine. Extensive brakes of swamp cane and tangles of vines are abundant. The Spanish moss of the Low-country abounds in these swamps, imparting that tropical aspect which so impresses observers. This growth is an outright air plant, and not parasitic as many think. It takes nothing whatsover from the tree on which it grows, and is a member of the Pineapple family.

Ricefield Area

The Carolina ricefields are reminders of a golden era upon which the sun has set forever. On the "glory that was rice" was founded the great plantation culture, which not only made its product known the country over, but contributed so much to the gracious manner of living of the ante-bellum Carolina Low-country. Although few of the splendid old manorial homes still stand, there are numerous examples of the fields which made them possible. Many of these are maintained now much as they used to be, but for a different reason. Instead of the golden rows of rice there are now open stretches of water and clumps of aquatic vegetation which attract ducks by the thousand, for many of the present owners are sportsmen. Fields, canals, trunks, and dykes are kept up because of duck shooting.

Ricefields fall into two categories, river and inland types. The former are those along the portions of the great coastal rivers in which the fresh water of these streams rises and falls because of tidal influence. The fields themselves are blocked off from the river by dykes, or banks, are criss-crossed by canals, and are capable of being flooded or drained by means of water-gates or "trunks" opening into the river.

The inland fields were redeemed swamp lands but the water, necessary to rice growing, instead of coming from rivers, was available from impounded reservoirs in the swamps, called "backwaters" or "reserves." These great lagoons form one of the most impressive and beautiful characteristics of the coast country. Often grown up in huge, buttressed, moss-bannered cypresses, the more open areas support masses of water-lilies, lotus, and wampee, together with clumps of willow and buttonbush.

Such a spot is Blake's Reserve on the property of the Santee Gun Club near McClellanville, the site of what is probably the oldest egret rookery in continued use in the country, records of it going back to 1823. Another such is the reserve at Dean Hall Plantation, Cooper River, now owned by Benjamin Kittredge and familiar to many thousands as Cypress Gardens. Still another is beautiful Mayrant Backwater, Fairlawn Plantation, Charleston County, the site of one of the largest White Ibis colonies in the State.

Mainland

This division is self-explanatory. Much of it consists of agricultural lands on which cotton and many kinds of vegetables are grown. Farms and plantations are numerous, as also are pastures and wide stretches of woodlands. A striking characteristic is the great reaches of pineland, once largely composed of the splendid long-leaf pine, now mainly loblolly. Undergrowth is at a minimum under these trees, long aisles stretching back between the trunks in the dim distance.

The heart of South Carolina is the Middle-country, geographically a part of the Low-country, culturally allied to both Tidewater and Piedmont. Here in ante-bellum times the great plantations gradually gave place to smaller holdings as one travelled toward the fall line. Nevertheless estates of a thousand acres or more were not unusual. There were fewer rice fields, yet ancient dams and trunks exist far up the Pee Dee and even the Wateree and Congaree. Indigo was for many years the chief money crop, then cotton. Hence there are numerous "old fields" now overgrown with sweet gum, sassafras, persimmon, and loblolly pine. Black-water streams, such as the Edisto, Black River and Black Creek, originating in the sand hills, flow through dark, peaty soil. Their swamps are relatively narrow but afford cover for wildlife. The great yellow streams, bringing down tons of silt from the Piedmont, flow through wide, fertile valleys, their vast swamps furnishing the last stand of the Wild Turkey. Here the noblest trees are cypress, black and tupelo gum. On the ridges are scaly-bark hickory, water and willow oak, ash and loblolly pine. A tangle of vines—smilax, wild grape, crossvine and poison ivy—often impedes the progress of the hunter or naturalist. Especially is this true where the timber has been recently cut.

No description of this section would be complete without mention of the bays, those peculiar depressions in the earth's surface thought by some to have resulted from meteoric action ages ago. These are most numerous in Horry and adjacent counties, but occur, in fact, all over the Coastal Plain. They are generally elliptical in outline, contain a lake of fresh water with a sandy beach at one end and a border of gum, cypress and very dense undergrowth. In places the smilax makes a veritable wall, to be penetrated only with briar hook or machete.

THE PIEDMONT

Just above the fall line we enter the Piedmont region, or Up-country. It must not be thought, however, that this transition is abrupt, for, except for the rocky shoals in the beds of the rivers, it is a tortuous, serrated line which divides the two regions. The sand hills extend far down into the Coastal Plain, like long boring fingers, and there are places where Spanish moss and the scrub palmetto grow well into the country of red clay and granite boulders. Nevertheless the typical Piedmont country is easy to recognize. Its surface is rolling and rocky, and the soil is chiefly a sticky red clay.

The geology of the Piedmont is exceedingly complex, its ancient rocks—some of them among the oldest in North America—being both igneous and sedimentary in origin. These rocks, except a few of the more resistant, were eventually worn down to form a level plain, very little above the sea level. Later the plain was uplifted and tilted and valleys were cut into it. Divides between the larger valleys are nearly level and represent the remnants of the old plain. Knowledge of this geological background is necessary to a full understanding of the Piedmont as it exists today.

The river valleys of the Piedmont are narrow, instead of forming wide swamps as in the Low-country. Rocks and boulders are everywhere. The gently sloping sand hills give place to rugged masses of iron-bearing red clay, many of them now, alas! bare and gullied from erosion. Where vestiges of the forest remain the dominant trees are the white oak, the hickory, and the loblolly pine, the latter gradually giving place to the shortleaf pine as one approaches the mountains. In the river valleys are black gums, sweet gums, maples, and willows. The chestnut once was plentiful over the upper part of this area, as well as in the mountains, but is now completely extinct. Except for artificial hydro-electric developments such as Lake Murray, Parr Shoals, and Buzzard's Roost, there are no large bodies of water. On these, however, and on the many ancient mill ponds, some migrating waterfowl are temporary residents. Even such typically Low-country birds as the coot and the marsh hen are occasionally found and gulls are fairly common along the shore of Lake Murray.

While by no means as rich in wild life as is the Coastal Plain, the Piedmont still offers much for the student of nature in general and of bird life in particular.

MOUNTAIN REGION

The mountain region is much the smallest division, being barely more than a narrow strip running north and east from the apex of the triangle at the North Carolina and Georgia lines. Here an outlying span of the Blue Ridge lies inside the Palmetto State. No great elevation is attained, but there are at least three peaks each in excess of 3,000 feet, the highest being Sassafras Mountain in Pickens County. Caesar's Head, a remarkable outcropping of rock, reminiscent of a gigantic human profile, is perhaps the best known spot in the mountain region, though Table Rock Park now rivals it as a vacation resort.

Here both flora and fauna are alpine rather than sub-tropical. The trees are more like those of New England than of coastal Carolina. The white pine abounds as do the Carolina and common hemlock, the sourwood, and the cucumber tree. As in New England the butternut tree, a relative of the black walnut, is found here. White oaks, chestnut oaks, and hickories are plentiful. Greybeard, leucothoe, philadelphus, mountain laurel, and rhododendron abound.

South Carolina's mountains are surpassed by few areas in interest and beauty. Their presence makes it possible for South Carolinians to boast of an amazing variety of scenery, flora, and fauna within the borders of their State. Indeed few other states offer such a wide range of delights to the lover of nature.

Such then is South Carolina, the avian hunting grounds of Catesby, Bachman, Loomis, and Wayne. This is the region to which American ornithology owes so much, where so many still come to see and enjoy the bounties which have made it what it is.

On Studying Birds

Birds can never be adequately understood unless considered in relation to their environment. This fact is so generally disregarded that it is important to call attention to it. After one has begun to study birds the fact becomes apparent that certain species cannot be expected to occur except under more or less definite conditions and in a suitable locality. One cannot expect to find a covey of Bobwhites in a salt marsh or a brace of Mallards nesting in a chimney. Nevertheless, so little importance is attached by many people to this simple fundamental that they are often disappointed and become discouraged. A working knowledge of habitat is therefore essential.

By habitat is of course meant the immediate environment—the specific terrain a particular bird utilizes to find its food, build its nest, and rear its young. If a bird is adapted to a particular habitat it is unlikely to occur outside of it except under unusual conditions. However, the word habitat must be rather broadly construed, since there is always considerable latitude as to the sum total of conditions which constitutes this. For example, a particular wader may prefer salt water, accept brackish water, and tolerate fresh water. A woodland species may reach its greatest abundance in pine barrens, but be fairly plentiful in a hardwood forest.

Changes of habitat inevitably bring changes in bird life. This is one reason why birds become scarce in places which once harbored many, or abundant in localities where they had not been noted previously. Such changes are often the work of man. Clearing of forest lands and subsequent cultivation have resulted in greatly increasing the population of some birds while reducing that of others. The Mockingbird, for instance, a dweller of open bushy countryside, hedgerows, towns, and cities, is now probably more abundant than when it was observed by Mark Catesby in the vicinity of Charleston in 1722. This was then largely forest land which the Mockingbird does not frequent. The change was beneficial to the bird.

On the other hand there are, alas! many examples of a bird's disappearing from an environment which has not essentially changed at all, either by man's influence or otherwise. A case in point is the now extinct Great Auk. Funk Island off Newfoundland, where this bird once occurred in great numbers, has not changed as a result of our civilization. The bird itself, however, was the only flightless recent species in North America, performing its migrations along the Atlantic coast by swimming. Its feathers and its oil were desired by man and the vulnerable birds were slaughtered in such numbers as to wipe them from the earth. An even better example would be the disappearance of the Passenger Pigeon, except that in the latter case there was more change in the physical environment. Its fate was sealed by wanton commercial annihilation of the bird and by its inability to survive except in colonies. There are men still living in South Carolina who shot wild pigeons in their boyhood and still marvel at the bird's seemingly limitless numbers. There are hunters today who resent the decreasing bag limit on doves, who fight protective legislation, who resent the duck stamp. Can it be that their grandchildren will say, "There are no more doves; my father used to tell me about the big doveshoots he attended, how at the end of the day they'd count eighty, or a hundred or four hundred doves shot over a baited field"?

Again, a bird may become excessively rare or even extinct because of a man-made change in its environment, without having ever been an especial object of sport or persecution. An example is the Everglade Kite, now very rare in the United States. It is an inhabitant of the fresh-water marshes of Florida and is such a specialized feeder that it subsists on practically a single item of diet, a large snail of the genus *Pomacea*. Man appears with his bulldozers and draglines and drains a marsh where the snail lives and the kites congregate. The snail disappears and the kite vanishes, without an ounce of powder or shot having been expended. We too often disregard the kind of country we are dealing with in our so-called "improvements" and, in altering it to conform to our mechanical age, we do away forever with the great natural asset of wild life that it supported.

The kind of country inhabited by a given bird has been stressed in this book, yet perhaps, even here, not stressed enough. In direct relation to this thought it must be remembered that a bird or, indeed, any form of wild life occurs in a certain locality because that locality fills a definite need. Much of that need is connected directly with the vegetation of the area. Plants are absolutely vital to birds, as they are to human beings. Recently biologists have come to recognize localities harboring certain plants, animals, birds, reptiles, etc., under the term *wildlife community* or *association*. Everything in such a community is inter-related, each depending on the other to maintain a satisfactory balance of life. The terrain may be flat or hilly, wet, dry or damp; it may be grassy, bushy, grown in saplings or small trees, or it may be a dense forest. In each such habitat certain kinds of plants occur that are typical of the particular community and there, likewise, the birds belonging thereto will be found. Hence one will find Prairie Warblers in a dry, bushy community but will not encounter them in heavy forests.

These communities may change with time, with or without interference by man. Sometimes the open, dry, grass-covered stretches will become grown up with bushes and saplings. These, in turn, may give way to larger trees and eventually the area may become a forest. Thus the bird life in such areas will change also along with other differences, although such a change is generally a slow one, measured in decades or even centuries, rather than in years. Fallow land is first an "old field" overgrown with broomsedge and harboring Field Sparrows, Meadowlarks and a covey or two of Bobwhites. Then, when the boy who once roamed it with his slingshot is an old man and wanders back over it, he is likely to find loblolly pines covering the old field, with here and there a persimmon tree or a red haw. And crows are now nesting in the tallest of the pines and he hears the cheerful notes of the Flicker—only he has always called him a Yellow-hammer. And when his son, in turn, treads in his father's footsteps, there is scarcely a trace left to indicate that the place was once a field, except if he looks carefully he may still see signs of furrows. Then a sawmill will inevitably come and the pines, now larger than a stout man's body, will be cut down and their tops left to rot or burn. Then the wildlife community will change once more, perhaps duplicating again the condition of the "old field" with its broomsedge and its briars, its cottontails and its Field Sparrows.

The habitat of a given species is the setting, the background that enables one to know where to expect a particular bird. But all this is of little value unless the bird itself be identified. Late in the 19th century, when a wider interest in bird study was beginning to take hold of people, Dr. Frank M. Chapman published his splendid *Handbook of Birds of Eastern North America,* an excellent introduction to identification. Dr. Chapman, probably more than any other man in this century, popularized bird study as a sport or hobby. Since his day the tools of identification have increased both in number and in quality, excellent field guides, manuals and other useful books and magazines now being available to the student.

While identification is, of course, of prime importance, modern study goes a great deal farther than simply acquiring the ability to recognize species. After identification, the question "Why is that bird?" becomes nearly as important as "What is that bird?" What niche does it fill in the whole, balanced economy of nature? What relation does it bear to other forms of life?

Much work in recent years has been devoted to the study of "behavior." Why does a bird do this, or that? Why does it build its nest in a certain way, or in a certain place? Why are certain actions and procedures characteristic of one species but not of others? Concerning such questions we know comparatively little, but naturalists are beginning more carefully to investigate them.

Aristotle, Pliny, and many others among the ancients were interested in and studied the life histories of birds; in fact, this was the very first kind of bird study. The technical study of specimens began much later, but in time it largely supplanted the older form, and for centuries bird study has largely been concentrated on dead specimens. Such things as color changes, moults, measurements, color patterns, etc., can be determined only through collecting and examining the specimens themselves. Although much remains to be learned about the physical characteristics of birds, a great deal more is known about them than about the "why" of so many phases of bird life, the reasons which underlie so much bird behavior.

There are, however, many pitfalls in the consideration of bird behavior into which the uninformed are prone to fall. The most common of these is the tendency to endow birds with human characteristics, this often resulting in mawkish sentimentality. Birds are completely creatures of instinct and do not "think" about what they do or why they do it. The attributing of human characteristics to animals is as old as history, and has always been the chief stock in trade of the nature faker, who does a great deal of harm both to technical and popular study by spreading erroneous information.

Many people cannot view with anything but horror the killing of one bird or other animal by another. The hawk that seizes a young cardinal from a nest has done nothing more or less than the cat does when it catches a mouse; both acts are perfectly natural, carried out in accordance with the dictates of nature. And yet the hawk is branded as a murderer of innocents, an indefensible outlaw. Of course, even greater wrath is aroused when a bird's interests come in conflict with those of man; when, for instance, an eagle takes a duck which a hunter is trying to kill, the predator is condemned out of hand.

The term "biological balance" has been much used in recent years, and it is an important thing to comprehend. If depredations such as the taking of the cardinal by the hawk did not take place, the result would not be a wildlife Utopia but rather an inconceivably bad, perhaps an impossible situation. It is possible that if bird life were not kept in balance through this and other means the world would become literally smothered in birds.

The person who rids himself of sentimentality and who approaches the study of the behavior of birds in the spirit of true scientific investigation will find such study enormously rewarding. When interest in birds goes beyond their

PLATE III: WHITE IBISES OVER MARSH

Oil Painting by Francis Lee Jaques

physical appearance and seeks to penetrate the mysteries of behavior, then new and enchanting horizons appear.

Little equipment is necessary for bird study, but that little is essential. After outing clothes, which one may choose with a variety of tastes, one should possess a good pair of binoculars. Buying cheap binoculars is poor economy. Good ones are expensive but are a lifetime investment. The ideal glass is one having a magnification power of seven or eight. Thus the distance separating the observer from the bird is divided seven or eight times. If, for example, you are watching a warbler 35 feet away with a seven-power glass the bird will appear to be only 5 feet away. The immense advantage is obvious. All the better class modern binoculars have coated lenses, an improvement developed during World War II which greatly reduces reflection and gives brilliant illumination on the object.

Note taking is vitally important. It is impossible to remember all the things one observes in the field. Therefore take notes and plenty of them. Keep a "life list" and, as it grows, so will your interest and desire to add to it. Dates of arrival and departure of migrants, first nestings, species which come to your feeding tray, all such data should be written down and filed. As one progresses with such work increased knowledge and pleasure will result.

Sharing one's interest is another way to increase it. Kindred spirits naturally enjoy one another. It is good for enthusiasts in any line to get together and learn from each other. The existence of many bird clubs throughout the country is a healthy phenomenon and every student, no matter how young or how old, is advised to join such an organization.

There are national organizations of much wider scope than the local groups. These are more likely to be informed on conservation problems and methods. One or more should be selected and joined. For amateurs and professionals there is the American Ornithologists' Union, an old and honored group dealing somewhat more with the technical rather than the popular aspect of birds. The National Audubon Society is the foremost conservation organization of popular appeal. It has done, and is doing, much in the preservation of bird life. The South Carolina Academy of Science is another organization of more restricted regional interest. Finally there may be the local group in your town or city. Identify yourself with it and lend it your support. If there is no such club or society where you live, start one; much can be gained thereby.

Order Gaviiformes
Loons

Family Gaviidae: Loons

1. COMMON LOON: *Gavia immer immer* (Brünnich)　(7)

(Lat., *Gavia*, a bird, probably a gull; *immer*, Norwegian name of this bird.)

LOCAL NAMES: Big Diver.

DESCRIPTION: Length 28.00 to 36.00 inches. Bill long, stout, sharply pointed, black. *Summer.* Head, neck, and throat black, with narrow white streaks on throat and sides of neck; back black with numerous square white spots; under parts pure white. *Winter.* Back fuscous, the feathers edged with gray; head and neck sooty; under parts white.

RANGE: Breeds north to northern Alaska, Greenland, Iceland, and Jan Mayen Island; south to southern Alaska and Massachusetts. Winters north to the Great Lakes, Nova Scotia, and the North Sea; south to Washington, southern Louisiana, southern Florida, Madeira, and the Black Sea.

STATUS IN S. C.: Common winter resident, October 17 to May 13, casually July 5; in the coast region in winter, but in the interior mainly during migration. Recorded north to Chester County and Chesterfield County; east to Horry County; south to Beaufort County; west to Anderson County.

HISTORY: Through the cold months, off-shore beyond the breakers of the surf, one may see a large, dark-backed, white-breasted bird riding the waves and often disappearing beneath them in clean dives. It looks like a gigantic grebe and, in a sense, so it is, for the loons and grebes are closely related. The water is the Common Loon's natural element and there it excels; it is a strong flier as well, but on land it is comparatively helpless because of its peculiar structure. The feet are placed very far back, and as a result the bird cannot easily walk; it often simply pushes along on its breast in a most awkward manner. It must be in the water in order to take flight.

It is in no sense a game bird and is seldom shot locally, for the flesh is very rank and totally unfit for food. The bird is vulnerable to, and often suffers from refuse oil dumped at sea by ships. The plumage becomes so fouled that flight becomes impossible and starvation and disease result. Now and then one is found on a beach in emaciated condition due to such an accident, a very frequent occurrence in the days during the recent war when so much oil was released from torpedoed tankers.

The Common Loon sits low in the water with the head and beak in a parallel plane with the surface, a feature which always distinguishes it from the Red-throated Loon. In diving, it leaps forward and disappears in an instant, so quickly, indeed, that it is said to be able to dodge a load of shot. The flight is strong and attains considerable velocity. J. A. Pittman, flying a light plane between Huntersville and Davidson, N. C., on May 9, 1947, clocked a loon at 90 miles an hour, at 1200 foot altitude.

The weird quavering cry for which this species is famous, but which is not its common call, is seldom if ever heard here. During the breeding season this loon frequents fresh-water lakes and ponds of the far north, but in winter it resorts mainly to the ocean and bays of the coastline.

A remarkable instance of behavior was reported by T. A. Beckett: On the night of December 5, 1947, near Charleston a loon so persistently attacked a fisherman's lantern, hanging from the side of his boat, that the fisherman was obliged to kill it.

Food: The Common Loon is primarily an eater of fish and these include mullet, pickerel, black bass, smelt, and killifish. Crabs and crayfish are sometimes taken. It consumes only about half as many commercially valuable fishes as non-edible varieties. It is likely that, off this coast, this loon takes a good many menhaden (*Brevoortia*), but it seldom preys on what are known as food fish.

2. Lesser Loon: *Gavia immer elasson* Bishop (7a)

(Gr., *elasson*, less.)

Description: Length 28.00 to 31.00 inches. Like the Common Loon, but smaller.

Range: Breeds north to British Columbia and Manitoba; south to northeastern California and northern Indiana. Winters north to southeastern Alaska and Maine; south to California and northeastern Florida.

Status in S. C.: Fairly common winter resident, January 19 to May 2, in the eastern part of the State. Recorded north to Cheraw; south to John's Island.

History: While checking specimens in connection with this work Chamberlain noted a specimen of this race in the Charleston Museum collection (No. 7760). This bird was taken by L. M. Andrews on John's Island, Charleston County, May 2, 1924, and constitutes the first known record for the State. There is another specimen in the Museum collection (No. 33.7) that was taken in the vicinity of Cape Romain, South Carolina, on January 19, 1933, by H. F. West. The bird was found on the beach in a nearly dead condition. Still another specimen was obtained by Charles Webb at Cheraw on April 12, 1939, and identified by Dr. Harry C. Oberholser.

However, it may be pointed out that because of the small number of actual specimens examined this subspecies may prove to be more common along our coast than the present records indicate. The two are identical in appearance except for size, and therefore not identifiable in the field.

In habits and food the Lesser Loon does not differ from the Common Loon.

3. RED-THROATED LOON: *Gavia stellata* (Pontoppidan) (11,

(Lat., *stellata*, starred, relating to the spotted plumage.)

LOCAL NAMES: Diver.

DESCRIPTION: Smaller than the Common Loon; length 24.00 to 27.00 inches. Bill more slender and having an upturned appearance even at a considerable distance. *Summer*. Head and neck medium gray; the hind neck streaked with black and white; a long chestnut patch on the foreneck; rest of upper parts together with sides dark brown with numerous small white spots; rest of lower parts white. *Winter*. Above dark brown with small white spots; below white.

RANGE: Breeds north to Melville Island, northern Greenland, Spitzbergen, and New Siberia Island; south to British Columbia, New Brunswick, northern Russia, and Kamchatka. Winters north to the Aleutian Islands, Gulf of St. Lawrence, Great Britain, and Japan; south to Lower California, Florida, Mediterranean Sea, and southern China.

STATUS IN S. C.: Fairly common winter resident, October 15 to May 18, in coastal waters; but only occasional during migrations in the interior. Recorded north and west to Chester County; east to Horry County; south to Beaufort County.

HISTORY: Though this loon is smaller than the Common Loon, it can always be separated from it in the field by the way it carries the beak at an upward angle when sitting on the water. The Common Loon holds its beak parallel with the water. In flight, as on water, this species is much more slender and tapering, and looks much like a very large grebe.

It is almost totally confined to the ocean and is often seen from beaches, just beyond the surf line, where it appears and disappears in its continual diving operations. At times it comes into the larger estuaries and salt rivers, and is seen along stretches of the Inland Waterway. Though long thought to be very rare in our coastal waters (Wayne took but two specimens in twenty-five years), it has been established through numerous records as a regular and fairly common winter visitor. It arrives usually in late October or early November and remains until March. A specimen was taken in Chester County February 28, 1885 by L. M. Loomis (*Auk, 8*: 1891, 55).

Its habits and behavior are similar to those of its larger relative and to the grebes, it being a highly accomplished diver and swimmer.

FOOD: Largely fishes of non-commercial varieties such as the menhaden, silversides, killifish, etc.

Order Colymbiformes
Grebes

Family Colymbidae: Grebes

HOLBOELL'S GREBE
4. *Colymbus grisegena holböllii* (Reinhardt) (2)

(Gr., *Colymbus,* a diver; Lat., *grisegena,* gray-cheeked; *holböllii,* to C. Holböll.)

DESCRIPTION: Length 18.00 to 20.00 inches. *Summer.* Above black; throat and sides of head white; neck brownish red; rest of lower parts white. *Winter.* Blackish brown above; white below; front and sides of neck faintly reddish in adult, gray in immature.

RANGE: Breeds north to Kamchatka and northern Ungava; south to Ussuriland, northern Washington, and southwestern Minnesota. Winters north to southern British Columbia and Maine; south to China, southern California, and southern Florida.

STATUS IN S. C.: Rare winter resident, October 10 to March 16, mostly on the coast. Recorded north to Berkeley County; east and south to Charleston County; west to Aiken County.

HISTORY: It was not until 1912 that this grebe was definitely recorded in South Carolina. On January 25 of that year, one was secured in Aiken County by George N. Bailie and later presented to the Charleston Museum by Dr. Eugene E. Murphey of Augusta, Ga. It remains the only South Carolina specimen extant, but since it was secured there have been observations of the species as follows: one seen near Charleston on February 24, 1912, by Wayne; one seen in Charleston Harbor on March 16, 1928, by E. A. Smyth; one noted at Cape Romain Refuge on January 24, 1933, by F. M. Weston and Sprunt; another seen at Bull's Island on January 19, 1937, by Sprunt; several more recorded near Bull's Island on January 3 and 12, 1940, by A. D. Cruickshank; four found in the same locality on February 14, 1940, by Weston and Chamberlain; in a letter dated October 12, 1942, Dr. E. E. Murphey states that he had seen a specimen two days before near Augusta, which makes "about the seventh instance of this bird being found in the Savannah Valley . . ."; one more seen at Bull's Island on December 24, 1944, by Dr. R. C. Murphy; one seen near Cainhoy, Berkeley County, on February 22, 1947, by J. E.

Mosimann and G. B. Rabb; finally, one seen at McClellanville on March 15, 1948, by A. H. DuPre.

These observations seem sufficient to indicate that this grebe is a rare winter resident rather than of only accidental occurrence, as was long believed. Holboell's Grebe and the Horned Grebe resemble each other in the field, though the former is distinctly larger. In winter Holboell's Grebe is gray on the cheeks and sides of the neck, in contrast to the Horned Grebe, which is white in the same areas at the same season. Like all of the grebes, it swims and dives with amazing celerity, and is usually found in salt water during its winter sojourn in the South. It is strange that the only specimen thus far secured in the State was taken in fresh water.

Grebes are frequently mistaken for ducks, but on any reasonably close inspection the sharp, dagger-like bill will be seen to differ markedly from that of a duck.

FOOD: This species feeds largely on small fish of non-commercial varieties.

5. HORNED GREBE: *Colymbus auritus* Linnaeus   (3)

(Lat., *auritus*, having ears, with reference to tufts of feathers on head.)

LOCAL NAMES: Diver; Hell-diver; Diver Duck.

DESCRIPTION: Length 12.00 to 15.00 inches. *Summer*. Upper parts brownish black; chin and ruff black; a broad ochraceous patch on sides of head; neck and sides of body rufous; other lower parts white. *Winter*. Grayish black above; white below; throat and cheeks pure white in contrast to blackish crown.

RANGE: Breeds north to central Alaska, Ungava, and northern Russia; south to southern British Columbia, Nebraska, New Brunswick, and Denmark. Winters north to southern Alaska, Maine, northern Europe, and Japan; south to southern California, Florida, northern Africa, and eastern China.

STATUS IN S. C.: Winter resident, October 25 to June 5; abundant coastwise, rare inland. Recorded north to Chester County; east to Horry County; south to Beaufort County; west to Berkeley County.

HISTORY: Known as "Diver" in South Carolina, this grebe is often confused with ducks. There is actually little resemblance except for the fact that they both swim. Grebes and loons are among our most aquatic birds and are highly adapted to a watery existence. Though practically unable to take off from land because of the position of the legs, grebes swim and dive with ease. The feet are not webbed like those of a duck but are scalloped or lobed along the toes.

The Horned Grebe does not have its "horns" in winter, the tufts of feathers which give it this name being a characteristic of the breeding plumage, seldom attained in this latitude. The bird usually arrives late in October, in some seasons not until November, and it remains on this coast until April, sometimes later. Dr. Eugene E. Murphey secured a specimen in breeding plumage at Cape Romain, May 15, 1904.

The Horned Grebe is abundant during the winter months, occurring freely along the ocean beaches, bays, estuaries, and tidal rivers, but shunning fresh-water localities. It is seldom molested by hunters for it does not frequent the rice fields, and is not likely to be seen where much hunting takes place. Its flesh is unfit for food. In taking flight it is obliged to patter along the surface for a considerable distance, looking as if it were running on the water. When it finally gets into the air it presents a peculiar appearance; the head and neck are bent slightly downward, and the feet, which act as a rudder, protrude noticeably behind the almost absent tail. The conspicuous white wing-patch helps identify it in flight. It flies strongly with very rapid wing-beats, usually at low elevations, and skids into the water again with quite a splash.

The close, shining white feathers of the breast were once in great demand for trimming hats. In some places the plumage was almost as much in demand commercially as the plumes of the American Egret and Snowy Heron. Needless to say this practice is now illegal, and has virtually stopped.

FOOD: The Horned Grebe, though a fish-eater, is not exclusively so. Wetmore (1924) summarizes the food as nearly one-third fish, one-sixth crustaceans, and about one-half insects. Fish are taken mainly in winter, these being non-commercial varieties. It also takes many crayfish.

6. WESTERN GREBE: *Aechmophorus occidentalis* (Lawrence)   (1)

(Gr., *Aechmophorus*, bearing a spear, referring to the dagger-like beak; Lat., *occidentalis*, western.)

DESCRIPTION: Length 24.00 to 29.00 inches; largest of the grebes. Bill long, sharply pointed, and slightly upturned. Crown and back of neck black; back dark gray; entire under parts white.

RANGE: Breeds north to British Columbia and Saskatchewan; south to southern California and Utah. Winters north to British Columbia; south to central Mexico; casual in the eastern United States.

STATUS IN S. C.: Accidental in June in Charleston County only.

HISTORY: The occurrence of this large grebe so far out of its normal range is, of course, purely accidental but none the less interesting. One record is responsible for its inclusion among South Carolina birds. On June 22, 1936, a fisherman picked up a dead specimen floating in the Inland Waterway near McClellanville, Charleston County, and took it to Andrew DuPre, of the Cape Romain Wildlife Refuge, who, in turn, presented it to the Charleston Museum. Examination proved that the bird had been shot. It is preserved in the collection as No. 36.136, and was recorded in the *Auk*, 53: 1936, 438. The specimen is the first record of this far western species on the Atlantic Coast.

There is little likelihood that this grebe would be mistaken on sight, as it is far larger than the others of its family, and the long, almost swan-like neck gives it a grace of carriage which is highly characteristic. Its behavior and actions are similar to those of other grebes, and its complete mastery of the water is evidenced in every movement of swimming or diving.

PIED-BILLED GREBE
7. *Podilymbus podiceps podiceps* (Linnaeus) (6)

(Lat., *Podiceps* + *Colymbus*; *podiceps*, rump-headed.)

LOCAL NAMES: Diver; Hell-diver; Didapper; Dabchick; Waterwitch.

DESCRIPTION: Length 12.00 to 15.00 inches; bill short and thick. *Summer*. Above dull black; neck and cheeks gray; chin and throat black; rest of lower parts pale brown or white, with indistinct brown spots; a black band on bill. *Winter*. Similar but more brownish; no black on chin, throat, or bill.

RANGE: Breeds north to southern Mackenzie and Quebec; south to Mexico and Central America. Winters north to British Columbia and New York; south to Mexico, Central America, and Cuba.

STATUS IN S. C.: Common permanent resident in most of the State. Recorded north to Chester County; east to Horry County; south to Beaufort County; west to Anderson and Oconee counties.

HISTORY: This little grebe is by far the best known of the family in this State, though not under its correct name. To most people who recognize it at all it is known as the Hell-diver or Didapper.

Though it occurs in salt water in coastal areas, the Pied-billed Grebe prefers fresh water most of the time. It never breeds in salt water. It is a small grebe, very brownish in color, at times displaying usually concealed patches of pale buff or white at the sides of the rump. This grebe is the "duck" of many an inland farm boy. Its aquatic ability matches that of any member of its family and at times seems to exceed any other, for it is able to submerge vertically, sinking straight down with no forward plunge and leaving not a ripple. So much does it depend on its wonderful ability in the water that it is rare to see one in flight.

An unusual incident has been reported by John C. Ball, Jr. During the summer of 1948 he noticed a Pied-billed Grebe, its head under water, flapping wildly in a small pond at Old Town, near Charleston. Investigation disclosed that the bird (then dead) had been seized by the head by a large blue crab (*Calinectes*) and apparently drowned.

Mating takes place in late February in the coast region and somewhat later in the interior. The nest, which is usually started about mid-March, is placed in swamps, rice fields, small ponds, or bogs. At times the nest is a veritable little floating island, being constructed of rushes, aquatic grasses, and waterlogged debris, raised a few inches above the water, containing usually five to seven eggs which are of a buffy color, without markings, averaging 43.4 to 30.0 millimeters. But one brood is raised, incubation taking from twenty-three to twenty-four days. The young are covered with down, heavily streaked and very attractive in appearance. They are often carried on the backs of the adults, from which they peep about from under the wings, making an unforgettable picture. Typical egg dates are: April 11, Charleston County; June 7, Beaufort County; May 14, Richland County. A remarkably late nesting is a record of three eggs brought to Edward von S. Dingle, in Summerton, Clarendon County, September 18, 1922. These were addled but from the state of the contents could not long have been in such a condition. Birds, apparently mated, have been

Cypress Swamp, Berkeley County   CARL JULIEN

Rice Field Canal, Combahee River

CARL JULIEN

Peach Orchard, Lexington County   CARL JULIEN

Cotton Field, Barnwell County

CARL JULIEN

observed in Anderson County, March 16, and Oconee County, March 27 (F. Sherman).

FOOD: One hundred and seventy-four stomachs of this grebe have been examined by the U. S. Fish and Wildlife Service. The contents were: fish 24 per cent, crayfish 27 per cent, insects 46 per cent. Among the fish were perch, sunfish, eels, suckers, carp, and catfish. The insect content which, by the way, is surprising in such a bird, was made up of water boatmen, whirligig beetles, scavanger beetles, dragon flies, grasshoppers, and water bugs. The Pied-billed Grebe, like other members of its family, often has quantities of feathers in its stomach, occasionally amounting to more than half of the total contents.

Order Procellariiformes
Tube-nosed Swimmers

Family Procellariidae: Shearwaters and Petrels

8. Sooty Shearwater: *Puffinus griseus* (Gmelin) (95)

(Lat., *Puffinus*, from English puffin; *griseus*, gray.)

DESCRIPTION: Length 16.00 to 18.00 inches; about the size of a grebe. Head, wings, and upper parts blackish brown; under parts deep gray; lining of wings partly white.

RANGE: Breeds north to New Zealand and adjacent islands and southern South America. Ranges the Atlantic and Pacific oceans north to Greenland and Alaska; south to the Antarctic Ocean.

STATUS IN S. C.: Rare summer visitor in May, coastwise. Reported from Charleston County only.

HISTORY: Shearwaters are oceanic birds, so much so that they are virtually unknown to landsmen. They are long-winged birds, of rather somber plumage, almost black in this species, gray and white in others. Their habit of flapping and sailing, close over the waves, is characteristic and they are able to stay at sea for long periods even in severe weather.

Heavy storms sometimes drive them to the island beaches, or even into bays and harbors, and many are killed in this manner, their bodies sometimes being found on the sands. Voyagers on coastwise ships are able to see them in the summer months, and anyone going out with the fishing trawlers operating from South Carolina ports may well observe them. The best field mark of this species is its uniformly dark appearance.

Wayne (1910) speaks of this bird as "very abundant" off the coast in summer and possibly this is the case, but few indeed are seen from or near the shore. One was picked up dead on the beach of Bull's Island in May, 1916, by Clarence Magwood, and noted by Wayne (*Auk*, 35: 1918, 437). A more recent observation is that of a bird seen from Cape Island (Cape Romain Refuge) on May 10, 1946, by Allan D. Cruickshank. Most of the shearwaters nest in far southern oceans and therefore appear here locally in their winter which is our summer. The name "shearwater" is frequently given to the abundant Black Skimmer locally. The mistake results in much confusion, for many observers are sure they know shearwaters when actually they have never seen one.

FOOD: The diet of this species is oceanic life of various sorts, together with scraps thrown from ships, and fish offal from the trawlers.

AUDUBON'S SHEARWATER
9. *Puffinus lherminieri lherminieri Lesson* (92)

(Lat., *lherminieri*, to F. J. Lherminier.)

DESCRIPTION: Length 11.00 to 12.00 inches. Upper parts and wings black; under parts white; the lower tail coverts with some brown.

RANGE: Breeds north to Bermuda Islands; south to the West Indies. Ranges parts of the North Atlantic Ocean, north to New York and south to the Lesser Antilles.

STATUS IN S. C.: Rare summer visitor, May 19 to August 31, in the southern coast region. Reported only from Charleston County.

HISTORY: This small black and white shearwater is present during the summer months at sea. Like its larger relatives, it is seldom seen from land and practically all the known South Carolina specimens have been the result of tropical storms. Typical of such records are the following: one found dead on Sullivan's Island, August 10, 1911, by Chamberlain; about fifteen dead on Isle of Palms, August 2, 1926, by E. von S. Dingle; one found dead on Deveaux Bank (mouth of the Edisto River), July 24, 1935, by Dunbar Robb; one found dead on Edisto Beach, July 24, 1938, by Hugh M. Rutledge; five found dead on Isle of Palms, August 15, 1940, by Chamberlain and Lunz. However, two were seen off the Charleston Sea Buoy on May 19, 1939, by E. Milby Burton, and at that time normal weather conditions prevailed.

Ellison A. Smyth collected the first specimen of this species in South Carolina in Stono Inlet, August 4, 1888, in a very emaciated condition, and found the remains of another on Folly Island the same day. One specimen has been taken in Charleston Harbor (Wayne).

Audubon's Shearwater swims and dives freely, and has the characteristic flapping and sailing flight of birds of this family.

FOOD: Small marine organisms, fish, and refuse from vessels.

ALLIED SHEARWATER
10. *Puffinus assimilis baroli* (Bonaparte) (92.1)

(Lat., *assimilis*, like; *baroli*, name of man for whom bird was named.)

DESCRIPTION: About 11.00 inches. Upper parts slaty black; under parts, as well as sides of neck and face, all white.

RANGE: Breeds on the Canary Islands, Salvage Island, and Madeira. Ranges over the North Atlantic Ocean, mainly on the eastern side, but accidentally west to the coast of North America.

STATUS IN S. C.: Accidental in Charleston County.

HISTORY: This North Atlantic shearwater finds a place among South Carolina birds by reason of a tropical hurricane plus Arthur T. Wayne. Its history is of great interest. In August, 1883, a severe storm struck the coast. Shortly afterwards a specimen was picked up in an exhausted condition on the beach at Sullivan's Island and in some manner reached the hands of John Dancer, a taxidermist of Charleston. Wayne writes "I acquired the bird in 1884 . . . I recall the Shearwater in every detail and know that Mr. Dancer put white eyes in the bird, for I was by his side when he was mounting it."

Wayne, thinking that this bird was a specimen of the Audubon Shearwater, sold it in 1899 to William Brewster, who later gave it to the Museum of Comparative Zoölogy at Cambridge, Massachusetts. There Outram Bangs discovered, on close examination, that it was an Allied Shearwater and therefore constituted the first actual specimen for North America. One other has been recorded, by Jonathan Dwight in 1897, as having struck a lighthouse on Sable Island, off Nova Scotia. James L. Peters (*Auk, 41*: 1924, 337) considers Wayne's bird as the second published record.

11. GREATER SHEARWATER: *Puffinus gravis* (O'Reilly) (89)

(Lat., *gravis*, heavy.)

DESCRIPTION: Length 18.00 to 20.00 inches; somewhat smaller than the Herring Gull. Upper parts very dark brown, the feathers with gray edges; under parts white.

RANGE: Breeds on Tristan da Cunha. Ranges the Atlantic Ocean, north to Greenland; south to southern South America and southern Africa.

STATUS IN S. C.: Rare summer visitor, August 27 to September 4, along the coast. Reported from Charleston County only.

HISTORY: This rather large dark gray and white species is possibly the one most likely to be encountered off this coast. The hurricane of August 27, 1893, destroyed numbers of them and Wayne (1910) states that "A few days after the cyclone, I visited Long Island [Isle of Palms] and found the beach literally strewn with dead birds." Another violent storm struck this coast in 1911 on the same day as the 1893 hurricane, August 27. One week afterward, on September 4, 1911, a decomposed specimen of this bird was found on Sullivan's Island by Miss Laura M. Bragg. In neither instance was a specimen preserved, making it impossible to confirm the identification at this time.

12. CORY'S SHEARWATER: *Puffinus diomedea borealis* Cory (88)

(Lat., *diomedea*, of Diomedes, a mythological Greek hero; *borealis*, northern.)

DESCRIPTION: Length 20.00 to 22.00 inches. Upper parts brownish gray, darker on wings and tail; under parts white, sometimes washed with gray on breast; under tail coverts white, marked with gray.

RANGE: Breeds in the Canary Island, Salvage Islands, Madeira, and the Azores. Ranges the Atlantic Ocean, north to Newfoundland; south to central eastern Brazil.

STATUS IN S. C.: Rare summer visitor in August on the coast. Known from Charleston County only.

HISTORY: There were no definite records of Cory's Shearwater in South Carolina until 1940. During that summer large numbers appeared off the south Atlantic coast. On July 13 Dr. T. Gilbert Pearson, who was aboard a ship off the South Carolina coast, saw about a thousand of these birds in four separate flocks. The ship passed through one of the flocks and Dr. Pearson noted that some of the birds had fed so heavily that they dived rather than took flight, their movements under water being plainly visible from the deck.

On August 11, 1940, a severe storm occurred and a dead bird, picked up a week later by Edward von S. Dingle on the Isle of Palms, proved to be of this species, the identification being corroborated by Dr. Alexander Wetmore. This constitutes the first State record (*Auk, 58*: 1941, 251).

Family Hydrobatidae: Storm Petrels

LEACH'S PETREL
13. *Oceanodroma leucorhoa leucorhoa* (Vieillot)   (106)

(Gr., *Oceanodroma*, ocean-runner; *leucorhoa*, white-rumped.)

LOCAL NAMES: Mother Cary's Chicken.

DESCRIPTION: About the size of the Purple Martin; length 8.00 inches. Tail forked. Plumage very dark; upper parts blackish brown; under parts fuscous; a large white patch at base of tail above; feet black.

RANGE: Breeds in the Pacific Ocean, north to the Commander Islands, and south to the Kurile Islands; in the Atlantic Ocean north to Greenland and south to Maine. Ranges south to Hawaii and the Galapagos Islands, and in the Atlantic Ocean to Brazil and Liberia.

STATUS IN S. C.: Accidental.

HISTORY: The smaller petrels are known everywhere and collectively as "Mother Cary's Chickens," the world's literature containing many references to them. Though they are unknown to the vast majority of people by sight, their names and reputations are familiar. Like the shearwaters, they are oceanic birds, but because of their small size and apparent fragility they command even more attention and comment.

This species is more northerly than most of the family, and is seen in some of the roughest portions of the North Atlantic; it ranges at times, however, as far south as the Equator. The only record of its occurrence in South Carolina is a decomposed specimen picked up on the beach at the Isle of Palms, September 20, 1926, by Edward von S. Dingle. It was impossible to preserve it, but his identification of the bird was corroborated at the United States National Museum by Joseph H. Riley.

FOOD: Small oceanic life, together with scraps thrown from ships, and trawlers.

WILSON'S PETREL
14. *Oceanites oceanicus oceanicus* (Kuhl) (109)

(Gr., *Oceanites*, child of the sea; Lat., *oceanicus*, oceanic.)

LOCAL NAMES: Mother Cary's Chicken.

DESCRIPTION: Length 7.00 to 7.50 inches. Tail square. Above sooty black; under parts similar but somewhat lighter; upper tail coverts white; webs of feet yellow.

RANGE: Breeds on South Georgia, South Orkney Islands, and South Shetland Islands. Winters north to Labrador and Great Britain.

STATUS IN S. C.: Fairly common summer visitor, May 5 to October 15, along the coast. Recorded from Charleston County only.

HISTORY: This little sea bird is the common petrel of this coast. Those who have made coastal voyages will undoubtedly recall it, for the sight of any bird at sea demands attention, whether the observer is particularly interested or not. These little creatures, so oblivious to the dangers of the vast watery wastes where they live, appeal strongly to the imagination, and cause wonder in all who watch them.

They look very much like swallows, and the flight is similar also; indeed, one might think that he was observing a long-legged Purple Martin with a white rump. They swoop and swim over the waves with agile grace, sometimes appearing actually to walk on the water. The illusion is responsible for the name "petrel," in reference to St. Peter and his attempt to walk on the water to Christ.

Uniformly dark, except for conspicuous white tail patch, Wilson's Petrel should be recognized at once. Although this species is the one which is most likely to be seen off the South Carolina coast, it is well to note that, in contrast to the possible Leach's Petrel, Wilson's Petrel has a square tail, not a forked one, beyond which the *yellow-webbed feet* extend.

The sight of a petrel from a beach occurs but rarely: One was seen on June 15, 1913, on Bird Bank in Bull's Bay by Caspar Chisolm, and another was seen by Sprunt from Folly Island, July 29, 1947. Newton Seebeck also saw one from the same beach on October 15 of the same year. E. Milby Burton took a specimen off the Charleston jetties on August 14, 1938, and again on May 5, 1939.

FOOD: Small marine life and refuse from ships.

Order Pelecaniformes
Totipalmate Swimmers

Family Phaëthontidae: Tropic-birds

YELLOW-BILLED TROPIC-BIRD
15. *Phaëthon lepturus catesbyi* Brandt (112)

(Gr., *Phaëthon*, mythological character, once driver of the sun-chariot; *lepturus*, slender-tailed; *catesbyi*, to Mark Catesby.)

DESCRIPTION: Length 30.00 to 32.00 inches, including tail. Central tail feathers greatly lengthened. Plumage mostly white tinged with pink; wings marked with black; a black stripe through eye; bill yellow.

RANGE: Resident and breeds north to Bermuda; south to the Bahamas and Lesser Antilles. Accidental north to Nova Scotia.

STATUS IN S. C.: Accidental.

HISTORY: But one record exists for this beautiful bird, and that, astonishingly enough, comes from the foot of the Blue Ridge Mountains. On July 30, 1926, one was picked up alive by Miss Sarah Godbold, at Jocassee, Oconee County. She sent the bird to Clemson College, from there it went to Wayne. It is now in the Charleston Museum. Its presence in such an unusual place can only be accounted for as an accident possibly caused by adverse weather conditions.

Even to one not familiar with the species the bird can hardly be confused with anything else. The beautiful, streaming feathers of the tail are at once diagnostic. Young birds lack them, but they do have the white back barred with wavy, black lines. The bird nests as far north as Bermuda, which lies some five hundred miles due east of Charleston. It seems rather strange that more of these birds are not blown toward the South Carolina coast during the tropical storms. The explanation may be that the winds carry them northward rather than westward.

The note of the Tropic-bird is a shrill whistle, much like that of the boatswain's pipe of sailing ship days; hence the name "Bo'sun-bird" by which it is known to seamen. Like terns, Tropic-birds dive for their food of fish.

Family Pelecanidae: Pelicans

16. WHITE PELICAN: *Pelecanus erythrorhynchos* Gmelin (125)

(Gr., *Pelecanus*, a pelican; *erythrorhynchos*, red beaked.)

DESCRIPTION: Length 60.00 inches. Extent of wings 96.00 to 108.00 inches. White, except primaries black; bill and feet yellow to orange red.

RANGE: Breeds north to central British Columbia and southern Mackenzie; south to southern California and Texas. Winters north to northern California and Florida; south to Panama and Trinidad.

STATUS IN S. C.: Casual in the eastern half of the State, January 7 to December 10, chiefly in the coast region. Recorded north to Orangeburg County; east to South Island; south to the mouth of the Savannah River; west to the Savannah River near Augusta, Georgia.

HISTORY: This splendid species, one of the largest birds in North America, is rarely seen in South Carolina. Larger and more spectacular than the abundant Brown Pelican, it is a far western nester but migrates in part cross-country to spend the winter in Florida and along the Gulf coast. It now and then straggles as far as South Carolina. No one, however inexperienced, should mistake a pelican for anything else. The huge beak, with its great pouch, is an unmistakable characteristic, to say nothing of the size of the bird itself. The snow-white body, set off by the black-tipped wings, makes it a commanding object, worthy of attention by anyone anywhere.

Audubon quotes Bachman to the effect that "This bird is now more rare on our coast than it was thirty years ago . . . I saw a flock on the Bird Banks of Bull's Island on the 1st day of July, 1814, when I procured two full plumaged old birds . . . "

Nearly a hundred years passed before another specimen was taken in South Carolina. On October 26, 1910, one was secured in the Santee Swamp by a farmer, from whom it was purchased by W. C. Smith, of Charleston, and reported to the Charleston Museum. (*Bull. Chas. Mus.*, 6:57). It is possible that the bird had been blown north from the Gulf region by a hurricane which occurred a day or two prior to its capture. A third specimen was taken 4 or 5 miles above Orangeburg, November 26, 1935, by C. W. Pace, who presented the bird to the Charleston Museum (No. 35.373).

PLATE IV: DUCKS IN RICE FIELD

Oil Painting by Francis Lee Jaques

Flying ducks, upper right: top, two Green-winged Teals (male); below, Green-winged Teal (female). Flying ducks, left, left to right: Blue-winged Teal (female) and Blue-winged Teal (male). Ducks on ground, left to right: Shoveller (female), Shoveller (male), Pintail (female), and two Pintails (male).

In addition to the foregoing specimens, the following observations have been reported: May 12, 1929, one was seen at the mouth of the Savannah River, Beaufort County, and another a year or two later near Bluffton by I. R. Tomkins (*Auk, 47*: 1930, 577); June 13, 1934, ten seen at Folly Island flying south in single file about one-half mile offshore (Sprunt); January 7, 1939, one seen at Cape Island (A. H. DuPre and Sprunt); June 9 to 12, 1939, eleven seen at South Island, Winyah Bay (J. B. Gibson); June 30 to July 5, 1939, eleven seen at Cape Romain (W. P. Baldwin); August 21, 1944, one seen at Cape Romain on the ground in the midst of a colony of Brown Pelicans (Chamberlain and Baldwin); November 20, 1945, one seen at Cape Island (DuPre); October 13, 1947, one seen in Charleston Harbor (W. W. Humphreys); November 8 to 12, 1947, one seen over the Ashley River and on a mud flat on the western edge of Charleston (I. S. H. Metcalf, Chamberlain, and George Rabb). The groups of birds seen during June and July, 1939, in two localities were, in all probability, the same flock. The bird seen at Charleston in October and November, 1947, was probably the same individual. A number of these observations were made in good weather, and the birds' presence cannot be attributed to storms.

The feeding habits of this species are utterly unlike those of its smaller relative. Instead of diving for its prey, as the Brown Pelican does, the White Pelican swims along the surface, scooping up its food with the pouched beak. It seems strange that birds so closely related should exhibit such different feeding techniques.

This species is much given to soaring high in the air in flocks, wheeling in immense circles over land and water. Seen performing in this way, they constitute one of the most spectacular and thrilling sights in nature, the glistening plumage, framed by the black wing tips, standing out against the blue of the sky in beautiful contrast.

FOOD: Exclusively fish of various sorts, mainly carp and suckers. No commercial varieties appear to be taken in the winter range.

EASTERN BROWN PELICAN
17. *Pelecanus occidentalis carolinensis* Gmelin   (126)

(Lat., *occidentalis*, western; *carolinensis*, of Carolina.)

DESCRIPTION: Length 48.00 to 54.00 inches. Extent of wings 78.00 inches. *Summer adult.* Head white; hind neck mostly chestnut; rest of upper parts silvery gray; under parts grayish brown. *Winter.* Similar, but head and neck white. *Immature.* Head, neck, back, and upper breast brownish gray; under parts white partly tinged with brownish gray.

RANGE: Resident and breeds on south Atlantic and Gulf coasts of United States from South Carolina, casually North Carolina, to southern Texas.

STATUS IN S. C.: Common permanent resident coastwise. Recorded north to Horry County; south to Beaufort County.

HISTORY: These ponderous fishermen are among the most interesting of our coastal birds. The Charleston area constitutes the northern regular limit of the nesting range, and the colony at Cape Romain is one of the great avian sights of the State. Though Brown Pelicans have been recorded as nesting once on the North

Carolina coast (1929), the Cape Romain colony is the most northerly one used annually by the species.

For a long time the Eastern Brown Pelican was thought to be a summer resident only. It is practically permanent now, however, for it has been seen every month in the year, and it remains regularly until Christmas. Very few are to be seen in January and February. The first midwinter record was established at Folly Island, January 25, 1932, when nine birds were seen (Weston and Sprunt). This apparently constitutes the farthest north winter occurrence on the Atlantic coast to that time.

During recent years numbers of young pelicans have been banded in the Cape Romain area. There have not been a great number of returns, but of those reported the vast majority have come from Florida during the winter months, showing that there is a decided southward movement of pelicans during the fall. The returns also reveal that numbers of the birds continue to the West Indies and the Caribbean area. The greatest distance thus far reported is made known by one band from Cayo Cruz, Cuba.

Brown Pelicans add enormously to the interest of the Low-country. They may be watched almost daily by summer beach residents. Flocks of the birds scale along in file beyond the breakers off the beach as though they were playing follow-the-leader, flapping heavily, then sailing in perfect unison, their wing tips seeming to clear the water by only an inch. They are spectacular fishermen, plunging headlong from the air, turning into the wind just before they enter the water and striking the surface with a leaping fountain of spray. Nothing is more ridiculously dignified than a Brown Pelican perched atop a dock piling, beak on breast, giving the observer a most solemn stare.

In spite of its size the pelican apparently has enemies beneath the surface of the ocean. E. Milby Burton, on his way to Cape Island in July, 1930, flushed three adult pelicans which appeared to have been resting on the water. On his return he again flushed the group, but this time only two of them flew off; the third seemed crippled. With much difficulty Burton at last captured the bird and was then able to discover why the bird could not fly: Its left wing had been severed completely close to the body and the wound was bleeding freely, strong proof that the injury had just occurred. A reasonable presumption is that the bird had been attacked by a large shark. The bird was given to John P. DeVeaux of Charleston, who attempted to save its life by forced feeding, but after about ten days it died.

A visit to a nesting colony is something to remember, olfactorily as well as visually. When the eggs are hatching, the adults stand close by and may be seen in every detail. The nests are built on the ground. They are made of seaweed, marsh grass, and debris, and are often a foot or more high. Normally there are three eggs (sometimes two or four), of a dirty white, often much nest-stained. They average 73.0 by 46.5 millimeters, and require about twenty-eight days for incubation. Only one brood is raised.

Concerning the nesting habits of the Eastern Brown Pelican there is some discrepancy in the reports of even the most reliable observers. Sprunt says that the nests he has found have always been of the type just described. Wayne (1910), however, stated that "this species builds no nest upon this coast, but lays its eggs in a hole scooped out in the bare sand." Burton confirms Wayne's observation by actual photographs taken in 1928 of sand-hole nests. It is possible that as the pelican has come to enjoy a greater degree of protection it is changing its habits somewhat and is generally building the more substantial kind of nest.

At the Cape Romain colony the nesting dates vary. The earliest record is for March 27, 1935, when one hundred pairs were found at Sandy Point, Raccoon Key, Bull's Bay, with one to two eggs laid (H. F. West and Sprunt). Previous to that, the earliest record of nesting had been April 4, 1933, at the same place (West). On April 19, 1945, young birds were wandering about Sandy Point in droves, some well feathered, while many nests still held eggs. Five or six hundred birds were in evidence that season (Sprunt). Nesting must have been begun in mid-March that year. It is often stretched through many weeks, for the colony is not infrequently washed by high tides. During the breeding season of 1946, the Cape Romain colony reached the highest peak known, when nearly eight hundred nests were reported. Near the end of May, H. S. Peters counted 626 nests (eggs and a few young) on Sandy Point, and A. H. DuPre counted over 150 nests on Cape Island.

Newly hatched young are about as ugly as anything can well be—naked, black, blind, and helpless. Soon a white down appears, and the young birds, looking like creatures belonging to the age of dinosaurs, begin to waddle about the vicinity in bands and squadrons. The pouch is well developed, even at this early age. Lying about the nesting area are many fish in various stages of decomposition, having been regurgitated by the young. If the eggs are destroyed by high water, the birds will lay again and again. As a result, the season is often a protracted one.

Another colony nests at times on Bird Bank, St. Helena Sound, near Beaufort, where E. J. DeCamps has found eggs on June 20. This group, or perhaps another, has also nested on Deveaux Bank, at the mouth of the Edisto River. Pelicans are not very shy and often congregate around wharves or fish houses along the water fronts of coastal towns, and may often be seen off the Battery at Charleston. Most of the birds seen in the fall and early winter are immatures.

FOOD: Exclusively fish, for the most part silversides (*Atherina*) and menhaden (*Brevoortia*). The pelican rarely feeds upon any other species locally, though it is often accused of consuming fish that are commercially valuable. It also takes some pigfish, thread herring, and top minnows.

Detailed study of Atlantic and Gulf coast colonies in 1918 by Dr. T. Gilbert Pearson revealed that of 1276 fish picked up in one colony only thirty-nine were commercially valuable. Some 3428 fish were examined from Florida colonies, of which only twenty-seven were of kinds sold in the market. Despite such definite proof that pelicans do not compete with commercial fishermen, persecution of the birds continues in parts of the range.

Family Sulidae: Boobies and Gannets

ATLANTIC BLUE-FACED BOOBY
18. *Sula dactylatra dactylatra* Lesson (114)

(Norwegian, *Sula*, name of a similar bird; perhaps from Gr., *sule*, right of seizure; *dactylatra*, black-fingered.)

DESCRIPTION: Length 25.00 to 29.00 inches. *Adult.* White; the primaries, secondaries, and tail mostly brownish black; face blue. *Immature.* Head, neck, and upper surface dull brown, with some white on neck and rump; the remaining lower parts white.

RANGE: Resident and breeds north to Yucatan and the Bahama Islands (formerly); south to northern Colombia and the islands off the coast of northern Venezuela.

STATUS IN S. C.: Accidental in the coast region.

HISTORY: This tropical species is no more than an accidental wanderer even as far south as Palm Beach, Florida. Its inclusion among South Carolina birds rests on but one observation which did not include the taking of a specimen. On January 23, 1937, Sprunt saw two of these birds off the beach of Folly Island. He watched them for half an hour, as they swam, dived, and flew about. The day was bright and sunny, and the thermometer registered 74°. Both birds were in good plumage and the black tails showed in sharp contrast to the white body plumage. This occurrence appears to be the first observation of the species north of southern Florida. Though this bird is distinctive enough, whether known previously or not, the observer in this case had become familiar with it at the Dry Tortugas, where it occurs every year.

In general habits and food the Blue-faced Booby does not differ materially from other boobies.

WHITE-BELLIED BOOBY
19. *Sula leucogaster leucogaster* (Boddaert) (115)

(Gr., *leucogaster*, white-bellied.)

DESCRIPTION: Length 28.00 to 30.00 inches. Extent of wings about 50.00 inches. *Adult.* Dark brown but belly white; bill and feet yellow. *Immature.* Similar, but belly dull brown.

RANGE: Breeds north to southern Florida (formerly); south to Brazil and Ascension Island. Winters north to the Bahamas and Florida; south to the Straits of Magellan.

STATUS IN S. C.: Accidental in the coast region.

HISTORY: The history of this tropical sea bird in South Carolina is rather obscure. Actually, nothing is known about it except Wayne's reference (1910). Wayne states that "There were at least four specimens of this species in the Charleston Museum, labeled 'South Carolina' by Dr. John Bachman. All of these birds were in immature plumage."

The occurrence of White-bellied Boobies on this coast is purely accidental, but tropical storms may bring them. Boobies are similar in form and habit to the

Gannet, but may be distinguished by their black tails and (in this species) black upper parts, which contrast sharply with the white belly.

Normally, the White-bellied Booby reaches this country only at the Dry Tortugas, in the Gulf of Mexico, and is practically unknown to the vast majority of continental bird students. Like the Gannet, it dives for its prey of fish, from the air. It is a large bird, about the size of the cormorant.

20. GANNET: *Morus bassanus* (Linnaeus) (117)

(Lat., *Morus*, foolish, probably pertaining to tameness on nest; *bassanus*, for Bass Rock, England, famous nesting site.)

DESCRIPTION: About the size of the Canada Goose. Length 30.00 to 40.00 inches. *Adult*. White, tips of wings black; head washed with yellow. *Immature*. Mainly brown marked with white, paler on the under parts.

RANGE: Breeds north to Gulf of St. Lawrence and Iceland; south to Maine and northern Great Britain. Winters north to Massachusetts; south to Mexico and the Canary Islands.

STATUS IN S. C.: Fairly common winter resident, October 2 to June 18, on the coast. Reported north to Horry County; south to Beaufort County.

HISTORY: The status of this fine species in, or rather off, South Carolina has been found to vary from Wayne's conclusions (1910). Wayne wrote that, though the bird occurs regularly off shore during migrations, he had never observed it in winter. As a matter of fact, it winters regularly on the South Carolina coast in considerable numbers, often being visible from the beaches.

The length of stay in southern waters is prolonged, from October to June, nine months or more. In order to see this species to advantage, the observer should accompany off-shore fishermen; at times, however, excellent views may be had from one of the beaches.

To watch these great birds at their fishing is a memorable experience. They secure their prey by spectacular, plunging dives, often from considerable heights, and throw up veritable fountains of spray as they strike the water. Though terns feed in a similar manner, and the largest of this family, the Caspian Tern is present in winter, there is no possibility of confusing the two. The Gannet is far larger, the plumage is pure white in the adult, with the tips of the wings black and the beak yellow. The tern is grayer, and has a red bill.

There has always been, and still is, confusion locally in regard to the term "Gannet." Audubon stated that his co-worker, Dr. Bachman, had seen flocks of Gannets near Cole's Island (near the mouth of Stono River) in July, 1836, and that a friend of Bachman's, a Mr. Giles, had, during the preceding summer, "seen a pair of Gannets going to, and returning from, a nest in a tree!" This was, of course, a case of mistaken identity and directly traceable to the universal local use of the word "Gannet." It is unfortunately applied to the Wood Ibis. This bird is also white, and it has black-tipped wings. Sprunt recalls having been severely taken to task by local residents who "knew" Gannets, but who in reality were speaking of the ibis. It is hardly necessary to add that the Gannet does not nest in trees, and that the chief breeding locality in North America is on Bonaventure Island, in the Gulf of St. Lawrence. This spot harbors thousands of Gannets annually, and is one of the great bird sights of this continent.

FOOD: According to A. C. Bent (1922) the Gannet " . . . is a voracious feeder and undoubtedly consumes an enormous number of fish; it is not partial in its choice, though it feeds largely on herring and mackerel where they are abundant in schools; it also takes capelin and other species as well as small codlings." Probably menhaden (*Brevoortia*) form the bulk of its food on this coast.

Family *Phalacrocoracidae:* Cormorants

EUROPEAN CORMORANT
21. *Phalacrocorax carbo carbo* (Linnaeus) (119)

(Gr., *Phalacrocorax*, a cormorant; Lat., *carbo*, coal.)

DESCRIPTION: Length 34.00 to 40.00 inches. *Adult.* Black with a white patch on flanks and small whitish plumes on head and neck; gular pouch bordered behind with white. *Immature.* More brownish, with no white plumes; below partly white.

RANGE: Resident and breeds north to Greenland and Norway; south to Nova Scotia and the British Isles. Winters south to Florida and the Canary Islands.

STATUS IN S. C.: Casual winter visitor, October 19 to March 27, in the coastal region. Observed north to Charleston; south to the mouth of the Savannah River.

HISTORY: This old world species, the largest of the South Carolina cormorants, is included among South Carolina birds only as a casual wanderer, as this State is south of its normal range. In 1883 William Brewster stated that he had examined two specimens that were in the collection of the College of Charleston. " . . . I have lately examined two specimens of *Graculus carbo* which are labeled as having been captured near that city. The southward wanderings of the species on the Atlantic coast do not seem to have been traced beyond the Middle States" (*Bull. Nutt. Orn. Club 8*: 1883, 186).

On October 19, 1930, a specimen was taken by Ivan R. Tomkins near the North Jetty at the mouth of the Savannah River (*Auk, 48*: 1931, 279). He presented this bird to the Charleston Museum where it is preserved (No. 30.238). In addition to this specimen, one sight record has been reported on March 27, 1946, at the Charleston jetties, an adult seen at close range by H. S. Peters. In connection with records from the southeastern seaboard, it is pertinent to remark that the banding files of the U. S. Fish and Wildlife Service show that of birds of this species banded in Quebec, one has been taken in Virginia, and another in Florida.

This species is larger than the abundant Double-crested and Florida Cormorants. The adult has a white patch on the flanks, not possessed by the other species. Though the bird cannot, of course, be expected in this locality, constant watch may again reveal its presence probably during the fall and winter, particularly after northeast storms which may drive it down from its northern range.

COMORANTS

Double-crested Cormorant
22. *Phalacrocorax auritus auritus* (Lesson)   (120)

(Lat., *auritus*, eared.)

Local Names: Niggergoose.

Description: Length 29.00 to 33.00 inches. *Adult.* Greenish black, back and wings mottled with brown, lores and throat pouch orange; eyelids and mouth blue. *Immature.* Grayish brown.

Range: Breeds north to Alberta and Newfoundland; south to Utah and Maine. Winters north to Michigan and Maine; south to the United States coast of the Gulf of Mexico and Florida.

Status in S. C.: Abundant winter resident, November to May, mostly coastwise. Recorded north and west to Spartanburg County; east to Horry County; south to Beaufort County.

History: This species, and the following form, are the birds usually mistaken for geese in South Carolina by many. In flight they resemble geese, and indeed are known almost universally as "Niggergeese." Many of the reported observations of geese really relate to cormorants. Actually there are marked differences between the birds. Mature cormorants are uniformly dark-bodied; they fly with rather rapid wing-beats and rarely hold a formation for any length of time. When at rest, they sit in an upright position; in the water, they swim very low, the neck held erect with the head and beak carried point upward at a noticeable angle. These differences, aside from the fact that cormorants are far more common than geese, should serve to distinguish them.

A specimen taken on the Combahee River, Colleton County, November 23, 1940, had been banded as a nestling on June 27 of the same year in Nova Scotia, by H. S. Peters. A bird noted near Spartanburg by Gabriel Cannon and Ellison A. Williams on April 22, 1948, was probably of this race. While abundant in the tidal rivers, bays, and ocean, they may be seen at inland localities which possess large bodies of water, notably the Santee-Cooper Lakes, and the borders of river swamps and large ponds. In the coast region, they go to sea to spend the night and may be seen in large numbers as they pass over waterfront towns in the late afternoon.

Although Wayne (1910) notes that they are very shy birds, cormorants have become much more tame in recent years and often allow close approach, perhaps because they are no longer disturbed by shooting. Few, if any, are shot locally; every marsh-man knows that cormorants are totally unfit for food. The breeding plumage, which shows the tufts of feathers on the head and which gives rise to the name "double-crested," is seldom seen in this part of the range, as the birds migrate before it is attained.

On dissecting a sick bird taken near Charleston in December, 1913, Chamberlain noted a growth in the chest cavity. Examination by Dr. Kenneth M. Lynch, of the Medical College of the State of South Carolina, resulted in his finding that the " . . . right thorax was occupied by an ovoid tumor, about the size of a pullet's egg, arising from the lower half of the lung of this side, and, upon microscopical section, proving to be a cancer." (*Bull. Chas. Mus., 9*: 70).

FOOD: Largely fish, about 99 per cent. Sea-catfish, gizzard shad, herring, skipjack, sunfish, and toadfish have been found in stomach contents. Shrimp, crabs, and other crustaceans are taken, and sometimes frogs. It will be readily understood why the flesh of these birds is unpalatable.

FLORIDA CORMORANT
23. *Phalacrocorax auritus floridanus* (Audubon) (120a)

(Lat., *floridanus*, of Florida.)

DESCRIPTION: Length 22.00 to 30.00 inches. Similar to the Double-crested Cormorant but slightly smaller, with a larger bill.

RANGE: Breeds north to Louisiana and southeastern North Carolina; south to the Isle of Pines. Winters south to the Lesser Antilles.

STATUS IN S. C.: Fairly common permanent resident chiefly in the coast region. Reported north to the Santee River Delta; south to Beaufort County; and west to Coming-Tee in Berkeley County.

HISTORY: The Florida Cormorant is a permanent resident of South Carolina, and is presumed to breed there, but as yet all attempts to find its nest have proved fruitless. This is really an astonishing fact, since this form nests in North Carolina and also south of South Carolina. Wayne (1910) says that "This subspecies breeds . . . ," but he was never able to locate a colony and no observer since has been successful. While it is impossible to separate the two forms in the field in winter, when both occur in the State, any cormorant seen after May 1 is probably this subspecies. Specimens examined from South Carolina include a male taken at Coming-Tee on the upper Cooper River by E. Milby Burton on January 22, 1936, and a female collected in the Santee River Delta, also by Burton, on February 15, 1936.

In habits this bird is like the Double-crested Cormorant and the food is similar.

Family Anhingidae: Darters

WATER TURKEY
24. *Anhinga anhinga leucogaster* (Vieillot) (118)

(*Anhinga*, South American name of the bird; Gr., *leucogaster*, white-bellied.)

LOCAL NAMES: Snake-bird; Anhinga.

DESCRIPTION: Length 32.00 to 36.00 inches. *Male.* Glossy black, wings spangled with white and grayish white markings; tail tipped with brownish white. *Female.* Head, neck, and breast grayish buff; rest of plumage like that of male.

RANGE: Resident and breeds north to southern Illinois and North Carolina; south to Central America and Colombia, South America.

STATUS IN S. C.: Common permanent resident eastward. Recorded north to Mullins; east to Horry County; south to Beaufort County; and west to Bamberg, Clarendon, and Richland counties.

HISTORY: Certain birds are so inevitably connected with definite types of country that thought of one automatically produces vision of the other. Amid the gray-green reaches of the cypress lagoons, where still, dark water leads away between the soaring trunks; where the emerald foliage meets overhead like the roof of some vast cathedral, dwells this mysterious creature, seemingly an avian throwback to the Age of Reptiles.

Somber of plumage, silent of movement, the Anhinga seems to typify the brooding, inscrutable wilderness which is its home. Now and then it can be seen along rice-field canals, in willow swamps, or in other similar places, but the cypress swamp is its real home.

Though coastal in its distribution, the Anhinga shuns salt water. Only rarely does it visit the barrier islands, and to be certain of finding it, one must penetrate the fresh water rivers and swamps, or the old "backwaters" of the rice plantations.

Of very slender build, with long neck and tail, the male is jet black with silvery markings upon the back and wings. The female shows her fawn-colored neck and breast conspicuously and in practically any posture. The Anhinga is a wonderful flier and an adept swimmer and diver, being as aquatic as it is aerial. When swimming, as it does with its body submerged, the long, slender neck looks much like a snake looping along through the water; when soaring high over the trees, the long, fanned out tail appears much like that of a turkey.

The Anhinga nests in the swamps from late April through May, building a substantial home of twigs, sticks, and moss and often lining it with green cypress foliage. The nest is a much more finished product than that of the herons with which the Anhinga sometimes associates. The elevation of the nest above water varies from only a few feet to as much as 50 or more. The three to five eggs are plain, bluish white, often with a chalky coating which becomes nest stained as incubation advances. The eggs average 52.5 x 35.0 millimeters, and incubation requires twenty-five to twenty-eight days. Typical egg dates are: Beaufort County, May 10; Charleston County, April 19.

Bent states that this species "probably uses the same nest year after year." The bird certainly returns to approximately the same spot season after season, and sometimes new nests are built within a few feet of the old ones.

The young are even more reptilian looking than the parents; they are queer, snaky little creatures covered with beautiful buffy down which contrasts strongly with the dark feathers which later appear. Should they fall into the water, the young birds swim and dive with amazing celerity.

E. Milby Burton, while banding nestlings in June, 1929, at Coming-Tee Reserve, noted the remarkable diving ability of these young birds. Most of the nests were situated about twenty feet above the water. When Burton climbed a tree and neared one of the nests, the larger nestlings would poise on the edge of the nest and without any hesitation make a perfect dive into the water and come up 40 or 50 feet away. Others, when they struck the water would look around and then dive. This seems all the more remarkable because it was the first time that the nestlings had come in contact with water. After a few such incidents, banding was discontinued because it was impossible to capture these young birds in order to return them to their nests.

Most of the year the Anhinga is a completely silent bird, but during the nesting season it gives utterance to a peculiar, guttural note which would sadly puzzle any one unfamiliar with it. Sprunt recalls an occasion when, in company with Herbert R. Sass, he was investigating a Low-country backwater. They kept hearing a strange note for which they could in no way account; it had a weird, unearthly quality which fitted perfectly into the watery wilderness about them, and it was with difficulty that they finally traced it to an Anhinga, sitting motionless on a small cypress, like some fantastic idol.

The Anhinga was long considered a summer resident only, but in recent years has been found regularly in winter.

Food: Almost entirely fish. Some commercial varieties are included, but these are secured in swamps, where fishing is not commonly carried on. Typical of species consumed are mullet, sunfish, bream, and gizzard shad. Insects are taken at times and one stomach examined by the U. S. Biological Survey, contained a large quantity of caddis-fly larvae. The flesh of the Anhinga is unfit for food. Dingle (ms. 1948) states that he has observed this species feeding on berries of the hackberry (*Celtis*) and that excreta of the bird sometimes contains such seeds. This seems a remarkable departure from custom.

Family Fregatidae: Man-o'-war-birds

MAN-O'-WAR-BIRD
25. *Fregata magnificens rothschildi* Mathews (128)

(Ital., *Fregata*, a frigate; Lat., *magnificens*, splendid; *rothschildi*, to Walter Rothschild.)

LOCAL NAMES: Frigate Bird.

DESCRIPTION: Length 37.00 to 41.00 inches. Tail very deeply forked; bill strongly hooked. *Adult male.* Entirely black, glossed with purple reflections. *Female.* Dull black with a dull white patch on breast and sides. *Immature.* Back and wings brownish black, head and under parts brownish white.

RANGE: Resident and breeds north to the Bahamas; south to Honduras and northern Venezuela. Ranges also north to Texas and Florida, casually to Quebec.

STATUS IN S. C.: Casual summer visitor, May 12 to October 19, along the coast. Reported north to Cape Romain; south to Folly Island.

HISTORY: Few birds equal the Frigate Bird in power of flight, and none surpasses it except possibly the albatrosses. The body is of insignificant size, but the spread of the sable pinions is immense, some 7 feet or more. Able to float aloft indefinitely without a flap of the wings, it uses the air currents and drafts to an amazing degree. The eyesight of the bird is no less wonderful. It can drop with lightning swiftness to the water for the smallest morsel and, just as it seems about to crash, it arrests itself by a twist of the wings and picks up the object without wetting a feather.

Although the Frigate Bird cannot be expected on the South Carolina coast, there have been occurrences which cannot be accounted for by tropical storms, the bird appearing with no abnormal stress of weather whatever. It is rare, however, that it does so. The bird is common enough in south Florida, but it has never been found nesting there. Though perfectly capable of securing its own food, it indulges commonly in the practice of robbing other birds-—gulls, terns, pelicans, and boobies. From this habit it has gained the name of "Man-o'-war."

Apparently the first recorded specimen occurred in 1824 for in the *Charleston Courier* of September 24 the following is found: "A very large and singular variety of the *Frigate Bird* was sent yesterday by BENJAMIN WHITTER, Esq. of James Island, to the Museum of the Philosophical Society. The body of the bird is of the size of the Crane; from the head to the end of the wings, three feet in length extent of wings from tip to tip, seven feet. This is the second rare Bird MR. WHITTER has sent to the Museum, killed on his own premises."

Probably it did occur during the intervening years but it apparently was not again recorded until Wayne saw one on August 26, 1893, a few hours before the arrival of the great hurricane, which struck the next day.

Additional records of it in South Carolina are as follows: a specimen was taken on Sullivan's Island by George Aldret early in the morning of October 20, 1906, that afternoon the wind velocity reached 64 miles an hour; on October 19, 1910, Wayne saw a specimen near his home at Porcher's Bluff, the wind being 40 to 50 miles an hour; on May 24, 1925, Alex Mikell saw one over Charleston Harbor, and one at Folly Island on June 2. These two observations may have been of the same bird. Two were seen circling over South Battery in Charleston, September 22, 1926. Clear, calm weather prevailed before and after the two foregoing occurrences. Since these were recorded, about twelve more observations have been made.

The Frigate Bird often occurs about rookeries of herons, pelicans, and cormorants in the Florida Keys, and is always present at the great tern colonies of the Dry Tortugas. Although Watson, in his detailed studies there in 1908, stated that he never saw them molest the Sooty Tern young, other observers have since recorded considerable predation among these birds by the Man-o'-war-bird. Sprunt, studying there in 1946 and 1947, saw many young sooties seized and swallowed by the Frigate Birds.

Food: Mainly fish which are taken from other sea birds. Menhaden, flying fish, pinfish, sea-catfish, weakfish, and mullet have been found in stomachs. It is probable that the Frigate Bird seldom takes commercial varieties of fish.

Order Ciconiiformes

Herons, Storks, Ibises, Flamingos, and Allies

Family Ardeidae: Herons and Bitterns

GREAT WHITE HERON
26. Ardea occidentalis occidentalis Audubon (192)

(Lat., *Ardea*, a heron; *occidentalis*, western.)

DESCRIPTION: Length 45.00 to 54.00 inches. Legs and neck very long, the back of the head with relatively short plumes; plumage entirely white; bill and legs yellow.

RANGE: Resident and breeds north to the extreme southern Florida mainland; south to the Florida Keys; accidental in North Carolina, northwestern Pennsylvania, and South Carolina.

STATUS IN S. C.: Accidental in the coast region.

HISTORY: This fine bird, the largest of American herons, inhabits the most restricted range. It occurs regularly only in extreme southern Florida and the Keys and its normal range is roughly an area about one hundred miles long by fifty wide. It will be seen, therefore, that South Carolina is not a likely place in which to look for the Great White Heron. Only an accident places this species on the South Carolina list.

In the spring of 1943 a report from Mrs. Francis Bartow, of Brewton Plantation, near Yemassee, reached Sprunt that a Great White Heron was frequenting the rice fields of the plantation. Sprunt, Chamberlain, and Alexander Sprunt, IV, journeyed thither on May 29, 1943, and found the bird at once. Collecting was not advisable, but they succeeded in obtaining a photograph of the bird. This is the sole record for the State (*Auk, 61*: 1944, 150).

The Great White Heron is pure white and has a yellow beak. It is often confused, therefore, with the American Egret, but there is one infallible field characteristic which will always distinguish it: the legs of the Great White are greenish yellow; those of the Egret are jet black.

Sprunt has had much experience with the Great White Heron in the Florida Keys where he worked with it for years, following its fortunes from an all-time low population status of 146 birds in the fall of 1935 to about eight hundred in 1940, an increase due to the rigid protection afforded it by the National Audubon Society.

In general habits and food this bird does not differ materially from the Great Blue Heron.

GREAT BLUE HERON
27. *Ardea herodias herodias* Linnaeus (194)

(Gr., *herodias*, heron.)

LOCAL NAMES: Poor Joe (Po' Jo'); Blue Crane.

DESCRIPTION: Length 42.00 to 50.00 inches. A large, long-legged, long-necked wading bird. Mainly slaty gray with various markings of black, white, and chestnut.

RANGE: Breeds north of Alberta and Quebec; south to eastern Nebraska and central eastern South Carolina. Winters north to Texas and New York; south to Panama and Venezuela.

STATUS IN S. C.: Common permanent resident throughout State except in southern corner where found only in winter; less numerous elsewhere in winter. Recorded north to Spartanburg and Chester counties; east to Horry County; south to Charleston County (Porcher's Bluff); west to Pickens County.

HISTORY: This bird probably will continue to be the "Blue Crane" of the uninformed until the end of time. Known practically the country over in one or another of its several races, this big heron is the "Poor Joe" of the Low-country. It is a permanent resident over the entire State, with the exception of the southeastern corner. Its long, lanky form, majestic flight, and raucous squawks render it one of the most conspicuous of water birds. Birds that breed to the northward of South Carolina pass through the State on migration, as is indicated by the record of a bird banded in Wisconsin in July, 1932, and recovered near Summerville, Dorchester County, in September, 1933 (*Bird-Banding*, *9*: 80).

The species is particularly abundant in the coastal waters, but it makes its home in mill ponds, streams, and swamps anywhere in South Carolina. It has been reported from practically every county in the State. This big heron is rather a still-hunter in its feeding habits, often standing like a statue in shallow water until a frog, fish, or snake appears within range of its dagger-beak which it plunges downward like a flash to transfix the prey.

Nesting sometimes begins about the second week in March, but a more average date would be the latter part of the month. For one reason or another, in some years the season may be prolonged into summer. The placing of the rude platform of dead sticks which constitutes the nest varies with the locality selected. More often than not the nest is built in the tops of such tall trees as pines and cypresses, and it is not unusual for several nests to be in the same tree. Now and then, on marsh hammocks, nests are much lower, sometimes in the tops of heavy willows and myrtles no more than 8 or 10 feet high.

There are usually four eggs, sometimes five, sometimes but three. Like those of all herons, large or small, the eggs of the Great Blue Heron are unmarked and of greenish-blue color, averaging 64.5 x 45.2 millimeters. But one brood is raised each year (Wayne), and incubation consumes about twenty-eight days. Typical nesting sites in the Low-country are the pines of Bull's Island, and the great cypress trees of such backwaters as Blake's Reserve on the South Santee River. It has been found nesting sparingly on Buzzard Island in the Stono River, at very low elevations.

The young birds are very pugnacious when the nest is being examined; they strike at the observer viciously with sharp beaks, which can inflict a painful injury. The disgorged food and generally filthy condition of the nests make a rookery offensive to the olfactory senses.

FOOD: Findings of the U. S. Fish and Wildlife Service show the diet of the Great Blue Heron to consist of fish, 60 per cent; crustaceans, 14 per cent; insects, about 9 per cent; frogs, salamanders, and snakes, 9.5 per cent; and mammals (mainly field mice), 6 per cent. Approximately half of the fish were useful varieties such as catfish, pickerel, and sunfish; the rest were suckers, killifish, and gizzard-shad. Dragon-fly nymphs, water bugs, and water tigers, all destructive to fish, were among the insects.

28. WARD'S HERON: *Ardea herodias wardi* Ridgway (194b)

(Lat., *wardi*, to Charles W. Ward.)

LOCAL NAMES: Poor Joe (Po' Jo'); Crane.

DESCRIPTION: Length 48.00 to 54.00 inches. Similar to the Great Blue Heron but larger and paler, particularly on the hind neck and remaining upper parts.

RANGE: Breeds north to Kansas, southeastern Iowa, and southeastern South Carolina; south to southern Texas and southern Florida. Winters north to Texas and Alabama; south to central Mexico and Florida.

STATUS IN S. C.: Common summer resident from February, north to Charleston and south to Beaufort County.

HISTORY: This larger edition of the Great Blue Heron reaches its northern supposed nesting limit on the Atlantic coast in the southern portion of this State, and is the supposed breeding form about Hilton Head Island and the adjacent territory of Beaufort County north to Charleston County. There it is a summer resident, usually arriving in late February. Specimens examined by Dr. Harry C. Oberholser have been taken on Hilton Head Island May 10, 1864, by D. W. Prentiss, and near Charleston on March 27, 1939, by E. von S. Dingle.

No distinction can be made by most observers between this race and the Great Blue Heron, the two birds being so similar that identification in the field can be made only by experts.

The habits, haunts, breeding season, and nesting habits of Ward's Heron do not differ appreciably from those of the Great Blue Heron.

FOOD: Like the Great Blue Heron, this bird consumes numbers of snakes, these amounting to about 10 per cent of the total food.

AMERICAN EGRET
29. *Casmerodius albus egretta* (Gmelin) (196)

(Gr., *Casmerodius*, gaping heron; Lat., *albus*, white; *egretta*, French *aigrette*, egret.)
LOCAL NAMES: White Heron; White Crane.
DESCRIPTION: Length 36.00 to 42.00 inches. Plumage white; legs and feet black; bill yellow.
RANGE: Breeds north to Oregon and New Jersey; south to Patagonia. Winters north to Oregon and North Carolina; south to Patagonia. Moves north in summer to Manitoba and Quebec.
STATUS IN S. C.: Common permanent resident but far less frequent in winter and most numerous on the coastal plain. Recorded north to Chester and Lancaster counties; east to Horry County; south to Beaufort County; west to Oconee and Pickens counties.

HISTORY: The history of this beautiful bird in South Carolina closely parallels that of other parts of its range since the stoppage of the plume trade. It is a story of a "comeback" from the edge of oblivion to abundance, probably the outstanding proof of the efficacy of Twentieth Century conservation effort. Granting the importance of individual cooperation in many localities, the preponderance of credit for the saving of this species (and the following) should go to the National Audubon Society, its then president, Dr. T. Gilbert Pearson, and to Dr. Theodore Sherman Palmer of the Biological Survey. Without their efforts, it is altogether likely that the two "plume birds" would now occupy that sad category shared by the vanished Passenger Pigeon and Great Auk.

Arthur T. Wayne in 1910 had this to say about this egret: "The species has been, and still is, mercilessly shot for its plumes . . . for millinery purposes and the day is not distant when it will be absolutely extinct unless laws are made and enforced for its protection. These birds are now so very shy that the sight of a human being causes them to take wing when they are more than a quarter of a mile away."

The history of the fight to save the American Egret is too long for inclusion here, but it is a story which everyone interested in ornithology should read. Probably the best account is by Dr. Pearson, the man who led the fight.

One result of the American Egret's great increase in numbers has been its altered status, in South Carolina, from that of a summer resident, which it was long considered to be, to that of a year-round species. It occurs commonly throughout the twelve months near the coast and even in salt water localities. Localities in which the Egrets nest now include marsh hammocks such as Buzzard's Island, Stono River, and similar spots. There have been, therefore, noticeable changes not only in the number of the birds, but in their seasonal occurrence and nesting habits since Wayne's book appeared.

Of a number of American Egrets banded by Burton near Charleston on June 8, 1929, one was taken at Oglethorpe, Ga., July 19, 1929, and another in Lancaster County, August 1, of the same year. Also a bird banded in Florida in June, 1926, was taken in Kershaw County in August of the same year.

American Egrets, like most herons, nest together in large colonies, or rookeries. The most important one in the coastal region is at Blake's Reserve, on the South Santee River, in Charleston County. This beautiful backwater, with its great cypresses, waving moss, and miles of wine-brown water, is the oldest known egret colony in continued use in the country, unbroken records going back to the spring of 1823. Here, these ethereally beautiful birds live in surroundings suggestive of fairyland. This was the site used by the late Dr. Frank M. Chapman for the studies of the habitat group of these birds which is in the American Museum of Natural History in New York City.

The American Egret's nest is no great achievement of avian architecture. It is simply a platform of dead twigs and sticks, and it does no more than keep the eggs from falling out and give the young a precarious habitation. It may be placed in low bushes or on the tops of tall trees, depending on the locality. The eggs are usually three in number, of the typical heron color of greenish blue. They average 56.5 x 40.5 millimeters and require twenty-eight days for incubation. Nesting commences in late April or early May. The earliest seasonal record known for South Carolina occurred in 1945, when Lloyd Barber found young "standing in the nests" on April 16. These nests were started in March and eggs must have been laid at least by the middle of the month. American Egrets rear only one brood each season.

It is during the breeding season that the plumes, worn by both sexes, are at their finest; and to see the birds displaying at the nest, with the misty shower of delicate lace-like "aigrettes" raised like a bridal veil, is one of the most entrancing bird sights in nature. Later, the plumes begin to drop, and sometimes can be found floating under the rookery trees, usually water-stained and bedraggled.

Unlike the more active Snowy Egret, this species appears to prefer still-hunting, standing motionless amid the marshes or at the edge of ponds until prey comes its way. After the nesting season young and old scatter widely in feeding but come together at evening in communal roosts, either in fresh-water lagoons or on islands in the marshes.

Food: Strangely enough, little is known specifically regarding the American Egret's diet. Small fish predominate, such as gizzard-shad, sunfish, and minnows. Numerous frogs are taken, and at times, small alligators, lizards, mice, fiddler crabs, grasshoppers and other insects.

PLATE V: DUCKS OFF BEACH

Oil Painting by Francis Lee Jaques

Two topmost flying ducks, left to right: Buffle-head (female) and Buffle-head (male). The five ducks just below the Buffle-head, left to right: Old-squaw (female), two Old-squaws (male), American Golden-eye (female), and American Golden-eye (male). The pair at right, center, left to right: Surf Scoter (female) and Surf Scoter (male). Bottom, left, left to right: American Scoter (female) and American Scoter (male).

Among the snakes, the venomous water moccasin (*Agkistrodon piscivorus*) is often taken. Frogs make up a large percentage of the food brought to the young.

To imagine this species as preying upon other birds would seem fantastic, but Sprunt recorded at least one instance which would lead to the suspicion that egrets occasionally devour smaller birds. In May, 1938, an overseer on Cherokee Plantation in Colleton County saw an egret seize something on the edge of a rice-field ditch and take flight. He succeeded in making the egret drop its prey, which turned out to be a still living Red-winged Blackbird. Examination showed the blackbird had been previously wounded, although it could still walk (*Auk 56*: 1939, 469).

30. SNOWY EGRET: *Leucophoyx thula thula* (Molina) (197)

(Gr., *Leucophoyx*, white heron; *thula*, Chilean name of this bird.)

LOCAL NAMES: Snowy Heron.

DESCRIPTION: Length 20.00 to 27.00 inches. Plumage white; bill and legs black; feet yellow.

RANGE: Breeds north to Utah and New Jersey; south to Chile and Argentina. Winters north to Texas and South Carolina; south to Argentina. Moves north in summer as far as Alberta and New Brunswick.

STATUS IN S. C.: Common permanent resident largely on the coastal plain but less numerous in winter. Reported north to Florence County; east to Horry County; south to Beaufort County; west casually to Aiken County.

HISTORY: This exquisite bird was even more heavily persecuted during plume trade days than its larger relative, the American Egret, and in consequence came nearer to extermination. Wayne (1910) says of it that, "The Snowy Egret is now almost extinct on this coast . . . it is so rare a bird at the present day that I have not seen an example for more than ten years. . . ."

Today, happily, Wayne's statement is no longer true. The Snowy Egret is now a permanent resident and one may see it, in an appropriate environment, almost every day of the year, winter and summer. The return to abundance from the shadow of extinction is a wonderful illustration of concerted and determined conservation. The Snowy Egret was "rediscovered" in the coast region by Herbert R. Sass on May 15, 1908, and recorded by him in *Bird-Lore, X*: 160.

The Snowy Egret is one of the most active of the herons. It seems forever on the move, quick and graceful, the picture of animated beauty. It is no still-hunting bird. Rather it steps quickly along, poking here and there into marshy gutters and little pools, sometimes hovering over a school of minnows and jabbing downward with its beak, almost like a petrel above the waves. Its feeding habits are characteristic of no other members of the heron group.

The Snowy Egret seems much more partial to salt water than its larger relative and it is found in the marshes and among the barrier islands even more than in the cypress lagoons. The birds that winter in South Carolina do not seem to be affected by the occasional cold waves which visit the Low-country. The late E. A. Simons reported seeing a bird on the Country Club golf course, James Island, on January 2, 1928, a day on which the temperature dropped to 18° F. For many years a group of six to twelve birds wintered regularly in a small pond between Cannon and Spring streets, near the Ashley River Bridge, in Charleston. On several occasions this pond was frozen over and it was a remarkable sight to see Snowy Egrets walking on ice. It is thought that it was about 1928 that the Snowy Egret began appearing regularly in winter near Charleston.

Nesting takes place usually early in May, but may be earlier in some seasons and later in others. Typical dates are as follows: Heron Island, Charleston County, April 28, 1928, estimated 110 pairs, eggs just laid; same locality, May 31, 1929, 125 pairs, young hatching. On June 7, 1930, forty-seven young were banded at this spot.

The Snowy's nest is the usual frail affair of sticks, in bushes or occasionally on the ground. The blue-green eggs number four or five, occasionally three, and average 43.0 x 32.4 millimeters. Incubation requires about eighteen days. Button-bushes and small cypresses are used in fresh-water sites, cassine (*Ilex*), salt-water myrtle (*Baccharis*), and prickly pear (*Opuntia*) on the marsh islands. In nesting, Snowy Egrets commonly congregate with Little Blue and Louisiana Herons. During the past two or three seasons a thriving rookery has developed on Drum Island, in Charleston Harbor, crossed by the Cooper River bridge. The birds make a white blanket over the low bushes which surround an open, sandy area, which also supports a colony of Black Skimmers and Least Terns. Like the American Egret, the Snowy raises but one brood.

It is to be noted that the plumes of this species recurve at their tips, unlike the perfectly straight "aigrettes" of the larger egret. There are also short plumes on the head and breast of the Snowy. The outstanding field mark is the presence of bright yellow feet on the black legs.

Food: The Snowy Egret feeds principally on shrimp, small fish, fiddler crabs, snails, insects, lizards, and frogs. O. E. Baynard (1912) records that Florida birds consume suckers, grasshoppers, cutworms, crayfish, and small snakes.

Reddish Egret
31. *Dichromanassa rufescens rufescens* (Gmelin) (198)

(Gr., *Dichromanassa*, two-colored queen; Lat., *rufescens*, becoming reddish.)

Description: Length 27.00 to 32.00 inches. *Normal phase*. Plain slate color; head and neck cinnamon rufous. *White phase*. Plumage entirely white.

Range: Resident and breeds north to southern Texas, and southeastern Georgia (casually); south to Yucatan and Cuba.

Status in S. C.: Accidental in the coast region.

History: This species has been observed only once in South Carolina, on January 15, 1934, when Clarence E. Chapman saw two birds from a duck blind on his plantation, The Mulberry, in Berkeley County. One was in the normal slate-colored phase, the other in the white phase (which was once thought to be a distinct species, the Peale's Egret of Audubon). The record can be accepted as entirely authentic, for Mr. Chapman was an excellent observer as well as an ardent sportsman and made many valuable records during his many years of winter residence in the South Carolina Low-country.

The Chapman observation was recorded by Sprunt (*Auk, 52*: 1935, 77):

> On January 15, 1934, on his plantation "Mulberry," Cooper River, S. C., Mr. Clarence E. Chapman, of New York, saw two specimens of this species, and watched them for forty minutes. Seated in a duck blind in one of his rice fields, Mr. Chapman studied every detail of the strangers, sometimes at a range of from fifteen to twenty feet. He knew what they were at once, and his vivid description of them leaves nothing to be desired. One was in the dark, and the other the light phase of plumage.
>
> They were fishing, preening and resting, and finally disappeared into the saw-grass. Though realizing their rarity and with a gun in his hands at the time, Mr. Chapman did not attempt to take either. He was perfectly convinced of their identity and so is the writer. This is an addition to the avifauna of South Carolina.

The Reddish Egret resembles the Little Blue Heron but is larger and has a "mane" of feathers on the head and neck, which is capable of being erected or depressed at will. The two-colored bill (light at the base and dark at the tip) is an excellent field mark.

Louisiana Heron
32. *Hydranassa tricolor ruficollis* (Gosse)   (199)

(Gr., *Hydranassa*, water queen; Lat., *tricolor*, three colored; *ruficollis*, red-necked.)

LOCAL NAMES: Crane.

DESCRIPTION: Length 23.00 to 28.00 inches. Above bluish gray, with neck plumes maroon; chin and rest of lower parts white.

RANGE: Breeds north to Texas and Virginia; south to Ecuador and Venezuela. Winters north to Lower California and South Carolina; south to Colima, Panama, and Venezuela. Wanders north in summer casually to California and New York.

STATUS IN S. C.: Common permanent resident; most common along the coast, and less frequent in winter. Reported north to Timmonsville; east to Horry County; south to Beaufort County; and west casually to Aiken County.

HISTORY: Probably the most graceful of all the herons, this "Lady of the Waters" is the most abundant member of the family in the coastal region of South Carolina. It does not stray far inland, as a rule. To the uninformed, it is another of the numerous "cranes" of the blue, gray, or white varieties. To the bird student, it is the easiest of all the medium-sized herons to know, since it is the only one with dark plumaged neck and white belly. It wears a small, gray and white head plume in the nesting season.

Vying with the Snowy Egret in constant, graceful activity, the Louisiana Heron gives an impression of extremely slender build, more so than that of most herons. It is perfectly at home in fresh-water lagoons or salt marshes and nests in both. It can often be seen within the limits of the coast towns, from Myrtle Beach southward through Charleston and Beaufort. The mud flats near the Ashley River

Bridge in Charleston are favored feeding grounds, and there is no reason for the city dweller to be unfamiliar with it. The fact that it is a permanent resident furthers the opportunity for observation and for the study of its breeding rookeries and autumnal and winter roosts.

The complete dissimilarity of this bird's nesting locations is at times surprising. It is a far cry from the unearthly beauty of a cypress-grown, moss-draped, lotus-spangled lagoon, to the insignificant yard-high bushes of a tiny bank of oyster shells, surrounded by miles of salt water. And yet both places form the rookeries of this interesting and versatile heron. It commonly associates with Snowy and Little Blue Herons in nesting, and the rookeries of such groups, which may also contain Night Herons and White Ibises are animated and uproarious spectacles. The sights, sounds, and smells of a heron colony are memories that linger long with an observer.

From late April on, nesting is in full swing, and neither the construction of the nest, nor the four or five bluish eggs, differ much from those of the Snowy and Little Blue. Only when the owner is on the nest can accurate identification be made of it, until the young are hatched. A typical egg date is provided by a record made on Heron Island, May 3, 1928, eggs having just been laid. Delayed nesting at times extends into July, such an instance being recorded in field notes of Sprunt: "July 3, 1930, colony found on White Banks, Bull's Bay, nesting in very low bushes of sea lavender (*Tournefortia*). Some nests practically on the ground." The size of the eggs averages 44.1 x 33.7 millimeters, and incubation requires about twenty-one days.

During the past fifteen or twenty years hundreds of herons have been banded by staff members and associates of the Charleston Museum, under the direction of E. M. Burton, and by personnel of the U. S. Fish and Wildlife Service. Most of the work has been done in the vicinity of Charleston or on the Cape Romain Refuge, near McClellanville. A number of interesting returns have come in on Louisiana Herons, some showing the northward movement of immature birds into North Carolina and Virginia. Other birds have been recovered in Mississippi, Florida, British Honduras, Cuba, Puerto Rico, and the Bahamas. Recovery time has been from a few months to almost eight years.

One of our most interesting banding returns resulted from the discovery of five bands by Chamberlain in the stomach of an eight foot alligator killed at Porcher's Bluff, Charleston County, on August 9, 1929. These bands were from young Louisiana and Little Blue Herons banded June 13, 1929, in a colony situated a mile and a half from the point where the alligator was taken.

FOOD: Having examined forty-eight stomachs of this bird, the U. S. Fish and Wildlife Service has found the food to be composed of more than 68 per cent killifish, these being found in thirty-eight of the stomachs. Crustaceans, shrimp, and crayfish made up 20 per cent of the total, and other items included spiders, weevils, grasshoppers, giant water bugs, dragon flies, and beetles. Among the fish appeared only one "food" species, a sheepshead.

LITTLE BLUE HERON
33. *Florida caerulea caerulea* (Linnaeus)   (200)

(*Florida*, honoring that state; Lat., *caerulea*, blue.)

LOCAL NAMES: Blue Crane; Calico Crane.

DESCRIPTION: Length 20.00 to 29.00 inches. *Adult*. Slaty blue, the head and neck maroon; legs dull black. *Immature*. White with slaty wing tips.

RANGE: Breeds north to Texas and New Jersey; south to Mexico and Central America. Winters north to Texas and South Carolina. Moves northward in summer to Wisconsin and Quebec.

STATUS IN S. C.: Abundant permanent resident over much of the State but less common in winter and in the interior. Recorded north to Chester and Darlington counties; east to Horry County; south to Beaufort County; and west to Greenwood and Oconee counties.

HISTORY: This abundant heron is a permanent resident. It is one that is to be seen more often in the interior of South Carolina than the two preceding species, for it wanders widely after the nesting season and commonly penetrates into the mountain region. Almost invariably, such observations concern immature (white) birds. Usually they may be looked for from late July until early September in the mountain region, the earliest record at Clemson, Oconee County, being July 4 (G. E. Hudson).

The adult and immature plumages of this heron sometimes confuse observers. The adult is an all-dark bird; the immature, white. A white Little Blue Heron may seem a paradox, but white it is. Confusion with the Snowy Egret results, but it should be recalled that the latter has black legs and yellow toes, while this species has dark greenish legs and toes. The Snowy's beak is black; the Little Blue's is parti-colored, dark at the tip and light at the base. Immature Little Blues have dusky or bluish wing tips, a fact that may be noted even in nestling birds before the primaries are actually unsheathed. The transition from immature to adult plumage produces a rather startling, pied pattern of white and blue, resulting in the local name "Calico Crane."

In nesting and feeding the Little Blue frequents both fresh and salt water. There are at least four rookeries of Little Blue Herons in Charleston County that are on islands completely surrounded by salt water, which comes to within a few feet of many nests. One of these islands is more than five miles from the mainland, across marshes, mud flats, and open sounds.

Nesting in colonies with other herons, the Little Blue Heron does not differ in any way from the other herons in the nature of its nests and eggs, both of which are identical with Louisianas and Snowies. Four or five eggs are usually laid during the third week in April, but forward or backward seasons produce variations. The size of the egg averages 44.0 x 33.5 millimeters; only one brood is raised and incubation requires twenty-one to twenty-three days. On June 8, 1927, young had hatched in the rookery on Raccoon Key (Cape Romain); on June 12 of that year eggs at Heron Island had not yet hatched. On June 12, 1930, 113 young were banded at Youghal Plantation, Christ Church Parish, Charleston County, and many more have been banded there before and since.

It will be of interest to follow the trails of a few of these banded birds. Two banded in June 1929 were found two months later in the stomach of the same alligator mentioned in the account of the Louisiana Heron. Of two birds banded in June 1931, one was taken in Virginia the following August, and the other in Louisiana five years later. A bird banded in June, 1932, was recovered in Jamaica, B.W.I., in October, 1934. Four birds banded on June 12, 1932, show well the widespread movements of our herons. One was taken in Honduras, in January, 1934; another was found in the Bahamas, in October, 1935; the third in Tumaco, Colombia, South America, in April, 1938; and the fourth near its original banding point, James Island, S. C., in December, 1939.

As Wayne (1910) records, this heron breeds while in the immature white plumage, but pairs of blue and white birds are very uncommon.

FOOD: Crustaceans (mostly crayfish) appear to predominate in the food of this species, judging from examinations of some forty-six stomachs made by U. S. Fish and Wildlife biologists. The percentage reached 45 per cent, with fish forming 27 per cent. The fish were killifish, catfish, sunfish, and minnows. Insects amounted to 16.5 per cent of the total, and frogs, snakes, and turtles were represented. It seems clear enough that the Little Blue Heron is a highly useful species.

EASTERN GREEN HERON
34. *Butorides virescens virescens* (Linnaeus) (201)

(Lat. and Gr., *Butorides*, bitternlike; Lat., *virescens*, greenish.)

LOCAL NAMES: Skeow.

DESCRIPTION: Length 16.00 to 22.00 inches. Above dark metallic or glaucous green; neck and sides of head maroon; remaining lower parts plain gray.

RANGE: Breeds north to North Dakota and southern Quebec; south to southern Mexico and Honduras. Winters north to Texas and South Carolina; south to southern Mexico and Guatemala.

STATUS IN S. C.: Common permanent resident throughout the State, less numerous in winter. Observed north to Chester County; east to Horry County; south to Beaufort County; and west to Oconee and Pickens counties.

HISTORY: This smallest heron is an individualist, and remarkably unheronlike in some ways (as may be surmised from its generic name). Far more inclined to the solitary life than most of its family, it covers a large range, and is known to many a country boy and mill-pond angler. It is found in many parts of South Carolina where other herons do not occur, and is known by a variety of names. It nests within the limits of towns, and even cities, but it is so secretive that many people never know of its presence. Wayne (1910) mentions it as nesting in Charleston in the late 1880's, and it still does so.

Salt marshes, river swamps, creeks, ponds, and upland rivers,—all of these are its home in summer. A few spend the entire winter in the coast region, and are therefore permanent residents, but the bird is very local and is not at all common from November until late March.

Nesting commences in early April, eggs being laid during the second week of the month. The nests are very frail; some of them show the eggs through the bottom. For the most part, single pairs nest apart from other birds; now and then they breed in loose colonies or on the outskirts of other heron rookeries. Nests are sometimes only a few feet above the ground, but they may be at elevations of 20 or 30 feet if located in trees like the live oak. The eggs generally number four or five and can be recognized by their small size, averaging 38.0 x 29.5 millimeters, though the color, greenish blue, unmarked, is identical with that of the other herons. Usually one, sometimes two, broods are raised and incubation requires seventeen days.

In flight the Green Heron draws the neck in between the shoulders, in typical heron fashion, but when the bird is alarmed, it stretches the neck to its rather surprising length. This, with the crest flared, gives the bird a completely different aspect from that of the resting posture, when it seems much smaller. The usual single, explosive note much resembles the word "skeow," hence, that name for the bird is almost universal.

FOOD: Examination of over two hundred stomachs of this species resulted in the following analysis: fish 40 per cent; crustaceans 24 per cent; insects 27 per cent. Again killifish were the most numerous, with thirteen other species represented, such as carp, catfish, and eels. Dragon flies, katydids, grasshoppers, beetles, and damsel flies composed the insect diet.

BLACK-CROWNED NIGHT HERON
35. *Nycticorax nycticorax hoactli* (Gmelin) (202)

(Gr., *Nycticorax*, night raven; *hoactli*, Aztec name of bird.)

LOCAL NAMES: Indian Pullet.

DESCRIPTION: Length 23.00 to 26.00 inches. *Adult.* Crown and back black; forehead, sides of head, long head plumes, and lower surface white; rest of plumage gray. *Immature.* Light brown, spotted above and streaked below with white.

RANGE: Breeds north to Oregon and southern Quebec; south to Central America and Argentina. Winters north to Oregon and Massachusetts; south to Argentina.

STATUS IN S. C.: Common permanent resident throughout the State, most numerous on the coastal plain, less frequent in winter. Reported north to Chester County; east to Horry County; south to Beaufort County; and west to Greenwood and Oconee counties.

HISTORY: This species is known the year around, although adults are rare and local in winter. Immature birds are often seen and still roost at times along the Ashley River waterfront in Charleston. Another group, numbering perhaps two dozen birds, roosts regularly in the grounds of 32 Legare Street, in lower Charleston. The night herons deserve their name, for much of their feeding is done after dusk. As they leave their day-time roosts and wing out to the marshy creeks and mud flats, the hollow, resonant, "quock" which is so characteristic, may be heard by many a porch-sitter taking the evening coolness. The birds are much stockier in build than other herons, with shorter neck and shorter legs. The heavily streaked immature birds are utterly unlike the adults, except in contour and structure, but may always be recognized as night herons by their shape. Migrants from the northern colonies appear in the Carolinas in winter.

Of the comparatively few herons of this species banded near Charleston, returns have come in from North Carolina and Virginia within a few months of banding. One bird was found dead at Fort Pierce, Florida, two years after banding. Also of interest is a bird banded in July, 1932, at Gay Head, Massachusetts, and found in Beaufort County in September, 1938 (*Bird-Banding, 13*: 1942, 36).

Although early seasons will sometimes induce nesting in late April, a more average time is mid-May. The birds resort to both the fresh-water swamps and salt-marsh hammocks in the breeding season, and they associate freely with other herons in their rookeries. As a rule the nests are more substantial and bulky, less of the slovenly character exhibited by the rest of the family, and the three to five eggs are somewhat paler in their shade of greenish blue, and larger, averaging 51.5 x 37.0 millimeters. The incubation period is from twenty-four to twenty-six days. This species seems less inclined to congregate in the numbers common to the other herons; twenty to thirty pairs nesting with hundreds of Louisiana and Little Blue Herons would be a considerable percentage. However, there are many of these small colonies throughout the nesting range.

FOOD: W. L. McAtee has studied the food of this heron and has found that fish compose nearly 54 per cent of the total. Crustaceans (mainly crayfish) were 22 per cent, insects nearly 16 per cent, frogs 7 per cent, and meadow mice 1.66 per cent. Catfish, sunfish, suckers, shiners, carp, and killifish were represented, the majority of these having no commercial value.

YELLOW-CROWNED NIGHT HERON
36. *Nyctanassa violacea violacea* (Linnaeus) (203)

(Gr., *Nyctanassa*, night queen; Lat., *violacea*, violet colored.)

LOCAL NAMES: Indian Pullet.

DESCRIPTION: Length 22.00 to 28.00 inches. Bill stout. *Adult.* Gray, paler below; head and nape black, with crown, cheek patch, and most of head plumes yellowish white. *Immature.* Like that of the Black-crowned Night Heron but darker.

RANGE: Breeds north to Kansas and Massachusetts; south to Mexico, Costa Rica, and Trinidad. Winters north to Texas and Florida; south to Central America and Trinidad.

STATUS IN S. C.: Fairly common summer resident, March 23 to November 10, in southern and eastern parts of the State. Reported north and east to Horry County; south to Beaufort County; and west to Aiken County.

HISTORY: This beautiful and retiring species is far less familiar than the Black-crowned Night Heron. Its range is much more restricted, for one thing, and its habitat in that range is more selective. In the nesting season it is a bird of the cypress swamps, where its soft gray plumage, and silent, unobtrusive ways seem to suit perfectly the gray-green obscurity of its watery haunts.

It is a summer resident in South Carolina, and occurs but rarely at any great distance from the coast. Immatures appear inclined to remain later than adults.

Foothill Country, Oconee County

RUSSELL MAXEY

Blue Ridge Vista, Spartanburg County

Table Rock, Pickens County   CARL JULIEN

Caesar's Head, Greenville County   CARL JULIEN

The young of the two night herons are so strikingly similar that much difficulty is experienced in field identification. The young of the Yellow-crowned Night Heron are generally darker than those of the Black-crown, and the legs are more yellowish, but these are characters not easily seen. Peterson (1947) gives as the best field mark the fact that the feet of this species extend beyond the tail when the bird is in flight, whereas those of the Black-crown do not.

Even in its nesting the Yellow-crown is rather solitary. Now and then five or six pairs will build in a loose colony, but generally speaking each pair prefers to nest apart from other birds. Although it does not congregate with other herons, it may nest on the outer fringes of a populous rookery. It is very likely to return to the same spot in a swamp, year after year. The nest is saddled on a limb of a cypress or gum, sometimes overhanging one of the "leads" or aisles of water amid the tree trunks. Care must be used in approaching it; otherwise the bird will slip silently away like a gray ghost, to sit quietly in some nearby tree. There are, as a rule, three or four eggs, of the usual shade of blue-green; and they average 51.3 x 36.9 millimeters. Two broods are raised and incubation requires twenty-four days. May is the nesting month, although late April records exist. Wayne (1910) lists April 20 as "very early" for eggs.

After the nesting season, the Yellow-crowns leave the cypress lagoons and congregate in the salt marshes until they migrate southward. Many can then be seen on the barrier islands.

FOOD: Examination of ninety stomachs by E. R. Kalmbach revealed the food to be almost wholly crayfish (this reflecting their fresh-water preference). Wayne states that small fiddler crabs are taken in late summer. A few fish and aquatic insects are also taken. Audubon listed a more varied diet, consisting of small snakes, lizards, snails, small mammals, and young birds which had fallen from their nests.

37. AMERICAN BITTERN: *Botaurus lentiginosus* (Montagu)   (190)

(Lat., *Botaurus*, combination of *bos* and *taurus*, bull; *lentiginosus*, freckled.)

LOCAL NAMES: Stake-driver; Thunder-pumper.

DESCRIPTION: Length 23.00 to 34.00 inches. Upper surface ochraceous, much mottled with brown, black, and white; lower parts pale buff striped with brown.

RANGE: Breeds north to British Columbia, southern Mackenzie, and southern Ungava (Quebec); south to southern California and Florida. Winters north to British Columbia and Massachusetts; south to Guatemala and Panama.

STATUS IN S. C.: Uncommon local permanent resident over much of the State but more numerous in winter. Recorded north to Rock Hill (York County); east to Horry County; south to Beaufort County; and west to Oconee County.

HISTORY: The American Bittern is an unfamiliar bird. It is a strange, secretive creature, more like an animated piece of vegetation than a bird. It shuns dry land completely, making its home amid boggy marsh and swampland, either fresh or salt. Unless blundered upon, it seldom flies but rather slips away among the cat-tails and bullrushes in noiseless, invisible retreat.

One of the most protectively colored of birds, the bittern can be gazed upon at very short range and still not be seen. Head and neck erect, it stands like a brown statue among the reeds, and it will actually sway with the waving grasses if a breeze is blowing. When suddenly flushed, it springs upward with a guttural croak and flies away like a brown phantom.

This bittern is a permanent resident in South Carolina, but it is much more likely to be seen in winter, when its numbers are augmented by migrants from the north. In summer it seems rare and local, but this is probably due to its retiring habits. That it nests seems beyond question, but the strange fact remains that the breeding record by Dr. John Bachman in 1833 is the only one in existence from South Carolina (*Audubon, Vol. 6*: 96).

Wayne (1910) found young birds near Yemassee in June, 1887, but could find no nests. Though they are partial to interior fresh water at this season, the ponds on some of the barrier islands such as Bull's Island harbor them at nesting time and the birds undoubtedly breed there.

Two of the local names of the bittern refer to its unique calls, namely, "Thunder-pumper" and "Stake-driver." Such terms are descriptive of the weird, unearthly sounds it makes, to an accompaniment of violent contortions of the head and neck. Unless these efforts are part of the courtship (as they very well may be) the purpose and the bird's method of producing the call are unknown. Peterson (1947) renders the pumping call as "oong-ka-choonk" (with accent on the middle syllable), which is as good as any; the effect of the other common call is much like that of hammering a stake into boggy ground. To hear either of these peculiar notes on the still air across a marsh or swamp is an experience the hearer does not forget quickly. They are undoubtedly two of nature's queerest sounds.

FOOD: Twenty-five per cent of the bittern's food consists of crayfish. This makes the bird highly regarded by rice growers and agriculturists. Frogs make up about 16 per cent; fish 15 per cent; snakes 5 per cent; insects 7 per cent; and small rodents 8 per cent. Dragon-fly nymphs, water tigers, and bugs, are included among the insects, and catfish, suckers, and killifish occur in the fish content. The foregoing percentages are based on the examination of 128 stomachs.

EASTERN LEAST BITTERN
38. *Ixobrychus exilis exilis* (Gmelin) (191)

(Gr., *Ixobrychus*, a reed bellowing, referring to voice and habitat; Lat., *exilis*, small.)

DESCRIPTION: Length 11.00 to 14.00 inches. *Male.* Hind neck chestnut; rest of upper surface black; sides of head and neck ochraceous; lower surface buffy white. *Female.* Like male but black areas replaced by brown.

RANGE: Breeds north to Saskatchewan and southern Quebec; south to southern Mexico and the West Indies. Winters north to Texas and South Carolina (casually); south to Brazil.

STATUS IN S. C.: Fairly common summer resident, March 3 to October 20, chiefly in the middle and southern parts of the State; casual in winter. Known north to Greenwood County; east to Horry County; south to Beaufort County; and west to Aiken County.

HISTORY: Unlike its larger relative, this tiny representative of the bitterns is normally only a summer resident in South Carolina. It has been noted in winter only on December 23, 1937, when E. Milby Burton saw a bird on Hallidon Hill Plantation, Upper Cooper River, Berkeley County.

This species is found in both fresh- and salt-water marshes, swamps, rice fields, and boggy spots. Black and buff are its predominating colors, and the black back will always distinguish it from a rail, as it flushes and flies weakly away among the grasses and reeds. It is, however, capable of long flights; its summer home extends into Canada and it winters as far south as Brazil. To see one fly a short distance, the observer would never believe it capable of such distances.

One of the notes of this little marsh-dweller is rather dove-like, and the bird is at all times inconspicuous and retiring. It also trusts much to its protective plumage, but its camouflage methods are not, perhaps, so remarkable as those of the larger bittern.

The nest is attached to the upright stems of aquatic reeds, a sort of shallow platform, holding four or five pale bluish-white eggs, which average 31.0 x 23.5 millimeters. Usually these are laid in late April or early May, although W. W. Elliott has found fresh eggs as early as April 10 (1936) near Beaufort. Two broods are raised, since Wayne (1910) has seen young in August, and A. J. C. Vaurie found two nests of three eggs each at Santee Gun Club on July 19, 1945. The incubation period is fifteen to seventeen days.

Though one can see this bittern by penetrating its watery haunts during the day, it seems to be largely nocturnal in its feeding and, as a result, is even less known than its larger relative. Now and then, the birds will be seen in unusual places during the migratory seasons, in city gardens and yards, for example, where the sight of one always attracts comment and wonder.

FOOD: Wetmore has found, by examination of 93 stomachs, that fish form nearly 40 per cent of the food. Crustaceans amounted to 10 per cent, and aquatic insects, nearly 12 per cent. The bird seems to be very fond of dragon flies, these constituting 21 per cent of the total. The fish taken are, of course, always small, and are of a kind frequenting fresh-water marshes and ponds: top minnows, mud minnows, and sunfish.

Family Ciconiidae: Storks and Wood Ibises

39. WOOD IBIS: *Mycteria americana* Linnaeus (188)

(Gr., *Mycteria*, snout; Lat., *americana*, of America.)

LOCAL NAMES: Gannet; Gourdhead.

DESCRIPTION: Length 35.00 to 47.00 inches. Head bare; bill stout and curved down at tip. Plumage white with black tail and wing tips.

RANGE: Resident and breeds north to southwestern Mexico and possibly South Carolina; south to Peru and Argentina.

STATUS IN S. C.: Permanent resident in the middle and eastern sections, mainly coastwise; common in summer, occasional in small numbers in winter. Known north to Lancaster

County; east to South Island (Georgetown County) and Charleston; south to Beaufort County; and west to Aiken and Lexington counties.

HISTORY: The Wood Ibis is another misnamed bird. Actually it is not an ibis, but a true stork, the only such representative of regular occurrence in the United States.

A large, spectacular species, awkward and clumsy looking at rest, the Wood Ibis is a grand performer in the air. The flight is strong and well-sustained, the neck carried fully outstretched and bent slightly downward, while the long legs trail behind. It is fond of rising to great heights, there to wheel and swing in magnificent circles, sometimes indulging in aerial acrobatics of an astounding sort. It is one of the birds which sometimes fly upside down. This performance has been noted by Sprunt on two occasions, both at Fairlawn Plantation, Charleston County. In each case one bird of a soaring flock wheeled over, and proceeded for some distance in inverted flight, no wing movement being noted.

The Wood Ibis, locally called "Gannet," appears in both fresh and salt water, but is largely coastal in distribution. Most of the birds begin arriving in mid-April and remain into October. Although it is common most of the year, and really abundant in typical nesting localities in the very midst of the breeding season, no one has yet taken eggs or seen young birds in the nest. Young birds, apparently not long out of the nest, appear on the salt marshes and coastal islands in July, their light-colored heads and necks advertising their immaturity. While investigating egret-heron rookeries in the cypress backwaters of the Low-country, the writers have seen Wood Ibises perched in the surrounding trees or soaring overhead. In June, 1946, Herbert R. Sass saw a Wood Ibis carrying a stick in its bill at Mayrant Backwater, on Fairlawn Plantation, but could not successfully follow the bird into the swamp. E. Milby Burton has also noted a similar incident.

There is a distinct movement from the fresh-water lagoons to the salt marshes in July, where the birds feed throughout the rest of the summer. At times they are to be seen on the mud flats near the Ashley River Bridge, within the city limits of Charleston.

One interesting fact about the feeding habits of the Wood Ibis is that a number of the birds will seek out a pool and, by stirring up the mud and water by shuffling their big feet, bring food to the surface where it can be picked up.

FOOD: This species consumes fish in some numbers, mostly minnows of various kinds, together with frogs, small turtles, snakes, fiddler crabs, and wood rats. Young of such birds as rails and grackles have been found in the diet (Audubon).

Family *Threskiornithidae:* Ibises and Spoonbills

EASTERN GLOSSY IBIS
40. *Plegadis falcinellus falcinellus* (Linnaeus) (186)

(Gr., *Plegadis*, scythe; Lat., *falcinellus*, sickle.)

DESCRIPTION: Length 22.00 to 25.00 inches. Bill long and decurved. Plumage chestnut with green and purple reflections on the upper surface.

RANGE: Breeds north to Louisiana, South Carolina, France, and Turkestan; south to Florida and Madagascar.

STATUS IN S. C.: Rare, perhaps only casual, summer resident, May 1 to November 24, in the southeastern section. Recorded north to Santee National Wildlife Refuge; east to South Island (Georgetown County); south to the mouth of the Savannah River; west to Berkeley County.

HISTORY: This species is a straggler from south central Florida, where a large rookery is guarded annually in Lake Okeechobee by Audubon wardens. It is an all-dark bird, whose long, decurved beak is diagnostic at a glance. Somewhat smaller than the White Ibis, it is a bird which prefers open situations such as lakes and marshes rather than the cypress lagoons.

Our knowledge of this bird's occurrence in South Carolina rests on less than a dozen records, but the species sometimes wanders far northward from Florida, and future records are to be expected. The first state record was definitely established by Edward von S. Dingle, when he saw two birds, and secured one on Middleburg Plantation, Cooper River, Berkeley County, on May 1, 1928. The other specimen remained in the area for at least six weeks (*Auk, 45*: 1928, 499). Ivan R. Tomkins saw one on Turtle Island, at the mouth of the Savannah River, November 24, 1929, a very late instance which he recorded in the *Auk, 47*: 1930, 577. On June 15, 1941, Herbert R. Sass observed a bird at French Quarter Creek, on the east branch of the Cooper River, Berkeley County; and a small flock of eight individuals was noted at the Santee-Cooper lakes (Santee Wildlife Refuge), in May, 1943, by William P. Baldwin. Another was seen by him on October 13, 1943, at the same place. On June 15, 1947, Sass saw a pair of these ibises in a large colony of herons and White Ibises, in Blake's Reserve, South Santee River, Charleston County. He was convinced by their actions that the pair was nesting, but because of the dense growth did not find the nest. On July 3, Sass, together with E. A. Williams, Sprunt, and Chamberlain went to the reserve and made a special effort to locate the nest. They saw one of the birds as soon as they reached the rookery, located in a cypress tree. After the observers had spent hours perched in cypress trees, checking the area to which one of the birds kept returning, they narrowed the search down to a small spot near one edge of the rookery. Finally in a myrtle bush, about 4 feet above the water, the nest was located. It contained two pin-feathered young about a week or ten days old, both dead. No marks of any kind were found on them, and death had been very recent, as decomposition had not set in. The black down with which they were scantily covered, as well as the noticeable green color of the opened tips of the pin feathers was in marked contrast to the markings of the many young White Ibises of similar age in the same area.

The eggs of this ibis are entirely different from those of its relative, the White Ibis; they are plain, unmarked, greenish blue (like a heron's). The average measurement is 52.1 x 36.9 millimeters, and incubation requires twenty-one days.

On June 26, 1947, H. J. Harllee collected two specimens from a flock of sixteen, on South Island, Georgetown County. On April 29, 1949, at least five birds were seen at Blake's Reserve, Santee River, by J. H. Dick, Carol and Stuart Roesler, and E. Milby Burton.

FOOD: The Glossy Ibis feeds for the most part on crayfish and grasshoppers, but it also takes small snakes, including the cottonmouth moccasin. O. E. Baynard has said that this bird has " . . . a clear record of 100 per cent good; not a bad thing can be laid to his door."

41. WHITE IBIS: *Guara alba* (Linnaeus) (184)

(*Guara*, Brazilian name; Lat., *alba*, white.)

LOCAL NAME: Curlew.

DESCRIPTION: Length 22.00 to 27.00 inches. Bill long and decurved. Plumage white with black wing tips; legs red.

RANGE: Resident and breeds north to Lower California and South Carolina; south to Nicaragua and Peru.

STATUS IN S. C.: Summer resident, March 13 to late September, casually to December 15. Reported north to Richland County and Waccamaw River; east to Charleston County; south to Beaufort County; west to Aiken County.

HISTORY: This spectacular bird annually causes excited wonder and speculation among those unfamiliar with it. Actually the White Ibis is an abundant summer resident in the coast region, but inhabits localities visited by comparatively few people. It is a bird of the cypress lagoons, like the Anhinga, Yellow-crowned Night Heron, and the Prothonotary Warbler. There one must go to see it, but a visit is well worth while.

When Wayne wrote in 1910, he was certain that the White Ibis nested in the State, but, at that time, he had never found a colony. A decade and more passed before that memorable spring day when, on May 20, 1922, he and Sprunt discovered about seventy-five pairs nesting in Penny Dam Backwater, Fairlawn Plantation, Charleston County. Since that time, with some intermission, increasing numbers have populated these cypress bird cities, and have now progressed northward along the coast to the Santee River, and probably beyond that. Curiously enough, the original site in Fairlawn has been abandoned by the birds in favor of another backwater on the same plantation (Mayrant), and this colony has increased from two to three hundred pairs in 1939 to nearly three thousand birds in 1947.

The nests are usually built in small cypresses, some trees holding as many as a dozen homes. The nests are constructed of sticks and twigs, and lined with moss and cypress leaves. Eggs, which usually number three or four, are laid in early May. These have a greenish-white ground color, and are splashed and dotted with dark, brownish markings. They average 57.6 x 38.3 millimeters, and incubation requires about twenty-one days.

A very successful colony now utilizes Blake's Reserve, South Santee River, the famous egret rookery known since 1823. The first report of White Ibises using this rookery was in the spring of 1943, when A. H. DuPre saw six or eight breeding pairs. Birds seen about Georgetown and the Waccamaw River plantations each spring indicates additional colonies in that area. On April 17, 1944, a flock of some eight hundred to a thousand birds were seen milling about over Pawley's Island, Georgetown County, in bad weather (D. W. Green). This appears to be the farthest north record for so many birds.

After the young are on the wing (July) these ibises appear in the salt marshes and on the ponds of the barrier islands. Flocks noted at Bull's Island in August 1942, were the first to be seen there.

Immature birds are very unlike the adults, being of a greyish-brown color, with the lower back and underparts white. They retain this plumage through the succeeding nesting season, but apparently do not breed until adult.

Ibises feed at considerable distances from the rookery, traveling in long files, V's, and other formations, flapping and sailing alternately. The sight of incoming birds at sundown is a remarkable picture, hundreds dropping into the rookery amid the croaking clamor of the youngsters. During the spring migration they often travel in large flocks, progressing in a spiral, circling flight, appearing and disappearing like great snowflakes as the sun alternately lights up and loses their white plumage.

The great majority arrive usually by the beginning of March, and early September sees the southward departure of most of them, although stragglers, mainly immature birds, remain later. A very late bird was seen on November 29, 1942, when one adult was observed on Richmond Plantation, Cooper River, by Edward Manigault. However, E. von S. Dingle saw one at Middleburg, Cooper River, on December 15, 1946.

FOOD: The principal food of the White Ibis is crayfish. This item outweighs all else and rendered the species highly regarded by rice growers, as crayfish play havoc with banks and dikes. They also eat insects in considerable quantities, notably cutworms and grasshoppers. In addition to crayfish, they feed upon crustaceans, mainly small fiddler crabs which they secure in the salt marshes in late autumn.

42. ROSEATE SPOONBILL: *Ajaia ajaja* (Linnaeus)   (193)

(*Ajaia*, Brazilian name of the bird.)

DESCRIPTION: Length 28.00 to 35.00 inches. Bill broadly flat and spoon-shaped. Neck, breast, and back white; most of remaining plumage rose pink.

RANGE: Resident and breeds north to Mexico, Louisiana, and Florida; south to Nicaragua and central eastern Argentina.

STATUS IN S. C.: Casual visitor, June 16 to October 14, in the southern section. Reported north to South Island (Georgetown County); east to Bull's Island; south to Hunting Island; west to Aiken County.

HISTORY: This brilliantly distinctive bird is of only casual occurrence in South Carolina. While its normal range is south Florida and the Gulf Coast, tropical storms may blow it north at times, and wanderers may even appear without that impetus. Whatever the cause, no one need be under any delusions should a specimen be seen, for its pink plumage, and amazing, spatulate beak constitute a combination without parallel in South Carolina.

There are several records of the Spoonbill in South Carolina; each one worthy of separate citation. Audubon states that Dr. John Bachman saw only three in twenty years, and secured one within 10 miles of Charleston. No dates are given, but we may be quite certain Dr. Bachman at least saw the bird mentioned by the *Charleston Courier* on October 1, 1822: "A beautiful specimen of that splendid bird, the *Roseate Spoon-bill*, shot on Saturday, near town, has been sent to the Museum for preservation . . . " The day before the bird was taken Charleston was visited by a "Dreadful Hurricane." Unfortunately, this specimen no longer exists. The next record, in point of time, appears to be that recorded in 1905 by Henry L. Barker (*Bull. Chas. Mus. I*:44), who states, "In the early sixties Elias A. Ball, then the owner of Dean Hall plantation [Berkeley County] killed one on the edge of a duck pond and identified it by the plate and description in Audubon." Dr. Eugene E. Murphey (1937) records a specimen taken in the summer of 1867, in Aiken County, by George Twiggs. In 1931, E. A. Preble, of the U. S. Biological Survey (now Fish and Wildlife Service), called attention to an article by Professor James Orton, published in the *American Naturalist* (*4*:716). Among certain birds listed as being in the museum of Vassar College we find: "*Platalea ajaja* Linn. This specimen was obtained by Dr. Trudeau. It was shot on the plantation of his father, near Charleston, S. C." We suspect an error in the locality, since we have been unable to connect the name Trudeau with the Charleston region. Indeed, reference to Audubon seems to clear the matter up, when we read that he named "Trudeau's" Tern for his friend "J. Trudeau, Esq., of Louisiana."

In June, 1879, a Spoonbill was taken in Charleston, near the present site of the Museum, by Dr. T. Grange Simons, and prepared as a skeleton by Dr. Gabriel Manigault; and this specimen remains in the Charleston Museum collection (No. 518). In the autumn of 1885, a specimen was secured by Eugene Gregorie, on Retreat Plantation, Beaufort County (Wayne, 1910). In 1935 Herbert R. Sass tells of another occurrence, related to him by the late Washington Seabrook, of Edisto Island, Charleston County. Seabrook had recounted that a short time before, an aged feather-stuffed cushion in his living room popped open, disclosing a number of pink feathers. Mrs. Seabrook was puzzled, but Seabrook immediately recalled that as a boy or young man he had shot a Roseate Spoonbill on the mud flats opposite Rockville, Charleston County, and that the soft feathers had gone toward stuffing the cushion. When this story was related, Seabrook was well along in his sixties; the killing of this specimen may be conjecturally placed in the 1880's.

PLATE VI: HAWKS AND EAGLE

Oil Painting by Francis Lee Jaques

Flying birds, top to bottom: Red-tailed Hawk (immature), Bald Eagle (adult), Marsh Hawk (female), and Marsh Hawk (male). Perching, left to right: Red-tailed Hawk and Red-shouldered Hawk.

The remaining records are based on observations. On September 20, 1905, the late Dr. Robert Wilson reported seeing a Spoonbill on South Island Causeway, Georgetown County (*Bull. Chas. Mus., 1*: 31-32). A number of years ago Dr. H. C. Oberholser mentioned that he had seen a Spoonbill in this State and under date of February 4, 1949, he wrote: "My record of the roseate spoonbill in South Carolina was made on the northern end of Hunting Island, Beaufort County, near the lighthouse, on June 16, 1923. . . . I watched the bird for some time through a high-power glass. . . ." Further records: one seen among a flock of Wood Ibises on July 26, 1934, in Bull's Island Narrows, by Clarence Magwood; another, on September 12, 1935, with fourteen Wood Ibises, at Price's Inlet (between Bull's and Capers Islands). The last record is that of a bird first noted in Summerhouse Pond, Bull's Island, on September 29, 1943, by Leroy Hills. This bird remained through October 14 of that year, often in the company of Wood Ibises, and during this period was seen by many competent observers.

It is to be noted that in the last three observations recorded above the Spoonbills were in the company of Wood Ibises. There is a decided affinity between these species.

The spoonbill nests in the United States only in southern Florida, Texas, and in western Louisiana. In former years it was shot for its plumage, used in the making of feather fans and for other purposes.

Food: The food of the Roseate Spoonbill consists largely of killifish, water boatmen, and shrimp.

Family Phoenicopteridae: Flamingos

43. Flamingo: *Phoenicopterus ruber* Linnaeus (182)

(Gr., *Phoenicopterus*, red winged; Lat., *ruber*, red.)

Description: Length 42.00 to 48.00 inches. Legs and neck very long and slender; bill with terminal half turning sharply downward. Plumage uniform light vermillion; wing quills black.

Range: Resident and breeds north to Yucatan and the Bahamas; south to the Galapagos Islands and Brazil.

Status in S. C.: Accidental. Recorded only from Georgetown and Charleston counties.

History: It can hardly be gainsaid by anyone that this remarkable bird, together with the Spoonbill, forms a combination of strangeness scarcely equalled by any other two American species. Brilliant in color, fantastic in structure, and possessed of beaks which border on the incredible, the Flamingo and the Spoonbill seem to belong to prehistoric times.

The Flamingo is, essentially, a tropical species. Its place among South Carolina birds is accidental, and based on very few occurrences. One of these is mentioned in Audubon's *Birds of America*, which states that it was procured near Charleston (*Vol. VI*: 170). Another was recorded by Wayne (1910: 25) as having been taken on Debidue Island, Georgetown County, in September of 1876, after a storm.

The very first reference to this species in the State antedates both foregoing ones. It comes from the files of the *Charleston Courier,* under the date July 20, 1818. Commenting on a large migration of "ricebirds" (Bobolinks) that had passed through, the article continues: "We hope that they will meet with better reception than the unfortunate flamingo who recently paid us the honor of a visit from South America, but before he arrived in the metropolis [Charleston], was slain at John's Island by a man who mistook him for a British soldier. It is now mouldering in the Museum along with the other ornithological specimens." The specimen thus referred to must have mouldered to complete oblivion, for no record of it remains.

Many people seem to think that the Flamingo is a common bird in Florida, but that is not true. It is no more than accidental, even there. There is, of course, a large flock of captive birds maintained at the Hialeah Race Track, these birds being known to thousands all over the country. They have nested there for some years, and this is the only known instance of their breeding in the United States.

FOOD: The food of the Flamingo consists wholly of small mollusks that are of no value to man. Captive birds, seen in parks and zoos, are almost invariably disappointing in the pale, washed-out appearance they present. This is due to the lack of correct diet. The flock at Hialeah Park however, is an exception, for great care is taken to provide nutriment of a natural sort, and the color is therefore retained.

Order Anseriformes
Swans, Geese, and Ducks

Family Anatidae: Swans, Geese, and Ducks

44. MUTE SWAN: *Cygnus olor* (Gmelin) (178.2)

(Lat., *Cygnus*, a swan; *olor*, a swan.)

DESCRIPTION: Length 50.00 to 61.00 inches. Bill knobbed. Carries its neck in an S-curve rather than straight like the Whistling Swan. *Adult.* Plumage entirely white. *Immature.* Dull gray.

RANGE: Breeds north to Sweden and Mongolia; south to Asia Minor and Persia. Winters north to northern Africa and northwestern India. Naturalized in southeastern New York and New Jersey.

STATUS IN S. C.: Accidental. Known from Charleston County only.

HISTORY: This European species has been rather successfully introduced and naturalized in a few parts of this country. It furthermore is the common "park" swan seen in numerous places. It has become wild in portions of Long Island, the lower Hudson Valley, and into New Jersey, nesting in suitable localities. Its status, therefore, is somewhat similar to that of the Starling and the English Sparrow, with the obvious difference in population figures.

Its inclusion among South Carolina birds rests on the capture of one specimen. On December 28, 1926, a boatman shot a swan in the Ashley River, opposite the Battery in Charleston. He had mistaken it for a goose. The bird was skinned out rather roughly and brought to the Charleston Museum where it is now preserved (No. 7854). This is the bird referred to in the *Supplement to the Birds of South Carolina* as a Trumpeter Swan. Re-examination proved it to be a Mute Swan. Doubtless it was a wanderer from the New York region, there being no sign whatever that it had been a captive, or domesticated bird.

45. WHISTLING SWAN: *Cygnus columbianus* (Ord) (180)

(Lat., *columbianus*, of the Columbia [River].)

DESCRIPTION: Length 47.00 to 58.00 inches. Neck makes right angle with head when carried erect. *Adult.* Entirely white, with small yellow spot at base of the black bill. *Immature.* Light gray.

RANGE: Breeds north to northeastern Siberia, Victoria Island, and Baffin Island; south to southern Alaska and Southampton Island. Winters north to southern Alaska and Massachusetts; south to California and Florida.

STATUS IN S. C.: Rare winter resident, October 22 to April 2, mostly coastwise. Reported north to Chester County; east to Horry County and Georgetown; south to Beaufort County; west to Edgefield and Aiken counties.

HISTORY: This regal member of the wildfowl family is a rare bird in South Carolina, despite the high winter population in North Carolina. It is safe to assert that even a school child would know a swan, for its frequent occurrence in zoos, parks, and estates has rendered it as well known as any waterfowl in existence. That domesticated specimens are not of this species makes little difference, for, to most people, a swan is a swan.

When Chamberlain and Sprunt issued the *Supplement to the Birds of South Carolina* (1931), this great bird was classed as an accidental visitor. That status must now be changed to rare winter resident, for records of it are increasing steadily. Wayne (1910) mentions it as appearing "occasionally" on the Waccamaw and Combahee Rivers, an immature bird having been secured on the Combahee in 1905. Others were already in the Charleston Museum collection. On November 26, 1907, one was taken at Ridge Springs, Edgefield County; this Wayne secured for his collection. The Museum has another, taken at Rice Hope, Berkeley County, November 21, 1909, by D. S. Lesesne, and Wayne saw one near his home in Christ Church Parish, January 17, 1921.

Since then, records have been made on a number of occasions from Huger, John's Island, South Edisto River, Georgetown, and Bull's Island. A dozen of the great birds spent as much as a month in the winter of 1947 in the rice fields owned by Lionel K. Legge, near Rantowles, Charleston County. One bird was seen in late November, 1939, at Long Bay Plantation, Horry County, by Richard G. Kuerzi. The winter of 1944-45 produced more than the usual number of birds, with reports ranging from one to four birds from Charleston, Clarendon, Colleton, and Aiken counties, to twenty-one in Georgetown County.

Swans congregate with ducks and geese, feeding in both fresh and salt water. They do not dive, but "tip-up," reaching for the bottom with their long, graceful necks. It is well to have in mind the field characters of this swan as compared with those of the Mute Swan which may, at times, escape from parks, or wander south from the New York region. The Whistling Swan has a black bill, with a yellow spot at its base, and it usually holds the head quite straight, at right angles to the equally straight neck. The Mute Swan has an orange bill, with a knob at the base, and carries the neck in a curve with the bill pointed downward. The immature swan is a dingy gray.

Because of their great size, swans are obliged to assist themselves in taking flight by heading into the wind, and pushing against the water for some distance with the big, webbed feet, before rising into the air. The neck is carried fully outstretched, and the bird makes a magnificent appearance in the air. The voice, which is loud and resonant, carries for a long distance.

FOOD: The Whistling Swan is a vegetable feeder, consuming the roots and seeds of wild celery (*Vallisneria*), pondweeds (*Potomogeton*), and aquatic grasses. Some insects are taken.

COMMON CANADA GOOSE
46. *Branta canadensis canadensis* (Linnaeus) (172)

(Lat., *Branta*, from English brant; *canadensis*, of Canada.)

LOCAL NAMES: Wild Goose.

DESCRIPTION: Length 34.00 to 43.00 inches. Head and neck black; throat white, extending up to a point on sides of head behind eye; back and wings brown, the primaries darker; rump and tail black; upper tail coverts white; under parts light drab and white.

RANGE: Breeds north to northern Manitoba and northern Quebec; south to California, Tennessee, and southern Quebec. Winters north to British Columbia and Nova Scotia; south to southern California, Tamaulipas, and Florida.

STATUS IN S. C.: Fairly common winter resident, October 7 to May 1, over most of the State. Recorded north to Chester County; east to Horry County; south to the Ashepoo River; west to Oconee and Pickens counties.

HISTORY: Although the Common Canada Goose occurs every winter in scattered localities, it cannot be considered very common in South Carolina. Reported occurrences probably outnumber actual ones, as cormorants are frequently mistaken for true geese. The establishment of the Cape Romain Refuge, and the construction there of fresh-water ponds on Cape Island, has, however, brought Canada Geese to that area annually and in considerable numbers. The geese congregate in like manner at the Santee Refuge, near the great power development of Santee-Cooper. The rice fields of the Combahee River also appear to have considerable attraction for this bird, and flocks of varying size are reported there every winter on one or another of the plantations. For years, flock have been reported from the Columbia area. The species winters regularly in the Clemson region (Pickens-Oconee counties), feeding in oat fields. G. E. Hudson and F. Sherman record its stay as from early January to late March.

In the migrations a considerable number must pass through South Carolina. An article in the Winnsboro (Fairfield County) *News and Herald* for March 18, 1943, provides what appears to be the earliest migratory record for the State: Hugh S. Wylie, writing of bird life around Winnsboro in the early 1870's, says, "About that time and for years later I saw during the late fall and early spring thousands of wild geese . . . in [flocks of] twenties and thirties. . . ." The earliest records of the appearance of the birds in autumn come from an observation (H. R. E. Hampton) of a flock at Lake Murray, near Columbia, October 7, 1939; and from a report of sixteen birds at Pawley's Island, Georgetown County, on October

10, 1938 (William Ancrum). The latest spring record is for May 1, 1940, when a flock of thirty-eight was seen flying over Wappoo Creek, near Charleston (Chamberlain).

Its famous V-formation, resonant honking, and proverbial wariness, are too well known to need further comment. The term "goose" as a synonym for dullness and stupidity certainly did not derive from this bird.

Food: The Canada Goose is for the most part a vegetable feeder. Roots, tubers, and seeds of aquatic plants such as wild celery (*Vallisneria*), wild rice (*Zizania*), sedges, grasses, and the like make up most of the diet. The bird eats a considerable amount of grain in some localities and is at times detrimental to rice and other crops in the west.

47. American Brant: *Branta bernicla hrota* (Müller) (1732)

(Lat., *Bernicla*, from Old English *bernekka*, a barnacle; *hrota*, Icelandic name for brant.)

Description: Length 22.00 to 30.00 inches. Head, neck, and upper breast black, with narrow white streaks on sides of neck; back and wings brownish gray; tail brownish black with upper and lower coverts white; rest of under parts slaty gray.

Range: Breeds north to Axel Heiberg Island, northern Greenland, and Spitzbergen; south to the Gulf of Boothia and south central Greenland. Winters north to British Columbia, Massachusetts, and the Baltic Sea; south to California, Florida, and Egypt.

Status in S. C.: Rare winter resident, November 30 to January 31, in the coast region. Reported north to Horry County; south to Beaufort County.

History: This small goose has made less than half a dozen appearances in South Carolina, but it may occur more frequently than such records indicate. It was unknown in South Carolina until 1924, when on December 28 of that year, an adult female was shot by Edward Manigault near Fort Sumter, in Charleston Harbor. It was presented to the Charleston Museum (No. 7686) and recorded in the *Auk*, 42: 1925, 265. Although in good plumage, the bird was very thin, its stomach containing three ounces of sea lettuce (*Ulva lactea*).

It was thus removed from the Hypothetical List on which it had been placed by Wayne (1910) because of the uncertainty attaching to statements of Elliott Coues and Wells W. Cooke regarding the species in this State. A little more than six years later, on January 2, 1930, two birds were seen in almost exactly the same place by Richard Grant, who took one of them and gave it to the Museum (No. 30.4); on November 30, 1932, one was shot on Tibwin Plantation, near McClellanville, by the owner, George Haas. It was an immature female and, like the two former specimens, exceedingly thin; on January 31, 1935, Sprunt watched an adult for nearly an hour at Cape Island (Cape Romain Refuge). It came to within two hundred yards of the boat while swimming, and later went ashore on the sandy beach and walked about, pecking here and there; on December 24, 1939, Richard G. Kuerzi saw a flock of thirty-five of these birds, flying south, at Long Bay Plantation, Horry County. This is the only record of a flock, and, with the above instances, constitutes all that is known of the Brant in South Carolina.

The Brant is a small goose, only a little larger than the Mallard Duck. In the adult, the white streaks on the dark neck form a good field mark, but these are almost lacking in the immature bird. It feeds on aquatic vegetation which, in its winter range in North Carolina, seems to be largely eelgrass (*Zostera marina*).

GREENLAND WHITE-FRONTED GOOSE
48. *Anser albifrons flavirostris* Dalgety and Scott (171)

(Lat., *Anser*, goose; *albifrons*, with white forehead; *flavirostris*, yellow-billed.)

DESCRIPTION: Length 26.00 to 30.00 inches. Largely grayish brown; a white patch on forehead; lower parts grayish white blotched with black; bill yellow; feet orange yellow.

RANGE: Breeds in Greenland and winters south along the Atlantic coast of North America to Georgia.

STATUS IN S. C.: Rare winter resident, December 15 to February 3, in the eastern part of the State, chiefly in the coast region. Reported north and east to Berkeley County; south to Beaufort County; west to Edgefield County.

HISTORY: This northern goose is of rare occurrence only. Wayne (1910) stated that in the Charleston Museum " . . . there were at least five mounted specimens . . . which were taken in the interior of the State." Neither date nor locality was given for any of these mounted specimens and their whereabouts now is unknown. Murphey (1937) recorded that a White-fronted Goose was killed "in the Savannah River, seven miles above Augusta, February, 1891." Wayne mentioned another, identified by Dr. Murphey in the winter of 1903 or 1904, which was taken in the same river "opposite Edgefield county, S. C."

Additional records have been made since the appearance of Wayne's book (1910). Two of these are specimens that antedate those of the Murphey records. One was secured January 29, and another February 3, 1866, near Pocotaligo, Beaufort County, by George H. Mackay (*Auk, 45*: 1928, 368). It was not until 1920 that this goose was again definitely recorded in the State. On December 15 of that year one was shot at South Mulberry, on Cooper River in Berkeley County, by F. A. Dallet (*Auk, 44*: 1927, 559). Another was secured on the same plantation, January 5, 1927, by Richard A. Monks. This specimen has been identified by Charles E. O'Brien of the American Museum of Natural History as the Greenland White-fronted Goose, *Anser albifrons flavirostris*, described in 1948 by Christopher T. Dalgety and Peter M. Scott (*Bull. Brit. Ornith. Club, Vol. 68*: 1948, 115). Furthermore it is the only specimen now available from the State. Since this subspecies is the one of most probable occurrence in South Carolina, all the records of the species not based on specimens very recently identified are placed under this race.

The White-fronted Goose is known as "Speckle-belly" in most of its winter range because of the broken bars on the belly.

LESSER SNOW GOOSE

49. *Chen hyperborea hyperborea* (Pallas)   (169)

(Gr., *Chen*, a goose; Lat., *hyperborea*, far northern.)

DESCRIPTION: Length 23.00 to 31.00 inches. *Adult*. Body plumage entirely white, sometimes stained with rust about the head; primaries black. *Immature*. Light gray.

RANGE: Breeds north to Victoria Island and Baffin Island; south to northern Alaska and Southampton Island. Winters north to British Columbia and Rhode Island; south to Central Mexico and Florida.

STATUS IN S. C.: Rare winter resident, October 16 to February 23, along the coast. Reported north to Cape Romain National Wildlife Refuge; south to the Combahee River. No certain record for the interior of the State.

HISTORY: This beautiful little goose is about the size of the brant, and, except for the Greater Snow Goose, could hardly be mistaken for anything else even if the observer were unfamiliar with its characters. Pure white, with black-tipped wings, it is a small edition of the Greater Snow Goose, although size is often deceptive in the field and cannot always be accepted as certain in the identification of birds.

Although most of the snow goose field records from South Carolina identify the birds observed as Greater Snow Geese, it is more than probable that they were actually Lesser Snow Geese. The conjecture is reasonable because there is a general though erroneous impression that practically all birds of this species along the Atlantic Coast are Greater Snow Geese. As a matter of fact, it is the Lesser Snow Geese which exist in greater number, according to Dr. H. C. Oberholser. Consequently any records not substantiated by existing specimens may be referred to Lesser Snow Geese. For this reason the following records, though originally made as observations of the Greater Snow Goose, have been transferred to the Lesser.

Wayne (1910) stated that this white goose is known to occur regularly in the interior, along the Wateree, Congaree, and Saluda Rivers. There are no actual specimens from those areas, and it is very unlikely that the birds still occur there. Audubon mentioned a specimen in Dr. Bachman's possession, but the next record of the bird does not occur until two were shot by L. W. Boykin on the Wateree River some time between 1905 and 1910.

On October 27, 1914, four were seen near Mt. Pleasant and one secured on the following day by a Negro. It was again collected in South Carolina on October 16, 1916, by Lucian L. Porcher, who took one on Porcher's Plantation in Christ Church Parish. This bird was given to Wayne, who recorded it (*Auk*, 35: 1918, 437). Several years elapsed before it was again noted; then, for several days, an individual was seen at Mulberry Plantation, Berkeley County, by Clarence E. Chapman, who first saw it on Thanksgiving Day, 1927. Another specimen was obtained by J. Thompson Brown on November 11, 1931, at the Grove Plantation, South Edisto River (*Auk.* 49: 1933, 343).

On January 23, 1934, one bird was seen on Myrtle Grove Plantation (Combahee River), by Dr. Harry C. Oberholser and the authors. One bird was seen on Bull's Island, November 19, 1938, with four Blue Geese, during the field trip of the second meeting of the A. O. U. at Charleston. It was seen by many participants in that outing. Two birds were seen in the Santee Delta, on February 23, 1949, by Harold S. Peters.

Food: The Lesser Snow Goose is a vegetable feeder consuming quantities of grain during its sojourn in the United States.

GREATER SNOW GOOSE
50. *Chen hyperborea atlantica* Kennard (169a)

(Lat., *atlantica*, of the Atlantic [Ocean].)

DESCRIPTION: Like the Lesser Snow Goose but larger; length 29.00 to 38.00 inches. Plumage entirely white except for black primaries; head at times tinged with rust.

RANGE: Breeds north to Ellesmere Island and northern Greenland. Winters north to Delaware Bay; south to South Carolina.

STATUS IN S. C.: Casual winter visitor in November in the coast region. Certainly determined only from the Combahee River to the mouth of the Savannah River.

HISTORY: As explained under the Lesser Snow Goose, the majority of snow geese on the Atlantic coast belong to that subspecies. The two probably have, however, the same general range in this region.

Three of these geese were taken at Longbrow Plantation on the Combahee River in Colleton County, on November 25, 1933, by Dr. William H. Frampton. He brought one of these birds to the Charleston Museum where it is still preserved as a skin, the only one of the Greater Snow Goose now in existence from South Carolina. Another specimen was taken 3 miles east of Savannah, Georgia, by I. R. Tomkins on November 24, 1931.

In habits, including food, this bird does not differ from the Lesser Snow Goose.

51. BLUE GOOSE: *Chen caerulescens* (Linnaeus) (169.1)

(Lat., *caerulescens*, bluish.)

DESCRIPTION: Length 25.00 to 30.00 inches. *Adult.* Dark brownish gray, with wing coverts bluish gray and head and neck white. *Immature.* Head and neck grayish brown.

RANGE: Breeds north to northern Keewatin and southwest Baffin Island; south to Southampton Island. Winters casually north to Nebraska and Ohio; south chiefly to the coast of Texas and Louisiana, casually to Florida and Cuba.

STATUS IN S. C.: Rare winter visitor, first week in October to April 26, chiefly in the coast region. Reported north to Georgetown County; south to Colleton County; west to Clarendon County.

HISTORY: The recurring records of this handsome species in recent years have established it as a rare winter visitor. Much mystery surrounded it for years. Audubon considered it an immature Snow Goose (today the Blue Goose is known to interbreed occasionally with the Snow), and it was not until June, 1929, that the first nest and eggs were discovered. This distinction goes to J. Dewey Soper, of the Canadian Department of the Interior, who found the Blue Goose breeding on Baffin Island. The next spring G. M. Sutton found another breeding area on Southampton Island, Hudson Bay.

The principal wintering ground is the coast of Louisiana, to which great numbers resort annually. During the migrations, and occasionally in winter, it appears on the Atlantic seaboard. The name "Blue" is somewhat of a misnomer, for the adult bird is dark brown or slate color with white head and neck, and uniformly dark when immature.

The Blue Goose was unrecorded from South Carolina until about the winter of 1908, when one was taken at the Santee Gun Club, near McClellanville, Charleston County, by Frank Carnegie, and identified by Wayne (*Auk*, *35*: 1918, 438). Several years passed before the next recorded observance; on October 26, 1925, two birds were seen off Edingsville Beach, Charleston County, by Herbert R. Sass and Charles L. Bull (*Auk*, *43*: 1926, 228). The third instance occurred during the winter of 1927, when three were killed by members of the Santee Gun Club. Since that date, records have multiplied and it seems unnecessary to list them in detail. Practically all records in recent years have been made during the months of November and December. However, three birds were seen by many observers from March 12 to April 26, 1949, on the mud flats near the Ashley River Bridge in Charleston. This constitutes the latest spring record.

FOOD: Largely vegetable, the roots and tubers of sedges and grasses, as well as grain. The so-called "goose grass" (*Scirpus robustus*) is a favorite food. Small crustaceans and other marine life are taken on the Atlantic coast.

COMMON MALLARD
52. *Anas platyrhynchos platyrhynchos* Linnaeus (132)

(Lat., *Anas*, a duck; Gr., *platyrhynchos*, broad-billed.)

LOCAL NAMES: English Duck; Green-head; Gray Mallard.

DESCRIPTION: Length 21.00 to 27.00 inches. *Male.* Head and upper neck metallic green; below this a narrow white ring; speculum (wing patch) violet, bordered in front and behind by a white bar; rest of upper parts mostly grayish brown; breast chestnut; abdomen grayish white; under tail coverts black. *Female.* Mottled brown streaked with darker shades; speculum similar to that of male.

RANGE: Breeds north to northwestern Alaska, Hudson Bay, northern Europe, and Siberia; south to northern Lower California, Texas, Virginia, and northern Africa. Winters north to central Alaska, Nova Scotia, central Europe, and Japan; south to southern Mexico, Florida, Africa, and India.

STATUS IN S. C.: Common winter resident, September 19 to April 24, casually June, over all the State, but more common in the coastal section. Reported north to Chester County; east to Horry County; south to Jasper County; west to Greenwood and Oconee counties.

HISTORY: Familiar or not as one may be with the ducks, this species is more likely to be known than any other. It is, in truth, *the* wild duck of the country. Its British name is Stock Duck, for it is from the Mallard that many domesticated strains come.

The Mallard arrives in South Carolina in middle to late October, and remains until mid-March. Variations in arrival and departure depend upon seasonal conditions.

This species is one of the fresh-water ducks, a group of the wildfowl sometimes known as river ducks. Not only does it frequent the great rice fields which lie along the tidal rivers, but it is fond of the cypress backwaters, where it occurs in numbers. Like others of this class, it feeds by "tipping-up," reaching to the bottom of shallow waters by up-ending the body and maintaining a perpendicular position by paddling the feet. It does not ordinarily dive.

Few sights in nature are more spectacular than a full plumaged drake against a backdrop of gray-green cypress trunks and wine-brown water. The wonderful iridescence of the green head catches the light in shining reflections and the white neck-ring seems to set the glossy head off as a crowning climax to the soft grays and browns of the body plumage.

Naturally, it is highly prized by sportsmen, and comes readily to well placed stands of what the Low-country Negroes call "duck image" (decoys). Many are taken during the open season. This is one of the few ducks that really quack in the conventional sense, and a flock can set up a great clamor as they paddle and splash about in their feeding. Many specimens weigh between 3 and 4 pounds, although the average weight of the male is 2 lbs. 11 oz., the female 2 lbs. 6 oz.

The flight of the Mallard is strong and well sustained. The bird springs almost perpendicularly into the air from the surface of the water; it does not patter along to gain a start as do the diving ducks. The speed of flight is often exaggerated; actually it is slower than it is popularly supposed to be, usually between 45 and 60 miles an hour. While not one of the fastest flying ducks, it is capable of sustained speed. An example is provided by a Mallard that was banded in Green Bay, Wisconsin, and shot five days later near Georgetown, S. C. The air line distance between these two points is about 900 miles.

Mallards and Black Ducks sometimes interbreed. The resulting hybrid is a peculiar looking bird, combining characteristics of both. The Charleston Museum has several specimens, most of them from the Kinloch Plantation, North Santee River, through the courtesy of Richard Stanland. This locality is visited by Mallard x Black Duck hybrids practically every winter, at least in recent years. Probably they are bred in as restricted an area as that in which they winter, and these repeated occurrences at Kinloch Plantation may represent "related" individuals which resort to the same winter range annually.

On October 9, 1930, Dr. Henry Norris reported in a letter to Dr. F. C. Lincoln of the Bureau of Biological Survey that some two dozen Mallards spent the summer near Waverly Mills, Georgetown County, and that he "had been told" several broods of young were raised on the nearby Baruch estate. We believe such cases of breeding to be due to the presence of "decoy" stock. Mallards have also been reported by W. M. Levi as breeding near Sumter, in April, 1943. It is probable that these too were "decoy" stock.

Food: The Mallard feeds largely on vegetable matter, a fact that renders it so acceptable on the table. Examination of over fifteen hundred stomachs by W. L. McAtee of the U. S.

Fish and Wildlife Service, revealed that nine-tenths of the food was of such nature. Sedges, wild rice, millet, switch grass, cordgrass, smartweed, pondweeds, widgeon grass, eel grass, duckweeds, coon-tail, wild celery, and duck potato are eaten. Acorns, hickory nuts, cypress balls, as well as the fruits of gum, water elm, holly, dogwood, and poison ivy form a part of its diet. The little animal food consumed is made up of mollusks, a few fish, and insects.

53. BLACK DUCK: *Anas rubripes* Brewster (133)

(Lat., *rubripes*, red-footed.)

LOCAL NAMES: Black Mallard; Skiddler; Black English Duck.

DESCRIPTION: Length 21.00 to 26.00 inches. Much like the female Mallard but darker. Dark sooty brown, head and neck buffy with much fine streaking; speculum metallic blue, bordered behind by only a very narrow white line; under surface of wings silvery white; bill greenish yellow; feet red to orange.

RANGE: Breeds north to northern Manitoba and northern Quebec; south to northern Iowa and eastern South Carolina. Winters north to Nebraska and Nova Scotia; south to Texas and Florida.

STATUS IN S. C.: Common winter resident, August 31 to May 1, throughout much of the State; occasional in summer; rare or accidental in the western portion. Reported north to York and Lancaster counties; east to Horry and Georgetown counties; south to Beaufort County; west to Edgefield and Anderson counties.

HISTORY: There is much confusion in the common names of this fine species which is commonly called the "Black Mallard." Though clearly related to the Mallard, it is entirely different in appearance and bears no resemblance to the male Mallard at all except in size, which is about the same. Nor is it literally black. Audubon's name for it of Dusky Duck is really much more descriptive and preferable.

Along with other species, many Black Ducks have been banded in this country and Canada, and the files of the U. S. Fish and Wildlife Service show that Black Ducks banded in Ontario have later been recovered in South Carolina in the following counties: Charleston, Berkeley, Georgetown, Barnwell, Laurens, Anderson, and Edgefield.

The Black Duck occurs in both fresh and salt water, feeding in both, but more commonly in fresh. The birds which winter on the coast often resort to the salt marshes to spend the night. It is one of the wariest of the ducks, possessing amazing eyesight and being credited by hunters with the ability to "see through a brick wall." The gunner in a blind must be very careful when these ducks come in to the decoys. They often circle several times, and one can see them craning their necks as they search the scene below. The slightest movement is enough to send them on their way.

The uniformly dark plumage of the Black Duck is set off sharply in flight by the silvery white undersurface of the wings, a field mark which is unmistakable and which renders this duck one of the easiest to identify. No other ducks, except the oceanic scoters, are nearly as dark in appearance. On the water it sits high, is always alert, and leaps upward into flight as though propelled by a strong spring. Speeds over 60 miles an hour are probable only when the bird has the advantage of a tail wind. It is a very noisy duck, and utters the well known "quack," almost identical with that of the Mallard, and much more energetically given than that of the Gadwall, another quacking species.

Sometimes when ducks (Black Ducks in particular) are being prepared for the table, the cook is alarmed to discover in the body tissues what appear to be small, white worms. These have been critically examined by pathologists and found to be parasites which are harmless to human beings and which do not at all affect the table qualities of the duck. They have been identified as *Sarcocystis rileyi*, there being no common name.

The Black Duck is markedly nocturnal in habit and often feeds after dark, particularly on moonlight nights. It employs the tipping-up method in feeding.

The supposed race of this bird known as the Red-legged Black Duck is now understood to be based simply on an age character, and is no longer recognized. The sex of the adult is determinable by the markings of the feathers taken from the side of the chest; those with the U-shaped markings are male, while those with the V-shaped markings are female.

Over the years occasional instances of breeding have been reported in South Carolina. It is possible that the birds thus observed were of "decoy" stock. However, in view of the nesting of this species in eastern North Carolina and of its apparent tendency in recent years to extend its breeding range, it appears probable that these records are of wild birds. In the spring of 1948 a pair was reported breeding near McClellanville by J. B. Shuler, Jr.

Food: Though a vegetable feeder, this species takes more animal food than does the Mallard. The animal food amounts to about 25 per cent of the total, and consists of mollusks, crustaceans, fish, and insects. As many as 650 snails have been found in a single stomach. Shrimp, crayfish, crabs, and sand fleas make up the crustacean diet. Insects are represented by water beetles, dragon flies, crickets, grasshoppers, ants, and weevils. Vegetable matter amounts to 75 per cent and includes pondweeds, eelgrass, wild celery, rice, marsh grasses, and seeds of water lilies.

54. GADWALL: *Anas strepera* Linnaeus (135)

(Lat., *strepera*, noisy.)

LOCAL NAMES: Gray Duck; Gray Widgeon.

DESCRIPTION: Length 19.00 to 23.00 inches. *Male.* Head and neck pale brownish white, speckled with black; rest of plumage finely undulated with slate and white; under-tail coverts black and the speculum white. *Female.* More brownish than the male, but also with white speculum which is the best field mark.

RANGE: Breeds north to southern British Columbia, northern Manitoba, Iceland, and Kamchatka; south to southern California, northern New Mexico, England, Algeria, and the Caspian Sea. Winters north to southern British Columbia, Rhode Island (casually), the British Isles, and Japan; south to central Mexico, Jamaica, Abyssinia, and India.

STATUS IN S. C.: Common but local winter resident, November 7 to May 19, casually June 30, mostly along the coast. Reported north to Clarendon County; east to Horry County; south to Beaufort and Jasper counties.

HISTORY: Of this species, Wayne (1910) wrote that it "is very rare in South Carolina, and I have seen but four or five specimens." Doubtless many observers today will wonder at that statement and with good reason. No doubt the Gadwall was rare, and still is, about Wayne's home and in the territory where he made most of his observations. In this instance, at least, Wayne was making the mistake of judging the general situation by too local conditions. As the authors of this volume pointed out in the *Supplement to the Birds of South Carolina* (1931), the Gadwall is "much less rare than formerly supposed." It is, indeed, a common duck in many localities and is seen and taken regularly every winter.

Though one of the "big ducks," it is well known only to experienced observers, but there is no good reason why this should be true. The drake is an easy bird to identify, but the female, like many others of the sex, is notoriously difficult at times because of its resemblance to others. When on the water, the drake shows a jet black area under the tail, an excellent field mark. When in flight, the white speculum always shines out and is very helpful for purposes of identification.

Gadwalls inhabit rice fields, fresh-water ponds, and to some degree the cypress backwaters. Though not abundant and though somewhat locally distributed, they are well scattered about the whole of the coast region and may be seen throughout the winter. There are more of these ducks in some seasons than others.

Occasionally, though a tip-up duck, the Gadwall will dive for its food. It utters a "quack" similar to that of the Mallard and Black Duck, but in a more subdued tone and volume. It is a good table bird.

FOOD: The vegetable content of the food of the Gadwall is nearly 98 per cent. Pondweeds and widgeon grass form about 42 per cent; sedges, bullrush, and saw-grass seeds about 20 per cent; algae 10 per cent. It also eats water-lily seeds and duck potato, one stomach containing as many as twelve hundred water-lily seeds.

55. AMERICAN PINTAIL: *Anas acuta tzitzihoa* Vieillot (143)

(Lat., *acuta*, acute, referring to pointed tail; *tzitzihoa*, Aztec name of the species.)
LOCAL NAMES: Sprig; Sprig-tail; Widgeon.

DESCRIPTION: Length 21.00 to 30.00 inches. Slender, with long neck and much elongated central tail feathers. *Male.* Mainly gray above and white below, with dark brown head and a white stripe up the sides of the neck. *Female.* Mostly brown, and much more plainly colored than the male.

RANGE: Breeds north to northern Alaska and New Brunswick; south to southern California, northern Illinois, and New Jersey (casually). Winters north to British Columbia and Massachusetts; south to the Hawaiian Islands, southern Mexico, and Panama.

STATUS IN S. C.: Common winter resident, September 5 to April 30, in most of the State. Recorded north to Chester County; east to Horry County and the lower Santee River; south to Beaufort County; west to Greenville County.

HISTORY: This beautiful species, so graceful in form and carriage, is one of the most distinctive of the wildfowl. The long central tail feathers of the adult male are always noticeable, and the slender brownish neck with its white streak is conspicuous. Even the brown female is comparatively easy to recognize because of the general shape. The white breast of the drake shines out at long distances, and a flock on the water reminds one of a mass of water-lily blossoms.

The Pintail arrives in some seasons as early as the first week of September but does not appear in any numbers until October, typical dates being October 22 in Richland County, and October 9 in Colleton County. It remains until mid-March in some numbers, and uncommonly into April. Always preferring fresh water, Pintails congregate in rice fields and open ponds, as well as on the cypress lagoons, where they tip-up in feeding, showing the sharply pointed tail with its black under coverts, in marked contrast to the white belly. In some seasons, Pintails outnumber all other ducks on the rice plantations of the coast country, but the first large flights usually proceed southward as cold weather advances.

Many people consider this the most graceful of all ducks. It sits lightly on the water, and often comes ashore to preen, rest, and even walk about on grassy edges and gravel bars. It decoys readily and is a favorite with many gunners. The flight is swift and strong, the initial spring from the water being almost vertical. The streamlined body is made for speed and actual timing has shown velocities well in excess of 65 miles an hour when the bird is alarmed (airplane data). Normal flight is about 45 to 50 miles an hour. Kortright (1942) states that a flock paralleled a train for some time at a speed of 52 miles an hour.

Hybrids between this duck and the Mallard have been known to occur but, of course, are highly unusual. Sprunt secured such a specimen in the rice fields of the South Edisto River, Colleton County, in December, 1942.

The Pintail stands high as a table bird, for its food is mainly vegetable and the flesh has fine flavor.

FOOD: Eighty-seven per cent is made up of seeds of pondweeds and sedges, smartweed being a favorite, as illustrated by the fact that as many as four thousand to twelve thousand five hundred seeds have been found in a single stomach. The 13 per cent animal food consists of shrimp, crabs, crayfish, and some insects such as beetles and flies. The Pintail is sometimes accused of eating cultivated rice in damaging quantities, and undoubtedly does so now and then; but in the southeast, this grain is taken only in winter and much of it is waste.

56. EUROPEAN TEAL: *Anas crecca* Linnaeus (138)

(Lat., *crecca*, formed to indicate the bird's quack.)

DESCRIPTION: Length 12.00 to 16.00 inches. Like the Green-winged Teal except that the male lacks the white bar in front of the wing, and the inner webs of scapulars are conspicuously white.

RANGE: Breeds north to the Aleutian Islands, Iceland, northern Europe, and northern Asia; south to the Mediterranean Sea and Mongolia. Winters north to the Aleutian Islands, western Europe, and Mongolia; south to the Canary Islands, Abyssinia, and India. Accidental in eastern United States.

STATUS IN S. C.: Accidental, November 28 to February 13, in the coast region. Known only from the lower Santee River and Bull's Island.

HISTORY: This Old World duck is of purely accidental occurrence in South Carolina, and is rare anywhere in eastern North America. There is one secured specimen from this state and three or four sight records. On February 13, 1930, Richard E. Bishop shot one at the Santee Gun Club, South Santee River. It was identified and recorded by the late Witmer Stone, and is preserved in the Philadelphia Academy of Science (*Auk, 51*: 1934, 227). On January 22, 1940, Allan D. Cruickshank reported seeing one bird on Bull's Island, and five days later A. H. DuPre and James Silver, of the U. S. Fish and Wildlife Service, saw on the lower Santee River two pairs of teal which they believed to be this species.

In December 1946, Sprunt, while conducting the Audubon Tours on Bull's Island, saw one of these birds, a drake. Nearly a year later, another was observed there on November 28, 1947. Several members of the Tour party saw the specimen clearly.

Though it closely resembles the Green-winged Teal, the European species may always be instantly recognized by the absence of the characteristic white bar in front of the wing, as well as by the additional field mark of a horizontal white bar *above* the wing. Females of these two teal are indistinguishable in the field.

It may be that this bird occurs now and then among the multitudes of Green-wings which visit the South Carolina coast every winter, and it should be looked for among flocks of them.

57. GREEN-WINGED TEAL: *Anas carolinensis* Gmelin (139)

(Lat., *carolinensis*, of Carolina.)

LOCAL NAMES: Teal; Green-wing.

DESCRIPTION: Length 13.00 to 16.00 inches. *Male.* Largely gray above; head chestnut; a white bar in front of wing. Speculum and a patch on sides of head metallic green. Breast tinged with vinaceous and spotted with black. *Female.* Brownish white mottled with brown; wing as in the male.

RANGE: Breeds north to Alaska, northern Manitoba, and southern Quebec; south to central California and southeastern Ontario. Winters north to southeastern Alaska and Nova Scotia; south to southern Mexico and Tobago Island.

STATUS IN S. C.: Common winter resident, October 5 to May 1, in most of the State, but more numerous in the coast region. Reported north to Chester County; east to Horry County; south to Beaufort County; west to Aiken County.

HISTORY: This is the smallest of the South Carolina ducks, except the similarly sized Buffle-head, and is one of the handsomest of the fresh-water group. It is a

---

PLATE VII: HAWKS

Water Color by Roger Tory Peterson

Flying, top to bottom: Pigeon Hawk, Duck Hawk, Cooper's Hawk, and Sharp-shinned Hawk. On post: Sparrow Hawk (male).

miniature species, clean-cut and attractive. Though arriving later and departing earlier than the Blue-wing, it outnumbers that species considerably in midwinter. Severe cold does not seem to affect it in any way. Some few years ago, immense numbers of Green-winged Teal frequented the ricefields of the Santee Delta, great flocks coming every day; but, like most of the ducks, they have shown decreases in the last few seasons. The Green-wing arrives by mid-October and stays usually until late March.

Green-wings are remarkable for their mass flights, wheeling and turning like formations of sandpipers, as if each bird anticipated the movement of another by the fraction of a second. It is astonishing that collisions do not occur more often; as a matter of fact, they are rare.

The Green-wing prefers fresh water, but occasionally may be found in the salt marshes and tidal rivers nearby. The very small size serves to identify it under almost any conditions, but the white bar in front of the wing of the drake marks it infallibly. The Green-wing is reputed to be the fastest of the ducks and there are many hunting stories which have this characteristic as their theme. The belief in the Green-wing's speed may be based on the fact that gunners so frequently miss them. Actually, some of the much larger ducks are faster fliers. The quick get-away of the Green-wing, together with the rapidity of its twists and turns, is mislead-ing. Kortright (1942) states that an English falconer had flown his hawk at Mallard and teal flushed simultaneously, and that the teal were always overhauled by the falcon before the Mallards. Canvasbacks are known to fly faster. There is no doubt Green-wings attain 50 to 60 miles an hour, and sometimes probably exceed that speed. Forty miles an hour would be nearer the average, though this will be hard for many people to believe. The old-time estimates were nothing but pure speculation, and there are few limits to that. Both automobiles and airplanes have done a great deal to establish concrete facts about bird speed.

These little ducks feed on land at times, and run nimbly about with none of the awkwardness one usually associates with ducks when walking. The note is a shrill piping sort of whistle that is not unlike the call of some of the shore birds. They feed by tipping-up.

FOOD: Ninety per cent of the Green-wing's food is vegetable. This exceeds the amount eaten by the Blue-wing, and makes the Green-wing more acceptable as a table bird. Sedge seed forms about 38 per cent of the total, with pondweeds, eelgrass, and widgeon grass amounting to 11 per cent. Wild rice and millet are often taken. The small amount of animal food consists of flies, beetles, snails, and crustaceans.

58. BLUE-WINGED TEAL: *Anas discors* Linnaeus (140)

(Lat., *discors*, discordant.)

LOCAL NAMES: Teal-duck.

DESCRIPTION: Length 14.00 to 16.00 inches. *Male.* Head dark gray with white crescent between bill and eye; rest of upper parts brown with numerous lighter markings; lower parts pale cinnamon with round black dots; a large patch of blue on fore part of wing which is conspicuous in flight; and a white patch on each side of the black under-tail coverts. *Female.* Rather obscure and mottled with brownish gray but with the blue wing patch.

RANGE: Breeds north to southern Mackenzie and southern Quebec; south to northern Nevada, Louisiana, and Florida. Winters north to southern California, Maryland, and Rhode Island (casually); south to Chile and Brazil.

STATUS IN S. C.: Common winter resident, August 5 to June 6, in most of the State but more numerous in the coast region. Recorded north to York and Florence counties; east to Horry County; south to Beaufort County; west to Aiken County and Columbia.

HISTORY: This handsome little duck is the earliest of the family to arrive in autumn and one of the latest to depart in spring. Indeed, in many years it comes before autumn, as there are records for August. September, however, is the regular arrival month. It is abundant during every season, early and late, but is often scarce and hard to find in midwinter. The majority proceed southward to spend the coldest part of the year. This, of course, varies with the seasons. In a mild winter, many Blue-wings remain in South Carolina.

The Blue-wing is larger than other teal but, when compared to the "big" ducks, its size is always diagnostic. The blue shoulders cannot be seen when the bird is on the water, but the moment it leaps into the air, this mark leaves no doubt of its identity. The mark is worn by both sexes, which helps a great deal in the identification of the otherwise very obscure-looking female. The white crescent of the head of the drake is visible at considerable distances.

The Blue-wing is an active bird, quick in its movements. It can frequently be seen feeding along banks and out on mats of vegetation. It has long held a reputation for great speed, but actually the facts do not support the belief; it is the small size of the bird and its quick turns and mass movements which give an illusion of considerable velocity. Usual normal speed in the air is about 45 to 50 miles an hour unless the bird is hard-pressed. At such times, the speed can be, and undoubtedly is, accelerated. Old writers have asserted that the Blue-wing can attain 130 miles an hour; such a notion is, of course, pure fancy. F. C. Lincoln states that migrating Blue-wings travel at about 30 to 40 miles an hour.

Blue-wings are fresh-water ducks and feed by tipping-up. They may be found in rice fields, and in bodies of water of almost any size in the migrations. They sometimes appear in salt water.

FOOD: Because it prefers vegetable food, the Blue-winged Teal is a delectable bird for the table. The body is very small but the flesh has an excellent flavor. Seeds of sedges, pondweeds, wild rice, and smartweeds are favorites. Cultivated rice is taken also, but probably most of this is waste grain. The vegetable proportion of the food amounts to about 70 per cent. Animal matter consists of snails, insects, crustaceans, caddis-fly larvae, dragon-fly nymphs, beetles, and damsel flies.

59. CINNAMON TEAL: *Anas cyanoptera cyanoptera* (Vieillot)   (144)

(Gr., *cyanoptera*, blue-winged.)

DESCRIPTION: Length 15.00 to 17.00 inches. *Male.* Head, neck, and lower parts chestnut; scapulars and tertials striped with buff or white; bend of wing light grayish blue; speculum green. *Female.* Similar to the female Blue-winged Teal but somewhat larger and plumage somewhat more rufescent.

RANGE: Breeds north to southern British Columbia; south to northern Lower California and Texas; also in South America north to central Peru and northern Argentina; south to southern Chile and the Falkland Islands. Winters north to central California and southern Louisiana; south to Chile and Patagonia.

STATUS IN S. C.: Accidental in the coast region.

HISTORY: This handsome far-western duck is of purely accidental occurrence in South Carolina. To any one familiar with waterfowl, the appearance of the drake is unmistakable, but the female is very similar to the female of the Blue-winged Teal.

Its inclusion among the birds of this State is due to an observation by Francis M. Weston who, on January 28, 1933, saw a drake and a female in the rice fields of Cotton Hall Plantation, Beaufort County. He watched them at a distance of no more than 50 yards with a six power field glass. The manager of the plantation had been seeing these "Red Teal" throughout January and had wondered what they were. The record appears in the *Auk, 50*: 1933, 219. It is possible that a close examination of gunners' bags in future will reveal additional specimens of the Cinnamon Teal.

The specimen mentioned by Wayne (1910) on page 17 of his *Birds of South Carolina*, which he referred to this species because of the narrowness of the bill, has since been determined to be a female of the Blue-winged Teal.

In general habits and food this bird does not differ essentially from other teals.

60.   EUROPEAN WIDGEON: *Mareca penelope* (Linnaeus)   (136)

(*Mareca*, Brazilian name for a kind of duck; Gr., *penelope,* the wife of Ulysses in Greek mythology.)

DESCRIPTION: Length 17.00 to 21.00 inches. To be distinguished from the Baldpate by the rufous brown head and buff crown, instead of a gray head and white crown; and axillars mottled with gray, instead of wholly white as in the Baldpate.

RANGE: Breeds north to Iceland, northern Europe, and northern Siberia; south to southern Europe and central Asia. Winters north to Great Britain, Japan, British Columbia, and Greenland; south to northern Lower California, Florida, Abyssinia, and India.

STATUS IN S. C.: Rare winter visitor, November 28 to March 9, in the eastern part of the State. Recorded north and east to the lower Santee River; south to the Combahee River.

HISTORY: The distribution of this duck is peculiar. An Old World species, it appears to be increasing in this country, most of the records coming from the northeast. It was naturally thought to be of accidental occurrence in South Carolina, upon its first appearance, but observations have increased in such numbers that the bird may now be properly classified as a rare winter visitor.

The first South Carolina specimen we know of was taken on March 9, 1912, at the Bugbee Hunting Club, on the Ashepoo River, Colleton County, and sent to the Charleston Museum (No. 7126). The next preserved specimens are a pair of birds in the collection of E. von S. Dingle, taken by him on January 2 and 14, 1927, at Middleburg on Cooper River, Berkeley County. In the meantime, C. E. Chapman, of Mulberry Plantation, on the same river, took a bird on December 27, 1926 (and another on December 1, 1938), and Andrew Simons, of Charleston, took one about 1926 in this region. On March 4, 1931, E. Milby Burton banded a male caught in a trap at Long View Plantation, Combahee River, Colleton County, and on December 14, 1937, George A. Haas secured another at Tibwin Plantation, Charleston County, presenting it to the Charleston Museum (No. 37.213). In the latter part of November of the preceding year, A. H. DuPre reported seeing a single bird on the Santee River, near McClellanville.

From November 28, through the whole of December, 1941, a drake was seen on Bull's Island by members of the Audubon Wildlife Tours, conducted by Sprunt, covering a period of nine separate trips. This species has also been observed on that island during the Christmas Bird Count in recent years.

The European Widgeon's habits and food are the same as those of the Baldpate.

61. BALDPATE: *Mareca americana* (Gmelin)   (137)

(Lat., *americana*, of America.)

LOCAL NAMES: Widgeon; Brown Widgeon.

DESCRIPTION: Length 18.00 to 23.00 inches. *Male.* Mostly vermiculated above with brownish gray; patch on side of head green; crown white; fore part of wing white; black patch under tail preceded by a white patch; chest and sides vinaceous; axillars white, unmarked; speculum green; bill dull blue. *Female.* Brown with speckled gray head and neck; much white in wings and under parts. In flight the dark breast contrasts sharply with the white belly.

RANGE: Breeds north to northern Alaska and northern Mackenzie; south to northeastern California and northern Indiana. Winters north to southern British Columbia and Massachusetts; south to Costa Rica and Trinidad.

STATUS IN S. C.: Common winter resident, September 13 to June 6, over much of the State, but most common coastwise. Recorded north to Chester County; east to Horry County; south to Beaufort County; west to Aiken County.

HISTORY: The Baldpate, or American Widgeon, is a strikingly handsome duck. It is often called a "Widgeon," a term that has come to have little meaning, since it is very loosely applied to practically any wildfowl whose identity is not certain. The drake Baldpate is an unmistakable species and even the female is easier to identify in the field than most of her relatives of that sex. The amount of white in the forepart of the wings is always diagnostic, and the sharp line of demarcation between the dark breast and white belly is also an excellent identification mark. As for the drake, the marking which gives it the name of "Baldpate" is enough. The top of the head is not, of course, bare but bald in the sense of white, as in the Bald Eagle.

The Baldpate is a very active, noisy bird, the note being a sort of peeping whistle, very characteristic, and often heralding its presence or approach. It does not sound unlike the peeping of "biddies" in a barnyard. Baldpates sometimes appear to be very fast in the air, but this is an illusion created by their medium size and their ability to make sudden twists and turns. Actually, the air speed seldom exceeds 40 to 50 miles an hour.

Baldpates are often piratical in their behavior toward other waterfowl; they wait at the surface until some diving duck pops up with a succulent morsel and, attacking it at once, snatch the food away. Being surface feeders, though capable of diving, these ducks when tipping-up show the white belly against the black tail in striking contrast.

Most of the Baldpates usually arrive in South Carolina in November, early or late, according to the season. The spring migration is sometimes rather late; large numbers can be seen through all of April in some years. However, on May 30, 1940, and again in 1945 a high-plumaged drake was noted at Bull's Island, a month behind usual schedule. Neither showed sign of any injury.

Practically confined to fresh-water situations, this duck is a rice-field dweller and often appears in the cypress backwaters and lagoons. Here, amid the trunks of the great trees, hung with moss banners reflected in the still brown water, a cruising flock makes a striking picture of wilderness beauty.

FOOD: Baldpates limit themselves almost entirely (93 per cent) to vegetable forms of food. Favorite foods are pondweeds (*Potamogeton*) 42 per cent; wild rice 14 per cent. Algae, wild celery (*Vallisneria*), water milfoils, smartweeds, and duckweeds (*Lemna*) make up the rest. Animal food, about 7 per cent of the total, comprises small mollusks and insects. The Baldpate has not been found to be destructive to grain.

62. SHOVELLER: *Spatula clypeata* (Linnaeus)   (142)

(Lat., *Spatula*, a spoon, referring to bill; *clypeata*, shield-shaped.)

LOCAL NAMES: Spoon-bill; Shovel-billed Widgeon.

DESCRIPTION: Length 17.00 to 22.00 inches. Bill long, very broad and shovel shaped, with many bristles along edges. *Male*. Head and neck black glossed with green; back fuscous; breast white; sides and belly reddish chestnut; posteriorly grayish white; a blue patch on fore edge of wing. *Female*. Mottled brown; wing patch blue as in male.

RANGE: Breeds north to northern Alaska, central New York, northern Europe, and northern Asia; south to southern California, Texas, Turkey, and Turkestan. Winters north to southern British Columbia, Virginia, New Jersey (casually), Turkey, and Turkestan; south to Hawaii, Colombia, Abyssinia, and Australia.

STATUS IN S. C.: Common winter resident, September 4 to June 6, over most of the State, though more numerous in the coastal region. Recorded north to Chester County; east to Horry and Georgetown counties; south to the Combahee River; west to Aiken County.

HISTORY: Were it not for the Shoveller's great, misshapen beak, which gives it its name, it would rival the best of the duck family for looks. Its plumage is strikingly handsome, and a drake in his adult dress is something to remember. But because of its specialized bill the bird presents an overbalanced and clumsy appearance.

The Shoveller is a common, sometimes abundant, winter visitor and arrives early. From November well into March it occurs regularly, both in salt and fresh water, though it prefers the latter.

Although it is one of the river ducks, the Shoveller does not tip-up as much as the others but frequently feeds by extending the neck and swimming along with the beak half-submerged. Again, it may be seen feeding with the head fully under water, whirling around in aimless circles, and giving one the impression that it has no head. It takes in its food with a considerable amount of water, which is strained out through the comb-like fringe along the mandible.

Since the Shoveller consumes a good deal of animal food at times, its flesh is not always palatable and a good many hunters rather scorn it for that reason. One rather wonders at Audubon's statement that "no sportsman who is a judge will ever pass a Shoveller to shoot a Canvass-back." The birds he referred to undoubtedly had been feeding on vegetable matter, and were, therefore, good on the table.

The color of the beak differs between the sexes, being black in old males, and yellowish below in the females. One look at it is enough to distinguish the species either on the water or in flight. The flight speed of the Shoveller has been clocked by automobile at from 47 to 53 miles an hour (Kortright). It is capable of long flights, for it is one of the few birds that brave the long 2,000 mile trip from Alaska to the Hawaiian Islands.

It is not a very shy duck and will allow a close approach at times. Now and then Shovellers congregate about inlets and the mouths of tidal rivers where they empty into the sea, and gabble and feed about the sandbars with mergansers, cormorants, and other maritime birds.

Polyandry is very prevalent among the Shovellers and this unusual matrimonial arrangement seems to be accepted by both husbands without any jealousy. The second male, which is usually a young bird, takes up with the pair after they are mated.

Food: The rather high animal content of the Shoveller's food (34 per cent) consists chiefly of small mollusks. It also eats insects such as water bugs, water beetles, caddis-fly larvae, dragon-fly nymphs, small fish, crabs, and crayfish. Vegetable matter is made up of pondweeds, smartweed, and water-lily seeds. The Shoveller is economically valuable because of its destruction of highly injurious insects such as dragon-fly nymphs, water scorpions, back swimmers, and crayfish.

63. Wood Duck: *Aix sponsa* (Linnaeus) (144)

(Gr., *Aix*, a water-bird; Lat., *sponsa*, bride, referring to the brilliant [bridal] plumage.)

Local Names: Summer Duck; Acorn Duck.

Description: Length 17.00 to 21.00 inches. *Male.* Crested head purple, green, and white; upper surface black; breast purplish chestnut; belly white; flanks barred with black and white. *Female.* Head gray; a conspicuous eye-ring, and patch behind eye white; upper surface of body mostly olive brown; breast brown marked with buff; abdomen white.

Range: Breeds north to southern British Columbia and central eastern Labrador; south to southern California, Texas, and Cuba. Winters north to southern British Columbia and Massachusetts (casually); south to central Mexico and Jamaica.

Status in S. C.: Permanent resident, common locally in the coast region; fairly common in the interior. Recorded north to York County; east to Horry County; south to Beaufort County; west to Oconee County.

HISTORY: To many people, the Wood Duck is the ultimate among wildfowl. Even prosaic science unbends somewhat toward this lovely bird and has named it *sponsa*—bride, an avian bride adorned. Peterson (1947) says that "descriptive words fail" to describe this bird's plumage, and surely he is right. The Wood Duck is a natural masterpiece. It is one of the very few ducks in South Carolina that alights in trees.

Thoroughly appropriate also, is its name of "Wood," for it is essentially a forest bird. Equally applicable is its local name "Summer Duck," for it is one of the few ducks which remain the whole year in the South. Catesby found it here in 1722, and, amid the fairyland of cypress lagoons and moss-hung swamp lands, it occurs today to delight the eyes of any who penetrate the gray-green gloom and sun-splashed retreats that are its chosen home. Like that other exquisite dweller of the dark backwaters, the American Egret, the Wood Duck has paid for being beautiful. The feathers of the Wood Duck are much in demand for the making of trout flies. This, together with the desire for specimens by collectors, the annual hazard of the open season plus the shooting by lawbreakers at any season, and the destruction of much of its habitat has reduced the Wood Duck population to an alarmingly low level in recent years. Closed seasons for many years have helped to restore it, but it is still in danger.

In South Carolina, the Wood Duck resides chiefly in the coastal area. It lives among the great river swamps, rice fields, and ponds of the barrier islands, as well as along the rivers which penetrate the interior, but always near forested lands. It is one of the very few American ducks that do not nest on the ground, always using a cavity in a tree or stump. Now and then a pair will build in a prepared box or in an old building, but the nest is never exposed in open surroundings.

Mating usually takes place early in March, and in some forward seasons the eggs may be laid in that month, but they are more likely to be found in April. Wayne found a nest on April 7 that contained seven eggs. An early nesting record was made by the late Allard Heyward on April 29, 1938, when he saw a female and several young near Bacon's Bridge, Ashley River. E. von S. Dingle has seen young on May 5, and observed six ducklings "a week or so old" on June 8. Sprunt and Burton examined a nest in Blake's Reserve, Santee River, on June 29, 1929. The nest was in a dead stump, 10 feet from the water, and held nine eggs. This nest must have been subsequent to one which met with an accident, for the date is late. A female with three young, about three to four days old, was seen in the same locality, May 3, 1932. Other late nestings include the observation of a nest of fourteen eggs in a piling on a salt water creek, on August 11, 1941 (E. M. Burton), and of a female with ten young on August 25, 1944 (W. P. Baldwin).

The nest sometimes has bits of moss as lining, but is always provided with down from the breast of the female. Elevations vary from only a few feet to as much as 50 or more. The eggs usually number ten to fifteen, and are buffy white, averaging 51.1 x 38.8 millimeters. Incubation is by the female only, and consumes twenty-eight to thirty days. Only one brood is raised.

To see a Wood Duck fly into her nesting hole is something to make one rub one's eyes. She approaches the tree in headlong flight and without seeming to hesitate at all simply disappears into the opening. How it is accomplished with such apparent ease is a mystery. How the young descend from the nest is a never-ending cause for conjecture; but the usual, normal method is, without any question, to flutter or fall to the water or ground by themselves. Some nests have been found more than a mile from water. There are reports that the female sometimes carries the young down from the nest in her beak, but this is not usual. It is perhaps unnecessary to say that, once out of the nest, the young never return to it, despite entrancing stories to the contrary.

Even after gaining the water, however, the life of a duckling is ever in danger, for turtles, black bass, snakes, and other predators are always on the alert to seize it. There are few sights that can compare in serene beauty with that of a female and drake convoying a brood of downy youngsters through a cypress lagoon.

The Wood Duck feeds both in the water and ashore, where it walks easily and gracefully and runs well. The flight is a marvel of accurate speed, and the manner in which it can thread its way through dense swamps is astonishing. The note of the bird is just as characteristic as its exquisite plumage, a high, squealing sort of whistle, usually rendered as "o-eek, o-eek." One can be quite certain of the identity of the bird the moment he hears the call.

While the Wood Duck is a permanent resident and is the only duck that breeds regularly in South Carolina, a great number migrate north in the spring. These migrants are probably raised in the north and come south for the winter. A specimen that had been banded at McBee, S. C., on November 26, 1941, was killed the following September in the Province of Quebec.

FOOD: The high vegetable content of the Wood Duck's food (90 per cent) makes the bird excellent eating and is one reason for its decline in numbers, for lawless gunners shoot it the year 'round. Duckweed (*Lemna*) appears to be the favorite item at all times and forms 10 per cent of the total. Cone scales of the cypress form another 10 per cent. The Wood Duck likes wild rice (*Zizania*), pondweeds, water-lily seeds, wild grapes, buttonbush, and water-elm seeds, as well as nuts among which are acorns, beechnuts, and water hickory. Wild fruits figure to some extent in the Wood Duck's diet. The animal matter (10 per cent) is chiefly bugs, beetles, dragon flies, grasshoppers, and crickets, with small crustaceans occasionally.

64. REDHEAD: *Aythya americana* (Eyton) (146)

(Gr., *Aythya*, a sea bird; Lat., *americana*, of America.)

DESCRIPTION: Length 17.00 to 23.00 inches. Forehead rather high and abrupt. *Male.* Finely barred with black and white above, but head and upper neck chestnut; chest black; belly white; bill light blue. *Female.* Brown with a gray wing patch (speculum); and bill dull light blue.

RANGE: Breeds north to central British Columbia and southern Manitoba; south to southern California and southeastern Michigan. Winters north to southern British Columbia and Massachusetts; south to southwestern Mexico and Jamaica.

Brown Pelicans at Nesting Colony

ALLAN D. CRUICKSHANK
National Audubon Society

Adult Anhingas and Young

Young Anhingas in Nest   ALEXANDER SPRUNT, JR.

American Egret at Nest

JAMES J. CARROLL

STATUS IN S. C.: Uncommon winter resident, October 27 to March 30, over most of the State though more frequent along the coast. Reported north to Chester County; east to Horry County; south to Beaufort County; west to Aiken and Oconee counties.

HISTORY: This is one of the lesser known ducks of South Carolina. It is an uncommon winter visitor and so erratic in its movements that few hunters ever become acquainted with it, even though it may fall to their guns. Astonishingly enough, Wayne (1910) states that he never saw it alive in the State. It probably is true that the Redheads have been more numerous in South Carolina in recent years, but the scarcity of records in the past may have been due to a lack of observers and to an unfamiliarity with the bird on the part of those who did observe it.

Most of the secured specimens of the Redhead seem to have been taken from December through February. It frequents both salt and fresh water and is a representative of the diving ducks, those that literally dive for their food rather than tip-up as the river ducks do. Superficially, it resembles the much more famous Canvas-back, but there are differences which anyone can with care easily note. The back of the Redhead is distinctly gray instead of white and the shape of the head is at once characteristic. The forehead rises abruptly from the base of the beak, and does not slope gradually as does that of the Canvas-back. The female looks much like a scaup but lacks the white face patch of those species and does not have the light eye ring that marks the female Ring-neck.

Though traveling in large flocks throughout much of its southern winter range, the Redhead is often a solitary bird in South Carolina. Now and then a pair or a small group may be seen, but the majority of observations cover single birds. It is likely to remain for several days in a very restricted locality. Some winters pass in which not a single one is reported. It leaves probably in early March though there are not many definite data on this part of its history. In 1947-48, during the period of the Audubon Wildlife Tours to Bull's Island, which took place between mid-November and mid-January, Redheads were often seen, and as many as eight to a dozen were found in certain ponds during almost all of that time.

The Redhead appears to be a swift flier, but actual velocities rarely exceed 45 to 50 miles an hour.

FOOD: The fact that the Redhead is a diving duck would suggest that it searched for animal rather than vegetable forms of food. As a matter of fact, about 90 per cent of its food is vegetable—wild rice and celery, pondweeds, coon-tail, duckweed, and water-lily and smartweed seeds. In consequence, the flesh is excellent, and the Redhead is a fine table bird. The animal matter in its diet is composed of clams, snails, fish, frogs, lizards, and insects, amounting to no more than 10 per cent.

65. RING-NECKED DUCK: *Aythya collaris* (Donovan) (150)

(Lat., *collaris*, collared.)

LOCAL NAMES: Blackhead; Bullhead; Ring-bill; Ring-neck; Moonbill.

DESCRIPTION: Length 14.00 to 18.00 inches. *Male.* Like the scaup ducks, but with the back black; a conspicuous white bar in front of wing; a dull chestnut collar; back banded with black and gray; wing speculum gray. *Female.* Obscure brown, but with a whitish eye ring; banded beak; and gray speculum.

RANGE: Breeds north to southwestern Mackenzie, western Ontario, and southeastern Maine (casually); south to northeastern California, central eastern Arizona, and northern Illinois. Winters north to southern British Columbia and Massachusetts; south to Guatemala, southern Florida, and the Bahama Islands.

STATUS IN S. C.: Locally abundant winter resident, October 21 to May 7, over most of the State though more numerous in the coast region. Reported north to Chester County; east to Horry County; south to Beaufort County; west to Aiken and Oconee counties.

HISTORY: Wayne (1910) records that he secured only one in all his many years of field work in the coastal area and that he had been unable to verify the assertions that it is abundant in this State. Wayne simply did not look in the right places for it and was handicapped by working a very restricted locality.

The Ring-neck is one of the commonest of our ducks, arriving in late October. While somewhat locally distributed and prone to frequent particular areas, it is abundant in those areas. During migration it is frequently seen on the small ponds in the Piedmont region. It is often mistaken for a scaup duck, and is grouped with that species by its local name of "Blackhead." Though a diving duck, it occurs more frequently in fresh water than salt and lives in the cypress backwaters, rice fields, island ponds, and tidal rivers during its stay in South Carolina. It is capable of diving to a depth of 40 feet for its food. Occasionally, it appears in Colonial Lake in Charleston and near the Ashley River Bridge, both salt-water areas.

The Ring-neck does resemble the scaup at a glance, for the head is black and the belly white but that is about as far as the similarity goes. The differences are obvious. The banded beak, which can be seen from a distance, alone is enough to distinguish the species. Moreover, the black back (as compared with the very light colored scaup), the gray sides, the white bar in front of the wing (all of which markings the scaup lacks) are easy field marks. The Ring-neck gets its name from an indistinct band of chestnut around the glossy black neck, a mark that is impossible to see at any distance at all and worthless to the field observer as an identification mark. The banded beak of the female is enough to distinguish her.

The speed of the Ring-neck is considerable, and it can weave and twist in a most disconcerting manner, making it a difficult mark for the gunner. To see a flock come in at high altitude, then suddenly side-slip down into the water, with a series of breath-taking "falling leaf" and "fish-tail" maneuvers, is a wonderful experience. Accurate data are lacking, but it is likely the duck attains speeds up to 60 miles an hour or more. "Blackhead" shooting is a sport which will test the skill of any marksman.

The Ring-neck is a jaunty duck, and the drake in full plumage is very handsome indeed. The note is a low, guttural sort of croak.

Several years ago several hundred Ring-necks were banded at Lavington Plantation on the Ashepoo River. Returns show that a number had been taken as far north as Manitoba and Saskatchewan.

FOOD: This is another diving duck with vegetable preferences; hence it is a good table bird. Seeds of the water lily, water shield, bindweed, and spike rush compose most of the food, forming about 80 per cent. Animal is made up of minnows, frogs, crayfish, snails, and some insects.

66. CANVAS-BACK: *Aythya valisineria* (Wilson) (147)

(Lat., *valisineria*, from *Vallisneria*, generic name of the wild celery, a favorite food; to Vallisneri, an Italian naturalist.)

DESCRIPTION: Length 19.00 to 24.00 inches. In both sexes the gently sloping profile of the bill is distinctive. *Male*. Head and neck dark reddish chestnut; breast and lower neck black; back white; bill black. *Female*. Brown, more reddish on head and neck.

RANGE: Breeds north to Alaska and northern Mackenzie; south to eastern Oregon and southern Wisconsin. Winters north to southern British Columbia and Massachusetts; south to Guatemala and Cuba.

STATUS IN S. C.: Fairly common winter resident, October 31 to April 18; occurs mostly coastwise but also inland. Recorded north to Chester County; east to Horry County; south to Beaufort County; west to Aiken and Oconee counties.

HISTORY: The Canvas-back excels the Mallard in popular fancy, and epicures hold it in highest regard. It is in the very forefront of American wildfowl. It eluded observation by Wayne, who considered it to be very rare in South Carolina (1910). Actually, it occurs regularly every winter, but in varying numbers, and the indications are that it has increased locally in recent years. In any event, one now has no difficulty in seeing it in considerable numbers in suitable locations.

The Canvas-back is a diving duck. It occurs in both salt and fresh water, usually feeding in fresh water and going out to sea to spend the night. On certain of the barrier islands, one may see flocks moving in from, and going out to sea at various hours during the day. Canvas-backs arrive in South Carolina usually in late November or early December. The first severe cold in the north sends them southward as soon as the ponds and streams become frozen.

Wild celery is so much a favorite food in most of the Canvas-back's southern (North Carolina and Virginia) range that the name of this plant was given to the bird. The plant is not as abundant in South Carolina as are some other duck foods, and the duck is attracted to some of its favored haunts by an introduced growth known as the banana water lily (*Castalia flava*). This is luxuriant in ponds on Bull's Island of the Cape Romain Refuge, and Canvas-backs resort there every winter to remain the entire season.

The Canvas-back is a distinctive duck afloat, ashore, or in flight. The white back of the drake shines out, and the reddish head against the black breast makes a striking color combination. The gently sloping line of the bill and forehead is different from that of any other closely related duck, and is one of the surest means of identification at a distance, for it can be picked out when no color at all is distinguishable. Females are unimpressive birds except for the characteristic outline of the head, which is a dull brown with no more than a wash of red. The Canvas-back sits rather low in the water. It springs forward as it dives, a feat it performs with ease, and descends to considerable depths. Baldpates and Coots, waiting at the surface, often snatch from the Canvas-back the roots and tubers it brings up from below.

The Canvas-back is a speed flier, one of the fastest of the ducks. It has been timed by airplane at 72 miles an hour. A flock in the air is an impressive and thrilling sight.

The flavor of the flesh of wild ducks is determined, of course, by the kinds of food they have eaten. Birds taken in the same rice field, for example, are almost impossible to distinguish when they have been prepared for the table. A Mallard, a Pintail, and a Canvas-back fattened on rice will taste very much alike.

FOOD: In addition to wild celery, the Canvas-back eats many other plant foods, which compose about four-fifths of the total. Water lily, water milfoil, foxtail grass, pondweeds, wild rice, widgeon grass, and saw grass seeds are in its diet. It also eats some insects, beetles, and fish.

GREATER SCAUP DUCK
67. *Aythya marila nearctica* Stejneger (148)

(Gr., *marila*, charcoal; Lat., *nearctica*, of the New World.)

LOCAL NAMES: Blackhead; Big Blackhead; Bluebill; Broadbill.

DESCRIPTION: Length 16.00 to 21.00 inches. *Male.* Head, neck, and upper breast black; the head glossed with metallic green; back finely barred with white and black, appearing white at a distance; speculum white; bill dull light blue. *Female.* Brown with a white speculum; area around base of bill white; bill dull light blue.

RANGE: Breeds north to northern Alaska, northern Manitoba, and southeastern Quebec; south to central British Columbia and southeastern Michigan. Winters north to the Aleutian Islands and Maine; south to southern California and Florida.

STATUS IN S. C.: Rare winter resident, October 31 to early April, in both coastal and interior sections. Reported north to Chester County; east and south to the Isle of Palms; west to Aiken County.

HISTORY: The "Big Blackhead" is a real diver. It is not familiar to most persons, since commonly it is not distinguishable from the Lesser Scaup. Its exact status on the South Carolina coast is rather uncertain at best, apart from the well established fact that it winters here. Not many are taken, for its decided preference for salt water makes it difficult to know with certainty when the bird arrives and departs. However, both the Greater and Lesser Scaups probably come at the same time, late in October, and they remain into April. An occasional specimen of one or the other may be seen in early summer.

The scaups are easy to recognize as such but the field differences between Greater and Lesser Scaups are puzzling. Both are black-headed, light-backed birds, as Peterson (1947) puts it, "black at both ends and white in the middle." The blue bill gives rise to one of the local names, but an observer must be very keen of eye to note the greenish gloss on the head of the Greater, as against the purplish sheen of the Lesser. The white wing area, present in both, is usually larger in the Greater than in the Lesser, but this is difficult to see. The females of these two species are all but inseparable in the field except by size and flight. The name scaup is generally supposed to be derived from the bird's habit of feeding on beds of shellfish which Europeans call scaup beds, this word having the same derivation as the word scallop.

The Greater Scaup in South Carolina seldom visits fresh water; it prefers the large bays, estuaries, and the ocean itself. At times, it congregates there in large flocks or "rafts," as they are called. The diving and submarine swimming abilities of the scaups are great. They are powerful fliers, and probably attain speeds of from 45 to 50 miles an hour, more if pressed. The white belly shows well in flight, the line of demarcation between it and the black breast being very sharply drawn. Like all diving ducks, the scaups have to paddle along the surface for some distance before rising into the air.

FOOD: This duck appears equally fond of vegetable and animal food, consuming widgeon grass, wild rice, pondweeds, wild celery and buttonbush seeds, as well as oysters and insects such as dragon flies, beetles, May flies, etc. As a rule the flesh is too fishy for general table use.

68. LESSER SCAUP DUCK: *Aythya affinis* (Eyton) (149)

(Lat., *affinis*, allied.)

LOCAL NAMES: Blackhead; Bluebill; Broadbill.

DESCRIPTION: Length 15.00 to 19.00 inches. Like the Greater Scaup Duck but smaller; head glossed with purple.

RANGE: Breeds north to central Alaska and northern Manitoba; south to central western California (casually) and northern Ohio. Winters north to southern British Columbia and Maine; south to Panama and Trinidad.

STATUS IN S. C.: Abundant winter resident, October 20 to June 19, occasionally July; somewhat more numerous coastwise. Reported north to Chester and Lancaster counties; east to Horry County; south to Beaufort County; west to Aiken and Oconee counties.

HISTORY: The Lesser Scaup is an abundant species, well known under the term "Blackhead." Much more inclined toward fresh water than its larger relative, it also resorts to salt water and rafts off the island beaches. The differences between the Lesser and the Greater Scaup have been discussed in the history of the Greater Scaup.

The Lesser Scaup is one of the least shy of the ducks and responds readily to any kind of protection. It is the duck which many winter visitors feed at such places as St. Augustine, Daytona Beach, and elsewhere in Florida, and it could be attracted in exactly the same way on the South Carolina coast if anyone would take the trouble to provide regular feeding. Every winter, numbers of these ducks appear at the city end of the Ashley River Bridge at Charleston, feeding about the sewers there, in close proximity to motor traffic. A few years ago, one could expect them there about mid-February, but in recent times, they have appeared in early January and remain well into March. The only persons appearing to pay much attention to them are small boys with air rifles and sling shots. Occasionally, a few scaups will spend a day or two in Colonial Lake, a perfectly ideal situation for municipal or private feeding. In January, 1943, some twenty thousand birds were estimated to pass the

Cape Romain Refuge, and in the same month, 1944, a like number appeared in and near Charleston Harbor.

The Lesser Scaup's habits and behavior are much like those of its larger relative, but the duck is not a favorite with sportsmen, who consider it a poor table bird. This is true enough when the bird has limited itself to animal food, but the flesh may be very palatable if the bird has been feeding in fresh-water localities. This it often does, consuming vegetable matter to the extent of 60 per cent of the total amount of food.

These Scaups are active, fast flying birds, small enough to give an impression of high speed which is frequently exaggerated in hunting stories.

During February of 1930, E. Milby Burton banded several hundred of these birds on the Combahee River. Without going into details on recoveries, it is interesting to point out that returns have come in from the upper Tanana River, Alaska, and the Canadian provinces of Alberta, Manitoba, Ontario, and Saskatchewan, as well as a dozen states, including Alabama, Missouri, Michigan, Minnesota, Wisconsin, and Pennsylvania.

FOOD: The Lesser Scaups eat seeds of the water lilies, pondweeds, water milfoil, and widgeon grass, together with mollusks, insects, and crustaceans. Curiously enough, the duck is something of a scavenger, feeding at mouths of sewers, as indicated above, and as examination of stomach contents has definitely proven.

AMERICAN GOLDEN-EYE
69. *Bucephala clangula americana* (Bonaparte) (151)

(Gr., *Bucephala*, bull-headed; Lat., *clangula*, a little noise, referring to wings; *americana*, of America.)

LOCAL NAMES: Whistler.

DESCRIPTION: Length 16.00 to 23.00 inches. *Male.* Largely white; head black, glossed with metallic green, with a round white spot between bill and eye; back black; eye yellow. *Female.* Grayish brown with head reddish brown and collar white; a large white patch in the wing.

RANGE: Breeds north to central Alaska and northern Labrador; south to southern British Columbia and New Hampshire. Winters north to the Aleutian Islands and Newfoundland; south to Sinaloa (Mazatlan), Florida, and Cuba (casually).

STATUS IN S. C.: Fairly common winter resident, November 4 to April 20, chiefly coastwise. Known north and east to Horry County; south to Beaufort County; west to Greenwood and Oconee counties.

HISTORY: The Golden-eye is a diving duck unfamiliar to most people, even old-time hunters, as it is not a table bird and is in South Carolina largely confined to salt water. Because of its black and white plumage the drake is a handsome bird. The species is a very hardy one; it comes to South Carolina only after cold weather has set in.

Though occasionally taken in the large backwaters, the Golden-eye is really a sea duck, preferring ocean bays, estuaries, and inlets. In some ways it appears to be a glorified edition of the smaller Buffle-head. The color pattern of the drake is unmistakable, and the yellow eye and snuff-brown head of the gray female is diagnostic.

The local name of "Whistler" is well chosen; it comes from the high, shrill music made by the wings of the duck in flight, a sound which carries far and announces the presence of the bird sometimes even before it is seen. It is a strong, fast flier, having been timed from trains at 50 miles an hour. No doubt it is capable of greater speeds.

The great salt marshes of the coastal area, with their many winding creeks and openings, are favored haunts of the Golden-eye, and those who travel the Inland Waterway have many opportunities to see it. Now and then it occurs in harbors and along waterfronts of fishing villages and towns. Occasionally, the Golden-eye appears on Colonial Lake, in Charleston.

This is one of the few ducks that nest higher than the ground, using the natural cavity in a tree or stub in its northern breeding range.

Food: Though in some localities the Golden-eye takes considerable vegetable food, in the southeast it prefers animal food. This amounts to as much as 75 per cent. Hence the flesh is rather rank and fishy. It eats mussels, clams, small fish, and insects with a good many fiddler crabs (*Uca*). Wild celery, nut grass, water lilies, and pondweed seeds figure in the vegetable diet.

70. Buffle-head: *Bucephala albeola* (Linnaeus) (153)

(Lat., *albeola*, whitish.)

Local Names: Butterball.

Description: Length 13.00 to 16.00 inches. A small black and white duck with puffy head. *Male.* Back black; upper neck and head glossy green and purple; hind head with a large white patch; a large white area on wings. *Female.* Dark brown above, with a white mark on cheeks and a white wing patch.

Range: Breeds north to central Alaska and western Ontario; south to northeastern California, southeastern Wisconsin, and southeastern Maine (casually). Winters north to the Commander and Aleutian islands and Maine; south to central Mexico, Florida, and Cuba (casually).

Status in S. C.: Fairly common winter resident, November 16 to April 24, largely coastwise. Reported north to Chester and Lancaster counties; east to Horry County; south to Beaufort County; west to Aiken County.

History: The Buffle-head shares with the Green-winged Teal the distinction of being the smallest of the South Carolina ducks. It is one of the most handsome of the whole wildfowl family, alert, dainty, and altogether pleasing. Because of its striking black and white plumage and diminutive size, it is easily distinguished from any other duck except perhaps the Golden-eye. The female, too, despite her plain olive-brownish and white plumage, is not difficult to know; she is set apart by her size and by the conspicuous cheek patch.

The Buffle-head arrives in early November and sometimes lingers until late April. It is a diving duck and in South Carolina prefers salt water. The Inland Waterway, marshes, bays, and tidal rivers are its home, but it occasionally comes into rice fields and fresh-water ponds. The females and immatures outnumber the adult drakes, but the drakes appear regularly each winter. A pair of these tiny ducks, seen in a still pond rimmed by trees or tall rushes, is a memorable sight.

The Buffle-head is a great diver and under-water swimmer, being able to remain submerged for a surprising time. Its flight is very swift, with extremely rapid wing-beats, almost creating a blur about the bird. Sometimes it emerges from the water in full flight, without first pattering along the surface as other ducks seem forced to do before they can rise. It often flies at very low elevations.

Few of these little ducks are shot locally. The flesh is unpalatable, and the small size does not attract hunters, nor does its habit of resorting to open salt water encourage its pursuit. When alighting on the water, the Buffle-head does so under considerable momentum, and comes to a sliding and gradual stop. It is another tree-nesting duck, but of course does not breed anywhere near South Carolina; its nesting grounds are in western Canada.

FOOD: Largely animal matter (crustaceans, mollusks, small fish, and insects) amounting to about 80 per cent. Its vegetable diet is composed of seeds of the pondweeds, wild celery, and various sedges.

71. OLD-SQUAW: *Clangula hyemalis* (Linnaeus)   (154)

(Lat., *Clangula*, a little noise; *hyemalis*, pertaining to winter.)

LOCAL NAMES: Long-tailed Duck; South-southerly.

DESCRIPTION: Length, male, 19.00 to 23.00 inches; female, 15.00 to 18.00 inches. *Male*. Middle tail feathers greatly lengthened. *Summer*. Mostly dark brown, but patch on side of head, also posterior lower parts, white. *Winter*. Back, wings, and breast dark brown; sides of head gray and brown; rest of plumage mostly white. *Female*. Dark brown above, white below; head white, with brownish black crown and cheek patch.

RANGE: Breeds north to northern Melville Island, northern Greenland, Spitzbergen, and the Arctic islands of Siberia; south to the Aleutian Islands, southern Labrador, the Faeroe Islands, and the Kurile Islands. Winters north to northern Alaska, southern Greenland, and Japan; south to southern California, Florida, Italy, and China.

STATUS IN S. C.: Uncommon winter resident, November 6 to April 3, chiefly along the coast. Recorded north and east to Horry County; south to Beaufort County; west to Hampton and Aiken counties.

PLATE VIII: TIDAL CREEK SCENE
Oil Painting by Francis Lee Jaques

Flying: Wood Ibises. Alighting on piling: Osprey. Left center: Pied-billed Grebe. Right center: upper, Common Loon (winter plumage); lower, Common Loon (breeding plumage). Bottom, left to right: Lesser Scaup (female), Lesser Scaup (male), Greater Scaup (male), Horned Grebe (breeding plumage), and Horned Grebe (winter plumage).

HISTORY: The Old-squaw is essentially a sea duck. It rarely comes into fresh water. Probably it is as little known as any of the wildfowl that visit South Carolina. It does, however, occur practically every winter in varying numbers, particularly when the northern winter has been cold. Because it lives on the ocean and the larger bays, and delights in rough water, wind, and cold, there is nothing surprising in the fact that few people are acquainted with it. Yet it is an interesting bird, and has been taken within a hundred yards of East Battery in Charleston; it has also appeared at times in Colonial Lake. Now and then a specimen will be taken in a cypress backwater or rice field. It has been taken in Berkeley County by E. Milby Burton (at Otranto) and by E. von S. Dingle (at Middleburg). Sprunt has seen it near Yemassee in the headwaters of the Combahee River, and Dr. E. E. Murphey has secured it in the Savannah River, near Augusta.

Among the dead trees along the beach on Capers and Bull's Islands, this duck feeds on a mussel which adheres to tide-washed trunks and branches. It probably feeds in the same manner on other barrier beaches south of Charleston Harbor. It is perfectly at ease in the roughest surf, and is an excellent diver and submarine swimmer, and there are definite records of their having been caught in gill nets at depths of over 150 feet.

The Old-squaw is usually a noisy duck. This characteristic is implied in the scientific name which, when translated, means "a little winter noise." Some of its numerous local names are derived from supposed resemblance to its calls, as "South-southerly." However, on the South Carolina coast, it seems to be a rather silent species. Occasionally, an individual will remain about a restricted area for days at a time, this having been noted on more than one winter, when visitors to the Audubon Tours at Bull's Island have been shown one which stayed in the boathouse cut for days.

FOOD: The diet of the Old-squaw is about 90 per cent animal matter. It is not a table bird. Mollusks, insects, fish, crustaceans, and marine seaweeds make up the bulk of its food, with a small amount of vegetable food consisting of seeds of pondweeds and various grasses.

EASTERN HARLEQUIN DUCK
72. *Histrionicus histrionicus histrionicus* (Linnaeus) (155)

(Lat., *Histrionicus*, stage-playing, *i. e.*, like a harlequin.)

DESCRIPTION: Length 15.00 to 21.00 inches. *Male.* General color bluish plumbeous, varied with white stripes and spots; a broad stripe on each side of the crown, together with flanks and the sides of the body, rufous. *Female.* Mostly dull brown with two white spots on each side of head. *Immature.* Similar to the adult female.

RANGE: Breeds north to southern Greenland and Iceland; south to northern Ungava and Newfoundland. Winters north to Iceland; south accidentally to Louisiana and South Carolina.

STATUS IN S. C.: Accidental winter visitor to the coast. Reported only from Charleston County.

HISTORY: The first record of the Eastern Harlequin Duck for South Carolina consists of four birds observed at Porcher's Bluff near Mt. Pleasant by Arthur T.

Wayne on January 14, 1917, and two more on January 16. The weather was very cold. Wayne's account of this occurrence (*Auk*, *35*: 1918, 437) is as follows:

> During the intensely cold weather which began on December 30, 1917, and continued through the third week of January, 1918, I was constantly on the lookout for far northern birds. On January 14, I saw four of these ducks, and on the 16th, I saw two more near the place where the first were seen on January 14. These ducks were probably not more than 75 or 80 yards from me and the identification was established without a doubt despite the fact that I was unable to shoot one. All the examples were in the plumage of the female and must have been that sex or else young males of the first winter plumage. Near at hand were small flocks of Buffle-head (*Charitonetta albeola*), Old-squaw (*Harelda hyemalis*), and Ruddy Ducks (*Erismatura jamaicensis*), and the Harlequin's [*sic*] were easily identified. This is an addition to the avifauna of South Carolina.

Nineteen years later, on February 1, 1936, Andrew H. DuPre saw two drakes and one duck on the Cape Romain Refuge, a few miles north of the place where Wayne made the first record. These birds were observed in the Inland Waterway a few miles from McClellanville.

Although no specimen was obtained by either observer, the circumstances indicate that the records are valid. The male of this strangely plumaged waterfowl could scarcely be mistaken for any other. It is one of the far northern species and also one of the rarest.

The habits and food of the Harlequin are very much the same as those of other northern diving ducks.

73. KING EIDER: *Somateria spectabilis* (Linnaeus) (162)

(Gr., *Somateria*, body down; Lat., *spectabilis*, conspicuous.)

DESCRIPTION: Length 19.00 to 25.00 inches. *Male.* Back and abdomen black; wings black with white patches; breast cream buff; head gray; cheeks tinged with pale green; neck white; bill and frontal shield orange. *Female.* Brown, barred and streaked with ochraceous.

RANGE: Breeds north to Melville Island, northern Greenland, Spitzbergen, and northern Siberia; south to northern Alaska, northern Labrador, Anadyr (northern Siberia), and Kamchatka. Winters north to Bering Sea, southern Greenland, northern Europe, and northern Asia; south to California (casually), southeastern Georgia, Italy, and the Kurile Islands.

STATUS IN S. C.: Casual winter visitor, December 26 to January 2, along the coast. Known from only Charleston County.

HISTORY: This big boreal sea duck is of accidental occurrence in South Carolina waters, and is very rare anywhere along the middle or south Atlantic seaboard. It belongs to the famous group which furnishes the eiderdown of commerce, none of which ever comes very far south, even in winter.

On December 26, 1936, E. Milby Burton secured an immature female at the Charleston Jetties, and three days later, at the same place, took another. These specimens now bear Nos. 36.240 and 36.241.1 in the Charleston Museum collection.

On January 2, 1947, James Mosimann and Thomas Uzzell, Jr., saw a single adult male bird off the Isle of Palms, near Charleston. These are the only records for the State.

The eiders, which are heavy-bodied sea ducks, are fond of rocky shores. The food is about 95 per cent animal matter, and the flesh is rank. The birds dive to a depth of 8 or 10 fathoms (48-60 feet). The bills are very distinctive, being enlarged in the drake of this species into a broad lobe which forms a kind of shield on the forehead.

WHITE-WINGED SCOTER
74. *Melanitta deglandi* (Bonaparte) (165)

(Gr., *Melanitta*, a black duck; *deglandi*, to C. D. Degland, a French naturalist.)

DESCRIPTION: Length 19.00 to 24.00 inches. *Male.* Black, but with wing patch and spot below eye white. *Female.* Brown, with white wing patch, and two white patches on each side of head.

RANGE: Breeds north to northern Mackenzie and Labrador; south to central North Dakota and southern Quebec. Winters north to the Great Lakes and Newfoundland; south to Louisiana and Florida.

STATUS IN S. C.: Rare winter resident, coastal, November 3 to May 15, casually June. Reported north to Horry County; south to Charleston.

HISTORY: This species, with the two following, are unfamiliar birds, even to coast dwellers. The scoters are off-shore ducks and rarely indeed in winter does one appear anywhere else. All of them are large, heavy birds with bulbous beaks and black plumage. Two of them, the White-winged Scoter and the Surf Scoter, have white markings here and there, so placed as to be very distinctive and to provide excellent field characters. The White-winged Scoter, as its name indicates, has the white in the wings and may be seen at a considerable distance when the bird is in flight. It constitutes a distinguishing mark.

The occurrence of the White-winged Scoter in South Carolina was thought for long to be no more than accidental. Wayne (1910) included it in the Hypothetical List on the basis of observations by Coues, but he himself saw one in the Wando River, Charleston County, on January 20, 1911. On January 31, 1918, E. A. Simons took an adult male on the Cooper River, the first to be secured in South Carolina. Curiously enough, it was shot in fresh water.

On May 15, 1926, Dr. Thomas Smyth and J. D. Corrington saw three birds off the Isle of Palms beach. On January 20, 1934, fifteen of these birds were seen off the South Jetty, Winyah Bay, by Dr. H. C. Oberholser, Chamberlain, and Sprunt. Since that time, eight or ten observations have been made, including a bird taken in Charleston Harbor on January 30, 1936, by E. Milby Burton (No. 36.17.1). On June 10, 1939, A. H. DuPre and W. P. Baldwin found a bird, unable to fly, on Bull's Island. Such observations in recent years seem to indicate that the White-winged Scoter deserves the status of rare winter resident rather than that of an accidental wanderer.

Food: The White-winged Scoter's food is largely animal (94 per cent) and the flesh is usually unfit for the table, though it is eaten as a stew in New England, where the ducks are known as "Sea Coots."

75. Surf Scoter: *Melanitta perspicillata* (Linnaeus) (166)

(Lat., *perspicillata*, conspicuous.)

Description: Length 17.00 to 22.00 inches. *Male.* Black, with a white patch on crown and another on the nape. *Female.* Brown, with two white patches on each side of head, but no white on the wings.

Range: Breeds north to northern Alaska and Labrador; south to Alberta and James Bay. Winters north, to the Aleutian Islands and the Bay of Fundy; south to Lower California and Florida.

Status in S. C.: Fairly common winter resident, October 24 to June 7, in coastal waters. Observed north to Horry County; south to Folly Island.

History: The Surf Scoter is far more common than the White-winged, for it is a regular winter visitor. A late record was made on June 7, 1942, when twelve were seen off Folly Island by Dr. R. B. Rhett. Like the other scoters, it is a sea duck and its appearance in fresh water is very unusual. Apparently it was far more abundant in years past than it is at the present, but this difference can hardly be accounted for by the recent duck "shortages." It has, to some extent, simply changed its range and does not appear as commonly as it once did.

The drake of the Surf Scoter is easily recognized by the white patches on the head and back of the neck; otherwise it is jet black. These white markings show at great distances. Flocks of Surf Scoters, in varying numbers, can be seen from any of the ocean beaches along the coast, usually flying low over the waves in long lines. Their large size and black plumage are distinctive.

At many places on the beaches of the barrier islands (notably Bull's, Dewees, Botany Bay, and Seabrook's Islands) fallen trees, toppled over by erosion along the high-water line, are washed by the surf and become covered by barnacles, mussels, and other forms of shellfish. Such places make excellent feeding grounds for various kinds of sea and shore birds, among them the Surf Scoters. Their sea-food diet renders the flesh of the scoters unpalatable; hence these ducks are not regarded as game birds in South Carolina and are rarely shot.

Food: Like others of this family, the Surf Scoter prefers animal food. Mussels, clams, scallops, small crabs, and fish compose 90 per cent of the diet. The small amount of vegetable food which it eats consists of wild celery, pondweeds, and widgeon grass.

76. American Scoter: *Oidemia nigra americana* Swainson (163)

(Gr., *Oidemia*, a swelling, referring to the bulbous bill; Lat., *nigra*, black; *americana*, of America.)

Description: Length 17.00 to 21.00 inches. *Male.* Plumage all black; base of bill orange yellow. *Female.* Brown, with light cheeks that contrast with the dark crown.

RANGE: Breeds north to northern Siberia, northern Alaska, and northern Quebec (northern Ungava); south to the Kurile and Aleutian Islands and southern Quebec. Winters north to the Pribilof Islands and Newfoundland; south to China, southern California, and Florida.

STATUS IN S. C.: Abundant winter resident, October 11 to May 28, casually July 3, in the coast area only. Reported north to Horry County; south to Beaufort County.

HISTORY: The American Scoter might properly be called the "Black Duck" for it is of an unrelieved black, with not a feather of another shade. Only the base of the bulbous bill, so characteristic of the scoters, is at variance, being a bright orange-yellow. At reasonable ranges therefore, the American Scoter can be confused with no other duck, not even its close relatives, which show white in some parts of their plumage.

The American Scoter was once all but unknown on this coast. Indeed, it was not until 1884 that the first record occurred, when one was taken by Henry Hunter, in January of that year, in Charleston Harbor. Wayne was not familiar with this record, for he gives a male secured by Dr. E. E. Murphey in Bull's Bay, May 7, 1903, as the first State record.

Years passed before the bird was observed again, even longer than the interim between the Hunter and Murphey specimens, which was nineteen years. Twenty-six years later, eight birds were seen by Weston and Sprunt off Seabrook's Island, January 31, 1929. Since then, records have multiplied, and the species is now listed as a regular winter visitor. It is, indeed, the most common of the scoters frequenting the South Carolina coast. In the American Scoter we have an instance of a shift in population status which has been noted at times among other species. It compares, in reverse, with the decline of the population of the Surf Scoters in South Carolina.

On November 17, 1934, E. Milby Burton saw about one thousand birds off Charleston Harbor, and on November 21, 1938, Weston, DuPre, and Sprunt saw flocks in Bull's Bay estimated at about twelve thousand birds. Beverly Howard stated that he saw what he considered to be at least ten thousand from a plane between Beaufort and Savannah, in January, 1947. These are the largest numbers thus far reported.

Specimens of the American Scoter have been secured in December (Bull's Bay, by Burton), in February (Bull's Island, by G. G. Dominick), and in April (Seabrook's Island, by I. H. Grimball). The latest date of the bird's occurrence in spring is May 28, from a specimen (a sick bird, weighing only 1 pound, 6 ounces) found by Edward Hyer on Sullivan's Island. There are two summer records. On June 24, 1944, W. P. Baldwin observed an American Scoter which it is believed had been forced to remain so late in the season either because it was moulting or because it had been injured. The other summer record was established by Burton and Sprunt, who observed a scoter at Bull's Bay on July 3, 1930. The bird would not fly, and the observers conjectured that it had been wounded, possibly by Burton himself in the previous winter when he had taken several specimens in the same area.

These black ducks are to be seen off the coast either from boats or beaches. They fly in typical scoter style, low over the water in long lines. They are not inconvenienced by rough weather but seem rather to delight in it. They dive deeply and feed on mollusks and shellfish, like others of the family. They are seldom shot in South Carolina.

FOOD: The food consists of about 90 per cent animal matter (mussels, clams, oysters, and fish.) This scoter sometimes eats pondweeds, wild celery, and musk grass, taken in the seldom frequented fresh-water areas. The stomach of a sick, very thin, bird taken at Charleston in December contained the remains of a small mussel (*Mytilidae*).

77. RUDDY DUCK: *Oxyura jamaicensis rubida* (Wilson) (167)

(Gr., *Oxyura*, sharp-tailed; Lat., *jamaicensis*, of Jamaica; *rubida*, ruddy.)

LOCAL NAMES: Spiketail; Bumblebee Coot; Butterball; Dicky; Leatherback; Leather Breeches.

DESCRIPTION: Length 14.00 to 17.00 inches. *Male.* Crown black; rest of upper surface and neck rich chestnut; a broad patch on cheeks white; posterior lower parts dull white; bill light blue. *Female.* Dull brown above, sides of head brownish white, with a dark horizontal line; most of lower parts white.

RANGE: Breeds north to central British Columbia, southern Mackenzie, and northern Quebec (Ungava); south to central Mexico, Guatemala, and Carriacou Island. Winters north to southern British Columbia and Massachusetts; south to Guatemala, Costa Rica, and Grenada Island in the West Indies.

STATUS IN S. C.: Common winter resident, October 5 to May 1, mainly coastwise. Recorded north to Oconee and Richland counties; east to Horry County; south to Beaufort County; west to Aiken County.

HISTORY: There is so much of the comical about the little Ruddy Duck that it might be called the clown of the wildfowl family. Its general appearance, movements, flight, and much of its behavior are genuinely amusing as well as interesting. It is well known over the entire country, a fact attested by the great number of local names applied to it, amounting to more than a hundred.

In South Carolina the Ruddy Duck is not very well known. Hunters scorn it because of its small size. There is a general though erroneous belief that it is not a table bird. Being largely coastal in distribution, it is not often observed in the interior.

The Ruddy is a typical diving duck. It prefers fresh water in South Carolina, and mingles freely with Mallards, Pintails, Teals, Baldpates, and other river ducks. It secures its food by diving and is wonderfully adept both in diving and in submerged swimming. The Ruddy is unmistakable in appearance, short, squat, and dumpy; it has a remarkably thick neck and broad bill, but its characteristic feature is the rather long, stiff tail which is often carried in a perpendicular position, not infrequently pointing forward over the back and giving the illusion of a huge, aquatic wren. The crown of the head of the male (in spring plumage) is very dark and contrasts strongly with the white cheeks. These are good markings for the identification of the bird in the field. The handsome reddish breeding plumage of the male, from which comes the name "Ruddy," is not often seen locally, as the bird migrates before attaining it. In South Carolina the Ruddy usually appears in rusty brown and gray.

The Ruddy is obliged to patter along the surface for a considerable distance before rising into the air; the short little wings seem inadequate for the chunky body. It seeks safety by diving, but it is not shy and often allows close approach. Like the grebe, it has the power of submerging vertically, without any suggestion of the forward plunge so characteristic of the diving ducks. Indeed, it resembles the grebes structurally, for the feet are very far back on the body, and it is practically helpless out of the water, waddling and floundering along on its breast in a most awkward manner.

The Ruddy resorts to selected ponds or backwaters during its stay in South Carolina, and stays away from nearby waters which to the human eye are entirely similar to the ones they have chosen. As many as a hundred usually spend the entire winter in Summerhouse Pond on Bull's Island.

FOOD: Contrary to general belief, this little duck is excellent eating, for 75 per cent of its food is vegetable. Wild celery, arrowhead, pondweeds, eelgrass, water lilies, hornwort, and bindweed are all taken and render it most palatable. Animal food consists of snails and mussels.

78. HOODED MERGANSER: *Lophodytes cucullatus* (Linnaeus) (131)

(Gr., *Lophodytes*, a crested diver; Lat., *cucullatus*, wearing a hood.)

LOCAL NAMES: Hairyhead; Sawbill; Fish Duck; Mosshead.

DESCRIPTION: Length 16.00 to 19.00 inches. *Male.* Upper parts largely black, including head and neck; head with a fan-shaped white crest; breast white with two black bars in front of wing; sides and flanks reddish brown; rest of upper parts largely white. *Female.* Head, neck, and back grayish brown; under parts dull white; crest small and ragged.

RANGE: Breeds north to southeastern Alaska and northern Maine; south to Oregon and Florida. Winters north to southern British Columbia and Massachusetts; south to central eastern Mexico and Cuba.

STATUS IN S. C.: Common winter resident, October 29 to May 11, very rare in summer, occurring in nearly all parts of the State. Recorded north to Chester County; east to Horry County; south to Beaufort County; west to Aiken County.

HISTORY: This strikingly handsome duck, one of the most colorful of all wildfowl, is found in more localities over South Carolina than are the other two mergansers, because of its liking for fresh water situations. It is as much at home in the mill ponds and small streams of the interior as on the salt marsh creeks and cypress lagoons of the coast. Few pictures in nature are more memorable than the sight of a drake cruising the still waters of a woodland pool with a back drop of willows or cat-tails along the shore. The beautiful crest, dark back, and chestnut sides seem to glow with living color as the bird appears and disappears amid the waters.

The Hooded Merganser is the smallest of the three mergansers. It usually arrives in South Carolina in early November and remains through the winter into the second week in April. It is very active in its movements and the flight is rapid, the wings moving almost in a blur, the head and neck bent somewhat downward. Hooded Mergansers are to be seen in pairs frequently during the winter.

One does not think of South Carolina as duck-nesting territory. The Wood (Summer) Duck is the only species which nests here regularly. However, the Hooded Merganser does occasionally breed in southern states, and has done so in at least two known instances in South Carolina. The records are separated in time by practically one hundred years.

Until recently, there was but one reference to the nesting of the Hooded Merganser in the State, that quoted by Audubon from Bachman's observation in 1838 (*Birds of America*, 4: 404). The record was made at Mexico Plantation, Berkeley County, when Bachman in that year found broods of young. Ninety-nine years later, another nesting was observed, the details of which were related to the writers by E. J. DeCamps of Beaufort. On April 6, 1937, workmen, felling trees at Gray's Hill, Beaufort County, cut a tree which fell against an adjacent dead pine. In the ruins of the pine, they picked up a dead female Hooded Merganser, killed on her nest in an old hole of a Pileated Woodpecker. There were six eggs, five of which had been mashed; the sixth was saved through careful treatment by DeCamps, who secured it from William Elliott, of Beaufort, to whom it had been taken. The egg measures 53.5 x 44.0 millimeters. This is the second and only other record of the breeding in South Carolina of this beautiful little duck which, like the Buffle-head and Wood Duck, nests in cavities in trees (*Auk, 61*: 1944, 306).

FOOD: Stomachs of eighty specimens of the Hooded Merganser have revealed that the food is composed of 37 per cent fish; 58 per cent crayfish, crustaceans, insects, and frogs. Vegetable matter included pondweeds, wild celery, acorns, and other seeds. Crayfish destruction compensates for the Hooded Merganser's destruction of commercially valuable fish.

AMERICAN MERGANSER
79. *Mergus merganser americanus* Cassin (129)

(Lat., *Mergus*, a diver; *merganser*, diving goose; *americanus*, of America.)

LOCAL NAMES: Fish Duck.

DESCRIPTION: Length 21.00 to 27.00 inches. *Male.* Mostly white, with black back and greenish black head; bill and feet orange. *Female.* Mostly gray above, with reddish brown head and foreneck; otherwise chiefly white below; a large white patch on wing.

RANGE: Breeds north to southern Alaska and Labrador; south to California and North Carolina; south to northwestern Mexico and Florida.

STATUS IN S. C.: Uncommon winter resident, November 24 to April 16, in most of the State. Reported north to Oconee and Richland counties; east to Berkeley County and Charleston; south to Beaufort County; west to Aiken County.

HISTORY: This largest of the three Mergansers, or "Fish Ducks," is the least numerous in South Carolina. It was not until 1911 that the first known specimen was taken, although this species was previously recorded by W. J. Hoxie near Beaufort. On January 2 of that year, an adult male was taken on Back River, Berkeley County, by Caspar S. Chisolm (*Auk, 28*: 1911, 254). Eleven years later, another drake was secured on Chee-ha River, Beaufort County, January 29, 1922, by James Henry Rice, Jr., and presented to the Charleston Museum. During the winters of 1924-25 and 1926-27, specimens were killed by Clarence E. Chapman at Mulberry Plantation, Cooper River. B. F. Taylor saw one bird near Columbia on April 16, 1916, and another was observed at Clemson, Oconee County, March 9, 1926 (Sherman). Sight records were made by Burton in 1936 on several occasions in January, and E. von S. Dingle saw four on February 10, and nine on February 16, at Huger, Berkeley County, the same year. Since then additional records have been made.

It appears that this duck is decidedly uncommon, but because of the similarity between the females of the American and the Red-breasted Mergansers, it is possible that individual American Mergansers are sometimes overlooked or mistaken for their related species. The drake shows a greater amount of white than the male Red-breast, and the head of the latter has much more of a ragged crest. Females are very difficult to separate at any distance, both being gray above and white beneath, with white wing patches; but the rufous colored head of the American is sharply defined against the white of the throat, whereas that of the Red-breast blends gradually into the throat color. This fine species, like all its relatives, is a wonderful diver.

FOOD: The food of the American Merganser is made up largely of fish (80 per cent) and crustaceans. At fish hatcheries it commits depredations on small fry and sometimes takes game and food fish where these are abundant. It occurs so infrequently and irregularly in South Carolina, however, that the amount of damage it does to commercially valuable fish is negligible.

RED-BREASTED MERGANSER
80. *Mergus serrator serrator* Linnaeus (130)

(Lat., *serrator*, a sawyer.)

LOCAL NAMES: Sawbill; Hairy Head; Fish Duck.

DESCRIPTION: Length 19.00 to 26.00 inches. Head conspicuously crested. *Male.* Head, neck, and back black; a cinnamon band speckled with black on chest; under parts otherwise white. *Female.* Gray above, but head and bill rufous; white patches on wings; lower parts dull white.

RANGE: Breeds north to northern Alaska, Greenland, northern Europe, and northern Siberia; south to southeastern Alaska, Nova Scotia, Denmark, and the Kirghiz Steppes. Winters north to British Columbia, Maine, central Europe, and central Asia; south to southern Lower California, Florida, Cuba (casually), northern Africa, and northwestern India.

STATUS IN S. C.: Abundant winter resident, October 2 to June 23, casually July 19, chiefly coastwise. Known north and east to Horry County; south to Beaufort County; west to Aiken County.

HISTORY: One of the most numerous of the wildfowl in the winter months, the Red-breasted Merganser usually arrives in South Carolina late in October. It is common all through the winter and until early April, when most of them migrate northward. Stragglers continue through May, sometimes throughout the summer.

As easy of observance as this bird is, comparatively few people are familiar with it. It is not popular with hunters because of its ill-flavored flesh, and since salt water is its home, where not much hunting occurs, it is seldom molested. It is, however, one of the most common birds of the marshes and waterways; hundreds may be seen in such localities, either in small bands or large flocks. The gray and white plumage, white wing patches, and the long, torpedo-shape (when the bird is in flight) make it easy to identify.

Years ago, mergansers were better known than they are now because, when game was sold on the streets, many a housewife bought a brace of what were called "Canvas-backs" or "Brown Widgeon" or any other name that the vendor might happen to know. But when the birds appeared on the table and the carving commenced, all doubt about the birds' true identity disappeared, for both the taste and odor of a merganser are unmistakable.

Any one unfamiliar with birds may be excused for failing to identify a Red-breasted Merganser in the field, but there is no reason for failure when the bird is in the hand. The bill gives it away immediately. Completely unlike the flattened, conventional duck-shape, that of a merganser is long, very narrow and serrated, a line of "teeth" appearing along the mandible from tip to base. This, of course, explains the name Sawbill, which is very descriptive.

The Red-breast in South Carolina is a salt water dweller and rarely appears anywhere else. Apparently the only definite inland record is Murphey's statement (1937) that the species is occasional in winter on the Savannah River bordering on Aiken County. The drake is a handsome bird, black, white, and reddish, with the feathers of the crest lengthened rather raggedly, thus giving rise to the localism "Hairy Head." Specimens of this duck occur now and then in Colonial Lake in Charleston, and are not uncommon along waterfronts of both the Ashley and Cooper Rivers.

Food: Examination of ninety-nine stomachs shows that fish comprise 77 per cent of the food. Thirty species were identified, eleven of which were food varieties, though but five had commercial value. Crayfish made up 16 per cent of the stomach content. It will be readily understood why this bird is unpalatable as food. E. Milby Burton shot a male on January 22, 1936, which contained 295 top minnows (*Gambusia*).

Order Falconiformes
Birds of Prey

Family Cathartidae: American Vultures

81. Turkey Vulture: *Cathartes aura septentrionalis* Wied   (325)

(Gr., *Cáthartes*, purifier; *aura*, South American name of this bird; Lat., *septentrionalis*, northern.)

Local Names: Turkey Buzzard.

Description: Length 26.00 to 32.00 inches; extent of wings 68.00 to 72.00 inches; end of tail rounded; head bare. Head red, plumage blackish brown; the entire hind under-surface of wings light brown.

Range: Breeds north to southern Ontario and central New York; south to Louisiana and Florida. Winters north to Indiana and New Jersey; south to Louisiana and Florida. Casual in New England.

Status in S. C.: Common permanent resident throughout the State. Reported north to Greenville, Spartanburg, Cherokee, and Darlington counties; east to Horry County and Georgetown; south to Beaufort and Jasper counties; west to Oconee and Pickens counties.

History: Few birds have ever been so closely associated with a specific city as the "Buzzard" has been with Charleston. Happily that association is a matter of history. In the days when garbage disposal and sanitary conditions were not as they are now, the butchers in the old City Market of Charleston were accustomed to throw scraps of meat out on the cobbled street. Both Turkey Vultures and Black Vultures gathered there daily, awaiting these hand-outs and did away with them virtually under the feet of passers-by. Thus grew up many an exaggerated tale of the prevalence of buzzards in Charleston, some of which are still heard.

Though the term "Buzzard" is universally applied to both species of vultures, the birds do not deserve it. It is, correctly, the name of some of the European *buteo* hawks, which are, of course, very different birds.

The Turkey Vulture is a permanent resident throughout South Carolina. This does not necessarily mean that all individuals remain in a given region constantly. Illustrative of this fact is the case of a bird banded at Hampton, Virginia, April 27, 1935, and recovered near Conway about February 5, 1937 (*Bird-Banding, 12*: 1941,

151). As common as the species is, few people have ever seen its nest or young. It is abundant enough near towns and cities but retires to woodlands and swamps to breed, and nests there on the ground or in a hollow log or stump. An unusual nesting site was found near Saluda, Saluda County, in June, 1948, by J. M. Eleazer. It was in a deserted and tumble-down house, on the second floor, under the roof of a rear porch. There was one young bird. Two, rarely three, eggs are laid in early April, typical dates being April 15 (small embryos) and April 25 (eggs on verge of hatching) (Wayne, 1910). The earliest record we have is the discovery of eggs by E. A. Williams, at Dixie Plantation, Charleston County, February 20, 1943. The eggs are white, spotted and splashed with chocolate and purplish markings, averaging 71.3 x 48.6 millimeters. Incubation takes about thirty days.

The young are clothed in whitish down. They resent intrusion by ejecting the stomach contents and as this is semi-digested carrion, the result is better imagined than experienced. The home of a vulture is not an attractive place.

As ugly and awkward as the vulture is at close range, no one can but admire its mastery of the air. In flight it shows much light brown on the undersurface of the wings, from body to tip. The long, rounded tail is a capable rudder. The bird flies with deep, deliberate strokes and soars with no apparent effort, the wings raised at a wide V-shaped angle. Its utilization of varying air currents is amazingly efficient.

The endless argument as to whether vultures find their prey by sight or smell still goes on, but many now agree that both senses play a part, with sight predominating. Certainly, the eyesight is almost beyond belief and compared to this bird, human beings are nearly blind.

Before taking flight, the Turkey Vulture is obliged to hop along the ground for several feet before rising into the air. It is virtually a silent bird, the only note being a hiss. The accusation that, together with the Black Vulture, it is a carrier of anthrax is not based on any exact data.

FOOD: Almost entirely carrion of any sort. Occasionally it eats small snakes. Reports that it may seize the young of domestic animals seem to have some authenticity. The vulture's value as a scavenger is not to be questioned.

82. BLACK VULTURE: *Coragyps atratus* (Meyer) (326)

(Gr., *Coragyps*, a raven-vulture; Lat., *atratus*, black.)

LOCAL NAMES: Buzzard; Charleston Buzzard; Carrion Crow.

DESCRIPTION: Length 23.00 to 27.00 inches; extent of wings 54.00 to 59.00 inches; tail square at tip. Head unfeathered, black; plumage dull black; undersurface of wings silvery gray becoming dull white near tips.

RANGE: Resident and breeds north to Kansas and Maryland; south to Chile and Argentina; casually in the northwestern United States and southeastern Canada.

STATUS IN S. C.: Abundant permanent resident throughout the State, but less common in the mountainous section. Observed north to Greenville, Spartanburg, Lancaster, and Florence counties; east to Horry County; south to Beaufort County; west to Oconee and Pickens counties.

HISTORY: The Black Vulture, like the Turkey Vulture, is a permanent resident throughout South Carolina but is much more abundant on the coast than in the interior. Wayne (1910) considered that it out-numbered the Turkey Vulture, on the coast, in the ratio of " . . . at least forty to one." This seems an exceedingly high estimate, but it is true that the Black Vultures are more numerous.

The Black Vulture, which is a smaller and much blacker bird than its relative, is sometimes known as the "Carrion Crow." The tail is short and square. This is one characteristic by which it can be distinguished from the Turkey Vulture, but the best of all is the manner of flight. The Turkey Vulture flies with slow, deep strokes, the Black with short, heavy, labored flappings as though the wings were about to drop off. So marked is this difference that the two birds can be recognized as far off as they can be seen in the air. It seems strange that this reliable means of identification has not been stressed in the literature.

The Black Vulture is also a ground nester, but it breeds earlier than the Turkey Vulture. Mating occurs in February and in some seasons the eggs are laid about the third week in March. There are, however, variations in dates. The earliest nesting record is February 15, 1920, when C. E. Chapman found an egg at Mulberry Plantation, Cooper River. It was left for over a week to see whether another would be laid, but the set was not increased. This very early record is all but matched by E. von S. Dingle, who found one egg on February 18, 1938, at Middleburg Plantation, also on the Cooper. On March 26 Wayne found two eggs which were on the point of hatching, and since incubation requires about twenty-eight days, these eggs must have been laid about March 1.

The usual number of eggs is two, averaging 75.6 x 50.9 millimeters. They are handsomer than those of the Turkey Vulture in that the markings of dark brown are more sharply defined, on a greenish white ground. Wayne noted that it is an "almost constant" habit of the bird to place china or pearl buttons, and pieces of glass and china about the eggs. This, he says, he has never seen mentioned in literature. Bent (1937) quotes Wayne on the matter, but the habit appears to be a local one. The bird returns year after year to the same spot to nest. J. M. Eleazer reported a nest found in June, 1948, in an abandoned barn, on the farm of E. A. Corley, near Saluda, in that county.

Both of these vultures spend much time soaring over woods, fields, and marshes in their search for prey. Now and then, many of them can be seen in a dead tree, with their wings spread out, drying or airing the plumage. In order to rise into the air from the ground the Black Vulture is forced to take several awkward running hops.

Persistent reports occur of their attacking young stock animals. The experience of observers varies in this regard, and many statements deal with generalities rather than specific instances. Wayne (1910), for instance, says that in all his years of field work he never saw the Black Vulture attack a living animal. Other observers have. Mrs. W. H. Faver of Eastover reported Black Vultures eating three new-born pigs (March 10, 1948) before being driven off. Sprunt has seen the bird carrying snakes which were still alive but never saw an example of attack on a farm animal.

Both "buzzards" are also periodically accused of spreading hog cholera. It has been definitely proved that they do not, but it seems hard to dispel the belief. Findings of the State Board of Health of Florida show that " . . . the virus of hog cholera is digested in the intestinal tract of buzzards and the droppings of buzzards fed on the flesh of hogs dead from cholera do not produce cholera when mixed in the feed of hogs."

The beak and claws of the vultures are not as strongly developed as those of hawks but the birds do not on this account always wait for decomposition to be advanced before feeding on the carcasses of animals.

Food: A large percentage is carrion, and valuable service is rendered by the bird in disposing of it. However, the Black Vulture, to a greater degree than its relative, varies its diet with other food. It is often found about colonies of birds such as herons and pelicans, where it preys not only on the fish dropped there, but on the eggs and young birds as well. Small pigs, lambs, and chickens have been known to be taken at times.

Family Accipitriidae: Kites, Hawks, and Eagles

WHITE-TAILED KITE
83.   Elanus leucurus majusculus Bangs and Penard   (328)

(Lat., *Elanus*, a kite; Gr., *leucurus*, white-tailed; Lat., *majusculus*, somewhat greater.)

DESCRIPTION: Length 15.00 to 17.00 inches. Plumage above light gray; head, tail, and under parts white; a large black patch on bend of wing.

RANGE: Resident and breeds north to central California and central Florida; south to north central California and southern Florida.

STATUS IN S. C.: Accidental, February 8 to May 7, in the coast region. Recorded north to the mouth of the Santee River; east and south to Charleston; west to 40 miles west of Charleston (Colleton County).

HISTORY: The history of this beautiful species in South Carolina is brief but most interesting. As it is a western bird, it can hardly be considered anything other than a wanderer to South Carolina and is very rare anywhere east of the Mississippi Valley. None the less, it has occurred in the past as well as in the last few years, and an instance of its breeding in the State has been noted.

Audubon wrote that he had " . . . traced the migration of this beautiful Hawk from the Texas as far east as the mouth of the Santee River in South Carolina." He received a live specimen from Dr. Ravenel, of Charleston, on February 8, 1834. Another was sent to him on the twenty-third of the same month by Francis Lee, who had taken it on his plantation 40 miles west of Charleston. Audubon recorded that his field companion in Florida, H. Ward, found this kite nesting in March (1834) on the plantation of Alexander Mazyck on the Santee River, and shot three, two of which were in Audubon's possession. Finally in his account of the bird in South Carolina, he wrote that his friend Dr. Bachman had seen this species flying at very great heights in early March and thought that it was only in recent years (1830's) that it had begun to make an appearance in the State.

Chamberlain has discovered an interesting letter in the collection of the Charleston Museum from Dr. Bachman to Audubon's son, Victor, which throws light on the parts played by Bachman and Ward in the Santee River occurrences. It is dated March 9, 1840, and in the part concerning this species reads: "The black winged hawk was obtained not on Mazycks but on Wm. Lucas plantation — the rascal Wards name ought not to have been mentioned for he stole the specimens afterwards . . . "

Nearly a hundred years passed before this bird was seen again in South Carolina. Early in May, 1929, Chamberlain saw what he is certain was a White-tailed Kite flying over Youghal Plantation, Charleston County. Because of its rarity and because he did not collect it, he said nothing of it in print. On May 7, 1929, Edward M. Moore watched, for an hour, a White-tailed Kite in company with a Swallow-tailed Kite, soaring over the house on Bull's Island. At times the bird was "just above the roof" of the house. He studied it with and without seven-power glasses. Moore was able to see and note every field character.

Bull's Island and Youghal are diagonally opposite each other across a stretch of marsh, and the observations of Chamberlain and Moore occurred in the same week. It seems as certain as anything could be without actual proof that both saw the same bird. Months passed before either had any idea that the other had made the observation. It is certainly true that a species can appear and disappear in a given locality over a long period of time.

FOOD: The food of this kite consists of insects, snakes, and small mammals. The bird is unquestionably valuable from every viewpoint.

SWALLOW-TAILED KITE
84. *Elanoïdes forficatus forficatus* (Linnaeus)   (327)

(Lat. and Gr., *Elanoïdes*, kite-like; Lat., *forficatus*, forked.)

LOCAL NAMES: Swallow-tail Hawk.

DESCRIPTION: Length 19.00 to 26.00 inches. Like a huge barn swallow but tail deeply forked. Head and under parts white; back, wings, and tail black.

RANGE: Breeds north to northern Minnesota (formerly) and North Carolina; south to eastern Mexico and southern Florida. Winters north to Louisiana (casually) and Florida; south to Ecuador.

STATUS IN S. C.: Uncommon summer resident, March 5 to November, formerly over most of the State, now chiefly in the swampy areas of the eastern section. Recorded north to Gaffney (Cherokee County) and Chester County; east to Georgetown County and Charleston; south to Beaufort County; west to Aiken and Pickens counties.

HISTORY: One's first sight of this magnificent bird is something never to be forgotten. Comparisons are hard to draw and may be inadvisable, but of the entire avian family of this country, it is difficult to think of a bird more graceful than the Swallow-tailed Kite in form and movement, more completely a master of the air, or clothed in more attractive plumage. "Aristocrat" is the word that comes most naturally to mind at any mention of this exquisite creature. Aside from the steely-blue back (black at a distance) and the white underparts, the best field character of this bird is the long, deeply forked tail. Its aerial evolutions are at times spectacular in the extreme, for it may turn over and over in the air and sweep into breath-taking dives, side-slips, and zooms. Several of the birds may perform at the same time. Murphey (1937) has counted as many as a hundred in the air at once, on the Carolina side of the Savannah River near Augusta, Georgia. The Swallow-tailed Kite seizes its prey on the wing, eats it aloft, and even drinks by skimming low over the water and scooping up the liquid in a swallow-like manner. It spends most of the day in the air and seems to be almost independent of a perch or rest.

It is unfortunate that it is not common in South Carolina. A dweller of the cypress swamps and lagoons of the Low Country, of heavy woodlands and river bottoms, it occurs mainly near the coast but seldom over salt water. The most recent record from the interior of the State was made by Gabriel Cannon, who examined a specimen killed near Gaffney, Cherokee County, on March 10, 1937. This kite is a summer resident, usually arriving by the first part of April, though it has been observed as early as the fifth of March, near Charleston. It migrates south rather early in the fall, usually leaving by late August. A very late date is November (1933), when C. V. Boykin saw a bird near Lambs, Charleston County. Wayne speaks of it as being "very abundant," but Wayne was writing in 1910, and the bird is certainly not abundant today. It comes regularly, but is locally distributed and decidedly uncommon.

The birds are mated by mid-April and, according to Wayne (1910) "breed abundantly." Wayne, however, never saw a nest in this State, and Sprunt has seen but one. This was found in the Santee Swamp (Wadmacaun River) in June of 1935 by W. F. Welch. The kite could be seen sitting on it; later the three young were several times seen on the edge of the nest. It was no more than 40 feet up in a large loblolly pine (*Pinus taeda*), near the bank of the river.

Murphey (1937) saw a nest which contained young birds in Aiken County years ago, but it was about 90 feet from the ground in a slender tree and could not be reached.

Usually, the Swallow-tailed Kite nests in the tops of very tall trees, often cypresses or pines. The eggs usually number two (sometimes three), and are white, beautifully

PLATE IX: LOW-COUNTRY WOODLAND SCENE

Oil Painting by Francis Lee Jaques

Foreground, left to right: Bobwhite (male), Bobwhite (female), and Bobwhite (male). Center, left to right: Wild Turkey (male), Wild Turkeys (two females), and Wild Turkey (male). Flying: top, Mourning Dove; below, Ground Dove. Perching: two Mourning Doves.

splashed with hazel brown, chestnut, and blackish markings. They average 46.7 x 37.4 millimeters. Accurate incubation data are lacking.

FOOD: Largely insects, together with snakes, frogs, and lizards. Grasshoppers and dragon flies are favorite food. It sometimes eats cottonworms. The stomach of a bird taken in August near Charleston contained insect remains, including one smooth caterpillar. Audubon's plate of this species shows it with a garter snake in its talons. It is never known to attack poultry or native birds.

85. MISSISSIPPI KITE: *Ictinia misisippiensis* (Wilson) (329)

(Gr., *Ictinia*, a kite; Lat., *misisippiensis*, of Mississippi.)

DESCRIPTION: Length 13.00 to 15.00 inches. Head, neck, and lower surface light gray; back bluish slate; tail black.

RANGE: Breeds north to Kansas and South Carolina; south to southern Texas and northern Florida. Winters north to Texas and Florida, casually South Carolina; south to Guatemala.

STATUS IN S. C.: Fairly common summer resident, March 12 to October 23, in much of the State, but more frequent in the coast region; accidental in winter (February) coastwise. Recorded north to Richland and Marlboro counties; east to Georgetown County; south to Beaufort County; west to Aiken County.

HISTORY: Though a regular summer resident in lower South Carolina, which may be seen if one looks for it in the right habitat, this bird is unknown to most people. Big woods are its home, woods with occasional clearings, fields, and brushy pastures. The old phosphate diggings along the South Carolina coast and up the tidal rivers, grown now to forests of gum, pine, and cypress, harbor this handsome bird of prey, with its pale gray head, dark back, light under parts and square, black tail.

As a rule it arrives in late April. The earliest record is that of a bird seen at Twickenham Plantation, Combahee River, March 12, 1941, by R. J. Turnbull and F. M. Hutson.

The Mississippi Kites arrive about a month before they begin to lay their eggs. Wayne observed the species breeding near his home and noted that a single pair would return to the same tree year after year. The birds build their nests in the tallest trees, and thus make them inaccessible to all but the hardiest climbers. Wayne, for example, writes that on May 28, 1898, he discovered the nest of the Mississippi Kite in a pine tree, 111 feet, 7 inches from the ground. Wayne himself did not undertake the climb and he had some difficulty in finding a Negro who would do so. The single egg which the nest contained was the first to be collected in South Carolina; it is now in the United States National Museum. Another nest, also reached by a Negro climber, was 135 feet above the ground. These records probably represent the greatest elevations at which birds' eggs have been secured from trees in South Carolina.

The nest of the Mississippi Kite is no masterpiece of avian architecture. It is rather small and frail, made of twigs, leaves, and moss. The kite lays one or two (sometmes three) eggs, which average 41.3 x 34.0 millimeters. Incubation requires about thirty-one or thirty-two days.

An instance of the ease with which this kite can be seen in suitable localities was the experience of Ivan R. Tomkins on May 22-23, 1948. From a boat on the Savannah River, for a distance of 52 miles beginning at a point 12 miles below Augusta, he "saw a Kite or so very frequently." He saw none, however, along the lower reaches of the river. The kite is found regularly along the east bank of the Ashley River, at Lambs. In late summer it occasionally occurs on the barrier islands and has been noted at Bull's, Kiawah, and Seabrook's Islands, and even over the city of Charleston. Most of them leave in September, but stragglers occur well into October, the latest record being October 23 (Dingle).

On February 2, 1936, Dr. Robert Cushman Murphy saw an individual of this species at Hasty Point Plantation, Georgetown County, over the rice fields of the Waccamaw River. It is the sole record of the occurrence of the bird in winter in the State. To make it more strange, the weather was unusually severe and there was snow on the ground, the temperature being 38° (*Auk, 54:* 1937, 384).

FOOD: Almost wholly insects. Among all the birds of prey, the kites are the greatest insect destroyers and are not known ever to take poultry, game birds, or native song and insectivorous species of birds. Grasshoppers, beetles, katydids, and crickets form the bulk of this kite's diet. It occasionally eats small snakes and frogs. The species deserves all the protection that can be given it.

SHARP-SHINNED HAWK
86. *Accipiter striatus velox* (Wilson)　(332)

(Lat., *Accipiter*, a hawk; *striatus*, striped; *velox*, swift.)

LOCAL NAMES: Little Blue Darter.

DESCRIPTION: Length 10.00 to 14.00 inches; tail long and square at end. *Adult.* Above bluish gray; below white, barred with rufous. *Immature.* Above dull umber brown; below white striped with brown.

RANGE: Breeds north to northern Alaska and Newfoundland; south to southern California and northern Florida. Winters north to southeastern Alaska and southern Quebec; south to Guatemala and Panama.

STATUS IN S. C.: Common permanent resident, but rare in summer, over the entire State. Reported north to York County; east to Horry County and Georgetown; south to Beaufort County; west to Greenwood and Oconee counties.

HISTORY: The activities of this little Hawk, together with those of Cooper's Hawk, have created the evil reputation which so many of the birds of prey have. The Sharp-shin is popularly known as the "Little Blue Darter" and it may be said at once that it is a killer. It is, of course, only obeying a law of its nature when it kills, but because its appetite so often clashes with man's interests it has been labelled "vermin."

In South Carolina it was long thought to be only a winter visitor, but it can now be definitely included as a breeding species of the State.

Normally, it arrives in numbers in early October, at the time of the regular hawk migration. It is fairly common throughout the winter and remains until the last of April. Near Mt. Pleasant, Charleston County, on August 18, 1896, Wayne secured an immature bird which he said must have "bred not far away." On July 22, 1911, one was recorded by F. M. Weston near Charleston, and since that time several spring and summer records have been made in the coastal region. In all probability, these records are of breeding adults, or young birds hatched locally. This is strongly indicated by the actual discovery of a nest and eggs near Beaufort, Beaufort County, on May 14, 1937, by E. J. DeCamps. The nest was 30 feet from the ground in a second-growth pine woods, 8 miles northwest of Beaufort, and when first found contained one egg. After two more eggs had been laid, the bird deserted the nest and the eggs were taken. This gives the first nesting record for the strictly coastal area (*Auk, 61:* 1944, 306). It has been supposed that the Sharp-shin breeds now and then in the mountains, but the only other instance of nesting below the fall line was provided by H.'L. Harllee, who says that "about the year 1898" Henry E. Davis shot a male on a nest while it was feeding its young. This incident occurred near Salters, Williamsburg County, the nest being in a long-leaf pine (*Pinus palustris*) about 100 feet from the ground. Above the fall line the Sharp-shin has been reported as breeding in Chester County, and doubtless it breeds in other Piedmont counties.

Though its usual habitat is any sort of woodland, the Sharp-shin prefers conifers in the nesting season. Along the coast it nests in pine trees; in the mountain regions, in hemlocks, spruce, and balsam. The nest is composed of small sticks. The eggs number from three to five, more rarely seven. They are very handsome, being white, nearly spherical, splashed with dark brown; they average 37.5 x 30.4 millimeters. Incubation requires from twenty-one to twenty-four days.

In view of its destructive proclivities and remarkable fearlessness, it is perhaps as well for small poultry and song birds that the Sharp-shin is no larger than it is. Even so, it takes prey fully as large as itself. Occasionally it attacks birds larger than itself, definite records noting the Wood Duck and the Black-crowned Night Heron as prey. A South Carolina instance of such an attack was observed by James E. Mosimann and Thomas Uzzell, Jr., on October 25, 1947, in Bear Swamp, Charleston County. They saw a Sharp-shin chasing a squawking Snowy Egret back and forth over the swamp road for about a minute.

Haunting the edges of clearings and woodlands, the Sharp-shin makes bold forays into barnyards and even into city gardens. Its flight is amazingly swift, and the bird can thread its way through trees and branches like a wood duck. The name "darter" suits it well, and woe betide the warbler, sparrow, or thrush which it singles out. So swift and lightning-like is its attack that it may come and go without being seen at all. It is this secretiveness and ability to keep out of sight which has brought condemnation upon the much slower *Buteo* hawks, for they get much of the blame for what the Sharp-shin actually does. It will return again and again to a feeding station or poultry yard and often the only remedy for the loss of chickens is a shotgun and a very quick eye.

Food: Mainly small birds and poultry. In over one thousand stomachs examined, 860 contained bird remains of one sort or another. Sparrows, warblers, vireos, thrushes, and bluebirds were represented, as well as numerous others. The Sharp-shin also eats insects and small mammals.

87. COOPER'S HAWK: *Accipiter cooperii* (Bonaparte)   (333)

(Lat., *cooperii*, to William Cooper.)

LOCAL NAMES: Big Blue Darter.

DESCRIPTION: Length 14.00 to 20.00 inches. Tail rounded instead of nearly square. Similar to the Sharp-shinned Hawk but larger.

RANGE: Breeds north to British Columbia and New Brunswick; south to lower California and Florida. Winters north to northern Oregon and southern Maine; south to Mexico and Costa Rica.

STATUS IN S. C.: Common permanent resident throughout the State, less numerous in summer. Observed north to Cherokee, Lancaster, and Darlington counties; east to Horry County; south to Beaufort County; west to Oconee and Pickens counties.

HISTORY: Everything that has been said about the Sharp-shinned Hawk can be said about Cooper's Hawk in enlarged terms. The "Big Blue Darter," as it is called, is a much more powerful, rapacious, and capable killer than the "Little Blue Darter." In behavior, tastes, and habitat, it is almost exactly a counterpart of its smaller relative, and indeed it is difficult at times to tell them apart at a quick glance, for even size is not a criterion. A small specimen (and there is much individual variation) of Cooper's Hawk may be about the same size as a large Sharp-shinned Hawk. However, the tail is always a good mark, for that of the Sharp-shin is squared off at the end while that of Cooper's is distinctly rounded.

Wayne (1910) says that it breeds in mid-April. The writers have never succeeded in finding a nest. E. J. DeCamps, of Beaufort, found it nesting in that vicinity on April 24, (four eggs); April 27, (four eggs); May 5, (four eggs); May 6, (five eggs). Murphey (1937) records a nest of three eggs in Edgefield County on April 4, 1892.

The nest is built of sticks and twigs and lined with bark strippings. It is usually against the trunk of a pine tree, often in a crotch. The elevation varies, but it is likely to be high. The three to five eggs are plain bluish white and average 49.0 x 38.5 millimeters. Incubation requires about twenty-four days.

Cooper's Hawk employs the sneak method of attack on prey, appearing and disappearing like a streak. It is adept at flying through remarkably thick cover. Alexander Sprunt, IV, once saw a Green Heron escape from a hawk by diving headlong into the waters of a salt creek, with the hawk virtually on its tail. On another occasion, he saw a Cooper's Hawk dive upon a Ring-necked Duck as the latter was flying below tree-top level over a road on Bull's Island. The hawk "rode" the duck to the ground, but on seeing the observer, at once released its hold and flashed away. Only a day of two later, Alexander Sprunt, Jr., flushed a Cooper's Hawk from the still warm body of a Clapper Rail on Bull's Island.

This species may easily be attracted by a "squeak," the noise made by kissing the back of the hand. In response to such a noise the Hawk appears from nowhere, through the woods, darts within inches of the caller's head, and nearly turns wrong side out when it discovers the real source of the sound.

Because of its amazing speed, Cooper's Hawk is seldom seen to take poultry, and the larger hawks which happen to be in the neighborhood get the blame. The term "Chicken Hawk," so loosely applied to other birds of prey, really belongs to Cooper's Hawk and to the Sharp-shin.

FOOD: Poultry, game and song birds, with some mammals, reptiles, and insects. Occasionally, curiously enough, it takes small fish. J. B. May (1935) quotes A. R. Smith as saying that when mountain streams in Arkansas begin to dry up, Cooper's Hawk will take the stranded minnows. H. L. Stoddard (1931) says that it is very destructive to the Bobwhite.

EASTERN RED-TAILED HAWK
88. *Buteo jamaicensis borealis* (Gmelin) (337)

(Lat., *Buteo*, a buzzard; *jamaicensis*, of Jamaica; *borealis*, northern.)

LOCAL NAMES: Hen-hawk; Rabbit-hawk.

DESCRIPTION: Length 19.00 to 25.00 inches. *Adult*. Dark brown above, white beneath with streaks of brown on breast, and almost a band of these on abdomen; tail rufous above with a subterminal black band. *Immature*. Similar to adult, but tail grayish brown with nine or ten darker bars.

RANGE: Breeds north to northern Manitoba and southeastern Quebec; south to eastern Texas and northern Florida. Winters north to South Dakota and southern Maine; south to southern Texas and Florida.

STATUS IN S. C.: Common permanent resident throughout the State, more numerous in winter. Recorded north to Spartanburg and Chester counties; east to Horry County; south to Beaufort County; west to Oconee and Pickens counties.

HISTORY: This fine species, a very handsome bird, is the so-called "Hen-hawk" of the hunter and the farmer who go by the principle that the only good hawk is a dead one. Actually, it is a highly valuable species as a control on swarming numbers of rodents, mainly rats and mice.

It will be noted that the Red-tail's scientific name is *"Buteo"* or buzzard. Strange as this may seem, it is entirely correct, for the birds we usually call buzzards are actually vultures, and the term buzzard properly belongs to some of the Old World hawks, of which this one is typical. It would be correct, therefore, to call this species the Red-tailed Buzzard.

Much has been learned of its real status in South Carolina since Wayne's book appeared in 1910. Wayne considered the bird a winter visitor only, for he wrote that he had "never detected it in the breeding season anywhere near the coast." By the time the authors' *Supplement* was published (1931), there were several spring and summer records, and since then it has been found nesting. In the interior of the State, particularly in the Piedmont region, it has long been known to occur both in winter and summer. It therefore deserves the status of permanent resident over the entire State.

The first nest in the coast region was discovered near Beaufort on April 24, 1932, by H. L. Harllee. It contained two eggs. He found two more nests in this locality in 1933, March 19 and 20, each with two eggs. On March 28, 1933, Chamberlain found a nest with three eggs on Pine Island, Stono River, Charleston County. E. J. DeCamps of Beaufort has found eggs on March 10, 11, 20, and 23.

The nest of the Red-tail is often built in pines, 30 to 40 feet above ground, and is made of sticks, twigs, moss, and bark. In the East, the eggs almost invariably number two, rarely three, and are white, marked sparingly, sometimes heavily, with brownish splashes. They average 59.0 x 47.0 millimeters. The incubation period is about twenty-eight days. The sitting bird remains close on the nest as incubation advances, and will refuse to leave until one beats on the trunk of the tree with a stick.

This big hawk is one of the "soaring" group. It never hunts through the edges of thickets or heavy growth like the *Accipiters* (darters), but patrols fields, meadows, and marshes from the air, and searches out the terrain below with its piercing eyesight. As it swings in great circles on set wings, the red color of its tail flashes out clearly. At rest, it picks out a conspicuous perch such as the top of a dead tree in a field, the top of a telephone pole, or a similar eminence. From such points, it can maintain a vigilant watch in all directions.

The note of this hawk is rather inadequate for a bird of its size, a high, shrill whistle which has been rendered as "kree-e-e." Its habit of keeping out in the open has brought much mistaken condemnation upon it for, because it is easy to see, it receives blame for making inroads on poultry really committed by the unseen "darters." It does occasionally take chickens, but such destruction is negligible in comparison with the harmful rodents it destroys.

Albinos of this hawk are sometimes noted. Albinism seems to occur more frequently among the Red-tails than among other birds of prey. Wayne (1910) mentions an albino which wintered regularly on Dewees Island from 1901 to 1905 but which eluded all efforts to secure it. There is an excellent specimen of partial albinism in the Charleston Museum.

Sprunt has, on two occasions, seen this hawk hover motionless in the air, on rapidly beating wings, scanning the ground below. This is a common habit of the Osprey, American Rough-legged Hawk, and Sparrow Hawk, but not of this species. However, on these occasions, so pronounced was this manner of flight that for a few minutes the bird was mistaken for a Rough-leg.

FOOD: An analysis of 754 stomachs of this hawk from many localities, by W. L. McAtee, showed that *654 contained remains of rats, mice, and rabbits.* This should certainly end arguments about the destructiveness of the "hen-hawk." Rat-hawk would be a far better name. Injurious rodents make up 80 to 86 per cent of the Red-tail's food.

FLORIDA RED-TAILED HAWK
89. *Buteo jamaicensis umbrinus* Bangs (337f)

(Lat., *umbrinus*, dark.)

DESCRIPTION: Similar to the Eastern Red-tailed Hawk but smaller, length about 20.00 inches; darker above and with more extensive dark markings below, especially posteriorly.

RANGE: Resident and breeds north to southern Florida; south to Cuba and the Isle of Pines. Accidental north of Florida.

STATUS IN S. C.: Accidental in the coast area.

HISTORY: The only record of the Florida Red-tailed Hawk for South Carolina is a single adult female obtained near Charleston on February 9, 1926, and brought to the Charleston Museum where this specimen now bears the number 7797.

In habits and food this race does not essentially differ from the Eastern Red-tailed Hawk.

90. KRIDER'S HAWK: *Buteo jamaicensis kriderii* Hooper (337a)

(Lat., *kriderii*, to John Krider.)

DESCRIPTION: Length 19.00 to 25.00 inches. Similar to the Eastern Red-tailed Hawk but lighter, particularly head and lower parts more whitish, the latter with very few or no dark brown markings.

RANGE: Breeds north to southern Alberta and southern Manitoba; south to Wyoming and Missouri. Winters south to Texas and southeastern Georgia.

STATUS IN S. C.: Accidental visitor to the western part of the State.

HISTORY: This very pale form of the Red-tailed Hawk is a bird of the northern Great Plains region, but it sometimes wanders southeastward in winter. There is but one instance of its appearance in South Carolina. It is, therefore, to be regarded only as an accidental visitor. Dr. E. E. Murphey obtained a specimen on the Savannah River below Augusta, January 25, 1909. The bird was first seen on the South Carolina side of the river, but was actually secured in Georgia. No other individual has been reported.

The habits, behavior, and food of this race do not differ from those of the Eastern Red-tail.

91. HARLAN'S HAWK: *Buteo harlani* (Audubon) (337d)

(Lat., *harlani*, to R. Harlan.)

DESCRIPTION: Length 19.00 to 24.00 inches. Upper parts sooty black, sometimes marked with white; lower parts sooty black, occasionally entirely white but usually more or less heavily marked with black; tail confusedly mottled, not regularly barred, with gray, white, and dull brown; sometimes almost all white.

RANGE: Breeds north to northwestern British Columbia and southern Yukon; south to Alberta. Winters south to Texas, southern Louisiana, and southern South Carolina (accidentally).

STATUS IN S. C.: Accidental winter visitor to southern South Carolina.

HISTORY: Only one record of this hawk exists for South Carolina. A single individual, apparently an adult, was observed in the Savannah National Wildlife Refuge on January 24, 1946, by Dr. John W. Aldrich and T. D. Burleigh of the U. S. Fish and Wildlife Service. It was not collected, but since it was carefully watched by two such good field men, there can be no reasonable question regarding its identity.

The habits and food of the Harlan's Hawk are not materially different from those of the closely allied Red-tailed Hawk.

NORTHERN RED-SHOULDERED HAWK
92. *Buteo lineatus lineatus* (Gmelin)   (339)

(Lat., *lineatus*, lined or striped.)

LOCAL NAMES: Chicken Hawk.

DESCRIPTION: Similar to the Florida Red-shouldered Hawk but larger; length 18.00 to 24.00 inches. Upper and lower parts darker, more richly rufous.

RANGE: Breeds north to Manitoba and Nova Scotia; south to Kansas and North Carolina. Winters north to Oklahoma, Iowa, and New Hampshire; south to Texas and Georgia.

STATUS IN S. C.: Uncommon winter resident, September 23 to April 16, over much of the State. Recorded north to Chester County; east to Horry County; south to Yemassee; west to Aiken and Oconee counties.

HISTORY: Wayne (1910), in a list of species from the interior of the State, says that "The Red-shouldered Hawk is a permanent resident of the interior of the State, the subspecies *B. l. alleni* being restricted to the coast region." While this northern form may yet be found as a breeding bird, at present we do not know of any specimens that would prove the point. Murphey (1937) considers this form a winter visitor along the fall line, in the Aiken-Augusta region. Dr. H. Friedmann recently examined a specimen in the collection of the United States National Museum, taken by W. M. Perrygo and J. S. Y. Hoyt at Chester, September 23, 1940, and others at Conway, April 16, 1940, and McClellanville, November 28, 1940. The Charleston Museum possesses specimens of this race collected at several localities, among which may be mentioned an immature bird taken by Edgar Marvin, December 11, 1935; another at Tomotley Plantation, Yemassee, by Theodore Blake, March 6, 1935; another at Huger, by Edward von S. Dingle, November 20, 1926; another by William Humphreys, January 2, 1931; an adult at Mulberry Plantation in Berkeley County by Leon Jordan, November 10, 1930; and an immature by B. R. Chamberlain on Wadmalaw Island, December 30, 1910. These specimens have been identified by Dr. Harry C. Oberholser. Sprunt examined a bird taken at Clemson College by R. E. Ware, October 30, 1933.

In habits and behavior this species does not differ from the Florida Red-shouldered Hawk. Its food is also similar.

Snowy Egret Displaying   S. A. GRIMES

Yellow-crowned Night Heron   JAMES J. CARROLL

Resting Wood Ibis   S. A. GRIMES

Eastern Glossy Ibis

FLORIDA RED-SHOULDERED HAWK
93. *Buteo lineatus alleni* Ridgway   (339a)

(Lat., *alleni*, to J. A. Allen.)

LOCAL NAMES: Chicken Hawk.

DESCRIPTION: Length 17.00 to 19.00 inches. *Adult.* Above dark brown, varied with buff or white, the head paler; bend of wing more or less chestnut; beneath dull white barred with light rufous; tail black, barred with white. *Immature.* Breast heavily streaked with brown, wings with light spots toward the tips; tail brown barred with buff.

RANGE: Breeds north to Oklahoma and South Carolina; south to southeastern Texas and central Florida. Winters north to Oklahoma and South Carolina; south to southern Texas and southern Florida.

STATUS IN S. C.: Common permanent resident over all the State. Reported north to Spartanburg County; east to Horry County; south to Beaufort County; west to Greenwood and Oconee counties.

HISTORY: The Florida Red-shouldered Hawk is even more valuable than its larger relative for its destruction of injurious rodents. It is a strange but indisputable trait of human nature that what is not seen is not believed. Because the great amount of benefit which agriculture derives from the activities of the *Buteos* is not plainly evident to the eye, many people refuse to believe that the *Buteos* are beneficial at all.

The birds of prey, particularly the hawks, seem to be very difficult for beginning observers to identify. This is understandable, for the birds require a great deal of study in the field, especially when they are in their immature plumages. The adult of the Red-shoulder presents no trouble since it is unlike any other hawk. In addition to the bright rusty color of the "shoulders," it shows plainly the conspicuous black and white barring of the tail, and these constitute field marks that few can miss. The immature birds, though they lack the red shoulders and brightly barred tail, always show very light patches in the wing near the tips, "windows" as they are sometimes appropriately called.

The note is very characteristic, if difficult to render into words. Peterson (1947) gives it as "*kee—yer*," which may or may not bring the call to one's mind. It is perfectly imitated by the Blue Jay, so perfectly that it is impossible to tell which bird is giving it unless the bird can actually be seen.

Red-shoulders may usually be seen in February indulging in spectacular courtship tactics, diving upon each other from considerable heights and uttering the characteristic cries. The nest is built late in February or early March or even as late as April in backward seasons. Pine, gum, or cypress trees are favorite nesting places. Cypress backwaters are favorite habitats for this hawk. The nest is built of sticks, shreds of bark, weed stalks, and moss woven into a substantial structure to hold two or three eggs. These are whitish and may be marked either lightly or heavily with splashes of reddish brown and lilac, or they may show no markings at all. The eggs average 52.6 x 42.7 millimeters. Incubation requires about twenty-eight days.

This species will return to the same nest year after year, making repairs or additions to it. Typical egg dates for Charleston County are March 14, April 4; for Beaufort County, March 8 and 27, April 13; for Marion County, April 6.

The Red-shoulder often shows remarkable tameness; it will sit on a tree or the cross arm of a telephone pole and allow an observer to approach close underneath. It becomes timid, of course, when it is constantly persecuted.

FOOD: Very rarely does this species take poultry and wild birds. Examination of 444 stomachs have shown mammal remains in 287, poultry in seven, and other birds in twenty-five. It will be seen at once that the preponderance of take is mammalian, and rats and mice compose much of it. It eats a few frogs, insects, and snakes.

BROAD-WINGED HAWK
94. *Buteo platypterus platypterus* (Vieillot) (343)

(Gr., *platypterus*, broad-winged.)

DESCRIPTION: Length 13.00 to 19.00 inches. Upper surface brown; entire lower parts brown with transverse white spots; below white barred with rufous; tail brownish black broadly banded with gray or white.

RANGE: Breeds north to Alberta and southern Quebec; south to Texas and Florida. Winters casually north to Illinois, New Hampshire, and Rhode Island; south to Peru and Venezuela.

STATUS IN S. C.: Uncommon permanent resident, but rare in winter; occurs over all the State. Observed north to York County; east to Horry and Charleston counties; south to Beaufort and Jasper counties; west to McCormick and Oconee counties.

HISTORY: This small *Buteo* is both uncommon and comparatively unknown in South Carolina. Even so, records of its occurrence have been increasing and the bird may prove more common than actual observations indicate. The best field mark, aside from the small size, which is hardly greater than that of a crow, is the white and black banded tail, the bands being of nearly equal width. The general outline and the shape of the wings are like those of the Red-tailed Hawk.

It is usually considered a summer resident in South Carolina and is found chiefly in the Piedmont region. However, Murphey (1937) considered it a winter visitor in the Aiken-Augusta region, on the basis of specimens seen or taken in September, January, and February. It is rare on the coast, and until recent years knowledge of its occurrence there in winter had been based on only one record. Indeed, this little hawk is rare anywhere in the South in winter, for most of them spend that season in the tropics.

Wayne saw only two of these hawks during his life on the coast, one of which he secured on January 15, 1889. He conjectured that it occurred in the interior, and subsequent observations have proved that he was correct. The nest and eggs of a Broad-wing were found on July 20, 1925, in Greenwood County, by William Hahn, Jr. Another nest was found by him on April 21, 1926, in the same county (*Auk*, *44*: 1927, 428). On June 12, 1927, a pair of adults and two young were taken at Easley, Pickens County, by J. O. Pepper. These remain the only known records of nesting in South Carolina, possibly because of the scarcity of observers in the breeding range. Two spring records of interest are those made April 27, 1926, near the South Edisto River, Charleston County (Sprunt and L. L. Walsh), and April 25, 1947, in Calhoun County (George Rabb and James Mosimann). A specimen of this hawk was taken in Anderson County, July 1, 1935, by Paul Earle.

The nest, composed of sticks and twigs, is normally in some forest tree. The two or three eggs are of a light ground color, beautifully marked with lilac. They average 48.9 x 39.3 millimeters and require twenty-one to twenty-five days for incubation.

The Broad-wing is a woodland bird and is somewhat more inactive than many of its kin. It often sits motionless for long periods on a perch, but of course, shares with its family the ability to soar, sometimes at great heights. Its movements are however, sluggish; in consequence, it can be and doubtless is overlooked now and then. About half a dozen recent records exist for the coast country, three of them concerned with winter birds. Sprunt saw one in a small tree near his home in St. Andrew's Parish on January 19, 1934. He watched the bird for some time at no more than 50 feet and checked its identity from every possible angle. He did not, however, secure the bird. Familiarity with the bird from observations during the breeding season in the North Carolina mountains was of assistance in this observation. Sprunt and Robert Holmes saw another of these hawks briefly on the Christmas Count, at Fairlawn Plantation, Christ Church Parish, December 26, 1946, but because of the hawk's rarity at that season and the rather brief opportunity afforded for observation, the record should perhaps not be given the same value as the record of the 1934 bird, about which there was no doubt at all. A later winter observation was made when two birds were noted on February 22, 1947, near Mt. Pleasant by Rabb and Mosimann. The tameness of the Broad-wing is proverbial and helps a great deal in observation.

FOOD: Judged by its food habits, the Broad-wing is one of the most valuable of all birds of prey. The bulk of the diet consists of insects, small mammals, and reptiles, with now and then a disabled bird. Field mice, shrews, chipmunks, wood mice, and small squirrels compose the mammal content; grasshoppers, crickets, and beetles make up much of the insect diet. Eighteen of sixty-five stomachs examined contained mammal remains, whereas only two held small bird remains.

95. SWAINSON'S HAWK: *Buteo swainsoni* Bonaparte (342)

(Lat., *swainsoni*, to William Swainson, English ornithologist.)

DESCRIPTION: Length 19.00 to 22.00 inches. Upper parts dark brown somewhat varied with paler brown; tail barred with dark brown and dull white; below white with a broad band of cinnamon on the chest.

RANGE: Breeds north to northeastern Alaska and Manitoba; south to Illinois. Winters north to northern Argentina; south to central Argentina; accidentally north to Iowa.

STATUS IN S. C.: Accidental visitor in the coast region. Reported from only Charleston County.

HISTORY: Swainson's Hawk occasionally strays to the east and thus occurs as an accidental wanderer in places far out of its normal range. Such is its status in South Carolina. On Bull's Island, November 27, 1935, Edward M. Moore saw a hawk being mobbed by crows; he identified the bird as a Swainson's Hawk. Two days later, Sprunt was on the island and saw the same bird or one precisely similar fly over the yard of Dominick House, again pursued by crows. Having become familiar with Swainson's Hawk in its western home, Sprunt at once recognized this individual and thus corroborated Moore's original identification. This unique instance of the presence of Swainson's Hawk in South Carolina was recorded in the *Auk, 53*: 1936, 209. Although it was impossible to secure the bird, the species is so easily recognized at close range that this record may be considered valid.

In its habits the Swainson's Hawk, which formerly was one of the most abundant large species of the western United States, is unusually beneficial. It lives to a considerable extent on grasshoppers; as many as seventy-seven of these insects have been found in one stomach.

AMERICAN ROUGH-LEGGED HAWK
96. *Buteo lagopus s. johannis* (Gmelin) (347a)

(Gr., *lagopus*, hare-footed; Lat., *s. johannis*, of St. Johns [Newfoundland].)

DESCRIPTION: Length 19.00 to 24.00 inches. Legs feathered to toes. *Adult, normal phase.* Above dark brown, varied with light brown, gray, and dull white; tail white terminally, barred with dark brown; lower parts white, spotted and otherwise marked with dark brown. *Immature, normal phase.* Similar to the adult but terminal part of the tail plain brown; a broad dark brown band across the posterior lower parts. *Adult* and *immature, dark phase.* Almost entirely brownish black, with basal bands on the tail dull white.

RANGE: Breeds north to northwestern Alaska and northeastern Labrador; south to central British Columbia and Newfoundland. Winters north to southern British Columbia and southeastern Ontario; south to southern California and southern Georgia.

STATUS IN S. C.: Rare winter resident, November 17 to April 7, in the coast region. Observed north to the Santee Refuge, Clarendon County; east to McClellanville; south and west to the South Edisto River, Charleston County.

HISTORY: This large northern Hawk is now known to winter irregularly in the East and South. It has been observed on several occasions in South Carolina both by resident and visiting ornithologists but as yet no specimen has been secured.

The first observation of the bird in South Carolina was made by Wayne and Sprunt, who saw one on Capers Island, January 18, 1927 (*Auk, 44*: 1927, 249). Almost exactly one year later, on January 14, 1928, two were observed on Little Edisto Island by H. R. Sass and Sprunt. Some years intervened before the next observation, which was made at the Grove Plantation, South Edisto River, January 3, 1934, by Wilcox Brown and Sprunt. In the following winter, on November 29, 1935, one was seen on the Cape Romain Refuge near McClellanville, by Edward M. Moore and Sprunt. Since that time, there have been other records which give additional support to the status of this species as a rare winter resident in South Carolina, including a sight record made by Allan D. Cruickshank on January 8, 1940, at Bull's Island. These sight records may be accepted without question.

The Rough-leg is a very large, soaring hawk, with the habit of hovering in the air, on rapidly beating wings like the Osprey.

FOOD: In its food habits this bird is exceedingly beneficial, since it rarely takes birds and contents itself chiefly with various kinds of mammals and insects.

GOLDEN EAGLE
97. *Aquila chrysaëtos canadensis* (Linnaeus) (349)

Lat., *Aquila*, eagle; Gr., *chrysaëtos*, golden eagle; Lat., *canadensis*, of Canada.)

DESCRIPTION: Length 31.00 to 41.00 inches. Extent of wings 78.00 to 84.00 inches. Legs completely feathered to the toes. *Adult*. Dark brown, the head and neck streaked with light tawny. *Immature*. Similar but base of tail white.

RANGE: Resident and breeds north to northern Alaska and northern Quebec (Ungava); south to Durango (Mexico) and northwestern South Carolina. Winters south also to southern Louisiana and northern Florida.

STATUS IN S. C.: Rare permanent resident in the mountains of the northwestern section. Rare winter visitor, November 16 to February 15, elsewhere in the State. As a permanent resident recorded from Oconee, Pickens, and Greenville counties. As a winter visitor, recorded north to Anderson County; east and south to Charleston County; west to Aiken County.

HISTORY: This is a magnificent bird. Essentially of the West, it occurs sporadically in the eastern mountains and now and then straggles to the coast. Except for the huge California Condor, it is the largest North American bird of prey, and though it is not as imposing as its relative, the Bald Eagle, in contrasting plumage, it is by all odds the finest of the raptors.

Its status in South Carolina is rather uncertain. Several have been taken in the coastal area over a period of years, all of them in winter. Wayne never saw the bird alive but says (1910) that it "may breed in the mountainous parts." There is, as far as we know, no authentic record of its ever having nested in the State, but any such record in the future will not come as a surprise. In the authors' *Supplement to the Birds of South Carolina* (1931) it is designated as a "rare permanent resident in the Mountain Region; occasional on the coast." This may still stand, in spite of the few additional records since that time, as they do not alter the status of the bird.

An adult was taken at Middleton Gardens, Charleston County, in January, 1933, by Eugene Johnson, and one was caught in a steel trap at Witherbee, Berkeley County, in February, 1934. The bird was kept alive for some days and finally sent to the Charleston Museum on February 19 by Henry Dwight. One was seen near Charleston on December 22, 1941, by E. Milby Burton. There are three recent records of specimens secured in the northwestern section of the State, near the mountains: one was found dead under a power line (evidently electrocuted) at Townville, Anderson County, November 16, 1934, by J. E. Whitfield; one was taken in Pickens County in November, 1935, by W. MacFall; and one was reported by A. L. Pickens as having been shot near Greenville in the spring of 1926 (*Auk*, 44: 1927, 428).

The Golden Eagle is a very powerful bird and a far more predatory species than the Bald Eagle. It is uniformly dark and presents none of the spectacular contrast of plumage characteristic of the latter, but is much more capable of dealing with larger prey. The Bald Eagle is, of course, largely a fish eater; the Golden is a mammal killer, and does not confine itself to wild species. It bears a hard name in parts of the West because of its inroads upon lambs, goats, pigs, and even calves, although there is doubtless considerable exaggeration in some of the stories told of its destructiveness. It is known to attack successfully the young of mountain sheep and other game animals. It seizes birds to the size of geese and turkeys. At least two of these eagles taken in the Low-country were shot while eating Wild Turkeys they had killed. It is able to lift weights of more than 12 pounds. Stories of eagles carrying off children or even attacking them are usually sheer fabrication but occur persistently.

Some confusion may result in distinguishing this species from the immature Bald Eagle, which is also uniformly dark. A close view of the two birds, however, will reveal that the legs of the Golden Eagle are feathered to the toes, whereas the tarsus (shank) of the Bald Eagle is perfectly bare.

The nest of the Golden Eagle is almost invariably placed on cliffs in mountain regions. It is a great pile of sticks, trash, and debris, in an inaccessible position. The eggs usually number one or two, are white, variously marked with brown splashes, sometimes lightly, sometimes heavily. The eggs average 74.5 x 58.0 millimeters. The incubation period is not definite but probably runs from twenty-eight to thirty days.

Food: Mammals of varying size, from prairie dogs, gophers, and rats to the young of domestic stock and game animals. Because the Golden Eagle is rare in the East, the economic damage it does is negligible. An analysis of eighty stomachs showed mammal remains in sixty, non-game birds in fourteen, poultry and game birds in seven.

Southern Bald Eagle
98. *Haliaetus leucocephalus leucocephalus* (Linnaeus) (352)

(Gr., *Haliaetus*, sea eagle; *leucocephalus*, white-headed.)

Local Names: American Eagle; White-headed Eagle.

Description: Length about 32.00 inches; extent of wings about 75.00 inches. Lower parts of legs unfeathered. *Adult.* Uniformly dark brown; head, neck, and tail white; bill and feet yellow. *Immature.* Entire plumage blackish brown with much dull white mottling; white head and tail not attained until at least fourth or fifth year.

Range: Resident and breeds north to California and South Carolina; south to northern Lower California and southern Florida.

Status in S. C.: Fairly common permanent resident, more frequent in the coastal region. Reported north to Chester County; east to Horry County; south to Beaufort County; west to Greenwood and Oconee counties.

History: This bird should be known to every American citizen in view of its distinction as the national emblem. Unfortunately, it is unfamiliar to most people, and there is a widespread notion that a mere glimpse of an eagle is a rare experience.

While such a sight is always memorable, it is not a novelty, and though the Bald Eagle is not as abundant as it was in former years, it still occurs in many parts of the State and may often be seen.

The Bald Eagle is a strikingly handsome bird. It is almost universally misnamed *Bald-headed* Eagle. But it is not bald-headed. The term "bald" simply signifies whiteness, a perfectly correct use of the word. It should be said at once that all Bald Eagles are not white-headed. The immature bird is uniformly dark all over, with much mottling as it changes the plumage annually. Between four and five years elapse before it attains its white head and tail. Because of the colors it may wear in the years of its immaturity, one hears of "black" eagles and "gray" eagles.

The Bald Eagle is predominantly a coastal species, but it may be seen anywhere throughout South Carolina and it is a permanent resident. Not infrequently, one is seen about towns and cities as it flies over, particularly in coastal communities such as Beaufort, Charleston, Georgetown, and Myrtle Beach. It travels to the mountains, and one was taken in Pickens County on May 24, 1930, by T. J. Baskin.

The nesting season is in midwinter, a fact that never ceases to surprise those familiar with ornithology. The eggs are laid in November, December, or early January. Wayne found eggs on November 20, December 20, and January 6.

The nest is usually built in a large pine, sometimes at great heights. One of Wayne's nests was 112 feet, 6 inches from the ground. The nest is a huge mass of sticks, bark, grass, moss, and other debris. The birds return to it year after year. After many seasons' use, it attains enormous proportions. Actual measurements have revealed nests which were 15 feet high and 9 feet across the top. The strangest and most incongruous articles are found in them at times, such things as tennis balls, old shoes, candles, electric light bulbs, artificial minnows (fishing lures), and various sized bottles.

The eggs almost invariably number two; sometimes there is only one, very rarely three or even four. They are pure white (thus differing from those of the Golden Eagle), and are rather small for such a large bird, averaging 70.5 x 54.2 millimeters. Incubation requires about thirty-five days, and both sexes share the labor of incubating the eggs as well as the duty of feeding the young. Many stories are told of the fierceness of eagles at the nest and of their attacks upon climbers, but such stories are nonsense. Most parent eagles, when their nests are invaded, simply wheel about at a very safe distance, uttering a high, shrill, and utterly inadequate yelping cry. A nesting Brown Thrasher in one's yard is much more apt to attack an intruder.

It sometimes happens that eagle nests afford home sites for other birds, strange as this may seem. Boat-tailed Grackles occasionally build in the sides of the huge structure, and, though it is almost incredible, the Great Horned Owl will do the same thing. Bent quotes J. Warren Jacobs (1908) to the effect that he saw one of these owls nesting in a cavity in the side of an eagle's nest in Florida (*Life Hist. N. A. Birds of Prey*, 1937, 324). Charles Broley, of St. Petersburg, Florida, told Sprunt that he had found a Great Horned Owl sitting on its egg in the same nest with an incubating eagle. The nest was some 7 or 8 feet across, and about 3 or 4 feet separated eagle and owl. Such behavior appears completely inexplicable.

The Bald Eagle mates for an indefinite time, a pair remaining together season after season. This, of course, has given rise to the supposition that, if one bird is killed, the other never mates again, a notion which is totally erroneous.

The courtship of Bald Eagles is, as might be expected, spectacular. The birds make breath-taking dives on each other, wheel suddenly, and turn themselves completely over. Chamberlain saw such a flight involving an adult and an immature, over Folly Island in October, 1944. Wayne never observed the mating of an adult and an immature, but it does occur now and then. Bent (1937) states that observers "all seem to agree that it seldom occurs."

Although reported attacks of Bald Eagles upon children and adults are to be completely discounted, there are authentic accounts of attacks upon domestic animals. In such instances the birds may be prompted by hunger or a desire to protect their nest territory. The following incidents are illustrative: A. B. Nimitz writes that at Coming-Tee Plantation, Berkeley County, "in late September or early October," he was resting one day at the base of a loose hay stack in an open field. A small dog was with him, lying in the open about 10 feet away. Suddenly there was a noise "as of a gust of wind" and Nimitz sat up to see an eagle swoop low over the dog "hardly four feet above it." His movement was seen by the bird, which at once made off, but that it had intended to seize the sleeping dog seems certain, as "its talons were plainly visible and wide open."

Glenn Allan, of Summerville, witnessed an attack on two of his bird dogs while hunting on Captain's Island, in the month of January. The eagle dived and raked one of the dogs with its talons, and though Allan says the wounds thus inflicted were not serious, " . . . it was weeks before they (the dogs) loosened up and hunted freely again."

In spite of its adoption as our national emblem, it was not until 1940 that the eagle was afforded any protection. In that year, Congress passed a law prohibiting the shooting of the bird, and providing severe penalties for its violation. That there is such a law appears to be little known, however, for newspapers often carry accounts of the killing of eagles, giving names, localities, and dates. These are outright violations and the lawbreaker is open to serious trouble. The sooner the law becomes generally recognized and obeyed, the better.

There is a decided migration in midsummer of eagles which have nested in the Southeast to the northern states and into Canada. This has been definitely proved by the banding of young in the nests, and ornithological science owes a tremendous

PLATE X: SHOREBIRDS ALONG INLAND WATERWAY

Water Color by Roger Tory Peterson

Flying bird: Willet. Standing, right center: Marbled Godwit. Foreground, left to right: Semipalmated Plover, Oyster-catcher, Ruddy Turnstone (breeding plumage), and Black-bellied Plover (breeding plumage).

Roger Tory Peterson —

debt to Charles Broley, of Florida and Ontario, for this outstanding work. Broley has banded over a thousand Eagles in Florida, and has had returns from several northern states, Nova Scotia, Prince Edward Island, and other Canadian localities. Eight of his birds have been recovered in South Carolina. One of these was banded at Bradenton, Florida, on March 23, 1944, and was shot exactly a month later at White Pond, Aiken County. Broley has set forth his highly interesting work in a paper (*Wilson Bull.*, *59*: 1947, 3-20).

The birds return south in fall and early winter and remain from November until May. As many as eight at a time are often seen at Bull's Island from November through January.

The weight of the Bald Eagle varies from 7 to more than 10 pounds, and the wing-spread from 6 to 7 feet. The bird is able to carry a weight equal to its own. In soaring, the wings are held at right angles to the body, the bird being perfectly flat across the wings and back, with nothing of the "v" shape so characteristic of the Turkey Vultures, with which it is sometimes confused by observers. Few sights in nature can equal a soaring eagle in splendor, the sun glinting on the white head and tail as the great bird swings in magnificent circles through a cobalt sky.

Food: In South Carolina the Bald Eagle limits its diet almost entirely to fish. It seems to prefer sea catfish and seldom takes species of fish which have commercial value. It often raids the Osprey instead of fishing for itself. In winter it sometimes takes wounded ducks. It is known also to seize upon Coots, the eagle forcing its victim to dive again and again by hovering closely over it and pouncing upon it when it becomes exhausted and floats to the surface. The eagle also preys upon herons and small mammals such as rabbits, but it seldom touches poultry. At times it eats carrion, usually dead fish.

99. Marsh Hawk: *Circus cyaneus hudsonius* (Linnaeus)   (331)

(Gr., *Circus*, a kind of hawk; *cyaneus*, blue; Lat., *hudsonius*, of Hudson [Bay].)

Local Names: Rabbit Hawk; Bullet Hawk.

Description: Length 17.00 to 24.00 inches *Adult male*. Light bluish gray above, with white upper tail coverts; white below, with dark wing tips. *Female*. Dark grayish brown above, lighter beneath, much streaked with brown; upper tail coverts white. *Immature*. Similar to adult female but much more richly rufous.

Range: Breeds north to northern Alaska and southeastern Quebec; south to northern Lower California and northern Florida. Winters north to southern British Columbia and southern New Hampshire; south to Hawaii (casually), Guatemala, and Colombia.

Status in S. C.: Common permanent resident in all the State, but rare in summer, possibly breeds. Reported north to Spartanburg and Chester counties; east to Horry County; south to Beaufort County; west to Greenwood and Oconee counties.

History: The Marsh Hawk occurs throughout South Carolina and should be familiar to anyone, for it is certainly one of the easiest of the birds of prey to identify. In this respect it presents a sharp contrast to other hawks, which are often confusing to beginners in bird study.

Though there is a difference in the plumages of male and female, the bird may always be known instantly in whatever plumage by the very conspicuous white patch on the upper tail coverts (base of tail). This mark shows plainly in flight, and since the Marsh Hawk is rarely seen perching, the mark serves as a sure guide in quick identification. The manner of flight is also diagnostic, as the bird flies low over fields and marshes, quartering back and forth at no great distance above the grass tops, stopping occasionally to hover, then dropping downward as it sights its prey.

In South Carolina the Marsh Hawk is a permanent resident, having been seen in one locality or another every month in the year. There is as yet no positive evidence of its nesting. It is always present by late August and becomes increasingly common as fall advances and winter arrives, when it is abundant. It begins to drop off again in April and May. Summer records include one seen by Ivan R. Tomkins on June 13, 1937, 6 miles east of Savannah, Georgia, in South Carolina; one observed at the Santee Gun Club, Charleston County, on July 19, 1945, by A. J. C. Vaurie and his wife; and one seen at Huger, Berkeley County, by E. von S. Dingle on August 11, 1930.

The Marsh Hawk, which is a bird of the open, is equally at home in the great salt marshes of the coast and the cotton fields of the Piedmont. Its low flight is marked by frequent tiltings and veerings, the wings maintaining a decided "v" shape when not flapping. Its downward drop, when it sights its prey, is almost a pounce.

It is quite noticeable that the brown females and immatures far outnumber the blue-gray and white adult males. Wayne (1910) put the preponderance of the former over the latter at "fifty to one." Sprunt has found this to be true throughout the whole of the Southeast, until one reaches the Lake Okeechobee area of Florida, where the adult males are far more common.

The Marsh Hawk is one of the most silent of the birds of prey, at least in winter, and except during its spectacular courtship flight, it is practically voiceless. It roosts on the ground and often returns to the same spot in an old field or marsh, night after night.

FOOD: Like all the hawks, this species has been condemned, vilified, and persecuted on circumstantial evidence or no evidence at all. While it preys upon birds at times, notably the Clapper Rail (Marsh Hen), wounded ducks, and to a lesser extent, the Bobwhite, and poultry, its main dependence is upon rodents, rats, mice, and rabbits. In the southeast it appears particularly fond of the cotton rat (*Sigmodon hispidus*), this rodent being the No. 1 enemy of the Bobwhite. Examination of over a thousand pellets, picked up and analyzed at a roost of this hawk by H. L. Stoddard, showed remains of Bobwhites in four, and bones of the cotton rat in 925. Thus, for every Bobwhite taken, the hawk had consumed 231 cotton rats. Cotton rats destroy innumerable Bobwhite eggs and young.

Family Pandionidae: Ospreys

100. OSPREY: *Pandion haliaëtus carolinensis* (Gmelin) (364)

(Gr., *Pandion*, a king of Athens; *haliaëtus*, sea eagle; Lat., *carolinensis*, of Carolina.)

LOCAL NAMES: Fish Hawk; Fish Eagle.

DESCRIPTION: Length 21.00 to 25.00 inches. Above dark brown; neck and undersurface white; head white with brown markings on crown and also on nape; a broad stripe through eye; tail gray with dark bars.

RANGE: Breeds north to Alaska and Labrador; south to Mexico and southern Florida. Winters north to middle California and South Carolina; south to Mexico and Chile.

STATUS IN S. C.: Permanent resident, most numerous on the coast and in summer. Recorded north to Spartanburg and Chester counties; east to Horry County; south to Beaufort County; west to Aiken and Oconee counties.

HISTORY: The Fish Hawk is well known. It is a common sight in much of South Carolina. It was long considered a summer resident only, and Wayne (1910) thought that it did not occur in midwinter. While it is uncommon at that season, there are now definite records of its occurrence for every month in the year. It ranks, therefore, as a permanent resident. January is the month in which it is most rare. Late February sees its return in numbers, and until Christmas it is a common sight along the beaches and marshes, and the streams, rivers, and ponds of the interior. It sometimes carries on its spectacular fishing activities in Colonial Lake in Charleston, a few yards away from a closely built residential district. It goes up to the very border of the State, and has been secured at Clemson by R. E. Ware, on May 1. It is not uncommon along the Seneca River.

Ospreys begin to nest soon after they arrive, and they return year after year to the same nest, making repairs and additions until it eventually attains large proportions. Should winter storms cause the tree to fall, the birds build another nest nearby. On the coast islands and nearby mainland they build in dead pines; along the freshwater backwaters, in dead cypress stubs of varying heights. The Osprey becomes very much excited if its nest is molested, circling about with high, shrill cries. The eggs, almost always three, sometimes two or four, are laid in early April. They have a buffy color and are heavily marked with splashes of reddish brown and chocolate. They are among the handsomest eggs laid by the birds of prey. They have a peculiar odor which is imparted from the bird's plumage and which remains even after many years in a collector's cabinet. The average measurement is 61.0 x 45.6 millimeters. Incubation requires about twenty-eight days.

The Fish Hawk well deserves its name. It lives only on fish and secures its prey unaided but not without persecution from its larger relative, the Bald Eagle, which often robs it of a catch. The Osprey's technique on sighting a fish is to hover on heavily beating wings, then to plunge headlong into the water. It is one of the few birds which indulge this beating-wing-hovering habit. The bird may dive from as high as 50 feet, throwing up a cloud of spray as it strikes the water, and at times it entirely submerges. Stories are told of its attacking fish of such size as to be dragged under the water and drowned, but authentic instances of this are rare. The Osprey always carries its catch's head into the wind so that it offers a minimum of resistance to the air currents. It often carries fish for considerable distances when the young are being fed.

Though it is normally not an aggressive bird, attending to its own affairs in an exemplary manner, the Osprey does attack other birds, but not to kill them for food. E. Milby Burton in July, 1948, witnessed a determined pursuit of a Snakebird by an Osprey, which ended when the Snakebird flew headlong into the water of a cypress lagoon, and so escaped whatever was intended by the Hawk. Doubtless the reason for this attack was that the Snakebird was flying too close to the nest of the Osprey, which contained young. Burton also once saw an Osprey make several attacks on a Bald Eagle, which threw itself on its back in the air, in the characteristic defensive attitude. It is probable that the eagle had just robbed the hawk of a fish. This was certainly a reversal of the usual encounter between these birds.

FOOD: Entirely fish of various kinds consisting of menhaden, gizzard shad, catfish, perch, mullet, weakfish (Audubon's plate of the Osprey shows it carrying one of these), a few bass, carp, etc. Reports are made now and then of attacks on chickens by this species, but such reports appear upon investigation to be without foundation.

Family Falconidae: Caracaras and Falcons

AUDUBON'S CARACARA
101. *Polyborus cheriway audubonii* Cassin (362)

(Gr., *Polyborus*, very voracious; *cheriway*, the South American name of the bird; Lat., *audubonii*, to John James Audubon.)

DESCRIPTION: Length 20.00 to 25.00 inches. Top of head and general color brownish black, but foreback, throat, and breast dull white, barred with dull brown or brownish black; tail and its coverts mostly white, the tail barred with blackish brown.

RANGE: Resident and breeds north to southern Arizona and central Florida; south to Panama.

STATUS IN S. C.: Accidental in the coast area.

HISTORY: This remarkable hawk-vulture does not normally occur closer to South Carolina than the Kissimmee Prairie region of south central Florida, some five hundred miles to the south. It remained for a visiting ornithologist in the army to find the Caracara as a South Carolina bird. On May 1, 1943, Southgate Y. Hoyt and his wife for several minutes watched a Caracara flying and feeding near the Stark General Hospital in Charleston County, on what is known as the Old Dorchester Road. The two observers knew the bird from having seen it on the Florida prairies. The Hoyt observation, which is undoubtedly valid, constitutes the sole record for the State (*Auk, 61*: 1944, 145).

The Caracara eats both carrion and living prey, largely turtles, snakes, etc.

102. Duck Hawk: *Falco peregrinus anatum* Bonaparte   (336a)

(Lat., *Falco*, a falcon; *peregrinus*, wandering; *anatum*, of ducks.)

Description: Length 15.00 to 20.00 inches. *Adult.* Above slate color, back barred with black; undersurface white or pale buff heavily spotted and barred with blackish brown. *Immature.* Above fucous; below buff, streaked with dark brown.

Range: Breeds north to northern Alaska and western Greenland; south to Lower California and South Carolina. Winters north to British Columbia and Massachusetts; south to Mexico, Colombia, and Trinidad.

Status in S. C.: Rare summer resident in the mountains of the northwestern part of the State; uncommon winter visitor, August 14 to May 9, in the remaining section, most frequent along the coast. Recorded as a summer resident in Greenville and Pickens counties; a winter visitor north to Clarendon County; east to Horry County; south to Beaufort and Jasper counties; west to Aiken County.

History: Of all the birds of prey, the Duck Hawk most nearly approaches perfection in fearlessness and efficiency.

Unfortunately for those who wish to study it, the Duck Hawk is far from common. Strangely enough, one of the best places to see it is a big city. Above teeming Fifth Avenue or Riverside Drive in New York, about City Hall in Philadelphia, at the Custom House in Boston, this bird may be watched as it takes its toll from the swarming pigeons of the streets, and it may even be studied at its nesting on the jutting ledge of some soaring skyscraper.

Its status in South Carolina is peculiar. In the mountains it nests on the rocky crags of the higher peaks, and it is therefore listed as a summer resident. On the coast it is a winter visitor only, usually appearing from early September until the first part of March. It has been noted in Charleston on several occasions, where it is to be seen now and then on the steelwork of the Cooper River Bridge, on the lookout for shore birds or ducks.

Though summer observations of the bird in the mountain area have long led to the belief that it breeds there, actually known instances are few. An authentic record of recent years was an observation by R. E. Ware of a pair bringing food to young birds at Caesar's Head, Greenville County, in April, 1933. He saw the adults come in to the cliff several times, the nest being below him on a narrow ledge. At each approach of the parents, the young could be heard squealing loudly.

On the coast, the Duck Hawk shows a decided preference for the barrier islands and salt marshes, perching frequently on driftwood along a sea beach, or flying on extended aerial patrols. Personnel of the Cape Romain Refuge have noted that it sometimes deliberately follows a patrol boat in the waterways of the marshes, and when grebes or ducks are flushed ahead of the boat, the Duck Hawk swoops upon them with astonishing swiftness. The speed of this splendid hunter is one of its outstanding characteristics and has excited comment and wonder for generations. Audubon (1831) says that the Duck Hawk "pursues the fugitive with a rapidity scarcely to be conceived." Wayne, on shooting at a specimen which he saw strike a dove, says that "never have I seen a bird fly faster than this hawk."

Accurate data on specific velocities are difficult to obtain, but Bent (1938) cites the experience of D. D. McLean, who timed a Duck Hawk with a stop watch, and found it to fly at a rate of between 165 and 180 miles an hour. He also quotes the testimony of a pilot in a pursuit plane which was traveling at 175 miles an hour when a Duck Hawk flashed by him in a dive "as though the plane was standing still." The pilot estimated that the bird was traveling two feet to his one. It was certainly moving with a velocity "much greater than 175 m. p. h., and perhaps not far from double that rate." It has on many occasions been seen to overtake the fastest ducks. This characteristic, combined with others, accounts for the thrill which one cannot fail to experience when watching the Duck Hawk in action.

The Duck Hawk is a counterpart of the famous Peregrine Falcon of Europe, the ownership of which in the days of falconry was restricted to royalty. In recent years, there has been a revival of interest in this sport in the United States, and several species of hawks are trained for it. This has resulted in trapping or otherwise securing many individuals of the Duck Hawk, a practice hardly conducive to its increase.

Many instances of the fearlessness of this species are on record, particularly those which report its taking wounded game birds from under the hand of a hunter. Such exploits usually so astonish the sportsman that the hawk is gone with its prey before a gun can be brought to bear on it. Though it is natural for the hunter to be angered by the robbery, he can hardly fail to admire the hawk's daring.

This falcon's disposition being what it is, one may well expect it to be particularly dangerous in the vicinity of its nest. Although it has been repeatedly stated that the Duck Hawk will not attack an intruder, there are very definite records to the contrary. A recent instance is related in detail by G. B. Hendricks (*Auk, 52*: 1935, 446). He tells of a nesting Duck Hawk in Massachusetts which attacked and wounded four people who were photographing the nest.

This species is essentially a mountain nester; it places its eggs on ledges of sheer cliffs, many of them inaccessible except by rope climbing. Three or four eggs are laid with little nesting material about them. The eggs are of a buffy ground color, splashed and marbled with reddish brown, and are strikingly handsome. They are eagerly sought by collectors. The average measurement is 52.0 x 40.0 millimeters. The incubation period is about thirty-three days.

FOOD: Almost entirely birds, most of which seem to be waterfowl of various species, shore birds, and pigeons. The hawk also seizes poultry and will often return again and again to the same chicken yard. Petrels, terns, gulls, doves, ducks, coots, and the smaller insectivorous and song birds are among its victims. Though undoubtedly destructive to bird life, this superb feathered buccaneer has so many admirable qualities that it is hard to begrudge it any type of food, and the fact that it is not common keeps it from being a serious menace anywhere.

EASTERN PIGEON HAWK
103. *Falco columbarius columbarius* Linnaeus (357)

(Lat., *columbarius*, dove-keeper, referring to its bird-killing habits.)

DESCRIPTION: Length 10.00 to 14.00 inches. *Adult male.* Upper parts slate gray; tail with bands of grayish white; undersurface buffy white, streaked with brown. *Female* and *immature.* Above dark brown; tail bands buffy white; below buffy white with streaks of dark brown.

RANGE: Breeds north to northern Ontario and northern Quebec (Ungava); south to Iowa and Maine. Winters north to Nebraska and Maine; south to Peru and Trinidad.

STATUS IN S. C.: Fairly common winter resident, August 29 to May 16, over most of the State though more frequent coastwise. Observed north to Chester County; east to Horry County; south to the mouth of the Savannah River and Jasper County; west to Aiken County.

HISTORY: This daring little falcon is a miniature of its larger relative, the Duck Hawk. It is not at all well known but this is not surprising, since a hawk is a hawk to most people, and worthy of nothing but quick death. To the holder of briefs for the birds of prey, however, this species presents some problems.

Though it is not much larger than a robin, the Pigeon Hawk's spirit and dash makes it a veritable avian pirate. As far as small birds are concerned, it is just as well that the hawk is no larger than it is. The bluish gray male is distinctive because of its small size and banded tail; the female, always the larger, is very brownish and also heavily streaked below.

This falcon was long thought to be only a transient visitor in South Carolina. It is now known to occur locally throughout the winter. All sight records are included under this race.

The first observation made in winter was by Wayne, who, on January 14, 1911, saw one in his yard. He saw the "same bird" two days later. Other winter records, though by no means all of them, are: November 29 (Wayne); December 15 and 29 (Sprunt); January 24 (Tomkins); February 26 (Julian Mitchell, Jr.). Southbound fall flights are particularly noticeable along the barrier beaches, often at some distance from land. As an example, a steady though not great flight including Pigeon and Cooper's Hawks was noted on October 9, 1944, some 75 miles offshore, headed toward Charleston (F. L. Newman).

The Pigeon Hawk frequents open country, fields, beaches, and marshes and sometimes sits for long periods atop a high branch or stake, like a Sparrow Hawk. It can often be closely approached. Its flight is extremely fast, always exciting comment, and is marked by alternate periods of flapping and sailing. Despite its small size it does not hesitate to attack and destroy birds larger than itself such as flickers, pigeons, and even teal. It does not, however, often attack poultry.

FOOD: As indicated above, the food is chiefly birds, usually warblers, sparrows, vireos. However, it also takes insects and small mammals in greater amounts than does the Duck Hawk. Dragon flies, grasshoppers, and beetles are consumed. Since it rarely molests poultry, the Pigeon Hawk affects man's interests but little.

WESTERN PIGEON HAWK
104. *Falco columbarius bendirei* Swann (357c)

(Lat., *bendirei*, to Charles Emil Bendire.)

DESCRIPTION: Length 10.00 to 14.00 inches. Similar to the Eastern Pigeon Hawk, but lighter above, and in immature plumage also more brownish.

RANGE: Breeds north to northwestern Alaska and northwestern Mackenzie; south to northern California and northern Saskatchewan. Winters south to southern Lower California and southern Florida.

STATUS IN S. C.: Casual winter visitor in October to the southern coast region. Reported from only Charleston County.

HISTORY: In 1903 Wayne recorded (*Auk, 20*: 1903, 67) as Richardson's Pigeon Hawk a bird which he had taken at Mt. Pleasant on October 15, 1895, and later (1910) mentioned another that he had obtained there on October 7, 1896. These two specimens have been recently examined by Dr. Harry C. Oberholser and found to be referable to the Western Pigeon Hawk. Still another, also examined by Dr. Oberholser, proves to belong to this race. It was collected by B. M. Badger at James Island on October 26, 1935. These specimens are in the Charleston Museum collection. There are no other records for the State.

In habits and food this bird is not materially different from the Eastern Pigeon Hawk.

EASTERN SPARROW HAWK
105. *Falco sparverius sparverius* Linnaeus (360)

(Lat., *sparverius*, pertaining to sparrows.)

LOCAL NAMES: Killy Hawk.

DESCRIPTION: Length 9.00 to 12.00 inches. *Male.* Crown rufous, bordered with slate gray; back rufous, with broken black cross bars; sides of head white with two black vertical stripes; throat white; breast and belly buff to ochraceous, with small round black spots; tail rufous, with a broad black subterminal band of black; wing coverts slate color. *Female.* Like the male but back, wing coverts, and tail duller and with many bars of dull black; under parts streaked with brown.

RANGE: Breeds north to eastern Alaska and Newfoundland; south to Mexico and middle South Carolina. Winters north to British Columbia and Nova Scotia; south to Panama.

STATUS IN S. C.: Permanent resident in the northern part of the State, common in winter, rarer in summer; common winter resident in the remainder of the State. Reported north to Spartanburg, York, and Kershaw counties; east to Horry County; south (in winter only) to Beaufort County; west to Oconee and Pickens counties.

HISTORY: This beautiful little falcon, smallest of the South Carolina hawks, is sadly misnamed. Grasshopper Hawk would be much more apt, for grasshoppers (plus many other insects) are its principal food, not sparrows. Its small size, reddish tail, and habit of hovering in the air like a Kingfisher will always identify it. It frequently pumps its tail after alighting on a post, tree, or telephone wire. The oft-repeated, shrill cry of "killy-killy-killy" gives rise to the local name of "Killy Hawk."

The Sparrow Hawk is present over South Carolina the year around, though much more in evidence during the fall and winter. During this latter season a considerable number of birds come down from areas north of South Carolina. This is well evidenced by the fact that birds banded as nestlings in Massachusetts, New York, Pennsylvania, and New Jersey have been recovered in winter in Horry, Georgetown, Beaufort, Sumter, and Richland counties.

The Sparrow Hawk is an open country bird, frequenting fields, meadows, marshes, and the sea beaches. The perch is always conspicuous, a high stub, flagpole, wires, or the top twigs of a tree. From such perches the hawk makes sallies when it sights its prey, then it often returns to the same perch, much like a flycatcher. The hovering habit is strongly developed in this little hawk. The wings move very rapidly, but the body remains suspended in the air, almost motionless.

Brush fires attract numbers of Sparrow Hawks, along with other birds of prey, for there they can seize insects attempting to escape the flames. Smoke does not appear to inconvenience them at all, and as many as a dozen may congregate at such a fire, darting back and forth through the smoke and uttering the characteristic call.

This species is not uncommon even in towns and cities, and it is sometimes caught, tamed, and trained in falconry. It makes a fascinating pet. No better insect insurance could be imagined than a pair of these little falcons about a garden or farm. Most rural dwellers are aware of this fact, and encourage the birds to live in the neighborhood.

Nesting is rather irregular, and may take place in April or May. Murphey (1937) records a pair nesting in a Pileated Woodpecker hole in Edgefield County. He says that the species usually breeds in the third and fourth weeks of April. Unlike most other hawks, the Sparrow Hawk uses natural cavities in trees, abandoned woodpecker holes, and at times even bird boxes erected about dwellings. The eggs, which are nearly spherical in shape, usually number four or five. They are of a buffy ground color, lightly or heavily covered with reddish-brown markings, and average 35.0 x 29.0 millimeters. Incubation takes about twenty-nine or thirty days. They are miniature editions of Duck Hawk eggs.

Food: The record of the Sparrow Hawk's food habits is heavily on the right side of the ledger. Analysis of 320 stomachs is illustrative. Two hundred and fifteen contained insects; 118, spiders; ninety-nine, mice; twelve, other mammals; twelve, reptiles; and fifty-four, birds. In an additional lot of twenty-five stomachs, twenty-four held insects, most of which were grasshoppers. Other insects were crickets, katydids, dragon flies, caterpillars, and carrion beetles. Lizards and mice, together with frogs and small snakes, are sometimes taken. Birds, when taken at all, are small and of abundant species such as warblers, sparrows, and small flycatchers. The predominance of an insect diet shows how valuable this little hawk is to agriculture.

LITTLE SPARROW HAWK
106.   *Falco sparverius paulus* (Howe and King)   (360b)

(Lat., *paulus*, small.)

DESCRIPTION: Length about 10 inches. Similar to the Eastern Sparrow Hawk but smaller.

RANGE: Resident and breeds north to eastern Texas and southern South Carolina; south to southern Louisiana and southern Florida.

STATUS IN S. C.: Rare permanent resident in the southeastern part of the State. Reported north and east to Berkeley County; south to Beaufort County; west to Aiken County (probably).

HISTORY: This smaller form of the Eastern Sparrow Hawk is credited to South Carolina through the active interest of Ivan R. Tomkins (*Oriole*, 7: 1942, 13). For some time Tomkins had suspected that the Florida form ranged farther north along the southeastern coast than was generally recognized. He learned that two birds taken at Mt. Pleasant by A. T. Wayne, a female on May 14, 1902, and a male on the following day, were in the collection of the Museum of Comparative Zoölogy at Cambridge, Mass. These had been identified as the Little Sparrow Hawk, and re-examination by A. C. Bent, at Tomkins' request, confirmed this finding.

Three other specimens are in existence, a male from Mt. Pleasant obtained by Wayne on November 29, 1902, now in the collection of the Charleston Museum; one from Huger, Berkeley County, collected on December 30, 1926, by E. von S. Dingle; and one in the collection of the Cleveland Museum of Natural History that was taken on March 30, 1937, by H. M. Woods at Gray's Hill, Beaufort County; these have been identified by Dr. Harry C. Oberholser.

That this form breeds here is shown by the fact that Wayne noted on the label of the May 14 female, "Large egg in oviduct." The label of the male taken the following day says, "Mate to female."

In habits and food this race does not differ appreciably from the Eastern Sparrow Hawk.

Order Galliformes
Gallinaceous Birds

Family Tetraonidae: Grouse and Ptarmigans

APPLACHIAN RUFFED GROUSE
107. *Bonasa umbellus monticola* Todd   (300)

(Gr., *Bonasa,* bison, referring to the drumming of the bird; Lat., *umbellus,* umbrella, *i. e.,* the ruffs; *monticola,* a mountaineer.)

LOCAL NAMES: Pheasant.

DESCRIPTION: Length 16.00 to 19.00 inches. Neck with prominent tufts of black feathers; upper surface reddish brown or gray, mottled with black and buff; lower parts white or buff barred with brown; tail rufous or gray, with a broad subterminal black band.

RANGE: Resident and breeds north to southeastern Michigan and northeastern Pennsylvania; south to northeastern Alabama, northern Georgia, and northwestern South Carolina.

STATUS IN S. C.: Rare permanent resident in the mountain area of the northwestern section; casual elsewhere. Recorded in the mountains north to Greenville County; east to York (casually); south and west to Oconee County. Casually at Camden and Mt. Pleasant in the eastern part of the State.

HISTORY: This fine game bird is resident in the mountain area but sometimes descends into the Piedmont valleys in winter. Wayne (1910) states that it "used to be abundant" in Oconee, Pickens, and Greenville counties, and mentions Caesar's Head as a center of concentration. Hudson (1930) includes it as a permanent resident about Clemson, on the authority of the late Franklin Sherman, stating that it now occurs only in the mountains. Only under exceptional circumstances does the Ruffed Grouse occur below the fall line or even that far. N. C. Brown records one killed at Camden, December 27, 1904 (*Auk, 23*: 1906, 336), and Wayne says that a specimen identified by "several sportsmen who were acquainted with the species" was shot near Mt. Pleasant, Charleston County, in the autumn of 1874.

The Ruffed Grouse is the "Pheasant" of the mountain people; a bird of heavy forests, where its wonderfully protective coloration is so like its surroundings that a passerby can virtually step on a bird before it rises on thundering wings to thread a swift way between the tree trunks.

The distinctive name of this grouse is derived from the presence of the tufts of feathers, or ruffs, on the neck. By a corruption of the term the bird is sometimes incorrectly called a "Ruffled Grouse."

The courtship season is marked by the famous drumming of the cock bird, a far carrying, resonant sound produced by a rapid beating of the wings while the drummer stands on a log or stump. It was long disputed whether this sound was the result of contact with the wings against the perch, against each other, or against the sides of the bird. Slow-motion moving pictures, however, have proved that the sound is produced only by the action of the wings on the air as they are moved rapidly forward and backward.

The nest of the Ruffed Grouse is always on the ground, simply a depression lined with leaves at the base of a stump or beside a log. The eggs number about nine to as many as twelve or fourteen and are creamy buff in color, unmarked. They average 38.9 x 29.6 millimeters and are laid during late May and early June. Incubation requires about twenty-one days.

The chicks are protectively clothed and, like the young of the Bobwhite, lie close when any danger threatens. The old bird will attempt to lead an intruder away by feigning a broken wing.

FOOD: Seeds and berries of various sorts, acorns, nuts, and insects make up the diet. The grouse eats grasshoppers and crickets at some seasons, but prefers vegetable foods.

Family Perdicidae: Partridges and Quails

EASTERN BOBWHITE
108. *Colinus virginianus virginianus* (Linnaeus)   (289)

(Lat., *Colinus*, from French *colin*, quail; *virginianus*, of Virginia.)

LOCAL NAMES: Partridge; Quail.

DESCRIPTION: Length 8.00 to 10.50 inches. Tail short; bill stubby. *Male.* Above reddish brown mottled with black, white, and buff; throat and stripe above eye, white; band on upper breast black; rest of lower parts buffy white, narrowly barred with black. *Female.* Similar to the male, but throat and stripe over eye buff.

RANGE: Resident and breeds north to central North Dakota and southwestern Maine; south to southeastern Texas and northern Florida.

STATUS IN S. C.: Common permanent resident in all parts of the State. Observed north to Spartanburg, Chester, and Darlington counties; east to Horry County; south to Jasper County; west to Oconee County.

HISTORY: This familiar bird, a favorite with practically everybody, hardly seems to need description. Even the city dweller knows the clear, mellow whistle which so plainly says the name by which it is known. The Bobwhite is no respecter of city limits and often turns up in the most unexpected places—vacant lots, parks, even streets and large gardens. It is a permanent resident in virtually every part of South Carolina but is most abundant in the coast region. There, great plantations are maintained for the sport afforded by these highly regarded game birds. Some of these estates support as many as one hundred and fifty coveys of these birds, the hunting of which is carefully and systematically managed.

The name "Bobwhite" is the correct one for the South Carolina bird, though it is often called "quail," "partridge," or even "Bobwhite quail." Northern sportsmen introduced the name "quail" into the South. The Bobwhite, however, should be distinguished from other American species which are properly called quails, and from the Old World quails and partridges which belong to groups distinctly different from Bobwhites.

In an effort to increase its numbers, birds have been imported to some of the plantations from Mexico and Texas, these being of a geographical race called the Texas Bobwhite. Such individuals never do well and are great wanderers; some have been shot only three or four days after liberation, many miles from where they were set free. Native birds are highly sedentary. Specimens brought in from places like Mississippi and Tennessee are found to be more nearly like the Carolina birds in that they do not wander widely.

The Bobwhite is a late nester, full sets of eggs usually being completed during the last ten days in May. The nest is always on the ground, often arched over with grasses, in brushy fields and under fences or hedgerows. There may be as many as a dozen to twenty eggs in a single nest. E. J. DeCamps of Beaufort, once found a nest in Colleton County containing twenty-four eggs. The eggs are sharply pointed at one end and rounded on the other, so that they fit snugly into the depressed nest, and can be covered by the small-bodied bird. They are pure white though frequently nest-stained. They average 30.0 x 24.0 millimeters. The incubation period is about twenty-three or twenty-four days.

The nesting season is very long because the Bobwhite has many enemies and natural mortality is high. Dogs, cats, foxes, snakes, rats, and men take the eggs whenever they are found, and the birds must lay again and again in order to raise a brood. This doubtless led Audubon to say that the Bobwhite raises two broods in South Carolina. Wayne (1910) states that he found some very young birds during the second week in November.

DeSaussure Dehon reported three half-grown chicks seen near Summerville, April 27, 1941, an exceptionally early date. At the other extreme, W. P. Baldwin saw some young that could have been only a few days old, near McClellanville, September 7, 1940, and G. R. Lunz, Jr., found a Bobwhite incubating twelve eggs on October 5, 1944, at Estherville Plantation, Georgetown County. The chicks are attractive little creatures, clothed in down. They are adept at keeping still and avoiding observation.

Few people who have spent any time in the field can have failed at some time to flush a covey of these fascinating birds and to experience the sudden thunder of rising wings and the scattering of small, brown bodies like the parts of a dis-integrating bomb. The sport of shooting this famous game species is generations old and claims many enthusiastic adherents. Readers who would have further details about the Bobwhite are referred to Herbert L. Stoddard's, *The Bobwhite Quail,* a work which sets forth practically everything known about the bird by a man who knows it better than anyone else.

FOOD: The Bobwhite is of high value to agriculture, as every thinking farmer knows. Analysis of nearly a thousand stomachs by the U. S. Fish and Wildlife Service showed vegetable matter as 83 per cent of the total food, and animal matter 17 per cent. Weed seeds, grain, berries, and fruit are among the vegetable content; grasshoppers, boll weevils, army worms, tobacco worms, cutworms, potato beetles, cucumber and squash beetles, were among the insects. A glance at such a list will at once reveal the value of the Bobwhite to agriculture.

Family *Meleagrididae:* Turkeys

EASTERN TURKEY
109. *Meleagris gallopavo silvestris* Vieillot (310a)

(Lat., *Meleagris*, a guinea-fowl; *gallopavo*, from *gallus*, a cock, *pavo*, pea-fowl; *silvestris*, of woodland.)

LOCAL NAMES: Wild Turkey.

DESCRIPTION: Length, male, 48.00 to 50.00 inches; female, about 36.00 inches. Like the domestic turkey, but more stream-lined and slender; tip of tail and upper tail coverts chestnut instead of white; the bare head more bluish.

RANGE: Resident and breeds north formerly to southeastern South Dakota and Maine; south to southeastern Texas and northern Florida. Now extirpated in much of its former range.

STATUS IN S. C.: Uncommon but local permanent resident throughout the State though more frequent in the coast region. Recorded north to Greenville, Chester, and Florence counties; east to Horry County; south to Hilton Head Island; west to Aiken and Oconee counties.

HISTORY: The Eastern Turkey is the king of American game birds. Its great size, beautiful color, and imposing carriage all combine to make it a regal creature. Alarm is felt for its safety today, for its numbers have sadly decreased with the passing years, but with reasonable conservation there is no reason why it should not live on indefinitely in the swamps and woodlands.

Once occurring from the mountains to the sea, it is much reduced in range now and it lives mainly in the coastal area. The great plantations, many maintained by northern sportsmen, have given it refuge, in spite of poaching. On the Cape Romain Refuge it is completely protected and there will probably always be Wild Turkeys on Bull's Island. A part of the Francis Marion National Forest has very recently been set aside as a refuge for this bird particularly and with good patrol and management will go far toward insuring its perpetuation.

The Turkey is, of course, a forest bird and is at home in rather heavy woods, often bordering large swamps. It occurs on some of the heavily wooded barrier islands where it comes out into the comparatively open area between the sea dunes and the forest, feeding among the wax myrtles and the sea oats which crown the dunes. Bull's Island is one spot where one can be virtually certain of seeing a Wild Turkey during the course of a day afield.

TURKEYS

The Turkey is a ground nesting bird and therefore open to attack by such predatory animals as foxes, raccoons, wildcats, and the semi-wild hogs of the Low Country. The myriad ticks which infest many localities are serious enemies also. But of all its enemies man is the greatest, and in season and out of it, many birds are shot annually. Calling them by imitation of the gobbling of the cock is not difficult, and many are lured to destruction by such means as well as by illegal baiting.

The Eastern Turkey differs from the barnyard fowl by being much more alert and vigorous, slenderer, longer-legged, and with a brilliant metallic bronze shade of plumage for which it is famous. The ends of the tail feathers are a rich chestnut rather than white like those of the tame turkey, and both gobbler and hen wear the "beard," coarse, hair-like tufts which protrude from the breast, much more developed in the cock.

The nest is usually placed at the foot of a forest tree or by a log or on the barrier islands, in open situations such as the sides of grass-grown banks and dams. It is simply a depression in the soil, lined with leaves or grass. The eggs usually number from eight to fifteen. They are whitish or light buff with numerous small, reddish spots. They average 62.6 x 44.6 millimeters. The period of incubation is twenty-eight days, and only one brood is raised.

The range of laying is rather wide and varies with forward or backward seasons. Wayne (1910) lists "an exceptionally early date" as March 30, a date on which he found fifteen eggs already under incubation. Mid-April is a more normal time, and yet eggs have been found as late as May 22. W. P. Baldwin reports nests on Bull's Island on April 26 with six and thirteen eggs and a hen with eight chicks about four days old on May 11. J. F. Ariza found nine eggs on Hilton Head Island, Beaufort County, May 5, and E. J. DeCamps took seven eggs near Beaufort on May 22.

There have been very few reports of nesting in the interior. As a matter of fact, the interior parts of the State contain very few wild turkeys. Reports from Clemson College note observations at Jocassee, March 7, 1927, and at the old C. C. C. camp in Oconee County on April 25, 1937.

From time to time discussion arises about the weights of gobblers. The best information is that the maximum weight of an entirely wild male bird is 40 pounds; but Henry E. Davis records in his excellent work *The American Wild Turkey*, a gobbler, reared in captivity from an egg laid in the wild, which actually weighed 47 pounds at the time of its accidental death. There are authentic records of wild birds killed in South Carolina weighing 22½ pounds.

Food: Seeds, grain, acorns, and insects make up much of the diet. At times, acorns amount to as much as 60 per cent of the total. A good deal depends on the type of range, but mast is a staple item. Turkeys eat quantities of wax myrtle berries, with some poison ivy, black gum, greenbrier, and huckleberries. It is hardly necessary to comment on the value of the turkey as a table bird.

Order Gruiformes
Cranes, Rails, and Allies

Family Gruidae: Cranes

110. WHOOPING CRANE: *Grus americana* (Linnaeus) (204)

(Lat., *Grus*, a crane; *americana*, of America.)

DESCRIPTION: Length 49.00 to 56.00 inches. Legs and neck very long. *Adult*. Plumage pure white, with black wing tips; fore part of head bare, bright red. *Immature*. Similar to the adult, but many feathers marked with ochraceous.

RANGE: Bred formerly north to southern Mackenzie and northern Manitoba; south to Nebraska and Iowa, now extirpated from much of its former breeding range. Winters north to Texas and southern Georgia; south to southern Florida.

STATUS IN S. C.: Accidental in coastal area. Recorded north to the Waccamaw River; south to Charleston.

HISTORY: The Whooping Crane, one of the largest American birds, is on the verge of extinction. It once occurred in multitudes, but it has been reduced in numbers and is rapidly approaching the vanishing point and seems about to parallel the sad history of the Passenger Pigeon. A joint effort of the National Audubon Society and the U. S. Fish and Wildlife Service is now under way to save what few remain and to build up the pitifully small population, which has been accurately checked as twenty-nine individuals at the last report from the Texas wintering grounds (1947-48). Aerial search of its former breeding range during the seasons of 1947 and 1948 failed to reveal any birds.

PLATE XI: RICE FIELD SCENE

Water Color by Roger Tory Peterson

Flying: Wilson's Snipe. Left center: Woodcock. Foreground, left to right: Pectoral Sandpiper, Killdeer, Greater Yellow-legs, and Solitary Sandpiper.

Roger Tory Peterson—

Always a bird of the great open spaces and normally a species of the West and Midwest, it strayed to the East in many localities years ago. It occurred in South Carolina in colonial days and up to about one hundred years ago. A specimen was taken on the Waccamaw River about 1850 which was in the Charleston Museum when Wayne wrote of it in 1910. Audubon refers to a bird kept in captivity by Simon Magwood, near Charleston. These are the only two records we know of in the last century.

The Whooping Crane is a giant among birds, standing almost 5 feet high, with pure white plumage and black wing-tips, the top of the bare head being bright red.

LITTLE BROWN CRANE
111. *Grus canadensis canadensis* (Linnaeus) (205)

(Lat., *canadensis*, of Canada.)

DESCRIPTION: Length 33.00 to 39.00 inches. Neck and legs very long. Plumage mainly gray; the forepart of the bare head red.

RANGE: Breeds north to northeastern Siberia and Baffin Island; south to southern Alaska and Southampton Island. Winters north to central California and Texas; south to Mexico.

STATUS IN S. C.: Accidental in Charleston County.

HISTORY: There is but one record for the Little Brown Crane in South Carolina, that being a specimen secured by Wayne near Mt. Pleasant, October 21, 1890. It was originally recorded as a Sandhill Crane (*Auk, 8*: 1891, 308) but the error was corrected in a later issue of that journal (*Auk, 11*: 1894, 324). It was then only the second record for the Atlantic seaboard and remains the sole instance of its occurrence in this State. The mounted bird is now in the collection of the Charleston Museum (No. 226), and Wayne's identification has recently been corroborated by Dr. Harry C. Oberholser.

112. SANDHILL CRANE: *Grus canadensis tabida* (Peters) (206)

(Lat., *tabida*, wasting away, that is, becoming scarcer.)

LOCAL NAMES: Kronky; Whooping Crane.

DESCRIPTION: Length 40.00 to 48.00 inches. Largely gray with bare forepart of head red.

RANGE: Breeds north to British Columbia and Manitoba; south to California and northern Ohio (formerly). Winters north to central California and Texas; south to Mexico.

STATUS IN S. C.: Casual in the eastern and southern parts of the State. Recorded from Georgetown and Aiken counties.

HISTORY: A specimen of the Sandhill Crane was taken at Rice Hope Plantation on the North Santee River on December 19, 1941, and because of its rarity sent to the Charleston Museum, where it has been examined by Dr. Harry C. Oberholser. On November 23, 1928, one of these birds was seen at Hasty Point Plantation, Georgetown County, by Dr. R. C. Murphy (*Auk, 46*: 1929, 248). Dr. E. E. Murphey (1937) saw two at close range in the Aiken-Augusta region in May, 1894.

It is probable that the Sandhill Crane occurred in South Carolina much more frequently in former times than it does today. Unfortunately, only one specimen appears to be now extant. Since this individual is the true Sandhill Crane it is probable that the other records from the State are of the same subspecies. The conclusion is strengthened by the fact that there is now no proof that the Florida Crane (*G. c. pratensis*) occurs in South Carolina, though its occurrence here is not inherently improbable, since it breeds no farther away than the Okefinokee Swamp in southern Georgia.

Because the Sandhill Crane and the Florida Crane are so similar in appearance, it is difficult to distinguish between them in the field.

Family Aramidae: Limpkins

113. LIMPKIN: *Aramus guarauna pictus* (Meyer) (207)

(*Aramus*, derivation undetermined; *guarauna*, Brazilian name of the bird; Lat., *pictus*, painted.)

DESCRIPTION: Length 25.00 to 28.00 inches. A rather long-legged, long-necked marsh bird. Plumage dark brown streaked with white both above and below.

RANGE: Resident and breeds north to northwestern Florida and southeastern Georgia; south to the Isle of Pines and Jamaica.

STATUS IN S. C.: Casual in the eastern and southern sections. Recorded north to Georgetown County; west to Aiken County.

HISTORY: This strange tropical bird is at home in the United States only in certain fresh-water marshes of Florida and southeastern Georgia. It is one of the most peculiar of our birds, combining characteristics of the rails and the cranes.

The inclusion of the Limpkin among South Carolina birds rests on the capture of three birds and the observation of another. These were all stragglers from the south. Wayne (1910) mentions the three secured specimens, two taken in Aiken County, in October, 1890, and one killed in a yard on Water Street in Charleston in July, 1904. A single bird was seen in the rice fields of Hasty Point Plantation, Georgetown County, November 23, 1928, by the late Dr. Frank M. Chapman. One of the Aiken specimens, taken by W. H. Twiggs, is in the Charleston Museum collection, in addition to the Water Street bird.

The Limpkin is unmistakable in its brown and white-flecked plumage. Its astonishing cry is something never to be forgotten. Such local Florida names as "Crying-bird" and "Niggerboy" are indicative of its character. The bird has a habit of incessantly jerking its tail, and its name arises from the gait, which is very loose-jointed and limping. It subsists largely on a species of fresh-water snail (*Pomacea caliginosus*), which is not known to occur north of the Altamaha River in central Georgia.

Family Rallidae: Rails, Gallinules, and Coots

114. KING RAIL: *Rallus elegans elegans* Audubon (208)

(Lat., *Rallus*, a rail; *elegans*, elegant.)

LOCAL NAMES: Fresh-water Marsh Hen; Indian Pullet.

DESCRIPTION: Length 15.00 to 19.00 inches. Above olive brown heavily streaked with black; eyebrow stripe and throat brownish white; breast, belly, and sides of neck reddish brown; flanks barred with white and dark brown; wing coverts chestnut.

RANGE: Breeds north to eastern Nebraska, southern Minnesota, and Connecticut; south to Texas and southern Florida. Winters north to southern Wisconsin (formerly) and central New York (casually); south to Vera Cruz (Mexico) and southern Florida.

STATUS IN S. C.: Fairly common permanent resident over most of the State. Known north to Greenville County; east to Georgetown County; south to Beaufort County; west to Oconee County.

HISTORY: The King Rail, which is the largest of the South Carolina rails, is a very handsome bird. It is a permanent resident and breeds regularly in South Carolina. Though not so well known as its salt-water relative, the Clapper Rail, because of the popularity of the latter as a game bird, it is an easy rail to know, if this can be said of any rail. As a family, rails are so secretive, so adept at skulking among grasses and reeds, and so disinclined to flight that they are difficult to study to advantage.

It is true of all rails that they are much more apt to be heard than seen. The King Rail voices its "bup-bup-bup" from a home of cat-tails, rushes, and aquatic growth in fresh-water situations, rarely being seen in the salt marshes except during the migrations. Now and then, however, one may be seen picking here and there on a muddy spot, unobstructed by growth, and at such times the brown and white barred flanks and bright reddish breast show to good advantage.

Nesting usually takes place in the early part of May; full sets of a dozen eggs appear by the sixth of the month. A very early record was established on March 22, 1913, when Francis Porcher found a brood of ten young at Oakland Plantation, Christ Church Parish. The eggs must have been laid about the middle of February, an extraordinarily early date. A mid-State breeding date is April 9, 1909, when B. F. Taylor found a nest with eggs near Columbia. More typical dates are nests found by F. W. Hahn at Greenwood on May 14, 1924, and May 2, 1926.

The nest is a shallow platform of grasses, attached to the stems of aquatic plants, and the eggs vary in number, eight to eleven being most common. They are a warm buff color, speckled with brownish markings and average 41.0 x 30.0 millimeters. Incubation requires fourteen days. The young, which are covered with black down, are able to leave the nest almost at once. Occasionally an adult and brood may be seen crossing a road or open space, making an attractive picture of a wildlife family.

During spring and fall, the King Rail now and then appears in salt marshes, or even in the streets of towns and cities where it has doubtless become confused by lights in its migratory journey.

FOOD: Very largely animal matter. Small fish, crabs, crayfish, frogs, beetles, weevils, and grasshoppers have been found in the stomachs. Vegetable food consists of grains, mostly oats.

NORTHERN CLAPPER RAIL
115. *Rallus longirostris crepitans* Gmelin   (211)

(Lat., *longirostris*, long-billed; *crepitans*, clattering.)

LOCAL NAMES: Marsh Hen; Salt-water Marsh Hen; Mud Hen.

DESCRIPTION: Similar to Wayne's Clapper Rail but larger (13.00 to 16.00 inches), lighter, more brownish, particularly on the upper parts and flanks.

RANGE: Breeds in the salt-water marshes of the Atlantic Coast north to Connecticut; south to North Carolina. Winters north to southern Massachusetts (casually); south to northern Florida.

STATUS IN S. C.: Common winter resident, September 9 to March 15, casually June 8, in the coast region. Recorded north to Bull's Island; south to Beaufort County.

HISTORY: This subspecies augments the resident population of the Wayne's Clapper Rail in winter, so that at that season the birds are abundant. The earliest definite record for South Carolina is September 9, 1943, when A. R. Phillips secured a specimen on the front beach of Bull's Island.

The Northern Clapper Rail is hunted along with Wayne's Clapper Rail during the fall. In typical birds the differences between the two are easily seen, but it must be pointed out that intermediates occur between the races, and such individuals may be difficult to identify with certainty.

In habits, nesting, and food the two races do not vary to any extent.

WAYNE'S CLAPPER RAIL
116. *Rallus longirostris waynei* Brewster   (211c)

(Lat., *waynei*, to Arthur T. Wayne.)

DESCRIPTION: Length 12.00 to 14.00 inches. Upper parts dark brown, the feathers margined with grayish olive; wing coverts brown; lower surface grayish buff; the flanks barred with black and white. Plumage darker than that of the Northern Clapper Rail.

RANGE: Resident and breeds north to the coast of North Carolina; south to the coast of central eastern Florida.

STATUS IN S. C.: Abundant permanent resident in the salt marshes of the coast region. Recorded north to Murrells Inlet (Georgetown County); south to Beaufort County.

HISTORY: To any South Carolina coast dweller familiar with bird life, and to many who are not, this is a well-known bird though probably not by its correct name. "Clapper Rail" may elicit only a blank stare, but "Marsh Hen" produces instant understanding. It is the characteristic bird of the salt marshes, where it lives amid the thickly growing stems of the marsh grass (*Spartina alterniflora*).

It is hunted assiduously every fall and killed by the thousands, yet it persists in relatively large numbers up to and within the very corporate limits of towns and cities. Not the least remarkable thing about this bird is its amazing ability to reproduce itself and withstand the heavy inroads upon its population by man and nature. Illustrative of the species' ability to survive natural catastrophes is the fact that, though A. H. DuPre and W. P. Baldwin, of the U. S. Fish and Wildlife Service, estimated that fifteen thousand were killed on the South Carolina coast by the hurricane of August 11, 1940, they soon returned to their normal numbers.

The Clapper Rail is a permanent resident but lives strictly in salt water. The Latin name of the Northern Clapper Rail, *crepitans*, means clattering, and nothing could be more appropriate, for its notes resound through the marshes day and night. Usually rather quiet at high water, it is anything but quiet when the tide falls. There is hardly an hour of daylight or darkness in which the bird cannot be heard. Any sudden noise such as a shout, the clapping of the hands, or a boat whistle is enough to set off the clamorous, clacking chorus which is taken up by one bird after another until the marshes ring.

Nesting begins in the middle or latter part of March, sometimes not until April. A typical date is April 11, when Sprunt found a new made nest. On the sixteenth it held three eggs, on the twenty-third, six eggs. Two nests found in the Wappoo marshes, Charleston County, April 16, each held seven eggs by the twenty-fifth. An early breeding date is April 14, 1948, when E. B. Chamberlain, Jr., saw an adult with three or four downy young, near Charleston. The nests are depressed platforms of sedge and grass, attached to the stems of the marsh, a few inches to a foot or two above water. The eggs vary in number, but nine to twelve is usual. They are creamy buff, marked with brown and lilac spots. They measure 41.5 x 29.1 millimeters, and incubation requires about fourteen days. The young are attractive little creatures, covered with jet-black down, as are all young rails; they are able to leave the nest soon after hatching.

High tides and storms frequently destroy the eggs, and crows, minks, crabs, and other natural enemies take a heavy toll. The birds raise two broods and will lay again and again if the eggs are lost. Thus the season is often greatly prolonged. The shooting season is in the fall (September to November) at the time of the "spring" tides. Boats are poled through the marsh at high water, the birds flushing in front and making a target that few hunters miss. It is astonishing how the rails can stand the annual slaughter, for bag limits are frequently ignored by unscrupulous hunters who gather in as many as seventy-five to one hundred birds.

Wayne's Clapper Rail becomes very tame when unmolested, particularly in late summer.

Probably the outstanding characteristic of the bird is its voice; and the wide variety of clacks, grunts, groans, and shrieks which it emits is remarkable. There is one high, grating call which may be given by a bird for fifteen or twenty minutes at a time, repeated with monotonous regularity. The flesh is excellent on the table but its preparation must be well understood to eliminate a fishy flavor. A well cooked "marsh hen" prepared by a Low-country Negro has no peer among the game birds.

FOOD: Largely animal matter, such as crabs, small minnows, shrimp, fiddlers, and marsh insects. It also eats a few marine worms.

117. VIRGINIA RAIL: *Rallus limicola limicola* Vieillot (212)

(Lat., *limicola*, mud-dweller.)

DESCRIPTION: Length 8.00 to 11.00 inches. Above olive brown, streaked with black; under parts cinnamon, the flanks brown barred with white.

RANGE: Breeds north to southern British Columbia and Nova Scotia; south to Yucatan and North Carolina. Winters north to southern British Columbia and Massachusetts (casually); south to Guatemala and southern Florida.

STATUS IN S. C.: Fairly common winter resident, August 8 to April 5, in most of the State, but more frequent in the coast region. Reported north to Chester County; east to Horry County; south to Beaufort County; west to Greenwood County.

HISTORY: This medium-sized rail might almost be called a miniature edition of the King Rail. The two species are very similarly marked. The Virginia Rail is not as shy as most of the family and can be seen with some frequency if one hunts for it. It lives both in salt-water marshes and fresh-water swamps but feeds in the open where it can be easily seen.

It arrives early, sometimes in August, and is present until early April. Many are to be seen in suitable localities in winter. Some people believe that it nests in South Carolina, but no supporting evidence has been discovered. The bird is not even present during the nesting season. Like other members of the family, it appears in populated areas during migration, and often excites comment and wonder among those who are unfamiliar with birds.

The deep, weird, guttural notes have been described as "cutta-cutta".

FOOD: A mixture of animal and vegetable matter, consisting mostly of seeds, berries, and insects, with some snails and small crustacea.

118. SORA: *Porzana carolina* (Linnaeus) (214)

(*Porzana*, an Italian name; Lat., *carolina*, to Carolina.)

LOCAL NAMES: Carolina Rail; Ortolan; Railbird; Coot.

DESCRIPTION: Length 8.00 to 10.00 inches. Bill short and rather stout. *Adult*. Above olive brown, streaked with black; below gray, the sides and flanks barred with white and brownish olive; a black patch on the face and throat; beak yellow. *Immature*. Similar to the adult but lacks the black on face and throat.

RANGE: Breeds north to central British Columbia, southern Mackenzie, and southeastern Quebec; south to northern Lower California and Maryland. Winters north to central California, South Carolina, and Bermuda; south to Peru and Brazil.

STATUS IN S. C.: Fairly common winter resident, August 14 to May 14, over most of the State, though more numerous coastwise. Observed north to Chester County; east to Horry County; south to Beaufort County; west to Oconee County.

HISTORY: This little rail is seen more often in the open than are the other species of rails. It is an excellent skulker, however, and its habitat makes it hard to study. During freshets, many of the birds are forced out of grassy retreats and are then easily seen and secured, for it is a game species.

Although most of the literature states that the Sora winters from Florida southward, such statements need revision so far as South Carolina is concerned, for the Sora occurs in this State throughout the winter in considerable numbers. It is more apt to be seen in migration, of course, and Wayne (1910) considered it a transient visitor, since he failed to observe it after November 10. Wayne states, however, that it arrives very early in spring and gives March 4 as his earliest observation date.

Since the appearance of Wayne's book, it has been definitely established that the Sora winters locally. Some records may be of interest as typical. T. G. Samworth found this bird at his plantation in Georgetown County on December 18 and 23, 1943. Sprunt saw one at Cotton Hall, Beaufort County, on February 4, 1933. Several were seen on the South Edisto River by Wilcox Brown and Chamberlain on December 23, 1931. One was shot by E. Milby Burton at Edisto Island on December 19, 1937. Murphey (1937) records it in every month from September into April in the Aiken-Augusta region. It is present on some of the barrier islands every winter, notably Bull's Island. It has been noted on several of the Christmas Bird Counts.

The Sora occurs in both fresh- and salt-water marshes. For some inscrutable reason it carries the local name of "Coot." There is not the remotest resemblance between the Sora and the real Coot, and to account for such a term in connection with it is impossible.

FOOD: Largely seeds, snails, and insects. It also eats small mollusks and it appears fond of the seeds of wild rice (*Zizania*), which render it very fat and therefore desirable as food, despite its very small size.

YELLOW RAIL
119. *Coturnicops noveboracensis noveboracensis* (Gmelin) (215)

(Lat. and Gr., *Coturnicops*, face of a quail; Lat., *noveboracensis*, of New York.)

DESCRIPTION: Length 6.00 to 8.00 inches. Above black, the feathers margined with buff and barred with white; a white patch on each wing; lower surface ochraceous to white; the sides dark brown barred with white.

RANGE: Breeds north to southern Mackenzie and Nova Scotia; south to central California and Ohio. Winters north to Oregon and Rhode Island (casually); south to southern California and southern Florida.

STATUS IN S. C.: Rare winter resident, October 15 to March 21, throughout the State. Reported north to Chester County; east to Charleston County; south to Beaufort County; west to Greenwood County.

HISTORY: This little rail, in spite of its extensive range, which embraces much of Canada and of the United States, is one of the least known birds of the country. Many experienced ornithologists have never seen it, even though they have lived in its range all their lives and done much field work. It is about as easy to find in the grasses of its home as a mouse.

In its habits the Yellow Rail is much more like a small mammal than a bird. It slips silently through the grasses like a phantom, barely keeping out of the way of one's feet. The observer may be within inches of the birds and yet never catch a glimpse of them.

The Yellow Rail is a handsome bird in its mottled buffs, blacks, and whites, and it blends wonderfully with the light and shadow of the grass. The only real chance of seeing it, other than by sheer accident, is to employ the services of a good bird dog. Wayne (1910) did not have much trouble finding this secretive bird, for he had a well-trained hound which was very adept at seizing the bird from the grasses. The bird lies very close, and will only flush when absolutely obliged to. Occasionally during migration it flies into lighthouses, buildings, or street lights, and appears in the most unlikely situations. The flight is typically rail-like, apparently very weak and ineffective, but the bird accomplishes tremendous distances none the less.

FOOD: As might be supposed, little is really known regarding the diet of this elusive bird. However, it has been established that it seems fond of small, fresh-water snails and certain insects.

BLACK RAIL
120. *Laterallus jamaicensis pygmaeus* (Blackwell) (216)

(Lat., *Laterallus*, a broad, or distinguished, rail; *jamaicensis*, of Jamaica; *pygmaeus*, pygmy.)

DESCRIPTION: Length 5.00 to 6.00 inches. Bill short and rather stout. Head, neck, and under parts slate color, blackish on the crown; back brown, neck and back black with many fine white flecks. Posterior lower parts barred with white.

RANGE: Breeds north to east central Minnesota and Massachusetts; south to Kansas and northern Florida. Winters north to Louisiana and southern Georgia; south to Guatemala.

STATUS IN S. C.: Rare summer resident, March 31 to October 6, over much of the State. Reported north to Chester County; east to Charleston County; south to Beaufort County; west to Aiken County.

HISTORY: The Black Rail is the smallest of the South Carolina rails, and everything that has been said about the Yellow Rail can be repeated for this one. Little known, little seen, no bird is more secretive or harder to find. It is not as large as some of the warblers.

Although known to be a summer resident in South Carolina, it is difficult to state with any accuracy the status of the Black Rail in terms of population figures.

The Black Rail differs from the other members of its family in choice of habitat, in that it prefers dry fields to the low, wet marshes and swamps which the others delight in. Hayfields and patches of grain such as oats are good places in which to look for Black Rails. Harvest time is best, when the reaper is working, for as the area of standing grain is diminished, the possible cover is reduced and as it is narrowed down to a small circle, the Black Rails which may have retreated thither will be flushed as the last stand is levelled. The actual nesting of the Black Rail in South Carolina is represented by one instance. The nest was found by a Negro boy and reported to Wayne, whose account is fully set forth in his *Birds of South Carolina*, 1910: 39-40. The nest was located in an oat field on Oakland Plantation,

White Ibises Resting   S. A. GRIMES

The Widely-known Mallard

Female Gadwall

Cruising Baldpate

Charleston County, and contained eight eggs which were near hatching. It is of further interest to note that the field was being cut, and, Wayne writes, "It seems almost miraculous that none of the eggs were injured, as the hoof-prints . . . were all around the nest and one had actually lifted the nest from the ground, but despite the fact that a huge mowing machine, drawn by three mules, had passed over the nest twice and cut the stubble close above it, not an egg was broken."

The eggs usually number six to ten; they are creamy white, much speckled with reddish brown and lilac markings, and average 25.6 x 19.8 millimeters. Incubation requires twelve to fourteen days.

Little is known about the Black Rail's food, which probably consists of insects and seeds.

121. PURPLE GALLINULE: *Porphyrula martinica* (Linnaeus) (218)

(*Porphyrula*, a diminutive of *Porphyrio*, Old World gallinule, or reedhen; Lat., *martinica*, of Martinique.)

LOCAL NAMES: Bluepeter; Pondchicken; Marsh Hen.

DESCRIPTION: Length 12.00 to 14.00 inches. *Adult*. Head, neck, and anterior lower parts dark purplish blue; back olive green; wings greenish blue; under tail coverts white; bill carmine tipped with yellow; frontal plate blue; legs yellow. *Immature*. Brown above; under parts varied with lighter brown and white.

RANGE: Breeds north to southeastern Texas and South Carolina; south to Mexico and Argentina. Winters north to southern Texas, northern Florida, and casually South Carolina; south to Argentina.

STATUS IN S. C.: Fairly common, though local, summer resident, April 10 to October; casual in winter; occurs only in the southern part, mostly in the coast region. Recorded north and west to Aiken County; east to the mouth of the Santee River; south to Beaufort County.

HISTORY: If the Florida Gallinule could be considered the commoner of its family, the Purple Gallinule is royalty. One of the most exquisite of water birds, the Purple Gallinule is an aristocrat. Far less abundant and widespread than the Florida Gallinule, it is a regular summer resident of South Carolina and nests in localities frequented by both species.

In South Carolina the Purple Gallinule almost invariably makes its home in an area generously supplied with pickerel weed (*Pontederia cordata*), locally known as "wampee." Few sights in nature can equal in beauty a little flock of these birds swimming and chasing each other about in a cypress lagoon, amid a stand of yellow lotus (*Nelumbo lutea*), which blooms in the Low Country in June. The bright blossoms, standing well up out of the water, the intense green of the leaves and the iridescent, glowing plumage of the birds, combine to make a picture which will stir the admiration of the dullest observer.

Nest building takes place in early May and full sets of eggs are usual by the twenty-first of that month. DeCamps has found them on May 28 and July 1, 1941. The eggs generally number from six to eight, and are very different in appearance from those of the Florida Gallinule, being more elongated and of a pale, cream color with finer markings, almost dots of reddish brown and lilac. They average 39.2 x 28.8 millimeters, and incubation requires twenty-three to twenty-five days.

The nest is a depressed platform of rushes and grass, attached to stems of the wampee or settled into ricks of drifting weed. Some are completely exposed, others are well hidden. It is a habit of this bird to start but not complete one or more nests, for there are nearly always two or three incomplete nests near the one containing the eggs. The season is a prolonged one; Wayne (1910) mentions that a young bird still in downy plumage was sent to him alive on September 17. Wayne expressed the opinion that "the eggs are hatched by the decomposition of the vegetable matter which composes the nest." Certainly it is difficult to find a bird on the nest, unless the bird happens to be laying.

Murphey (1937) calls this species a rare but regular summer resident in the Aiken-Augusta region and says that young of the year have been taken as late as November. Along the coast, most of the birds depart well before cold weather and all are gone by frost. However, one was taken at Mulberry Plantation, Cooper River, on December 12, 1916, by Clarence E. Chapman; this constitutes the only known instance of its occurrence in winter in the State.

Aside from the brilliance of its plumage, the Purple Gallinule may at once be known by the bright yellow legs which dangle conspicuously as it is flushed. One does not always have to go to the cypress backwaters or rice fields to get occasional glimpses of the bird. During migrations, it sometimes appears in strange situations. Sprunt recalls that several years ago, an excited neighbor telephoned him to say that there was a "young peacock" in her garden eating her strawberries. Hastening to the garden, Sprunt found that the peacock was a Purple Gallinule.

Food: In South Carolina this species formerly consumed a great deal of rice in late summer but such diet is now inconsequential. Examination of stomachs from Florida show animal matter to make up 42 per cent of the food; vegetable, 58 per cent.

FLORIDA GALLINULE
122. *Gallinula chloropus cachinnans* Bangs (219)

(Lat., *Gallinula*, little hen; Gr., *chloropus*, green-footed; Lat., *cachinnans*, laughing.)

LOCAL NAMES: Bluepeter; Pondchicken.

DESCRIPTION: Length 12.00 to 15.00 inches. *Adult.* Head, neck, and most of lower parts gray; the flanks with white streaks and a white patch on each side of the tail; bill red tipped with yellow; frontal plate red. *Immature.* Similar to the adult but lighter in color, more brownish, and bill without red.

RANGE: Breeds north to central California and southern Quebec; south to Mexico, Panama, and Florida. Winters north to southern California and central North Carolina; south to Panama.

STATUS IN S. C.: Common permanent resident in the whole State, less numerous in the interior. Observed north to Spartanburg and Chester County; east to Horry County; south to Beaufort County; west to Oconee and Pickens counties.

HISTORY: The Florida Gallinule is practically unknown by that name except to those who make a study of ornithology. Even observers who are acquainted with many land species seem mystified when confronted with the name "Gallinule." This seems strange, for the species is common over much of the country and easy to know. True, it is a water-loving bird, but so are many others that are much better known.

"Pondchicken" is a name often applied to the Florida Gallinule, and the name is not inappropriate, for gallinules do remind one of barnyard chickens gone wild and aquatic. They are well adapted to a watery habitat, the toes being very long and slender, enabling them to walk easily over lily pads and other floating vegetation. They swim well, can dive, and nod the head while swimming. They twitch and jerk their tails frequently, and the astonishing medley of clucks, clacks, grunts, squawks, and shrieks sound like a barnyard gone crazy.

Gallinules are fresh-water dwellers but may be found very close to salt water; they often inhabit ponds on the sea islands, where they congregate with ducks and coots. During the migrations, they appear in utterly incongruous situations such as dry mountain valleys, city boulevards, or dusty fields. In South Carolina this species is a permanent resident, occurring every month. Wayne (1910) considered it less common than the Purple Gallinule, but that is not true today.

Nesting takes place in early May, and is conducted much like that of the Purple Gallinule, the nest being placed in a clump of rushes or grass. But the birds may build their nests also in willows, buttonwood bushes, and even climbing vines, and now and then a dilapidated duck blind. The eggs are numerous, usually ten to a dozen. They are buff colored with many markings of dark brown and black, and average 44.0 x 31.0 millimeters. In a large rice field or a backwater, it is not unusual for a persistent searcher to find as many as half a dozen nests in a morning. Incubation requires about twenty-one days. Two broods may be raised, for fresh eggs were found by Murphey (1937) in August, 1897, and young were seen on August 5, 1934, by E. Milby Burton.

Newly hatched Florida Gallinules are clothed in jet-black down, like the rails, and are attractive little creatures.

In spite of their association with ducks, few Florida Gallinules are killed locally. Most of the duck hunters know the bird well enough to refrain from killing it, though it is an "official" game bird, and is included in the open season listings. Consuming the amount of vegetable food that it does, there is no reason why it should not be a good table bird, but the usual attitude toward it is one of scorn on the part of the sportsman.

Though the Florida Gallinule is not as shy as the rails and comes out into open water readily, it will retreat speedily to the reeds and grasses at the sight of a too-obvious observer. When the bird is swimming on the surface the white streaks of its flanks are very noticeable, as is the red beak of the adult, both marks which aid in differentiating it from the Coot.

FOOD: A combination of animal and vegetable matter. Aquatic plant seeds, univalves, caddis fly larvae, snails, and insects are represented. On the coast it takes the banana water lily (*Castalia flava*) and pondweed (*Potamogeton*).

123. AMERICAN COOT: *Fulica americana americana* Gmelin (221)

(Lat., *Fulica*, coot; *americana*, of America.)

LOCAL NAMES: Bluepeter; Mudhen; Crowbill.

DESCRIPTION: Length 13.00 to 16.00 inches. Head and neck dull black; body slate color, paler beneath; back washed with olive; lateral under tail coverts white; bill white.

RANGE: Breeds north to British Columbia, southern Mackenzie, and New Brunswick; south to Mexico and Panama. Winters north to southern British Columbia and Massachusetts; south to Panama.

STATUS IN S. C.: Permanent resident, fairly common in summer; abundant in winter throughout the State. Reported north to Union and Chester counties; east to Horry County; south to Jasper County; west to Greenwood and Oconee counties.

HISTORY: Because it is one of the most abundant water birds in winter, the Coot need be a stranger to no one. It frequents both fresh and salt water, and during the migrations often is seen far inland. A companion of ducks and gallinules in winter, this species is generally rather despised by hunters and is seldom shot in South Carolina. Its flesh is perfectly acceptable on the table, especially if the bird has fed in the same situations as ducks. The Coot is often mistaken for a duck, but there is no good reason for such confusion. The Coot is easy to identify in the field; the outstanding characteristic is the white beak. No other North American bird except the all-but-extinct Ivory-billed Woodpecker has a white beak, and Coots are not apt to be mistaken for woodpeckers.

The Coot swims with a nodding motion of the head; ducks seldom do this. The feet are lobed or scalloped along the toes; ducks' feet are fully webbed. The Coot's beak is chicken-like, not flattened like a duck's.

The Coot lives in rice fields, backwaters, ponds, lakes, and streams. The universal local name for it is either "Bluepeter" or "Mudhen," and by these it is known to many a country boy. It is unable to take to the air until it has pattered along the surface for a considerable distance. But once on the wing, its flight is strong and fairly rapid, though most people are surprised to hear that it migrates from Canada to Panama. It is much more at home on land than are most ducks, walking strongly about with none of the waddle and awkwardness which is common to ducks. It often "grazes" on shore or on floating masses of vegetation and is a much larger looking bird out of water than in it.

In South Carolina the Coot is a permanent resident, occurring every month of the year. In spite of long and assiduous search by ornithologists, no nest of the bird has as yet been found. The writers have found the Coot in situations ideal for nesting, in the very height of the nesting season, yet for all their efforts they have never discovered any eggs. The nearest evidence yet gathered was the observance, on June 23, 1927, in a rice field of the Ashepoo River, Colleton County, of two half-grown young following an adult. This instance was noted by the late Dr. Charles P. Aimar, of Charleston, and Sprunt. That the young birds had been hatched in the vicinity is, of course, beyond question.

Like gallinules, the Coot has a variety of notes that baffles description. It is very noisy and the marshes and ponds ring to a medley of sound when Coots, ducks, and gallinules utter their various calls. Coots, though they are capable of diving, secure most of their food from the surface and sometimes rob diving ducks of their food as it is brought to the surface.

Food: Mainly vegetable, such as the seeds, roots, and leaves of pondweeds, water milfoil, burweed, smartweed, and banana water lily. It takes wild celery at times from ducks. It also eats small fish, tadpoles, snails, and aquatic insects.

Order Charadriiformes
Shore Birds, Gulls, Auks, and Allies

Family Haematopodidae: Oyster-catchers

AMERICAN OYSTER-CATCHER
124. *Haematopus palliatus palliatus* Temminck (286)

(Gr., *Haematopus,* red-footed; Lat., *palliatus,* wearing a cloak.)

LOCAL NAMES: Oyster Bird.

DESCRIPTION: Length 17.00 to 21.00 inches. Bill long and stout; legs robust. Head and neck black; back and wings dark brown, the latter showing conspicuous white patches in flight; under parts white; bill bright red; legs flesh color.

RANGE: Breeds on the Atlantic coast of the United States north to Virginia; south to the West Indies and Brazil; on the Pacific coast of North America north to Mexico and south to South America. Winters north to southern Virginia; south throughout its breeding range.

STATUS IN S. C.: Permanent resident, fairly common in summer and in winter along the coast. Known north to Winyah Bay entrance; south to Beaufort County.

HISTORY: This species, the aristocrat of the shore bird tribe, is a permanent resident of South Carolina and commonly nests in the State. Curiously enough, however, it occurs in greatest numbers not during the summer but in the winter months. The reason is that most of the birds breeding to the northward of South Carolina, along the North Carolina and Virginia coasts, come to South Carolina in the winter, and probably much of our summer population remains. That the North Carolina birds largely migrate in winter is supported by Pearson and Brimleys (*Birds of North Carolina,* 1942: 124), in noting flocks of as many as 120 birds seen in North Carolina in November, that "Evidently the oyster-catchers had gathered for the long migration trip southward." However appearances would indicate that the trip is not very long after all.

The Cape Romain area is certainly the wintering grounds for the great proportion of this species inhabiting the Atlantic coast, for the Oyster-catcher is now a rare bird in Florida and it is not very common on the coast of Georgia, from Brunswick south. It is believed that a peak population was reached during the winter of 1940, when an estimated fifteen hundred birds were reported for the Cape Romain Refuge. A few years prior to this, the population was set at eight hundred to one thousand.

The Oyster-catcher is another "unmistakable." Whether familiar with it or not, the observer, seeing his first specimen, need have no doubt about the bird he is looking at. It is one of the largest South Carolina shore birds. The striking black and white plumage, brilliant red beak, and flesh-colored legs will identify it at a glance. The large white patches in the wings shine out in flight, and the loud, clear, far-carrying whistle is as diagnostic as the bird's appearance.

The Oyster-catcher usually nests on the ocean beaches, but not necessarily near an inlet. It evidently has a considerable territory, for only a few pairs will inhabit miles of beach, and they usually do not colonize. Breeding begins in April, and varies from early to late in that month. Because high tides sometimes destroy the eggs, the season may be prolonged over many weeks in some years. The birds build no nest but lay the eggs in a depression in the sand amid bits of shell. Wayne states that the bird's eggs "invariably number three," but sometimes only two are laid, and Sprunt has found nests containing but one, these not being added to later. The ground color of the egg is creamy white or buffy white, with many markings of dark brown and lavender, and the eggs are very difficult to see against the background of sand and shell. They average 55.7 x 38.7 millimeters. Incubation requires twenty-four or twenty-five days.

Typical egg dates follow: for Charleston County, April 12, 20, and 30 (Wayne); for Beaufort County, April 19 and 28 (DeCamps). Occasionally, eggs are found in early May or even later in that month though this is probably due to the fact that earlier clutches have been destroyed. Other dates are May 9, 14, 19, and 30 (Sprunt).

In winter the Oyster-catcher changes its semi-solitary habits radically and goes about in large flocks.

At half tide, on the Inland Waterway, scores of Oyster-catchers are often seen at ranges of no more than 50 feet, as the boat slides by the bank on which they stand. Since the establishment of the Cape Romain Refuge the birds have become very tame and their behavior is utterly at variance with their reputation, which Wayne (1910) gave them when he described them as "at all times very shy." At times on the Christmas Bird Count in this region, flocks of three to four hundred are seen.

The species well deserves its name, although it is not much of a feat to catch an oyster. The bird does not pry the shell open but, when it finds a gaping oyster, it plunges the beak between the shells and cuts the adductor muscle, whereupon the shells fall apart and the oyster is easily obtained. Now and then the oyster is the quicker, however, and the shells clamp upon the beak. Held thus as in a vise the bird is drowned by the rising tide. Sprunt knows of at least two instances of this, and W. P. Baldwin has also recorded it (*Auk, 63*: 1946, 589).

Food: Exclusively animal matter. Mollusks, including oysters, clams, and other bivalves, are the usual diet, which is varied by the addition of a few aquatic insects, sea worms, fiddler crabs (*Uca*), and other marsh life. So fond of oysters is the Oyster-catcher that it has been claimed by collectors that by simply holding a bird by its legs and shaking it, oysters will fall from its mouth. The great majority of these shellfish are of the small, irregularly shaped type known as "raccoon oysters."

Family Charadriidae: Plovers, Turnstones, and Surf-birds

125. LAPWING: *Vanellus vanellus* (Linnaeus) (269)

(Lat., *Vanellus*, a little fan; in reference to its winnowing wings.)

DESCRIPTION: Length 11.00 to 13.00 inches. Head with a conspicuous pointed crest; top and front of head, throat, and breast black; sides of head, and of neck together with the hind neck white or gray; rest of the upper parts metallic green or blue; tail white with a black bar near its end; upper and lower tail coverts chestnut; remainder of lower parts white.

RANGE: Breeds north to Finland, northern Russia, and northern Siberia; south to Andalusia, western China, and Transcaspia. Winters north to Great Britain, southern Europe, and Japan; south to the Canary Islands, northern Africa, and India; accidental in eastern North America.

STATUS IN S. C.: Accidental in the coast region.

HISTORY: On Tuesday, December 3, 1940, Bryan Walpole called the Charleston Museum to say that he had just seen a strange bird on John's Island, Charleston County, where he farms. It was said to be in company with several Killdeer, the whole group following closely behind a tractor which was working a field. Knowing it to be a bird he had never before seen, Walpole described it as being approximately the size of the Willet, white below and greenish above, with a dark tail which was basically white. The head was dark and adorned with one or two dark-colored "spiky" feathers, two to three inches long. When the bird was flushed, it revealed a tan color "either in the wings or the hinder part of the body."

Such a description could fit only the Lapwing. Chamberlain went at once to John's Island and met Walpole and W. M. Hamilton, the owner of the field where the bird had been seen. Hamilton corroborated the Walpole description in all particulars. Walpole added that the driver of the tractor had said the bird "looked green as a parrot" and that it had come so close to the machine at times that it could have been killed with a stick.

PLATE XII: SHORE BIRDS ON BEACH

Water Color by Roger Tory Peterson

Flying: two Sanderlings. Alone on upper beach: Wilson's Plover. Group of four birds in left foreground, left to right: Wilson's Plover, Knot (winter plumage), Knot (breeding plumage), and Sanderling. Group of four birds in right foreground, left to right: Red-backed Sandpiper (winter plumage), Red-backed Sandpiper (breeding plumage), and two Semipalmated Sandpipers.

Roger Tory Peterson —

Though Chamberlain hunted the field carefully that afternoon and the next he failed to discover the bird. He later showed Walpole a color plate of the Lapwing in spring plumage, which of course, shows black on the throat. Walpole said at once that in all particulars except the black throat patch the bird in the plate was the one he had seen. Thus, it seems certain that his bird was the Lapwing in winter plumage. Several days later, the same bird or another exactly like it appeared on the John's Island farm of John Andel, who saw and reported it.

The authors have no hesitation in placing this species on the South Carolina List on the evidence just cited.

126. PIPING PLOVER: *Charadrius melodus melodus* Ord (277)

(Lat., *Charadrius*, a plover; *melodus*, musical.)

LOCAL NAMES: Ringneck.

DESCRIPTION: Length 6.00 to 7.75 inches. Forehead, collar about neck, and under parts, white; patches on sides of breast and band across head black; back, and most of wings pale brownish gray; bill orange at base.

RANGE: Breeds on the Atlantic coast of North America north to Nova Scotia; south to North Carolina. Winters north to southern Alabama and the Bermuda Islands; south to Jamaica and the Bahama Islands.

STATUS IN S. C.: Fairly common winter resident, August 2 to May 22, on the coast. Recorded north to Horry County; south to Beaufort County.

HISTORY: This little gray ghost of the sands is a beautiful, ethereal bird, almost a drifting phantom. As if above drab, earthly things, it never soils its feet on mud banks but keeps to the clean, wind-swept beaches of the sea, where it flits ahead of the observer. The whistling call is appealingly mellow and has a peculiar wild quality which brings to mind the tremendous distances of wave-lashed ocean which it navigates so well.

For long, this little plover was considered only a transient in the spring and fall. However, it now appears to be a fairly common winter resident. During 1929, 1930, and 1931, it was seen throughout the entire winter season and specimens were secured at that time. The altered status of this plover in South Carolina has been noted by Sprunt (*Auk*, 47: 1930, 250).

The species is, of course, much more in evidence during the migrations than any other time, and the normal dates of its appearance are from the second week in March to the middle of May in spring, and from August to October, in fall.

The Piping Plovers occur in small flocks or singly, running ahead of the observer on the beach, or flying out over the surf and circling behind to alight again on the sands. They exhibit the thoroughly characteristic habit of the plovers of running a few steps, then stopping suddenly, as if they had encountered some invisible barrier. Though rather a shy bird when approached on foot, the Piping Plover can be seen to wonderful advantage from a car.

Food: Small marine life and beach insects. Locally the Piping Plover eats the butterfly shell (*Donax variabilis*) in numbers. It also feeds upon marine worms, fly larvae, and some beetles.

BELTED PIPING PLOVER
127. *Charadrius melodus circumcinctus* (Ridgway) (277a)

(Lat., *circumcinctus*, surrounded, *i. e.*, belted.)

DESCRIPTION: Similar to the Piping Plover, but black patches on sides of breast united to form a band that is nearly or quite complete though sometimes mixed with white.

RANGE: Breeds north to southern Alberta and the Gulf of St. Lawrence; south to Nebraska and northwestern Pennsylvania. Winters north to southern Louisiana and probably South Carolina; south to southern Texas and southern Alabama.

STATUS IN S. C.: Rare spring transient, April 22 to May 14; probably also a winter resident. Occurs only along the coast.

HISTORY: Thus far there are but two records of the Belted Piping Plover for South Carolina. Both of these records are based on specimens in the Charleston Museum collected by Wayne on Long Island (Isle of Palms), and identified by Dr. Harry C. Oberholser. The dates are May 14, 1907, and April 22, 1922.

In its habits and choice of food the Belted Piping Plover does not materially differ from the Piping Plover.

SEMIPALMATED PLOVER
128. *Charadrius hiaticula semipalmatus* Bonaparte (274)

(Lat., *hiaticula*, diminutive of hiatus, an opening, or gape; *semipalmatus*, half-webbed.)

LOCAL NAMES: Ringneck; Ringneck plover.

DESCRIPTION: Length 6.50 to 8.00 inches. *Summer*. Upper surface hair brown; hind portion of forehead, nucal collar, and under parts white; band across forehead as well as a line from bill to eye black; legs and feet orange yellow. *Winter*. Similar to the summer plumage but the black areas brown like back.

RANGE: Breeds north to northern Alaska and Baffin Bay; south to British Columbia and Nova Scotia. Winters north to central western California and South Carolina; south to Chile and Argentina.

STATUS IN S. C.: Common permanent resident but does not breed; most numerous along the coast. Reported north to Florence County; east to Horry County and Cape Island; south to the Savannah National Wildlife Refuge; west to Aiken County.

HISTORY: While the Semipalmated Plover comes by its rather formidable name rightfully enough, by reason of its half-webbed toes, it would perhaps have been as fully appropriate to give it the name of "Ringneck." It is called that, anyway, and certainly that characteristic is easy to see, whereas the semipalmation of the toes is not.

This species is found throughout the entire year in South Carolina, and is therefore classified as a permanent resident, but it does not breed within a thousand miles or more of the State. This is true of many species of the great shore bird group, represented by an unusual number of immature, unmated, or wandering individuals.

Unlike the Piping Plover, the Semipalmated Plover prefers the mud banks and oyster flats rather than the sea beaches, though it may be seen on the beaches at times. It appears occasionally even in upland fields where rain pools collect, and it is more likely to be seen in the interior than some of its kin. Like all the plovers, it moves about by fits and starts. It is a much darker bird than the Piping Plover, and this, together with the orange-yellow feet and legs and an orange-yellow spot at the base of the bill, will identify it.

During the migrations, great flocks of Semipalmated Plovers pass along the wide, sandy flats of the coastal region. Murphey (1937) found the bird as a regular transient in the Aiken-Augusta region, frequenting mud flats, the margins of clay pits, wet ploughed fields, and river sand bars. They often associate with sandpipers as well as with the larger shore birds; a good feeding flat will at times reveal as many as a dozen species all busily engaged in picking up a living. An excellent observation spot exists within the city limits of Charleston, on the mud flats near the Ashley River Bridge, where as many as fourteen species of shore birds have been seen in an hour, at the right stage of the tide and the right season. This can doubtless be duplicated at Beaufort, McClellanville, Georgetown, and Pawley's Island.

Shore birds, particularly the sandpipers, are notorious for giving the amateur ornithologist headaches from his effort to identify them. But this Plover need cause no such discomfort. A reasonably good view of the bird will reveal its characteristic markings so clearly as to make it unmistakable.

Food: Largely small mollusks, crustaceans, marine organisms, and some insects.

129. Wilson's Plover: *Charadrius wilsonia wilsonia* Ord   (280)

(Lat., *wilsonia*, of [Alexander] Wilson.)

Local Names: Ringneck; Stuttering Plover.

Description: Length 6.50 to 8.00 inches. Bill relatively large and heavy. *Male.* Forehead, line over eye, and lower surface white; front of crown and band across the breast, black; back and wings grayish brown; bill black. *Female.* Similar to the male, but black markings replaced by brown.

Range: Breeds north to the coast of New Jersey; south to Texas and Florida. Winters north to southern Texas and eastern South Carolina.

Status in S. C.: Common summer resident, March 3 to October 17, occasional in winter. Occurs only along the coast. Reported north to Horry County; south to Beaufort County.

History: No summer beach resident who is at all aware of nature can have failed to notice this brown-backed, white-bellied, ring-necked dweller of the dunes. Even in thickly populated resorts, Wilson's Plover still persists, though of course it is much more common where human habitations are scattered. Though ring-necked like the Semipalmated Plover, the two birds need never be confused. The Wilson's Plover is distinctly larger and its oversized, heavy black bill is an excellent field mark. The female is of a duller brown, and her breast band not so well defined as that of the male.

Though it occurs on mud flats, spoil banks, and the sandy strips of marshy waterways, it is predominantly a beach bird and seems to prefer the shores of the inlets between the barrier islands.

Only on rare occasions has Wilson's Plover been observed in winter. Wilcox Brown and Sprunt established the first winter record on the third day of January, 1934, on Big Bay Island (Edisto Beach). The bird was a female. The temperature of the day was 40° F. (*Auk, 51*: 1934, 252).

This Plover nests commonly on the beaches, shelly flats, and even the mainland in suitable localities. On the Inland Waterway, near Wappoo Bridge, there is a sandy flat bordering a heavily traveled road to one of the local beaches. The flat, created by dredging operations, was appropriated almost at once, and has been for three seasons, by Least Terns, Willets, and Wilson's Plovers. Grass is now beginning to cover the area and the birds were not so numerous this season (1948), but until that occurred, nests of all of them could be found within a hundred feet of heavy traffic. A more typical nesting locality, however, is the area on a sea beach above high-water mark.

Wilson's Plover makes no nest but lays the eggs in a slight depression in the sand, which may have a few bits of shell about it. The eggs usually number three, though sometimes only two and ocasionally four, and, like shore bird eggs, they are very large for the size of the bird. They have a buff ground color, and are spotted with numerous small black markings. They are marvels of protective coloration, very difficult to see, even from a distance of a few feet. Laying usually starts in early May, though in forward seasons, eggs can be found in late April. Typical dates: Morris Island, May 11, three eggs; same locality, May 4, three eggs; Wappoo Creek, May 6, three eggs. If the eggs are lost, the birds at once lay again; illustrative of this fact are such dates as June 3, Dewees Island, three eggs each in seventeen nests; June 30, Kiawah Island, three eggs each in two nests; June 6, Folly Island, three eggs each in three nests. The first laying had evidently been lost to high water. On two occasions Sprunt has found eggs of the Least Tern in nests of the Wilson's Plover, and Burton has also noted the same thing. The eggs average 35.7 x 26.2 millimeters. Incubation requires twenty-four or twenty-five days.

A very young bird was banded on July 6, 1931, at Bird Bank, Stono River, by E. Milby Burton. Twenty-eight days later it was captured after much effort. Although it was well feathered, it could not actually fly. On September 22, 1932, this same bird was taken at Rose Hill Village, Berbice, British Guiana.

The young are just as hard to see as the eggs, but if made to move, they do so with great celerity and are hard to catch. They are beautifully clothed in grayish buff down. The parents become frantic when the nest is approached, and their attempts to lead an intruder away by feigning a broken wing are most convincing exhibitions. Fluttering and sprawling over the sand, they appear to be quite hopelessly injured, but always able to stay just out of reach. When a safe distance has been attained, up they spring and circle away.

The note of this Plover is very clear and penetrating, a sort of half whistle, half chirp, as Coues describes it. It is certainly one of the most characteristic sounds of the Low-country beaches in summer. The bird is not shy and can be fairly closely approached, even when not nesting.

FOOD: Wilson's Plover subsists on beach and marsh life in the form of small crabs, shrimp, crayfish, scallops, and other mollusks. Insects figure in the diet also, these being beetles, flies, ants, and occasionally spiders.

130. KILLDEER: *Charadrius vociferus vociferus* Linnaeus   (273)

(Lat., *vociferus*, noisy.)

LOCAL NAMES: Cheweeka.

DESCRIPTION: Length 9.00 to 11.00 inches. Above grayish brown; the rump, upper tail coverts, and base of tail rufous; forehead and lower parts white; two black bands across breast, the upper circling the neck; tail edged with white and with a subterminal black bar.

RANGE: Breeds north to northern British Columbia and southeastern Quebec; south to southern Lower California, Florida, and the Bahama Islands. Winters north to southern British Columbia and southeastern New Hampshire.

STATUS IN S. C.: Common permanent resident over the entire State; rare in summer and occurring on the coast mainly in winter. Known north to Greenville, Spartanburg, Chester, York, and Lancaster counties; east to Horry County; south to Beaufort County; west to Oconee County.

HISTORY: The Killdeer is doubtless the best known of the shore bird family in South Carolina. It is abundant in the coastal area but it occurs also in the interior counties, and every farm boy knows its cry of "Kill-dee-e-e," though he probably calls the bird "Cheweeka."

Distinctly larger than the preceding plovers, the Killdeer may be known at once by the two black bands on its breast. The reddish tan color of the rump shows well when the bird takes flight and is an added confirmation of its identity. Beaches, marshes, and open uplands are the home of the Killdeer, but never wooded areas. It also frequents pools in the barnyard, pond edges, dry fields, and roadsides. The bird is by no means shy about making itself known, and its specific name of *vociferus* is well chosen.

It is a permanent resident of South Carolina, but very local and scarce on the coast in summer in marked contrast to its winter abundance there. Wayne (1910) stated that it does not breed at all on the coast, but since he wrote, it has been found to do so. There are records from Ladies Island, and Frogmore, Beaufort County (W. J. Hoxie); and Charleston County, May 31, 1930, by W. W. Humphreys. G. E. Hudson found downy young in Oconee County on May 25.

The nest is a depression in the open ground, lined with shell, pebbles, or grass and the eggs usually number four, though sets of three and five occur. They are buff colored, heavily speckled with blackish brown. They have very sharp ends, and are placed in the nest with the sharp ends together so that the small-bodied bird can successfully cover them, for they are large in size, averaging 36.3 x 26.6 millimeters.

The birds sometimes nest in extraordinary places: between the ties of railroad tracks, on gravelled driveways, and on the roofs of buildings. Normally, they choose an open field, and lay the eggs between furrows. The incubation period is about twenty-four or twenty-five days.

Like many of its relatives, the Killdeer becomes greatly excited when its nest is endangered and seeks to protect it by feigning injury. It runs well and gracefully, and possesses the plover habit of jerky feeding, running, and stopping. Its flight is rapid and well sustained, often accompanied by the well known cry, which can frequently be heard at night.

FOOD: The Killdeer is probably of greater economic interest than any of the other shore birds. Its wide range over the country makes it very valuable to agriculture, for it consumes many insect pests. Often the bird follows a plow when furrows are being turned, and most farmers are aware of its importance in destroying their insect enemies. Almost 77 per cent of the food is insects. Among these, it has been found that beetles alone compose 37 per cent. Others are grasshoppers, dragon flies, ants, bugs, and caterpillars. Centipedes, spiders, ticks, snails, small marine life, and crustaceans occur in its diet on the coast.

AMERICAN GOLDEN PLOVER
131. *Pluvialis dominica dominica* (Müller) (272)

(Lat., *Pluvialis*, pertaining to rain; *dominica*, of Dominica.)

DESCRIPTION: Length 9.50 to 11.00 inches. Head small and bill slender. *Summer*. Upper surface brownish black, heavily spotted with yellow; the lower parts solid black except for a white patch on each side of the breast and neck extending up over eye to forehead. *Winter*. Upper parts fuscous, spotted with dull white; lower surface pale brownish gray.

RANGE: Breeds north to Melville Island and North Devon Island; south to northern Alaska and northeastern Manitoba. Migrates mainly over the Atlantic Ocean to South America in autumn returning in spring chiefly through the Mississippi Valley. Winters north to Bolivia and Brazil; south to Argentina.

STATUS IN S. C.: Rare transient. In spring, March 16 to May 9; in autumn, September 19 to December, mostly coastwise; occasional in the interior of the State. Reported north to Chester County and Murrell's Inlet; east to Charleston County; south to the mouth of the Savannah River; west to Aiken County.

HISTORY: This handsome plover is one of the rare shore birds of South Carolina. It is a transient visitor only and even during the migrations one cannot expect it with any degree of assurance. Practically everything depends on weather conditions at such times, for the usual southward flight from the Arctic is over the Atlantic Ocean, well out from shore. The fall flight of the Golden Plover stands out as a marvel in the miracle of bird migration for it traverses the longest known regular overwater route followed by any bird in the Atlantic Ocean, though it may occasionally be exceeded by the phenomenal wanderings of the Arctic Tern. Taking off from Newfoundland and Nova Scotia, the Golden Plover flies straight south, making landfall in the West Indies or South America, non-stop. The longest route is as much as 2750 miles over the sea.

Normally, therefore, the Golden Plovers pass South Carolina by, but adverse easterly winds sometimes cause them to appear on this coast. In all of Wayne's work on the coast he took but four specimens. Any records of its occurrence are of more than casual interest: One seen on Ladies Island October 6, 1869 (W. J. Hoxie); one taken September 19, 1877, in Chester County (L. M. Loomis); one taken in December, 1880, near Charleston (Wayne); one taken November 4, 1911, Charleston County (Wayne); two taken November 27, 1912, Charleston County (Wayne); one seen, October 15, 1932, injured leg, Slann's Island, Charleston County (E. A. Simons, Burton, and Sprunt); two seen, one taken, November 19, 1932, James Island, Charleston County (Sprunt); one taken, November 20, 1937, James Island (B. M. Badger, Jr.); one seen, October 9, 1946, Isle of Palms, Charleston County (J. E. Mosimann and G. B. Rabb). Murphey (1937) writing of the Aiken-Augusta region, considered this species formerly a regular but scarce autumnal migrant.

These records all relate to the fall migration. In spring, the Golden Plover returns from South America through the Mississippi Valley, and again only appears on the east coast as a result of abnormal weather or other unusual conditions. Records of it at this time of year are even rarer than in the fall, and are as follows: One seen, April 4, 1931, Sol Legare Island, Charleston County (E. A. Williams and Sprunt); one seen, April 23, 1931, Middleburg Plantation, Berkeley County (E. von S. Dingle); two seen, one taken April 23, 1931, Sol Legare Island (Sprunt); one taken March 16, 1935, Beaufort County (I. R. Tomkins); one seen, May 8 or 9, 1946, Murrell's Inlet, Georgetown County (W. B. Ward).

The Golden Plover can be confused with only the Black-bellied Plover which in spring has a pale gray back and white tail, and in winter black axillars under the wings where they join the body. The Golden Plover lacks these markings.

It frequents field, pond, and marsh edges; it may indeed be encountered anywhere, if it occurs at all, except in wooded areas. It was once shot as a game bird but this practice was stopped years ago by law.

Food: Insects, small marine life such as crustaceans and mollusks, and, in the far north, some vegetable matter such as berries.

BLACK-BELLIED PLOVER
132. *Squatarola squatarola* (Linnaeus) (270)

(*Squatarola*, Venetian name of this species.)

Local Names: Bull-head Plover; Black-breast.

Description: Largest of our plovers; length 10.50 to 15.50 inches. *Summer*. Upper surface with small, broken bars of white, gray, and black. Most of tail, a stripe over eye and down neck from forehead to breast, white; throat and breast black; abdomen white. *Winter*. Upper parts brownish gray, finely marked with white and darker gray; below white marked on neck, breast, and sides with gray.

Range: Breeds north to Wrangel Island and Baffin Island; south to central western Alaska, Southampton Island, and the Arctic coast of Europe and Siberia. Winters north to southern

British Columbia, Virginia, the Mediterranean Sea, and southern Asia; south to Chile, southern Africa, and Australia.

STATUS IN S. C.: Common permanent resident, but does not breed. Occurs chiefly along the coast. Most numerous during migration and in winter; less common in summer. Recorded north to Horry County; south to Beaufort County; west to the Santee Wildlife Refuge.

HISTORY: The Black-bellied Plover is a fine bird. Spectacular, handsome, alert, and musical, it is an aristocrat, a prince of the shore bird tribe. No coast dweller need be in ignorance of it, for it is a permanent resident, though it nests no nearer South Carolina than the Arctic. It is really a world species, for its range extends around the globe.

A Black-bellied Plover in full nuptial plumage is a memorable sight. There is nothing unusual in such an experience for the bird occurs within the city limits of any coastal village, town, or city. The bird is misnamed. It is not black-bellied at all, but black-breasted, the belly being white at all seasons. It is the largest of the South Carolina plovers, and when seen among its lesser kin or with sandpipers or turnstones, it towers like a giant above them. Beaches, mud flats, oyster banks, and at times the coastal fields harbor it, but unlike the Golden Plover and Killdeer, it is not often seen in agricultural country.

Years ago, when the shore birds were lawful game, it was shot in great numbers, for it came readily to decoys and its size made it desirable.

Many authors describe the Black-bellied Plover as a very shy bird, but the writers have never found it more shy than many of its smaller kin. Certainly, in protected areas such as the Cape Romain Refuge, one can easily approach it closely, particularly in boats and often when walking the beach. It is to be seen on the mud flats near the Ashley River Bridge in Charleston, feeding and resting within a few yards of scores of passing motor cars.

To many people, the note of the Black-bellied Plover is the most musical and appealing call of all shore birds. It is a clear, mellow, far-carrying whistle, with a plaintive quality reminiscent of the Bluebird. It has a wild freeness about it which brings to mind the vast reaches of Arctic tundra, the heaving wastes of mighty waters, windy beaches, and sun-drenched marsh. It is as unmistakable as the bird itself, and can often be heard downwind, before the bird appears. It is easily imitated, and effective as a decoy.

Because it is a large bird, the Black-belly strikingly exhibits the typical plover characteristic of sudden starts and stops. It is interesting and amusing to see a flock of a dozen or more feeding on a mud flat, their intermittent stops and runs suggesting the spasmodic moving of checkers on a vast board.

FOOD: The diet of the Black-bellied Plover in South Carolina consists mainly of marine life, largely various crabs, small fish, "fiddlers," and mollusks. It takes a few insects such as fly larvae and grasshoppers, and sometimes roundworms. It is certainly not in the remotest sense detrimental, and its destruction of insects, though not extensive, is beneficial.

RUDDY TURNSTONE
133. *Arenaria interpres morinella* (Linnaeus) (283a)

(Lat., *Arenaria*, pertaining to sand; *interpres*, a go-between; *morinella*, an old name of the turnstone.)

LOCAL NAMES: Calico-back.

DESCRIPTION: Length 7.75 to 10.00 inches. *Summer*. Neck and head white, marked with black; back mixed cinnamon rufous and black; breast black; abdomen and rump white; wings black, marked with cinnamon rufous. *Winter*. Duller than in summer, with little cinnamon rufous.

RANGE: Breeds north to Melville Island (probably) and western Baffin Island; south to northwestern Mackenzie and Southampton Island. Winters north to Texas and South Carolina; south to Brazil.

STATUS IN S. C.: Common permanent resident on the coast, but does not breed; rare in midsummer. Observed north to Horry County; south to Beaufort County.

HISTORY: The Turnstone is unlike any other shore bird. While the red, black, and white summer plumage is the more handsome, even the duller winter dress is contrasting enough to make an impression, and the pied appearance of the bird in flight is an excellent identification character. The Turnstone is an Arctic nester which is to be found the year round in South Carolina; therefore, it must be called a permanent resident, though it does not breed here. The name arises from the habit of turning over pebbles and small stones on rocky shores to get at whatever small marine life lies beneath. During much of the year, locally, it is seen in the winter plumage, which is a sort of washed-out version of the spring splendor.

The Turnstone is a bird of ocean beaches and tidal mud flats, and is one of the least shy of all shore birds, except, perhaps, some of the little "peeps," as the smallest sandpipers are called. It will often alight on the bow of a boat as it winds it way through the marshy creeks. On the barges which carry loads of oysters up and down the Inland Waterway, many of the birds busily walk about the mounds of shellfish, picking among them for food. The bird seems to have considerable curiosity about boats and will frequently circle around one at a few yards range, giving excellent opportunities for observation.

Since there are no rocks along the South Carolina coast, except those which form the jetties at harbor mouths, the Turnstone can not here engage in the occupation which gives it its name, though it does use its bill to turn over shells or other debris along the beaches and marshes. It is fond of breakwaters, and it is to be found on some of the barrier islands where tree trunks which were once part of forest growth now loom starkly as bleached skeletons in the surf, as the result of beach erosion. It is not uncommon to encounter the bird along any waterfront of coastal communities.

Wayne reported taking a specimen of the European form on Dewees Island, May 30, 1918 (*Auk*, 35: 1918, 439). This specimen is now in the collection of the Charleston Museum and has been reidentified by Chamberlain as being a specimen of the Ruddy Turnstone. This identification has been confirmed by Dr. Alexander Wetmore (*Auk*, *53*: 1936, 441).

FOOD: Small crustaceans, mollusks, etc. Bent (1929) says of the birds he watched in South Carolina that they fed on raccoon oyster banks, and chased the fiddler crabs (*Uca*) which abound in the marshes. The Turnstone secures its food by probing in the sand, as well as by turning over shells, sticks, and other material. Turnstones and Sanderlings have been seen digging up the small eggs of the king crab (*Limulus*) from an inch or two beneath the wet sand of the Bull's Island beach.

Family Scolopacidae: Woodcock, Snipe, and Sandpipers

134. AMERICAN WOODCOCK: *Philohela minor* (Gmelin) (228)

(Gr., *Philohela*, bog-loving; Lat., *minor*, smaller.)

DESCRIPTION: Length 10.00 to 12.00 inches. Body very stout; eyes near top of head; bill very long and straight. Upper parts cinnamon, mottled with black, gray, and brown. Lower surface cinnamon.

RANGE: Breeds north to southern Manitoba; south to southeastern Texas and central Florida. Winters north to northern Indiana and Maine (casually); south to southern Texas and southern Florida.

STATUS IN S. C.: Fairly common permanent resident, rare in summer, more common, even sometimes abundant, in winter, over the entire State. Recorded north to Chester County; east to Horry County; south to the Savannah National Wildlife Refuge; west to Aiken and Oconee counties.

HISTORY: There are those who insist that the Woodcock is the real king of American game birds and will listen to no argument to the contrary. In some ways, it is easy to agree with them, for, despite its queer appearance of misplaced eyes, inadequate legs, and enormously long bill, there is much about the bird to arouse interest and enthusiasm, not the least of which is its quality on the table.

The Woodcock is a permanent resident of South Carolina, but is steadily becoming scarcer. It has always been rather erratic in its distribution and movements, but in recent years there has been such a marked decline in Woodcock population that ornithologists have become alarmed and have expended much effort to secure a closed season on the bird, thus far without success.

Years ago, in severe spells of cold weather, there were veritable invasions of Woodcock in Charleston. The Battery and gardens in the lower part of the city swarmed with them on such occasions, and they were killed with sticks or any other handy weapon. Wayne vividly describes the great invasion of February, 1899 (*Auk*, *16*: 1899, 197). Murphey (1937) describes similar invasions as occurring in the Aiken-Augusta region. These descents upon towns and cities came because heavy freezes made it impossible for the bird to bore and probe into the soil of the swamps for food, and they congregated everywhere in confused, starving multitudes.

This species provides a remarkable example of protective coloration. Living in low, wet, and boggy ground of wooded areas, the bird allows itself to be all but trodden upon before bounding into flight, which is accompanied by a peculiar whistling noise of the wings. It is a master at dodging behind tree trunks, and soon drops to earth again, to become invisible. The eyes, which are near the top of the head, enable it to keep a vigil while it is probing into the ground, and the short legs also aid it in its peculiar manner of feeding. The bill is from $2\frac{1}{2}$ to 3 inches long, and the tip of the upper mandible is very flexible, providing the bird with a probing, as well as a feeding tool. Holes made by the Woodcock's search for food may often be found in the territory it inhabits. It seems strange to think of the Woodcock as a shore bird, in view of its forest loving nature.

Though the Woodcock nests regularly in South Carolina, there are few records of actual nests. The eggs are very hard to see, and the nesting bird will not leave them until the intruder is almost close enough to touch it. Then, too, the Woodcock breeds very early, at a time when one would hardly think of looking for eggs, unless he were familiar with the bird's habits. Wayne found but two nests in all his experience, the dates being February 13 and March 4, 1903, the first on Capers Island, Charleston County. He records young just hatched on February 25, 1915.

Other records for the coastal area are as follows: Woodcock and brood of young seen on March 24, 1911, by John Gadsden near St. Stephens, Berkeley County; a nest with four eggs found on March 1, 1931, near Harleyville, Dorchester County, by A. H. Webb; a nest with two eggs at Cherokee Plantation, Colleton County, February 28, 1933, and another with four eggs on the same plantation, February 25, 1935, both found by J. T. Jenkins; two young just able to fly seen on South Island, Georgetown County, on April 10, 1936, by James Gibson; a nest with four eggs found March 1, 1933, near Charleston by Charles Webb; an adult and four young, about two days old, seen on Richmond Plantation, Berkeley County, February 23, 1945, by T. K. Ellis; an adult and three young at Witherbee, Berkeley County, seen on March 18, 1946, by H. L. Guerard.

The nest is simply a depression in the ground lined with leaves, in low, wet woods. The eggs, almost invariably four, are grayish buff, beautifully marked with brown and lavender. They average 38.0 x 29.0 millimeters. Incubation requires about twenty or twenty-one days. The courtship of the Woodcock is a spectacular performance, involving a flight "song," the male rising from the ground for as much as 300 feet, peeping as he goes. Then he flutters slowly down again, uttering a musical, three-syllabled whistle, until he alights practically at the spot from which he took off. This performance is repeated over and over.

Large flights of Woodcock still occur in fall from the northern parts of the breeding range, which extends into Canada. It is at this time that northern sportsmen pursue it, and the concentrations lead them to believe that reports of its diminution are exaggerated; therefore, they object to any curtailment of the season. However, these flights are certainly not what they once were, and steady pressure should be brought to bear for the greater protection of this interesting bird.

FOOD: Entirely insects and worms. The bulk of the diet is earthworms, cutworms, and wireworms, together with flies, beetles, grasshoppers and grubs.

135. WILSON'S SNIPE: *Capella gallinago delicata* (Ord) (230)

(Lat., *Capella*, a star in constellation Auriga; *gallinago*, from *gallina*, a hen; *delicata*, delicate.)

LOCAL NAMES: Jack Snipe; English Snipe.

DESCRIPTION: Length 10.00 to 12.00 inches. Bill long and straight. Upper surface blackish brown, mottled with buff and cinnamon; middle of crown and eyebrow striped with buff; lower surface mostly white, the sides barred, the breast streaked and spotted with dark brown; throat and belly white; tail black with a broad bar of cinnamon rufous.

RANGE: Breeds north to northern Alaska and central eastern Labrador; south to California and Pennsylvania. Winters north to southeastern Alaska and Nova Scotia; south to Colombia and Brazil.

STATUS IN S. C.: Common winter resident, August 15 to May 20, throughout the State. Reported north to York County; east to Horry County; south to Beaufort County; west to Oconee County.

HISTORY: Although one hears of various and sundry kinds of snipe here and there throughout the country, there is in South Carolina only one snipe as such, by name, and that is this species. Though known by local names in different localities, Jack Snipe seems to be a favorite. Actually, it takes its common name from Alexander Wilson, one of our early ornithologists.

Superficially, it resembles the Woodcock, but is a much more slender bird, and the short, partly fox-colored tail is a good field mark. The localities inhabited are very different from those of the Woodcock's haunts, for the snipe is an open country bird, never found in woodlands. It prefers low, damp meadows, grassy fields and the edges of marshes, ponds, and streams, but always in the open. Its flight is erratic and twisting. Often, it will circle back to the starting point after a flight. It is highly regarded by sportsmen, who follow it with the greatest enthusiasm, some of the Low-country plantations having what are known as "snipe bogs," tracts of land especially prepared for the bird's requirements.

The peak of abundance is in January through March, in some seasons the bird being abundant, in others scarce. Like the Woodcock, it lies very close and flushes under one's feet, nearly always giving the explosive and characteristic "scaipe" note. Now and then it can be seen squatting in the grass, or even in the open, at which times it is very difficult to point out unless one's companions have also spotted it. The bill is very long, and used as a probing tool, like that of the Woodcock.

FOOD: Largely earthworms, cutworms, and grasshoppers, together with leeches; also locusts, beetles, mosquitoes, and other insects.

LONG-BILLED CURLEW
136. *Numenius americanus americanus* Bechstein (264)

(Gr., *Numenius*, name of some bird, supposedly a curlew; Lat., *americanus*, of America.)
LOCAL NAMES: Sickle-bill; Spanish Curlew.

DESCRIPTION: Largest of our shore birds. Length 20.00 to 26.00 inches. Bill very long, 5.50 to 8.75 inches, with sweeping downward curve. Upper parts and wings pinkish cinnamon, streaked and barred with brown; primaries barred; lower surface light pinkish cinnamon; the neck and breast with narrow brown streaks.

RANGE: Breeds north to northeastern Nevada and southern Michigan (formerly); south to central Utah and southeastern Kansas (formerly). Winters north to central California and South Carolina; south to southern Lower California and Cozumel Island (Yucatan).

STATUS IN S. C.: Uncommon permanent resident, only occasional in summer; known from only the coast. Recorded north to Georgetown County (Plantersville); south to Beaufort County.

HISTORY: This magnificent species is the largest North American shore bird. Its history in South Carolina is an interesting one of earlier abundance, virtual extinction, and recent reappearance. Wayne (1910) said that "it once swarmed in countless multitudes" on the South Carolina coast. He also said, however, that, in 1910, the bird was "now almost extinct." At that time he had not seen a specimen for eleven years, nor did he see one again until January 10, 1927, twenty-eight years later.

From that year, however, records began once more and have since multiplied until the Long-bill today is listed as an uncommon though regular winter visitor. It has been recorded at Cape Romain from July 31 (A. H. DuPre) and August 28 (Sprunt), to March 31, and occasionally later. The area about the Cape Romain Refuge appears to be the center of the population, as many as seventy-five birds frequenting that region during the season of 1938. At Platersville, Georgetown County, some 50 miles north of Romain, T. G. Samworth reported nine birds on October 10, and forty on November 16, 1944. It appeared on the Christmas Bird Counts of 1943 and 1945 in the Bull's Island area.

Past reports concerning the nesting of the Long-billed Curlew in South Carolina have been questioned. Audubon states:

> It is well known by the inhabitants of Charleston that it breeds on the islands on the coast of South Carolina; and my friend the Reverend JOHN BACHMAN has been at their breeding grounds. . . . Unlike the Ibis, however, which always breeds on trees, and forms a large nest, the Curlew breeds on the ground, forming a scanty receptacle for its eggs; yet, according to my friend BACHMAN, the latter, like the former, places its nests "so close together, that it is almost impossible for a man to walk between them, without injuring the eggs" (*Birds of America*, 6: 1843, 35).

Elliott Coues states that it ". . . formerly nested aboundingly on the South Atlantic coast" (*Key to N. A. Birds*, 2: 1903, 842), and C. W. Wickersham states that "On our Atlantic seaboard it is famous for its littoral habits, nesting in the Carolinas, Georgia and Florida, on the beaches and keys, . . ." (*Auk, 19*: 1902, 353).

Apparently Coues and Wickersham merely accepted Audubon's statement that the Long-bill nested on the South Carolina coast. Wayne took complete exception to Bachman's statement for he says:

> It may appear hypercritical to question Dr. Bachman's statement that this species bred on the coast islands, but the eggs were not described by either Audubon or

himself, and as far back as 1879 there were no eggs of *N. americanus* in the Charleston Museum, while the eggs of the "Stone Curlew" (*Catoptrophorus semipalmatus*) were well represented and were classified as eggs of the Long-billed Curlew, I have been unable to obtain any evidence, even from the "oldest inhabitants," that this species ever bred anywhere on the South Carolina coast. . . . It will thus be seen that the Long-billed Curlew must be excluded from the list of birds which breed in the South Atlantic states (*Birds of S. C.*, 1910, 56).

Wayne may have been right, but there is an article (*Wilson Bull.*, *46*: 1934, 169) by W. G. Fargo which quotes an unpublished manuscript of W. J. Hoxie as follows:

> In 1867 Long-billed Curlew, locally known as Spanish Curlew, were plentiful on Lady's Island, S. C. In the spring following my arrival there, that is in the spring of 1869 I saw a pair of these birds walking about on Distant Island sands feeding their young which could not fly. The bills of the young were straight. I watched them several days.

Hoxie was an outstanding ornithologist and worked for many years in the vicinity of Beaufort. He further writes on its abundance on the sea islands near Beaufort at that time, "A very common resident. Can be procured at evening when going to roost or in the morning when going to feed or in any quantity at Egg Bank in St. Helena Sound. In 1879 this bird had become quite rare about the Sea Ids." (mss. in collection of Charleston Museum).

From about 1879 until approximately 1930 the Long-billed Curlew was practically nonexistent along the South Carolina coast. While it has become more numerous, no evidence has been found of its breeding here in recent years.

The Long-bill can always be distinguished from the abundant Hudsonian, by its greater size, enormously long, sickle-like bill and its buff color, cinnamon wing linings, and lack of a middle light stripe on the top of its head. It frequents extensive mud flats, oyster banks, and sandy bars.

FOOD: Small mollusks and crustaceans, shrimps, crabs, etc., as well as some insects.

NORTHERN CURLEW
137. *Numenius americanus parvus* Bishop (264a)

(Lat., *parvus*, small.)

DESCRIPTION: Similar to the Long-billed Curlew, but smaller, particularly the bill.

RANGE: Breeds north to southern British Columbia and southern Manitoba; south to northeastern California and northern South Dakota. Winters north to central California and Georgia; south to Mexico.

STATUS IN S. C.: Accidental in the coast region. Known only from Beaufort County.

HISTORY: So far as is known there is but one record of this Curlew for South Carolina. This is a specimen, collector unknown, from Egg Bank, Ladies Island, May 27, 1867 (Oberholser, *Auk, 35*: 1918, 194).

In habits and food this subspecies does not differ from the Long-billed Curlew.

WOODCOCK, SNIPE, AND SANDPIPERS

HUDSONIAN CURLEW
138. *Numenius phaeopus hudsonicus* Latham (265)

(Gr., *phaeopus*, dusky footed; Lat., *hudsonicus*, of Hudson [Bay].)

LOCAL NAMES: Jack Curlew.

DESCRIPTION: Length 15.00 to 19.00 inches. Bill decurved. Upper surface grayish brown, the crown with a pale buff middle stripe; a dull buff superciliary stripe; rest of upper parts varied with pale buff and white. Lower surface dull buff, the neck, breast, and sides streaked with dark brown; the throat plain white; primaries barred.

RANGE: Breeds north to northern Alaska and northern Mackenzie; south to central western Alaska and northeastern Manitoba. Winters north to southern California and eastern South Carolina; south to southern Chile and eastern Brazil.

STATUS IN S. C.: Permanent resident but does not breed. Uncommon in winter and summer but abundant during migrations. Known only in the coast region. Reported north to Horry County; south to the mouth of the Savannah River.

HISTORY: This is the most abundant curlew of the Low Country. Since it occurs every month in the year it must be considered a permanent resident, but it does not nest and it is still uncommon in midwinter. This was not true when Wayne wrote in 1910, for up to that time he had not seen it in winter, though he did later. Thus Audubon's observation that he saw this species in December near Charleston is substantiated. When the authors' *Supplement to the Birds of South Carolina* appeared in 1931, there were but five winter records, but these have multiplied since then and the Hudsonian Curlew is now seen regularly at that season, though in comparatively small numbers.

It appears in largest numbers during the migrations. From about mid-April until mid-May and from early July till mid-September it is present in great numbers and may be seen practically anywhere in the coast region, including the corporate limits of towns and cities. It frequents the mud flats, oyster banks, and beaches, and much of the area traversed by the Inland Waterway is excellent country for the bird. A very large flight, estimated at forty thousand birds, was reported in early May, 1946, by A. H. DuPre of the U. S. Fish and Wildlife Service at Cape Romain.

The Hudsonian Curlew is rather noisy, though its notes have a pleasing quality characteristic of shore birds generally. The usual call is a rolling, flute-like whistle. The decurved bill marks it as a curlew and the conspicuous striping of the head is a good field mark.

Wayne (1910) believed that this species supplanted or displaced the Long-billed Curlew on this coast for he says that, prior to 1883, the Hudsonian was rare while the Long-bill was common. Exactly the reverse is true now. He further thought that the explanation lay in the food supply: both curlews live largely upon the fiddler crab (*Uca*) and since there was not enough for both, the smaller Hudsonian, by sheer weight of numbers, drove off the Long-bill. When one sees the millions of fiddler crabs today, it seems strange that their numbers in 1910 would not have been large enough to support both these birds, as well as many others.

Curlews are interesting shore birds, always attractive to local and visiting students. Their tremendous migrations, pleasing calls, far northern breeding habits, and unusual appearance combine to make them a spectacular species. It is astonishing that the fall migration begins as early as it does, and that the birds which appear in early July have already completed their nesting in the Arctic and are on the way south again.

FOOD: Small mollusks, crustaceans, marine worms, and some insects. The fiddler crab appears to be a favorite food of the Hudsonian on this coast.

139. ESKIMO CURLEW: *Numenius borealis* (Forster) (266)

(Lat.. *borealis*, northern.)

DESCRIPTION: Smallest of our curlews; length 12.00 to 15.00 inches. Bill short and slender with little downward curve. Crown brown, streaked with buff but lacking a median stripe; stripe over eye buff; rest of upper parts dull black varied with buff; primaries plain brown, not barred; lower surface buffy white to buff; the breast streaked with dark brown, the sides with broad v-shaped markings.

RANGE: Bred formerly to northern Alaska and northern Mackenzie; south to central western Alaska. Wintered north to Brazil; south to Chile and Argentina. Now nearly extinct.

STATUS IN S. C.: Formerly a casual transient along the coast.

HISTORY: This smallest of the curlews is now supposed to be extinct. A few years ago, it was reported that two were seen on Galveston Island, Texas, April 29, 1945, by J. M. Heiser, Jr., *et al.* (*Auk, 62*: 1945, 635). None has been taken in this country since 1915.

All that is known of it in South Carolina is Wayne's statement (1910) that he never saw it but that, in the Charleston Museum, there were "many mounted specimens that were labeled by Dr. Bachman as follows: 'South Carolina, Winter.' All of these specimens were dust-stained and somewhat moth-eaten, and when Dr. Gabriel E. Manigault became curator they, among other birds, were thrown away as trash."

Dr. Manigault became curator in the 1870's and as far as we know, these "moth-eaten" specimens were the last Eskimo Curlews taken in South Carolina.

Like the Passenger Pigeon, the Eskimo Curlew was shot in multitudes for food and, like the Pigeon, it has become only a sad memory. It was much smaller than

—

PLATE XIII: GULLS OVER SURF

Oil Painting by Francis Lee Jaques

Two top birds, left to right: Ring-billed Gull (adult) and Ring-billed Gull (immature). Four center birds, left to right: Herring Gull (adult), Herring Gull (immature), Laughing Gull (winter plumage), and Laughing Gull (breeding plumage). Lower right: Laughing Gull (immature).

the Hudsonian, the bill but slightly down-curved, and the lack of a median light line on the head was noticeable. The fall migration was largely offshore and the spring route was through the Mississippi Valley and the Great Plains.

140. UPLAND PLOVER: *Bartramia longicauda* (Bechstein) (261)

(Lat., *Bartramia*, to William Bartram; *longicauda*, long-tailed.)

DESCRIPTION: Length 11.00 to 13.00 inches. Legs and tail long. Upper surface dark brown mottled with buff and white; undersurface buffy white to buff; the breast streaked with black.

RANGE: Breeds north to northern Alaska and central Maine; south to southern Oregon and South Carolina. Winters north to northern Argentina and Brazil; south to central Argentina.

STATUS IN S. C.: Rare transient in spring from March 11 to May 19; in autumn from the middle of July to October 28; breeding accidentally; and occurring all over the State. Recorded north to Chester and Florence counties; east to Horry County and Mt. Pleasant; south to the Combahee River; west to Aiken and Oconee counties.

HISTORY: The Upland Plover is one of the rare shore birds of the State. At one time it was not an uncommon bird, but in the years when shore birds were hunted it suffered greatly; thousands were killed not only by individual sportsmen but by commercial hunters for sale in the open markets. As recently as 1932 Arthur E. Howell wrote in his *Florida Bird Life* that the Upland Plover was "rapidly approaching extinction." Since that time, happily, the number seems to be increasing; it is gratifying to note that the bird is again appearing with a fair degree of regularity in many places.

As its name implies, this Plover is essentially a dweller of upland grasslands and fields. It is sometimes called "Field Plover." Since it is virtually unknown in South Carolina it seems to have no local names in the State. Its real home is in the upper Mississippi Valley, and it was never common along the Atlantic Seaboard, though it occurred there during migration. In South Carolina, Wayne (1910) observed it as arriving in late March and being most numerous between the beginning and middle of April, a few remaining until May. On the return flight in fall, it appeared in mid-July and remained until late October. Occasionally it occurred in June, and Wayne gives an account of what must have been an instance of nesting near his home, in May-June, 1901. He had watched a pair about a cotton-field for some time, and on May 11, one of them followed him in a very excited state, "as the Willet . . . does in the breeding season." Try as he would, he could not find the nest, which must have been well concealed or "destroyed the previous day as the field was ploughed." Knowing Wayne's methods, the writers cannot doubt the correctness of his report: that is, it had been destroyed by the working of the field. Wayne lists this observation as "the most southerly record for the breeding of this species." It is recognized in the 1931 Edition of the A. O. U. Check-List.

Sprunt has seen this species but once in South Carolina, sighting a group of four birds on Combahee Plantation, Colleton County, April 15, 1926. Records are still rare today, but fairly recent ones include the following observations: G. E. Hudson found it in Oconee County, April 24, 1928, and in Florence County on August 9 of the same year. On March 20, 1930, C. S. Chisolm took one at the Charleston Airport. On September 22, 1935, a single bird was noted near Charleston by Chamberlain. Murphey (1937) recorded that the species had been increasing in the Aiken-Augusta region since 1926. Herbert L. Stoddard saw one on September 6, 1937, at Friendfield Plantation, Georgetown County. R. G. Kuerzi saw one at Long Bay Plantation, Horry County, on July 28, 1940. During the fall of 1943, a flock estimated at between seventy-five and one hundred birds was reported at an airport near Camden, Kershaw County.

The Upland Plover is a buff-brown bird. It occurs in open country, and often alights on a fence post or telegraph pole, holding the wings elevated over the back for an appreciable time after touching the perch. The legs and neck are long. The head seems distinctly small, and the bill rather short. One of the most likely situations in which to look for it, one from which many records in various localities have come, is an airport. The wide stretches of grass between the runways seem to attract it, and with the ever increasing number of such spots, more may be expected.

The note is distinctive, a rolling whistle, melodious and pleasing; there is also a kind of "whinnying" call which, in North Carolina, gives rise to the local names of "wild mare" and "flying colt."

Food: The Upland Plover, like the Killdeer, being a meadow-loving bird and occurring in the interior, does much more for agriculture than most shore birds. Half of its food is insects, some of which are most destructive to crops, such as the cotton boll weevil, grasshoppers, crickets, beetles, cutworms, army and cotton worms. It also consumes horseflies and cattle ticks in numbers.

141. Spotted Sandpiper: *Actitis macularia* (Linnaeus) (263)

(Gr., *Actitis*, shore frequenter; Lat., *macularia*, spotted.)

Local Names: Tip-up; Spotty.

Description: Length 6.75 to 8.00 inches. Upper parts grayish brown with a green tinge, and marked with dull black; lower surface white, heavily spotted with black; wing shows a conspicuous white bar in flight; bill flesh color tipped with black.

Range: Breeds north to northern Alaska and northern Labrador; south to southern California, central Mississippi, and North Carolina. Winters north to southern British Columbia and southern Virginia; south to Bolivia and southern Brazil.

Status in S. C.: Common permanent resident over the State but not yet known to breed. Observed north to Greenville, York, and Chesterfield counties; east to Horry County; south to Beaufort County; west to Pickens County.

History: The sandpipers are notorious stumbling blocks to the beginner in field identification. So many are alike, small, active, and hard to watch, that many observers throw up their hands over the problem of ever getting them straight. The Spotted Sandpiper, however, offers no particular difficulty. It is one of the easiest to learn. It is the only sandpiper with a distinctly spotted breast (like a thrush). Though these markings are not present in immature birds, there are others of equal importance to its identification. The bird teeters constantly, jerking up and down, its body tilted at an angle; and it flies with the wings bent downward and moving in a very rapid, tremulous manner, alternated by periods of sailing.

The Spotted Sandpiper has a great range covering practically all of the United States and it nests almost everywhere. Though a permanent resident in South Carolina, there is as yet no definite record of its nesting in the State. This is a fact hardly to be accounted for, especially since the ranges given in several books include South Carolina in the nesting territory. Perhaps the difficulty may be explained by a general scarcity of observers, particularly in the Piedmont section, where the bird would be likely to nest. At any rate, the first nesting record, when it is made, will not come as a surprise.

The Spotty, as the bird is called, occurs along the edges of ponds, streams, and watercourses common in the interior as well as on the salt marshes of the coast. It is one of the most active birds imaginable; it appears never to keep still an instant. Unlike many of its kin, it both swims and dives, and is as adept at swimming and diving as that strange little water sprite of western canyons, the Ouzel, or Dipper.

The note is a clear "peet-weet," often given as the bird takes wing, and the Spotty is called the "peet-weet" in some localities.

Food: As might be expected from its interior range, the Spotted Sandpiper is another insectivorous shore bird. Feeding in fields as well as along waterways, it takes numerous grasshoppers, caterpillars, cutworms, beetles, grubs, and cabbage worms. These, of course, are destructive pests and the Spotted Sandpiper should be given protection for the valuable service it renders.

EASTERN SOLITARY SANDPIPER
142. *Tringa solitaria solitaria* Wilson   (256)

(Lat., *Tringa*, a sandpiper; *solitaria*, solitary.)

DESCRIPTION: Length 7.50 to 9.00 inches. Upper surface brown with an olive tinge, speckled and streaked with white; lower parts white, the throat and breast streaked with brown; tail white, barred with black; legs and bill olive green.

RANGE: Breeds north to northern British Columbia and central Labrador; south to central Alberta and central Manitoba. Winters north to southern Louisiana and southeastern Georgia; south to Bolivia and Argentina.

STATUS IN S. C.: Fairly common transient, April 1 to June 4, July 8 to November 18, throughout the State. Recorded north to Spartanburg and Darlington counties; east to Horry County; south to Beaufort County; west to Oconee County.

HISTORY: The Solitary Sandpiper is well named, for it never goes in large flocks and is seldom seen except by itself. It would have been just as appropriate to call it "woods sandpiper" too, for it is a bird of forest pools, wooded streams, and timbered areas of any sort which hold water, as well as marshes. It is very apt to be overlooked, not only because of its unusual habitat but because it is very inconspicuous. If at the edge of a woodland pond, an olive-colored bird arises ahead of the observer and springs away with a flash of white and black tail and a ringing "peet-weet," it will probably be of this species.

The Solitary has the habit of bobbing the head, like the yellow-legs, which except for its size it resembles. After alighting, it often holds the wings elevated over the back for a few moments.

However unfamiliar the Solitary is to most people, the bird has an outstanding place in ornithology because of its remarkable nesting habits, which are radically different from those of other North American shore birds. The Solitary was described by Alexander Wilson in 1813, but it was not until 1903 that the first nest was found, an interim of ninety years. This was not because the nest was not looked for. Many searchers spent much time in the effort, until the question of the bird's nesting habits grew into a mystery which was both fascinating and tantalizing. In searching out nests of shore birds, one always looks to the ground, never up in trees, and the search for the Solitary's nest followed the traditional method. There lay the reason for the mystery.

Almost by accident, Evan Thompson, working in the Province of Saskatchewan, Canada, found the first known eggs of the Eastern Solitary Sandpiper in an old Robin's nest. Since that time, many nests have been found, for the secret was out. It uses the abandoned nests of passerine birds, as strange a departure from family custom as could be imagined. Nests of the Bronzed Grackle, Cedar Waxwing, Kingbird, and Canada Jay are also among those which it has appropriated and elevations have varied from 4 to 40 feet. Before Thompson's discovery, there were several records of eggs found on the ground and "positively identified" as those of the Solitary. None of these records has been substantiated and, as Bent (1929) says, "The solitary sandpiper may occasionally nest on the ground, but it is yet to be proven."

Food: As might be supposed from the localities it inhabits, the Solitary's diet is mainly insectivorous, with some small crustaceans and frogs. Grasshoppers, caterpillars, beetles, dragon fly nymphs, water boatman, spiders, and worms are mainstays.

Western Solitary Sandpiper
143. *Tringa solitaria cinnamomea* (Brewster) (256a)

(Lat., *cinnamomea*, of cinnamon.)

Description: Similar to the Eastern Solitary Sandpiper, but larger; markings of upper parts in immature birds more buffy or cinnamomeous.

Range: Breeds north to northern Alaska and central Mackenzie; south to central Alaska and southern Mackenzie. Winters south to Peru and Argentina.

Status in S. C.: Accidental spring visitor in the coast region.

History: At present, there is but one record of the Western Solitary Sandpiper for South Carolina—an adult male taken by Wayne at Mt. Pleasant on May 21, 1921, and identified by Dr. Harry C. Oberholser. The specimen is in the collection of the Charleston Museum.

This race is not particularly different from the Eastern Solitary Sandpiper in its behavior and choice of food.

EASTERN WILLET
144. *Catoptrophorus semipalmatus semipalmatus* (Gmelin)   (258)

(Gr., *Catoptrophorus*, carrying a mirror, referring to the white wing patch; Lat., *semipalmatus*, half-webbed.)

LOCAL NAMES: Stone Curlew; Will-willet.

DESCRIPTION: Length 14.00 to 16.00 inches. *Summer.* Upper parts brownish gray marked with dark brown; neck and breast spotted and barred with brown; wing with a large white patch. *Winter.* Upper parts plain brownish gray; below white; the neck and breast faintly washed with gray.

RANGE: Breeds north to Texas and Nova Scotia; south to southern Texas, Grand Cayman Island, and the Bahama Islands. Winters north to southern Texas and eastern Virginia; south to Costa Rica, Bolivia, and Brazil.

STATUS IN S. C.: Permanent resident, rare in winter, only along the coast. Recorded north to Horry County; south to Beaufort County. No winter specimens have actually been taken but this Eastern subspecies undoubtedly winters occasionally.

HISTORY: If ever a bird can be said to blow its own horn, consistently and vociferously, this is the one. The Willet is one of the completely unmistakable birds of the South Carolina coast, and the shrill, incessantly repeated notes which give it the name are certainly the characteristic sound of the summer marshes. The words "pill-will-willet" give a reasonably good impression of the sound, though the bird does have other calls.

It is an abundant summer resident, arriving by the middle of March and remaining into September. It is difficult to distinguish between the Eastern and the Western Willet, which occurs in winter, because of the overlapping periods of time at which they occur. However, in winter plumage the two are rather easily separated, for the Western is much paler above than the Eastern race. Some individuals of *Catoptrophorus* occasionally winter in South Carolina, and Wayne (1910) considered it a permanent resident. At any rate, summertime is willet-time on the South Carolina coast, where they are to be found on the mainland as well as on the barrier islands and marshes.

Few birds appear so utterly different at rest and in flight as this one. When standing or feeding, the Willet is a plain, nondescript, grayish-brown and white bird, with rather long, bluish legs and a long, stout bill. As soon as it rises into the air, however, its appearance changes remarkably, for the wings show large, contrasting black and white patches which flash out like a beam from a lighthouse. These markings, together with the call which the bird usually gives in action, will always distinguish it.

Nesting begins in late April, sometimes earlier, and incubation of the eggs is under way by the first week in May. Typical egg dates: for Beaufort County, April 26; for Charleston County, May 4, 10 and 11. The young hatch about the last of May, dates being May 29 and June 1. Forward and backward seasons have some effect on egg-laying.

The nest is a depression in the ground, lined with grass. The eggs are normally four; they are very large, sharply pointed, and placed with the ends together. They are greenish olive, spotted and splashed with dark brown and averaging 52.5 x 38.0 millimeters. Incubation requires twenty-one to twenty-three days. Though usually built in heavy grassy places, the nest is sometimes placed on a perfectly open sea beach, where the writers have found several. The sitting bird remains close on the nest and can sometimes be touched. One nest, found by Sprunt on Dewees Island, June 4, 1926, held six eggs; another, on Sullivan's Island in May, 1912, contained eight. Probably each of the nests represented clutches of eggs laid by two females.

The young are pretty little creatures, covered with down and able to run almost as soon as they are out of the shell. Few birds become so excited when the nest is approached. They often nest in loose colonies and the din which greets an observer as he walks through the grass is deafening. Willets hovering close overhead on fluttering wings give piercing cries and frequently dive or swoop within a few inches of one's head. The birds seem to go berserk, and if a bird could be said to use profanity, Willets are wonders of the art. One actually feels sheepish at times, so vituperative is their condemnation of the intruder.

Sometimes, when they have been alarmed, the parents transport the young birds to a safer place. This is unusual but has been witnessed by Wayne, who says that the adult picks up the chick between its thighs and flies off with it. The Woodcock is known to do this also. Wayne's date for his observation is May, 1899, when he watched an adult Willet carry four young fully a quarter of a mile, one after the other.

The almost universal name for the Willet on the coast is Stone Curlew, but it seems almost unnecessary to say that the Willet is utterly unlike the real bird of that name. The error is the more remarkable because there are no stones on the South Carolina beaches.

Food: The Willet feeds on small mollusks and crustacea, and other marine life found on the beaches and in the marshes. Fiddler crabs (*Uca*) are a staple. It also eats crayfish, beetles, crickets, grasshoppers, and small fish.

Western Willet
145. *Catoptrophorus semipalmatus inornatus* (Brewster) (258a)

(Lat., *inornatus*, unadorned.)

Description: Length 15.00 to 17.00 inches. Similar to the Eastern Willet but larger and paler.

Range: Breeds north to southern Oregon and southwestern Manitoba; south to northeastern California and northern Iowa. Winters north to northern California and South Carolina; south to the Galapagos Islands and Peru.

Status in S. C.: Common winter resident, October 1 to July 12, in the coast region only. Recorded north to McClellanville; south to the mouth of the Savannah River.

HISTORY: This paler form of the willet occurs on the South Carolina coast during every month in the year, except August and September, but is far more common in winter.

The Western Willet is notably paler in color than the Eastern one. The plumage of its back is particularly striking in winter, when it takes on the color of dry sea sand.

Ivan R. Tomkins secured eight specimens of this form from 1930 to 1933 at the mouth of the Savannah River on both sides of the South Carolina-Georgia line. He reported it as common there from October to February. Seven more specimens were secured by E. Milby Burton at Bullyard Sound in Charleston County on February 8, 20, and 22, 1936, and still another at McClellanville on April 12, 1937. Chamberlain collected one on Dewees Island, October 13, 1934, and Wayne took specimens at Hamlin Sound near Mt. Pleasant, March 26, 1913, and at Porcher's Bluff, Copahee Sound, July 11, 1911, April 16, 1913, and May 15, 1913. All these specimens have been identified by Dr. Harry C. Oberholser.

The habits and food of this race are the same as those of the Eastern Willet.

GREATER YELLOW-LEGS
146. *Totanus melanoleucus* (Gmelin) (254)

(Lat., *Totanus*, from Italian name of some bird; Gr., *melanoleucus*, black and white.)

LOCAL NAMES: Tattler; Tell-tale Snipe.

DESCRIPTION: Length 12.00 to 15.00 inches. Upper surface brownish gray, spotted, streaked, or barred with white; upper tail coverts white; undersurface white, largely streaked and barred with brownish gray. Legs and feet bright yellow.

RANGE: Breeds north to central southern Alaska and central Labrador; south to southern British Columbia and Newfoundland. Winters north to western Washington and central eastern North Carolina.

STATUS IN S. C.: Common permanent resident along the coast, though rare in summer, and does not breed. Transient in the interior of the State. Recorded north to Chester County; east to Horry County; south to Beaufort County; west to Oconee County.

HISTORY: If all birds were as descriptively named and exhibited the described characteristic as well as this one, observers could be thankful. The two Yellow-legs are distinctive among shore birds, chiefly because of the characteristic which gives them their name. It cannot be missed.

The Greater Yellow-legs is a permanent resident of South Carolina, but breeds only in the far north. It is a bird not only of mud flats and marshy ponds, the Inland Waterway, and the coast islands but of the interior as well. Its voice is almost as distinctive as the leg color and is an infallible aid to identification, for the bird can often be located by its call before it is even seen. The call is a clear, three or four-syllabled whistle which has been given as "whew-whew-whew," but this does not adequately express its penetrating, far-carrying quality. It is not difficult to imitate and can be used to great advantage in luring the birds closer to the observer.

Duck hunters dislike the Greater Yellow-legs for they believe, as did the shore bird hunters of a few years ago, that it gives alarm to other birds; hence the term "Tattler" or "Tell-tale Snipe." There is probably some truth in the belief, for the Yellow-legs is a very noisy bird. The writers have often noted that feeding ducks give attention to it. Flocks often frequent the rice fields and ponds where ducks congregate. The bird has the habit of bobbing the head as though bowing. The plain gray and white plumage is rather nondescript, but the color of the legs is striking and may be seen even when the light is poor.

Its food consist of small fish, mollusks, crustaceans, and aquatic insects.

147. Lesser Yellow-legs: *Totanus flavipes* (Gmelin) (255)

(Lat., *flavipes*, yellow-footed.)

Local Names: Tell-tale Snipe.

Description: Length 9.00 to 11.00 inches. Similar to the Greater Yellow-legs but smaller; also its bill is straight, not slightly upturned as in the latter.

Range: Breeds north to northern Alaska and central western Quebec; south to central Alberta and New York (formerly). Winters north to southern Texas and South Carolina; south to Chile and Argentina.

Status in S. C.: Winter resident, July 10 to May 20; uncommon in midwinter, fairly common at other times throughout most of the State, although more frequent coastwise. Reported north to Chester County; east to Horry County; south to Beaufort County; west to Aiken County.

History: The Lesser Yellow-legs is, except for its smaller size, practically a duplicate of the Greater Yellow-legs. The two species frequent the same places and are often seen together. At such times, the observer wonders how there could ever be any doubt about the distinction between the two, even when they are seen separately, for the difference in size is startlingly obvious. Yet experienced students are sometimes misled.

The notes of the Lesser Yellow-legs are very like those of its larger relative but are usually of only one or two syllables instead of three or four or more. Though this is a good general rule, it is not infallible.

The Lesser is mostly a transient visitor to South Carolina, but may be seen throughout the winter. Wayne (1910) said that he never saw one in the winter months, but in recent years there have been numerous records. February 17, 1940 (Charleston County); November 30, 1943 (Pinopolis Reservoir); and January 21, 1934 (Georgetown County) are representative dates for these records. The bird has appeared on several Christmas Bird Counts made in late December. Dates of its common occurrence run from early March to late May, and early July through August. It seems somewhat less shy than its larger relative.

Food is the same as that of the Greater Yellow-legs—practically all animal matter.

The Graceful Pintail

ALLAN D. CRUICKSHANK
National Audubon Society

Blue-winged Teal

ALLAN D. CRUICKSHANK
National Audubon Society

Male Ring-necked Duck

Male Lesser Scaup Duck

148. AMERICAN KNOT: *Calidris canutus rufus* (Wilson)   (234)

(Gr., *Calidris*, a sandpiper; Lat., *canutus*, to King Canute; *rufus*, reddish.)

LOCAL NAMES: Robin Snipe.

DESCRIPTION: Length 10.00 to 11.00 inches. *Summer*. Upper parts light gray, varied with brown; undersurface cinnamon with posteriorly some white and markings of brown. *Winter*. Upper surface gray with indistinct dark streaks; lower parts white, the breast faintly streaked with brown.

RANGE: Breeds north to northern Ellesmere Island and northwestern Greenland; south to Victoria Island and Melville Peninsula. Winters north to South Carolina and southeastern Massachusetts (casually); south to Tierra del Fuego.

STATUS IN S. C.: Fairly common winter resident, July 20 to June 17, more numerous during migrations, and occurs only along the coast. Recorded north to Horry County; south to Beaufort County.

HISTORY: Many people give a high place to the American Knot among the shore birds. Inevitably associated with the ocean beach, the never ceasing surf, and waving sea oats on the dunes, the bird connotes an untrammeled wildness and freedom that is equalled by few and surpassed by none.

For many years it was thought to be no more than a transient visitor in South Carolina, and so Wayne (1910) considered it; but recent years have shown that it is properly to be listed as a winter resident. Sprunt was the first to establish this fact and to secure the first specimen ever known at that season in South Carolina and north of Florida. Twenty-nine were seen and three taken on Big Bay Island, January 14, 1928. After that date sight records increased rapidly as numbers of specimens were taken along the South Carolina coast. From 1930 to 1933 the Knot was seen regularly throughout each winter, and fact of its occurrence at that season was firmly established. The numbers are highest from late April to early June, and late July to the last of October. Audubon quotes Dr. Bachman to the effect that he had never seen the Knot in South Carolina in full (spring) plumage. This is astonishing, for in South Carolina the Knot attains the highest perfection of plumage in the spring.

In its winter plumage, the Knot is plain gray above and white beneath. But in the spring it turns into a very handsome bird, with a beautiful cinnamon-red breast and soft gray back. It is a rather chunky bird, with a short, stout bill which at once sets it apart from the very long-billed Dowitcher, with which it may associate. American Knots are very gregarious, flocking together in great numbers on migration. They fly tremendous distances, for they breed along the Arctic Ocean and winter as far south as Tierra del Fuego. It was not until 1909 that the eggs were first taken; in that year two sets were found in northern Greenland by Admiral Peary.

FOOD: Wayne (1910) stated that the food of the American Knot on this coast is "a small bivalve which is found a few inches under the sand" which the bird eats "almost exclusively." This is the butterfly shell (*Donax variabilis*).

149. PURPLE SANDPIPER: *Erolia maritima* (Brünnich) (235)

(Lat., *Erolia*, from French *erolie*, name of a sandpiper; *maritima*, maritime.)

DESCRIPTION: Length 8.00 to 9.50 inches. Above dark gray to black; slightly varied with buff or white; lower parts white, streaked or spotted with dark gray except on belly.

RANGE: Breeds north to Melville Island, Ellesmere Island, Spitzbergen, and Franz Josef Land; south to Baffin Island, Norway, and Siberia. Winters north to Greenland, Iceland, and the Baltic Sea; south to Ohio, Florida, the Azores, and the European coast of the Mediterranean Sea.

STATUS IN S. C.: Casual winter visitor along the coast, December 29 to May 27. Reported north to Cape Romain; south to Charleston.

HISTORY: This far northern shore bird has no normal place among South Carolina avifauna, for this coast is far south of its usual winter range. Its inclusion rests upon two occurrences.

On December 29, 1939, Dr. Robert Cushman Murphy and E. Milby Burton saw three of these Sandpipers on the rocks of the Charleston Jetties. On the next day they returned to the place, saw two of the birds, and secured one. It was an adult male and is now in the Charleston Museum (No. 39.278.1). The stomach contained remains of small bivalve mollusks, a conch (*Anachis*), and fragments of a sponge (*Auk*, 57: 1940, 401). The Sandpipers seen on this occasion were in the company of Ruddy Turnstones. The weather had been very cold and continued so, snow falling at Myrtle Beach two days after the bird was taken.

Surprisingly enough, Chamberlain recently found that the files of the U. S. Fish and Wildlife Service at Patuxent, Maryland, contain the record of a Purple Sandpiper seen at Cape Romain Light Station, McClellanville, on May 27, 1929. The observer is listed as F. H. Oastler. In view of the records established by Murphy and Burton this sight record may be accepted as valid.

The Purple Sandpiper is a chunky species with short legs, a dark gray breast and back, and white under parts. The yellowish legs are a good field mark provided the observer can get close enough to see them. Its occurrence at the Jetties was true to the bird's habit of frequenting rocky shores, and on this rockless coast jetties form the only localities which would appeal to any wandering specimen. Close watch in the future, during severe winter weather, may prove productive of more records.

150. PECTORAL SANDPIPER: *Erolia melanotos* (Vieillot) (239)

(Gr., *melanotos*, black-backed.)

DESCRIPTION: Length 8.00 to 9.50 inches. Upper parts light drab, heavily streaked and spotted with black, the rump dark; lower parts white, but neck and breast buff heavily streaked with dark brown.

RANGE: Breeds north to northeastern Siberia and Southampton Island; south to central western Alaska and northeastern Manitoba. Winters north to Ecuador and central eastern South Carolina (casually); south to Chile and Patagonia.

STATUS IN S. C.: Fairly common transient, March 20 to May 3, and July 15 to October 30; casual in winter; most frequent along the coast. Known north to Chester County; east to Horry County; south to Beaufort County; west to Aiken County.

HISTORY: The Pectoral Sandpiper is not at all well known in South Carolina. It occurs in numbers in late summer and fall but is rather rare in spring. The proper place to look for it is in grassy fields and meadows, but it blends so well with such surroundings that it may easily be missed. It resembles Wilson's Snipe in its choice of habitat. The conspicuously banded breast, in contrast to the white belly, is a good field mark.

The Pectoral Sandpiper is most common from mid-July to late October; many of them may be seen in favorable localities in this period. There are only a few records for the spring: March 20, 1915, James Island (L. M. Bragg); March 20, 1915, Beaufort County (H. W. Abbott); April 17, 1931, April 1, 1935 (Sprunt); May 3, 1935 (E. von S. Dingle). Wayne (1910) listed but one spring record (March 26, 1886). The writers know of but one winter record for this species in South Carolina made on December 27, 1944, when Dr. R. C. Murphy and H. S. Peters saw four birds on the north end of Bull's Island.

The Pectoral Sandpiper possesses a gular sac which, during the season of courtship in the Arctic breeding grounds, it inflates to produce a booming sound. In this respect it resembles the Prairie Chicken.

151. WHITE-RUMPED SANDPIPER: *Erolia fuscicollis* (Vieillot) (240)

(Lat., *fuscicollis*, dusky-necked.)

DESCRIPTION: Length 6.75 to 8.00 inches. *Summer*. Upper parts mainly black, the feathers edged with buff or cinnamon; the upper tail coverts white; lower surface white, the breast with many small dark brown markings. *Winter*. Upper parts brownish gray, marked with brown; otherwise similar to summer plumage, but undersurface white, lightly streaked with brown.

RANGE: Breeds north to Victoria Land and Greenland; south to northern Alaska and Southampton Island. Winters north to northern Florida (casually), Paraguay, and Uruguay; south to Tierra del Fuego and the Falkland Islands.

STATUS IN S. C.: Uncommon transient, May 5 to June 1, and August 30 to October 20, chiefly in the coast region. Reported north and east to Middleburg Plantation in Berkeley County; south to the mouth of the Savannah River; west to Aiken County.

HISTORY: With the little White-rumped Sandpiper we come to a group of shore birds known collectively as "peeps." The term, of course, suggests their characteristic notes. Applied generally, it also indicates the observer's difficulty in distinguishing between the various species of sandpipers. And it must be admitted that identification is not always easy.

The marking which best identifies the White-rumped Sandpiper is that which gives it its name—a white patch above the tail, specifically, the upper tail coverts. No other sandpiper has this marking.

The White-rump is found on beaches, flats, and often in the short grass around rain water pools and permanent ponds, where it probes busily in the soft soil. Its movements are somewhat more deliberate than those of the other sandpipers. An observer, by walking slowly, can come within 20 or 30 feet of a feeding flock. When the bird flushes, the white patch is plainly visible. It is frequently found in company with other species of sandpipers.

The migratory flights cover immense distances, for the bird nests in the far Arctic and winter south to the Falkland Islands, these being about ten thousand miles apart. It is astonishing that birds so small are able to cover such great distances, much of the journey over ocean wastes.

The White-rump is a transient visitor in South Carolina, but is never common. It appears from early May to early June, and again from the last of August to mid-October. Murphey (1937) has recorded it as a straggler in the Aiken-Augusta region.

FOOD: The diet of the White-rumped Sandpiper is not at all well known, but there is no reason to believe that it differs to any extent from that of its relatives.

152. BAIRD'S SANDPIPER: *Erolia bairdii* (Coues) (241)

(Lat., *bairdii*, to Spencer F. Baird.)

DESCRIPTION: Length 7.00 to 7.50 inches. Similar to the White-rumped Sandpiper but upper tail coverts dark (fuscous); throat and chest less distinctly streaked.

RANGE: Breeds north to northern Alaska, Herschel Island (Yukon), and Baffin Island; south to central western Alaska and Southampton Island. Winters south to Chile and Argentina.

STATUS IN S. C.: Casual transient, May 5 to June 1, and July 29; accidental in winter. Reported only from Charleston County.

HISTORY: Baird's Sandpiper offers real difficulties of identification. Plain and obscure, and without any striking character, it is very similar to the White-rump, but it has a dark patch where the White-rump shows a light one. It is so rare in South Carolina, no more than an accidental wanderer, that one is certainly not likely to encounter it. Its past history, however, is worthy of note.

It was not until 1928 that Sprunt established the first record for South Carolina. On June 1 of that year he secured a specimen on Morris Island, at the mouth of Charleston Harbor (*Auk, 48*: 1931, 260).

Its history since that time is brief, amounting to three additional records, one of them most unusual. On December 13, 1928, what was thought to have been another Baird's was seen at Edingsville Beach, Charleston County, by H. R. Sass and Sprunt. The remarkable thing about this record is that it was made so late in the year, for at that time the species should have been in South America, since it does not winter in this country. Unfortunately the specimen was not secured, but the field identification was reasonably certain. It is an unusual record for the entire United States. The bird was probably a belated migrant.

A Baird's Sandpiper was seen at the Port Terminals on the Cooper River, near Charleston, on May 5, 1929, by Philip A. DuMont (*Auk, 46*: 1929, 539), and on July 29, 1947, one was watched from a distance of hardly more than 25 feet, on Sol Legare Island, Charleston County, by Sprunt, his son, and James A. Pittman, Jr.

Baird's Sandpiper frequents the same kind of habitat as the White-rump and is sometimes seen in company with it, as well as with other small species.

FOOD: Little is definitely known; probably small aquatic life, insects and seeds.

153. LEAST SANDPIPER: *Erolia minutilla* (Vieillot) (242)

(Lat., *minutilla*, very small.)

LOCAL NAMES: Sandchicken; Peep.

DESCRIPTION: Smallest of the South Carolina sandpipers; length 5.00 to 6.75 inches. Upper surface brownish black; feathers edged with buff; lower parts white, the fore neck and chest pale buff streaked with brown; legs dark greenish yellow.

RANGE: Breeds north to northwestern Alaska and Labrador; south to northern British Columbia and Sable Island (Nova Scotia). Winters north to central California and North Carolina; south to Peru and central western Brazil.

STATUS IN S. C.: Common permanent resident throughout the State, but does not breed; most numerous coastwise. Observed north to Chester and Darlington counties; east to Horry County; south to Beaufort County; west to Aiken and Oconee counties.

HISTORY: As may be inferred from its name, the Least Sandpiper is the smallest South Carolina member of its family. Its size might suggest that its identification would be easy, but this is not true. Several other sandpipers are close to it in size and very similar in general appearance. However, the olive color of the legs is a characteristic which at once identifies it if one can come close enough to see it clearly in a good light. The other sandpipers which so closely resemble this one have black legs.

The Least Sandpiper is a permanent resident of South Carolina, but it does not nest here. It is more common in June and July that at other times. It is a bird of mud flats and beaches as well as of ponds and rain water pools in upland fields. It is very tame and one can come surprisingly close to it at times. These Sandpipers will often come so close to a car on the beach that they will disappear beneath the running board.

The Least Sandpiper penetrates far into the interior of the State and may even be found in the mountains.

FOOD: The Least is quite a consumer of insects. Howell (1924) found stomach contents to consist largely of the larvae of small flies and aquatic beetles.

154. DUNLIN: *Erolia alpina alpina* (Linnaeus) (243)

(Lat., *alpina*, alpine.)

DESCRIPTION: Similar to the Red-backed Sandpiper, but smaller, the length about 7.50 inches; light markings of upper parts paler; breast much more heavily streaked.

RANGE: Breeds north to Iceland, Spitzbergen, and Nova Zembla; south to the Faeroe Islands, northern Norway, and northwestern Siberia. Winters south to northern Africa and southwestern Asia.

STATUS IN S. C.: Accidental in the coast region.

HISTORY: There is only one known occurrence of the Dunlin in South Carolina, a specimen collected by Wayne, on Sullivan's Island, May 17, 1888. This record is published here by courtesy of W. Earl Godfrey of the National Museum of Canada, who, as well as Dr. John W. Aldrich of the U. S. Fish and Wildlife Service, identified this specimen. It should be mentioned, however, that they noted it as not typical of the European race. Not only is it the first record of the Dunlin for South Carolina, but also the most southern occurrence in North America.

RED-BACKED SANDPIPER
155. *Erolia alpina pacifica* (Coues)　(243a)

(Lat., *pacifica*, of the Pacific [Ocean].)

LOCAL NAMES: Sandchicken; Peep.

DESCRIPTION: Length 7.50 to 9.25 inches. Bill long with tip distinctly down-curved. *Summer.* Head and back cinnamon, with black markings; lower surface white, mostly streaked with dark brown, a large black patch on the abdomen. *Winter.* Upper parts plain gray; lower parts white, the breast but lightly streaked with gray.

RANGE: Breeds north to northern Alaska and the Boothia Peninsula (northern Keewatin); south to central western Alaska and northeastern Manitoba. Winters north to southern British Columbia and Massachusetts; south to southern Lower California and central Florida.

STATUS IN S. C.: Common permanent resident, but rare during the summer and does not breed; observed mostly coastwise. Recorded north to Santee National Wildlife Refuge; east to Georgetown County; south to Beaufort County.

HISTORY: The identifying characteristics of the Red-backed Sandpiper make it a bird relatively easy to recognize among its fellow species. Certainly, the bright spring plumage is highly distinctive, for no other sandpiper has the large black patch on the belly or the reddish underparts. In winter, it presents a totally different appearance, being plain gray above and white beneath, but even in winter one can always identify it by its bill, which is much longer than that of most of the sandpipers and has a pronounced downward droop at the tip. Naturally, the Red-back is seen more often in this winter plumage than in the breeding dress, but that is put on before the bird leaves South Carolina and is very handsome. The Red-back is larger and more stocky than other small sandpipers.

It is an abundant bird in South Carolina. It winters in the State, and now and then a wanderer may be seen in the summer months. It frequents the extensive tidal mud flats and oyster banks more than it does the beaches. On winter days hundreds of the birds are to be seen along the Inland Waterway route or among the multitudinous marshy creeks of the Low-country. It is not at all shy and it allows boats to approach within a few yards. At times it feeds with the head totally submerged, probing busily in the soft mud at the edges of banks or pools. It comes freely to the waterfronts of towns and cities and is to be seen in numbers on the flats near the Ashley River Bridge in Charleston, as well as at other coastal towns such as Beaufort, McClellanville, and Georgetown. It has also been found around the Santee-Cooper lakes in Berkeley and Clarendon counties. Its mass flights are spectacular, hundreds of the birds wheeling in compact flocks as if at some command, suddenly twisting and turning at most unexpected intervals. Collisions appear inevitable but they seem never to occur.

FOOD: Small mollusks and crustaceans, insects and their larvae. Now and then the birds eat the seeds of aquatic plants but the bulk of the diet is animal matter.

EASTERN DOWITCHER
156. *Limnodromus griseus griseus* (Gmelin) (231)

(Gr., *Limnodromus*, a marsh-runner; Lat., *griseus*, gray.)

LOCAL NAMES: Red-breasted Snipe; Robin Snipe.

DESCRIPTION: Length 10.00 to 11.00 inches. *Summer*. Upper surface black, mottled with buffy white and cinnamon; rump white; upper tail coverts barred with black; lower surface pinkish cinnamon, spotted with brown, the abdomen partly white. *Winter*. Upper parts plain gray; below white, the breast and sides clouded with gray.

RANGE: Breeds from Hudson Bay to northern Ungava. Winters north to southern California, South Carolina, and casually North Carolina; south to central eastern Brazil.

STATUS IN S. C.: Common permanent resident but does not breed; occurs only along the coast. Most numerous in migration. Reported north to Horry County; south to Beaufort County.

HISTORY: The Eastern Dowitcher is about the size of the well-known Wilson's Snipe. In its summer plumage it is a handsome bird. The breast is cinnamon-red, mottled with small dark spots. The rump (lower back) is white, which shows as a conspicuous streak when the bird is in flight. This white streak and the bird's disproportionately long bill are excellent characteristics for identification of the Dowitcher in the field. The bright colors of its spring dress give way in winter to dull brown and white, but the white rump remains. Though the Eastern Dowitcher and Wilson's Snipe resemble each other in general appearance, the two are not likely to be confused if one will remember that the Dowitcher habitually frequents beaches and mud flats.

The breeding area for the Eastern Dowitcher is not yet thoroughly known, but some authorities believe it lies in the Ungava peninsula. Dowitchers are less in evidence in spring and early summer than at other seasons. All sight records not substantiated by specimens are included under this race. A number of specimens in the collection of the Charleston Museum have been identified by Dr. Harry C. Oberholser and F. A. Pitelka, as the Inland Dowitcher (*L. g. hendersoni*), a form which has not been recognized by the American Ornithologists Union.

Winter finds them in abundance, and a cruise along the tidal flats and extensive reaches of oyster territory will reveal hundreds of Dowitchers. The birds pay little attention to boats and feed at very close range to passing craft, for they are seldom if ever disturbed by human beings. At such times the excessively long bill can be easily noted, and the birds probe to the full length of it. Like other shore birds, they fly in large flocks with absolute precision, turning and wheeling with split-second accuracy.

Food: Much like that of other maritime shore birds, mollusks, crustaceans, and insects, such as beetles, grasshoppers, flies, water bugs, and the like.

LONG-BILLED DOWITCHER
157. *Limnodromus griseus scolopaceus* Say (232)

(Lat., *scolopaceus*, snipe-like.)

DESCRIPTION: Length 10.00 to 12.50 inches. Similar to the Inland Dowitcher but bill very much longer. Lower parts of a deeper cinnamon; the dark spots below much more concentrated on the breast; the sides and flanks more heavily barred.

RANGE: Breeds north to northern Alaska and northern Mackenzie; south to central western Alaska and north central Yukon. Winters north to southern California, Louisiana, central Florida, and South Carolina (casually); south to Argentina.

STATUS IN S. C.: Accidental coastwise in November.

HISTORY: The Long-billed Dowitcher, long thought to be fairly common in South Carolina, is now found to be no more than accidental. Much work has been done on the classification of the dowitchers since the appearance of Wayne's book in 1910, and recent data decidedly alter the known status of these birds in South Carolina. The only positive record of the Long-bill in South Carolina is a specimen secured on Turtle Island at the mouth of the Savannah River on November 30, 1929, by Ivan R. Tomkins. It is now in the collection of the Charleston Museum.

In habits and behavior the Long-billed Dowitcher is like the other dowitcher; as a matter of fact, to the casual observer the differences between the two are inconsequential. More collecting may prove this race to be of more frequent occurrence than present knowledge indicates.

PLATE XIV: TERNS AND SKIMMER

Water Color by Roger Tory Peterson

Flying in background, left to right: Least Tern and Black Tern (fall plumage). Flying in foreground, left to right: Forster's Tern (breeding plumage), and Forster's Tern (winter plumage). Foreground on beach, left to right: Black Skimmer, Royal Tern, Cabot's Tern, and Gull-billed Tern.

Roger Tory Peterson —

STILT SANDPIPER
158. *Micropalama himantopus* (Bonaparte) (233)

(Gr., *Micropalama*, small-palmed, *i. e.*, small-webbed; *himantopus*, a wading bird.)

DESCRIPTION: Length 7.50 to 9.25 inches. Legs long. *Summer.* Above varied with black, gray, and pale buff; below white to pale brown, streaked anteriorly, barred posteriorly with brown; legs yellow-olive. *Winter.* Upper parts largely gray; lower surface white; the neck and breast faintly streaked.

RANGE: Breeds north to northern Mackenzie; south to northeastern Manitoba. Winters north to Texas (accidentally) and Cuba, also Bolivia and Paraguay; south to northern Chile and Argentina.

STATUS IN S. C.: Rare transient, March 22 to May 11, and August 8 to October 20, occurring only along the coast. Recorded north to Pawley's Island (Georgetown County); south to the mouth of the Savannah River.

HISTORY: The Stilt Sandpiper is one of the rare shore birds of South Carolina. It was first taken by Dr. John Bachman about 1830. Then, W. J. Hoxie, working in the Beaufort region, recorded at least two "Flocks" in April during the period from 1868 to 1890. His only fall record was made at Trenchard's Inlet, near Frogmore, Beaufort County, on August 8, 1887.

On August 22, 1912, a Stilt Sandpiper was shot from a flock of Yellow-legs on Pawley's Island, Georgetown County, by C. P. Webber, and it is now in the Charleston Museum (No. 7171). Nineteen years went by before another was taken, that being a female by Sprunt on Sol Legare Island, Charleston County, April 17, 1931. This bird was also in company with Yellow-legs, feeding in a shallow pond. On May 11 of the same year, another specimen was seen in the same pond by Sprunt.

On April 20, 1934, two were watched for some time on Capers Island, Charleston County, by Charles A. Urner, John H. Baker, John B. May, and Sprunt. Ivan R. Tomkins has taken three specimens in Beaufort County, at the mouth of the Savannah River. The first was secured on October 20, 1935 (*Auk, 53*: 1936, 80), and the other two on March 22 and 29, 1936. The Capers Island birds and at least one of the Beaufort County specimens were in the company of Yellow-legs.

The Stilt Sandpiper gets its name from its long legs, and though it is similar to the Yellow-legs with which it associates so closely, it may be distinguished, in winter plumage, by its unspotted back, smaller size, and slender greenish legs. It is a wader, getting much of its food in the water, often at belly-depth, and it feeds in ponds rather than along the edges. It is more likely to be seen in grassy ponds and wet meadows than on open beaches and mud flats.

FOOD: About 70 per cent animal, and 30 per cent vegetable matter (Howell, 1932).

SEMIPALMATED SANDPIPER
159. *Ereunetes pusillus* (Linnaeus) (246)

(Gr., *Ereunetes*, a searcher; Lat., *pusillus*, small.)

LOCAL NAMES: Peep; Sandchicken.

DESCRIPTION: Length 5.50 to 6.75 inches. Upper parts light grayish brown, varied with black and light cinnamon; lower surface white, the breast indistinctly streaked with dull gray; legs and feet black.

RANGE: Breeds north to northeastern Siberia and southern Baffin Island; south to central western Alaska and Labrador. Winters north to Mexico and South Carolina; south to Chile and Patagonia.

STATUS IN S. C.: Abundant permanent resident but does not breed. Occurs mainly along the coast. Reported north and east to Horry County; south to Beaufort County; west to Aiken County.

HISTORY: The Semipalmated Sandpiper is the most abundant and best known of the "peeps" in the east. It is another non-breeding permanent resident of South Carolina, though for many years it was thought to be transient only. Recent records show it regular in winter, and though commoner in migration, it is to be seen every month.

The name of this little sandpiper, which is practically the same size as the Least, is derived from the partial webbing of the toes. This characteristic cannot, of course, be seen in the field. It often associates with other sandpipers of about the same size, sometimes two and three species being seen in the same feeding flock. At such times the Semipalmated, the Least, and the Western Sandpipers all look so much alike that many inexperienced observers fail to distinguish among them. However, close attention to the varying characteristics of the three makes identification easier than one might expect.

There are two marks to distinguish the Semipalmated: the black legs (olive in the Least), and the very short bill (as compared with the distinctly longer one of the Western).

The Semipalmated is a bird of both the open beach and mud flats, and sometimes comes into settled communities. In stormy weather the birds alight on wet highways and even in streets, where they huddle in close groups, often allowing very close approach. On the ocean beaches the Semipalmated associates with the Sanderling, running along at the edge of the tide, probing industriously in the sand, the twinkling legs moving so rapidly that it seems to skim the sands rather than to touch them. It is a remarkable formation flier, performing aerial evolutions of breath-taking quickness and precision in compact flocks. It frequently utters its mellow, two-noted whistle in flight.

FOOD: According to Bent (1927) an analysis of the food of this species showed it to be composed of small mollusks and crustaceans, worms, bits of seaweeds, and insects, including beetles.

160. WESTERN SANDPIPER: *Ereunetes mauri* Cabanis (247)

(Lat., *mauri*, to Maur.)

LOCAL NAMES: Peep.

DESCRIPTION: Length 5.75 to 7.00 inches. *Summer*. Like the Semipalmated and Least sandpipers but bill longer; upper parts heavily marked with cinnamon. *Winter*. Gray above and white beneath.

RANGE: Breeds north to the central northern coast of Alaska; south to central western Alaska. Winters north to northwestern Washington and eastern North Carolina; south to Peru and Trinidad.

STATUS IN S. C.: Abundant permanent resident but does not breed, occurs only in the coastal counties. Recorded north to Horry County; south to Beaufort County.

HISTORY: Despite its geographical name the Western Sandpiper is one of the commonest shore birds of the South Carolina coast. It is virtually the western form of the Semipalmated Sandpiper, but shows differences which are recognizable in the field. Wayne (1910) called it the "most abundant of all the waders that winter on this coast." Perhaps Wayne's statement is not true today, but the Western is certainly a common bird at times. It has been seen every month in the year, and should be classed as a permanent resident, but it does not breed in South Carolina.

It associates freely with other members of the family on the tidal flats and beaches. From its relatives of similar size, the Western can always be picked out by the distinctly longer bill.

FOOD: Similar to that of its close relatives and of a nature to be expected from its haunts. Marine worms, snails, fly larvae, and aquatic insects form the bulk.

BUFF-BREASTED SANDPIPER
161. *Tryngites subruficollis* (Vieillot) (262)

(Gr., *Tryngites*, concerning an unknown bird; Lat., *subruficollis*, reddish under neck.)

DESCRIPTION: Length 7.50 to 8.90 inches. Upper parts dull grayish brown or buff varied with blackish; under parts buff, often streaked or speckled on chest with dusky spots.

RANGE: Breeds along the Arctic coast from Siberia to Hudson Bay. Winters in Argentina and Uruguay; most abundant in migration in the Mississippi Valley.

STATUS IN S. C.: Accidental. Known only from Beaufort County.

HISTORY: South Carolina is outside the regular range of this Sandpiper, and it has never been seen by contemporary students. Wayne (1910) states that W. W. Worthington told him that Walter Hoxie secured a specimen on St. Helena Island "many years ago," and that he (Worthington) had identified it as this species. This specimen was taken near Chaplin Village, on St. Helena Island by Hoxie on May 5, 1884 (Hoxie mss. in collection of Charleston Museum).

This mid-western migrant has been taken in Currituck County, North Carolina (*Birds of N. C.*, 1942: 154).

162. Marbled Godwit: *Limosa fedoa* (Linnaeus)   (249)

(Lat., *Limosa*, muddy; *fedoa*, old name of godwit.)

DESCRIPTION: Length 16.00 to 20.00 inches. Bill very long and turned upward a little. Upper parts dark brown, varied with cinnamon; undersurface light cinnamon, paling to buff or white on the throat, and mostly barred narrowly with dark brown.

RANGE: Breeds north to central Alberta and southern Manitoba; south to Utah (formerly), South Dakota, and southern Wisconsin (formerly). Winters north to Lower California and South Carolina; south to northern Chile and Argentina.

STATUS IN S. C.: Fairly common winter resident, September 7 to June 28, casually August; occurring only along the coast. Known north to the mouth of the Santee River; south to the mouth of the Savannah River.

HISTORY: This fine species is one of the larger shore birds, exceeding the Willet in size though smaller than the Oyster-catcher and Long-billed Curlew. It towers above the plovers and sandpipers like a giant and is always conspicuous on the great tidal flats and oyster banks where it feeds. The brownish buff plumage is very distinctive, but even more so is the long bill which has a pronounced upward turn along its length, being the reverse of the curlews, whose bills curve downward. This characteristic, together with the plumage, is so distinct that the veriest beginner in shore-bird study should have no trouble with the species.

The status of the Marbled Godwit in South Carolina has changed both since Wayne wrote in 1910 and since the present authors produced their *Supplement* to his work in 1931. From transient visitor, as it was then thought to be, it has now definitely been established as a regular winter resident and is steadily increasing in numbers.

The Marbled Godwit arrives in early September (occasionally August), and remains through the winter and spring migration until mid-May. There are even later records: three birds were seen June 28, 1930, on Cape Island (Burton and Sprunt) and five were seen on June 26, 1941, on Hunting Island, Beaufort County (Dr. Irving Phinizy). There are now numerous records for November, December, January, and February.

Although W. J. Hoxie found it "common" in the 1870's in the vicinity of Beaufort, Wayne (1910) considered it "one of the very rarest of birds at the present time on this coast." Even as late as 1930 it was rare, but since then records have multiplied steadily, and today one can be reasonably sure, at certain seasons, of seeing the bird in numbers. The general area of the South Carolina coast about and south of the Santee River, is the farthest north point on the Atlantic seaboard where the Marbled Godwit may be seen in winter.

When half-tide exposes the great mud flats along the Inland Waterway and the flocks of shore birds whirl down to feed, this fine species congregates with Oyster-catchers, curlews, plovers, turnstones, and sandpipers. It is hardly ever seen on an open sea beach, for it is essentially a bird of the flats. Now and then one may hear the note, which is said to resemble the word "god-wit," but usually it is a silent bird.

FOOD: Consists of mollusks, crustaceans, roundworms, weevils, fly larvae, grasshoppers, May flies, caddis fly larvae, and various beetles. Seeds and tubers of some pondweeds, sedges, and musk grass, constitute the vegetable matter.

163. HUDSONIAN GODWIT: *Limosa haemastica* (Linnaeus) (251)

(Gr., *haemastica*, bloody, with reference to the ruddy lower parts.)

DESCRIPTION: Length 14.00 to 17.00 inches. *Summer*. Above brownish black, varied with white, buff, and rufous; upper tail coverts mostly white; tail black, its base buffy white; lower parts chestnut, barred with black. *Winter*. Above pale gray, paler below; upper tail coverts white.

RANGE: Breeds north to northwestern Mackenzie; south to northeastern Manitoba and Southampton Island. Winters north to central Arizona; south to southern Chile and the Falkland Islands.

STATUS IN S. C.: Accidental in spring in the coast region.

HISTORY: There is but a single record of the Hudsonian Godwit in South Carolina. E. von S. Dingle, one of the most careful observers in the State, reports that on May 8 or 10, 1941, he had a close view of a single bird near Charleston and plainly noted its characteristic markings. This record, although not substantiated by a specimen, is so evidently authentic that it should be regarded as the first definite record for South Carolina. Dr. Coues (1868) stated that the species occurs in winter in this State. He did not (as he said in his *Birds of the Northwest*) see the bird himself, and his inclusion of it in his list of the birds of South Carolina seems to rest on only hearsay.

The Hudsonian Godwit is one of the rarest of the North American shore birds, and one of the least known. In general habits and probably in choice of food it does not differ materially from the other godwits.

164. SANDERLING: *Crocethia alba* (Pallas) (248)

(Gr., *Crocethia*, a seashore runner; Lat., *alba*, white.)

LOCAL NAMES: Sandchicken.

DESCRIPTION: Length 7.00 to 8.75 inches. *Summer*. Upper surface light cinnamon; throat and breast cinnamon, all marked with brown; rest of lower surface white. Bill and legs black. *Winter*. Upper parts pale gray, the head nearly white; under parts pure white.

RANGE: Breeds north to northern Greenland and Spitzbergen; south to northern Alaska, and the coast of northern Siberia. Winters north to northwestern Washington, southeastern Massachusetts, Great Britain, and Japan; south to southern Chile, Argentina, and Australia.

STATUS IN S. C.: Abundant permanent resident, but does not breed; occurs mostly along the coast, being almost wholly confined to the sea beaches. Observed north and east to Cherry Grove Beach (Horry County); south to Beaufort County; west to Aiken County.

HISTORY: The Sanderling is, without doubt, one of the most attractive of the sandpipers. Many people are familiar with it, even if they do not know it by name.

Every beach resident in summer and every one who ventures along the wind-swept winter inlets and dunes will recall seeing this busy little white runner of the seashore. So abundant is it, so easily seen on any beach at any time of year, so tame and unsuspicious, that anyone can make its acquaintance. It is the palest of the sandpipers in winter, and the one most likely to be seen on any open beach. They stop abruptly to probe the sand in the brief interim between a receding wave and the coming of the next, feed hurriedly, and then, as the water rushes toward them, rise lightly into the air, and circle back to the beach again. In flight, a vivid white stripe appears in the wing, which is otherwise dark.

Birds of this species, like the other sandpipers, often rest and sometimes even hop on one leg. So conspicuous is this habit that it would lead an inexperienced observer to be certain that the birds were crippled.

Oddly enough, this beach-loving species has been recorded by Murphey (1937) as a regular, although not abundant, fall migrant "on the sand bars and mud flats" of the Savannah River, between Aiken and Augusta.

Food: Confined as it is to beaches, the Sanderling eats practically nothing but animal food.

Family Recurvirostridae: Avocets and Stilts

165. Avocet: *Recurvirostra americana* Gmelin (225)

(Lat., *Recurvirostra*, upcurved billed; *americana*, of America.)

Description: Length 15.00 to 20.00 inches. Bill long and markedly upturned toward the tip. Body mainly white; neck and rest of head cinnamon; wings black with large white patches; rest of under parts white.

Range: Breeds north to Washington and southern Manitoba; south to southern California, northern Iowa, and central eastern New Jersey (formerly). Winters north to California, southern Texas, and northeastern North Carolina (casually); south to Guatemala and Tobago Island.

Status in S. C.: Rare winter visitor, October 5 to June 6, only along the coast. Reported north to South Island (Georgetown County); south to the mouth of the Savannah River.

History: This strikingly handsome species, one of the most spectacular of the shore birds, is as rare in South Carolina as it is elsewhere in the East, but records of the past twenty years indicate that its former status of accidental visitor should be changed to that of rare winter visitor.

When one sees an Avocet he need never be in doubt about its identity. It is one of the larger shore birds, black and white (in winter), and with a three- to four-inch bill which is very slender, delicate, and distinctly turned upward toward the tip. In summer the neck is a beautiful pinkish cinnamon color.

Wayne was never fortunate enough to see an Avocet, but he quotes Audubon regarding Dr. Bachman's observation, which was to the effect that the Avocet is rare on this coast. That Dr. Bachman was correct is well proved; nearly a century went by before the bird was again recorded. On November 14, 1923, W. H. Magwood took one specimen and saw another, at the mouth of the Santee River, on South Island, Georgetown County. The bird collected was presented to the Charleston Museum (No. 7635).

The next records came from the southeastern corner of the State, near the mouth of the Savannah River. Here Ivan R. Tomkins secured one on March 7, 1929; saw another on November 9 and 10 of the same year; secured a female on October 5, 1930; saw two from November 14 to 24 and took a male on December 24, 1930.

During the field trip of the American Ornithologists' Union meeting to Bull's Island, November 19, 1937, Dr. Clarence Cottam pointed out an Avocet to several participants. Two winters later, William P. Baldwin and others noted that a single bird remained on the Island from November 16, 1939, to March 14, 1940. During December, 1942, an Avocet remained at Summerhouse Pond for two weeks, and was seen by many observers. In October, 1946, "about 50 of these birds" were seen on South Island Plantation, Georgetown County, by William E. Phelps, who continued to observe small groups of them until early March, 1947. This observation confirms that of Baldwin, already cited, that Avocets actually spend the entire winter on this coast.

The foregoing records cover a period from October 5 to March 14. Additional records show that Avocets occur in spring and summer also. On or about May 20, 1940, Charles C. West saw two birds in St. Helena Sound, Beaufort County, and on May 27 of the same year A. H. DuPre saw one on Cape Island, Romain Refuge. On June 2, 1947, DuPre saw fourteen birds, also on Cape Island. Four were seen by H. S. Peters at South Island on May 24, and six on June 6, 1949, the last being our latest record.

The Avocet frequents both fresh and salt water but seems to prefer the former. It feeds by walking through the shallows and sweeping the bill rapidly from side to side, often with the head submerged. This habit is very similar to that of the Roseate Spoonbill. Bent (1927) says that the Avocet "tips up" like the river ducks at times. It swims well and is capable of diving. It is not shy and often allows close approach.

FOOD: About 65 per cent animal and 35 per cent vegetable matter. Such insects as dragon fly nymphs, water boatmen, aquatic beetles, and fly larvae compose the animal diet. The seeds of marsh and water-loving plants make up the vegetable content.

166. BLACK-NECKED STILT: *Himantopus mexicanus* (Müller) (226)

(Gr., *Himantopus*, a wading bird; Lat., *mexicanus*, of Mexico.)

DESCRIPTION: Length 13.00 to 15.50 inches. Bill long and slender; legs very long. Upper parts black, glossed with green; lower surface white; legs rose pink.

RANGE: Breeds north to central Oregon, southeastern Saskatchewan (casually), and New Jersey; south to southern Mexico, northern Peru, and central Brazil. Winters north to Lower California and North Carolina (casually); south to Brazil.

STATUS IN S. C.: Rare summer resident, March 29 to August 16, only in the coast region. Known north to South Island, Georgetown County; south to Bull Point, Beaufort County; west (inland) to Middleburg Plantation in Berkeley County.

HISTORY: This is one of the most distinctive birds of the United States. Because of its wide range, doubt about its identity need never occur. In South Carolina it has increased steadily during recent years though it was once very rare. Audubon noted that it was "rather scarce along the shores of the Carolinas" and his statement remained true for the next hundred years. Wayne saw but one pair during his life, in mid-May, 1881, on Sullivan's Island, and he was convinced that the birds were nesting, though he did not press his search about the pond they frequented "on account of moccasin snakes, which were abundant." In the light of later discoveries, there can be little doubt that his birds were indeed a breeding pair. Three years later, W. J. Hoxie reported a bird at Bull Point, April 24, 1884. It was nearly half a century after Hoxie's record before the species was found again. On August 16, 1928, E. von S. Dingle took one at Middleburg Plantation, Berkeley County.

The first known breeding record was established when Ellison A. Williams found three eggs on Sol Legare Island, Charleston County, July 10, 1938. For some reason these eggs were deserted, and on July 12 they were collected and deposited in the Charleston Museum.

Since then, the Stilt has appeared regularly, in small numbers, in the Cape Romain area and elsewhere. Though in some instances birds have been seen which gave every indication of nesting, no additional breeding records occurred until June 26, 1947, when two nests with four eggs each were found on South Island by H. L. Harllee and Wray Nicholson.

The Stilt is a black and white shore bird with very long, thin, red legs. The pattern of the head gives the impression that the bird is wearing spectacles. The neck is long and slender and the bill straight, sometimes with a slight upturn. The Stilt, which frequents ponds and wet grassy flats, walks with a peculiar, high-lifting stride.

The nest, which is built on the ground, is simply a depression lined with bits of shell and dried grass. There are usually four eggs, of a buff color, heavily marked with blackish spots and blotches. They average 44.0 x 30.5 millimeters, and their incubation requires about twenty-one days.

FOOD: Practically all animal matter, 98.9 per cent (Wetmore, 1925). Aquatic bugs make up a large portion, 35 per cent; beetles and weevils, 32 per cent; and flies, 10 per cent. Small fish, snails, crawfish, May flies, caddis fly cases and dragon fly nymphs constitute the remainder. It will be readily seen that the bird is a valuable one.

Family Phalaropodidae: Phalaropes

167. RED PHALAROPE: *Phalaropus fulicarius* (Linnaeus) (222)

(Gr., *Phalaropus*, coot-footed; Lat., *fulicarius*, cootlike.)

DESCRIPTION: Length 7.50 to 9.00 inches. Bill short and rather stout; toes lobed or scalloped like those of the Coot. *Summer.* Top of head and chin black; sides of head white; back cinnamon buff streaked with black; sides of neck and lower parts purplish cinnamon; wing with a white bar. *Winter.* Head and undersurface white; upper plumage gray.

RANGE: Breeds north to Greenland and Spitzbergen. Winters north to California, southeastern North Carolina, the Mediterranean Sea, and the coast of Arabia; south to Chile.

STATUS IN S. C.: Accidental, April to December, in the coast region. Recorded from Charleston County.

HISTORY: Phalaropes might well be called oceanic sandpipers, for although they are shore birds in the nesting season, they spend much of their lives at sea. Unlike the sandpipers, they swim freely, and take their food from the surface of the water. They seldom run along the beaches or flats. They are unique among American birds in that the female is more brightly colored than the male, and does nothing whatever toward the reproduction of the species except to court and to lay the eggs.

The Red Phalarope is about the size of the familiar Sanderling of the sea beaches, but it is maritime much of the year, covering many thousands of miles of oceanic wandering. For that reason, records of it on this coast are few. A male was caught in exhausted condition at Mt. Pleasant, December 4, 1900, by W. D. Hamlin, and given to Wayne (*Auk, 18:* 1901, 271). Before that time, all that was known of the bird was that it occurred offshore. There is a specific note to that effect by Gerald H. Thayer (*Auk, 19:* 1902, 286). With the ornithological artist, Louis A. Fuertes, Thayer saw "enormous flocks" some 50 miles off the northern South Carolina coast on March 17, 1898.

Since the 1900 record of a specimen secured, there has been but one definite identification, that of a bird near the Charleston Lightship on April 22, 1934. It was identified by the late Charles A. Urner, one of the country's leading authorities on the shore birds. It is the second record for the State (*Auk, 51:* 1934, 374).

FOOD: Minute marine organisms which it takes from the surface of the ocean while swimming, often in a rapidly circling manner like a spinning top.

168. WILSON'S PHALAROPE: *Steganopus tricolor* Vieillot (224)

(Gr., *Steganopus*, covered footed, *i. e.*, web-footed; Lat., *tricolor*, three-colored.)

DESCRIPTION: Length 8.25 to 10.00 inches. *Summer female.* Crown pale gray; nape white; broad stripe on side of neck black; back gray with stripes of chestnut; upper tail coverts white; foreneck and chest cinnamon; rest of lower parts white. *Summer male.* Similar, but much duller than the female. *Winter female* and *winter male.* Upper parts light gray; lower surface white.

RANGE: Breeds north to Washington and southern Manitoba; south to central California and southeastern Ontario. Winters north to Peru and Bolivia; south to Chile, Argentina, and the Falkland Islands (casually).

STATUS IN S. C.: Rare transient, May 5 to 15, in autumn from September 7; occurs only on the coast. Reported only from Charleston County.

HISTORY: Wilson's Phalarope is less oceanic than its two relatives. It occurs in the northern parts of the United States and the prairie provinces of Canada as a nester and migrates mainly through the central states, but at times it appears on the coast. It is a rare transient visitor to South Carolina. It was added to South Carolina's avifauna on September 7, 1910, when Chamberlain took a male on Sullivan's Island (*Auk, 28*: 1911, 109).

On May 5, 1929, another was seen on Morris Island, at the mouth of Charleston Harbor, by P. A. DuMont, and from May 11 through 15 of the same year a female remained on Sol Legare Island, where it was seen by H. R. Sass, E. A. Williams, and Sprunt. It is possible that this was the specimen noted some days earlier by DuMont, since the localities are not far apart. A female in very high plumage was taken in a pond on Sol Legare Island, May 15, 1931, by Sprunt, accompanied by Peter Gething (*Auk, 48*: 1931, 597).

Wilson's Pharlarope feeds like the others. It frequents ponds, where it sits lightly on the water and whirls rapidly about like a living top; the movement is supposed to stir up the small aquatic life on which it subsists. The breast and belly plumage is very dense and, like that of the ducks, is underlaid with down, which renders it impervious to water. The bill is delicate and needle-like. Wilson's Pharlarope often associates with Lesser Yellow-legs, but the actions of the bird are so characteristic and so different from those of other shore birds as to render it unmistakable.

FOOD: Animal matter, about 93 per cent. The bulk is composed of aquatic insects, water boatmen seeming to be favorites.

169. NORTHERN PHALAROPE: *Lobipes lobatus* (Linnaeus)   (223)

(Lat., *Lobipes*, lobe-footed; *lobatus*, lobed.)

DESCRIPTION: Length 6.50 to 8.00 inches. *Summer female*. Above slate gray, the back striped with ochraceous; wings with a white bar; lower parts white, but foreneck, chest, and sides of neck cinnamon rufous. *Summer male*. Similar, but much duller. *Winter female* and *winter male*. Upper surface gray, the head mainly white, with a black spot before and behind the eye; under parts white.

RANGE: Breeds north to central Greenland and Spitzbergen. Winters, chiefly at sea, north to southern California (casually), Costa Rica (casually), Ecuador, the northwestern Indian Ocean, and Japan; south to the ocean off the coast of Peru.

STATUS IN S. C.: Rare transient, May 17 to June 3, and September 25 to October 25, mostly in the coast region. Recorded north to Chester County; east to Cape Romain and Mt. Pleasant; south to the Savannah River.

HISTORY: Although, as Wayne (1910) states, this species "undoubtedly occurs abundantly off the coast during the migrations," it is virtually unknown ashore. Strangely enough, the first specimen for South Carolina was not from the coast at all but was taken in Chester County, 150 miles from the ocean, by Leverett M. Loomis on May 17, 1880.

Bent (1927) lists two records, one from Frogmore, Beaufort County, and one from "Sea Islands," September 25 and October 25 respectively. These are observations by Walter J. Hoxie; the September record was made in 1885 and the other probably about the same time. The first known specimen for the coast region was secured by a cat. The animal, which belonged to Wayne, brought a Northern Phalarope into his house on June 3, 1903, and, Wayne said, "Before I could secure it, she had eaten all except a wing." Wayne later saw a Northern Phalarope off Mt. Pleasant, on May 28, 1913, and considered his record "positive."

It was twenty years before another bird was recorded. On May 30, 1933, E. A. Simons, Andrew Simons, and Sprunt were on Cape Island, in company with Harold F. West, then in charge of the Cape Romain Wildlife Refuge. They saw a small bird in the surf, just beyond the breakers; Sprunt had barely identified it as a phalarope, when it rose and flew directly toward the beach, alighting about 25 feet away. It was a female Northern Phalarope in high plumage. One of her legs dangled loosely, and as the bird stood, the head drooped noticeably. The observers approached to within 10 feet; then the bird rose, circled a little, and came to rest again. This was repeated until finally it flew out over the surf and alighted there.

One year later on May 29, 1934, an adult female was taken on Bull's Island by Edward M. Moore and presented to the Charleston Museum. On the night before this specimen was secured, the highest tide recorded on this coast in twenty-three years occurred, with a wind of 53 miles an hour. The weather had doubtless blown the bird ashore.

The habits, feeding methods, and general characteristics of this species are in general like those of the other two. Great flocks, sometimes running into thousands, are seen during migrations from coastwise steamers or fishing craft.

Family Stercorariidae: Jaegers and Skuas

POMARINE JAEGER
170. *Stercorarius pomarinus* (Temminck) (36)

(Lat., *Stercorarius*, pertaining to excrement, as a scavenger; Gr., *pomarinus*, flap-nosed.)

DESCRIPTION: Length 20.00 to 23.00 inches. Middle tail feathers broad and more or less twisted. *Adult, light phase.* Top and sides of head dark slate color; the hind head, nape, and lower parts white; ear coverts straw yellow. *Immature, light phase.* Above dark brown varied with buff, the head, neck, and lower parts dull buff barred with dark brown. *Adult* and *immature, dark phase.* Entirely sooty slate color.

RANGE: Breeds north to central Greenland and Spitzbergen; south to northern Alaska, Baffin Island, and northern Russia. Winters north to southern California, Virginia, the Orkney Islands, and Japan; south to Peru, southern Africa, and Australia.

STATUS IN S. C.: Accidental in the coast region.

HISTORY: There is but one record of this species in South Carolina waters, that made by Allan R. Phillips near Charleston on November 4, 1943. The bird was seen from shipboard and came close enough to be readily identified. The occurrence is thus authenticated, even though the bird was not collected. W. C. Starrett records having seen two Pomarine Jaegers from shipboard, March 23, 1945, "200 miles SE of Cape Lookout, N. C." This would place the locality off the South Carolina coast (*Auk, 64:* 1947, 320).

The peculiar twisted appearance of the broad, elongated middle tail feathers of this bird is sufficient for identification. In food and general habits this Jaeger does not differ materially from our other jaegers.

PARASITIC JAEGER

171. *Stercorarius parasiticus* (Linnaeus) (37)

(Lat., *parasiticus*, parasitic.)

DESCRIPTION: Length 15.00 to 21.00 inches. Central tail feathers pointed and tapering but not twisted. *Adult, light phase.* Crown dark brown; neck white; rest of upper parts brownish gray; sides of head white tinged with straw yellow; lower surface white. *Adult, dark phase.* Uniformly grayish brown, but neck often tinged with yellow. *Immature.* Dull colored and much mottled with brown, cinnamon, white, and buff.

RANGE: Breeds north to Melville Island, northern Greenland, and Spitzbergen; south to southwestern Alaska and northern Labrador. Winters north to southern California, South Carolina, the Mediterranean Sea, and northwestern India; south to Tierra del Fuego, southern Africa, and New Zealand.

STATUS IN S. C.: Rare winter visitor, November 5 to April 26, mainly in the coastal area. Reported north to Horry County; south to Charleston County; west to Aiken County (probably).

HISTORY: Besides a few sight records, there is one actual specimen of the Parasitic Jaeger extant from South Carolina. This is a bird secured off Charleston Harbor, April 26, 1935, by E. Milby Burton and now in the Charleston Museum. Another bird was taken by D. Henderson on November 7, 1936, on the Savannah River, three miles below Augusta, and is in the collection of Dr. E. E. Murphey.

It is not because the species is rare on this coast that more have not been seen or taken, but simply because it occurs at sea and is rarely seen from the shoreline. Collecting, therefore, is difficult for obvious reasons. At long intervals these piratical birds may appear in harbors or close to beaches, but unless an observer happens to be on hand at such a time with the means of securing it, the chance is lost.

Sprunt has seen the Parasitic Jaeger but once from shore; on March 10, 1932, he watched one chasing gulls at Big Bay Island. Wayne stated that he had "occasionally" seen it pursuing gulls in Charleston Harbor in November. Its presence offshore is well known to the crews of trawlers or coastwise vessels, and its stay in South Carolina waters runs from November to late April.

Jaegers are swift, powerful, hawk-like sea birds of dark and light plumage and peculiar, elongated middle tail feathers. They go through two distinct color phases. They often attack gulls, terns, and other marine birds and force them to give up their catches of fish.

LONG-TAILED JAEGER
172. *Stercorarius longicaudus* Vieillot (38)

(Lat., *longicaudus*, long-tailed.)

DESCRIPTION: Length 20.00 to 23.00 inches. Middle tail feathers very long and slender. *Adult, light phase.* Cap brownish black, the rest of head and neck straw yellow; remainder of upper parts slate color, the wings and tail darker; lower parts anteriorly white, posteriorly slate color. *Immature, light phase.* Similar to the adult but middle tail feathers nearly as short as the remainder and the entire plumage similar to that of the immature Parasitic Jaeger. *Adult* and *immature, dark phase.* Wholly brownish black varied a little with buff or ochraceous.

RANGE: Breeds north to northern Alaska, northern Greenland, Spitzbergen, and the Arctic coast of Siberia; south to central western Alaska, northern Labrador, northern Norway, northern Russia, and St. Lawrence Island. Winters north to California and South Carolina; south to Chile, Argentina, the Mediterranean Sea, and Japan.

STATUS IN S. C.: Accidental in the coast region.

HISTORY: Thus far, only two records of the Long-tailed Jaeger exist for South Carolina. It was observed from the Low-country beaches by Wayne on two occasions. The first was on December 21, 1896, when Wayne saw a single individual chasing a flock of gulls off Capers Island. Wayne saw it again on February 3, 1908, off Dewees Island. Although no specimen of this species has yet been taken in the State, Wayne seems to have been familiar with the Parasitic Jaeger, the only species with which the Long-tail would likely be confused. Wayne saw a number of Long-tails in Florida before his observations were made in South Carolina. Therefore, Wayne's records appear to be authentic.

In habits and food the Long-tail is very similar to the Parasitic.

Family Laridae: Gulls and Terns

GLAUCOUS GULL
173. *Larus hyperboreus hyperboreus* Gunnerus (42)

(Lat., *Larus*, a gull; *hyperboreus*, far northern.)

DESCRIPTION: Length 26.00 to 32.00 inches. Back and wings pale gull gray; rest of plumage white; head and neck sometimes streaked with gray; no dark wing tips.

RANGE: Breeds north to Melville Island, northern Greenland, Franz Josef Land, and New Siberia Island; south to Mackenzie, Newfoundland, Iceland, northern Europe, and Kamchatka. Winters north to southern Alaska, Greenland, central Europe, and Japan; south to central California, Florida, the Azores, and the Caspian Sea.

STATUS IN S. C.: Casual winter visitor, November 19 to April 6, only on the coast. Observed north to Charleston; south to the mouth of the Savannah River.

HISTORY: This pale gull of the Arctic seas occurs only casually in South Carolina. The first intimation of its occurrence was due to the vigilance of Ivan R. Tomkins who, while attached to the U. S. Dredge "Morgan," secured a specimen on February

28, 1931, at the Savannah River entrance. A little more than a month later, on April 6, he took another at the same place, both birds being shot on the Georgia side of the river.

Twelve years later, on November 19, 1943, a white-winged gull was seen on the Cooper River waterfront in Charleston by William Humphreys. He reported it at once, and Chamberlain made an unsuccessful attempt to collect it. On November 26, Alexander Sprunt, IV, saw what may have been the same bird from the Ashley River Bridge at Charleston. Since identification between Glaucous and Iceland Gulls is notoriously difficult in the field, it is not possible to be definite regarding this specimen but the likelihood is that it was the Glaucous Gull.

On November 22, 1947, Alexander Sprunt, IV, again saw a large white-winged gull on the Cooper River waterfront, at the foot of Elliott Street, Charleston. He promptly called Chamberlain, who secured the bird two days later. Examination proved it to be a Glaucous Gull. It is the first specimen taken in South Carolina.

Since that time there has been one additional record. A bird in second year plumage was seen on Bull's Island on April 4, 1949, by Mr. and Mrs. G. W. Cottrell, Jr., and Governor and Mrs. Robert F. Bradford of Massachusetts. It was observed at close range among Herring Gulls, Royal and Forster's Terns resting on the beach at the south end of the Island. These observers are familiar with the bird in Massachusetts.

The Glaucous Gull is a powerful, rapacious bird, preying upon other sea birds and capable of swallowing entire birds as large as the Black-bellied Plover. In addition to being noticeably larger than the abundant Herring Gull, the Glaucous Gull lacks the black wing tips of that bird. Northern fishermen and sailors refer to it as "Burgomaster."

174. GREAT BLACK-BACKED GULL: *Larus marinus* Linnaeus (47)

(Lat., *marinus*, marine.)

DESCRIPTION: Length 28.00 to 31.00 inches. *Adult.* Back and wings blackish gray; rest of plumage white. *Immature.* Resembles a young Herring Gull, but is paler, particularly on head, neck, and lower parts.

RANGE: Breeds north to central western Greenland and Iceland; south to southeastern Quebec, Massachusetts, Scotland, and northern Russia. Winters north to southern Greenland and Great Britain; south to central Ohio, northern Florida, Canary Islands, and the Caspian Sea.

STATUS IN S. C.: Rare winter visitor, January 8 to May 12, only on the coast. Known north to South Island (Georgetown County); south to Beaufort County.

HISTORY: This large Gull, unmistakable in adult plumage, occurs only as a rare winter visitor to South Carolina. However, there is a probability that it will be seen more frequently in the future, for it appears to be extending its winter range regularly to North Carolina and may eventually come down in numbers to the South Carolina coast at that season.

W. J. Hoxie appears to have been familiar with this bird in the Beaufort region for he speaks of it as being a "rare winter visitor" (*Orn. and Ool., 10*: 1885, 29). He later collected one in Chatham County, Georgia, which is along the Savannah River. This specimen is now in the collection of the University of Georgia.

An excellent photograph of a Black-back was secured on Bull's Island, in January, 1940, by Allan D. Cruickshank, who observed it there on January 8, 10, and 18. On May 12, 1935, Lester L. Walsh and Sprunt saw an immature on Bull's Island. It was checked thoroughly by Walsh, who is very familiar with the species about Long Island, New York. On January 21, 1936, Robert P. Allen and Sprunt saw another in Oyster Bay, Cape Romain Refuge, Allen knowing the bird well.

It is entirely possible that this gull is overlooked at times, especially when it is in its immature plumage. Observers are few and the general similarity between the Black-back and the Herring Gull may be confusing. The adults, of course, cannot be mistaken.

HERRING GULL
175. *Larus argentatus smithsonianus* Coues (51a)

(Lat., *argentatus*, silvery; *smithsonianus*, of [James] Smithson.)

LOCAL NAMES: Sea Gull.

DESCRIPTION: Length 22.00 to 26.00 inches. *Adult*. Back and wings pale gray, the wings tipped with black; rest of plumage white; bill yellow. *Immature*. Grayish brown, the upper parts mottled with white; bill flesh color at base, dark brown terminally.

RANGE: Breeds north to central Alaska and southern Baffin Island; south to central British Columbia and Massachusetts. Winters north to southeastern Alaska and the Gulf of St. Lawrence; south to Yucatan and Cuba.

STATUS IN S. C.: Permanent resident, but does not breed; common in winter, less common in summer; most numerous along the coast. Observed north to Greenville and Lancaster counties; east to Horry County; south to Beaufort County; west to Aiken and Pickens counties.

HISTORY: Most of the Herring Gulls arrive about mid-October, a few days earlier or later, depending upon seasonal variation; and they remain until early May. In recent years many have extended their stay into and through the summer. Most of these birds are immature. The latest Piedmont date is a record from Six-mile Creek, Pickens County, June 4, 1931 (F. Sherman).

Adult birds are easy to know, but immatures are very different in appearance, being dark brown all over. In the second-year plumage, this dark color gives place to a much lighter tone, rendering the bird very mottled. The rump is then white and the tail is dark-tipped.

Large numbers of these gulls frequent the water fronts of all coastal towns. They are also common in the salt marshes and on the barrier beaches, tidal rivers, and large lakes. Waterfront birds often become very tame and are easy to study. There are marked differences between the behavior of waterfront gulls and that of birds seen on the remote beaches. Now and then one may watch gulls take shellfish aloft and drop them on the hard packed sands of the beach in order to break them. The technique is characteristic but it is not a common practice locally. The notes made by Sprunt on his first observation of this habit locally state that "For the first time on this coast, I saw birds indulging in dropping shellfish on Folly Island, March 1, 1929. There were at least twenty gulls in the flock but all were not active. The beach was strewn with smashed shells, all of which were yellow cockles (*Cardium muricatum*)."

The Herring Gull has an astonishing life span as is evidenced by the history of a specimen kept in captivity at Morehead City, N. C. At its death, it had attained a known age of forty-nine years.

FOOD: The role of scavenger played by most gulls is well recognized. This species takes practically any animal food it can find. It eats garbage and carrion as well as mice, mollusks, crustaceans, squid, marine worms, starfish, and insects. Marine algae appears to be the main vegetable item. About 50 per cent of the total food is fish, largely in carrion form. The value of gulls as harbor and beach "clean-up squads" is, of course, high.

176. RING-BILLED GULL: *Larus delawarensis* Ord (54)

(Lat., *delawarensis*, of the Delaware [River], whence it was first described.)

LOCAL NAMES: Sea Gull.

DESCRIPTION: Length 18.00 to 20.00 inches. *Adult.* A smaller edition of the Herring Gull, but with a black band on the yellow bill. *Immature.* Mottled gray, white, and brown; tail gray to white, with a wide blackish brown band near the tip.

RANGE: Breeds north to southern Alaska and southeastern Quebec; south to northern California and northwestern New York. Winters north to southern British Columbia and the Gulf of St. Lawrence; south to Cuba.

STATUS IN S. C.: Permanent resident, but does not breed; abundant in winter, less common in summer; occurs largely on the coast. Observed north to Horry County; south to Beaufort and Jasper counties; west to the Santee National Wildlife Refuge.

HISTORY: The Ring-billed Gull is very like the Herring in the adult plumage, except that it is noticeably smaller and has the banded beak which gives it its name. Size is again a criterion in separating the immatures of the two species, though the Ring-bills are much lighter in color than young Herring Gulls and are marked by the dark, banded tail.

Most of the Ring-bills arrive with the Herring Gulls in mid-October, and stay about the same length of time. Many stay through the summer; immatures far outnumber adults at this time. This is true also of the Herring Gulls.

The Ring-bill frequents similar situations and exhibits the same behavior as its larger relatives.

PLATE XV: CAROLINA PAROQUETS

Oil Painting by Francis Lee Jaques

FOOD: Though a water-front and beach scavenger, the Ring-bill may be seen following plows and tractors during field cultivation and picking insects from the ground and air. Stomach analysis has revealed the presence of weevils, grasshoppers, crickets, locusts, cockroaches, and bugs, such food amounting to one-fifth of the total. Fish compose about 50 per cent of the entire diet.

177. LAUGHING GULL: *Larus atricilla* Linnaeus (58)

(Lat., *atricilla*, black-tailed, referring to young birds.)

LOCAL NAMES: Sea Gull; Black-headed Gull.

DESCRIPTION: Length 15.00 to 17.00 inches. *Adult in summer.* Head and upper neck dark gray; back and wings neutral gray, the latter with black tips; tail and undersurface white; bill red. *Adult in winter.* Similar to the summer plumage, but head and upper neck white. *Immature.* Brownish gray; wing tips dull black; tail darker toward the end and tipped with white.

RANGE: Breeds north to Maine; south to the coasts of Texas, Honduras, and Venezuela. Winters north to Louisiana and North Carolina; south to Peru and southeastern Brazil.

STATUS IN S. C.: Abundant permanent resident, mostly in the coast region. Reported north to Horry County; south to Beaufort and Jasper counties; west to the Santee National Wildlife Refuge.

HISTORY: Since the appearance of Wayne's *Birds of South Carolina* in 1910, much has been learned about the status of the Laughing Gull in the State. It was long supposed to be only a winter visitor, but it is definitely established as a permanent resident which nests regularly. When the authors of this volume prepared the *Supplement to the Birds of South Carolina* (1931), it was known that the Laughing Gull was a permanent resident but there was no nesting record. However, a record did exist in an unpublished manuscript of Walter J. Hoxie, now in the collection of the Charleston Museum. In it, after giving the date of April 8, 1884, for this species at Bull Point, Beaufort County, he says that it breeds there.

Nearly half a century passed before the Laughing Gull was again recorded nesting in the State. On May 23, 1933, a pair with a nest and two eggs was found on White Banks, Bull's Bay, Charleston County, by E. M. Burton, G. R. Lunz, and Chamberlain.

Since that time, the Bull's Bay colony has grown with fluctuating fortune. Three nests were found in May, 1935, and from small beginnings the birds have numbered up to two hundred pairs. Only one other locality in the State has been known as a nesting site, this being Egg Bank in St. Helena Sound, Beaufort County, now washed away. Here, E. J. DeCamps found a few pairs nesting on June 16, 1945. Incubation was well advanced.

The nest is composed of seaweeds, grasses, and sedge, raised a little off the sand or built up from a muddy bottom on grassy banks. The eggs almost invariably number three, though there may be two or four. They are very dark in color, scrawled and splotched with black. They average 53.5 x 38.5 millimeters. They are laid in late May and early June as a rule, and require about twenty days for incubation.

This gull is easy to recognize in summer, mainly because of its size, blackish hood, and dark mantle. The much smaller Bonaparte's Gull, which also has a black hood, leaves for the north in late April and early May, before the Laughing Gull nests. Immature birds in winter may cause trouble in identification, but in this species, the white upper tail coverts combined with the dark breast are diagnostic. Otherwise, the plumage is of a dusky, mottled gray. The name of the bird is derived from its peculiar cackling cry, which resembles high-pitched laughter. It is a very noisy bird on its nesting grounds, filling the air with an incessant din.

The Laughing Gull, like other gulls, frequents water fronts, marshes, and beaches. It is rather piratical: it sometimes robs the Brown Pelican of its prey by watching it dive, alighting on the Pelican's head and as it comes to the surface, snatching the fish. No other local gull seems to practice this kind of thievery.

FOOD: The Laughing Gull is an insect eater in certain localities. It takes beetles, grasshoppers, and ants. Flocks of the birds follow tractors breaking ground and pick up insects. As a scavenger this bird renders distinct service.

178. BONAPARTE'S GULL: *Larus philadelphia* (Ord) (60)

(Lat., *philadelphia*, to Philadelphia.)

LOCAL NAMES; Sea Gull; Surf Gull.

DESCRIPTION: Length 12.00 to 14.00 inches. *Summer adult.* Head and upper neck dark gray; back and wings pale neutral gray, the latter with black tips; legs red; bill black. *Winter adult.* Similar to the summer plumage but head and upper neck white with a black spot on the side of the head near the eye. *Immature.* Similar to the adult in winter, but back and lesser wing coverts grayish brown; tail with a subterminal dark brown band.

RANGE: Breeds north to northern Alaska and northern Mackenzie; south to central British Columbia and central Alberta. Winters north to southeastern Alaska and Maine; south to Mexico and Florida.

STATUS IN S. C.: Common winter resident, early October to June 9, casually August 20, mostly in the coast region. Recorded north to Horry County; south to Beaufort and Jasper counties; casually west to Pickens County.

HISTORY: The graceful little Bonaparte's Gull is one of the most attractive of the family of gulls. It usually arrives later in South Carolina than the others. It remains through the winter and departs just after attaining the breeding plumage, when it appears like a tiny edition of the Laughing Gull. This plumage appears during the latter part of April. In some seasons it occurs earlier and black-headed birds have been seen in late March (Wayne). The latest record is an immature bird seen at Dean Hall, Cooper River, on June 9, 1934 (Sprunt). Another late instance was that of a bird caught at Six-mile Creek, Pickens County, June 4, 1931, and banded by O. L. Cartwright and David Dunavan.

During the period when the Bonaparte's Gull is common locally, no one need confuse it with any other gull, though it associates with them all. It is, by far, the smallest, exceedingly light and airy in its movements; and the presence of the conspicuous blackish spot on the side of the head will always distinguish it. Any waterfront situation, but particularly near a sewer outlet, will reveal gulls, and size comparisons are often a simple matter.

FOOD: Contents of seventy-eight stomachs of Bonaparte's Gull, examined by the U. S. Fish and Wildlife Service, showed the food to be about 33 per cent insects, 50 per cent fish, and 17 per cent snails and crustaceans. The fish were small species, mostly of minnow size, and of no commercial value.

GULL-BILLED TERN
179. *Gelochelidon nilotica aranea* (Wilson) (63)

(Gr., *Gelochelidon*, laughing swallow; Lat., *nilotica*, of the River Nile; *aranea*, pertaining to the spider.)

DESCRIPTION: Length 13.00 to 15.00 inches. Bill heavier than that of the other terns; tail not deeply forked; crown and occipital crest black; back pearl gray; wings darker; under-surface and tail nearly or quite white; bill black.

RANGE: Breeds locally along the Atlantic coast of the United States north to Virginia; south to south central Florida, and on the coast of the Gulf of Mexico from Mississippi to Texas; also to Cuba and the Bahama Islands. Winters north to Texas and northern Florida; south to Peru.

STATUS IN S. C.: Fairly common summer resident from the middle of April to September 19, only in the coast region. Recorded north to Cape Romain; south to Beaufort County.

HISTORY: Much has been learned about the Gull-billed Tern since Wayne wrote, in 1910, that it "does not breed" in South Carolina. He considered it a transient visitor, but it is now established as a regular summer resident and it nests here, if only sparingly.

The Gull-bill is not hard to recognize, for its stout, black bill is very different from that of any other tern and the tail is not deeply forked. The best means of identification in the breeding season is the call, which sounds very much like "katydid-katydid." Indeed, if terns were as vociferous during the rest of the year as they are on their nesting grounds, much of the confusion regarding their identity would be eliminated, for the notes of all South Carolina terns are markedly different and one can differentiate the various species overhead, even while walking along the sands with head down. The notes of the Gull-bill are as completely unlike the buzz of Forster's, the nasal "tee-ar" of the Common, or strident "cack" of the Royal, as anything could well be.

It was not until 1929 that the first eggs of this tern were found in South Carolina. On May 28 of that year, Dr. Frank Oastler, of New York, discovered a few pairs breeding on Cape Island, off McClellanville, now a part of the Cape Romain Refuge. Nesting does not occur regularly in this locality, but there are other records. One is for July 17, 1934 (Chamberlain and H. F. West). Another is for June 18, 1936 (E. Milby Burton); still another for June 8, 1941, when A. H. DuPre, of the Refuge staff, found three nests with eggs. DuPre also recorded nests there in 1942. In June, 1944, W. P. Baldwin, also of the staff of the Cape Romain Refuge, found twenty-five nests there, with young birds on June 24. Others were noted there in June, 1947, by Chamberlain and Burton. It is entirely possible that this tern breeds far more regularly than recorded observations indicate.

The two or three eggs are laid in a slight hollow in the sand, among bits of shell, and may be close to those of the Royal and Least Terns and the Black Skimmer. They are distinctive enough to those familiar with oölogy, but can easily be overlooked by an observer not familiar with the difference in tern eggs. They are of a greenish-buff color, spotted with dark brown and lilac, and average 47.0 x 34.0 millimeters. Incubation requires eighteen to twenty days. The Gull-billed Tern raises only one brood.

FOOD: This species takes more insects than most of the other terns except the Black Tern. It feeds extensively over marshes. Some observers maintain that it takes nothing but insects, but stomach contents have revealed remains of crabs and other crustaceans. However, grasshoppers, locusts, dragon flies, and beetles form the bulk of the diet. Burton and Chamberlain examined a downy young bird in the colony on Cape Island in 1947, which had about two inches of the tail of a lizard (*Cnemidophorus*) protruding from its beak.

180. FORSTER'S TERN: *Sterna forsteri* Nuttall (69)

(Lat., *Sterna*, from Old English sterne, a tern; *forsteri*, to John R. Forster.)

LOCAL NAMES: Sea-swallow.

DESCRIPTION: Length 14.00 to 15.00 inches. *Summer*. Top of head and nape black; rest of upper surface pallid gray; lower surface and outer edge of outermost tail feather white. *Winter*. Head and nape white, with a dark stripe through the eye.

RANGE: Breeds north to central Washington, central Alberta, and central eastern Virginia; south to central California and southeastern South Carolina. Winters north to southern California and North Carolina; south to Guatemala and the coast of Brazil (casually).

STATUS IN S. C.: Common permanent resident along the coast. Reported north to Myrtle Beach (Horry County); south to Beaufort County; west to Santee National Wildlife Refuge.

HISTORY: The exact status of Forster's Tern in South Carolina is something of a puzzle. A really abundant bird much of the year, especially in winter, it falls off sharply at other seasons, but occurs during every month of the year.

There are only two records of Forster's Tern breeding in the State. In marginal notes in a personal copy of S. F. Baird's *Birds*, volume IX of the *Pacific Railroad Report* (now in the Charleston Museum), W. J. Hoxie gave its status on the sea islands of the Beaufort region as a breeding resident (*c.* 1870). He apparently had "Eggs with a greenish ground color nearly as dark as Mockingbirds." Of the eggs he further said, "The Ethiopian who had my specimens in charge sat on them but they did not hatch." However, it must be mentioned that Hoxie gave Havell's Tern (*Sterna havelli* Audubon) the same status as Forster's and noted that its eggs had a creamy ground color. These two names apply to the same bird, and Hoxie indicated his doubt by writing (1875), "It is unfortunate that I did not secure a larger number of skins & eggs of this species & forsteri. As it is I hardly know whether to differ with Coues or agree." Coues believed, correctly, that Havell's

Tern, as described by Audubon, was merely the adult winter plumage of Forster's and not a distinct species.

The other breeding record came to light in a conversation between Dr. E. E. Murphey and Sprunt. A cousin of Dr. Murphey, Elwood Murphey, had collected a set of three eggs on June 24, 1904, at Bird Bank in Bull's Bay, Charleston County. A companion had identified them as those of Forster's Tern. Dr. Murphey secured them and notified Wayne, who was a great friend of his. Since Wayne doubted the identification, the set was sent to the Smithsonian Institution in Washington, where the determination was confirmed. Dr. Murphey presented the eggs to Sprunt in 1937.

Usually, Forster's Tern varies the family custom of nesting by constructing a real nest of grass, in rank growths of grass or on drifted mats of sedge. The eggs usually are three or four in number, are buffy brown in color with splashes of dark brown or black. They average 43.0 x 31.0 millimeters. Incubation takes about twenty-three days. Forster's Tern raises only one brood.

The note of this species is unmistakable, a peculiar buzzing "za-a-ap." Once learned it is a great help in picking out this species among the swirling multitudes of birds over a nesting ground. The adult bird is often confused with the Common Tern, but a good field mark is the fact that the tail is of the same gray as the back not a contrasting white, as with the Common. The immature bird has a conspicuous black patch through the eye and ear; the adult in winter plumage also has a black spot near the ear. There is no black cap in winter, and the bird is generally silent then.

Forster's Tern patrols ocean beaches, marshy bays, rivers, and estuaries, securing its prey by plunging headlong into the water. The flight is very airy and graceful, the head often held down with the bill at a right angle to the body, as it searches the surface below.

Occasionally Forster's Tern is blown inland. W. P. Baldwin recorded a number seen at the Santee Refuge in Clarendon County on September 18, 1945, following strong winds on the coast.

FOOD: Forster's Tern eats insects, particularly grasshoppers and various insect larvae. It also consumes such fish as carp, perch, pompano, anchovies, killifish, and menhaden.

181. COMMON TERN: *Sterna hirundo hirundo* Linnaeus (70)

(Lat., *hirundo*, a swallow.)

LOCAL NAMES: Sea-swallow.

DESCRIPTION: Length 13.00 to 16.00 inches. *Summer.* Crown and nape black; back and wings pale gray; upper tail coverts, neck, lower tail coverts, and most of tail white, the outer edge of outermost tail feather dark gray; breast and belly pale gray; bill red. *Winter.* Similar to the summer plumage but anterior part of head mostly white.

RANGE: Breeds north to southern Mackenzie, Newfoundland, Norway, and northwestern Siberia; south to southern Texas, the Virgin Islands, the Canary Islands, and Persia. Winters north to Lower California and South Carolina; south to the Straits of Magellan, southern Africa, and the coast of western India.

STATUS IN S. C.: Common ~~winter~~ resident, August to June 22, more numerous during migrations, and occurring mostly on the coastal plain. Recorded north to Lake Murray (Lexington County) ; east to Horry County; south to Beaufort County; west to Aiken County.

HISTORY: The Common Tern well deserves its name for it is one of the terns most frequently seen. It is very much like Forster's Tern, and many people have difficulty in distinguishing between the two birds in the field. It should be recalled that the tail in this species is white, in contrast to the back; whereas the tail of Forster's Tern is gray like the back. In the winter plumage, which lacks the usual black cap, a line through the eye continues around the back of the neck. The corresponding mark of Forster's Tern is confined to the region of the eye, before and behind.

In South Carolina, the Common Tern is for the most part a transient visitor. It appears in both spring and fall and remains from May 5 to June 22, and again in August to September 21. Now and then, a few appear in winter, but South Carolina is the northern portion of its winter range, and it is then very sporadic and uncertain. Three were seen on December 24, 1939, in Horry County by Richard G. Kuerzi.

The only inland record to date is that made by Chamberlain in September, 1948, at Lake Murray in Lexington County. The bird has been recorded several times at Augusta, however, and at various other localities in the interior of Georgia.

There is nothing in the behavior and habits of the Common Tern which differs very much from other members of its family. It is a graceful, attractive species, and an active, spectacular fisherman. The note is highly distinctive, a strident "tee-ar-r-r," the latter part very guttural. Unfortunately, during the time it is present in South Carolina it is a silent bird as a rule.

FOOD: This is one of the really fish-eating terns. The great majority of 185 stomachs examined showed nothing but fish remains. Non-commercial varieties make up the bulk— menhaden, sand lances, and minnows. Anchovies and sticklebacks were also represented, as well as a few perch, small mackerel, and carp. Larvae of May flies, water beetles, ants, moths, and crustaceans were found in some of the stomachs.

182. ROSEATE TERN: *Sterna dougallii dougallii* Montagu   (72)

(Lat., *dougallii*, to Dr. McDougall, of Scotland.)

DESCRIPTION: Length 14.00 to 17.00 inches. *Summer.* Top of head and nape black; upper tail coverts and tail white; remainder of upper surface pale gray; bill mostly black; undersurface white with a rosy tint. *Winter.* Similar to the summer plumage, but forehead and fore part of crown white.

RANGE: Breeds north to Nova Scotia, Great Britain, and Jutland; south to British Honduras, the Grenadines, and Trinidad. Winters north to eastern North Carolina (casually), the Bahama Islands, and the Mediterranean Sea; south to central eastern Brazil and southern Africa.

STATUS IN S. C.: Rare transient, March 29 to May 14, and July 28 (casually) to October; occurs only along the coast. Reported north to Horry County; south to Beaufort County.

HISTORY: The Roseate Tern is not very well known in South Carolina chiefly because its migrations pass offshore, where few observers have opportunity to see it. Walter J. Hoxie recorded it from Egg Bank, St. Helena Sound, May 14, 1870. Wayne (1910) states that "Mr. Ellison A. Smyth, Jr., has taken it near Charleston in October." This apparently is the only definite time that it has been taken. Unfortunately Wayne did not give the year when it was secured.

In company with Charles Urner and John B. May, Sprunt saw three of these terns off the beach of Dewees on April 19, 1934. A. H. DuPre and Dr. E. P. Maynard got excellent views of a Roseate on March 29, 1937, at Cape Romain. On the following day, Dr. Maynard and C. C. West again saw the bird at close range. On April 16 and July 28, 1940, a Roseate Tern was seen near Long Bay Plantation, Horry County, by Richard G. Kuerzi. The most recent record for South Carolina was made by Lester L. Walsh, who saw a Roseate on April 5, 1948, at Bull's Island.

The Roseate takes its name from the rosy tint of the breast during the nesting season. The tail is very deeply forked, and it is among the most graceful of a graceful group. The note is different from that of all other terns, a very musical, mellow double call, suggestive of a shore bird. It has been described by Peterson as "*chivy*."

Its diving tactics are spectacular in the extreme, and the bird at times disappears beneath the surface with the violence of its plunge.

FOOD: Nothing of a very specific nature is known regarding the food, but it is probably chiefly composed of small fish.

EASTERN SOOTY TERN
183. *Sterna fuscata fuscata* Linnaeus   (75)

(Lat., *fuscata*, dusky.)

DESCRIPTION: Length 15.00 to 17.00 inches. Top of head and nape black; rest of upper parts and wings fuscous black; forehead white; undersurface white; bill black.

RANGE: Breeds north to southern Texas, Florida, the Bahama Islands, and the islands in the Gulf of Guinea (western Africa); south to British Honduras, Trinidad, and the Island of St. Helena in the south Atlantic Ocean. Winters south to Patagonia and the Falkland Islands.

STATUS IN S. C.: Casual summer visitor, June 14 to September 25, mostly coastwise. Recorded north to Florence County; east to Horry County and Cape Island (Cape Romain); south to Charleston; west to Clarendon County.

HISTORY: Though some of the terns give trouble to the amateur because of their similarity in appearance, this species is unmistakable. It is the only one which is dark above and light beneath, and it can be expected to occur only during or after a tropical storm. South Carolina is far north of its normal range.

It was added to the State List on July 29, 1926, when, during a heavy blow, Sprunt saw three birds over the Boulevard section of Charleston (*Auk 43*: 1926, 535). The next day a dead specimen was picked up at Mt. Pleasant, across the

Harbor, by a Negro and brought to Ellison A. Williams, who presented it to Wayne (*Auk, 43*: 1926, 534). Other live birds seen about this time include two observed at Porcher's Bluff, Charleston County, by Philip Porcher; one taken alive at Myrtle Beach by Hugh Belser, Jr.; and one caught at Pawley's Island July 30, by Wayne. E. von S. Dingle found several dead ones on the Isle of Palms at this time.

On September 18, 1928, one was secured alive at Windermere, St. Andrew's Parish, Charleston County, by V. L. T. Cooper and presented to the Charleston Museum. Two dead birds were found on the Isle of Palms two days later. The presence of all these can be accounted for by a heavy storm.

On July 18, 1931, while banding Royal Terns, E. Milby Burton saw an Eastern Sooty at Cape Island. The bird was in sight for some hours. The weather was clear and mild and this is the only record for the species during normal atmospheric conditions. Burton recorded the species again on October 13, 1933, when he found a dried specimen on Raccoon Keys, Charleston County. This one may have been blown there by the storm of September 6 of that year.

Three dead birds, and one living specimen, which was later released, were found on the Isle of Palms by E. von S. Dingle during the period of September 6-11, 1935. William Humphreys found another dead specimen on Sullivan's Island on September 8, 1935. These birds came as a result of the terrible hurricane which swept the Florida Keys a few days before.

During the hurricane of August 11, 1940, Richard G. Kuerzi saw a group of three, and another of eleven flying south, at Long Bay Plantation, Horry County. W. P. Baldwin saw five birds at the Santee Refuge on September 17-19, 1945, after a hurricane on the seventeenth. One dead adult and one immature, alive, were examined in the hand. An immature was seen being fed by an adult.

On September 25, 1947, both the writers happened to be in Florence, S. C., visiting H. L. Harllee, when D. B. Boswell brought to them a living immature Sooty Tern. It had been picked up on Highway 76, some 8 miles east of Florence a short while before, and appeared to be suffering from a lung ailment. It must have been blown northward by the tropical storm of the day before, which travelled up Florida from the region of the Keys, and struck the coastal region with diminished intensity on the twenty-fourth. These records constitute the history of the species in this State.

FOOD: The Sooty Tern subsists almost wholly on minnows and small fish.

BRIDLED TERN

184. *Sterna anaethetus melanoptera* Swainson (76)

(Gr., *anaethetus*, stolid, stupid; *melanoptera*, black-winged.)

DESCRIPTION: Length 14.00 to 15.00 inches. Top of head and nape black; back and upper surface of wings fuscous black; forehead, stripe over head, around neck and undersurface white.

RANGE: Resident and breeds north to the Bahama Islands; south to British Honduras and Aruba Island (coast of Venezuela).

Pintails Feeding

ALLAN D. CRUICKSHANK
National Audubon Society

Black Vulture Leaving Nest   S. A. GRIMES

Bob White Returning to Nest   S. A. GRIMES

Incubating Wild Turkey   ALEXANDER SPRUNT, JR.

STATUS IN S. C.: Accidental summer visitor, June 17 to September 20, mostly coastwise. Recorded north to the Isle of Palms; south to St. Helena Island; west to Orangeburg.

HISTORY: The Bridled Tern is another tropical wanderer of accidental occurrence. It was first taken in South Carolina by Walter J. Hoxie, at Frogmore, St. Helena Island, Beaufort County, August 25, 1885. The specimen was recorded by William Brewster (*Auk, 3*: 1886, 131).

Over a quarter century later, one flew aboard the SS "City of Memphis" when the vessel was 35 miles northeast of Tybee Island, Georgia, September 12, 1912. The bird was secured by a Mr. Jones, was eventually presented to Wayne and is now in the collection of the Charleston Museum (No. 30.147.384). The position of the ship at the time was off the South Carolina coast (*Auk, 30*: 1913, 105).

After the hurricane of late July, 1926, E. von S. Dingle found a dead specimen on the beach at the Isle of Palms, on August 2. He recorded the discovery (*Auk, 44*: 1927, 93). Again, after the 1928 storm, one was found on the same beach, September 20, by E. B. and B. R. Chamberlain and Sprunt.

A very curious occurrence took place on June 17, 1932, at Orangeburg, some 70 miles inland. A specimen of the Bridled Tern flew into the wire backstop of a tennis court and was killed by a small boy. Robert Furchgott secured the bird and sent it to the Charleston Museum. The weather at the time was rainy but not stormy (*Auk, 50*: 1933, 104).

Finally a dead bird was found September 7, 1935, by E. von S. Dingle on the Isle of Palms. The bird had undoubtedly been blown north by the famous Labor Day Hurricane (September 4) of the Florida Keys.

185. LEAST TERN: *Sterna albifrons antillarum* (Lesson) (74)

(Lat., *albifrons*, white foreheaded; *antillarum*, of the Antilles.)

LOCAL NAMES: Sea-swallow.

DESCRIPTION: Smallest of the South Carolina terns. Length 8.50 to 9.75 inches. Forehead, sides of head and neck, together with the lower surface white. Crown, nape, and stripe from bill to eye black; rest of upper parts pale gray.

RANGE: Breeds north to central Texas, southern Louisiana, and Massachusetts; south to British Honduras and central Venezuela. Winters north to southern Louisiana; south to Argentina and southern Brazil.

STATUS IN S. C.: Abundant summer resident, March 15 to October 28, mostly coastwise. Observed north to Horry County; south to Beaufort and Jasper counties; west to the Santee National Wildlife Refuge.

HISTORY: To contrast what Wayne (1910) had to say of this exquisite little tern, and what may be said of it today is to realize something of the strides made in wildlife conservation in the past quarter century. It is an illuminating and gratifying picture. Wayne said, when he wrote, that "As a result of the custom of adorning women's hats with birds, these beautiful little terns have become practically, if not absolutely, extinct on this coast . . . " That was a sad fact. Today the Least Tern is one of the most abundant and characteristic birds of the summer coast country;

sea islands, beach resorts, waterways, spoil banks, and even the mainland support colony upon colony of dozens, scores, and hundreds.

The establishment of laws prohibiting the wearing of wild bird plumage and the greatly increased sentiment for protection and encouragement of wildlife have saved the Least Tern, even though they were too late to save other birds. But when Wayne wrote, the situation, desperate as it was, had a slightly better aspect than he realized, for even then there were small colonies of about fifty pairs on Morris Island, Charleston Harbor, and on Raccoon Key in Bull's Bay (*Auk*, 27: 1910, 305). By the summer of 1927, at least six hundred pairs were found nesting within 50 miles north and south of Charleston. Since then the increase has been steady and now the situation is completely satisfactory. Small colonies are frequently found a few yards from heavily travelled highways.

The only inland record to date was made by W. P. Baldwin, who recorded a number on September 18-19, 1945, at the Santee Refuge after the hurricane of the seventeenth of that month.

The Least Tern builds its nest about the middle of May, and lays from one to four eggs, usually three. The nest is simply a slight hollow scraped in the bare sand and lined with bits of shell. The eggs, no two of which are alike in markings, vary from a light to a dark ground color and are mottled with spots, dots, and twisted marks ranging from lilac, through brown, to a color that it almost black. The result is a protective coloration so effective as to make the eggs almost invisible on the sand. The eggs measure, on the average, 31.0 x 23.5 millimeters. Incubation requires from fourteen to sixteen days, and the Least Tern raises one or two broods in a season. The young birds are clothed with a sand-buff brown and are very attractive.

FOOD: For the most part, small fish—killifish, anchovies, silversides, and menhaden. Examination of stomach contents reveals that shrimp, marine worms, and even ants form part of the Least Tern's diet.

186. ROYAL TERN: *Thalasseus maximus maximus* (Boddaert) (65)

(Gr., *Thalasseus*, of the sea; Lat., *maximus*, largest.)

DESCRIPTION: Length 18.00 to 21.00 inches. *Summer*. Crown black, the feathers lengthened into a crest; back and wings pale gray; undersurface white; bill red or orange. *Winter*. Similar, but the fore part of the top of the head all white.

RANGE: Breeds north to southern Texas and southeastern Virginia; south to the West Indies. Winters north to southern Louisiana and South Carolina; south to Argentina.

STATUS IN S. C.: Abundant permanent resident, but uncommon in winter. Reported north to Hamer (Dillon County) casually; east to Horry County; south to Beaufort County; casually west to Barnwell and Santee National Wildlife Refuge.

HISTORY: Caspian and Royal Terns are so much alike in appearance and size (though the Royal is actually the smaller), that in the field many people find it hard to distinguish between the two. The Royal Tern has a more deeply forked tail, the primaries are less dusky, and the whole contour of the bird is more elongated and streamlined; the Royal does not have the stout chunkiness of the Caspian.

Since the Royal Tern occurs every month in the year, it must be considered a permanent resident. It appears in greatest numbers in late March and early April. Only from about Christmas until late March is it relatively rare; though as a matter of fact it may now be seen at almost any time during the winter months. Its occurrence in winter has long been established by records; as early as 1888 E. A. Smyth stated that he had seen it in that season. Typical records for winter include a bird taken by E. Milby Burton off Charleston, January 27, 1933, this bird having been banded by him July 10, 1930; six seen in the Bull's Bay area during the Christmas Bird Count of December 22, 1939; and fifteen observed off Edisto Beach by George B. Rabb and Thomas M. Uzzell, Jr., January 8, 1949.

The nesting season usually starts early in June, and incubation requires twenty days. Eggs and nests are sometimes destroyed by high tides, and since the terns make new nests and lay new eggs to replace those that have been destroyed, the nesting season may be prolonged into August. Under normal circumstances the newly-hatched young birds will be found in greatest numbers in late June and in July. These dates are confirmed by summer banding records. Burton, who has banded almost ten thousand Royal Terns over a period of many years, notes that July 10-15 is nearly always the best time for such work.

One of the largest colonies ever examined on the South Carolina coast was investigated in 1947, when, on June 4, the authors estimated eleven thousand "nests" on Cape Island. This nesting had escaped a full moon tide of the night before. The birds were very tame and almost bewildering in numbers. The great majority of this colony, however, were destroyed by high water in July. Trips made there afterwards revealed about twenty-five hundred young which had escaped drowning; nine hundred of these were banded on July 25.

The Royal Tern usually lays but one egg, in a nest which is nothing but a slight depression in the sand. It is unusual to find two eggs in a nest, and still more unusual, three. An interesting count was once made by E. J. DeCamps, of Beaufort who, in a colony in St. Helena Sound numbering three thousand nests, found twenty-nine sets of three, three hundred sets of two, and the rest singles.

The eggs have a light ground color, sometimes almost white, with many spots which are normally rather small and well defined. However, the color variation is great, and one can find eggs with such large splashes of color as to make them appear almost wholly dark. Occasionally, eggs have no markings at all. The average measurement is 63.0 x 44.5 millimeters.

Egging was once practiced extensively on this coast, but is now practically, if not entirely a thing of the past. The sand crab (*Ocypoda arenaria*) sometimes destroys numbers of eggs, such damage being noted at Cape Romain in the 1947 season by Chamberlain. It is difficult to understand exactly how one of these crabs manages to break an egg so large and thick-shelled.

From the extensive banding of Royal Terns on the South Carolina coast interesting returns have been secured. One bird was recovered at Port Arthur, Texas; one bird, at Tule Lake, California (the long distance champion of a South Carolina banded tern). It was one year and four months old. One was taken at Hamer, South Carolina, a considerable distance inland, in August, 1940. This bird was undoubtedly blown there by the hurricane of that month. The ages of birds so recovered run anywhere from one year, to six, eight, and ten, the oldest being ten years eight months. Most of the returns have come from Florida, as might be expected. Birds have been taken there in late summer and fall as well as in winter, indicating a decided southward movement soon after the nesting season. Birds banded in South Carolina have been recovered in Cuba, Dominican Republic, Haiti, Jamaica, Colombia, and Mexico.

Wayne records that Royal Terns were shot in Barnwell County in August, 1893 (*Auk*, *11*: 1894, 85). W. P. Baldwin saw a number of these birds along with other terns at the Santee-Cooper Refuge, Clarendon County, on September 18-19, 1945. These two records and the Hamer, Dillon County, record already mentioned constitute the known inland occurrences.

FOOD: The Royal Tern eats menhaden, silversides, perch, bluefish, and shrimp. The young birds, when they are being banded, often regurgitate squid.

187. CABOT'S TERN: *Thalasseus sandvicensis acuflavidus* (Cabot) (67)

(Lat., *sandvicensis*, of Sandwich, England; *acuflavidus*, slender-pointed, yellowish, referring to bill.)

DESCRIPTION: Length 14.00 to 16.00 inches. Top of head, short crest, and nape black; back of wings pale gray; neck, rump, upper tail coverts, tail and under parts white; bill black with a yellow tip.

RANGE: Breeds north to southern Texas and southeastern Virginia; south to British Honduras, Cuba, and the Island of Dominica. Winters north to southern Texas and southern Florida; south to Oaxaca and southern Brazil.

STATUS IN S. C.: Fairly common summer resident, April 8 to October 30, only along the coast. Known north to Horry County; south to Beaufort County.

HISTORY: In 1910 Wayne considered Cabot's Tern to be an extremely rare visitant, but a few years later he himself found it less rare than he had supposed. In June, 1916, he discovered "at least 12 or 15 pair" nesting in Bull's Bay. Since that time it has proved to be a regular though uncommon summer resident. Most of them arrive about mid-May and remain through the summer, but it is unusual to see this species after mid-August. The earliest record is that of a bird seen at Bull Point, Beaufort County, by W. J. Hoxie on April 8, 1884. The only fall records are of one secured, and another seen, on Folly Island by E. Milby Burton on October 23, 1934, and a later sight record of one by James E. Mosimann and George B. Rabb on October 30, 1946, at the Isle of Palms.

Cabot's Tern nests in small numbers in at least two locations, the Cape Romain area and St. Helena Sound. Egg dates for both localities are usually in the second week of June. On June 4, 1947, the authors examined the large Royal Tern colony at Cape Romain, and among the approximately eleven thousand eggs of that species, they found eighteen nests of Cabot's Tern.

Cabot's Tern lays two or three eggs which, though smaller than those of the Royal Tern, are not otherwise unlike them. The markings are generally small and well defined, dark brown and black on a creamy-white ground. The eggs average 51.1 x 36.0 millimeters. They are laid directly on the sand and may or may not be surrounded by bits of shell. There is endless variation in the number and arrangement of the markings. The incubation period is twenty-one days.

Cabot's Tern is not difficult to identify in the field. Its distinctive characteristic is the bill, which is black, sharply tipped with yellow.

FOOD: Almost entirely fish. In stomachs examined by the U. S. Fish and Wildlife Service, only small fish and shrimp were found. Menhaden and anchovies seemed to be favorite fish.

188. CASPIAN TERN: *Hydroprogne caspia* (Pallas) (64)

(Gr., *Hydro*, water, +Lat., *Progne*, Pandion's daughter, who was turned into a swallow; thus a water swallow; Lat., *caspia,* of the Caspian [Sea].)

DESCRIPTION: Largest of our terns. Length 19.00 to 23.00 inches. Bill thick; tail short and not much forked. *Summer.* Top of head with crest black; rest of upper surface pale gray; upper tail coverts white; tail grayish white; lower parts white. *Winter.* Similar to the summer plumage but crown streaked with white.

RANGE: Breeds north to southern Mackenzie, southeastern Quebec, the Baltic Sea, and southern Siberia; south to central Lower California, southeastern South Carolina, southern Africa, and Ceylon. Winters north to central California and South Carolina; south to Mexico and southeastern Africa.

STATUS IN S. C.: Fairly common permanent resident but only along the coast. Reported north to Horry County; south to Beaufort County.

HISTORY: The Caspian Tern is so like the Royal Tern that many observers find difficulty distinguishing between the two in the field. As compared with the Royal, the Caspian has less of a fork in the tail; the wing tips are much darker; the body is heavier, not so streamlined and elongated. The large coral-red beak of the Caspian, as opposed to the orange or orange-red beak of the Royal, serves for an excellent field mark.

The Caspian nests in the Cape Romain area, in company with the Royal Tern, though never in such large numbers. The eggs, which usually number two, sometimes one or three, are laid in early June. They so much resemble the eggs of the Royal Tern both in size and color that the eggs of the two species are practically indistinguishable. Generally speaking, however, the markings on the eggs of the Caspian are smaller. The eggs average 64.5 x 45.0 millimeters. They require twenty days for incubation.

High tides often wash the eggs from the sandy banks used as nesting sites. The birds, however, will lay again and again until a hatch is attained. For this reason the season is sometimes very much prolonged.

Because of its great size, equalling that of some gulls and exceeding others, the Caspian Tern's methods of fishing are more than usually spectacular. It descends like a living spearhead, throwing up a cloud of spray and seldom is the aim not accurate. In the winter months, when most of the Royals have drifted to the southward, this is the large tern of the ocean beaches and the salt estuaries. The note is a far-carrying cry, with a peculiar rattling quality which is not unlike that made by some of the mechanical toy noise-producers.

Food: Entirely fish, some of considerable size. Those which it takes are usually mullet, menhaden, suckers, and various minnows.

189. Black Tern: *Chlidonias niger surinamensis* (Gmelin) (77)

(Gr., *Chlidonias*, a swallow; Lat., *niger*, black; *surinamensis*, of Surinam.)

Description: Length 9.00 to 10.00 inches. *Summer adult.* Head, neck, and under parts except the white lower tail coverts, black; upper surface dark gray. *Winter adult* and *immature.* Head and lower parts mostly white with some dark brown markings on the head.

Range: Breeds north to southern Mackenzie and central Manitoba; south to southern California and northwestern Pennsylvania. Winters north to Mexico and southern Louisiana (accidentally); south to Chile and Surinam.

Status in S. C.: Abundant summer resident, May 4 to October 9, mostly coastwise, but does not breed. Known north and west to Greenville County (casually); east to Horry County; south to Beaufort and Jasper counties.

History: While the adult plumage of the Black Tern fully justifies its common name, immature birds and the adult in winter plumage present a problem to anyone interested in bird study. As easily recognizable as the summer adult is, in winter it looks like a young bird in plumage, which is dark gray above and mottled white below. Dark markings appear about the eye, ear, and neck as well. These mottled birds are often seen on migration.

The Black Tern is abundant in South Carolina in late spring and again in late summer and fall. So early does the southward migration from its nesting grounds begin that it is considered a summer resident in South Carolina. Wayne (1910) said that the species is "very rarely seen in the spring migration" but his observation no longer holds true.

Although Murphey (1937) found it regularly in the middle Savannah River Valley, and it is recorded commonly in interior Georgia, this bird is not definitely recorded from the interior of South Carolina except from Greenville County (Pickens, *Auk, 44*: 1927, 428).

On its nesting grounds in the north, the Black Tern is a fresh-water bird entirely, but in the migrations it frequents both salt and fresh bodies of water.

Food: Inland, the food of the Black Tern is composed largely of insects, on the coast fish appear to be the mainstay. Examination of 270 stomachs showed that fish make up 19 per cent of the food. Minnows, killifish, and menhaden form the greater part of the diet.

190. Noddy Tern: *Anoüs stolidus stolidus* (Linnaeus) (79)

(Gr., *Anoüs*, stupid; Lat., *stolidus*, stolid.)

DESCRIPTION: Length 13.00 to 16.00 inches. Tail broad and fanshaped, only a little forked. Entire body and wings sooty brown; forehead white, shading to silvery gray on the crown and nape; bill black.

RANGE: Resident and breeds north to southern Florida and the Bahama Islands; south to British Honduras, Trinidad, and the Island of St. Helena in the southern Atlantic Ocean.

STATUS IN S. C.: Casual summer visitor, May 5 to September 19, only along the coast. Recorded north to Myrtle Beach (Horry County); south to Charleston.

HISTORY: The history of this beautiful, dove-like tern in South Carolina closely parallels that of both the Sooty and Bridled Terns. Its appearance locally is only casual.

Curiously enough, though hurricanes have occurred on the South Carolina coast since very early times, there was no evidence of the presence of either the Sooty or the Noddy until 1926, when both birds arrived, apparently as a result of tropical storms. On July 29, 1926, a Noddy was secured by T. M. Evans near Myrtle Beach, Horry County, and given by him to Clemson College (*Auk, 44*: 1927, 94). This is the first State record. Following a storm several dead birds and a few living ones were found on Bull's Island, Charleston County, on September 19, 1926, by E. M. Moore.

In the storm of September 18, 1928, B. R. Chamberlain picked up an exhausted Noddy at Porcher's Bluff, Christ Church Parish. It was released some hours later, after examination and study, the wind still being high from the southeast.

On June 16, 1929, three Noddies were seen on a piece of driftwood at the mouth of Charleston Harbor, between Fort Sumter and the Jetties, by Allan D. Cruickshank. There was no storm to account for their presence, and the observation for that date is particularly remarkable because in mid-June the Noddy is in the midst of its nesting on the Tortugas (*Auk, 52*: 1935, 309). J. A. Bruce found an exhausted bird on the Isle of Palms, August 14, 1939, and presented it to the Charleston Museum.

The Noddy is unlike any other South Carolina tern, even the all-dark Black Tern. Its flight and general appearance are remarkably like those of a pigeon. The food is small fish.

Family Rynchopidae: Skimmers

191. Black Skimmer: *Rynchops nigra nigra* Linnaeus (80)

(Gr., *Rynchops*, beak-faced; Lat., *nigra*, black.)

LOCAL NAMES: Shearwater; Sea-dog.

DESCRIPTION: Length 16.00 to 20.00 inches. Upper mandible shorter than the lower; plumage above black, below white, including most of tail; basal half of bill red, the remaining portion black.

RANGE: Breeds on the Atlantic and Gulf of Mexico coasts north to southern Texas and southeastern Massachusetts; south to Yucatan and Florida. Winters north to southern Louisiana and central eastern North Carolina; south to El Salvador and the northern coast of Venezuela.

STATUS IN S. C.: Common permanent resident, mostly coastwise. Reported north to Chester (casually); east to Horry County; south to Beaufort and Jasper counties; west to Aiken County.

HISTORY: Sometimes as he steps ashore on a sandy bar of an inlet or the end of a barrier island beach, the observer is greeted by a charging host of long-winged, yelping sea birds. Coming head-on, in a close-knit phalanx this aerial formation suddenly splits aside and sweeps by in a whirling, gyrating mass of black and white pinions, outlandish beaks, and deafening cries. Walking through this amazing assemblage, one finds the sand spotted all about with hundreds of depressions, each holding three to five beautifully marked eggs—a typical nesting colony of Black Skimmers.

This remarkable looking bird is common on the South Carolina coast, where it is almost invariably called "Shearwater." It is unlike the oceanic birds which have a right to that name, but the practice of misnaming it is so general that it parallels the error of calling herons "cranes." It is true that the Black Skimmer shears the water, but it is not a shearwater.

Wayne considered the Black Skimmer a summer resident only, but since he wrote (1910) it has been found to winter regularly in South Carolina in considerable numbers. It decreases in abundance during the winter but if looked for it can usually be found. The Skimmer is strictly a species of ocean beaches, salt marsh creeks, and wide estuaries and it rarely penetrates inland, though occasionally it may be blown there by tropical storms. A young female of this species was taken by L. M. Loomis on September 10, 1882, at Chester (*Auk*, 2: 1883, 193). Murphey (1937) records it in the Savannah River in the Aiken-Augusta region in 1888, following a northeast blow.

Its outstanding characteristic is its amazing beak, unlike that of any other American bird. The upper mandible is much the shorter. In feeding, the bird immerses the tip of the lower mandible beneath the water, and with rapidly beating wings literally skims along, scooping up the small fish on which it subsists. Thus arises its name. Any bird easier to identify than this would be hard to imagine, assuming that the observer gets a good view of it.

Though it often nests on remote islands, the Skimmer by no means shuns human habitation. It frequents waterfronts of towns and cities, populous beach resorts, and busy harbors. With its black and white plumage and unique beak it is highly

PLATE XVI: OWLS

Water Color by Roger Tory Peterson

Upper left: Great Horned Owl. Upper right: Barred Owl. Lower left: Short-eared Owl. Lower right: top, Barn Owl; below left, Screech Owls (gray and red phases).

individualistic. On the wing, it is a picture of grace, but at rest it looks clumsy and top-heavy. This is largely because of the beak, and the small, very short legs and feet. Flocks are often seen within the city limits of Charleston, Georgetown, and Beaufort, either fishing or resting on mud flats, all the birds facing into the breeze.

Nesting occurs in June, though in some seasons it may be earlier or later. The second week of June normally sees the eggs laid. A typical early record is June 4, 1938, St. Helena Island (DeCamps). The bird does not build a nest but simply makes a depression in the sand in which to deposit the eggs. These number from three to five, and are creamy white, with an endless variety of brown, black, and lilac markings, spots, dots, splashes, and blotches. Eggs have been found without a mark on them, some with only one or two, but these are unusual. They are among the very handsomest of sea-bird eggs, a series of them making a very attractive display. Average measurement is 54.0 x 33.5 millimeters, and the incubation takes twenty-one to twenty-three days. The Black Skimmer raises only one brood a season.

Skimmer nests were once heavily egged throughout much of the breeding range, but today the chief enemies of skimmer colonies are the wind and tides. The low-lying banks on which they nest are often swept by spring and storm tides, and the birds will lay again if the first eggs are destroyed.

Young skimmers are covered with buffy down. They begin to run about very soon and roam over the nesting ground in gangs. It is astonishing that the parents can tell one young bird from another. If the nest is endangered by an intruder, the adult bird will feign injury, flopping about over the sand in an effort to lure the intruder away.

Skimmers are nocturnal; they often feed after dark and on moonlit nights. The familiar, yelping note, so like that of a small dog that fishermen often call the Skimmer "Sea-dog," is a characteristic sound of the night marshes.

Food: Small fish, for the most part killifish, menhaden, and minnows.

Family Alcidae: Auks, Murres, and Puffins

192. Razor-billed Auk: *Alca torda torda* Linnaeus (32)

(Lat., *Alca*, from Icelandic *alka*; *torda*, Swedish name of this bird.)

Description: Length 15.00 to 18.00 inches. Bill high and very thin. *Summer.* Head and neck dark brown; remainder of upper surface slate black; lower parts white; bill black with a narrow white bar. *Winter.* Similar to the summer plumage, but whole under portion of head and neck white.

Range: Breeds north to southern Greenland and Lapland; south to southern New Brunswick, Iceland, and the Baltic Sea. Winters north to northeastern Ontario, southern Labrador, and the Baltic Sea; south to South Carolina (casually), the Canary Islands, and the Mediterranean Sea.

Status in S. C.: Accidental, recorded only from Georgetown County.

History: The term "auk" almost invariably suggests extinction because it is so well known that the Great Auk is an extinct species. Nevertheless, there are several existing species of auks and auklets, though such birds are relatively unknown in South Carolina. They are far northern birds of the Arctic and sub-Arctic coasts, rare in the United States south of New England.

However, on January 12, 1948, a specimen of the Razor-billed Auk, covered with oil but still alive, was picked up on the beach at Pawley's Island, by Julius S. McDonald. He took the bird to R. M. Ford, of Georgetown who, in turn, sent it by C. H. Sellers to the Charleston Museum, where it was prepared and preserved. It is the sole record for the State and much credit is due McDonald for making his remarkable discovery known and thus adding the species to the birds of South Carolina.

FOOD: The food of this species and its relatives is composed entirely of marine organisms.

193. BRÜNNICH'S MURRE: *Uria lomvia lomvia* (Linnaeus) (31)

(Gr., *Uria*, a water bird; *lomvia*, a Faeroese name.)

DESCRIPTION: Length 17.00 to 20.00 inches. *Summer*. Head, neck, and rest of upper surface slate black; secondaries (of wing) tipped with white; remaining under parts white. *Winter*. Similar to the summer plumage but whole lower surface white.

RANGE: Breeds north to northern Greenland, Spitzbergen, and Franz Josef Land; south to Hudson Strait, Iceland, northern Lapland, and Nova Zembla. Winters north to Hudson Bay and southern Greenland; south to central Iowa, South Carolina (casually), Great Britain, and the Baltic Sea.

STATUS IN S. C.: Accidental, recorded from Anderson County and probably Charleston County.

HISTORY: Brünnich's Murre, a far northern sea bird of Greenland and Labrador, has no regular place among the birds of South Carolina. Only one certain instance of its capture is on record. On December 19, 1896, a specimen was taken by J. R. Nowell near Anderson, in the northwestern part of South Carolina. The only explanation of such an extraordinary occurrence is that in the winter of that year, there was a decided southward movement of these birds from the far north and that this specimen was either blown much off course or wandered hopelessly across country, confused as to direction. It was recorded in the *Auk, 14*: 1897, 203, by Elliott Coues.

Wayne found the decomposed remains of a murre in a cornfield near Mt. Pleasant in January, 1897. Practically no feathers remained, so that absolute identification was not possible, but there is every reason to believe that the bird was of this species, and another individual of that great winter flight of 1896-97.

194. DOVEKIE: *Plautus alle* (Linnaeus) (34)

(Lat., *Plautus*, flat-footed; *alle*, Swedish name of this bird.)

DESCRIPTION: Length 7.00 to 9.00 inches. Body plump and compact. Bill very short and stout. *Summer*. Upper parts, including the head, neck, and chest, clove brown and black; rest of under parts white; a narrow white bar on the wings. *Winter*. Anterior lower surface together with sides of neck white.

RANGE: Breeds north to Ellesmere Island, Greenland, and Spitzbergen; south to Baffin Island, Iceland, and Nova Zembla. Winters north to southern Greenland, Great Britain, and the North Sea; south to Florida, Cuba, and the Canary Islands.

STATUS IN S. C.: Casual winter visitor, October 29 to February, only along the coast. Recorded north to Myrtle Beach (Horry County); south to Beaufort County.

HISTORY: The Dovekie, which is one of the smallest of the auks, is another Arctic bird normally out of place in South Carolina but with considerably more history than that of the murre. There are several specimens and numerous observation records.

Before 1932 there was but one instance of this little ocean wanderer in the State. A specimen was found dead at Beaufort in February, 1909. It was sent to Dr. L. C. Sanford of New York, who later presented it to Wayne. This extraordinary incident added the Dovekie to the South Carolina list and extended its known range 200 miles southward.

In November, 1932, dwellers along the Atlantic coast from Maine to Florida were amazed to encounter on beaches, inlets, islands, and mainland, great numbers of tiny black and white sea birds, hardly larger than Starlings, though much heavier and stouter in build. In some places they swarmed by hundreds; at others only a few appeared. Dead and living birds were picked up, many others were seen, and the newspapers carried accounts of the "invasion." The little birds were Dovekies, or as they are sometimes known, Little Auks, normally at home on the rugged coast of Greenland. There is little doubt that the vast majority of the birds went unobserved on this coast. Because it was winter, the beaches were deserted and comparatively few specimens were found. However, the following 1932 records are of interest: one picked up on Folly Island, December 2 (Mrs. Beverly Mikell); one picked up on Big Bay Island, December 4 (H. R. Sass, Jr.); two picked up on Folly Island, December 4 (C. C. West and Elizabeth Lowndes); one picked up on Pawley's Island, December 3 (C. P. Lachicotte). The pilot boat and the crew of the Charleston Lightship reported hundreds at and near the Charleston Jetties.

This great movement of Dovekies which extended even to the north coast of Cuba, gained scientific as well as popular attention, and a full account of it by Dr. R. C. Murphy and William Vogt appeared in the *Auk, 50*: 1933, 325. Most of the birds were exhausted, thin, stomachs empty, and their strength reduced. Thousands of them died. The basic reason for the invasion was believed to be the unusual atmospheric conditions off New England and northward, with winds which forced the birds out of their range.

Ten years later, Frederick Wehman and Edward Manigault saw four Dovekies in the North Santee River, on December 10, 1942 (*Auk, 60*: 1943, 598). One was killed with a boat paddle; the bird was very thin, and the stomach was empty. None of the four birds attempted to fly, but all dived well.

On December 8, 1944, E. O. Mellinger picked up two dead Dovekies at Myrtle Beach. Two days later, Mrs. Joseph Fisher brought him two more and reported seeing another pair. Mellinger prepared the four birds and presented three to the Charleston Museum. The birds were very thin. On November 17, 1945, a

Dovekie was seen at Myrtle Beach by Fred K. Garvey (*Chat*, *10*: 1946, 38). The most recent record was made on October 29, 1948, when Dr. Harry G. Jopson picked up a dying bird at Pawley's Island, Georgetown County (*Chat*, *13*: 1949, 17).

FOOD: Plankton, shrimps, crabs, and other small crustacea.

Order Columbiformes
Pigeon-like Birds

Family Columbidae: Pigeons and Doves

195. ROCK DOVE: *Columba livia* Gmelin (313.1)

(Lat., *Columba*, dove; *livia*, from *liveo*, I am of a bluish color.)

LOCAL NAMES: Domestic Pigeon; Pigeon.

DESCRIPTION: Length about 11 inches. Above bluish gray, the head darker, the neck glossed with metallic green or purple, the rump white, the tail with a broad black terminal band; lower parts gray, paler than the upper surface. There is much variation because of domestication.

RANGE: Naturalized and permanently resident in much of the United States and southern Canada.

STATUS IN S. C.: Common permanent resident locally over the State.

HISTORY: The well-known Domestic Pigeon has in recent years become so thoroughly naturalized that it is now fully able to take care of itself. While it prefers the vicinity of buildings, particularly in towns and cities, in many places outside South Carolina and perhaps even here it has reverted to its natural wild habit of nesting in caves, the crannies of cliffs, and similar places.

The nest, a crude platform of twigs and straws, is placed in the eaves and crannies of large buildings. Two white eggs, averaging 39.1 x 28.7 millimeters, are laid, and their incubation consumes about fourteen days. The young of pigeons and doves are hatched practically naked and are fed for a short time on "crop milk" or "pigeon's milk," which is secreted in the internal organs of both parents. The Rock Dove raises two or more broods each year, and nesting probably takes place throughout the year in South Carolina.

In Charleston some of the Rock Doves have the habit of resting on the exposed mud flats in the western part of the city.

FOOD: Its diet consists of various kinds of vegetable matter.

EASTERN MOURNING DOVE

196. *Zenaidura macroura carolinensis* (Linnaeus) (316)

(*Zenaidura*, from *Zenaida*, a related genus, named in honor of Madame Zenaide Bonaparte; and Gr., *ura*, tail; *macroura*, long-tailed; Lat., *carolinensis*, of Carolina.)

LOCAL NAMES: Turtle Dove; Carolina Dove; "Moaning" Dove.

DESCRIPTION: Length 11.00 to 13.00 inches. Hind head bluish gray; forehead fawn color; rest of upper parts grayish brown; lower parts fawn color; a dark spot on the side of the head; tail pointed and edged with white.

RANGE: Breeds north to Wisconsin and Nova Scotia; south to southern Louisiana, southern Florida, and the Bahama Islands. Winters north casually to Wisconsin and Maine; south to Mexico and Panama.

STATUS IN S. C.: Common permanent resident throughout the State. Observed north to Greenville, Spartanburg, York, and Dillon counties; east to Horry and Georgetown counties; south to Beaufort and Jasper counties; west to Oconee and Pickens counties.

HISTORY: The Eastern Mourning Dove is one of the best known birds in South Carolina. It was originally made known to science from this state by Mark Catesby in 1731 under the name of "The Turtle of Carolina," and even today it is sometimes called the Carolina Dove. It is a permanent resident and a favorite game species; its plaintive cooing notes and the characteristic whistling noise of the wings are known to farm boy and city dweller alike.

It is a bird of open woodlands and fields, often seen on telephone wires along roads, but it is also common among the sand dunes of the barrier islands. It inhabits the entire coastal plain, the sandhills, the Piedmont, and the mountains. In fall and winter Mourning Doves gather in flocks, augmented by birds from the north, and provide sport for hundreds of hunters, who are enthusiastic about the difficult target made by the bird in its swift, erratic flight, especially on windy days. There is, today, some diminution in its numbers, and a curtailment or at least a revision of the open season seems highly advisable.

The nesting season varies with locality. In the coastal area mid-April is the normal time for the bird to lay its eggs, but forward seasons advance nesting and backward seasons retard it. The earliest record is from Bishopville, two eggs, February 10, 1949 (T. Perry). For the interior, typical dates for eggs, incubation, and fledglings are provided by the following records: Columbia, incubation, March 8; Ridge Springs, March 9; Batesburg, incubation, March 10 (D. E. Etheredge); Barnwell County, March 12 (E. E. Crow); Aiken County, newly hatched young, September 20 (Crow); Lexington County, two fledged young, September 28 (Mrs. P. B. Hendrix). A record of most abnormal nesting was established in the last week of December (1946), when T. A. Beckett found a nest with two eggs at Boone Hall Plantation, Charleston County.

The Mourning Dove normally raises two broods (less frequently three) during a season. The nest is simply a shallow platform of twigs and pine needles, a very frail structure through which the eggs may sometimes be seen from below. The nest is built either on the ground or in bushes and trees preferably pines, 20 or 30 feet from the ground. Like the eggs of all species of pigeons and doves, those of the Mourning Dove are pure white. There are always two eggs in a nest. In 1943 Mrs. E. C. von Treschow reported finding at Camden a nest containing four eggs, all of which hatched, but it seems very probable that this particular nest was being used by two females. The eggs average 28.4 x 21.5 millimeters. Incubation requires from twelve to fourteen days. On occasion the parent bird feigns injury in order to lead an intruder away from the nest. The bird is not particularly shy, however, and frequently builds its nest close to human habitations.

Bob-tailed Mourning Doves are not unusual. One explanation, offered to account for the phenomenon in winter, is that on cold nights the birds, which make a habit of roosting on the ground, lose their tails when the tips freeze to the surface of the ground. The feathers are set loosely in the skin, so that when the bird takes flight in the morning it simply leaves its tail behind. T. Gilbert Pearson (1942) once observed that of 250 doves which he saw during a 10 mile drive in Mississippi two-thirds were without tails.

The Mourning Dove has been hunted for generations; its flesh is excellent on the table. In some parts of the country, however, it is regarded as a song bird and is never shot.

FOOD: Because of the Mourning Dove's status as a game bird and its prevalence in agricultural districts, its diet takes on particular significance. Examination of some 237 stomachs has shown the food to be over 99 per cent vegetable. Animal matter amounts to less than 1 per cent. Weed seeds make up the great bulk of the diet (64 per cent). Thus it will be seen that benefit results from this one item. The bird also eats grain—wheat, oats, corn, rye, and buckwheat; but it should be noted that three-fourths of these grains are waste, picked up in fields after harvest. Wheat was the only grain taken while growing, most of it in July and August. Corn was old, damaged grain. On our coast, the dove is very fond of benne seed, which is often planted on some of the plantations as an attraction.

197. PASSENGER PIGEON: *Ectopistes migratorius* (Linnaeus) (315)

(Gr., *Ectopistes*, a wanderer; Lat., *migratorius*, migratory.)

LOCAL NAMES: Wild Pigeon.

DESCRIPTION: Length 15.00 to 18.00 inches. Tail long and distinctly graduated. Head bluish gray without any black spot; rest of upper parts similar; sides of neck glossed with bronze; anterior lower parts reddish vinaceous; abdomen white.

RANGE: Now extinct everywhere. Bred formerly north to central Mackenzie and southeastern Quebec; south to northern Mississippi and Pennsylvania. Wintered north to Arkansas and North Carolina; south to Texas, Louisiana, Florida, central Mexico (casually), and Cuba.

STATUS IN S. C.: Formerly a very abundant winter resident throughout the State; casual in summer in the northwestern region. Reported north to Caesar's Head and Chester County; east to Williamsburg County and Mt. Pleasant; south to 13 miles north of Charleston and Blackville (Barnwell County); west to Anderson and Walhalla (Oconee County).

HISTORY: The history of the Passenger Pigeon is, for South Carolina, a brief one. There is no room here to recount the sad story of human persecution which wiped this splendid bird from the earth. Suffice it to say that it was human persecution, not disease, natural disaster, or any other of the explanations which are offered for its disappearance. The last known specimen taken in the field was killed in 1904; the last authentic observation was made in 1907. Captive specimens lived after that, but the last Passenger Pigeon on earth died at the Cincinnati Zoological Park in 1914. Thus it vanished behind the same black curtain which hides forever the Great Auk and the Labrador Duck.

Wayne (1910) says it "occurred in enormous numbers on the coast." He was fortunate enough to see two pairs in the upper part of the State, at Caesar's Head, Pickens County, in the summer of 1882; but on the coast, where he spent his life, he never saw a living specimen. One dead bird came under his notice, a specimen killed by a Negro on a deer stand, November 21, 1885, a few miles north of Charleston. Even the preservation of this bird was denied him, for it had been shot with buckshot and could not be saved.

L. M. Loomis in the *Bulletin of Nuttall Club* (1879) says of the Wild Pigeon in Chester County, "Migratory. Common; *very* abundant during the latter part of the winter and spring of 1874." Other records include that of the late C. W. Pitchford, who told Chamberlain in 1925 that some fifty to sixty years earlier (*c.* 1865) a "pigeon roost" 3 to 4 miles from Walhalla (Oconee County) held "clouds" of Passenger Pigeons. In the early 1870's, according to letters by H. S. Wylie and T. C. Camak in the *News and Herald* of Winnsboro in March, 1943, hundreds of thousands of Wild Pigeons passed over Fairfield County in their eastward flight. S. B. Crayton, of Georgetown, told Chamberlain that in the fall and winter of 1888, a Negro hunter killed two Passenger Pigeons out of a flock of twelve to fifteen near Anderson. In the fall of 1889, Crayton, in company with his father, saw a smaller flock on his plantation at Anderson. Murphey (1937) reports that a Passenger Pigeon was killed at Blackville, Barnwell County, in 1890 by Reuben Wilson; Henry E. Davis reports one killed in Williamsburg County in the autumn of 1895 (*American Wild Turkey*, 1949, 34).

Reports of the Passenger Pigeon still occur, but are invariably traceable to the Mourning Dove. The two are similar in appearance, but the Passenger Pigeon was much larger, the plumage more iridescent and lacked the black spot behind the eye which the Mourning Dove plainly shows.

EASTERN GROUND DOVE
198. *Columbigallina passerina passerina* (Linnaeus) (320)

(Lat., *Columbigallina—columba*, dove, and *gallina*, hen; *passerina*, sparrowlike.)

LOCAL NAMES: Mourning Dove.

DESCRIPTION: Length 6.00 to 7.00 inches. Tail rounded. Back grayish brown; head and breast vinaceous, the latter with small fuscous spots; under wing surface rufous; feet pink or flesh color.

RANGE: Resident and breeds north to central Alabama and west central North Carolina; south to southeastern Texas and southern Florida.

STATUS IN S. C.: Common permanent resident in the southeastern half of the State, less frequent in the interior. Observed north to Richland County and Marion; east to Horry County; south to Beaufort and Jasper counties; west to Aiken County.

HISTORY: This gentle, confiding little bird is a general favorite throughout its range. It is so friendly that it comes freely into yards and often feeds with chickens. Years ago, it was abundant on Sullivan's Island, near Charleston, and still occurs there, but the removal of much of the vegetation has reduced the breeding sites and the birds are in consequence much less common today.

The Ground Dove is a permanent resident, though it is not common in the winter months. It seems to prefer the coastal region. There will probably always be confusion between the two doves which inhabit South Carolina. Both this species and the Mourning Dove were originally described from South Carolina by Catesby, but one often hears the Ground Dove referred to as "Mourning Dove" and the real Mourning Dove as either Turtle Dove or Carolina Dove. The term "mourning" arises, of course, from the cooing note, but since all doves utter such plaintive calls, it hardly follows that all of them are Mourning Doves.

The Ground Dove is well named, for it is one of the most terrestrial of birds. Its larger relative also spends much time on the ground but not as consistently as this tiny creature. It is not a game bird and is never molested except by juvenile hunters. Everyone welcomes it for its quick, graceful movements, soft plumage, and appealing voice.

Nesting usually begins in mid-April and lasts practically through the summer and into the fall, for it sometimes rears four broods. Remarkable extremes are noticeable in breeding dates. The earliest known is that recorded by Sprunt who discovered two fresh eggs in a ground nest on February 22, 1913, in Beaufort County. The latest (for eggs) is October 19, 1886, on Sullivan's Island (Wayne).

The nest, like the nests of all other doves, consists simply of a few twigs laid across one another with some grasses or pine needles. It may be on the ground, atop an old stump, in low bushes, or in small trees. On the sea islands, a favorite nesting shrub is the wax myrtle. The two eggs, which average 21.9 x 16.2 millimeters, are pure white. Incubation requires twelve to fourteen days. The bird will often attempt to lead an intruder away by feigning injury, flopping over the ground as if unable to rise, a trick which seldom fails to be effective.

Though it is a ground-loving bird, the Ground Dove may occasionally be seen on an elevated perch such as a telephone wire. In flight, the flash of rufous in the wings and the lack of white in the tail will always distinguish it.

FOOD: Like the Mourning Dove, this dove has a splendid record in the destruction of weed seeds, which form practically all of its food, together with a small amount of waste grain. Some of the plants represented in stomach contents are crab grass, wire grass, foxtail, purslane, ragweed, mallow, amaranth, and sedges of various kinds. One stomach was found to contain 1611 seeds of purslane.

Order Psittaciformes
Parrots and Paroquets

Family Psittacidae: Parrots and Paroquets

CAROLINA PAROQUET
199.   *Conuropsis carolinensis carolinensis* (Linnaeus)   (382)

(Gr., *Conuropsis,* having the appearance of the genus *Conurus;* Lat., *carolinensis,* of Carolina.)

DESCRIPTION: Length 11.00 to 14.00 inches. Tail long and graduated. Upper surface bright green; head and neck yellow, becoming orange on forehead and cheeks; lower parts apple green.

RANGE: Formerly resident and bred north to eastern Pennsylvania and central eastern New York; south to Georgia and southern Florida.

STATUS IN S. C.: Formerly abundant permanent resident over much of the State; now probably extinct. There are records north to the Santee River (possibly); south to the Combahee River; west to Aiken County.

HISTORY: The Carolina Paroquet is now generally believed to be as extinct as the Great Auk and the Labrador Duck. It is still possible, however, that a few remain in remote and little-known areas in the swamps and hammocks of the southeastern United States. Sprunt is acquainted with a venerable ornithologist who still stoutly maintains that the species yet lives, but he refuses to say anything about the locality except that it is in Florida.

Its history in South Carolina is somewhat parallel to that of the Passenger Pigeon; though the Paroquet was once abundant and seen by many observers, there are few specific records. It was described by Catesby from this State (1731) as the "Parrot of Carolina," and Wayne (1910) says of it that "it has become extinct within the past fifty years on or near the coast, as well as in the State at large." Murphey (1937) records observations made in 1840 in Aiken County, and in 1864 on the Combahee River and in the woods between Yemassee and the coast.

Of the many reports which have been received in recent years, one deserves special attention. In 1933-34, George M. Melamphy, who was working in the Santee

Swamp, Georgetown County, on a Wild Turkey project, talked to Sprunt and authorities of the Charleston Museum on several occasions regarding observations he had made on both the Ivory-billed Woodpecker and the Carolina Paroquet. Those on the Ivory-bill were fully substantiated later, as will be noted in the account of that species in this volume. Melamphy gave detailed accounts of watching paroquets from turkey blinds. He saw as many as nine at one time, feeding on the sunflower seeds which were part of the bait used to attract turkeys. He succeeded once in obtaining a photograph of a small flock, but the print was poor and the birds appeared simply as dark spots.

These reports were considered to be of so much value that the National Audubon Society undertook an investigation. To this end Robert P. Allen was sent from New York and joined Sprunt in a three weeks' stay in the swamp, from November 26 to December 18, 1936. The expedition was attended by almost incessant rain and mist. Nevertheless, the two observers discovered a flight-line of birds to and from a heavy cypress growth on an island in the Wadmacaun River, an arm of the Santee. At no time was the light sufficient to reveal anything but silhouettes of the birds as they passed over the narrow river, but Sprunt believes that they were parrots beyond question. This flight took place late in the afternoon day after day.

Blinds were erected and bait put out, and one morning Sprunt had a good glimpse of a parrot as it passed over the blind. Sprunt saw the brilliant green color of the bird from the rear but he did not see the head. On one other occasion, in the spring of the same year (1936) a small party of observers, of which Sprunt was a member, saw a wholly green bird fly at close range over an open field. The bird's plumage corresponded in every respect to that of the immature Carolina Paroquet.

Though the search in the Santee Swamp was conducted with great secrecy and as thoroughly as weather conditions permitted, the final results were unsatisfactory, for the observers never had a clear view of an adult bird. A warden, however, who had been placed on duty after the discovery of the Ivory-billed Woodpecker in the same area, reported on three occasions during the next two years a total of four fully adult paroquets.

It has been suggested by some ornithologists interested in this matter that the birds were escapes of an exotic species. Sprunt holds this opinion to be untenable. Though exotics which have escaped from tankers and banana ships from the tropics do occur at times, they are usually single birds. That nine should escape, proceed to the greatest river swamp in the State, set up a flight-line, and act in every way as Carolina Paroquets have acted since time immemorial, seems too much for him to believe. It is Sprunt's firm and considered belief that the Carolina Paroquet was in the Santee Swamp in 1936-38, a remnant of a population which probably had always lived there.

Chamberlain, who spent five days in the swamp with Sprunt and Allen when the investigation was being made, saw no evidence of Carolina Paroquets and does not believe that they were there then. *

The completion of the Santee-Cooper Hydro-electric Project since that time has so altered the character of the country that any paroquets present in the swamp in 1936-38 would have probably disappeared along with the Ivory-billed Woodpeckers. Persecution on the part of fruit growers, the demand of the feather market, and thoughtless shooting and collecting were factors in the reduction of the species to its present state of practical oblivion.

The Carolina Paroquet nested in the natural cavities of trees and stubs, but few authentic eggs were ever secured. Eggs laid in captivity (two or three in number) are white. They average 34.23 x 27.80 millimeters. Eggs hatched in captivity required nineteen or twenty days for incubation.

FOOD: The Carolina Paroquet seemed to be very fond of the seeds of the pine, maple, and elm. They often ate sandspurs or cockspurs, cypress "balls," pecans, beechnuts, pawpaws (*Asimina*), mulberries, wild grapes, and citrus fruits. Many paroquets were destroyed in Florida because of their depredations in the citrus groves.

---

* *Editor's Note*: From the foregoing account it is obvious that the occurrence of the Carolina Paroquet in the Santee Swamp as late as 1936-38 continues to be a matter of some uncertainty. While there can be no question of Sprunt's skill as an observer or of the weight which must be given to his conclusions, the Editor feels that on so controversial a point as this it is in the interest of ornithological science to offer as many authentic data and opinions as possible.

In a letter dater from Tavernier, Florida, June 5, 1949, Robert P. Allen (Sprunt's companion on the Santee Swamp expedition) disagrees with Sprunt's opinion. He writes that "though it is difficult to make a flat statement one way or the other" after a number of years, he is certain that the members of the expedition never "saw or heard paroquets in the Santee. It is perfectly possible, of course, that a final remnant survived there until around 1936, but the absence of any sound from even a small flock of paroquets is a point that cannot be overlooked." And he concludes, "Flying birds observed by us at dusk on several occasions were probably doves."

Lester L. Walsh who, along with Sprunt and Allen, was a member of the group making the investigation, in a letter dated July 24, 1949, writes in part as follows: "Personally, I never saw anything that looked like a paroquet in the Santee, unless it be a mourning dove. I joined Sprunt and Bob [Allen] after that reported but uncertain observation of their occurrence, and we spent many evenings at Bluff Landing in company with Old Man Shokes, but nothing nearer than a mourning dove did I ever glimpse. Roger [Tory Peterson] and I spent about a week in my kayak and exploring the cypress on both sides of the river from a point below the Wateree down almost to Winyah Bay in March, I believe it was, of 1937, with no trace of paroquets."

Gayer G. Dominick, who owned Bull's Island in the early part of 1936, writes (from New York, June 28, 1949) that at about the time Carolina Paroquets were reported in the Santee Swamp he had some small parrots, "larger than a paroquet," which he thinks came from Australia, and which were kept in a cage on the Island for a time. When they were released, "they stayed around 4 or 5 weeks, but began to fly higher, and then started to disappear." "It is likely," he continued, " . . . that these are the birds that are reported in the Santee Swamp. I remember the time when the rumor got about. I unfortunately cannot tell you the date as to when we had these parrots." (Bull's Island is about 25 miles from where the investigation was made.)

While such notes do not invalidate Sprunt's observations, they indicate that the positive identification of the Santee Swamp birds as Carolina Paroquets is still in the realm of doubt.

Order Cuculiformes
Cuckoo-like Birds

Family Cuculidae: Cuckoos, Roadrunners, and Anis

YELLOW-BILLED CUCKOO
200. *Coccyzus americanus americanus* (Linnaeus) (387)

(Gr., *Coccyzus*, from *coccyzo*, I cry cuckoo; Lat., *americanus*, of America.)

LOCAL NAMES: Rain Crow.

DESCRIPTION: Length 11.00 to 13.00 inches. Upper surface brownish gray with a bronzy gloss; under parts dull white; tail dark brown, the feathers broadly tipped with white; lower mandible yellow.

RANGE: Breeds north to North Dakota and New Brunswick; south to Mexico and the West.Indies. Winters north to Colombia and Venezuela; south to northern Argentina and Uruguay.

STATUS IN S. C.: Common summer resident, April 6 to November 12, over the entire State. Known north to Greenville and York counties; east to Horry County; south to Beaufort County; west to Oconee and Pickens counties.

HISTORY: The Yellow-billed Cuckoo is one of the birds which have been described as well by poets as by ornithologists. Wordsworth very properly asks, "O Cuckoo! shall I call thee Bird, Or but a wandering Voice?" Though it is a common species and widespread in its range the cuckoo remains little more than "a wandering Voice" to most people. The hollow, resonant "kuk, kuk, kuk," or "kaow, kaow, kaow," coming from the green depths of summer woodlands, has long been thought to herald bad weather. Many people no doubt recognize the name "Rain Crow," but comparatively few recognize the bird itself.

The Yellow-billed Cuckoo is a summer resident in South Carolina and occurs generally over the State. Arriving about mid-April, it remains until early November. A month usually elapses between arrival and nesting. The cuckoo is a woodland bird, though it sometimes appears in the shade trees of towns and cities. So secretive is it, however, that one seldom sees it slipping silently and unobtrusively through the foliage. Its brown plumage blends well with its leafy haunts. The body is trim and streamlined with a long tail. The thumb-nail patches of white on the tail are sometimes plainly visible, and a reasonably close observation reveals the yellow under mandible of the bill, which is noticeably decurved.

Many people are under the impression that the cuckoo builds no nest and always lays its eggs in the homes of other birds. The notion arises from the fact that this is the habit of the European Cuckoo, much publicized in literature. It does not apply to the Yellow-billed Cuckoo. The only South Carolina bird which habitually parasitizes other species is the Cowbird. It should be noted, however, that on May 30, 1947, Thomas Rivers, Johnson Cannon, and Thomas Uzzell, Jr., found the nest of a White-eyed Towhee on James Island, containing one egg of this cuckoo. It is the only instance of such parasitism reported in the State.

The nest of the Yellow-billed Cuckoo is nothing to brag of, but it is a nest. It is composed of a few twigs, a frail, shallow platform which barely supports the eggs. Favorite sites are oak trees and, on the coast islands, clumps of the wax myrtle. The eggs number two to four, usually three. They are a pale, greenish blue, unmarked, rounded at both ends. They average 30.4 x 23.0 millimeters and incubation requires about fourteen days. Two broods are raised, the eggs of the first being laid about the middle of May. An early record at Mt. Pleasant is May 2 (Wayne); a typical date in Beaufort County is May 12 (E. J. DeCamps). Eggs have been found on June 10 (Sprunt), and a bird was found incubating on the Isle of Palms on June 29 (J. E. Mosimann and G. B. Rabb). Wayne (1910) says the second set of eggs is laid in August.

FOOD: This cuckoo is highly valuable to agriculture. The food is composed almost entirely of insects, most of them injurious to crops. Caterpillars are a staple item, some of them being the hairy kind not usually taken by birds. The outstanding pest, the tent caterpillar, is an example. Caterpillars make up about 50 per cent of the total food. Other species of insects are grasshoppers, beetles, flies, katydids, and cicadas.

BLACK-BILLED CUCKOO
201. *Coccyzus erythropthalamus* (Wilson) (388)

(Gr., *erythropthalamus*, red-eyed.)

DESCRIPTION: Length 11.00 to 13.00 inches. Similar to the Yellow-billed Cuckoo, but tail feathers without conspicuous white tips, and bill entirely black.

RANGE: Breeds north to southeastern Alberta and Prince Edward Island; south to Oklahoma and South Carolina. Winters north to Colombia; south to eastern Peru.

STATUS IN S. C.: Fairly common transient, April 23 to June 13, and August 3 to October 25, over most of the State; also casual in summer and probably breeds. Reported north to Greenville, Spartanburg, and Chester counties; east to Horry County and Sullivan's Island; south to Beaufort County; west to Aiken, Oconee, and Pickens counties.

HISTORY: Few people make any distinction between the Black-billed and the Yellow-billed Cuckoos. Both are popularly known as "Rain Crows." They frequent similar places, and their calls are somewhat alike, except that the Black-bill omits the "kaow" sound at the end. There are evident points of difference in the appearance of the birds: The Black-bill has a red ring about the eye and a distinctly black bill, and there is not so much white in the tail.

The exact status of the Black-bill in South Carolina is not clearly established, and needs more observation and study. The bird is rare on the coast, no more than a transient visitor, as far as we know today, but it is commoner in the Piedmont, and probably breeds in the mountains. Definite records of nesting occur a short distance across the North Carolina line and in Georgia.

Wayne's experience with it was limited to the taking of two females, one on May 10, and another on May 11, 1911, near Mt. Pleasant. In each case, dissection showed that eggs had been laid but search of the vicinity failed to reveal the nest. Nevertheless, he lists this as "the first authentic breeding record for the State" (*Auk, 28*: 1911, 485).

Coastal records in addition to these Wayne birds now number about a dozen, and most of them are for mid-May. They include one killed by Kingbirds in a yard near Charleston, May 15, 1922, and presented to the Charleston Museum by Miss Marie Dwight. Two others flew into the Museum and were secured there (*Second Supplement*). Another in the Museum collection was taken by F. N. Irving on Sand Island, Beaufort County, on April 23, 1911. This is the earliest spring record by only one day, as W. J. Hoxie saw one at Frogmore, same county, on April 24, 1885. The extreme fall dates are records of single birds seen near Summerville, August 3, 1943, by J. S. Y. Hoyt and at Middleburg Plantation, Berkeley County, October 25, 1944, by E. von S. Dingle. Another autumnal bird was found floating dead in Copahee Sound, Charleston County, on September 23, 1922, by Wayne.

In the interior, the Black-bill is evidently not so rare a migrant as in the coastal region. Murphey (1937) records it as a regular spring and fall migrant in the Aiken region; Miss Marion J. Pellew gives specific dates, May 3 to 5, for the same area. Elliott Coues found it a rare migrant in the Columbia region in April and September. Two specimens were taken in Chester County by L. M. Loomis during migration. F. W. Hahn found it a rare migratory visitant in Greenwood County, while Gabriel Cannon records it from April 29 to May 5 at Spartanburg. A. L. Pickens noted it only in spring in Anderson, Greenville, and Pickens counties. The bird is probably resident in Oconee County, however, for John Kershaw saw it at Walhalla on June 13, 1909, and G. E. Hudson stated that it was more common than the Yellow-billed at Clemson.

Though the Black-bill constructs its own nest and rears its young, it sometimes follows the European Cuckoo's parasitic habit. There are instances of its laying eggs not only in the nest of the Yellow-billed Cuckoo but also in those of the Wood Pewee, the Catbird, and the Yellow Warbler. Its own nest and eggs (two or three) are similar to those of the Yellow-bill, but the eggs, averaging 27.18 x 20.57 millimeters, are darker and smaller. One or two broods are raised and incubation requires about fourteen days.

What points very strongly to a nesting record on the coast was made known by E. J. DeCamps, whose son collected the nest of a Yellow-billed Cuckoo with four eggs near Beaufort, in June, 1948. Two of the eggs were smaller and darker than the others. DeCamps did not himself see the nest until it was brought in. He has taken eggs of the Black-bill in the North, is familiar with them, and feels sure that these two small, dark eggs are of that species.

FOOD: Very much like that of the Yellow-bill, but it appears to take fewer beetles and more bugs.

PLATE XVII: GOATSUCKERS

Water Color by Edward von S. Dingle

Top flying bird: Nighthawk (male). Lower flying bird: Nighthawk (female). Foreground, left to right: Chuck-will's-widow (female), Whip-poor-will (male), and Chuck-will's-widow (male).

Order Strigiformes
Owls

Family Tytonidae: Barn Owls

202. BARN OWL: *Tyto alba pratincola* (Bonaparte) (365)

(Gr., *Tyto*, owl; Lat., *alba*, white; *pratincola*, a meadow inhabitant.)

LOCAL NAMES: Monkey-faced Owl.

DESCRIPTION: Length 15.00 to 21.00 inches. Face heart-shaped; legs long; each eye rimmed with feathers forming a disc. Upper parts, including wings, ochraceous buff, mottled with gray and white; undersurface ochraceous buff or white, spotted with black; face brownish white.

RANGE: Resident and breeds north to western Washington and Connecticut; south to Mexico and southern Florida.

STATUS IN S. C.: Common permanent resident over most of the State. Observed north to Chester County; east to Horry County; south to Jasper County; west to Oconee County.

HISTORY: As common as the Barn Owl is over much of the country, it always creates a sensation when seen by those unfamiliar with it. More often than not, it is considered either a new species or a stranger from some far country, and newspaper stories do nothing to discourage such errors. The name "Monkey-faced Owl" which is often applied to it is apt enough, for there is something about the bird's face and expression which is distinctly simian.

The Barn Owl is a nocturnal bird. This explains, of course, why so few people are familiar with it. By day, it remains quietly roosting in thick woodland cover, oak groves, and evergreens, or in old buildings. It need not be confused with any other South Carolina owl, for its strange face and pale coloration are unmistakable. In some places it likes to use telephone poles as lookout perches, where it can be seen in the glare of automobile headlights. Under such circumstances it appears almost completely white.

Although the Barn Owl is ordinarily seen only at dusk or when the bird is flushed from its roost in daytime, Chamberlain has recorded that on October 25, 1940, he saw the flight of a Barn Owl at 8:40 o'clock of a "bright, sunny morning." His attention had been attracted to the pigeons which were flying about the roof of the Charleston Museum. They were evidently much disturbed. Suddenly a Barn Owl, flying south, appeared about a hundred feet above the roof top. It paid no attention to the pigeons but continued in its flight until it disappeared over the roof tops.

Strange as it may seem, the Barn Owl is often found in towns and cities. So secretive is it, however, and so nocturnal, that a pair may reside for weeks or even months about a congested area without being noticed. Wayne (1910) mentions a pair which used the steeple of the Circular (Congregational) Church on Meeting Street in Charleston as a regular nesting site. Sprunt recalls that a pair often nested in the old West Point rice mill, at the west end of Calhoun Street, before the building was remodeled for military use. There is little doubt that in many towns of the State, Barn Owls are living undiscovered in the most populous areas.

The breeding season is another peculiarity of this peculiar owl. Breeding takes place at odd times. The eggs are laid at irregular intervals, and fresh eggs are often found in a nesting place with almost full grown young. Wayne provides an illustration by describing a set of six eggs taken on September 19, 1907, at Bossis Plantation, Berkeley County, one of which contained a large embryo, another a half developed one, the remaining four being in various stages of incubation. Another September breeding was noted by B. R. Chamberlain. He found a set of four eggs near Charleston on September 24, 1910, along with remnants of various animals, in a large box in the top of an abandoned building (*Auk, 28*: 1911, 112). Sprunt found two half grown young in the West Point Mill on November 20, 1921. On April 1, 1907, Dr. T. Gilbert Pearson and William Lowndes found a pair using an old rice mill on Lowndes' plantation on Cat Island, Georgetown County. The nesting place contained four eggs at the time. On May 20, when the observers visited the site again, there was only one young owl left. On February 7, 1927, one egg was found in an old rice mill at Prospect Hill Plantation, South Edisto River, a site which had been used for many years.

The Barn Owl builds no nest but lays the eggs on the bare floor in lofts, steeples, barns, grain chutes, or abandoned buildings. Sometimes the natural cavity of a tree or even a hole in a bank serves as a nesting place. The eggs number from four to nine, are almost spherical (as are all owls' eggs), and are pure white. They average 43.1 x 33.0 millimeters, and their incubation requires about twenty-one to twenty-four days.

Though the Barn Owl may be a city dweller, it hunts in rural districts, marshes, and farm lands, flying long distances for the purpose. In common with the other members of its family, it ejects the indigestible portions of its food in elongated pellets, these always being scattered about the roost. Exactly what the bird has been eating can be checked from an examination of these pellets.

Though the species remains in South Carolina permanently, there is a migratory movement among some of these birds, and the winter population is larger than that of other seasons.

FOOD: The Barn Owl is one of the most useful birds in the country. Every farmer who does not actively protect it is losing something. The great bulk of the diet consists of rats and mice. It also preys upon pocket gophers and shrews, and occasionally eats a bird. It very rarely molests poultry. Predominant in its prey is the cotton rat (*Sigmodon hispidus*), the chief enemy of the Bobwhite in the Southeast. Insects, mainly locusts and grasshoppers, also occur in its diet.

Family Strigidae: Typical Owls

203. Eastern Screech Owl: *Otus asio naevius* (Gmelin) (373m)

(Lat., *Otus*, a horned owl; *asio*, a horned owl; *naevius*, spotted.)

Description: Similar to the Southern Screech Owl but larger; upper and lower parts lighter.

Range: Resident and breeds north to northeastern Minnesota and New Brunswick; south to northern Kansas and northwestern South Carolina.

Status in S. C.: Resident and breeds in the northwestern section. Recorded from Oconee, Pickens, and Greenville counties.

History: Specimens of this owl were obtained from Caesar's Head by W. M. Perrygo and J. S. Y. Hoyt on July 10, 1940. Specimens were also taken at Clemson College on November 29, 1925, by E. J. Anderson; on May 14 and September 18, 1926, by F. Sherman; and on January 15 and 21, 1929, probably by Sherman. This seems to be without doubt the breeding race in the mountain region of the State.

In nesting and other habits, as well as in its choice of food, it does not differ from the Southern Screech Owl.

204. Southern Screech Owl: *Otus asio asio* (Linnaeus) (373)

Local Names: Squinch Owl.

Description: Smallest of the eastern North American owls except the Saw-whet Owl; length 8.00 to 10.00 inches. Head with conspicuous ear tufts. *Reddish phase.* Upper parts cinnamon rufous streaked with black; undersurface white heavily marked with rufous. *Gray phase.* Upper surface brown, streaked, vermiculated, and barred with black and brown; iris yellow.

Range: Resident and breeds north to Tennessee and southeastern Virginia; south to central Alabama and southern Georgia.

Status in S. C.: Common permanent resident in all but the northwestern part of the State. Reported north to York, Chester, and Lancaster counties; east to Horry County; south to Beaufort County; west to Greenwood and Abbeville counties.

History: This little owl is probably the best known of its family in the eastern and southern sections of the United States. It is a distinctly nocturnal bird, and though it is not shy and by no means avoids human habitation, is much oftener heard than seen. It is a permanent resident in the coastal plain and somewhat beyond, but gives place in the upper counties of South Carolina to the Eastern Screech Owl.

The Screech Owl manifests two distinct color phases, one largely reddish, the other gray. They appear to be about equally divided, one is as likely to be seen as the other, and some broods of young will contain both. The word "screech" in the name of this little owl seems rather inappropriate, for the bird, unlike its related species, rarely screeches. The characteristic note is a quavering, tremulous whistle, possessing a very eerie quality, distinctly plaintive and sad. It has given rise to much of the superstition and dread with which so many people view this inoffensive little bird.

Now and then one may see a roosting Screech Owl in a patch of woodland, sitting up close against the trunk of a sapling, or tree, with eyes wholly or partially closed. At such times the bird may be closely approached. It is seldom that the owl utters its cry in the daytime. Sprunt has noted but one instance, that of a bird heard at 8 a. m. on July 23, 1931. Another bird was heard at about 8 a. m., December 31, 1948, by M. L. McCrae and others.

The Screech Owl nests in cavities of trees, old woodpecker holes, and nest boxes. Elevation of the nest from the ground varies greatly: it may be from as low as 3 feet to more than 50. It has been noted that this owl often takes the nest boxes erected on Bull's Island for Wood Ducks, most of them being less than 20 feet high. The eggs are from two to six in number. They are practically round and are pure white, averaging 35.5 x 30.0 millimeters. Incubation requires about twenty-six days. But one brood is raised. The eggs are usually laid in early April, sometimes earlier. Typical dates: Beaufort County, March 28, 1936, three eggs, and April 10, 1942, four eggs (E. J. DeCamps); Charleston County, April 9, 1895, two eggs (Wayne). One egg was found on the ground in low wet woods on John's Island on April 4, 1948, by George B. Rabb and James E. Mosimann

The Southern Screech Owl hunts woodlands, farms, and the edges of marshes, almost wholly by night. With a good flashlight, one may sometimes see it at its hunting or perched atop a stump where it may be approached to within 3 or 4 feet if one is careful. When the bird leaves, however, not a whisper from the wings is audible; the flight is soundless.

If one of these owls ventures abroad by day, or is found roosting, the small birds of the vicinity—Mockingbirds, flycatchers, and jays—set upon it with great outcry. Sometimes it can be attracted by the "squeak" and will come within a few feet of the caller. An imitation of its note, which can be mastered to perfection, will nearly always result in bringing up numbers of small birds such as kinglets, Chickadees, Titmice, and the like.

Small as it is, the Screech Owl destroys a good many birds in some localities, but for the most part its food habits make it economically beneficial.

FOOD: Small rodents form the bulk of the food of the Southern Screech Owl, but it sometimes preys upon small birds, mostly sparrows and warblers. Examination of 255 stomachs by A. K. Fisher, showed the following results: forty contained bird remains; ninety-one held mice; eleven, other mammals; one hundred, insects; nine, crayfish; the rest, miscellaneous food.

GREAT HORNED OWL
205. *Bubo virginianus virginianus* (Gmelin)　(375)

(Lat., *Bubo*, a horned owl; *virginianus*, of Virginia.)

LOCAL NAMES: Hoot Owl; Cat Owl.

DESCRIPTION: Length 18.00 to 25.00 inches. Ear tufts very prominent. Above dark brown, finely mottled with ochraceous and white; under parts white or buff, with bars of dark brown or black, but these absent on middle of upper breast, thus forming a conspicuous broad white collar in front.

RANGE: Resident and breeds north to southeastern South Dakota, Wisconsin, and New Brunswick; south to southeastern Texas and Florida.

STATUS IN S. C.: Fairly common permanent resident over all the State. Recorded north to Chester County and Bennettsville; east to Horry County; south to Beaufort County; west to Anderson and Oconee counties.

HISTORY: The Great Horned Owl is the largest and most powerful of the owls, a capable and relentless bird of prey. The prominent ear tufts or "horns," the expression of the yellow and black eyes, the huge talons, and the large size of the bird all combine to make it an impressive creature.

In some respects, the history of this big owl and that of the crow parallel each other. The hand of man has been against both since earliest Colonial days. They have been shot, trapped, poisoned, vilified, and persecuted, yet both persist in numbers and are well able to take care of themselves in the midst of a mechanical civilization.

This "tiger among birds" is a woodland resident, but it often comes into the outskirts of towns. Stretches of pineland, live oak groves, and river swamps are its home as well as the barrier islands, the Up-country farms, and the mountains. It is much attached to the tree in which it habitually roosts and uses it for years if undisturbed.

Rather than constructing its own nest (though it sometimes does), this great owl usually takes over a deserted nest of a hawk or crow, or occasionally that of an Osprey (which continues to use it, as it breeds later than the owl). It has even been known to occupy parts of a nest with a Bald Eagle, the owl and the eagle incubating eggs in the same nest, a few feet apart. Again, eggs of the Great Horned Owl have been found on the bare wood of a deep crotch of a forest tree (Wayne).

Nesting takes place very early in the year. Usually two, sometimes three, eggs are laid, these being spherical and pure white. They average 56.1 x 47.0 millimeters. Typical egg dates are: January 19 and 26, Charleston County (Wayne); January 7, 17, and 29, Beaufort County (E. J. DeCamps); December 28, Newberry County (J. H. Burley). Incubation requires about twenty-eight days.

The voice of the Great Horned Owl is very deep and resonant; it comes forth in a series of four hoots, a repeated "hoo-hoo, hoo-hoo," with a rising inflection at the end. It may often be heard in broad daylight, particularly in the big cypress swamps of the Low-country.

The owl may occasionally be seen hunting in daytime. In pursuit of its prey it is determined and fearless. On February 9, 1940, R. E. Ware caught, banded, and released a Great Horned Owl which had followed a Black Duck it was chasing into a banding trap at Clemson College. The owl smelled strongly of skunk, a fact not particularly remarkable, since the Great Horned Owl consistently preys upon skunks. When food is abundant, several Great Horned Owls may congregate in a rather restricted area. Several seasons ago wardens on Bull's Island reported seeing as many as twenty of these owls on a night patrol of the sea beach along a 7 mile stretch. The abundance of rodents, wildfowl, and turkeys probably explains this unusual concentration.

The Great Horned Owl nests regularly on Bull's Island. A sitting bird has been seen on its nest in a slender pine tree not 20 feet from a road in December and January of 1946-47. There is another nest in a huge pine only a few hundred yards from headquarters, and a third one in an old eagle nest near Jack's Creek Basin. The owl's head, topped by the great ear tufts, is often visible over the rim of the nest.

This owl must be handled with great care when it is being banded, for its talons have tremendous power and can go through a man's hand like a knife.

FOOD: The diet of the Great Horned Owl is the subject of endless argument and contention. Some people maintain that the owl is valuable because of its destruction of harmful rodents, which it takes in numbers; others condemn it for attacks on poultry and game birds. There is, of course, something to be said on both sides. The owl consumes many rats, rabbits, squirrels, gophers, and mice; on the other hand, it also kills chickens, turkeys, ducks, and other game species. Its economic importance varies according to locality and conditions. The bird certainly performs meritorious service, but it also causes loss to the poultryman. Many owls are caught in pole traps, a nefarious device because it frequently catches everything except what it is set for.

206. SNOWY OWL: *Nyctea scandiaca* (Linnaeus) (376)

(Gr., *Nyctea*, nocturnal; Lat., *scandiaca*, of Scandia, *i. e.*, Scandinavia.)

DESCRIPTION: Length 20.00 to 27.00 inches. White, more or less barred or spotted with dark brown.

RANGE: Breeds north to northern Alaska and northern Greenland; south to central western Alaska, northern Quebec (Ungava), Lapland, and northeastern Siberia. Winters north to southern Alaska, Labrador, northern Europe, and northern Asia; south to central California, southeastern Georgia, Great Britain, and Japan.

STATUS IN S. C.: Rare and irregular winter visitor over most of the State. Reported north to Chester; east to Cape Romain; south to the mouth of the Savannah River; west to Aiken and Richland counties.

HISTORY: This beautiful, ghostly creature of the Arctic tundras seems more of a wraith than an actuality, as it drifts in silently on the wings of winter. It seems particularly unreal in South Carolina, which is far south of its normal range. In severe winters, invasions of these owls are expected in the northern states, but even there, years may pass between their visits. In years when the rodent population of the far north drops off and when frigid weather strikes the South, Snowy Owls may travel as far as South Carolina in search of food.

Its status in South Carolina has, of course, always been considered accidental; but there are now at least ten records of the Snowy Owl in the State. It would seem, therefore, that it is more than an accidental wanderer. At any rate, it is, as Wayne used to say, a *"rara avis"* here, though future winters may produce additional specimens. The Snowy Owl is unlike any other. Though many specimens are heavily cross-barred with brown, the markings vary to a degree and may be entirely absent, thus rendering the male bird pure white. It is the only white owl (with the exception, of course, of albinos) in South Carolina. The Snowy has no ear tufts or "horns."

Audubon lists three Snowy Owls from this state in his *Birds of America*, one from James Island, one from "Clarkson's Plantation," both Charleston County, and one from Columbia, Richland County. L. M. Loomis recorded the next bird. He saw one several times in early December, 1886, near Chester (*Auk, 8:* 1891, 55). G. E. Harris reported a wing-tipped Snowy Owl taken at Aiken, S. C., during February, 1891 (*Orn. and Ool., 16:* 1891, 108). A bird was secured at Winnsboro, Fairfield County, November 28, 1908, and was recorded by Wayne (*Auk, 27:* 1910, 454). Another was taken at the Savannah River entrance, February 8, 1931, by Ivan R. Tomkins (*Auk, 48:* 1931, 268, misspelled Lamkins). One was seen but not secured at the Grove Plantation, South Edisto River, December 29, 1931, by Wilcox Brown (*Auk, 49:* 1932, 351). In late winter of 1936-37, B. P. Rogers saw a "white owl" in a tree at a C. C. C. camp in Oconee County. This is probably another Snowy Owl record. One was seen on Bull's Island on October 26, 1943, by A. H. DuPre; and on January 24, 1946, a specimen was seen on the roof of the Charleston High School where it was watched for some time by the science teacher and his class.

The Snowy is a large, powerful bird, capable of dealing with sizable prey. However, it is not very shy, possibly because in its far northern haunts, remote from civilization, it has never learned to fear human beings. Therefore, during southern invasions many of them are killed.

FOOD: Largely rodents and birds of the northern tundras, rats, mice, lemmings, and hares, together with ducks, shore birds, grouse, and ptarmigan. Rabbits seem to be a favorite item.

WESTERN BURROWING OWL
207. *Speotyto cunicularia hypugaea* (Bonaparte) (378)

(Gr., *Speotyto*, a cave owl; Lat., *cunicularia*, a burrower; Gr., *hypugaea*, underground.)

DESCRIPTION: Length 9.00 to 11.00 inches. Legs long; head without ear tufts. Plumage above brown varied with white and buff; below white, barred or spotted with dark brown, but with collar plain white.

RANGE: Breeds north to British Columbia and southern Manitoba; south to Panama. Winters north to California and northern Texas; south to Panama.

STATUS IN S. C.: Accidental.

HISTORY: The sole record of this species for South Carolina rests on a bird seen by Ivan R. Tomkins on December 7, 1943, on the shore at Bay Point, near Beaufort, S. C. The bird was flushed from beneath a stranded barge lying on the beach, where it had apparently taken up residence. Tomkins was at the time without means of securing the bird. There can be no doubt whatever about the reliability of Tomkins' report and the record it establishes. The bird is so different from any other owl or indeed from any other bird that there is little likelihood of mistaking it in the field.

The Florida Burrowing Owl does not regularly occur north of central Florida and it is not known to be migratory, whereas the Western Burrowing Owl migrates more or less regularly southward after the breeding season. Therefore it seems to be more than probable that the bird reported by Tomkins was an individual of the western race.

In food and habits it is not injurous to man.

208. NORTHERN BARRED OWL: *Strix varia varia* Barton (368)

(Lat., *Strix*, a screech owl; *varia*, different.)

DESCRIPTION: Similar to the Florida Barred Owl, but with feathered toes.

RANGE: Resident and breeds north to Saskatchewan and Newfoundland; south to northern Arkansas and North Carolina; in winter casually farther south.

STATUS IN S. C.: Casual in winter in the northwestern part of the State.

HISTORY: This form of the Barred Owl is apparently only a casual winter visitor to South Carolina. There is only one record of its occurrence in this State, a typical specimen from Clemson College, Oconee County, obtained by R. E. Ware, December 11, 1939, and now in the collection of Clemson College. It has been identified by Dr. Harry C. Oberholser.

In behavior and food this race does not essentially differ from the Florida Barred Owl.

209. FLORIDA BARRED OWL: *Strix varia georgica* Latham (368a)

(Lat., *georgica*, of Georgia.)

LOCAL NAMES: Hoot Owl.

DESCRIPTION: Length 18.00 to 24.00 inches. Toes bare; head large and round with no ear tufts, or "horns." Upper parts dark brown, broadly barred with white or buff; lower parts white, buff, or grayish white, anteriorly barred, posteriorly streaked, with brown; eyes dark brown.

RANGE: Resident and breeds north to northeastern Texas and central eastern North Carolina; south to southeastern Texas and central Florida.

STATUS IN S. C.: Common permanent resident throughout the State. Recorded north to Cherokee County; east to Horry County; south to Beaufort County; west to Greenwood and Pickens counties.

HISTORY: The Florida Barred Owl is well known throughout South Carolina. It is a large owl and is responsible for the term "Hoot Owl," so often applied to all

Wild Turkey Gobbler

Wayne's Clapper Rail Incubating   S. A. GRIMES

Black Rail on Her Eggs   S. A. GRIMES

Incubating Woodcock   HUGH M. HALLIDAY

owls. It may be easily distinguished from the Northern Barred Owl by the fact that the toes are not feathered.

It frequents rather heavy woodland, stretches of pineland, mixed forest, and the river swamps, where its deep-toned call may at times be heard in full daylight. The call has an "aw" sound at the end which is very distinctive and which some northern visitors have referred to as a "southern drawl." Not at all shy, the Florida Barred Owl, rather unfortunately for its own safety, may be closely approached, and it often sits still and simply looks at an observer. Many of them, therefore, are shot, falling to that prejudiced persecution so commonly meted out to the birds of prey. It may be sometimes attracted by the "squeak" used in calling up small birds.

An owl taken at Central, Pickens County, December 8, 1925, by J. O. Pepper and another taken at Meredith, near Florence, by R. V. Segars on January 30, 1928, were identified by Dr. Harry C. Oberholser as the Florida form. Other specimens identified by Dr. Herbert Friedman are from Georgetown, January 4, 1891, and Conway, April 18, 1940.

The breeding habits of the Florida Barred Owl resemble those of the Great Horned Owl. Both birds nest early and often use the deserted nests of hawks and crows. Now and then they use a natural cavity of a tree. The eggs usually number two, sometimes three, and are pure white and round, like those of other owls. They average 51.4 x 43.5 millimeters, and incubation requires about twenty-eight days.

Typical nesting dates in the coastal region are Beaufort County, February 9 in 1936 and 1937, with two eggs in both cases (E. J. DeCamps); Charleston County, January 10, two eggs (Sprunt). A typical breeding date in the Piedmont area is March 15 (a nest with two young just hatched, in Pickens County, reported by F. Sherman).

FOOD: The Barred Owl is often accused of stealing poultry but actually seldom does so. It is difficult to persuade many persons to believe this, but examination of cast pellets or of the stomach contents of freshly killed specimens will furnish proof. The great bulk of the food is composed of rodents, insects, and some small birds.

Analysis of 109 stomachs by A. K. Fisher, of the U. S. Biological Survey, now the U. S. Fish and Wildlife Service, revealed that sixty-four contained mammals such as rats, mice, shrews, squirrels, and rabbits. Only five showed poultry remains; eighteen contained small birds. Frogs, lizards, fishes, and insects had been taken; and, curiously enough, among the birds were several screech owls. The cotton rat is often eaten. Protection of the Barred Owl about a farm is like taking out an insurance policy against the depredations of rats and mice.

210. LONG-EARED OWL: *Asio otus wilsonianus* (Lesson) (366)

(Lat., *Asio*, a horned owl; *otus*, horned owl; *wilsonianus*, to Alexander Wilson.)

DESCRIPTION: Length 13.00 to 16.00 inches. Ear tufts long. Upper parts blackish brown, mottled with white and buff; undersurface white or buff, streaked with dark brown, most heavily on breast, also narrowly barred on abdomen.

RANGE: Breeds north to central British Columbia, southern Mackenzie, and Newfoundland; south to northern Lower California and Virginia. Winters north to southern British Columbia and Massachusetts; south to Mexico and southern Florida.

STATUS IN S. C.: Rare winter resident, October 23 to March 16, over practically the entire State. Recorded north to Chester; east to Charleston; south to Beaufort County; west to Edgefield and Oconee counties.

HISTORY: The Long-eared Owl probably occurs with more frequency than the few records indicate. One is more likely to encounter it in the interior than on the coast. Murphey (1937) states that it is an uncommon winter resident in the Aiken-Augusta area; L. M. Loomis found it moderately common in the 1880's at Chester. Wayne met with it but once, on March 16, 1896, when he took two specimens near Mt. Pleasant, Charleston County. He mentions two records of birds taken by others, one from Edgefield County in the winter of 1905, the other near Mt. Pleasant, January 16, 1906.

On December 31, 1914, E. von S. Dingle saw what he thought was a Long-eared Owl near Summerton, Clarendon County. His note in the Charleston Museum file reads: "This single individual was flushed by a dog out of a brush heap, in a pine woods. He flew away and could not be secured." C. E. Chapman saw one of these owls at Mulberry Plantation, Berkeley County, January 16, 1917, and R. E. Ware of Clemson College secured a specimen in Oconee County on January 21, 1939, this being the last bird taken of which the writers have knowledge. It is now in the Clemson College collection, and has been examined by Sprunt.

The most recent record, and by far the earliest, is that of a bird which E. Milby Burton saw October 23, 1948, in downtown Charleston. The bird stayed all day in a tree and was approached to within 20 feet.

Though owls are almost universally regarded as nocturnal, they are not all entirely so; and the Long-eared Owl is one which may sometimes be encountered in daylight. It prefers thick cover at all times and is adept at the art of not being seen. This fact, together with its rarity, makes it a comparatively unknown bird in South Carolina.

FOOD: Almost entirely small mammals, particularly mice; occasionally, small birds such as sparrows. The Long-eared Owl rarely attacks poultry or game birds.

SHORT-EARED OWL
211. *Asio flammeus flammeus* (Pontoppidan) (367)

(Lat., *flammeus*, flame-colored.)

DESCRIPTION: Length 13.00 to 17.00 inches. Ear tufts very short. Plumage ochraceous buff, heavily streaked with dark brown above, lightly so below.

RANGE: Breeds north to northern Alaska, southeastern Baffin Island, Norway, and northern Siberia; south to California, New Jersey, northern Spain, and Sakhalin Island. Winters north to southern British Columbia, Maine, and the Mediterranean Sea; south to Guatemala, Cuba, Abyssinia, and southeastern China.

STATUS IN S. C.: Fairly common winter resident, October 26 to late April, in the eastern two-thirds of the State. Known north to Chester County and Marion; east to Bull's Island; south to Beaufort County; west to Aiken County and Columbia.

HISTORY: The Short-eared Owl is another unfamiliar species, most people being unaware of its existence. It is a winter resident in South Carolina but is rather locally distributed. It cannot be accounted common but is more numerous in some localities than others, and it seems to prefer the coast during its sojourn in the State. It is not an owl of the woods but rather of open prairie, grassy tracts, the salt marshes, and the barrier islands, where it lives among the dunes above high-water mark or on the grassy flats near the inlets.

It is a medium-sized owl. Its uniformly buff coloration and somewhat moth-like flight are good characters by which to identify it. The name arises from the fact that the ear tufts are very short, often so well concealed in the head plumage that they may be difficult to see even in a dead specimen. Sometimes Short-eared Owls are found in small flocks or bands, quite unlike the custom of owls in general. A note made by Sprunt mentions "five or six flushed at once from crest of a high dune on Long Island [Beaufort County] today, mouth of Savannah River on South Carolina side, January 23, 1931."

The Short-eared Owl is somewhat erratic in its occurrence; one season it will be almost common, the next very scarce. Another note made by Sprunt is illustrative: "Flushed one on Isle of Palms today, among sand dunes of front beach, November 7, 1930. It rose at a distance of about 6 feet. Though not having seen a specimen for over three years, this makes the second one within a week."

FOOD: This owl, which hunts by day as well as night, is a valuable check on injurious rodents. Its food is composed largely of rats and mice. Ivan R. Tomkins collected sixty-eight pellets of this owl on the dunes and marshes about the mouth of the Savannah River. These pellets contained the remains of ninety-six house mice, four rats, and thirty-eight birds. Some of the birds were the Sora Rail, Black-bellied Plover, Turnstone, and three other species of sandpipers as well as a number of passerines (*Wilson Bull.*, *48*: 1936, 77).

212. SAW-WHET OWL: *Aegolius acadicus acadicus* (Gmelin)   (372)

(Gr., *Aegolius*, a kind of screech owl; Lat., *acadicus*, of Acadia.)

DESCRIPTION: Smallest of the owls of the eastern United States. Length 7.50 to 8.00 inches. No ear tufts. *Adult.* Dark brown above, streaked and spotted with white; under parts white broadly striped with brown. *Immature.* Very different from the adult. Forehead, superciliary stripe, chin, and sides of throat white; rest of upper surface, throat, and breast plain dark brown; remainder of lower parts plain cinnamon buff.

RANGE: Breeds north to southern Alaska and southeastern Quebec; south to Maryland. Winters north to southern British Columbia and southeastern Quebec; south to Mexico and southeastern Georgia.

STATUS IN S. C.: Rare winter resident, November to February, over most of the State. Recorded north to Oconee and Richland counties; east to Charleston County; south to Beaufort County, west to Aiken County.

HISTORY: The Saw-whet Owl, which is not so large as a Robin, is the smallest of the owls in the eastern United States. Aside from its size, which is enough to distinguish it, the bird is so tame as to seem almost stupid. It spends the day sitting quietly in some thick shrub or small tree, and if it is detected there will sometimes allow an observer to approach close enough to catch it. It does not have the ear tufts or "horns" of the Screech Owl, the next South Carolina species in size to it. The streaked brown plumage blends well with its surroundings and it is only by accident that it is seen.

The Saw-whet is a rare owl in South Carolina, occurring only as a winter resident. Apparently the first specimen known from the State was secured on St. Helena Island, Beaufort County, by Alfred Cuthbert. Wayne (1910) says of it that the "data are incomplete" but he evidently had the specimen, for he says that he sent it to William Brewster. Wayne himself saw but one bird, that on December 24, 1885, at Hobcaw Plantation, Charleston County. It was in a dark piece of woods and, after watching it for some time, he "retreated some distance and fired at it, but could not find any trace of the bird except a few feathers."

A specimen was taken in Aiken County in February, 1899, and exhibited in a gunsmith's store in Augusta, Georgia, where Dr. E. E. Murphey saw it. It was destroyed in a flood in 1908. Another specimen from Aiken County was taken within a hundred yards of this one by the same collector (Thomas H. Sherman) in 1907, according to Murphey (1937).

A female taken on November 11, 1909, at Weston, Richland County, by J. P. Garrick, Jr., was sent to Wayne (*Auk, 28*: 1911, 112). Twenty years passed before another was noted. Then, on November 24, 1929, one was watched at close range at Mt. Pleasant, Charleston County, by Mesdames F. H. Horlbeck and F. Barrington.

On November 25, 1933, an adult bird was found injured in a garage on East Bay Street, Charleston, and given to the Charleston Museum by Miss Caroline Prince (No. 33.384). On November 30, 1939, a specimen was taken in a banding trap at Clemson, Oconee County, by R. E. Ware and is preserved in the Clemson College collection.

On the night of November 28, 1942, Sprunt heard a Saw-whet in his yard in St. Andrew's Parish, Charleston County. The peculiar character of the notes, which possess a metallic, ringing quality, are very distinctive and have been likened to the sound of a saw being sharpened; hence the bird's name. It will be noted that five of the nine foregoing records for this species have been made in November.

FOOD: Almost entirely mice; small birds only when mice are scarce or difficult to obtain. Meadow, white-footed, and house mice are the kinds usually taken.

Order Caprimulgiformes
Goatsuckers and Allies

Family Caprimulgidae: Goatsuckers

CHUCK-WILL'S-WIDOW
213. *Caprimulgus carolinensis* Gmelin (416)

(Lat., *Caprimulgus*, a goatsucker; *carolinensis*, of Carolina.)

LOCAL NAMES: Whip-poor-will; Dutch Whip-poor-will; Twixt-hell-and-the-white-oak.

DESCRIPTION: Length 11.00 to 12.00 inches. Tail rounded. *Male.* Upper surface dark brown, streaked, spotted, and vermiculated with black and buff; throat with a transverse white band; under parts varied with black, white, and buff; three outer tail feathers with large white patches at their ends. *Female.* Similar, but lacks the white on tail feathers.

RANGE: Breeds north to southeastern Kansas and southern Maryland; south to southeastern Texas and southern Florida. Winters north to southern Louisiana and northern Florida; south to Guatemala and Colombia.

STATUS IN S. C.: Common summer resident, March 11 to September 28, throughout the State. Reported north to Spartanburg and Chester counties; east to Horry County; south to Beaufort County; west to Edgefield and Oconee counties.

HISTORY: Much confusion attends the identity of the Chuck-will's-widow and the Whip-poor-will. Most people assume that any nocturnal bird they hear must be either an owl or a Whip-poor-will.

The Chuck-will's-widow seems to be a disembodied spirit rather than a creature of flesh and blood, and despite its abundance, its vociferous nature, and its State-wide distribution, it remains unknown to thousands of South Carolinians. This is a pity, for it is one of the most interesting of birds and has a considerable economic value. It is a summer resident in South Carolina, usually arriving from the tropics the third week in March. The males are the first to come, followed in a few days by the females, and courtship proceeds quickly.

Nesting begins, Wayne (1910) says, "as early as the last week in April." Since he wrote, however, even earlier dates have been recorded. Two fresh eggs were found by Sprunt on April 13, 1928, on James Island, thus advancing the former earliest record by two weeks. Somewhat later dates are typical of the interior; for example, June 10, near Columbia (A. A. Barden, Jr.). The eggs are laid without benefit of a nest, directly on the ground upon a carpet of leaves, in open woodlands. They invariably number two, and are, to quote Major Bendire (1895), "among the handsomest to be found in the U. S." The ground color is a deep cream, and the markings range from palest blue to dark brown, showing wide variation in size and distribution over the shell, some eggs being sparingly marked, others heavily. They average 35.56 x 25.57 millimeters. Both birds incubate and only one brood is raised. Incubation takes about twenty days (J. S. Y. Hoyt).

There are some very interesting facts about the Chuck-will's-widow's nesting habits. A pair will return year after year, to practically the same spot to nest, despite travelling perhaps thousands of miles in the interim. Sprunt found a set of eggs on May 8, 1926, on Folly Island, Charleston County, and marked the site carefully. He returned to it on May 12, 1927, and found another set within 5 feet of the earlier site. It is not possible, of course, to say positively that such a second nesting is by the same pair, unless the birds have been banded and can be caught a second time for identification.

If one handles the eggs, the birds remove them at once by carrying them away in the wide mouth. When the eggs are taken the female will lay again and again. Wayne noted four such successive layings. The young birds are clothed in down, like a barnyard "biddy," and match their surroundings amazingly, as, of course, do the parents. The parent bird resorts to feigning injury to lure an intruder away from the nest site. The eyes reflect light well, and the bird may be picked up by careful maneuvering while a flashlight is focussed upon it.

Like others of its family, the Chuck usually alights lengthwise upon a perch. Strange variations have been noted. One of the most remarkable and inexplicable was the action of a bird watched at sea by Gerald Thayer (*Auk, 16*: 1899, 273). It came aboard the ship off Cape Hatteras, and made dashes here and there, capturing warblers which had also come aboard during a migratory flight. This bird was seen to alight on the surface of the water, from which it took off with no apparent difficulty.

The voice of the Chuck is its primary characteristic. As clear-cut and incisive as the call is, many people identify it as the call of the Whip-poor-will in spite of the latter's three syllables as against the Chuck's four. Uninformed writers have contributed toward this error. "When the whip-poor-will calls, it's time to plant corn," wrote a famous contemporary novelist. The locality was Florida; therefore, it was actually the Chuck and its four-syllabled call of which the novelist was writing. Even reputable ornithologists have written about the "three-syllabled" call of this bird, possibly because the last note is not clear when the call is heard from a distance.

The bird begins the repetition of its name as soon as it arrives in spring, and the nights resound with it during the nesting season. Sometimes on cloudy days one may hear it in daylight hours. It ceases when the young hatch and are being raised but begins again during the fall migratory period. The Chuck disappears from South Carolina in September.

There is much variation in the rapidity and frequency of the call. The usual interval between the notes is about 2½ seconds; thus, about twenty-five calls a minute is normal. The total given at any one period varies from very few to very many. Hundreds of consecutive calls are not uncommon. E. von S. Dingle has counted three hundred straight calls, and Sprunt has records of several hundred. Quite the most remarkable number in Sprunt's experience was made by a Chuck in his yard, on the night of June 2, 1939. The bird called 834 times without stopping except for two periods of 3½ seconds between notes, instead of the usual 2½.

Other notes of this strange bird are a sort of "growl," like the twang of the bass string of a bull fiddle, uttered in flight while hunting; a peculiar croak, or "quak," given when flushed; a very guttural sound which sometimes precedes the typical call; and according to Dingle (ms., 1948) "a sing-song 'konk, konk, konk' repeated as many as 25 or 30 times." Dingle has also noted a lone, soft, murmuring call, apparently made in between the feeding flights.

The Chuck may sometimes be flushed in daytime when one is walking through open, leaf-strewn woodlands. It flies a short distance and alights on a limb of a tree. It is found in oak woods, deciduous growths, and even pineland.

Food: Chiefly night-flying insects such as moths, beetles, and winged ants, these making up 70 per cent of the total. The diet is strangely varied by inclusion of small birds such as sparrows and warblers. Whether this is accidental or illustrative of predacious activity is not entirely clear. Instances of the latter, however, seem positive. That the bird is very valuable in insect control is beyond question.

Eastern Whip-poor-will
214. *Caprimulgus vociferus vociferus* Wilson (417)

(Lat., *vociferus*, noisy.)

Description: Length 9.00 to 10.00 inches. Wings short and rounded; tail rounded and rather long. *Male.* Grayish brown above, much mottled with black and buff; lower parts brownish black; varied with buff; a white crescent on throat; broad end of three outer tail feathers white. *Female.* Like male but white of tail replaced by buff.

Range: Breeds north to central Saskatchewan and Nova Scotia; south to Arkansas and northwestern South Carolina. Winters north to southeastern Texas and central eastern North Carolina; south to Guatemala and Costa Rica.

Status in S. C.: Fairly common winter resident, August 27 to April 28, in the middle and eastern sections of the State. Fairly common summer resident, March 30 to September 18, in the northwestern third of South Carolina. In winter reported north to Florence County; east to Charleston County; south to Beaufort County; west to Aiken County and Columbia. In summer recorded north to Greenville and Cherokee County; east to Chester County; south to Edgefield; west to Oconee County.

History: Though the Whip-poor-will occurs throughout the year in South Carolina, there are sharp differences in its seasonal distribution. It does not appear at all in the coast region in summer but is present in winter. It is a summer resident in the Piedmont but is absent there in winter. Those who deny such a statement are confusing the Whip-poor-will with the Chuck-will's-widow.

There is no real reason why there should be any confusion between the Whip-poor-will and the Chuck-will's-widow. The Whip-poor-will has usually departed the Low-country before the Chuck arrives, and the latter migrates in fall before the Whip-poor-will returns. To complicate matters somewhat, however, both of the birds occur on the outskirts of the mountains in the nesting season.

The Whip-poor-will, like the Chuck, is almost wholly nocturnal and is therefore seldom seen. In winter it rarely utters the call which gives it its name. Sprunt has heard it on but three occasions in the Low-country. E. von S. Dingle has heard it frequently calling at Middleburg Plantation, Berkeley County, in February and March, and he also heard it on August 27, 1945, the latter being the earliest coastal record. E. Milby Burton heard it calling at Runnymede on the Ashley River on March 31, 1931. Wayne states that this bird is "not in the least inconvenienced by very cold weather." He recorded it on one occasion when the temperature stood at 6° F. (1899).

It arrives in upper South Carolina about the middle of April, the earliest record having been made on March 30, 1948, near Gaffney, Cherokee County (J. E. Mosimann, G. B. Rabb, and T. M. Uzzell, Jr.). The earliest record at Clemson College is April 9, 1927, with eggs having been found there on April 21. It probably leaves that area in mid-September.

Like the other goatsuckers, this species lays but two eggs, smaller but similar to those of the Chuck, in open woodlands. The eggs average 29.0 x 21.3 millimeters. The bird's wonderfully protective coloration is also characteristic of the family. The sharply enunciated call is three-syllabled and is a repetition of the name. The specific name of the bird, *vociferus*, is easily understood by anyone who has heard the call. The Whip-poor-will is distinctly smaller than the Chuck and is more grayish. The family name of "goatsuckers" arises from an old belief that these birds sucked goats of their milk, this fantastic supposition being based on the enormous size of the mouth. The base of the beak is provided with a fringe of bristles, which aid it in capturing the night-flying insects which are its prey.

FOOD: Nocturnal insects such as moths, beetles, and winged ants.

PLATE XVIII: WOODPECKERS

Water Color by Edward von S. Dingle

Upside down in center: Pileated Woodpecker (male). Above, left: Pileated Woodpecker (female). Four birds, top right, left to right: Downy Woodpecker (male), Downy Woodpecker (female), Yellow-bellied Sapsucker (male), and Yellow-bellied Sapsucker (female). Lower birds, left to right: Hairy Woodpecker (immature male), Hairy Woodpecker (male), Hairy Woodpecker (female), Red-bellied Woodpecker (male), Red-bellied Woodpecker (female), Red-headed Woodpecker (immature), and Red-headed Woodpecker (adult).

Ed Dimk.

GOATSUCKERS

EASTERN NIGHTHAWK
215. *Chordeiles minor minor* (Forster) (420)

(Gr., *Chordeiles*, an evening musical instrument, referring to flight performance; Lat., *minor*, smaller.)

DESCRIPTION: Length 9.00 to 10.00 inches. Tail a little forked, wings long and pointed. *Male.* Black above, barred and mottled with gray and buff; wing with a large white patch; a white subterminal band on the tail, except on middle feathers; throat and upper breast dark brown spotted with white and ochraceous; a white crescent on throat; belly cream buff, barred with dark brown. *Female.* Similar to the male but throat crescent buff; tail with no white bar; and wings with much less white.

RANGE: Breeds north to northern Yukon and central Labrador; south to northwestern Washington and northwestern South Carolina. Winters north to Colombia and Venezuela; south to central eastern Argentina and southeastern Brazil.

STATUS IN S. C.: Common summer resident, April 23 to October 9, in the mountain region of the northwestern section and in the central northern part of the State. Reported north to Chester; east to Florence; west to Oconee County. Probably a transient in the rest of the State, recorded definitely from Beaufort County.

HISTORY: This bird, indistinguishable in the field from the Florida Nighthawk, belongs to the mountain counties and northern South Carolina. The Florida Nighthawk frequents the rest of the State. Specimens taken by Franklin Sherman at Mountain Rest, Oconee County, June 12, 1934, are referable to this northern race. Three specimens secured by G. E. Hudson at Florence, June 10, July 16 and 22, 1926, proved to be of this subspecies. And one in the collection of the Cleveland Museum of Natural History was taken by R. J. Kula in Beaufort County on April 23, 1941. These specimens have been examined by Dr. Harry C. Oberholser.

The habits, nesting, and food of the Eastern Nighthawk do not differ from those of the Florida Nighthawk.

FLORIDA NIGHTHAWK
216. *Chordeiles minor chapmani* Coues (420a)

(Lat., *chapmani*, to Frank Michler Chapman.)

LOCAL NAMES: Bull-bat.

DESCRIPTION: Similar to the Eastern Nighthawk but smaller, somewhat paler and more spotted with white or ochraceous on the upper parts.

RANGE: Breeds north to southern Illinois and central eastern North Carolina; south to southeastern Texas and southern Florida. Winters north to central eastern Brazil and south to northern Argentina.

STATUS IN S. C.: Common summer resident, March 20 to December 1, in all of the State except the northern sections. Recorded north and west to Anderson County; east to Horry County; south to Beaufort County.

HISTORY: Almost everything about the authentic and local names of the Florida Nighthawk is misleading and ill-chosen. It is not a hawk, it is not particularly nocturnal, and it is certainly neither a bull nor a bat. Yet the names are fixed; "Nighthawk" or "Bull-bat" the bird is likely to remain.

The Florida Nighthawk is by no means confined to rural areas; it is also a dweller of towns and cities and often nests in the busiest districts. Afternoon brings them out, and their swooping, erratic flights weave intricate patterns through the warm summer evenings. The spectacular dives performed at high speed from considerable heights, the sudden upward turn just as it seems that the bird would dash itself to the ground, are breath-taking. As the bird swerves upward, the wings make a high, booming sound audible at some distance. High above field, beach, or teeming street, the familiar nasal "peenck" may drift thinly to the ear of a lonely field worker or of hurrying throngs of shoppers, even at the mid-day hour.

The Florida Nighthawk differs in its nesting habits from those of its relatives. It usually lays its eggs in open situations, seldom in woods or under any sort of cover. It constructs no nest. The site may range from the sand dunes of a barrier beach to furrows in a cornfield or the flat top of a city warehouse or store. The eggs blend remarkably well into their surroundings. They are two in number, thickly spotted and have a grayish white ground color. The average size is 29.97 x 21.84 millimeters. Incubation requires about nineteen days. The bird excels at feigning injury and the act is so convincing that many an observer is fooled by it.

Nesting occurs in May and early June. Early egg dates on the coast are May 7 (Sprunt); May 9 (E. von S. Dingle). Most eggs are laid after May 20. Typical is May 22, Beaufort County (E. J. DeCamps).

In the spring and particularly during the fall tremendous migration flights take place. Wayne tells of one that took place on September 6, 1905, "between 5:30 P. M. and sunset, these birds were migrating in dense flocks, which at times obscured the sky. As far as I have been able to ascertain, these flocks extended over an area of more than fifteen miles from east to west. The number of birds seen must have represented millions." Murphey (1937) relates another incident which took place in the Aiken-Augusta region, "In September, 1934, I counted over 2200 in the course of a thirty-seven mile ride, and several observers informed me that their numbers were equalled by these [those] seen over a distance of thirty miles in the opposite direction—a zone of migrating nighthawks, sixty-seven miles in breadth."

The Florida Nighthawk is far more diurnal than either the Whip-poor-will or Chuck-will's-widow. Its note can often be heard after dark, but it consistently hunts during the day.

Food: Insects exclusively, of which it devours great numbers. It is certainly one of the most valuable of birds. Winged ants form almost 50 per cent of its food. It also consumes May beetles, mosquitoes, gnats, grasshoppers, potato beetles, and the cotton-boll weevil. It is obvious that the bird has an exceedingly high economic value.

Order *Apodiformes*
Swifts and Hummingbirds

Family Apodidae: Swifts

217. CHIMNEY SWIFT: *Chaetura pelagica* (Linnaeus)   (423)

(Gr., *Chaetura*, bristle-tail; Lat., *pelagica*, nomadic.)

LOCAL NAMES: Chimney Swallow; Chimney Sweep.

DESCRIPTION: Length 4.75 to 5.50 inches. Wings long and narrow; tail short, tipped with sharp spines. Plumage sooty olive to deep hair brown, the throat pale gray.

RANGE: Breeds north to central Alberta and southeastern Quebec; south to southeastern Texas and southern Florida. Winters in Peru.

STATUS IN S. C.: Abundant summer resident, March 7 to November 5, throughout the entire State. Known north to Greenville and York counties; east to Horry County; south to Beaufort County; west to Oconee and Pickens counties.

HISTORY: It is probable that everyone knows the Chimney Swift, but it is equally probable that most people erroneously name it "Chimney Swallow." The Swifts are related to the hummingbirds and are not swallows at all. They are birds both of the city and of the country, and in the spring, summer, and autumn skies, they wheel, swoop, and circle endlessly in erratic, darting flight.

Swifts arrive in late March. They are abundant by April and remain so until late October when they leave. Despite their rather early arrival, they nest late. For two months they do nothing but fly and roost, and are apparently more often in flight than at rest. If any bird deserves the adjective *tireless*, it is the Swift. Round and round, hour after hour, they pursue their twittering way, and the miles they fly and insects they consume must reach astronomical figures. The value of Chimney Swifts, Nighthawks, and Purple Martins in the control of insects is incalculable.

When Swifts nest, they illustrate why the term "chimney" has come to be applied to them, for it is in chimneys that most of them breed and roost. Late in May they may be seen hovering about the dead twigs at the end of the branches; these dead twigs they break off in flight and carry to their chosen black abode. Distances of the nests from the top and bottom of the flue vary considerably and seem to follow no design.

The nest is a semi-circular basket of twigs, glued together and to the supporting bricks by the bird's saliva. The nest is not lined. There are three to six pure white eggs averaging 20.10 x 13.24 millimeters. Incubation requires about eighteen days. Full sets are usually found by June 15, but there are records of earlier dates. Chimneys in cities, towns and villages are utilized, but now and then instances of primitive nesting occur, for some Swifts still nest as they did before there were any chimneys—in hollow trees. In the great swamps along the Pee Dee, Santee, and Savannah Rivers, large, hollow-trunked cypresses harbor colonies of the birds. Sprunt found them in the Santee Swamp of Georgetown County in 1936-37. It is interesting to note that the birds nesting in such situations appear to show a more whitish throat than other birds of the same species.

A rather unusual nesting site was discovered by Sprunt on June 4, 1947. The nest, containing four eggs, was attached to the inside wall of a boathouse on the unused dock of the Cape Romain Lighthouse, Raccoon Key. It was about 5 feet from the floor, and the sitting bird was touched before it left the nest. On June 29, 1948, Hoyt Young and Henry C. Rucker, of the Cape Romain Refuge staff, found three nests in this boathouse, all containing young.

Rains sometimes loosen the nest attachment, and the eggs or young are precipitated into grates or to the floors of dwellings, usually to the consternation of the housewife. Aside from the cleaning-up job then necessary, no harm is done, though there is a widespread belief that the birds carry and distribute vermin. There is no ground whatsoever for this notion.

No doubt the most interesting thing about these birds, until very recently, was the mystery of their winter home. No one could say, with accuracy, where it was. While modern study had advanced beyond the old theory that the birds hibernated in hollow trees or in mud banks, no one could put a finger on a map and say that here was the area to which the Swifts migrated. Birds were known to leave the Gulf Coast in fall and to return in spring, but that was all. Many thousands were banded, year after year, about 375,000 in all, and at last the bands gave the answer. In May of 1944 word was received from the American Embassy at Lima, Peru, that thirteen bands had been "secured from some swallows killed by Indians" living on the border of Peru and Colombia. The report stated that the birds had been taken some six months previously, which would date the capture in December, 1943, Most of these birds, which were Chimney Swifts, had been banded in Tennessee, from 1938 to 1940 (*Auk, 61*: 1944, 604).

Food: Entirely insects, taken on the wing. Beetles, flies, and ants predominate. The Engraver beetles, very harmful to trees, potato beetles (*Lema trilineata*), and plant bugs (*Lygus*) are destroyed in great numbers. The value of these birds can hardly be overestimated.

Family Trochilidae: Hummingbirds

RUBY-THROATED HUMMINGBIRD
218. *Archilochus colubris* (Linnaeus) (428)

(Gr., *Archilochus*, a company chief; Lat., *colubris*, from South American name *colibri*.)

DESCRIPTION: Length 3.00 to 3.50 inches. *Male.* Upper parts metallic bronze green; throat brilliant metallic red; undersurface gray, the sides with some metallic green. *Female.* Similar to male but with throat grayish white, and outer tail feathers tipped with grayish white. *Immature.* Throat speckled with dark brown; otherwise similar to female.

RANGE: Breeds north to central Alberta and southeastern Quebec; south to central Texas and southern Florida. Winters north to southern Louisiana and northern Florida, casually South Carolina; south to Guatemala and Panama.

STATUS IN S. C.: Permanent resident, common in summer, very rare in winter, over the entire State. Reported north to Greenville, Cherokee, and Darlington counties; east to Horry County; south to Beaufort and Jasper counties; west to Aiken and Oconee counties.

HISTORY: Miniatures have a peculiar fascination. It is small wonder, then, that the hummingbirds are such attractive, magnetic bits of avian life. They are the smallest and certainly among the most interesting of American birds. Their tiny size, rapidity of movement, and brilliant plumage make them objects of wonder and admiration.

The Ruby-throat is the only member of its wide family occurring regularly in the eastern United States, and it is a summer resident in South Carolina throughout the length and breadth of the State. Migrants arrive from the south in late March, usually just before the end of the month in the coastal area and about mid-April in the Piedmont. Males come first but are soon followed by the less brilliant opposite sex. Mating takes place almost at once, and the courtship of the hummer is a spectacular performance. The male swings rapidly back and forth on the arc of a circle while the object of his attention either feeds at a blossom or sits on a twig and watches him. At such times, the ruby patch on the male bird's throat shines and glows like a living coal, and the vibration of his wings in a hazy halo about him produces a hum which seems out of all proportion to the maker.

The nest, which is surely one of the most beautiful creations of avian architecture, is constructed by the female, very rarely with any assistance from her mate. Pines, oaks, and dogwoods seem to be favorite nesting trees. The nest may be built at elevations of from 4 to 60 feet above the ground. It measures about an inch deep and an inch across and is made of wadded plant down, pressed almost to a felt, plastered with lichens bound on with cobwebs. The eggs almost always number two and are pure white, averaging 12.9 x 8.5 millimeters (about the size of cowpeas). They are laid in late April and early May, eggs of the second laying being deposited in late June. A very early breeding date is April 3, Beaufort County (E. J. DeCamps). Incubation requires sixteen days. The young are hatched naked, blind, and helpless, and are fed by regurgitation.

The males are the first to leave in autumn, usually by mid-September, but the females and immatures linger a month longer. Not the least interesting phase of this tiny bird's life is the tremendous distance which it covers on migration, for the greatest number leave the United States in winter. How such fragile bits of life can cross trackless miles of ocean and jungle between the Americas is one of the greatest marvels of nature.

Occasionally, hummers are found in South Carolina in winter. The known dates seem to indicate that some individuals simply remain during the cold season and are not belated migrants. It is not certain whether they are locally bred birds or birds which hatched much further north and have migrated this far only. The latter explanation seems the more probable. Winter records exist from Marion, November 5, 1911 (E. B. Wheeler); Charleston, December 18 and 30, 1910 [the same bird?] (H. R. Sass); and Charleston, February 20, 1933 (Hugh Rutledge).

Hummers are highly pugnacious and do not hesitate to drive away any intruder from the nest territory; they attack much larger birds without hesitation. Battles between males often take place but rarely end in injury.

FOOD: Though the popular conception is that hummers live on the nectar of flowers, and this is true to some extent, they consume large numbers of insects. The characteristic hovering about blossoms and probing into them represents a search for minute insects rather than for the more romantic and ethereal diet of nectar. Many authorities believe that the bird's fondness for sweets is an acquired taste. Tubular flowers attract it, particularly red ones, not so much because they are red, but because they are usually conspicuous against their background.

219. RUFOUS HUMMINGBIRD: *Selasphorus rufus* (Gmelin) (433)

(Gr., *Selasphorus*, light-bearing; Lat., *rufus*, reddish.)

DESCRIPTION: *Male.* Top of head metallic green; remainder of upper parts cinnamon rufous; chin and throat metallic scarlet; chest white; remaining lower parts cinnamon rufous. *Female.* Above metallic green; below anteriorly dull white; posteriorly buffy white, but cinnamon rufous laterally.

RANGE: Breeds north to southeastern Alaska; south to central California and southern Idaho. Winters north to Louisiana (casually) and South Carolina (accidentally); south to Mexico.

STATUS IN S. C.: Accidental.

HISTORY: The Rufous Hummingbird occurs normally in the Rocky Mountain region and westward and is purely accidental in South Carolina. There is but one record of its capture, at Charleston on December 18, 1909, by Edward A. Hyer. The bird was more or less automatically identified as a winter Ruby-throat and remained so labelled in the Charleston Museum collection for nearly twenty years. In November, 1928, a question was raised regarding its identity and it was sent to the United States National Museum in Washington, where J. H. Riley identified it as the Rufous Hummingbird. This is the specimen referred to in the editorial footnote on page 98 of Wayne's *Birds of South Carolina* (1910). It was recorded in the *Auk, 46*: 1929, 237-38.

Generally speaking, the Rufous Hummingbird and the Ruby-throat are very much alike in habits and choice of food.

Order Coraciiformes
Kingfishers and Allies

Family Alcedinidae: Kingfishers

EASTERN BELTED KINGFISHER
220. *Megaceryle alcyon alcyon* (Linnaeus) (390)

(Gr., *Megaceryle*, a large kingfisher; Lat., *alcyon*, a kingfisher.)

DESCRIPTION: Length 11.00 to 14.00 inches. Head large and crested. *Male*. Upper surface and a wide band across chest bluish gray; other under parts white. *Female*. Similar to the male but sides of body and an additional band on chest cinnamon rufous.

RANGE: Breeds north to Mackenzie and south central Labrador; south to southern Texas and southern Florida. Winters north to Wyoming and southern Maine; south to Guatemala, Colombia, and Trinidad.

STATUS IN S. C.: Common permanent resident throughout the State. Observed north to Greenville, Spartanburg, York, and Dillon counties; east to Horry County; south to Beaufort and Jasper counties; west to Oconee and Pickens counties.

HISTORY: One of the best known birds over the country generally, this noisy, jaunty, vigorous species is a permanent resident in South Carolina. It is one of the few land birds dependent on water areas, for it secures all of its food from water.

As if its plumage and general appearance were not conspicuous enough, the Kingfisher is endowed with a voice which it puts to frequent use, and which one is quickly aware of anywhere in the bird's range. It is universally described as a rattle, a description that can hardly be improved upon.

The Kingfisher is usually a solitary creature. It sits patiently upon an over-water perch until its quarry comes near, but sometimes it hunts from the air, hovering until it sights its prey, then plunging into the water. It often gives its characteristic cry as it flies off with the catch. Both the farm boy and the city dweller are familiar with the Kingfisher, for it seeks its food impartially in a shady creek near a rural barnyard or in a pond or lake surrounded by city streets and residences. The Kingfisher is often seen perched on telephone wires along ditches which parallel highways;

they fly from pole to pole at the approach of a car, swing around behind it and perch once more.

Winter is the time when it is most abundant in South Carolina; the population is then augmented by incoming migrants from northern points. When the nesting season starts the birds are much more quiet than at other times and attend strictly to domestic duties. They breed in holes which they dig in the faces of banks, cuts, or similar declivities. The burrow is nearly circular and about 4 inches across, varying considerably in depth, from hardly more than 3 feet to as much as 15. At the end of the excavation, five to eight glossy white eggs are laid, averaging 33.9 x 26.7 millimeters, these being deposited early in April. Incubation requires about twenty-three or twenty-four days. Only one brood is raised.

Relatively common as the Kingfisher is, the finding of a nest is really unusual. Wayne never succeeded in taking the eggs, as he was "invariably too early or too late." The early April laying date is determined by the fact that Wayne saw young birds faring for themselves on May 31, and that there is a record in the Charleston Museum files by B. F. Taylor of a bird digging a nest-hole on March 30, 1909, at Columbia. In the Low-country, banks for the construction of nesting burrows are not everywhere available, and the Kingfisher may possibly utilize other situations, such as natural cavities in stubs or trees (Bent, 1940).

Food: About three-quarters of the Kingfisher's diet is composed of various kinds of fish, mostly of inedible kinds. Two-fifths of the fish are commercially valuable, and are secured at fish hatcheries and rearing ponds. Such thievery has brought the bird under the wrath of the fish culturist. Though much of this depredation could be prevented by the screening of the pools, the less expensive method is to shoot the offender, and this is a method widely practiced, though not so frequently in South Carolina as elsewhere.

Order Piciformes
Woodpeckers and Allies

Family Picidae: Woodpeckers

221. NORTHERN FLICKER: *Colaptes auratus luteus* Bangs (412a)

(Gr., *Colaptes*, a chisel; Lat., *auratus*, golden; *luteus*, yellow.)

DESCRIPTION: Similar to the Southern Flicker but larger. Length 11.00 to 12.00 inches.

RANGE: Breeds north to Nebraska and Nova Scotia; south to central northern Texas and northwestern South Carolina. Winters north to about the northern limits of its breeding range; south to southeastern Texas and northern Florida.

STATUS IN S. C.: Common permanent resident in the northwestern edge of the State and a fairly common winter resident over the remaining portion, September 20 to April 30. Recorded in summer north to Greenville County and south to Walhalla (Oconee County). Winters also north to York and Chesterfield counties; east to Bennettsville and McClellanville; south to James Island and Allendale; west to Anderson County.

HISTORY: The Northern Flicker lives along the northwestern edge of South Carolina, a fact indicated by a series of specimens taken at Caesar's Head and Walhalla in the summer of 1940 by W. M. Perrygo and J. S. Webb and examined by Dr. Harry C. Oberholser. They are now in the United States National Museum. Two Charleston Museum specimens, taken by S. K. Johnson on July 15, 1927, at Caesar's Head have also been referred to this form. Though these vary toward the Southern Flicker, they seem better referred to the Northern Flicker, as has been done by Robert Ridgway with less material than is now available. A winter bird from Clemson College was recently identified as a Northern Flicker, but the breeding race in that locality is the Southern Flicker.

In winter the population of flickers in South Carolina is considerably augmented by migrants from northern parts of the country, indistinguishable in appearance but averaging a little larger. These are Northern Flickers. Further assurance of the bird's occurrence in South Carolina is made evident by such records as the following, all of which are verified by specimens examined by Dr. Oberholser: a specimen at Clemson College, collected December 31, 1925, by G. E. Hudson and Franklin

Sherman; other specimens are from Summerville, February 7, 1926, M. P. Skinner; James Island, January 4, 1938, W. W. McLeod; Charleston, October 24, 1942, Miss Mary Frost and January 18, 1946, Miss Margaret Miller; Berkeley County, October 16, 1939, E. von S. Dingle. Other specimens used in outlining the winter range are in the United States National Museum.

In habits, behavior, and food this bird does not differ from the Southern Flicker.

SOUTHERN FLICKER
222. *Colaptes auratus auratus* (Linnaeus)   (412)

LOCAL NAMES: Yellowhammer; Golden-winged Woodpecker.

DESCRIPTION: Length 10.00 to 11.00 inches. *Male.* Top of head and hind neck gray, the latter with a scarlet crescent; back grayish brown barred with black; rump white, conspicuous in flight; chin and foreneck dull vinaceous, with a black mustache at the corner of the mouth; chest with a broad black crescent; posterior lower parts pale pinkish buff to yellowish, grayish, or brownish white, with large round black spots; shafts of tail feathers and lining of wings yellow. *Female.* Similar but lacks the black mustache.

RANGE: Resident and breeds north to southern Missouri and southeastern Virginia; south to southeastern Texas and southern Florida.

STATUS IN S. C.: Common permanent resident throughout the State except the northwestern edge. Reported north to York, Lancaster, and Dillon counties; east to Horry County; south to Beaufort County; west to Anderson County, Clemson College, and Spartanburg (probably).

HISTORY: To most people the Southern Flicker is a Yellowhammer. It is a common, permanent resident of South Carolina except along the northwestern edge of the State. It is the best known member of its family. Active, vigorous, noisy, and withal a friendly bird, it is both a rural and urban dweller. Small boys once regarded it as game. It is not dependent upon any particular kind of country, though it is more likely to be found in open woodlands and at the edges of fields than in forests. It is common on the sea islands and mainland edges and penetrates all the way to the edge of the mountain region. It nests everywhere.

In typical woodpecker fashion, the flicker digs out a hole in a dead tree, and there lays its five to ten pure white glossy eggs. The eggs average 28.57 x 22.01 millimeters. The holes are often made in pines though not invariably. It also uses the softer, fibrous palmetto, and now and then telephone poles, dock pilings, and even fence posts and bird boxes. Elevation of the holes varies widely, from 4 feet above the ground or water to as much as 50 or more. Eggs may be found from early April to mid-May. The first week in May is typical. Incubation requires from fourteen to sixteen days.

The courtship antics of the Southern Flicker are very curious. A pair of birds will face each other on a tree branch or on a crossarm of a telephone pole and weave back and forth for some time with a pendulum-like motion, bobbing and bowing now and then. The far-carrying note, which sounds like "flica-flica" is familiar, but it has another call resembling the word "clape," which is a local name for the bird in some places.

More than any other woodpecker the Southern Flicker is a ground bird. It is often flushed from fields or roadsides and bounds away in characteristic, undulating flight, showing the yellow lining of the wings and the white patch at the base of the tail, which is its best field mark. This predilection for the ground is undoubtedly due to its excessive fondness for ants, though how such a taste should be so highly developed in one member of a family and not in others is not clear.

The Southern Flicker has a habit of drilling into the sides of wooden buildings to make a roosting hole. The clatter it thus produces becomes a nuisance, and its habit of drumming on a tin roof or gutter does not endear it to early morning sleepers.

Food: This bird is certainly one of the most valuable of the woodpeckers in relation to our economy. Its diet is composed of about 60 per cent animal and 40 per cent vegetable food. Ants are an outstanding item in the former, forming half the total animal food. Flickers eat them the year round. Of 684 stomachs examined, 524 contained remains of ants. Ninety-eight stomachs held nothing else, and as many as five thousand ants have been counted in a single one. Other insects include crickets, grasshoppers, beetles, caterpillars; spiders and snails are also taken. The vegetable food is usually wild fruit, mast, and corn. The corn is for the most part waste left in fields and eaten only in small quantities.

223. BOREAL FLICKER: *Colaptes auratus borealis* Ridgway (412b)

(Lat., *borealis*, northern.)

DESCRIPTION: Similar to the Northern Flicker but still larger. Length 12.00 to 13.00 inches.

RANGE: Breeds north to northwestern Mackenzie and northern Ungava; south to Wyoming and Quebec. Winters north to southern British Columbia and Maine; south to California and South Carolina.

STATUS IN S. C.: Rare winter resident, October 8 to January 24, over most of the State. Recorded north and east to Bennettsville; south to Edisto Island; west to Anderson.

HISTORY: The Boreal Flicker is a far northern subspecies which sometimes strays widely. There is a specimen in the Charleston Museum, presented years ago by H. T. Nowell, which carries no data on the label other than the notation "Anderson, S. C." This was Nowell's home, where he worked for years. Additional records have been recently obtained from specimens identified by Dr. Harry C. Oberholser. These are as follows: 14 miles northwest of Bennettsville, October 8, 1940, collected by W. M. Perrygo and J. S. Webb; a female, found by Mrs. C. H. Bailey on Edisto Island, November 12, 1945, not preserved but identified from measurements; and a male, taken at Huger, Berkeley County, January 24, 1938, by E. von S. Dingle.

In habits and food this subspecies does not materially differ from the Southern Flicker.

SOUTHERN PILEATED WOODPECKER
224. *Dryocopus pileatus pileatus* (Linnaeus) (405)

(Gr., *Dryocopus*, wood-cutting; Lat., *pileatus*, capped.)

LOCAL NAMES: Log-cock; Kate; Woodcock.

DESCRIPTION: Length 15.00 to 19.00 inches. *Male.* Head with large scarlet crest and cheek patch; rest of plumage black, except for white throat and white stripe from base of bill down sides of neck; lining of wings and a patch on the wing quills white. *Female.* Like the male, but fore part of crown and cheeks not red.

RANGE: Resident and breeds north to Missouri and southern Pennsylvania; south to southeastern Texas and northern Florida.

STATUS IN S. C.: Fairly common permanent resident in all the State. Noted north to Caesar's Head, Greenville, Chester County, and Florence County; east to Horry County and Mt. Pleasant; south to Beaufort and Jasper counties; west to Greenwood, Oconee, and Pickens counties.

HISTORY: The Pileated Woodpecker, often confused with the nearly extinct Ivory-billed Woodpecker, is in its own right a regal creature. Its history is in direct contrast to that of the Ivory-bill for it has been increasing over the country, whereas the Ivory-bill has been decreasing. The principal reason seems to be that it can adapt itself to changing conditions and the Ivory-bill cannot.

The Pileated Woodpecker is a great black and white bird, with a flaming red crest in both sexes. It prefers wooded country, of course—formerly, as Wayne (1910) says, of "a primeval nature"—but despite the disappearance of much heavy growth, the Pileated is still with us and actually seems to have become more common in recent years. It occurs close to settlements and sometimes within them. It lives also on the barrier islands, in the cypress swamps, and in river woods, up into the rolling hills of the Piedmont and the mountains.

Individual birds like particular places and will stay in a rather limited area year after year; they even return to the same trees to nest. They make roosting as well as breeding holes; the roosting holes often have more than one opening so that the bird may escape if cornered. The Pileated exhibits a curious combination of shyness and tameness. Sometimes it is almost impossible to approach, but occasionally it will work away on a tree, apparently oblivious of an audience. It is more often heard than seen, but there is no doubt whatever about its note. The voice of the Pileated, though some notes are flicker-like, is a wild, far-carrying cry, defying accurate translation but sounding something like "kuk, kuk, kuk." It also has a flight call which rolls and reverberates through the woods with startling effect. It often calls as it leaves a tree and while it is in flight. The hammerings on limbs and trunks can be heard for long distances and give the impression of being delivered with power by a large bird. In its search for food it dislodges large chunks of bark and rotten wood. In the nesting season it can be decoyed by tapping on a dead limb or the sides of a dugout in cypress country, in imitation of its strokes. Birds thus attracted give evidence of great excitement.

The Pileated usually mates in February and starts digging the nesting hole during the latter part of that month. Wayne says it "requires exactly a month for completion." It is not hard to observe the birds closely while the nest is under construction.

Egg time comes about April 20, although a complete set of eggs has been taken as early as April 9. There are three to five pure white eggs averaging 32.90 x 24.72 millimeters. Only one brood is raised and incubation requires about eighteen days. Though the birds may use the same tree in successive seasons, they always make a new hole; hence one can find large trees with two or three such apertures which are obviously Pileated Woodpecker holes because of their great size and elliptical shape. Elevation varies from hardly more than 10 feet (unusual) to 75, and the holes may be in either dead or living trees—cypresses, sweet and black gums, and long-leaf and loblolly pines. Occasionally on the barrier islands, the Pileated nests in a palmetto. Old holes often become the homes of other birds or of small mammals like the fox squirrels and flying squirrels.

When perched, the Pileated shows no white in the wings, except perhaps a thin streak, but in flight, the white patches or wing lining blaze out prominently in the forward portions. This character is infallible in distinguishing the Pileated from the Ivory-bill. The Ivory-bill shows much white in the wings when perched; and in flight the rear part of the wings is white. There is a belief that the white bill of the larger bird is an excellent field mark; actually it is a poor one, for in certain lights the Pileated's beak shines as white as that of the Ivory-bill's. The flight of the Pileated is undulating, while the Ivory-bill flies much like a crow, with steady flapping and no dipping.

Food: The Pileated Woodpecker is a most valuable asset to forests and timber. It destroys large numbers of wood-boring beetles, ants, and grubs. It also eats wild fruits and berries. E. von S. Dingle has frequently noted the Pileated feeding on the seed of the magnolia, as illustrated in his painting which appears in this volume.

RED-BELLIED WOODPECKER
225. *Centurus carolinus carolinus* (Linnaeus) (409)

(Gr., *Centurus*, prickle-tailed; Lat., *carolinus*, of Carolina.)

LOCAL NAMES: Zebra Woodpecker; Cham-chack.

DESCRIPTION: Length 8.50 to 10.00 inches. *Male.* Top of head and hind neck red; remainder of upper parts and wings black, barred with white; undersurface pale smoke gray tinged with yellow or red; abdomen pale red. *Female.* Similar to the male but top of head gray, only the back of the head and neck being red.

RANGE: Resident and breeds north to southern Pennsylvania and eastern Maryland; south to southeastern Mississippi and central Florida.

STATUS IN S. C.: Common permanent resident throughout the State. Recorded north to Greenville, York, and Marlboro counties; east to Horry County; south to Jasper County; west to Greenwood and Oconee counties.

HISTORY: People who see the Red-bellied Woodpecker for the first time almost invariably ask why the term "red-bellied" is applied to it. The question is a reasonable one for the term is certainly misleading. There is a reddish patch on the abdomen, but it is hard to see on the living bird and is sometimes (though very rarely) lacking.

This woodpecker was named by Catesby, back in the 1730's, as *Picus ventre rubro* (a woodpecker with a red abdomen). It is from this that the common name has come. As a matter of fact, the local name Zebra or Zebraback is much more descriptive.

This is the most common woodpecker in South Carolina. It occurs generally the year round and is equally at home in town or country, coast or inland, swamp or upland. It prefers deciduous woodlands but appears in pinelands also.

It is a noisy bird. Harsh, nasal, and penetrating, the calls sound more like "cham-chack" than any other word, and in some places the bird goes by this name. Its conspicuously white and black barred back and its shining red head and neck make it a showy bird, and it is approachable and abundant enough to be even better known than it is.

The nesting hole is usually excavated in dead trees from 12 feet to as much as 130 feet from the ground. It may on occasion nest in a palmetto or a stub of that tree. The eggs are generally four or five, white, and average 25.06 x 18.78 milli-meters. They are laid from mid-April to early May. E. Milby Burton has banded well-grown young on May 14. Mrs. G. E. Charles saw a bird beginning its hole in a maple at West Columbia, on March 21; by March 26 it was out of sight in the excavation. She also reported that a pair of these woodpeckers took 117 days to dig a nest and raise two broods to flight stage, the first appearing on May 19, the other on July 16. Incubation takes about fourteen days, and one or two broods are raised.

Food: In South Carolina, this woodpecker eats insects such as ants, caterpillars, borers, grubs, and grasshoppers for as much as 50 per cent of its diet. Nuts, berries, and other fruits make up the vegetable matter, with a considerable percentage of acorns and tupelo berries.

RED-HEADED WOODPECKER
226. *Melanerpes erythrocephalus erythrocephalus* (Linnaeus) (406)

(Gr., *Melanerpes*, black creeper; *erythrocephalus*, red-headed.)

LOCAL NAMES: Half-a-shirt; Shirt-tail Bird.

DESCRIPTION: Length 8.50 to 9.75 inches. *Adult*. Head, neck, and chest crimson; back, fore parts of wings, and most of tail blue-black; rump, broad ends of secondaries, and under parts white. *Immature*. Head, neck, and chest brownish gray streaked with black; posterior lower parts white streaked with gray; white on the wings marked with black bars.

RANGE: Breeds north to southern Manitoba and southern New Brunswick; south to Texas and southern Florida. Winters north to southeastern South Dakota and southern Maine; south to southern Texas and southern Florida.

STATUS IN S. C.: Common permanent resident locally distributed over the whole State, but less common on the coast than inland. Reported north to Spartanburg, Chester, and Chesterfield counties; east to Horry County; south to Jasper County; west to Greenwood and Oconee counties.

HISTORY: Though not the most abundant species in South Carolina, this striking woodpecker is probably one of the best known because of its unmistakable color pattern. Bluish black, white, and red are certainly an attractive combination, and the Red-head possesses all three in generous quantity. The arrangement of the white and black, particularly in flight, gives the bird the appearance of having white shirt tails fluttering out from a black coat; hence its local names.

The Red-head occurs throughout all of South Carolina at all seasons, but it is less common than in former years and is always local in its distribution. A pair will frequent a given area year after year. It is a bird of open situations, rural or urban, and it is often to be found in the shade trees of city streets or college campuses. It likes roadside telephone poles and the edges of fields in newly cleared land, where dead trees are standing. It is not to be found in heavy forests.

The automobile has become a hazard to the Red-headed Woodpecker and is responsible for some of the reduction of the population. Many Red-heads are killed when they swoop downward across the road in front of speeding cars.

The nest hole is dug into dead timber, usually a pine, and elevation may be any-where from a few feet to more than a hundred. Eggs are usually laid in the early part of May. They are pure glossy white, number four to seven, and average 25.14 x 19.17 millimeters. Two broods are often raised. Incubation takes about fourteen days.

The Red-headed Woodpecker becomes more common as one proceeds inland from the coast, and is encountered more consistently about the fall line and into the Piedmont. It is not a shy bird. It lives on the streets in towns, and sometimes like the flicker it drills on tin gutters or into the eaves of houses.

FOOD: The Red-head comes in for a good deal of adverse criticism because of its liking for grain and fruit. There is sometimes a real basis for such criticism, but its depredations appear to be strongly localized. Though severely condemned in one area, it may never be accused in another. Actually, its diet is about two-thirds vegetable and one-third animal matter. Grain, fruit, berries, and acorns compose much of the former. Animal matter is made up of eggs, sometimes the young of poultry and other birds. Prof. F. E. L. Beal, who studied its food intensively, concluded that "On the whole, there seems to be no reason to condemn the woodpecker except under very unusual conditions" (*U. S. Dept. Agri. Bull.*, 37: 1911).

PLATE XIX: FLYCATCHER GROUP

Water Color by Edward von S. Dingle

Flying birds, left to right: Kingbird and Crow. Perching birds, left to right: Kingbird, Crested Flycatcher, Phoebe, Acadian Flycatcher, and Wood Pewee.

.E.J. Dingle.

YELLOW-BELLIED SAPSUCKER
227. *Sphyrapicus varius varius* (Linnaeus) (402)

(Gr., and Lat., *Sphyrapicus*, a hammer + woodpecker; Lat., *varius*, different.)

LOCAL NAMES: Sapsucker.

DESCRIPTION: Length 7.25 to 8.75 inches. *Male.* Crown red, bordered behind with black; nape white; rest of upper parts varied with white; a white patch on wing; sides of head striped with black and white; middle of chin and throat red; a black patch on chest; rest of under parts pale yellow to white. *Female.* Like the male, but throat white and head without red.

RANGE: Breeds north to southern Mackenzie and southeastern Quebec; south to central Alberta, central Illinois, and southwestern North Carolina. Winters north to Kansas and Maine (casually); south to Mexico, the Virgin Islands, and Panama.

STATUS IN S. C.: Fairly common winter resident, October 4, casually August 24, to May 11, over practically all the State. Observed north to Greenville and York counties; east to Horry County; south to Beaufort County; west to Aiken and Oconee counties.

HISTORY: The Yellow-bellied Sapsucker is a winter bird in South Carolina. It is fairly well known by name, but the term "Sapsucker" is loosely applied to other woodpeckers and is therefore not always to be accepted.

The Sapsucker appears very regularly in early October and may remain until late April. Most of them, however, depart in late March. G. E. Hudson gives the stay about Clemson as October 9 to April 3.

The bird frequents deciduous woods. It is not often to be found in towns. Though it is not particularly shy, it is unobtrusive and goes about its way quietly and deliberately. Its call note is unmistakable, for its sounds startlingly like the mewing of a cat. The note provides a good means of tracing the bird.

Its manner of feeding differs sharply from that of other woodpeckers, for it will remain a long time on one tree, girdling it with a multitude of small holes which never penetrate very deeply beneath the bark. From these holes sap exudes, and on return trips the bird feeds both on the sap and the insects which have been attracted to it. At times, one can find a medium-sized tree with hundreds of such borings circling the trunk. The Sapsucker works particularly on such trees as sweet gum, cypress, long-leaf pine, holly, and hickory. One bird appears to have an extensive feeding territory, and it is unusual to encounter more than a single specimen in a large tract of woodland. It regularly frequents the barrier island jungles on the coast.

FOOD: The tree-girdling practice of the Sapsucker has brought the bird under severe criticism on the ground that it destroys valuable timber and fruit trees. No doubt this is often so, but it should not be forgotten that the sapsucker consumes many insects which come to the sap wells. Ants in particular are taken. Wild fruits and berries such as sour gum, dogwood, and frost grapes vary the diet. The bird is by no means universally harmful but only locally so.

EASTERN HAIRY WOODPECKER
228. *Dendrocopos villosus villosus* (Linnaeus) (393a)

(Gr., *Dendrocopos*, a tree-beater; Lat., *villosus*, hairy.)

LOCAL NAMES: Sapsucker.

DESCRIPTION: Length 7.50 to 8.75 inches. *Male.* Upper parts black with a white stripe on side of neck and another over the eye reaching to back of head; a red crescent across back of neck; middle of back with a broad white stripe; wings black with large squarish white spots; undersurface white, the four outer tail feathers mostly white, not dark-barred or spotted. *Female.* Like the male but lacks the red crescent on the back of the neck.

RANGE: Resident and breeds north to Minnesota and Nova Scotia; south to northern Texas and northwestern South Carolina.

STATUS IN S. C.: Fairly common permanent resident along the northwestern edge of the State. Rare winter resident in the remaining northern and central eastern sections. As a permanent resident, recorded north to Greenville County; south to Pickens and Oconee counties. As a winter resident elsewhere, recorded north to Lancaster and Cheraw; east and south to McClellanville; west to Anderson.

HISTORY: The Hairy Woodpeckers which occupy the northwestern edge of South Carolina in the mountain counties seem to be closely akin to the Eastern Hairy Woodpecker, as Ridgway noted many years ago (*Birds of North and Middle America, Pt. VI*: 1914, 204). The birds from this part of the State examined by Dr. Harry C. Oberholser, while not typical, are nearer this race than they are to the Southern Hairy Woodpecker.

In winter there is some movement of these northern birds southeastward into South Carolina, a movement also true of the flicker. Specimens of this subspecies were taken at Clemson College March 29, 1926, September 15, 1927, and November 10, 1927. These evidently represent the breeding bird of the northern part of the State. W. M. Perrygo and J. S. Y. Hoyt collected specimens from Caesar's Head at 3000 feet altitude, July 2 and 4, 1940; from Cheraw, October 10 and 15, 1940; from McClellanville, November 21, 1940; and Lancaster, September 19, 1940. There is also another example from the collection of H. T. Nowell in the Charleston Museum, taken at Anderson but without date. This probably does not represent the breeding form at that locality.

The habits and food of this bird do not vary from those of the Southern Hairy Woodpecker.

SOUTHERN HAIRY WOODPECKER
229. *Dendrocopos villosus audubonii* (Swainson) (393b)

(Lat., *audubonii*, to John James Audubon.)

DESCRIPTION: Similar to the Eastern Hairy Woodpecker but smaller, the lower parts less purely white, and the white markings on the wings smaller and less numerous.

RANGE: Resident and breeds north to southern Missouri and southeastern Virginia; south to southeastern Texas and southern Florida.

STATUS IN S. C.: Fairly common permanent resident over all the State, except the north-western edge. Recorded north to York County; east to Horry County; south to Beaufort County; west to Allendale and Anderson (probably).

HISTORY: This is probably the least known of the South Carolina woodpeckers. It is a permanent resident of South Carolina with a very general distribution, but it is not common anywhere and is easily overlooked. It does not like to be near human habitations and lives in the forests and river swamplands.

The Southern Hairy Woodpecker mates in February. Wayne found young hatched as early as March 24. Dates vary, of course; Wayne secured eggs on the seventh of April. The nest holes, which are usually in dead trees, are rather high and are difficult to find and difficult to reach. Wayne found one, however, which was dug into a living live oak. The three or four white eggs average 21.29 x 18.29 millimeters. Since few nests are ever found it is difficult to cite typical dates. E. J. DeCamps has taken eggs near Bluffton, Beaufort County, on March 30. Only one brood is raised and incubation requires about fourteen days.

The note of this bird is a sharp "peek" which sounds very like the note of the Downy Woodpecker but is louder and has a certain indefinite quality which identifies it as coming from a larger bird. Practice will enable one to separate the two notes almost without mistake. The Hairy gives another rattling call, much like the Downy's but harder to distinguish from it.

FOOD: The Hairy is one of the most valuable woodpeckers because it consumes such large numbers of insects. Ants predominate but the Hairy also eats the larvae of wood-boring beetles, caterpillars, and weevils. Wild fruits, seeds, and acorns, with waste grain (corn) make up the vegetable diet.

NORTHERN DOWNY WOODPECKER
230. *Dendrocopos pubescens medianus* (Swainson)   (394c)

(Lat., *pubescens*, becoming downy; *medianus*, in the middle.)

DESCRIPTION: Similar to the Southern Downy Woodpecker, but larger, length 6.00 to 7.00 inches; lower surface less brownish (more whitish); wings with larger and more numerous white spots.

RANGE: Resident and breeds north to southeastern Alberta and southeastern Quebec; and south to eastern Kansas and northwestern South Carolina.

STATUS IN S. C.: Fairly common permanent resident and breeds in the northwestern section; south in winter to other portions of the State. Recorded as resident north to Greenville County; south to Oconee County. As a winter resident, from September 21 to February 20, recorded from Anderson, Rock Hill, and Bennettsville.

HISTORY: The Northern Downy Woodpecker is the bird of the mountain counties in South Carolina, and while the individuals from this region are not typical, they seem nearer the northern form. Specimens identified by Dr. Harry C. Oberholser verify the occurrence of this bird as follows: Caesar's Head, July 12, 1927, collected by R. H. Coleman; same locality, July 5 and 11, 1940, collected by W. M. Perrygo and J. S. Webb; Bennettsville, October 5, 1940, and Rock Hill, September

21, 1940, by the same collectors; Sassafras Mountain in Pickens County, May 8, 1935, and Rocky Bottom in the same county, June 22, 1929, by Chamberlain; Anderson, January 7 and February 20, 1895, by H. T. Nowell.

In habits and food the Northern Downy is practically identical with the Southern Downy Woodpecker.

SOUTHERN DOWNY WOODPECKER
231. *Dendrocopos pubescens pubescens* (Linnaeus) (394)

LOCAL NAMES: Little Sapsucker.

DESCRIPTION: Length 5.50 to 6.00 inches. Like the Hairy Woodpecker in color and pattern, except that the white outer tail feathers and the under tail coverts are barred with black.

RANGE: Resident and breeds north to Oklahoma and southern Virginia; south to southeastern Texas and southern Florida.

STATUS IN S. C.: Common permanent resident throughout the State except the northwestern edge. Reported north to Spartanburg and York counties; east to Horry County; south to Jasper County; west to Greenwood and Anderson County (probably).

HISTORY: This is the smallest of the South Carolina woodpeckers. It is far better known than the Hairy, for it is a gentle, confiding bird which comes freely to feeding stations in one's yard or on one's kitchen window sill. It frequently travels in winter with bands of Chickadees, Titmice, and other birds, and may be attracted by squeaking. The Downy likes open woodlands, heavy swamps, roadsides, orchards, yards, and gardens.

It is a permanent resident of South Carolina, but is more noticeable in winter, when it is not scattered over nesting territories. The winter woods often echo to its sharp little call note, and it is so tame that one may approach to within a few feet of it.

Eggs have been found from early April to late May. The hole is made in dead willows and buttonwoods or in fence posts and stubs, either over land or water. It is fond of the cypress backwaters on the coast and commonly nests there. The elevation of the nest is usually under 15 feet. Four or five white, glossy eggs are laid, averaging 19.43 x 15.24 millimeters. Incubation requires about twelve days. Ernest A. Cutts, of Charleston, has reported seeing attempts by a Starling to take the holes of this little woodpecker, but the Downy put up such determined resistence that the larger bird was repulsed.

The Downy flies with the undulations typical of most woodpeckers, a kind of bounding through the air. It also has the habit of beating out a rolling tattoo on a dead limb. Sometimes the Downy clings to the underside of a branch or a pine cone like a Titmouse or nuthatch.

FOOD: Chiefly composed of insects; hence, the Downy is one of the most valuable of birds. Examination has shown that 76 per cent of the food is made up of insects. Beetles and ants predominate, but there are also caterpillars, cockroaches, grasshoppers, katydids, and crickets. Vegetable food such as fruits forms only 6 per cent of the diet, these being useless wild varieties.

RED-COCKADED WOODPECKER
232. *Dendrocopos borealis borealis* (Vieillot) (395)

(Lat., *borealis*, northern.)

LOCAL NAMES: Sapsucker.

DESCRIPTION: Length 7.00 to 8.50 inches. *Male*. Top of head black; a patch of white on cheeks; back and wings black with crossbars of white; under parts dull white, with black spots on sides; a red streak on each side of head above the ear. *Female*. Like the male but lacks the red streaks on the head.

RANGE: Resident and breeds north to northeastern Oklahoma and central Virginia; south to southeastern Texas and northern Florida.

STATUS IN S. C.: Fairly common permanent resident in the eastern and middle portions of the State. Reported north to Richland, Lee, and Dillon counties; east to Horry County; south to Beaufort County; west to Aiken County.

HISTORY: To most people the Red-cockaded Woodpecker is a stranger because of its rather limited and specialized range, and comparatively small numbers. So completely does it belong to the pinelands that one need not look for it anywhere else. The great open pine barrens of the Low-country form its home. Wherever it is found it is a permanent resident.

The Red-cockaded Woodpecker is an individualist. Its note, while at once recognizable as that of a woodpecker, is nevertheless so different that the hearer is at once aware that the bird is not a Hairy, Downy, or Red-head. The note is harsh, and querulous, with a sharpness in it which defies description or translation into words. Some writers call it a "churr."

Nesting takes place from late April to mid-May. A rather late date is the twenty-fifth of May, near Bluffton (E. J. DeCamps). Three to five eggs are laid, rarely more than four; they are characteristically pure white, averaging 24.04 x 17.86 millimeters. The nesting hole is another departure from woodpecker custom; it is always in a living pine, usually the loblolly (*Pinus taeda*), frequently one which is distorted in growth with a bend or crook in the trunk. Nests are never found in dead trees, at least not in coastal South Carolina. They can be rather easily located by the long streaks of pine gum on the trunk of a tree. This substance oozes not only from the excavation of the hole itself but from the many punctures around it, made by the birds. The birds return to the same nest hole year after year until they, as Wayne says, "can no longer make the gum exude." When this happens, the birds dig a new hole in the same tree which, by the way, always has a rotten center. But one brood is raised and incubation requires fourteen or fifteen days.

Because the young birds stay close to the parents into the fall, one often meets these woodpeckers in small groups. The Red-cockaded in not a shy bird and may be approached to within a few yards as it hitches its way around trunks or limbs. One of its most remarkable habits is its occasional method of descending a tree in backward, jerky hops.

It is regrettable that the Red-cockaded Woodpecker seems to be declining in numbers in recent years, the result of the destruction of a habitat which it refuses to leave.

FOOD: As might be supposed, the larvae of wood-boring insects, grubs, and beetles form the bulk of this woodpecker's food. In consequence it is a valuable asset to timber lands, and because of another habit, to agriculture as well. It has been noted by Dingle (*Bird-Lore, 28*: 1926, 124), that these woodpeckers commonly resort to cornfields when the grain is in the ear and extract the worms which so often bore into them. These worms are very destructive, and the value of this control factor is obvious.

IVORY-BILLED WOODPECKER
233. *Campephilus principalis* (Linnaeus) (392)

(Gr., *Campephilus*, caterpillar-loving; Lat., *principalis*, principal, referring to its large size.)

DESCRIPTION: Length 19.00 to 21.00 inches. *Male.* Glossy blue black, with a full red crest on back of head; a white stripe down each side of neck to the back; a large white area on hind part of wing; bill ivory white. *Female.* Like the male, but red of crest replaced by black.

RANGE: Formerly resident and bred north to central eastern Missouri and central eastern North Carolina; south to southeastern Texas and southern Florida. Still possibly exists in Louisiana, Texas, Florida, and South Carolina but apparently on the verge of extinction.

STATUS IN S. C.: Formerly a fairly common permanent resident over much of the eastern part of the State. Now probably extinct in South Carolina. Reported north to Greenville and Cheraw (Chesterfield County); east to the lower Santee River and Charleston; south to Hunting Island; west to Allendale County.

HISTORY: The recent rediscovery of the Ivory-billed Woodpecker, now a practically extinct species in South Carolina, has never been adequately related.

Records of the Ivory-bill's occurrence prior to this century are well set forth in the writings of Audubon, Wilson, and Wayne. Wayne never saw the birds in this State, but secured numbers of them in Florida. In commenting on his search for it in his native State he says (1910), "I have thoroughly explored, during the past twenty-five years, nearly all the great swamps from Charleston to the Savannah River with the hope of finding it." Had he gone north from his home instead of south, he would probably have found the Ivory-bill less than 40 miles from his house.

During 1933-35, George M. Melamphy was working on a Wild Turkey project in the Santee River Swamp, Georgetown County. He occasionally visited the Charleston Museum to study skins and secure other data, and several times mentioned that he had seen Ivory-bills in the swamp. It must be admitted that these reports did not receive immediate attention for the Museum staff had many such reports and had always found that the bird reported was the Pileated Woodpecker. However, at his insistence, on March 31, 1935, Herbert L. Stoddard and Sprunt joined Melamphy and examined, on foot and by boat, the area where he was working. Familiar with Ivory-bill country, Stoddard pronounced the surroundings ideal, but the expedition discovered no birds.

Later that spring, the National Audubon Society sent Lester L. Walsh, of the New York office staff, to join Sprunt in a thorough search. On May 11, 1935, they saw an Ivory-bill at close range, and heard two others the next day. As far as could be ascertained, the Santee birds numbered at least two pairs. A warden was placed on duty at once and a lease secured from the owners of that section of the swamp where the birds were found. For the next two years, Sprunt made many trips to the area, and several ornithologists from outside the State succeeded in seeing the Ivory-bill. They were the first of the species to be seen in South Carolina since about 1900. However, this discovery convinced both Sprunt and Herbert R. Sass that, on April 19, 1929, a bird seen by them on Fairlawn Plantation, Charleston County, had been an Ivory-bill. They were sure of it at the time but nothing was said by either of them publicly nor was the record published. On June 8, 1929, while visiting the same location E. Milby Burton saw an Ivory-bill, but like Sass and Sprunt he did not publish the record.

With the construction of the power dams of the Santee-Cooper Hydro-electric Project, some miles up the Santee River, in the late 1930's the area inhabited by these woodpeckers was changed and the birds probably disappeared. No recent investigations have been undertaken, but it seems useless to look for them there now.

For detailed information on the Ivory-billed Woodpecker, the reader should consult the work of James T. Tanner, in his *Research Report No. I, The Ivory-billed Woodpecker,* published by the National Audubon Society (1942).

Because the Ivory-bill and the Pileated Woodpeckers continue to be confused by those attempting to identify them, it is well to stress the differences between the two. At rest, the Ivory-bill shows much white on the lower half of the wings; the Pileated, none. The female Ivory-bill has a black crest, the female Pileated a red one. In flight, the Ivory-bill shows a great deal of white in the hinder parts of the wings; the Pileated shows less. The white bill of the Ivory-bill is its poorest field mark. Light conditions sometimes make the bill of the Pileated as white as any Ivory-bill's. The manner of flight of these two woodpeckers also differs markedly; that of the Ivory-bill is straight and non-undulating, much like that of a crow, whereas the Pileated dips deeply in its course, somewhat like other woodpeckers. The voice is perhaps the best characteristic of all, if a glimpse cannot be obtained, for that of the Ivory-bill is completely different from that of the Pileated. Many writers have rather aptly likened it to the sound made by a cheap tin horn, but Sprunt says that it reminds one of a large nuthatch. It has a nasal, tinny quality which is unmistakable, and it is not at all as far-carrying as the call of the Pileated.

The Ivory-bill nests in heavy forests, in holes of its own excavation, at varying heights. The eggs, like those of all woodpeckers, are pure white; they number three to five and average 34.87 x 25.22 millimeters. Only one brood a season is raised. In a recent conversation with E. J. DeCamps, of Beaufort, the authors were told that he saw a nest of the Ivory-bill on the banks of the Reedy River, Greenville County, in May, 1896. He and a companion secured the three eggs which the nest contained, and the birds were seen to leave the hole. The eggs were later lost in a fire. This is the only definitely known breeding record for the State.

Food: The food habits of the Ivory-billed Woodpecker have been responsible in part for the bird's decline. It is a specialized feeder, depending very considerably upon certain wood-boring insects which inhabit only decaying trees. Since only a large forest area can supply a sufficient number of such trees and since today large tracts are so rare as to be practically nonexistent, the bird has disappeared with the alteration of its habitat.

This fact is a striking illustration of what may result by a simple change of environment. Though many Ivory-bills were shot for one reason or another, it can fairly be said that the real reason for its virtual extinction was not powder and shot but the encroachment of civilization. The bird would not or could not adapt itself to such changes. It is perfectly possible that by the time this volume is published, there will be no more Ivory-bills, and that they will have joined the sad company of extinct birds which includes the Passenger Pigeon and the Great Auk.

Incubating Willet

ALLAN D. CRUICKSHANK
National Audubon Society

Royal Terns on Barrier Beach

ALLAN D. CRUICKSHANK
National Audubon Society

Great Horned Owl on Nest

S. A. GRIMES

Florida Barred Owl   S. A. GRIMES

Order Passeriformes
Perching Birds

Family Tyrannidae: Tyrant Flycatchers

234. EASTERN KINGBIRD: *Tyrannus tyrannus* (Linnaeus) (444)

(Lat., *Tyrannus*, a ruler, tyrant.)

LOCAL NAMES: Bee-bird; Bee-martin.

DESCRIPTION: Length 8.00 to 9.00 inches. Upper parts slate color, but a concealed orange spot on crown; head and tail black, the latter tipped with white; undersurface white.

RANGE: Breeds north to southern British Columbia and southeastern Quebec; south to southeastern Texas and southern Florida. Winters north to Costa Rica and British Guiana; south to southern Bolivia.

STATUS IN S. C.: Common summer resident, March 10 to October 16, over most of the State, uncommon in the northwestern corner. Recorded north to Greenville and Chester counties; east to Horry County; south to Beaufort; west to Oconee County.

HISTORY: The Eastern Kingbird is held in high regard by everyone except apiarists. It has a reputation for destroying bees and is therefore locally known as "Bee-martin." Neither the reputation nor the name is entirely justified.

It is a noisy, conspicuous bird. It likes to perch in open places—on telephone wires or in the tops of trees and bushes—from which it dashes in a flash of white and black plumage to catch insects on the wing. It is utterly fearless, chattering a warning to all invaders of its territory and without hesitation attacking crows, hawks, or eagles which blunder into its domain. The Eastern Kingbird's way of life is open to city and country dwellers alike, for it is at home everywhere.

The Eastern Kingbird may be present for a month before it begins to nest, but it raises two or even three broods in a season (Wayne). The nest is bulky but compact and well constructed of sticks, twigs, cotton string, and (in cypress lagoons) a good bit of Spanish moss. It is to be found in shade trees, bushes and low willows, buttonwoods, and small cypresses, often over the water. The elevation of the nest varies from a few feet to nearly a hundred.

The eggs, three or four in number, are very handsome, of a rich, creamy ground color, splashed and marbled with dark brown and lilac. The average measurement is 24.2 x 17.7 millimeters. Incubation requires thirteen or fourteen days. They are laid early in May, typical dates for Charleston County being May 5 (Sprunt) and May 10 (Wayne). From Beaufort County, there is a record for May 31 (E. J. DeCamps), probably representing a second nesting. In July, 1945, J. S. Thomas, of Smoaks, Colleton County, noted a pair of Eastern Kingbirds nesting in a Martin gourd on his farm. The young left this unusual nesting site "about July 25." Bent (1942) cites a similar instance of concealed nesting in a rain gauge, and two examples of the use of old nests of the Baltimore Oriole.

In the fall, large numbers of Eastern Kingbirds are sometimes noted in migration, which occurs by day. Wayne (1910) states that "it is not unusual to see thousands of these birds migrating southward—all following the coast line of the mainland." By the end of September most of them have gone, but a few linger into October. During the fall flight, the birds feed largely on the fruit of the magnolia.

There are two known winter records of the Eastern Kingbird for the State. Both were made in December, 1946. On December 8, Newton H. Seebeck, Jr., observed one on a telephone wire near Beaufort. On a Christmas Bird Count at Columbia December 26, B. Spencer Meeks, Jr., made the second record. During the same month and year, this species was seen in coastal Maryland and North Carolina although it normally winters southward from southern Mexico.

Food: Predominantly insects; hence the Eastern Kingbird is valuable to farms and gardens. The diet includes grasshoppers, beetles, wasps, flies, mosquitoes, caterpillars, and boll weevils. Locally, this bird sometimes consumes bees though in no very large numbers.

GRAY KINGBIRD
235. *Tyrannus dominicensis dominicensis* (Gmelin) (445)

(Lat., *dominicensis*, of Santo Domingo.)

DESCRIPTION: Length 9.00 to 9.80 inches. Bill very large, imparting to the bird a rather top-heavy appearance; upper surface gray with a concealed orange patch on crown; lower surface white; wings and tail grayish brown with no white on tail.

RANGE: Breeds north to southeastern South Carolina and the Bahama Islands; south to Colombia and Venezuela. Winters north to the Isle of Pines and Puerto Rico; south to Colombia and Venezuela.

STATUS IN S. C.: Rare summer resident, April 19 to September 8, in the coast region. Known only from Charleston County.

HISTORY: The history of the Gray Kingbird in South Carolina is an interesting one, but it can be told only briefly. The first record of its occurrence was made in Charleston in 1832 when a nest was found on the College of Charleston campus in the heart of the city, by a Mr. Lee, who reported the find to Dr. John Bachman. With Audubon, Dr. Bachman visited the campus, only to find the nest destroyed. Shortly after, the birds built another nest, and this also was found by Lee and reported to Dr. Bachman, who definitely identified the birds. For three successive years the Gray Kingbird returned to the same site and raised two broods each season; these facts are all set forth in Audubon's *Birds of America, I*, 1840, 203.

The second occurrence of the species in the State was "somewhere between 1881 and 1885" when Prof. John Gadsden secured a specimen on the grounds of the Porter Military Academy in Charleston. He took it to the Museum, where it was identified as the Gray Kingbird. In May, 1885, William Brewster and Wayne saw a pair on Sullivan's Island and on May 28 of the same year, Wayne found a nest there containing one egg and secured the female. On May 30, 1893, he found another nest, with two eggs, on the same island, and took both birds (*Auk, 11*: 1894, 178).

It was not until 1927 that the species was again reported. On May 17 of that year, Sprunt and Wayne saw a Gray Kingbird near Wayne's home on Oakland Plantation, Christ Church Parish. They failed to secure it and could not locate the nest. On August 11, 1942, E. von S. Dingle saw four birds near the western end of Sullivan's Island. Another recent occurrence was on April 19, 1945, when Sprunt saw a specimen at the Cape Romain Lighthouse. The bird seemed perfectly at home and settled, but search for a nest was unsuccessful. In 1947, Henry Kennan and J. B. Shuler, Jr., reported several observations of the Gray Kingbird near McClellanville. Together they observed the bird on August 4, and Kennan saw it later on August 18 and 19 and September 3 and 8. The most recent records are from the vicinity of Charleston. Lee Hagood and Mrs. Kate McIver reported seeing one bird about April 25, 1948, on Folly Island. Two days later, Newton Seebeck, Jr., reported one at Windermere, 8 miles from Folly.

Such records as these suggest that the Gray Kingbird must be considered an irregular and rare summer resident of the coastal region. The appearance of the bird, its notes, and its eggs, all of which are easily recognizable, distinguish it from the Eastern Kingbird. The nest is rather more slightly built than that of the Eastern Kingbird, and the eggs, three or four in number, are strikingly beautiful, even in a family noted for handsome eggs. They are pink in color, blotched with dark brown and average 25.1 x 18.2 millimeters. Incubation requires about fourteen days.

FOOD: Largely insects, with wasps predominating. These make up about 60 per cent of the total. The Gray Kingbird also eats wood borers, bugs, and dragon flies. Berries of various sorts compose the vegetable diet.

236. ARKANSAS KINGBIRD: *Tyrannus verticalis* Say (447)

(Lat., *verticalis*, referring to the vertex, or top of the head.)

DESCRIPTION: Length 8.00 to 9.50 inches. Upper surface gray, the crown with a concealed orange patch; throat white; breast and belly canary yellow; tail black, with outer webs of outer feathers white.

RANGE: Breeds north to southern British Columbia and southern Manitoba; south to northern Lower California and Texas. Winters north to Sonora and South Carolina (rarely); south to Colima and El Salvador.

STATUS IN S. C.: Rare winter resident, October 6 to January 18, in the coast region. Recorded north to Horry County; south to Edisto Island.

HISTORY: Long thought to be an accidental wanderer to South Carolina, the Arkansas Kingbird has occurred frequently enough in recent years to warrant its classification as a rare winter resident. It was added to the State List on December 16, 1913, by Chamberlain, who took a male at the west end of Tradd Street in Charleston. Practically a quarter century passed before the next recorded occurrence. Then, on the occasion of the second southern meeting of the American Ornithologists Union, at Charleston, in 1937, an individual of the species was seen during the field trip to Bull's Island, November 19. The bird remained about headquarters most of the day.

On November 14, 1938, F. M. Weston and Sprunt saw a specimen on James Island. Chamberlain secured it the next day. Three days later Weston and H. S. Peters saw a second individual within half a mile of the place where the first was discovered. Records multiplied in the following years. On December 16, 1939, Richard G. Kuerzi observed an Arkansas Kingbird in Horry County. Another was studied for some time on Edisto Island, November 15, 1941, by Sprunt. Eugene Eisenmann and John Bull, of New York, found one on Bull's Island on October 6, 1943, and again on October 13. Sprunt added another record from Bull's Island, November 24, 1945. The bird was seen on the same island three times in January, 1947, by Sprunt. The most recent record is for December 7, 1947, when J. E. Mosimann and G. B. Rabb saw an Arkansas Kingbird on a telephone wire on John's Island.

This kingbird is easily recognized; the outstanding field mark, as far as South Carolina birds are concerned, is the yellow belly in sharp contrast to the gray breast. It uses exposed perches like the other kingbirds, and is a typical flycatcher in habits, behavior, and food.

FOOD: Very largely insects, with a small percentage of vegetable food.

SCISSOR-TAILED FLYCATCHER
237. *Muscivora forficata* (Gmelin) (443)

(Lat., *Muscivora*, fly-eating; *forficata*, forked.)

DESCRIPTION: Length 11.50 to 15.00 inches. Tail long and deeply forked. Head, hind neck, and back pale gray, the back washed with pink; under parts mostly white, but breast pale gray, the sides of body and lining of wings deep salmon color; tail black, the outer feathers partly white, tinged with salmon pink.

RANGE: Breeds north to northwestern Oklahoma and southeastern Nebraska; south to southern Texas. Winters north to southern Texas; south to Panama.

STATUS IN S. C.: Accidental visitor, June 5 to November 6, in central and southern sections.

HISTORY: The Scissor-tailed Flycatcher is an accidental wanderer not only to South Carolina but to any place in the East. There are only three records of it for South Carolina.

On November 6, 1928, Herbert R. Sass saw a Scissor-tail perched on a wire fence on Edisto Island; this established the first record (*Auk*, *46*: 1929, 117). The first specimen actually secured was a bird taken near St. Matthews, Calhoun County, July 16, 1930, by F. M. Wannamaker. It was captured alive as it was unable to fly because of a wing injury. It lived for several days and at its death, it was sent to the Charleston Museum where it is preserved (No. 30.141). On June 5, 1933, G. R. Rossignol took a specimen at the Quarantine Station at the mouth of the Savannah River. Actually, the bird was shot in Georgia, the river being the dividing line, but it had been watched for some time as it flew across the river.

The greatly elongated tail feathers of this flycatcher will distinguish it from all others in South Carolina, as indeed from all other small South Carolina land birds.

FOOD: Insects, principally grasshoppers and crickets.

NORTHERN CRESTED FLYCATCHER
238. *Myiarchus crinitus boreus* Bangs (452a)

(Gr., *Myiarchus*, a fly ruler; Lat., *crinitus*, long-haired, *i. e.*, crested; *boreus*, northern.)

DESCRIPTION: Similar to the Southern Crested Flycatcher but larger; and the upper parts more brownish (less greenish) olive.

RANGE: Breeds north to southern Manitoba and New Brunswick; south to southern Texas and northwestern South Carolina. Winters north to southern Texas; south to Mexico and Colombia.

STATUS IN S. C.: Common summer resident, April 13 to August, in the northern part of the State; a transient elsewhere. Definitely recorded in summer north and east to York County; south to Newberry County; west to Oconee County. In migration, recorded east to Horry County.

HISTORY: The limits of the summer distribution of this race of the crested flycatcher in South Carolina remain yet to be definitely established on account of the lack of suitable specimens. The two forms of the species are so much alike that they are not identifiable in the field. Northern Crested Flycatchers were secured at Clemson College by G. E. Hudson and F. Sherman, April 24 and May 14, 1926 (*Auk*, *53*: 1936, 313). The following specimens were collected by W. M. Perrygo and J. S. Y. Hoyt, and identified by Dr. Alexander Wetmore: Walhalla, June 19, 1940; Whitmire, Newberry County, June 2 and 10, 1940; Wampee, Horry County, April 15, 1940; St. George, April 24 and 29, 1940; and another from McConnellsville, York County, June 10, 1940.

In habits and food this race is not distinguishable from the Southern Crested Flycatcher.

SOUTHERN CRESTED FLYCATCHER
239. *Myiarchus crinitus crinitus* (Linnaeus) (452)

LOCAL NAMES: Freight Bird.

DESCRIPTION: Length 8.00 to 9.00 inches. Head crested. Upper surface olive; throat and upper breast light gray; belly light yellow; wings fuscous with two buff bars; tail fuscous with inner webs mostly cinnamon rufous.

RANGE: Breeds north to southeastern Louisiana and southeastern South Carolina; south to southern Florida. Winters north to southern Florida and South Carolina (casually); south to Colombia (probably).

STATUS IN S. C.: Common summer resident, March 22 to October 26, in the eastern and southern parts of the State; casual in winter on the coast. Reported north to Greenwood; east to Horry County; south to Beaufort and Bluffton; west to Aiken County.

HISTORY: Ask the average farm boy what sort of a bird that is, perched on the top of a sycamore and showing a yellow breast and a top knot, and he will probably reply that it is a "Freight Bird."

The Freight Bird is a common summer resident in all parts of South Carolina (the Northern Crested Flycatcher is the race above the fall line). It arrives on the coast during the first week in April. Like others of the family, it is a bird of open woodlands, cypress swamps, farm yards, and the shade trees of city streets. It selects high, conspicuous perches from which it can command unobstructed sweeps in its alert watch for insects. The crested head, yellow belly, and characteristic call note are all good field characteristics. The crest is erected or depressed at will.

This flycatcher takes readily to man-made nesting sites. Frequently it will take possession of an open mail box or newspaper box, and carry in material day after day, even though unsympathetic human beings throw out the nest every morning. Grass, pine needles, feathers, and fur are common nest materials. But there is one strikingly unusual item which is practically always present—cast snake skin. Even when located in the middle of a city, the nest will contain such a skin. No one knows why.

A strange nesting behavior has been noted by E. Milby Burton, near Charleston. Some years ago he built a nesting box for Martins, consisting of four compartments in a row. Being erected rather late in the season it was not used by the Martins, but shortly after it was put up it was occupied by a pair of Southern Crested Flycatchers. They built their nest in one of the middle compartments and successfully raised a brood. In the other three sections they placed a great deal of nesting material, one of the false nests even containing a snake skin. Apparently this was done to keep other species from using the nesting box. Presumably the same pair returned for several seasons and always put nesting material in the other compartments.

The eggs number from four to six and are very easy to recognize because of their deep buff color, heavily streaked in longitudinal lines as if with dark purple ink. They average 22.4 x 17.6 millimeters. One brood is raised and the incubation period lasts about fourteen days. Eggs are laid from about mid-May to early June.

Most of the Southern Crested Flycatchers migrate in September, but a few stragglers may be seen in October. Very rarely a specimen is seen in winter. Wayne took one on December 11, 1914, and saw another on January 7, 1925, near his home at Mt. Pleasant.

FOOD: Mainly insects, in some variety. An examination of 265 stomachs revealed that animal matter comprises nearly 94 per cent. Among the insects were grasshoppers, crickets, katydids, weevils, horseflies, cicadas, beetles, stinkbugs, and leaf hoppers. Vegetable food (6 per cent) was represented by various berries and the fruit of dogwood and the Virginia creeper.

240. EASTERN PHOEBE: *Sayornis phoebe* (Latham) (456)

(Gr., *Sayornis*, [Thomas] Say's bird; *phoebe*, English name for this bird.)

LOCAL NAMES: Pewee.

DESCRIPTION: Length 6.25 to 7.25 inches. Back grayish olive; top of head dark brown; under parts white to pale yellow; sides of breast and body washed with grayish brown; wings without prominent bars; bill black.

RANGE: Breeds north to southwestern Mackenzie, Prince Edward Island, and Nova Scotia; south to south central New Mexico and northwestern South Carolina. Winters north to southern California (accidentally), southeastern Oklahoma, and New Hampshire (casually); south to Mexico and Cuba.

STATUS IN S. C.: Fairly common permanent resident in the northwestern section; common winter resident, September 3 to March 28, in the rest of the State. Breeds north to Greenville County; east to Cherokee County; south to Greenwood County; west to Oconee County. Winter resident also north to Florence County; east to Horry County; south to Beaufort and Jasper counties; west to Oconee County.

HISTORY: This little flycatcher, inconspicuous and unobtrusive, is so different in its habits from the noisy Eastern Kingbird and the Crested Flycatcher that it is not as well known. However, one can easily come to know it for, unlike the other members of its family, it is present in South Carolina the year round and is the only flycatcher which commonly winters in the State.

Coastal dwellers know it only in fall, winter, and early spring, but people who reside in the upper portion of the State see it the whole of the year, for it stays there always. It appears in the Low-country in late September and remains until late March. The Phoebe uses exposed perches, makes sallies for passing insects, and utters the call note which accounts for its name—"phe-be, phe-be," with the accent on the last syllable. One of the best recognition marks is the frequent pumping of the tail when it alights and while it remains perched on a dead twig.

The Phoebe is common during the coldest weather. It seems to find an abundance of insects on which it feeds almost exclusively, despite the fact that others of its insect-eating relatives go south for the winter.

The Phoebe evidently raises two broods in South Carolina. Egg dates at Clemson are May 4 and 23, 1926, and at Jocassee, April 4, 1927 (F. Sherman). Earlier Oconee County records were made by John Kershaw, Jr. He found a pair of birds using an old water mill at Walhalla for at least two seasons. On May 25, 1909, this nest contained four young birds, and on June 2, 1910, it contained five eggs.

A. L. Pickens found it building under bridges in the city of Greenville in 1931-32. G. E. Hudson recorded it as breeding commonly at Spartanburg about 1923. L. M. Loomis found it in Pickens County in 1887 and 1888. He states that he saw young birds just ready to leave the nest as late as June 23, 1887, in the higher sections of that county (*Auk, 7*: 1890, 39). F. W. Hahn said it breeds near Greenwood (1934). J. E. Mosimann, G. B. Rabb, and T. M. Uzzell, Jr., found a number of old nests under bridges in Cherokee County in the spring of 1948, and three nests of fresh eggs on April 19, 1949, on Caesar's Head.

The Phoebe builds its nest under eaves of porches, flooring of bridges, abutments, and in outbuildings, saddled on rafters, beams, or rock ledges. The nest is made of mud, grass, and moss. The eggs generally number four or five, and are usually pure white, but sometimes have fine dots of brown. They average 19.0 x 14.7 millimeters. Incubation requires about sixteen days. The nests of this bird are often so heavily infested with mites that the young birds suffer.

Food: A glance at the Phoebe's diet should convince every gardener of the bird's value. It consumes ants, flies, mosquitoes, beetles, boll weevils, grasshoppers, crickets, moths, caterpillars, ticks, and spiders. Insects comprise 90 per cent of its food.

Yellow-bellied Flycatcher
241. *Empidonax flaviventris* (Baird and Baird)   (463)

(Gr., *Empidonax*, gnat-king; Lat., *flaviventris*, yellow-bellied.)

Description: Length 5.10 to 5.80 inches. Above dull olive green with two wing bars of light olive yellow; below pale dull sulphur yellow tinged with olive on the breast.

Range: Breeds north to southern Mackenzie and Newfoundland; south to central Alberta, northern Minnesota, northern Pennsylvania, and southern New Hampshire. Winters north to central Mexico and Panama.

Status in S. C.: Rare or accidental transient.

History: The first reputed records of the Yellow-bellied Flycatcher were made by Wayne in October, 1912, and September, 1918 and 1920, when he secured birds which he referred to this species and recorded in the *Auk, 30*: 1913, 273 and *38*: 1921, 121. Later examination of these birds proved them to be immature specimens of the Acadian Flycatcher (Chamberlain and Allan R. Phillips). Murphey (1937) records two specimens of this species taken in the river swamp in Aiken County on

PLATE XX: Swallows
Water Color by Edward von S. Dingle

Four birds on left branch, left to right: Tree Swallow, Barn Swallow, Rough-winged Swallow (immature), and Rough-winged Swallow (adult). Three birds on right branch, left to right: Purple Martin (male), Purple Martin (female), and Bank Swallow.

September 3 and 6, 1904. Both of these specimens were subsequently destroyed by insects but there seems to be no reason to doubt the identification. The bird has recently been reported as occurring at Long Bay Plantation, Horry County, by Richard G. Kuerzi, who saw one individual and heard another calling on April 28, 1940. Kuerzi is familiar with the bird in the North, but at the time was not aware of its rarity in South Carolina and therefore made no attempt to obtain a specimen. There are apparently no further records for the State.

The Yellow-bellied Flycatcher is an interesting inhabitant of the northern coniferous woodlands, but aside from the fact that it builds its nest on or near the ground, it behaves very much like the other small flycatchers.

FOOD: This bird lives almost exclusively on insects and may be considered an exceedingly beneficial species.

242. ACADIAN FLYCATCHER: *Empidonax virescens* (Vieillot) (464)

(Lat., *virescens*, greenish.)

DESCRIPTION: Length 5.60 to 6.25 inches. Above grayish olive; under parts dull yellowish white, more yellowish on the abdomen; breast showing an indistinct gray band; two wing bars pale buff; eye ring white or yellowish white.

RANGE: Breeds north to northeastern Nebraska and southern Vermont; south to central Texas and central Florida. Winters north to eastern Colombia, casually to Mexico; south to eastern Ecuador.

STATUS IN S. C.: Common summer resident, March 24 to October 9, over most of the State. Recorded north to Greenville and Marlboro counties; east to Horry County; south to Charleston; west to Oconee County.

HISTORY: The Acadian Flycatcher is certainly the easiest species of this puzzling group to know. It is the greenest of them, and the notes and nest are distinctive. It is not difficult to become acquainted with, if one will penetrate its haunts, for it is a very common bird.

The Acadian Flycatcher is a swamp dweller; it is quite useless to look for it elsewhere. It arrives in early April on the coast, and toward the end of the month in the upper Piedmont (Clemson). It remains until late September. It is easier to hear than to see, but if one carefully follows up the recurring call note, ringing eerily through the green gloom, the singer will sooner or later be seen perched on a twig, sitting perfectly still until an insect passes. The note is highly characteristic but it is difficult to describe; it is usually interpreted as "wicky-up," which is fairly good, the syllables being very sharp and clipped.

Nesting usually takes place between the middle and last of May, although eggs have been found as late as July 8 near Charleston (N. H. Seebeck). The nest itself is about as frail and inadequate-looking as one can imagine, the antithesis of the well-made home of its larger relative, the Kingbird. It is really little more than a few strands of Spanish moss draped across the crotch or fork of a drooping limb, often over water. One may find it in a dogwood or sweet gum tree. Sprunt discovered a nest in a small cypress in a large backwater in Charleston County, June 5, 1928, through which the three eggs could be plainly seen from the dugout below.

There are from two to four eggs of a cream-buff color, marked about the large end with a few spots. They average 18.4 x 13.8 millimeters and incubation requires about thirteen days.

The Acadian Flycatcher is rather shy about its home, and unless one approaches noiselessly the bird is likely to take flight and leave the vicinity. The nest is seldom more than 20 feet above the ground.

FOOD: About 97 per cent insects. Ants, bees, and wasps make up nearly 40 per cent, moths and caterpillars about 20 per cent. Beetles, crickets, and grasshoppers compose the remainder, with a little wild fruit as vegetable matter.

ALDER FLYCATCHER
243. *Empidonax traillii traillii* (Audubon)   (466a)

(Lat., *traillii*, to T. S. Traill.)

DESCRIPTION: Length 5.20 to 6.00 inches. Head greenish olive above, dull white beneath with a tinge of grayish olive on breast and of yellow on abdomen; two wing bars olive white; and indistinct eye ring olive white.

RANGE: Breeds north to northwestern Alaska and central Labrador; south to Arkansas and northwestern Maryland. Winters north to Yucatan and Venezuela; south to Ecuador.

STATUS IN S. C.: Rare transient, August 15 to September 30, in the coast region. Recorded from only Charleston County.

HISTORY: The different species of small flycatchers are so similar that they are indistinguishable to most observers. Even good views of them, through excellent glasses, often result in bewilderment and uncertainty.

The Alder Flycatcher, a quiet and inconspicuous bird, is present in South Carolina only for about six weeks in late summer and autumn, when it passes through the State on its way to the tropics; apparently it does not appear at all in spring. Wayne (1910) secured the first specimen on September 6, 1900, in a spot where, he says, "innumerable alders grew." After this Wayne secured other specimens thus establishing it as a regular, though rare, transient in autumn.

The Alder Flycatcher likes low, wet places, often very difficult to penetrate. It utters a low, soft note, described as "pep." All the birds secured by Wayne were excessively fat.

FOOD: Almost exclusively insects.

LEAST FLYCATCHER
244. *Empidonax minimus* (Baird and Baird)   (467)

(Lat., *minimus*, least.)

DESCRIPTION: Length 5.00 to 5.75 inches. Upper surface brownish olive; wings and tail fuscous, two white or yellowish bars on the former; under parts dull white.

RANGE: Breeds north to southwestern Mackenzie and southeastern Quebec; south to southwestern Missouri and southwestern North Carolina. Winters north to Mexico; south to Panama and Peru (casually).

STATUS IN S. C.: A casual transient in May and September. Recorded only from the vicinity of Mt. Pleasant and Greenville.

HISTORY: This is the smallest of the South Carolina flycatchers and the State is largely out of its range, except for the highest mountains. It is known to occur at considerable altitudes in North Carolina, not far from the point at which the lines of North and South Carolina converge. Detailed search of the area about Caesar's Head and Mt. Pinnacle may yet reveal the presence of the Least Flycatcher in summer but thus far it is known only as a casual visitor.

Wayne secured two specimens, one on September 4, 1915, the other on September 8, 1920. Both birds were taken in the vicinity of Mt. Pleasant. P. M. Jenness, who was previously familiar with the bird, heard and saw one at Greenville on May 2, 1938.

245. EASTERN WOOD PEWEE: *Contopus virens* (Linnaeus) (461)

(Gr., *Contopus*, short-footed; Lat., *virens*, being green.)

LOCAL NAMES: Pewee.

DESCRIPTION: Length 5.90 to 6.75 inches. Upper surface olive, the head darker; under parts yellowish white, clouded on breast with gray; wings with two white bars; lower mandible and bill brownish white to yellowish white; an interrupted eye ring brownish white.

RANGE: Breeds north to southern Manitoba and southern Nova Scotia; south to southeastern Texas and central Florida. Winters north to Nicaragua and Colombia; south to Peru.

STATUS IN S. C.: Common summer resident, April 14 to October 30, throughout the State. Reported north to Greenville and Marlboro counties; east to Horry County; south to Beaufort County; west to Greenwood and Clemson College.

HISTORY: The Eastern Wood Pewee speaks its name as plainly as the Bobwhite or the Whip-poor-will. Its slender build and its two easily seen wing bars serve to distinguish it from the Phoebe, which it otherwise closely resembles. The Phoebe leaves the coastal region before the Pewee arrives; it is in the Piedmont that they occur together and may be confused.

The Pewee arrives in the coastal area by mid-April and in the upper Piedmont about a week later, remaining until the end of October. Its highly characteristic call, "pee-ah-wee," is heard on arrival, and continues pretty much through the summer. Records of its arrival should be based upon actual sight of the bird, not alone upon its call, for the Mockingbird imitates it perfectly.

The Pewee is a bird of open woodlands, orchards, and the outskirts of farmyards. It is not shy but gentle and approachable. Like the other flycatchers it perches on exposed places from which it watches for its insect prey, snapping it up in mid-air with audible clicks of the bill.

The Pewee raises two broods a season. The nest is one of the most beautiful of all passerine birds. It is a sort of enlarged, shallow edition of the Hummingbird's, made of grass, pine needles, and mosses, and covered on the exterior with lichens. It is saddled firmly either on a horizontal limb or in the fork of branches. Elevations vary from 30 to 90 feet above the ground.

The eggs, which number two to four, are of a deep cream ground color, wreathed about the large end with reddish, lilac, and almost black markings; they average 18.24 x 13.65 millimeters. There are usually three eggs in the first brood, two in the second according to Wayne (1910). Incubation requires about thirteen days. On May 27, 1910, John Kershaw found a nest containing five eggs in Clarendon County. He took a nest with four eggs in June, 1909, at Walhalla, Oconee County.

FOOD: The Pewee is one of the most exclusively insectivorous birds of the flycatcher group. Examination of 359 stomachs showed that 99 per cent of its food is animal matter, practically all insects. Wasps, ants, and sandflies make up 25 per cent; flies about 30 per cent; caterpillars, moths, beetles, and grasshoppers make up the remainder.

OLIVE-SIDED FLYCATCHER
246. *Nuttallornis borealis* (Lichtenstein) (459)

(Gr., *Nuttallornis*, [Thomas] Nuttall's bird; Lat., *borealis*, northern.)

DESCRIPTION: Length 7.00 to 8.00 inches. Above brownish slate color, the wings darker, the wing coverts edged with brownish gray; below white, but the sides and flanks, sometimes also breast, deep brownish gray.

RANGE: Breeds north to central Alaska and Newfoundland; south to northern Lower California, northern Wisconsin, and northwestern North Carolina. Winters north to northern Colombia and Venezuela; south to Ecuador and Peru.

STATUS IN S. C.: Casual autumn visitor in the coast country.

HISTORY: The only record of the Olive-sided Flycatcher in South Carolina is the one published by Wayne in his *Birds of South Carolina* (1910). Though Wayne includes it in the body of his text and not in the Hypothetical List, he did not collect the only specimen he ever saw, even though he knew it was a rare bird. Wayne saw the bird near Mt. Pleasant in the second week of September, 1904, but he was so close to it, that he feared it would be mutilated if he shot it. There had been a severe storm on the coast a few days before, and the presence of such an unusual species was possibly due to that disturbance. Wayne's familiarity with related birds and the relative ease with which this species can be identified in the field make certain that his record is valid. The Olive-sided has been recorded from both North Carolina and Georgia.

FOOD: Probably not different from that of related species and consists of insects of any kind which it can catch on the wing.

Family Alaudidae: Larks

NORTHERN HORNED LARK
247. Eremophila alpestris alpestris (Linnaeus) (474)

(Gr., *Eremophila*, desert-loving; Lat., *alpestris*, of the Alps, *i.e.*, of high mountains.)

DESCRIPTION: Length 7.00 to 8.00 inches. Anterior upper parts and upper tail coverts vinaceous cinnamon; back grayish brown, the edges of the feathers pale brown; crown and "horns" black; forehead and superciliary stripe yellow; throat yellow; a black crescent on chest; rest of under parts white; tail mostly black.

RANGE: Breeds north to northern Ungava; south to southeastern Ontario and Newfoundland. Winters north to Manitoba, southern Quebec, and Nova Scotia; south to southern Louisiana and southeastern South Carolina.

STATUS IN S. C.: Rare winter resident, December 6 to January 29. Recorded north to Chester County; east to Florence County; south to Charleston County; west to Richland County.

HISTORY: Horned Larks, representatives of the true larks of the Old World (unlike our so-called Meadowlarks) are northern in distribution, and South Carolina is south of the normal range. Therefore, the few existing records indicate that the species is of no more than rare occurrence, though strangely enough it was first described from South Carolina by Mark Catesby in 1731.

Wayne (1910) was under the impression that specimens which he secured in 1893 were the first for the State; he apparently overlooked the Catesby record. Wayne's records are also antedated by a male bird taken by L. M. Loomis at Chester Court House, December 6, 1886, now in the collection of the American Museum of Natural History (Spec. 53997). This bird was originally identified as the Prairie Horned Lark, but has since been determined to be the Northern Horned Lark by Allan R. Phillips.

During severe cold weather, Wayne took five birds of this race near Mt. Pleasant, on January 20, 1893. Their identification was verified by William Brewster. Nearly fifty years passed before another occurrence; Allan D. Cruickshank saw and identified a specimen in the field on Bull's Island, January 21, 1940, during very cold weather marked by a snowfall. On January 24, 1946, H. L. Harllee secured two females just west of the city of Florence, and five days later, took a male at the same place. Sprunt and Chamberlain examined these birds in the fall of 1947. A flock of at least fifty was seen in Richland County on January 1, 1949, by Mrs. W. H. Faver.

Horned larks get their name from the feather tufts on the head. They are trim, slender birds, white below and streaked like sparrows with a black band below a yellow throat. When flushed or seen flying overhead, they show a black tail. They inhabit open country, such as fields, airports, and golf courses. Instead of hopping as other small field birds do, they walk. They should be looked for in South Carolina during or just after any abnormally cold weather.

FOOD: About four-fifths vegetable.

PRAIRIE HORNED LARK
248. *Eremophila alpestris praticola* (Henshaw) (474b)

(Lat., *praticola*, an inhabitant of meadows.)

DESCRIPTION: Length 6.75 to 7.40 inches. Similar to the Northern Horned Lark, but smaller, more grayish, and more pinkish on nape and remaining upper parts; less yellow on forehead and superciliary stripe, which are usually white or nearly so.

RANGE: Breeds north to southern Manitoba and southwestern Quebec; south to eastern Oklahoma and northern North Carolina. Winters north to Nebraska and Maine; south to Arizona (casually), Texas, and southern Florida.

STATUS IN S. C.: Winter resident from the last week in November to March 8, locally common northward, less so southward. Reported north to Spartanburg, Chester, and Kershaw counties; east to Horry County; south to Charleston County; west to Anderson County.

HISTORY: The Prairie Horned Lark is more likely to be met with in South Carolina than the Northern Horned Lark. It has, however, been taken only in the Piedmont area. Records from other parts of the State are uncommon, not to say rare.

In the autumns of 1940 and 1941, Richard G. Kuerzi saw Horned Larks "usually flying over" at Long Bay Plantation, Horry County. He considered them "regular late fall and early winter visitors . . . never large flocks." Kuerzi did not make positive racial identification of the birds, but it seems logical to assume that they were Prairie Horned Larks, which occur much more regularly than the Northern Horned Larks. Another coastal record for which the subspecific form is uncertain is that made by R. J. Fleetwood, who saw one bird on Cape Island, March 8, 1948.

Murphey (1937) records the Prairie Horned Lark as occasional in the Aiken-Augusta region and the Misses Marion J. Pellew and Louise P. Ford noted three horned larks, which they thought were Prairies, near Aiken on December 27, 1929 (*Bird-Lore, 32*: 1930, 40).

Three Charleston Museum specimens, which were taken near Anderson on January 25, 1896, by J. R. Nowell, have been verified by Allan R. Phillips as the Prairie Horned Lark. On a Christmas Bird Count taken on December 26, 1919, in Spartanburg County, Gabriel Cannon, George Snowden, and Lewis Bailey identified a bird of this form in flight. Curiously enough, it has not been detected at Clemson.

L. M. Loomis found the bird in large flocks in Chester County and considered it a common, regular winter visitor there (*Auk, 8*: 1891, 56). The area seems to be a favored locality, and Loomis took many specimens. In nearby Kershaw County, two females were taken by N. C. Brown, one on January 10 and the other on February 7, 1906. These birds are now in the American Museum of Natural History, New York, as are those taken by Loomis. Dates of its stay in the Piedmont range from late November to the end of February, according to Loomis.

Prairie Horned Larks are, in all probability, more common in South Carolina than the records indicate. There are now few trained observers in the areas in which the bird is most likely to occur; again, the periods of cold weather most conducive to the bird's appearance in South Carolina are fairly rare.

FOOD: Similar to that of the Northern Horned Lark.

Family Hirundinidae: Swallows

249. TREE SWALLOW: *Iridoprocne bicolor* (Vieillot)   (614)

(Gr., *Iridoprocne*, iris, the rainbow, + *Procne*, daughter of Pandion, who was turned into a swallow; Lat., *bicolor*, two-colored.)

LOCAL NAMES: White-bellied Swallow.

DESCRIPTION: Length 5.00 to 6.25 inches. Tail slightly forked (emarginate). Steel blue or steel green above; pure white below.

RANGE: Breeds north to northern Alaska and northern Ungava; south to southwestern California and southeastern Virginia. Winters north to central California and southeastern Massachusetts; south to Guatemala and Cuba.

STATUS IN S. C.: Winter resident, common, at times abundant, July 7 to June 18, over most of the State, more numerous, however, in the eastern portions. Observed north to Greenville and Chester counties; east to Horry County; south to Beaufort and Jasper counties; west to Aiken County.

HISTORY: The Tree Swallow, one of the easiest of the swallows to know, spends so much time in South Carolina that it could almost be called a permanent resident but for the fact that it does not nest here. On the coast, where it seems most abundant, it is absent for only about three weeks of the year, from June 18 to July 7. In some years it is very abundant during the winter; in others, scarce and local.

The Tree Swallow is very fond of the berries of the wax myrtle and in the fall great flocks resort to the myrtle thickets on the sea islands and on the mainland. Often, gorged birds can be caught by hand.

Cold weather does not seem to inconvenience the Tree Swallow in the least, and when insects are difficult to find, it shifts to a vegetable diet. Thus it is able to winter farther north than other members of the swallow family. Sudden and severe cold, however, sometimes so reduces the food supply that these swallows starve in large numbers.

Records for the Tree Swallow near or above the fall line are rare. Murphey (1937) says that the time of its migratory appearance is uncertain; he lists it as an occasional winter visitor in the Aiken-Augusta region. L. M. Loomis records only two specimens from Chester County. B. F. Taylor recorded it at Columbia on September 6, 1910. It has not been noted at Clemson.

Adult Tree Swallows may always be recognized by the blue-black back and the pure white under parts which account for the name White-bellied Swallow. Immature birds are somewhat brown above and may show dingy areas on the sides of the throat; hence care is required not to confuse them with the brown-backed swallows, the

Bank and Rough-winged. The flight of the Tree Swallow is not as swift and darting as that of the Barn Swallow, but more deliberate and circling, the birds often coming close to a standing observer.

FOOD: Though the Tree Swallow is very fond of berries, it is, like the other members of its family, largely insectivorous. Eighty per cent of its food is animal matter, 20 per cent, vegetable. Of the latter, berries of the myrtle and bayberry make up more than nine-tenths. Insects, the bulk of the food, consist of flies, crane flies, horseflies, house flies, beetles, boll weevils, ants, leaf hoppers, plant lice, chinch bugs, and dragon flies.

250. BANK SWALLOW: *Riparia riparia riparia* (Linnaeus) (616)

(Lat., *Riparia*, riparian, *i. e.*, living on the bank of a river.)

DESCRIPTION: Length 4.75 to 5.50 inches. Plumage dark brown above, and white below with a distinct dark brown breast band.

RANGE: Breeds north to northern Alaska and northern Labrador; south to southern California and southern Virginia. Winters north to Colombia and Venezuela; south to Bolivia, Brazil, and Argentina.

STATUS IN S. C.: Uncommon transient, May 3 to 29, July 11 to September 29, in the eastern part of the State. Reported north to Clarendon County; east to Horry County; south to Jasper County; west to Aiken County.

HISTORY: The Bank Swallow is probably the least known of the South Carolina swallows. What we know of it up to the present indicates that it is only a transient visitor. A. L. Pickens writing of the birds of the Piedmont region (*Auk, 51*: 1934, 537) makes the somewhat ambiguous statement that "Further up among the mountains the Bank Swallow has at last dropped across the state line, attracted perhaps by the huge vertical sand cliffs left in building the earth dam of the Table Rock reservoir." He says nothing about nests, but the inference seems plain that the bird nests there; there is also the inference that this swallow breeds "across the state line," in North Carolina. On this point it is noteworthy that Pearson and Brimleys (*Birds of N. C.*, 1942: 234) consider the Bank Swallow simply a "rare transient" and mention but ten records of its occurrence. Present-day knowledge of the breeding range of the species in the southeastern United States is given by Bent (1942) as south to southern Virginia, southeastern Tennessee, and central Alabama.

The earliest spring record is May 3, 1947, when one was seen at Mulberry, Berkeley County, by E. Milby Burton. The latest spring date is May 29, 1934, when a male was taken by E. von S. Dingle at Huger, Berkeley County.

On the return migration in fall some birds reach this state in July, as is evidenced by observations made by Dingle on July 11, 1942, in Clarendon County, and by Allan R. Phillips on July 20, 1943, on Sullivan's Island, Charleston County. The latest fall date is September 29, 1946, when George B. Rabb and James E. Mosimann reported the birds near Charleston. On September 10, 1946, Rabb, Mosimann, and Newton H. Seebeck reported an enormous flock over the Rantowles marshes, near Red Top, Charleston County. They estimated that there were about two thousand birds, of which they believed nearly three-fourths to be Bank Swallows. Barn

Swallows made up the remainder of this great flock, except for a few Tree, Rough-winged, and Cliff Swallows. Observers in other parts of the United States have recorded Bank Swallows in huge flocks numbering up to ten thousand birds.

Great care must be taken to distinguish this little swallow in the field from its virtual counterpart, the Rough-winged Swallow. Seen in a good light, the brown band across the breast will serve to identify the bird, since the Rough-wing does not have such a band. One must bear in mind, however, that immature Tree Swallows are somewhat brown above and sometimes appear to have a dingy breast band, though it is not as dark and clear-cut as that of the Bank Swallow.

FOOD: The Bank Swallow is a very valuable destroyer of insects. Nearly all of its food is composed of insects, of which more than a fourth is flies.

ROUGH-WINGED SWALLOW
251. *Stelgidopteryx ruficollis serripennis* (Audubon) (617)

(Gr., *Stelgidopteryx*, scraper-wing; Lat., *ruficollis*, reddish necked; *serripennis*, saw-feathered.)

LOCAL NAMES: Sand Martin.

DESCRIPTION: Length 5.00 to 5.75 inches. Much like the Bank Swallow, and the tail similar. Plumage above plain brown; anterior lower parts pale grayish brown; remainder of the lower parts white.

RANGE: Breeds north to central British Columbia and New Hampshire; south to California and Florida. Winters north casually to southern Louisiana and South Carolina; south to Costa Rica.

STATUS IN S. C.: Common summer resident, March 9 to October 15, throughout the State. Accidental in winter on the coast. Observed north to Greenville, Cherokee, and Florence counties; east to Horry County; south to Jasper County; west to Oconee County.

HISTORY: Audubon was the discoverer of the Rough-winged Swallow, and since the type specimen was taken near Charleston, the bird should be of particular interest to South Carolinians. The first and last scientific names, as well as the common name, are based on the series of small barbs edging the first primary feather. It is much like the Bank Swallow in appearance, but it lacks the breast band. Except in good overhead views, however, this characteristic is difficult to see in the field.

Wayne (1910) observed "large numbers" of these swallows on January 26, 1884, and on December 22, 1894, took a specimen that had been in the neighborhood of Mt. Pleasant "since November." He stresses the fact (*Auk, 12*: 1895, 184) that severe cold had sent the temperature down to 8° F., an abnormal temperature for this region. Present-day observations lead to the belief that the bird is not a permanent resident, as Wayne considered it, but occasional or very local in winter. Murphey (1937) says the species is "Not common during December, January, and February," and G. E. Hudson reported the birds arriving at Clemson from mid-March to early April. J. E. Mosimann, G. B. Rabb, and T. M. Uzzell, Jr., noted several in Cherokee County on March 30, 1948. In September transients from the north pass through, and most of the local residents leave. However, Wayne took a specimen on October 12, 1906.

Some of these swallows, like the Kingfisher, dig burrows in banks to make their nests. It is obvious that more banks are found inland than on the coast, but suitable situations exist in the Low-country more frequently than one might at first imagine. Railroad cuts, low bluffs bordering tidal rivers and creeks, dredge cuts, and even the faces of sandhills make good nesting banks. Rough-wings also nest in or under buildings and in projecting pipes. As early as 1836 Dr. John Bachman sent Audubon eggs taken from scaffolding-holes in the walls of an unfinished brick house in Charleston. In 1906-1911, F. M. Weston, E. Milby Burton, and others found nests on the piazza of the old Isle of Palms hotel and on beams under nearby cottages. The burrows made in banks vary from 2½ to 6 feet in depth and are usually placed nearer the top of the bank that the center. Excavation usually begins about April 1, but may be earlier or later, depending on the season. Weston reported fresh eggs from April 30 to June 5, and heavily incubated eggs on May 11. Henry Dotterer observed well-grown young in the nest on June 6.

Rough-winged Swallows sometimes nest in small colonies, several pairs of birds using the same section of bank. The nests are usually crude affairs, made of grasses and rootlets. Eggs number six or seven, and are pure white, averaging about 18.3 x 13.2 millimeters. This swallow raises only one brood and incubation requires about fourteen days.

FOOD: Like that of the Bank and other swallows, almost exclusively insects of various sorts.

BARN SWALLOW
252. *Hirundo rustica erythrogaster* Boddaert   (613)

(Lat., *Hirundo*, a swallow; *rustica*, of the country; Gr., *erythrogaster*, red-bellied.)

DESCRIPTION: Length 5.75 to 7.75 inches. Tail deeply forked. Forehead chestnut; remainder of upper parts steel blue; lower surface chestnut to cinnamon.

RANGE: Breeds north to northern Alaska and southern Labrador; south to Mexico and northern Florida. Winters north to southern California (casually) and South Carolina (casually); south to Bolivia, Argentina, and southern Brazil.

STATUS IN S. C.: Permanent resident, rare in winter and summer, but abundant during migrations. Recorded north to Greenville and Darlington counties; east to Horry County; south to Beaufort and Jasper counties; west to Greenwood and Oconee counties.

HISTORY: This beautiful, graceful bird typifies the general conception of what a swallow should be. It is the only North American species having a "swallow-tail," that is, one deeply forked. The tail, together with the metallic steel blue of the back and the russet breast, make the bird easily recognizable.

The Barn Swallow is mostly a transient visitor to South Carolina. In spring the greater number of the northbound birds pass through the State from early April to early June. During the return migration to their South American wintering grounds, most of the birds are to be seen from late July to the end of September. Illustrative of the occasional winter records are observations made at the Navy Yard, Charleston, on December 17, 1912 (F. M. Weston), and on Seabrook's Island, Charleston County, on November 23, 1938 (Weston and Sprunt).

There is evidence that the Barn Swallow occasionally breeds along the southeastern coast. As early as June, 1898, Dr. T. Gilbert Pearson found two nests as far south as Wrightsville Beach, N. C., and later, in June, 1939, M. L. Davis, J. H. Grey, and Pearson found a nest a few miles below Southport, N. C. (*Birds of North Carolina*, 1942). Extending the breeding range some 300-odd miles southward, G. R. Rossignol (*Birds of Georgia*, 1945) stated that for years a colony of these birds nested under the eaves of a pavilion on Wassaw Island, Georgia. It came as no great surprise, therefore, when E. Milby Burton established the first known breeding record for South Carolina on June 24, 1946. On that date, Burton found a nest under an old boathouse dock at Cape Romain lighthouse, opposite McClellanville. The four young were resting on the beam beside the nest; although they were able to fly, they were still being fed by the parents. Visits to this locality in June and July of the following year disclosed the presence of two birds but no nest. However, on June 29, 1948, Henry C. Rucker and Hoyt Mills found two nests, one under the boathouse, the other inside the building. Both nests held young.

FOOD: Almost entirely animal matter, chiefly insects, with a few snails. The largest single item is flies, which compose nearly 40 per cent of the total. Beetles and weevils make up 16 per cent. The Barn Swallow consumes boll weevils in considerable numbers.

NORTHERN CLIFF SWALLOW
253. *Petrochelidon pyrrhonota pyrrhonota* (Vieillot) (612)

(Gr., *Petrochelidon*, rock-swallow; *pyrrhonota*, red-backed.)

DESCRIPTION: Length 5.00 to 6.00 inches. Forehead brownish white; remaining upper parts mostly metallic blue black, but the rump cinnamon rufous; upper throat chestnut; lower throat black; remainder of under surface dull white; belly gray or rufescent; the anterior part of the body laterally gray.

RANGE: Breeds north to Minnesota and southeastern Quebec; south to northern Alabama and Virginia. Winters north to Paraguay; south probably to Argentina.

STATUS IN S. C.: Uncommon transient, April 4 to May 29, August 10 to October 28, probably throughout the State. Reported north and east to Horry County; south to John's Island; west to Oconee County.

HISTORY: This is the rarest of the swallows that visit South Carolina. In recent years records of its presence have increased, but this may be due to an increase in the number of observers. Wayne secured the first specimens for the State in 1898, but during the next thirty years, he saw the bird less than half a dozen times.

The Cliff Swallow is an uncommon transient visitor in the State, passing through on both migrations. Records are so few, even yet, that they may be worth setting forth in detail.

Except for a record of a single bird seen by H. R. Sass in Charleston on August 15, 1910, the Cliff Swallow was not again reported until 1926. On April 20 of that year G. E. Hudson secured one at Clemson, Oconee County. He saw others on April 21 and May 4 of the same year (*Auk*, 47: 1930, 397), and again on April 4, 1927. The next record was for the coastal section, when E. von S. Dingle secured a female at Middleburg Plantation, Berkeley County, on May 29, 1934. On May 4, 1940, R. G. Kuerzi saw an adult male at Long Bay Plantation, near Myrtle Beach, Horry County. The year 1942 produced a number of records. On August 10, Allan R. Phillips observed at least one bird among Barn and Tree Swallows at Stark General Hospital near Charleston. On September 5-7, Chamberlain saw six to twelve birds, also with Barn and Tree Swallows, at Coburg Dairy, St. Andrews Parish, near Charleston. He also found them there on October 28 of the same year. On September 10, 1946, G. B. Rabb, J. E. Mosimann, and N. H. Seebeck noted six birds among thousands of other swallows at Red Top, Charleston County. On August 12, 1947, Sprunt and his son observed a flock which they estimated to be between eighty-five and one hundred Cliff Swallows circling over fields on Wadmalaw and John's Islands, Charleston County. Many of these birds, perched on wires over the road, allowed the car to stop directly under them. These records cover the known observations to date.

The Cliff Swallow is fairly easy to recognize, because of its square tail, buff-colored rump patch, light forehead, and dark throat.

FOOD: Almost wholly insects—beetles, ants, wasps, flies, and bugs, including the destructive chinch bug and boll weevil.

254. PURPLE MARTIN: *Progne subis subis* (Linnaeus) (611)

(Lat., *Progne* [Procne], daughter of Pandion, fabled to have been turned into a swallow; *subis*, old name of some bird.)

LOCAL NAMES: Martin.

DESCRIPTION: Length 7.25 to 8.50 inches. *Male*. Dark metallic blue or violet black above and below. *Female*. Similar to the male but duller above and gray below.

RANGE: Breeds north to southern British Columbia and Prince Edward Island; south to Mexico and southern Florida. Winters in Brazil.

STATUS IN S. C.: Abundant summer resident, February 6 (casually January 23) to November 3, throughout the State. Reported north to Greenville, Cherokee, and Dillon counties; east to Horry County; south to Beaufort County; west to Greenwood and Pickens counties.

HISTORY: The Purple Martin is one of the best known birds of South Carolina, but in all probability only a few South Carolinians realize that it is a swallow. From time immemorial, the Martin has been a "yard bird" in the Low-country; even the Indians encouraged it about their villages and settlements; it was they who originated the method of attracting the bird by erecting gourds for it to nest in. Their example was followed by slaves of the plantation era, and the method persists today not only in the old reliable gourd by the Negro cabin but in the elaborate many-gabled, chimneyed, and porticoed bird houses one sees in gardens, country estates, and city yards.

The Martin is a summer resident in South Carolina and occurs practically everywhere. The birds arrive in the coastal region in February and early March. Records for twenty-eight years, made by several observers, show an average arrival date of February 26 for the Charleston region. A phenomenally early record was established by E. A. Hyer, on January 23, 1911. As we go inland, arrival dates appear progressively later, on the average. Thus at Summerton, Clarendon County, E. von S. Dingle's records for four years give an average date of March 12. At Columbia there are records for thirty years, contributed for most of the period by R. H. Sullivan, and later by Mrs. G. E. Charles. These records indicate an average arrival date of April 4. At Clemson College, in the Piedmont, G. E. Hudson gives his earliest arrival date as March 30. They have also been recorded in Cherokee County on that date.

At times, temperatures drop considerably below freezing after the birds have arrived. Cold spells of short duration appear to cause little inconvenience to the birds, but protracted cold weather may result in starvation for many because of a shortage of insect food. Wayne (1910) cites one such instance in the first half of April, 1907.

The fall migration is a long-drawn-out affair. It usually starts in late July when the birds begin to gather in large flocks. Martins continue to be seen, however, through the rest of the summer and on into the fall, as they pass through from more northerly breeding grounds to their wintering areas in Brazil. The average departure date at Charleston is October 9.

Nesting takes place in late April or early May, and egg-laying occurs about the middle of the latter month. At Charleston an early date was recorded on April 19, 1912, when E. A. Hyer noted a nest with one egg. On one occasion a Martin was seen picking up several bits of oystershell from a nearby roadway, and taking these into its nesting gourd. There these fragments were checked again after the nesting season. No explanation can be offered for this behavior. There are usually four or five eggs; these are pure white and average 24.5 x 17.5 millimeters. Incubation requires twelve or thirteen days. In the days before settlement of the country, Martins used the natural cavities of trees, abandoned woodpecker holes, etc., as nesting sites, and Wayne (1910) speaks of having noted this habit. Thomas Rivers and T. M. Uzzell, Jr., found a nest of Martins in the top of a gasoline pump at a country store in Christ Church Parish, Charleston County in the spring of 1948. The pump was in use.

Nesting boxes erected for the birds are usually from 15 to 25 feet high. The birds will make use of much lower ones, however; we recall a box on John's Island, and a series of gourds strung on a wire in a Colleton County yard, scarcely more than 5 or 6 feet from the ground. If a nesting box has been taken down for cleaning and not erected by the time the first birds arrive in spring, they will flutter about in the air at the exact spot the box should be.

Martins raise only one brood, and most of the young are on the wing by the last of June. That Martins are of immense value as insect controls will not be doubted by anyone who has watched the adults of a nesting colony feeding their young. From dawn to dark they come and go, each trip carrying a supply of bugs and insects. Otto Widmann (*Forest and Stream*, *22*: 1884, 484) lists the visits of a colony of sixteen pairs, from 4 a. m. to 8 p. m., as 3277 trips, an average of 205 trips per pair. One hesitates even to guess at the number of insects which Martins destroy daily. Over the country as a whole, it must be astronomical.

FOOD: Entirely insects, particularly ants, bees, dragon flies, and wasps. Flies amount to 16 per cent; stinkbugs and tree hoppers, 15 per cent; beetles, 12 per cent, including May, ground, dung, boll and clover weevils, moths, and butterflies.

Family Corvidae: Jays, Magpies, and Crows

NORTHERN BLUE JAY
255. *Cyanocitta cristata bromia* Oberholser (477)

(Gr., *Cyanocitta*, blue jay; Lat., *cristata*, crested; Gr., *bromia*, noisy.)

DESCRIPTION: Similar to the Florida Blue Jay, but larger. Upper parts more bluish (less violet); white tips of the tail and wing feathers larger.

RANGE: Breeds north to northern Alberta and Newfoundland; south to southern Kansas and northwestern North Carolina. Winters south to southern Louisiana and central eastern South Carolina.

STATUS IN S. C.: Rare winter resident, January 12 to February 22, potentially throughout the State. Reported from Spartanburg, Sumter, Charleston, Orangeburg, and Lexington counties.

HISTORY: The Northern Blue Jay is probably more common than the records indicate. Banding in the northern United States has yielded records from Woodruff in Spartanburg County, February 20, 1940; from Sumter, January 12, 1930; and from Leesville in Lexington County, January 29, 1936. Specimens taken at McClellanville, February 2, 1936, by H. M. Rutledge and at Eutawville, February 22, 1936, by Chamberlain have been identified as this race by Dr. Harry C. Oberholser.

FLORIDA BLUE JAY
256. *Cyanocitta cristata cristata* (Linnaeus) (477a)

LOCAL NAMES: Jay; Jaybird.

DESCRIPTION: Length 10.00 to 11.50 inches. Head with a conspicuous crest. Upper parts grayish violet blue, with a black collar; wings and tail similar but barred with black, and the tips of secondaries and of their coverts together with the tips of the outer tail feathers, white; lower surface white with a black crescent on the chest.

RANGE: Resident and breeds north to northeastern Texas and the District of Columbia; south to southeastern Texas and north central Florida.

STATUS IN S. C.: Common permanent resident all over the State. Reported north to Greenville, York, Lancaster, and Dillon counties; east to Horry County; south to Jasper County; west to Greenwood and Oconee counties.

HISTORY: The Blue Jay is a jaunty brigand, known to every one by his conspicuous blue, black, and white plumage, his crested head, and his strident call of "jay, jay."

Abundant and noisy as the bird is for much of the year, it is astonishing how secretive and unobtrusive it becomes during the nesting season. A pair may nest in one's very yard and carry on their domestic activities busily without revealing their presence to any member of the human household. Once the young are abroad, however, they revert to their noisy and abandoned way of life. With the approach of cool weather, the birds assemble in small groups, hustling about in helter-skelter fashion, bedeviling hawk and crow or taking what appears to be a fiendish delight in routing out some somnolent owl.

The breeding season occurs in April and May. On the coast, sets of five eggs have been found on April 19 (E. J. DeCamps) and on April 23 (E. A. Cutts). R. H. Coleman discovered a bird incubating on April 27; still another pair began building on April 30 (Sprunt). From Columbia there is one report of building as early as April 4; another, of young birds awing on May 18 (Mrs. G. E. Charles).

Jays seem to prefer oaks as nesting trees; the nests are most likely to be found in live oaks in the coastal area. The nest is a bulky affair made of sticks, pine needles, grasses, cotton, and some mud. Elevation varies from about 20 to 50 or more feet. There is at least one instance in which a nest was used for two successive seasons, with little or no repair (R. H. Coleman).

The eggs usually number three or four. They are of an olive shade, heavily marked with dark brown, and average 27.1 x 20.4 millimeters. The incubation period is about seventeen or eighteen days, and two broods are raised.

FOOD: It is chiefly in connection with its food habits that there is real divergence of opinion regarding this bird. It is omnivorous, but the inclusion of eggs and other birds in its diet has brought down wrath from many. That the Jay preys upon other birds at times is an established certainty, but that all Jays do so consistently, or even generally, is not a fact. Nests of "yard" birds such as Cardinals, Painted Buntings, Towhees, etc., are sometimes broken up, but the consumption of eggs and birds probably does not exceed 2 per cent of the Jay's total food.

Vegetable matter furnishes 43 per cent, and consists largely of acorns. Beechnuts, hazelnuts, pecans, and wild fruits are also taken. Cultivated fruits amount to 15 per cent, in summer. Corn amounts to 18 per cent, and since it is eaten every month in the year, much of it is waste. Animal matter makes up 22 per cent, and three-fourths of this consists of destructive forms such as caterpillars, grasshoppers, and certain beetles. In addition to the insects, spiders, small mollusks, crustaceans, and small fish are taken.

257. NORTHERN RAVEN: *Corvus corax principalis* Ridgway (486a)

(Lat., *Corvus*, a crow; *corax*, a raven; *principalis*, principal.)

DESCRIPTION: Length 22.00 to 26.50 inches. Throat feathers pointed and narrow; tail graduated. Plumage entirely black.

RANGE: Resident and breeds north to northwestern Alaska and northern Greenland; south to Washington and northwestern South Carolina.

STATUS IN S. C.: Rare permanent resident in the northwestern part of the State; and a casual winter visitor to the eastern part. As a resident, reported north to Oconee, Pickens, and Greenville counties. In winter traced southeast to Berkeley and Beaufort counties.

HISTORY: Northern Ravens are now so reduced in numbers in South Carolina that they have become almost legendary, but a few persist in the mountain region and occasionally wander to the coast area. Years ago they were not uncommon in the northern counties and, as Wayne (1910) says, "The Raven has been known to breed in the mountains of Oconee, Pickens, and Greenville counties for more than one hundred years. . . ." The most recent records from that region are of a bird seen by M. B. Stevens in Oconee County in March, 1935, and the report by J. M. Sitton of two or three birds in the Walhalla section, also in Oconee County, in 1936. Ravens are increasing in the North Carolina Blue Ridge Mountains as a result of the establishment of the Great Smoky Mountains National Park, and in the future they may occur in South Carolina more regularly.

Curiously enough, there have been more records from the coast in recent years than from the upper part of the State. Two birds were seen by T. Kenneth Ellis, while he was on a deer stand at Richmond Plantation, near Cordesville, Berkeley County, about January, 1936. In 1938, Dr. R. B. Rhett of Charleston, reported seeing one between Port Royal and Lexington on May 20. On the last day of 1938 two were seen at Cote Bas Plantation, Cooper River, Berkeley County, by J. H. Walsh. T. K. Ellis made a later observation on April 17, 1943, 10 miles northwest of Monck's Corner. He saw a single Raven, in company with several crows, feeding on a dead goat on State Highway 311.

A specimen was captured on November 21, 1943, when Noel B. Wright found one with a broken wing on U. S. Highway 17, in Beaufort County. He kept the bird for over a month, then sent it to the Charleston Museum which in turn, gave it to the Hampton Park Zoo in Charleston. It is still there (1949), apparently in good

PLATE XXI: BRIGHT-COLORED GROUP

Water Color by John Henry Dick

Three upper birds, left to right: Blue Grosbeak (female), Blue Grosbeak (male), and Scarlet Tanager (male). Four lower birds, left to right: Indigo Bunting (female), Indigo Bunting (male), Scarlet Tanager (female), and Tufted Titmouse.

health. Wright stated that while he had the bird, it killed four of his chickens and on one occasion took food away from the family bulldog.

In appearance, the Raven is an oversized crow, with some variations. The neck feathers are lengthened and pointed, the tail is wedge-shaped, and the beak is very heavy. The flight is also different, consisting often of alternate flappings and sailings with the wings held in a horizontal position.

The Raven's voice is one of the bird's storied accomplishments—a deep, guttural "crok," very different from the well-known "caw" of its smaller relative. However, some of the notes are much like those of the crow, and Chamberlain, who studied the voice of the captive bird mentioned above, has found that one call is exactly like the "quok" of the Black-crowned Night Heron, so much so that he could detect no difference.

The Raven was once regarded with much superstition and dread, being considered a bird of ill omen. This, together with its propensity for preying upon young lambs or pigs, resulted in constant persecution and a consequent reduction of the Raven population. It is a powerful bird, fully capable of destroying creatures such as the larger hawks and owls prey upon.

FOOD: The Northern Raven is omnivorous in its tastes and consumes carrion. It often attacks small mammals, as well as game birds and sometimes poultry. However, it is so uncommon today that it presents no economic problem.

EASTERN CROW
258. *Corvus brachyrhynchos brachyrhynchos* Brehm (488)

(Lat., *Corvus*, a crow; Gr., *brachyrhynchos*, short-billed.)

DESCRIPTION: Similar to the Southern Crow, but larger, with longer and stouter bill.

RANGE: Breeds north to southwestern Mackenzie and Newfoundland; south to northern Texas and northern Maryland. Winters north to southeastern Ontario and southern Newfoundland; south to Texas and southern South Carolina.

STATUS IN S. C.: Probably fairly common winter resident, at least on the coast. Recorded north to Georgetown County; south to Charleston County.

HISTORY: In practically every respect the Eastern Crow is identical with the Southern Crow. It is the crow of the north generally, but it migrates southward in winter to South Carolina. In the field no distinction can be made between it and the Southern Crow, for it can be certainly identified only in the hand. Three specimens were taken in Georgetown County on February 9, 1935, by Dudley L. Vail, Jr., and another on John's Island on February 1, 1938, by Fred Wehman. These have been identified by Dr. Harry C. Oberholser and seem to be the only specimens now available from the State, although the Eastern Crow is probably more numerous in South Carolina than these few records indicate.

SOUTHERN CROW
259. *Corvus brachyrhynchos paulus* Howell (488c)

(Lat., *paulus*, little.)

DESCRIPTION: Length 16.00 to 20.00 inches. Plumage wholly black with purplish reflections.

RANGE: Resident and breeds north to southern Illinois and to the District of Columbia; south to southeastern Texas, northwestern Florida, and central eastern South Carolina.

STATUS IN S. C.: Abundant permanent resident in all the State excepting the southeastern corner where it is only a winter resident. Reported north to Spartanburg, York, and Darlington counties; east to Horry County; south (in winter) to Beaufort County; west to Oconee County.

HISTORY: It is altogether likely that the crow is the best known bird in South Carolina and, in one or another of its forms, in the entire country. It occurs from the Atlantic to the Pacific and from Maine to Mexico. The bird has given the language such expressions as "black as a crow" and "as the crow flies." It is probably the only species against which systematic and determined efforts at extermination have been made, and which thrives despite them. In all likelihood, there are more crows in the country today than when Columbus discovered America.

The Southern Crow is a permanent resident of South Carolina and occurs everywhere in the State. It is so obvious in fall and winter, when it flocks, and its familiar call is so universal, that the quietness and apparent scarcity of the bird in spring is a matter for wonder. This, however, is perfectly normal crow behavior, for it takes care that at the nesting season no one is advised of its presence. Around the nest it is one of the most secretive of birds, coming and going like a sable phantom.

The birds mate early in February and begin to build the nest about the middle of the month. The nest is usually high above the ground, in oaks or pines, and is well constructed of sticks, bark, and twigs and lined with pine needles or Spanish moss. The eggs number four to six. They are bluish green, with many spots and splashes of brown. They average 41.4 x 28.9 millimeters. One or two broods are raised, and incubation requires about eighteen days. Five fresh eggs were found by Thomas W. Perry at Rockville, Charleston County, on March 11. Another nest of five eggs was taken by E. J. DeCamps in Beaufort County on April 3—possibly the second brood.

A Southern Crow taken at Gray's Hill, Beaufort County, on March 22, 1937, by H. M. Woods, now in the Cleveland Museum of Natural History, has been identified by Dr. Harry C. Oberholser, showing that its winter range extends at least that far into the range of the Florida Crow.

FOOD: E. R. Kalmbach's extensive studies (1918) resulted in the discovery that the food is about 72 per cent vegetable and 28 per cent animal matter. In its choice of animal food, the crow is both an economic benefit and a detriment. It eats grasshoppers, crickets, beetles, cutworms, and caterpillars, as well as mollusks, crayfish, snakes, lizards, mice, rats, young rabbits, and the eggs and young of other birds. Wayne (1910) says that it destroys "innumerable eggs of the Clapper Rail" as well as those of the diamond-backed terrapin and yellow-bellied turtle. It certainly takes many eggs from the rookeries of various herons.

Of vegetable food, corn is the main item, being 38 per cent of the total. The crow eats wheat and oats in much smaller quantities. Wild fruits such as poison ivy, wax myrtle, sour gum, and dogwood, make up 14 per cent.

FLORIDA CROW
260. *Corvus brachyrhynchos pascuus* Coues (488a)

(Lat., *pascuus*, pertaining to pasture.)

DESCRIPTION: Similar to the Eastern Crow, but smaller except the bill.

RANGE: Resident and breeds north to southeastern South Carolina; south to southern Florida.

STATUS IN S. C.: Common permanent resident in the southeastern corner of the State, where it ranges north to Wadmalaw and John's islands in Charleston County.

HISTORY: The four specimens which determine the status of the Florida Crow in South Carolina have been identified by Dr. Harry C. Oberholser. Two are from John's Island, one collected December 15, 1934, by Chamberlain, the other February 1, 1938, by Fred Wehman; the third was taken on Wadmalaw Island, February 22, 1934, by E. Milby Burton; and a fourth at Beaufort, April 22, 1941, by E. P. McCullagh. These specimens, while not wholly typical of the Florida race, as they show some vergence toward the Southern Crow, the common race of South Carolina, are referable to this subspecies, and indicate that the northeastern range of the Florida Crow should be regarded as extending north to include the southeastern corner of South Carolina.

261. FISH CROW: *Corvus ossifragus* Wilson (490)

(Lat., *ossifragus*, bone-breaking.)

DESCRIPTION: Length 14.00 to 17.50 inches. Plumage entirely black with violet metallic reflections on back, and with greenish metallic gloss on the head and under parts.

RANGE: Resident and breeds north to central Arkansas and Connecticut, probably also to Massachusetts; south to southeastern Texas and southern Florida.

STATUS IN S. C.: Common permanent resident, chiefly in the coast region and for some distance inland. Reported north to Florence County; east to Horry County; south to Beaufort and Jasper counties; west to Aiken and Greenwood counties.

HISTORY: The Fish Crow is considerably smaller than the Southern Crow, but it can always be recognized by its voice, which is very hoarse and raucous as though the bird were suffering with a bad cold. The call is entirely unlike the characteristic "caw" of other crows.

This little crow is at home along the sea beaches, salt marshes, and mainland of the Low-country and frequents the cypress lagoons and fields as well. It sometimes raids the heron rookeries and the seabird colonies of the offshore banks, and it patrols the marshes for various sorts of aquatic life.

Inland Fish Crows are not numerous. Murphey (1937) regarded the bird as a permanent resident in the Aiken-Augusta region, but considered it sharply limited to the bottoms of the Savannah River and its tributaries. There is one report by F. W. Hahn of a nest in Greenwood County, April 1, 1925, the farthest inland record of occurrence and breeding. As Dr. Murphey indicates, Fish Crows follow the streams in from the coast for considerable distances. They are fairly common at times about the Santee-Cooper lakes.

The nesting season begins in late April and lasts through most of May. The eggs commonly number four or five. They are very similar in shape and color to those of the Southern Crow, but are smaller, averaging 37.17 x 26.97 millimeters. One brood is raised and incubation takes sixteen to eighteen days. The nest is built in pines or deciduous trees, often pecans, 30 or 40 to more than 100 feet above the ground. Fish Crows once nested in parts of Charleston, notably in the cemetery of St. Paul's Church on Coming Street, and on East Battery (Wayne), and on Broad Street (Chamberlain). A few pairs may still do so in some of the larger gardens where there are tall trees.

FOOD: The Fish Crow is well named for it consumes a good deal of marine life—fiddler crabs, small blue crabs, various kinds of minnows, and shellfish found on the beaches. Part of its diet consists of wild fruit and berries, among which are mulberries, hackberries, grapes, palmetto berries, holly, magnolia, and bay. In spring and early summer the Fish Crow, which is an inveterate thief, takes many eggs of herons and rails.

Family Paridae: Titmice, Chickadees, and Bush-tits

CAROLINA CHICKADEE
262. Parus carolinensis carolinensis Audubon (736)

(Lat., Parus, a titmouse; carolinensis, of Carolina.)

DESCRIPTION: Length 4.25 to 4.50 inches. Bill short. Head, nape, and throat black; sides of head white; back mouse gray; undersurface dull white, the sides and flanks washed with buff; tail dark gray.

RANGE: Resident and breeds north to northeastern Alabama and North Carolina; south to southern Alabama and southern South Carolina.

STATUS IN S. C.: Common permanent resident in the entire State. Reported north to Greenville and York counties; east to Horry County; south to Beaufort County; west to Aiken and Oconee counties.

HISTORY: One would hardly be wrong in saying that the Chickadee is a general favorite everywhere. Many people who know nothing of birds and have little interest in them are familiar with the Chickadee. Gentle, confiding, friendly, this little black-capped, black-bibbed ball of feathers seems to overflow with vitality and the joy of living, even when the winter is severe. It practically covers all of the United States (in a number of species), the range being as large as the bird itself is small.

The Carolina Chickadee, which looks very much like the others of its family, should be better known than it is, for it was described from near Charleston by Audubon and Dr. Bachman well over a hundred years ago (1833); it bears the State's name; and it is a permanent resident in every county.

Chickadees are woodland birds but they do not shun human habitation. Though perfectly at home in remote swamps and heavy forests, they come freely into yards of country and city dwellers alike, and many a kitchen-window feeding tray has them as regular boarders in winter. Their tiny size and black and gray plumage, together with the notes which so resemble the sound "chickadee . . . dee . . . dee," make them easy to recognize. Frequent companions are the Titmice, which are close relatives, Nuthatches, and Kinglets, all small birds.

Though Chickadees sometimes nest in bird boxes, they prefer a hollow; and in spite of the fact that abandoned woodpecker holes are a dime a dozen, Chickadees will often excavate their own nest cavities. The nest is never built in an exposed situation, and fence posts make as good a place as any. Male and female work at the job of home building, and if they excavate the hole it may be as much as a foot in depth. Plant down, fur, and feathers are used for lining, and a blanket of such material is drawn over the eggs when the bird leaves the nest. Full sets of eggs will have been laid between April 5 and 10, but earlier records are not uncommon. For example, Wayne has taken seven eggs as early as March 23, these being "heavily incubated." The nest which Wayne found was but 4 feet from the ground in a fence post. In backward seasons eggs may not appear until late April or even early May. The eggs vary from four to eight, and though eight is really an uncommon number, E. J. DeCamps has taken sets of eight several times. The eggs are white, heavily spotted with reddish brown and average 14.8 x 11.5 millimeters. One brood is raised (Wayne) and incubation requires eleven days.

Various observers have commented on the fact that Chickadees sometimes give a peculiar note when disturbed on the nest. E. von S. Dingle has noted it in regard to the Carolina Chickadee; he says that when the stub was tapped on the outside, the sitting bird uttered what sounded like "a little sneeze." It was repeated every time the stub was tapped (*Auk, 39*: 1922, 572). Other observers have characterized the sound as a hiss.

There is a marked difference between the song of the Carolina Chickadee and that of its northern relative. The latter's call is usually two syllabled, that of the Carolina, four. It is higher pitched and given more rapidly. Northern observers often comment on this variation when encountering the Carolina Chickadee for the first time.

FOOD: The animal content of the Chickadee's food amounts to 72 per cent; the vegetable, 28 per cent. Nearly half of the total is composed of moths and caterpillars. Stinkbugs, shield bugs, leaf hoppers, plant lice, tree hoppers, and scale insects occur in quantity. Ants, wasps, beetles, cockroaches, and katydids are consumed to a lesser extent; spiders make up 10 per cent.

263. TUFTED TITMOUSE: *Parus bicolor* Linnaeus (731)

(Lat., *bicolor*, two-colored.)

LOCAL NAMES: Tomtit; Peter Bird.

DESCRIPTION: Length 5.60 to 6.50 inches. Head crested; bill very short. Upper parts and tail slate gray; forehead brownish black; undersurface white, the sides and flanks light cinnamon rufous.

RANGE: Resident and breeds north to eastern Nebraska and Maine; south to southeastern Texas and southern Florida.

STATUS IN S. C.: Common permanent resident throughout the State. Observed north to Greenville, Cherokee, York, and Florence counties; east to Horry County; south to Beaufort and Jasper counties; west to Aiken and Oconee counties.

HISTORY: The Tufted Titmouse is as distinctive among small birds as the jay is among larger ones and for much the same reason; it is a crested species. No other small, grayish South Carolina bird is so adorned. Abundant over the State, it is a permanent and well-known resident. Few birds are more monotonously vociferous. The call is a clear, whistled "peto-peto-peto."

The Tufted Titmouse is a companion of Carolina Chickadees, Nuthatches, and Kinglets, and at times, warblers. It is one of the most satisfactory birds to "squeak," for it comes very readily to that sound, and often brings others along with it. The winter woods are much enlivened by its presence and one may be almost certain of seeing it anywhere in open woodlands and brushy tracts. It is by no means shy and comes freely into yards in towns and settlements.

The nesting season is usually late April and the nest is built invariably in a cavity of some sort, either natural or man-made or in an old woodpecker hole. The Tufted Titmouse does not excavate its own hole as the Carolina Chickadee often does. Elevations vary from 4 feet to as many as 50. The bird is a very close sitter and can sometimes be picked up off the eggs. Both sexes work on the nest. Cotton, hair, fur, feathers, and bark strippings go into its construction. In the Low-country a piece of cast snake skin is nearly always present. Wayne (1910) lists this material as "indispensable." The four to eight eggs are white, with many markings of reddish brown and lilac. They average 18.4 x 14.1 millimeters and incubation requires about twelve days. One brood is raised. Wayne once found a nest in a clump of Spanish moss, a very unusual situation which he recorded in the *Auk*, *14*: 1897, 98. J. S. Y. Hoyt recorded the bird breeding in Jasper County on May 12. Murphey (1937) has found a full set of eggs as early as March 23 in the Aiken-Augusta region.

Titmice come freely to feeding trays and exhibit a tameness which is hardly equalled or even approached by other small birds except the Carolina Chickadee and occasionally the American Redstart. They are jaunty birds, alert and active, the crested head no doubt adding a good deal to the general impression of these qualities. They are excitable and inquisitive and make very attractive feeding station boarders. Winter, of course, is much the best time for feeding them.

Food: The diet of the Tufted Titmouse is about two-thirds animal, and one-third vegetable matter. Caterpillars make up about 38 per cent; wasps, bees, and sawfly larvae, 12 per cent. Many insects are taken, among them the boll weevil. The birds have a liking for acorns, mulberries, and the berries of the wax myrtle.

CALIFORNIA BUSH-TIT
264. *Psaltriparus minimus californicus* Ridgway (743a)

(Lat., *Psaltriparus*, a musical titmouse; *minimus*, least; *californicus*, of California.)

DESCRIPTION: Length 4.00 to 4.50 inches. Tail long; top of head light brown; remainder of upper parts brownish gray; below pale smoky gray.

RANGE: Resident and breeds north to the interior of Oregon; south to the interior of south central California.

STATUS IN S. C.: Accidental.

HISTORY: There is only one record of the occurrence of the California Bush-tit in South Carolina. It is a record so remarkable, however, as to be almost unbelievable; and the fact that there are no specimens to substantiate the record, no material proof which the scientist can pick up and examine, admittedly increases the doubt. As Wayne wrote (1910), the record "seems to have been discredited by ornithologists generally. . . ."

Nevertheless the record cannot be ignored. Wayne himself credited it completely, and the present authors are entirely in agreement with him. There appears to be no reason to deny the authenticity of the account written by Leverett M. Loomis (*Auk*, 3: 1886, 137-138). That account is so important and so full of interest that it is here transcribed in full:

> In a letter received sometime since from Dr. C. Kollock, mention was made of the former breeding of the Least Bush-tit in the vicinity of Cheraw, South Carolina. Subsequently I wrote to him asking for further particulars concerning this interesting occurrence. His reply is as follows:—"As to the Chestnut-crowned Titmouse—*Parus minimus* of Townsend and Audubon—I never wrote anything on the subject except a short letter to the Rev. Dr. M. A. Curtis, who was then pastor of the Episcopal Church at Society Hill, about fifteen miles below Cheraw. When I first wrote him that I had found specimens of the Chestnut-crowned Titmouse near Cheraw, he wrote me promptly, saying that I must be mistaken, as that bird was never seen east of the Rocky Mountains. I had captured both the male and female, and the nest with six eggs in it. A few days later Dr. Curtis came to Cheraw, and when he saw the birds, nest, and eggs, he gave it up and said, 'You have discovered the first Chestnut-crowned Titmouse ever seen this side of the Rocky Mountains.' I saw perhaps six or eight others in the same locality. I have never seen any since that date, [the spring of] 1857, so it must have been an accident their appearing in this latitude."

> This account adds still another instance of that peculiar easterly migration of 'western' species toward the South Atlantic seaboard, which has so recently been revealed in the records of LeConte's Bunting, Painted Longspur, Nelson's Sharp-tailed Finch, and Yellow-headed Blackbird.

It is to be hoped that the constantly increasing band of ornithological workers, scattered over the State, will be able to throw the clearer light of later experience on this and other legacies of the Bachmanian epoch of South Carolina ornithology.

P. S.—Since writing the foregoing I have received a more detailed account from Dr. Kollock respecting the occurrence noted above, from which I add the following:

". . . The nest was suspended from low bushes, from three and a half to five feet from the ground; was in the shape of a long purse, from four to six inches in length, with a round hole at the top. The lower part or bottom of the nest was wider than the upper part. The nest was made principally of moss, lint, and down, and lined with feathers. There were several eggs—I do not now remember how many—four or five, I think, and were pure white. The nest was in a low place, not exactly a swamp or marsh, but a low bottom, grown up thickly with bushes of sweet-gum, hackberry, a bush known here as the spice tree. It was most beautifully and securely attached to the twigs.

"In 1857, Dr. Curtis was in the zenith of his reputation as a botanist and ornithologist. He died soon after the war. This is all I have to say on the subject of the *Parus minimus* being found in South Carolina. I had the male and female and a nest of eggs, all of which was burned in my office by Sherman's army in 1865. The birds and nest I procured in the very early part of May or latter part of April . . . I was not mistaken in my identification. I saw the birds before they were captured, knew they were rare in this region, having given some attention to the ornithology of this State. Having procured the specimens, I referred the matter to Dr. Curtis, who, when he saw them, admitted at once they were the *Parus minimus*, and said, 'You are the first to find this bird east of the Rocky Mountains.' Dr. Curtis doubted my correctness of identification till he saw the specimens." LEVERETT M. LOOMIS, *Chester, S. C.*

The validity of this extraordinary record rests, of course, entirely upon the testimony of the observers. They were not casual observers or amateurs in ornithology, however, but trained naturalists obviously confident of their knowledge. Although Drs. Kollock and Curtis identified the birds by the specific name *Parus minimus*, it seems unlikely that they were Coast Bush-tits (which was the first race of the species to be described and which inhabits only a narrow belt along the Pacific coast); it is more probable that they were of a related race, now called the California Bush-tit, which dwells in the interior.

The Bush-tits have habits similar to those of the Chickadees.

Family Sittidae: Nuthatches

FLORIDA NUTHATCH
265. *Sitta carolinensis carolinensis* Latham (727b)

(Gr., *Sitta*, a nuthatch; Lat., *carolinensis*, of Carolina.)

DESCRIPTION: Length 5.00 to 5.50 inches. Bill straight, thin, and pointed; tail short. Head and hind neck black; back and rump bluish gray; undersurface white, the under tail coverts light chestnut; most of tail black with large squarish white spots.

Acadian Flycatchers at Home   S. A. GRIMES

Captive Raven, Taken in South Carolina RONALD ALLEN REILLY

Nighthawk at Bay   S. A. GRIMES

Brown-headed Nuthatch

3. A. GRIMES

RANGE: Resident and breeds north to southern Missouri and central eastern North Carolina; south to southeastern Texas and southern Florida.

STATUS IN S. C.: Fairly common permanent resident throughout the State. Recorded north to Caesar's Head and Spartanburg, also to York and Florence counties; east to Horry County; south to Beaufort County; west to Aiken, Oconee, and Pickens counties.

HISTORY: Nuthatches are the acrobats of the bird world. A fly on a ceiling has nothing on these interesting little birds, for upside down is as natural to them as right side up. They are almost miniature woodpeckers, but they are capable of feats beyond the abilities of any woodpecker, and as a result have become known to many people who are not ordinarily interested in birds. At any rate, this little gray-backed, white-bellied, black-capped bird is easy to recognize and should be known without trouble. Even if the plumage were not diagnostic enough, the actions of the bird would establish its identity. It comes readily to feeding stations in winter.

Though a permanent resident in South Carolina, the Florida Nuthatch is never a common bird anywhere. Winter is the best season in which to see it, for the bird is more abundant then and easier to see in the leafless trees. Its presence is usually well advertised by the very distinctive note, described as "a nasal yank, yank." Certainly, when it has once been heard it will not be forgotten. This bird descends tree trunks head first, creeps easily about on the underside of limbs, and assumes every possible position of the body in its endless search for insects in the bark. Unlike its Brown-headed relative, the Florida Nuthatch is often a solitary bird or at best travels in pairs. It lives in dry, open woods, dense swamps, and pinelands, but it often appears in winter in the trees of towns and settlements. It is even more scattered in spring and summer than in winter; as Wayne (1910) says, a forest of as much as 300 acres seldom contains more than three or four pairs. In the Low-country, roughly, a single pair inhabits a hundred acres.

It nests in mid-February, much earlier than do most small birds. The male is very attentive to his mate. The eggs are laid from early March to early April, usually in a deserted woodpecker hole, for the nuthatch is a cavity nester. Bark strips, feathers, and caterpillar silk are carried into the hole and arranged into a bed for the eggs. These usually number four or five and are profusely spotted with reddish-brown and lavender markings. They average 18.3 x 14.3 millimeters. Incubation requires twelve days.

Study of the White-breasted Nuthatch of South Carolina indicates that the northeastern race (*Sitta carolinensis cookei*) does not occur in the State even in the mountain region. Specimens from Caesar's Head, Greenville County, taken July 12, 1927, by R. H. Coleman, and from Montreat, North Carolina, September 9, 1923, by Sprunt, have been found by Dr. H. C. Oberholser to be referable to the Florida Nuthatch. All other specimens examined from South Carolina apparently belong to the same race.

FOOD: The favorite food of the Florida nuthatch is mast, acorns, hickory nuts, and beechnuts. The bird wedges the nuts into a crevice and hammers upon them with the beak until they are broken; hence the name "nuthatch." Nuthatches also eat corn, pine seeds, and sunflower seed, beetles, weevils, bugs, ants, flies, and caterpillars. Undoubtedly the birds are highly valuable in keeping tree-destroying insects under control.

266. RED-BREASTED NUTHATCH: *Sitta canadensis* Linnaeus (728)

(Lat., *canadensis*, of Canada.)

DESCRIPTION: Length 4.10 to 4.75 inches. Bill straight, thin, and pointed; tail short. Upper surface bluish gray, the crown black with a black stripe through the eye and a white one over it; chin and throat dull white to pale cinnamon; rest of undersurface tawny buff to ochraceous.

RANGE: Resident and breeds north to southeastern Alaska and Newfoundland; south to Guadalupe Island in Lower California and to western North Carolina.

STATUS IN S. C.: Rare and irregular winter resident, September 17 to April 28, casually June 10. Reported north to Greenville, Spartanburg, and York counties; east to Charleston County; south to Beaufort County; west to Aiken and Oconee counties.

HISTORY: The Red-breasted Nuthatch is the most uncommon, or at least erratic, of the three nuthatches occurring in South Carolina. Winter is the time of year in which it occurs. The usual departure dates are from middle to late March. The bird has been recorded only twice from Clemson, April 13, 1927 (G. E. Hudson), and April 17, 1931 (H. A. Rankin). Unusually late is a record made by John Kershaw at Walhalla on June 10, 1910. However, since the bird is known to nest in parts of the high mountains of North Carolina, this is not strange.

The Red-breast is a handsome little bird and may always be recognized, apart from the plumage coloring responsible for its name, by the black band through the eye, which its relatives lack. It seems partial to the barrier island woods on the coast, and is found in coniferous growths, pines and cedars mainly, where it feeds on the seeds of these trees in the usual nuthatch manner. The notes are higher pitched than those of the White-breast.

FOOD: Chiefly seeds, mainly of the pines in the coastal region.

BROWN-HEADED NUTHATCH
267. *Sitta pusilla pusilla* Latham (729)

(Lat., *pusilla*, very small.)

DESCRIPTION: Length 3.75 to 4.10 inches. Head and hind neck light grayish brown; a prominent white spot on hind neck; back and rump bluish gray; under parts dull white washed with buff.

RANGE: Resident and breeds north to southern Missouri and southern Delaware; south to southeastern Texas and southern Georgia.

STATUS IN S. C.: Fairly common permanent resident in most of the State. Known north to Greenville, York, and Dillon counties; east to Horry County; south to Beaufort County; west to Oconee County.

HISTORY: This is the smallest of the nuthatches found in South Carolina, and the most abundant. It is a permanent resident. Since it occurs only in open pinelands, one need look for it in no other places. It is a thoroughly characteristic bird of such growth, and associates in the Low-country with the Red-cockaded Woodpecker and Bachman's Sparrow.

The Brown-head's notes are at once recognizable as those of the family but at the same time are completely different. They are frequently uttered and constitute the best means of locating the bird. The note is no more than a chatter, sounding something like "cha-cha," with a high, somewhat nasal, rather squeaky tone. Often several birds call at the same time.

The Brown-head is a common nester and much easier to find than the White-breast. Mating is early, sometimes in late January, though mid-February is more nearly normal. The nest is in a hole which both the male and female dig. They usually choose a dead stub but they may select a fence post or a stump. Several holes may be begun and abandoned before the real nest cavity is completed. Wayne found this bird digging a hole on an island in the Wando River as early as January 20. Elevation is anywhere between a few inches from the ground to many feet above it, as high as 90 feet being known. The usual height, however, is between 15 and 25 feet. Wayne's lowest nest was 6 inches from the ground.

When the nest is completed, the birds carry in their favorite building material, the thin, transparent sheath which covers pine seeds, innumerable trips being necessary to secure a sufficient quantity. The eggs usually number five or six. They are white, covered with splashes of brown and lavender. They average 15.5 x 12.3 millimeters and incubation requires about fourteen days. Dates for eggs in Charleston County are March 12, fresh eggs; March 30, fresh eggs; April 17, six eggs; May 2, four eggs (Wayne); May 10, four eggs (Sprunt); Beaufort County, five eggs, April 7 (E. J. DeCamps). It will be noted that considerable irregularity exists in the time of this bird's nesting. Only one brood is raised and the young remain with the parents for some time, the species maintaining the family unit long after the nesting season. In this it resembles the Red-cockaded Woodpecker.

FOOD: Largely pine seeds on the coast, but also insects such as leaf beetles, wood borers, click beetles, grasshoppers, moths, ants, and scale insects. The bird is of high economic importance.

Family Certhiidae: Creepers

BROWN CREEPER
268. Certhia familiaris americana Bonaparte (726)

(Gr., Certhia, the tree creeper; Lat., familiaris, domestic; americana, of America.)

DESCRIPTION: Length 5.00 to 5.75 inches. Bill long, slender, and curved; tail feathers long, narrow, and sharply pointed. Head and back sepia brown, streaked with grayish white; rump tawny ochraceous; lower surface dull white, posteriorly tinged with buff; wings fuscous with dull white markings.

RANGE: Breeds north to southern Manitoba, southern Quebec, and Nova Scotia; south to central western Nebraska, southeastern Missouri, and northwestern New Jersey. Winters north to central Minnesota and Nova Scotia; south to southern Texas and southern Florida.

STATUS IN S. C.: Fairly common winter resident, October 2 to April 14, throughout the State. Reported north to Greenville and Florence counties, east to Horry County; south to Beaufort County; west to Aiken and Oconee counties.

HISTORY: This quiet, unobtrusive little bird might be termed a woodpecker-nuthatch, though related to neither. In its habits and behavior it resembles both of these birds, but it is so easily overlooked that casual observers seldom see it.

It is a winter resident in South Carolina and is always associated with cold weather. Severe winters produce them in numbers, though they come regularly every year whether the weather is mild or severe. They usually arrive about mid-October and remain until late March.

The Brown Creeper lives in either swampy woods or highlands. It is fond of pines when pines occur in mixed woods, and on the barrier islands it resorts to these trees more than to any others. Very solitary in its habits, so far as its own species is concerned, it yet may be seen at times near Kinglets, Chickadees, and Titmice. Its note is thin, so high as to be inaudible to some listeners. The call is very similar to that of the Golden-crowned Kinglet, and the two calls are sometimes difficult to distinguish.

Few birds give the impression of working harder to make a living than does this little brown laborer. Literally creeping about the trunks and limbs of trees, probing here and there amid the crannies of the bark, right side up or down, crosswise, sideways, it searches a tree from bottom to top. It hitches its way up a trunk like a miniature woodpecker, and reminds one of a nuthatch in the manner it clings to the underside of branches. The sepia-brown, white-streaked plumage is good camouflage against the trunks, particularly of pines, and were it not for the bird's almost incessant movement, it would be very hard to find. When finished with one tree, it flies to the base of another, and performs all over again.

FOOD: The creeper is largely insectivorous, taking beetles, bugs, caterpillars, wood borers, sawflies, flying ants, and some spiders. In winter it may eat the seeds of pines.

SOUTHERN CREEPER
269. *Certhia familiaris nigrescens* Burleigh (726f)

(Lat., *nigrescens*, blackish.)

DESCRIPTION: Similar to the Brown Creeper, but upper parts darker.

RANGE: Breeds north to West Virginia; south to eastern Tennessee and the mountains of western North Carolina. Winters south to South Carolina.

STATUS IN S. C.: Casual winter visitor in the southeastern section.

HISTORY: To the present time the only record of the Southern Creeper for South Carolina is a male specimen taken at Otranto in Charleston County on March 1,

1927, by Sprunt, and subsequently identified by Dr. John W. Aldrich. This bird is in the collection of the Charleston Museum.

The bird has the same habits as other races of the species.

Family Troglodytidae: Wrens

EASTERN HOUSE WREN
270. *Troglodytes aedon aedon* Vieillot (721)

(Gr., *Troglodytes*, a cave dweller; *aedon*, the nightingale.)

DESCRIPTION: Length 4.25 to 5.25 inches. Upper surface dull warm brown; the rump more rufescent; under parts dull white, the sides and flanks tinged with chestnut; tail dark brown narrowly barred with black; wings brown with narrow bars of buff and black.

RANGE: Breeds north to southern Quebec and northern New Brunswick; south to Virginia. Winters north to southern Louisiana and South Carolina; south to southern Florida.

STATUS IN S. C.: Uncommon winter resident, December 11 to March 7. Recorded from only the coast at Mt. Pleasant.

HISTORY: The Eastern House Wren, formerly supposed to be the common race in South Carolina, now proves to be of rather uncommon occurrence. In fact, only two specimens from the State are now available. Wayne took these at Mt. Pleasant on March 7, 1891, and on December 11, 1911. They have been identified by Dr. Harry C. Oberholser. These birds are in the Charleston Museum collection. In general habits and food this subspecies does not differ from the race common in South Carolina, the Ohio House Wren.

WESTERN HOUSE WREN
271. *Troglodytes aedon parkmanii* Audubon (721a)

(Lat., *parkmanii*, to George Parkman, of Boston, Mass.)

DESCRIPTION: Similar to the other South Carolina house wrens, but duller, lighter, and usually more grayish.

RANGE: Breeds north to southern British Columbia and southern Ontario; south to northwestern Lower California and southern Illinois. Winters north to central California and southern South Carolina; south to Mexico, and southern Florida.

STATUS IN S. C.: Accidental in winter in the coast region.

HISTORY: The Western House Wren is given place among South Carolina birds because of a specimen secured at Port Royal, Beaufort County, January 29, 1891, by J. E. Benedict, and identified by Dr. H. C. Oberholser (*Ohio Jour. Sci., 34*: 1934, 95).

In habits and food it is not different from the other house wrens.

Ohio House Wren
272. *Troglodytes aedon baldwini* Oberholser (721b)

(Lat., *baldwini*, to Samuel Prentiss Baldwin, of Cleveland, Ohio.)

LOCAL NAMES: Jenny Wren.

DESCRIPTION: Similar to the Eastern House Wren but darker, duller, and less rufescent (more grayish).

RANGE: Breeds north to Michigan and southwestern Quebec; south to Kentucky and eastern North Carolina. Winters north to central Louisiana and South Carolina; south to Texas and southeastern Georgia.

STATUS IN S. C.: Winter resident, September 15 to May 5, common in the eastern, rare in the western portion of the State, in which latter area it is mostly a common transient. Reported north to Greenville and Chester counties; east to Horry County; south to Beaufort and Jasper counties; west to Aiken, Greenwood, and Oconee counties.

HISTORY: The Ohio House Wren is a winter resident in South Carolina, and it is much more common on the coast than in the interior, being positively uncommon in the upper Piedmont. Its stay in the State is lengthy, for it arrives in mid-September and remains until late April. It is abundant both on the coastal islands and on the mainland, frequenting tangles of vines, brush heaps, undergrowth, and hedgerows in either open or wooded country. It is by no means a shy bird but is often difficult to see, because of its constant dodging in and out of the thick cover which it always haunts. The characteristic, scolding notes sound as if the bird were greatly annoyed at being followed and peered at. The tail is frequently carried cocked over the back in typical wren fashion.

Recent years have added much to our knowledge of the distribution of this house wren. From present collections in South Carolina it now appears that this is the common house wren of the State, both the other races being rare or at least uncommon. Among the specimens that have been examined from the State and identified by Dr. Harry C. Oberholser these may be mentioned: Mt. Pleasant, March 8, and February 21, 1922, Wayne; Huger, October 10, 1941, and October 25, 1930, E. von S. Dingle; Charleston, January 10, 1891, J. E. Benedict; Charleston Navy Yard, April 12, 1907, H. R. Sass; Isle of Palms, November 20, 1924, Chamberlain; Allendale, October 22, 24, and 26, 1940, W. M. Perrygo and J. S. Webb; and Gray's Hill in Beaufort County, March 31, 1937, W. H. Corning.

FOOD: Its food habits are entirely beneficial, as it takes animal matter almost exclusively, the bulk of which is insects. Bugs (*Hemiptera*) compose the largest item, 30 per cent of the total, with stinkbugs and leaf hoppers in large numbers.

WRENS

EASTERN WINTER WREN
273. *Troglodytes troglodytes hiemalis* Vieillot (722)

(Lat., *hiemalis*, of winter.)

DESCRIPTION: Length 3.50 to 4.25 inches. The smallest species of the South Carolina wrens. Tail short. Upper parts rufescent brown; lower surface wood brown to cinnamon, vermiculated and speckled with dark brown, very heavily on the abdomen.

RANGE: Breeds north to central Alberta and Newfoundland; south to central Minnesota and Rhode Island. Winters north to central eastern Nebraska and southern Maine; south to Texas and central Florida.

STATUS IN S. C.: Fairly common winter resident, September 22 to April 24, over most of the State. Reported north to Greenville, Chester, and Florence counties; east to Horry County; south to Yemassee; west to Aiken and Oconee counties.

HISTORY: This tiny creature is so small that one can mistake it for a mouse darting into a brush pile. The very dark color and ridiculously short tail will distinguish it from all our other wrens.

It is, as its name indicates, a winter resident in South Carolina. It lives in the tangled thickets and underbrush of wooded areas. Because it is so diminutive and because it dwells in such inaccessible places, it is a difficult bird to observe. It can, however, sometimes be lured from its dense retreats by the "squeak." It sings occasionally during its South Carolina sojourn; its song is surpassingly beautiful.

FOOD: Like the other members of its family the Eastern Winter Wren subsists chiefly on insects.

SOUTHERN WINTER WREN
274. *Troglodytes troglodytes pullus* (Burleigh) (722g)

(Lat., *pullus*, dark-colored.)

DESCRIPTION: Length 3.50 to 4.25 inches. Similar to the Eastern Winter Wren, but upper surface darker, less rufescent, and posterior under parts more heavily barred and vermiculated.

RANGE: Breeds in the southern Allegheny Mountains north to western Virginia; south to northern Georgia. Winters south to Louisiana and southern Georgia.

STATUS IN S. C.: Rare winter resident, October 29 to January 30, in the middle part of the State probably also elsewhere. Recorded from Lee, Kershaw, and Allendale counties.

HISTORY: The only specimens of the Southern Winter Wren thus far available from South Carolina are as follows: Kershaw County, January 30, 1904, collected by N. C. Brown; Lynchburg, November 9, 1940, by W. M. Perrygo and J. S. Webb; and Allendale, October 29, 1940, obtained by the same two collectors. Since it breeds so near South Carolina, there is every reason to believe that it is more frequent in this State than the records indicate.

In habits and food it does not differ materially from the common race in South Carolina, the Eastern Winter Wren.

BEWICK'S WREN
275. *Thryomanes bewickii bewickii* (Audubon) (719)

(Gr., *Thryomanes*, reed-seeking; Lat., *bewickii*, to Thomas Bewick, the English ornithologist.)

DESCRIPTION: Similar to the Appalachian Bewick's Wren, but upper parts decidedly more rufescent.

RANGE: Resident and breeds north to south central Nebraska and central northern Illinois; south to northeastern Texas and northwestern Tennessee. Winters south also to southeastern Texas and northwestern Florida.

STATUS IN S. C.: Casual winter visitor. Recorded from only the coast region.

HISTORY: Evidence of the occurrence of Bewick's Wren in South Carolina rests at the present time on a single specimen, in the Charleston Museum, taken at the Charleston Navy Yard on October 17, 1907, by H. R. Sass and identified by Dr. John W. Aldrich of the U. S. Fish and Wildlife Service.

In habits and food it does not materially differ from the Appalachian Bewick's Wren.

APPALACHIAN BEWICK'S WREN
276. *Thryomanes bewickii altus* Aldrich (719m)

(Lat., *altus*, high.)

DESCRIPTION: Length 5.00 to 5.50 inches. Tail long and much rounded. Upper surface plain warm dark brown (mummy brown); lower surface grayish white; a white line over the eye; and the outer tail feathers tipped with grayish white.

RANGE: Resident and breeds north to central northern Ohio and northeastern Pennsylvania; south to central Alabama and central South Carolina. Winters also south to northeastern Texas and northern Florida.

STATUS IN S. C.: Uncommon permanent resident in the central and northwestern parts of the State; rare winter resident, September 22 to March 19, in the remainder of the State. As a breeding bird, reported north to Greenville; east to Chester; south to Aiken; west to Oconee and Pickens counties.

HISTORY: The Appalachian Bewick's Wren is the form of Bewick's Wren which breeds in South Carolina. Hence, all sight records of Bewick's Wren for the State are here listed as Appalachian. Because of the close similarity of the two subspecies,

---

PLATE XXII: WRENS AND KINGLETS
Water Color by Edward von S. Dingle

Six upper birds, left to right: Worthington's Marsh Wren, Wayne's Marsh Wren, Long-billed Marsh Wren, Prairie Marsh Wren, Golden-crowned Kinglet (male), and Golden-crowned Kinglet (female). Five lower birds, left to right: Carolina Wren, Short-billed Marsh Wren, House Wren, Ruby-crowned Kinglet (female), and Ruby-crowned Kinglet (male).

it is possible that a few of the wrens observed in the field and reported in the records were actually Bewick's Wrens.

Bewick's Wren, unlike the House and the Long-billed Wrens, belongs to the interior rather than to the coastal sections of the State. It is a permanent resident of upper South Carolina and nests there. Indicative of its rarity on the coast is the fact that Wayne established only six records of the bird in eighteen years (1907-1925). Five of these records were made in October, one in December. The latter is a specimen taken on December 27, 1925, near Mt. Pleasant, recently identified by Dr. John W. Aldrich. Other observers added to the records during the same period: F. M. Weston saw a Bewick's Wren on December 28; Edward A. Hyer, one on September 22; E. von S. Dingle, one on October 10.

Since 1925, the bird has been recorded near the coast on January 30 (Sprunt and F. M. Weston) and on December 29 (E. B. and B. R. Chamberlain). Such records give the bird a rare winter resident status on the coast. Actually, it is not common anywhere below the fall line.

What is known of Bewick's Wren as a breeding bird in upper South Carolina is based upon the work of L. M. Loomis, many years ago; on records made by John Kershaw, Jr.; on the work of Dr. E. E. Murphey; and on observations by George E. Hudson and the late Prof. Franklin Sherman in the vicinity of Clemson. Loomis recorded Bewick's Wren as an uncommon breeder in Chester County and found it in the summer at both Mt. Pinnacle and Caesar's Head. Kershaw recorded it as a summer resident at Walhalla, Oconee County, and discovered a nest in a hole in an apple tree in June, 1910. Hudson called it a permanent resident in the Clemson region (*Auk*, 47: 1930, 398). Murphey also called it a permanent resident, although uncommon, in the Aiken-Augusta section. He reported finding only two nests.

Like other wrens, Bewick's makes its home in thick tangles of vines, brush heaps, and hedgerows. However, it comes freely to dwelling houses and often nests near them, choosing nesting sites similar to those of the more familiar Carolina Wren. Though it is much like the Carolina Wren in appearance, it is smaller, and its long, rounded tail, the outer feathers of which are tipped with white, provides a characteristic which certainly distinguishes it.

Bewick's Wren builds its nest in natural cavities, bird boxes, fence posts, even in tin cans or discarded water pitchers or on the rafters of outhouses. There are usually five to seven white eggs, speckled with reddish brown. The eggs average 16.4 x 12.7 millimeters. The bird raises two broods a season and incubation requires about fourteen days.

Food: About 97 per cent animal matter, chiefly insects, among which are boll weevils, beetles, caterpillars, moths, grasshoppers, and flies. This wren is a valuable bird and deserves encouragement about homes, gardens, and farms.

CAROLINA WREN
277. *Thryothorus ludovicianus ludovicianus* (Latham) (718)

(Gr., *Thryothorus*, reed-jumping; Lat., *ludovicianus*, of Louisiana.)

DESCRIPTION: Length 5.00 to 6.00 inches. Upper parts plain chestnut brown; a white line over the eye extending back to the side of the nape; undersurface varying from buff to white; wings and tail with fine barring of dull black.

RANGE: Resident and breeds north to southeastern Michigan, eastern Ohio, and southern Virginia; south to southeastern Texas and northern Florida.

STATUS IN S. C.: Common permanent resident throughout the State. Recorded north to Greenville, York, and Marlboro counties; east to Horry County; south to Beaufort County; west to Aiken and Oconee counties.

HISTORY: The Carolina Wren is the official State Bird of South Carolina. It would be hard to imagine a better choice. It carries Carolina in its name; it is a permanent resident in every county; it is friendly and companionable; its song is melodious and universally appealing; and it sings practically the year round.

Bird songs are notoriously difficult to describe, but the song of the Carolina Wren sounds to many people like "tea-kettle-tea-kettle-tea-kettle." It must be admitted that the bird, tame as it is, is more often heard than seen, for it seems to object to close scrutiny and will scold from the midst of a thicket in tantalizingly close proximity to an observer.

The Carolina Wren raises three broods a year, most of them successfully. The high percentage of success which attends its reproduction is undoubtedly due to the fact that it trustfully builds its nest close to houses and that its sympathetic human neighbors give it scrupulous protection. A bird box in the yard, the rafters of the garage, a shelf in the tool house or on the back porch are all acceptable sites. Sprunt once saw a nest in a mayonnaise jar which had been placed on the window sill of a back porch at Bull's Island. The jar, with the bird in it, could be picked up, looked at, and replaced. Another remarkable nesting site, reported by Thomas Rivers, was a porch light. Unfortunately, when the light was turned on the eggs roasted.

In spite of its inclination to nest near human dwellings, the Carolina Wren lives also in the deepest swamps, the thick jungles of the barrier islands, and the edges of Piedmont cotton fields and woodlands.

The nest is made of grasses and leaves, pine needles, hair, and feathers. The eggs number from four to six and are of a whitish color, much spotted with lilac and brownish markings. They average 19.1 x 14.9 millimeters and incubation requires fourteen days. Chamberlain watched a nest in a flower stand on his porch, from the time the site was chosen to the leaving of the young, a period from April 2 to May 15. The bird spent eight days building the nest, then laid five eggs on successive days. Chamberlain noted that there were periods after 11 p. m. when the incubating bird was not on the eggs.

On the coast the Carolina Wren starts to nest in late March and early April; April 4 (Wayne) and April 6 (E. J. DeCamps) are typical dates. Eggs of the second and third broods appear in early June and mid-July respectively. Very early fall line dates are March 6 and 24, Richland County (Mrs. W. H. Faver). Breeding in the Piedmont is understandably later.

FOOD: The Carolina Wren is of immense value to agriculture. Nearly 95 per cent of the food is animal matter, practically all insects. Caterpillars and moths make up 21 per cent, and bugs 19 per cent. Beetles, grasshoppers, boll weevils, crickets, ants, and flies are included, and spiders account for 10.5 per cent. The bird also sometimes eats lizards, tree frogs, and small snails.

LONG-BILLED MARSH WREN
278. *Telmatodytes palustris palustris* (Wilson) (725)

(Gr., *Telmatodytes*, swamp-dweller; Lat., *palustris*, pertaining to a marsh.)

DESCRIPTION: Length 4.12 to 5.50 inches. Head, hind neck, and back brownish black, the back narrowly streaked with white; line over the eye white; under parts white, finely washed with pale brown on breast, the sides and flanks light brown; tail with narrow black bars.

RANGE: Breeds north to Connecticut; south to Virginia. Winters south to Texas and southern Florida.

STATUS IN S. C.: Common winter resident, September 29 to May 19, in the coast region. Recorded from Berkeley and Charleston counties. Probably occurs in all the coastal counties during the winter.

HISTORY: This is the species from which all other races of long-billed marsh wrens have been separated. Because of their variations in color and breeding range, these forms are of more interest to the advanced student than to the general observer. In the field, all are very similar in appearance; in most cases they can be identified only if they can be captured and compared with specimens already identified.

The Long-bill arrives in September and remains well into May. Living strictly up to the literal meaning of its scientific name, this tiny brown bird is a real marsh dweller. It inhabits fresh- and salt-water marshes, and it is quite useless to look for it anywhere else.

The bird is remarkably tame during the winter and in the coastal section has been known to come into duck blinds or boats and to hop about unconcernedly within arm's reach. Occasionally, it will perch on one's gun barrel, ammunition box, or even the toe of a rubber boot. It is vivacious and appears to be utterly fearless.

Since this wren is difficult to differentiate in the field from the other races of this species, the records of specimens are of primary importance. Some of these specimens, identified by Dr. Harry C. Oberholser, follow: Charleston, October 21, 1925, collected by J. R. Paul, Jr.; Huger, October 13 and November 13, 1930, by E. von S. Dingle; Mt. Pleasant, April 28, 1916, September 29, 1917, and May 19, 1921, by Wayne.

FOOD: The long-billed marsh wrens are almost wholly insectivorous. Diving and click beetles, weevils, water bugs, ants, wasps, damsel and dragon flies, spiders, and moths make up the bulk.

WORTHINGTON'S MARSH WREN
279. *Telmatodytes palustris griseus* (Brewster) (725b)

(Lat., *griseus*, gray.)

LOCAL NAMES: Tomtit.

DESCRIPTION: Length about 3.90 to 5.00 inches. Similar to the Long-billed Marsh Wren but above and below paler and much more grayish, the dark markings nearly absent or at least much reduced.

RANGE: Resident and breeds coastwise north to South Carolina; south to northeastern Florida.

STATUS IN S. C.: Common permanent resident on the coast. Recorded north to Horry County; south to Beaufort and Jasper counties; inland to Berkeley County.

HISTORY: Worthington's Marsh Wren is known to more people than any other member of the long-billed marsh wren group. To many a small boy in water-front towns it is the "Tomtit." But it is to be found only along the coast, and its home is the vast reaches of the salt marshes, where it lives in the company of the Clapper Rail and the Sharp-tailed Sparrow. It is a permanent resident of South Carolina from the mouth of the Santee River southward along the coast. It is a common bird in communities along the Inland Waterway and makes its home virtually in the back yards of residences in such towns. It breeds within the city limits of Charleston in the marshes near the Ashley River Bridge, within a few yards of heavy, steady traffic.

There is much variation in the breeding season. Wayne gives the usual egg-laying period as "the last few days in June," but he also says that in some forward seasons the eggs may be found in mid-May. The earliest recorded date for eggs is April 23 (Sprunt). Worthington's Marsh Wren raises three broods a season, hence eggs in July are not uncommon and Wayne has found them as late as August 9.

The nest is a globular structure of salt marsh grass with the entrance hole on the side, attached to the stems of growing marsh, often near the edges of creeks or "gutters" which wind through the grasses. It is a curious habit of the bird to construct several dummy nests in the vicinity of the one holding the eggs. The eggs, which are very small, number from four to six, and are a dark chocolate color, though occasionally one may be found that is practically white. The eggs average 15.4 x 11.2 millimeters. Incubation takes about thirteen days.

Nests, eggs, and young frequently come to grief because of natural catastrophes such as high spring tides, tropical storms, and, as Wayne points out, the predation of mice which live in the marsh. High water is the most frequent cause of loss. After such flooding, nests remain soggy, with mud on and around the eggs.

Anyone who cares to penetrate its haunts and is prepared to wade through mud can easily find this little wren. It comes to the "squeak" readily and can sometimes be studied dry-shod. Certainly it can be easily heard, for its voice is one of its outstanding characteristics. It is a persistent singer, not only through the day but often at night. It has been heard at practically every hour from dusk to dawn. Both the authors live in close proximity to salt marsh and have heard this wren singing at midnight as vivaciously as at sunrise or noon. The song is difficult to describe, but it has a distinctly bubbling character and is delivered with intensity and fervor, often on the wing. Worthington's Marsh Wrens are fairly gregarious and nest in what might be called loose colonies, though single nests are not uncommon. Tropical hurricanes at times destroy great numbers of the birds, and in seasons following there may be a comparative scarcity such as Wayne mentions after the severe storm of 1893. The 1911 hurricane was followed by a similar scarcity.

FOOD: Similar to that of the Long-billed Marsh Wren.

ALBERTA MARSH WREN
280. *Telmatodytes palustris iliacus* Ridgway   (725f)

(Lat., *iliacus*, pertaining to the flank.)

DESCRIPTION: Similar to the Prairie Marsh Wren but upper parts, flanks, and sides lighter, more ochraceous (less rufescent).

RANGE: Breeds in Alberta and western Saskatchewan. Winters south to Mexico, accidentally to South Carolina.

STATUS IN S. C.: Accidental winter visitor in the coast region.

HISTORY: The only specimens of this marsh wren that have yet been obtained within the confines of South Carolina are two collected by Wayne at Mt. Pleasant on October 24 and 31, 1914, respectively, and identified by Dr. H. C. Oberholser. They are in the collection of the Charleston Museum.

In habits and food it is similar to the other marsh wrens.

PRAIRIE MARSH WREN
281. *Telmatodytes palustris dissaëptus* Bangs   (725d)

(Lat., *dissaëptus*, having different young.)

DESCRIPTION: Similar to the Long-billed Marsh Wren but above and below darker, more rufescent.

RANGE: Breeds north to North Dakota and southern New Brunswick; south to Ohio and Massachusetts. Winters north to Massachusetts; south to Texas and southern Florida.

STATUS IN S. C.: Common winter resident, September 12 to May 26, in the extreme eastern part of the State; an uncommon transient, chiefly in April, in the western part. Recorded in the eastern section, north to Huger, Berkeley County; east to Charleston; south to Yemassee; west to Aiken County. In migration in the western section of the State, recorded north to Greenville County; east to Chester County; and west to Oconee County.

HISTORY: In South Carolina the number of Prairie Marsh Wrens is apparently exceeded only by Worthington's Marsh Wren. Unlike the Worthington's it lives in both salt water and fresh water habitats.

Some of the specimens of the Prairie Marsh Wren that have been recently identified by Dr. H. C. Oberholser are as follows: Huger, May 26, 1932, October 14 and

19, 1930, October 27, and November 3 and 8, 1942; Charleston, September 24, 1938, all collected by E. von S. Dingle; Yemassee, January 28, 1888, and Mt. Pleasant, September 12, 1917, Wayne; Clemson College, April 13 and 25, 1927, G. E. Hudson and F. Sherman; and McClellanville, November 30, 1940, W. M. Perrygo and J. S. Webb.

WAYNE'S MARSH WREN
282.   *Telmatodytes palustris waynei* Dingle and Sprunt   (725i)

(Lat., *waynei*, to Arthur Trezevant Wayne.)

DESCRIPTION: Similar to the Long-billed Marsh Wren of the eastern states but smaller and much darker, particularly on the upper parts and sides.

RANGE: Resident and breeds north to eastern Virginia; south to eastern North Carolina. Winters also south to southeastern Georgia.

STATUS IN S. C.: Winter resident, probably fairly common, September 14 to May 8, casually May 26, in the coast region. Identified north to McClellanville; south to Charleston.

HISTORY: The wrens of the genus *Telmatodytes* are, as Wayne said years ago, "a puzzling group." Specimens of this form he believed to be representatives of *T. p. marianae* (Marian's Marsh Wren) which is a race living and nesting on the west coast of Florida, from St. Marks to Tampa Bay (Howell). Wayne secured one near Mt. Pleasant, on April 16, 1897, which he recorded as the first for the Atlantic Coast; others followed in 1898-99 (*Auk, 16*: 1899, 361). It is one of the darkest races of the entire species, and, as Wayne then pointed out, nested on the North Carolina coast.

Wayne considered it a winter visitor to South Carolina, arriving in September, his earliest record being September 16. The birds remain through the entire winter as has been subsequently established, but Wayne thought that the majority migrated about November 1. His latest record in spring was May 8, but in 1932, E. von S. Dingle took one on the Cooper River on May 26, which is the latest date.

On the North Carolina nesting grounds, Dr. T. Gilbert Pearson took specimens in May and August, 1898, both of which were pronounced Worthington's Marsh Wren by Robert Ridgway and C. S. Brimley, each of whom had one bird for examination. Wayne differed with these authorities after seeing the birds himself, and stated that they were *marianae*. This identification stood for thirty-three years.

In 1932, E. von S. Dingle and Sprunt, after studying the matter and comparing specimens, concluded that the dark breeding bird of North Carolina could not possibly be *marianae*, as the range of that form had definitely been established as the coast of Alabama and west Florida (A. H. Howell and H. E. Wheeler). The Atlantic Coast bird was, therefore, without a name, and it was proposed that it be called for Wayne who had predicted in 1899 that the dark bird which he then secured would prove to be an Atlantic Coast breeder (*Auk, 49*: 1932, 454). Pearson and the Brimleys, as a result, recorded it as Wayne's Marsh Wren (*Birds of North Carolina*, 1942, 260).

Specimens from South Carolina recently identified by Dr. H. C. Oberholser include the following: Mt. Pleasant, October 20, 1918, collected by Wayne; Charleston, October 14, 1931, by R. N. S. Whitelaw; from the same locality, September 14, 1911, by Chamberlain; and McClellanville, November 25, 1940, by W. M. Perrygo and J. S. Webb.

The form breeds northward from the southern North Carolina coast into the Back Bay area of Virginia. It lives in the salt marsh, and its nesting, behavior, and food are not dissimilar to other members of the species.

SHORT-BILLED MARSH WREN
283. *Cistothorus platensis stellaris* (Naumann) (724)

(Gr., *Cistothorus*, shrub-jumping; Lat., *platensis*, of the Plata [River, Argentina]; *stellaris*, starry.)

DESCRIPTION: Length 3.75 to 4.50 inches. Upper surface largely light brown, narrowly streaked with brownish black, the head darker with a pale buff eyebrow stripe; under parts white with cinnamon on the chest, sides, and flanks.

RANGE: Breeds north to southeastern Saskatchewan and central Maine; south to southern Kansas and southern Maryland. Winters north to southern Illinois and southern New York; south to southeastern Mexico and southern Florida.

STATUS IN S. C.: Fairly common winter resident, September 12 to May 15, over most of the State; more numerous, however, coastwise. Reported north to Spartanburg and Chester counties; east to Horry County; south to Beaufort County; west to Aiken County.

HISTORY: The Short-billed Marsh Wren shares with the Winter Wren and the kinglets the distinction of being smaller than any other bird except the hummingbird. Unlike them, however, it is not as well known, for it dislikes the open and is sometimes as hard to find as any bird could well be.

Showing completely different choice of habitat from that of its long-billed relatives, the Short-bill lives only near fresh water, which on the coast may or may not be close to salt water. Sometimes it lives in densely grass-grown embankments which actually separate fresh from salt water, such as rice-field dykes or dams like those on some of the barrier islands. It will often respond to the "squeak" and at such times it seems to be entirely without fear, coming to within a foot or two of an observer when he stands perfectly still. Balancing on a grass stem, the tiny tail cocked up, and the bright, pin-point eyes peering inquisitively, it makes an attractive sight. Most of the time, however, all one can see of it is a flash of brown among the reeds.

The Short-bill is a winter visitor, arriving in the coast area, where it is most common, in September and remaining until the middle of May. R. G. Kuerzi listed it near Myrtle Beach "only as a rare migrant late fall and early winter." The Short-bill's known distribution in the interior is rather sketchy, probably because there are fewer suitable habitats and fewer observers inland. There are several records for the Santee Refuge in Clarendon County, where suitable marshes exist. The Short-bill has been recorded at Spartanburg by Gabriel Cannon. It has been found as early as

September 18 (L. M. Loomis) and as late as December 25 (William Neely) in Chester County. Murphey (1937) called it a winter visitor in the Aiken-Augusta region, and said that it stayed at least until the middle of May.

FOOD: Almost exclusively insects and spiders. Ants, weevils, beetles, moths, caterpillars, locusts, crickets, and grasshoppers make up the bulk of its diet.

Family Mimidae: Mockingbirds and Thrashers

EASTERN MOCKINGBIRD
284. *Mimus polyglottos polyglottos* (Linnaeus) (703)

(Lat., *Mimus*, a mimic; *polyglottos*, many-tongued.)

LOCAL NAMES: Mocker.

DESCRIPTION: Length 9.00 to 11.00 inches. Upper parts brownish gray; undersurface dull white or pale gray; wings and tail dull black, the wings each with a conspicuous white patch; outer tail feathers white.

RANGE: Resident and breeds north to eastern Nebraska and Massachusetts; south to southeastern Texas, southern Florida, and the Bahama Islands.

STATUS IN S. C.: Abundant permanent resident in all the State. Observed north to Greenville, Lancaster, and Marion counties; east to Horry County; south to Beaufort County; west to Oconee County.

HISTORY: If there is any bird in South Carolina which needs no introduction, it is the Eastern Mockingbird. Though the area of its greatest abundance is the coastal plain, it occurs everywhere in the State, from the coast to the mountain border. It is unrivalled in general popularity except, perhaps, by the Cardinal, and everyone will probably agree that as a singer the Mockingbird has no superior. Because it is so well known and well liked it is virtually inviolate even to the predatory small boy.

The Mockingbird is to be found everywhere—in country hedgerows, in woodland thickets, and in dooryards of villages, towns, and cities. The upland cotton fields and the magnolia and palmetto jungles of the barrier islands all resound with its melodies. Alert, trim, and vigorous, the mocker has no bright feathers, but it makes up, in overflowing measure, whatever it lacks in beauty by its superb ability in song. Its own song is enhanced and multiplied by that of any other bird which inhabits the same area, for no bird call seems beyond its power to imitate. There are few birds for which the translation of the scientific name is so appropriate or descriptive, for the Mocker is indeed a "many-tongued mimic."

It sings much of the year, even on mild days in winter. July and August are the months in which it is most likely to be silent. It often sings at night, especially in spring during moonlight. Cloudy nights do not deter it; Chamberlain, for example, heard a Mocker "singing persistently" a quarter of an hour before midnight on March 10, 1948, when the sky was dark and cloudy and the thermometer stood at 50° F.

The nesting season begins early in April, the first eggs of the first brood usually being laid about the second week of that month. The second brood appears in June and the third in late July or early August. There are, of course, seasonal variations. An instance of very early nesting was recorded in 1945, when on March 15 Fred Wehman found a completed but empty nest in his yard on Gadsden Street, Charleston. The first egg appeared on the seventeenth and there were three on the nineteenth. The nest had probably been started on March 8 to 10.

The nest is built at low elevations (usually between 3 and 10 feet above the ground) in bushes or trees, vines, hedgerows, and ornamental shrubbery. Small sticks, twigs, leaves, and vine tendrils provide building materials; the inner lining is formed of rootlets. The Mocker defends its nest with great vigor even against human intruders and invariably against mammals, other birds, and reptiles. The eggs number from three to five, are greenish blue, spotted and splashed with reddish brown, and average 24.3 x 18.3 millimeters. Incubation requires about fourteen days.

One curious and noteworthy bit of behavior on the part of the Mockingbird is its habit, when it is on the ground, of raising the wings repeatedly, in a kind of dance. Various theories have been advanced to account for the action; that it is a means of startling insects into activity; that it is a recrudescence of courtship performance; even that it is "an outflow of surplus energy and exuberance" (Eifrig, *Fla. Nat.*, *21*, 75).

Food: The Mockingbird's diet is chiefly vegetable; berries (of the palmetto, the wax myrtle, the gall berry, and the butterfly bush), figs, and wild fruit form the bulk of its food. On the coast in winter it subsists largely on the chinaberry (Pride of India). It consumes only a few insects (termites and spiders, on occasion).

285. Catbird: *Dumetella carolinensis* (Linnaeus) (704)

(Lat., *Dumetella*, a little thicket; *carolinensis*, of Carolina.)

Description: Length 8.00 to 9.00 inches. Crown black, the remaining upper parts slate gray; under tail coverts chestnut, the rest of the lower surface slate gray; tail black.

Range: Breeds north to British Columbia and Nova Scotia; south to southeastern Texas and central Florida. Winters north to northern Iowa (casually) and southern Maine (casually).

Status in S. C.: Common permanent resident in the eastern section; rare in summer coastwise; common summer resident, March 15 to October 14, in the western part of the State. As a permanent resident, reported north to Florence and Dillon counties; east to Horry County; south to Beaufort and Jasper counties; west to Aiken County and Columbia. As a summer resident recorded north to Greenville and Chester counties; east to Kershaw County; south to Greenwood County; west to Oconee County.

History: The Catbird is a familiar species and a permanent resident in South Carolina, but is not common in the Low-country in summer. It is not as conspicuous as either the Mockingbird or the Thrasher, its close relatives. It lives in thickets (the fact being reflected in its generic name), and is fond of tangles and underbrush, from which its rather querulous, mewing note is often heard before the bird is seen. It is abundant in the migrations and common in winter on the coast. Up-state, the Catbird is a summer resident. G. E. Hudson gave the dates of its stay at Clemson as April 17 to October 14. In winter the Catbird probably ranges no farther inland than the Columbia region; winter records increase from there to the coast.

The Catbird breeds but sparingly on the coast. Wayne found a nest with four eggs in a yard in Charleston in May, 1879 or 1880. W. S. Allan, Jr., found a nest with three fresh eggs on Sullivan's Island on June 30, 1910, and E. von S. Dingle found the bird breeding at Mt. Pleasant on June 10, 1940, and during the next two succeeding summers. A Greenville County date is May 14, four eggs (E. J. DeCamps).

The nest is made of twigs, lined with rootlets, and placed in low bushes, vines, or crotches of trees, usually at no great elevation. The greatest height for a nest in South Carolina was one at Manning which was 35 feet from the ground (W. M. Levi). There are normally four eggs, of a very dark, greenish blue, without marks, and averaging 23.3 x17.5 millimeters. As many as three broods are raised and incubation requires about twelve or thirteen days.

The song of the Catbird is pleasing but it is not heard very often on the coast. Occasionally one may hear what has been called its "whisper song," when the bird, sitting in a thicket, sings faintly but sweetly. The Catbird is sober-plumaged, its gray body very inconspicuous among the shadows of the sun-splashed undergrowth in which it lives. The patch of chestnut under the tail constitutes a good field characteristic.

Food: Examination of 645 stomachs of Catbirds by the U. S. Fish and Wildlife Service shows the food to be 44 per cent animal, and 56 per cent vegetable matter. It eats wild fruits and berries, together with some cultivated varieties.

Brown Thrasher
286. *Toxostoma rufum rufum* (Linnaeus) (705)

(Gr., *Toxostoma*, bow-mouthed; Lat., *rufum*, reddish.)

Local Names: Brown Thrush; Trasher.

Description: Length 10.25 to 12.00 inches. Upper parts, wings, and tail cinnamon rufous; undersurface white or buffy white, the breast and sides broadly streaked with dark brown.

Range: Breeds north to southern Manitoba and northern Maine; south to southeastern Texas and southern Florida. Winters north to southeastern Missouri, southern Michigan (casually), and Massachusetts (casually); south to southern Texas and southern Florida.

Status in S. C.: Common permanent resident throughout the State. Observed north to Greenville, Chester, and Dillon counties; east to Horry County; south to Beaufort County; west to Oconee County.

History: The bird which most people call the "Brown Thrush" should be one of the best-known birds of South Carolina, for it is a permanent resident, occurs everywhere in the State, and nests virtually at one's front door.

The Brown Thrasher, which is closely akin to both Catbird and Mockingbird, is an excellent songster. Wayne (1910) said that "To my ear the song . . . is sweeter, richer, and wilder than the Mockingbird, and as a musician he is simply incomparable." The bird has been heard in full song at Columbia, February 25, during snow (Mrs. G. E. Charles), and even as early as February 1 at Summerville (M. P. Skinner).

When it is singing, the Brown Thrasher selects an elevated perch; otherwise it is a low-ranging bird. It frequents bushes, vines, tangled thickets, and hedgerows, and spends much time on the ground. It expresses resentment of intrusion upon its haunts by a very harsh and unmusical scolding note. Howell (1932) renders it as "a sharp, smacking 'tchat'" sounding like the click of a hedge shears; Peterson (1947) calls it a "harsh chack." Certainly, it has a most impatient and annoyed quality.

The character of the bird is completely in keeping with the impression given by this scolding note, and it is also suggested by the yellow-white iris, which gives the bird a very forbidding expression. It does not hesitate to attack even human intruders about its nest, frequently flying full into one's face in the most determined manner and "cursing" vehemently.

The nest is at low elevations in bushes, tangled vines, shrubbery, and brier patches. It is made of twigs, and lined with black rootlets. The Thrasher lays three to five greenish-white eggs, thickly covered with fine, reddish dots, and averaging 26.5 x 19.4 millimeters. Full sets are normally laid by the middle of May, but there are wide variations in time. W. M. Levi reported a nest with one fresh egg as late as July 7 at Sumter. A nest and three eggs were brought to Wayne on April 7 in Charleston County. Day-old young have been seen on James Island, April 17, the parent taking food from the observer's hand and giving it to the young (Mrs. Francis Barrington). Three broods may be raised, Wayne said, and incubation takes eleven to fourteen days.

Numbers of Thrashers come south in the fall, so that the general population is much increased at that time and remains large through the winter.

FOOD: Examination of 636 stomachs by the U. S. Fish and Wildlife Service show that the diet is 64 per cent vegetable and 36 per cent animal matter. Acorns make up about a quarter of the vegetable food, wild fruit about one-fifth, and cultivated fruit, 12 per cent.

Family Turdidae: Thrushes and Bluebirds

EASTERN ROBIN
287. *Turdus migratorius migratorius* Linnaeus (761)

(Lat., *Turdus*, a thrush; *migratorius*, migratory.)

DESCRIPTION: Length 9.00 to 10.75 inches. *Adult.* Top and sides of head black; remainder of upper parts mouse gray; tail black, the outer feathers tipped with white; throat white streaked with black; posterior lower parts white; the remainder of the undersurface cinnamon rufous. *Immature.* Similar to the adult but duller, below paler or white, much spotted and streaked with dark brown.

RANGE: Breeds north to northwestern Alaska and northern Labrador; south to central southern Alaska, Kansas, western North Carolina, and New Jersey. Winters north to northeastern South Dakota and Nova Scotia; south to Texas and southern Florida.

STATUS IN S. C.: Common winter resident, October 25 to March 25. Positively recorded only in the southern and eastern sections, but doubtless occurs elsewhere in the State.

HISTORY: This is the robin of the northeastern part of the United States and southeastern Canada, except Newfoundland. It comes to South Carolina in winter, probably greatly augmenting the population of the local robins at that season.

Dr. H. C. Oberholser has examined and identified the following specimens: Mc-Clellanville, November 22, 1940, collected by W. M. Perrygo and J. S. Webb; Allendale, October 25, 1940, obtained by the same collectors; Huger, February 18, 1928, E. von S. Dingle; Mt. Pleasant, January 27, 1879, and January 27, 1899, Wayne; also March 25, 1924, Lee Royall, the last a partial albino.

In habits and food it is not materially different from the Southern Robin.

SOUTHERN ROBIN
288. *Turdus migratorius achrusterus* (Batchelder) (761b)

(Gr., *achrusterus*, pale-winged.)

DESCRIPTION: Similar to the Eastern Robin but smaller; length about 9.50 inches. Colors duller and lighter.

RANGE: Breeds north to southern Illinois and Maryland; south to southeastern Texas and southeastern Georgia. Winters north to Virginia; south to southern Texas and southern Florida.

STATUS IN S. C.: Common permanent resident except in the southeastern section and in the entire coast region. Common winter resident, October 17 to April 16, in the coast region. In its breeding range it has been traced north to Greenville and York counties; east to Florence County; south to Summerville; west to Aiken and Oconee counties. In its winter range it has been reported also north and east to Horry County; south to Beaufort and Jasper counties.

HISTORY: No doubt the robin is the best known bird of the United States. Its range covers much of the country, and its place in song and story has long been established. It is unlikely that many people are unfamiliar with the name of the bird, even though they may not know it by sight.

The robin is almost semi-domesticated. Certainly, it is a tame species in much of its range, feeding on lawns and using the shade trees as nesting sites. A robin searching for earthworms on a shady lawn after a summer shower is almost as common a sight as chickens in the back yard.

The Southern Robin is a permanent resident in South Carolina, though the distribution is somewhat peculiar. It is a common lawn bird in the Piedmont area, where it nests, but below the fall line the Southern Robin population drops sharply off in summer, and the bird breeds less commonly as one nears the coast. As yet, there is no record of its nesting directly on the coastal strip, but it appears to be coming closer steadily.

Wayne (1910) stated that it "breeds in the interior," by which he meant above the fall line, mentioning Greenville specifically; since Wayne wrote, however, it has penetrated almost to salt water. In 1937, J. S. Dantzler reported it nesting at Elloree,

Orangeburg County, within 60 miles of the coast, and sent Sprunt a nest for examination. The next year (1938) it had reached Summerville, Dorchester County, only 25 miles inland. Mrs. M. J. Bischoff reported adults feeding young in her yard there in July (*Auk, 56*: 1939, 87).

At Columbia (fall line) the Southern Robin nests early. Mrs. L. B. Stanton reports that nests were begun there March 26. She saw four fledged young on April 28. At Clemson, young birds out of the nests have been seen on May 19; four eggs on June 6. On June 3, 1947, Dr. J. R. Claussen of Florence found a young bird in his yard "just about to fly."

The nest is built in the crotch of a tree, usually at a low elevation, but it may be in old buildings, or under the roofs of porches, and the beams of bridges, like the nest of the Phoebe. Mud is the principal building material, with grass woven into and about it, the whole hardening into a firmly compact structure. Four eggs are the usual complement. They are a greenish blue, unmarked, of the color known to commerce as "robins-egg blue." The average measurement is 28.9 x 20.3 millimeters. Three broods are sometimes raised. Incubation requires about fourteen days.

The robin's song, a series of warbling whistles, is not unpleasant if heard occasionally, but day after day it becomes monotonous. There is no comparison between its song and that of the other thrushes, and it is inferior to the songs of the Mockingbird and the Thrasher.

Winter is the season for robins on the coast. Countless thousands of them appear then, the first arrivals coming at the end of October and remaining until late April or early May. Many of them are doubtless Eastern Robins. Curiously enough, the bird does not then frequent towns or settled communities. As a matter of fact, coastal dwellers are pretty generally unfamiliar with it. It lives largely in the great river swamps and wide woodlands, and though abundant there, it avoids other localities. Numbers on the Christmas Bird Counts often run into the thousands. The song is unknown in much of the Low-country, but the explosive call note is heard all winter.

Wayne (1910) says that great numbers used to frequent the large grounds of a private dwelling near Charleston between 1878 and 1883 and that thousands were shot by men from the city for "robin pie." Robin shooting was once prevalent over much of the South and in some remote localities still occurs. However, times have changed. The conservation efforts of the U. S. Fish and Wildlife Service, the National Audubon Society, garden clubs, and other organizations have done much to create a better understanding of the value of bird life, and a slaughter of robins today would not be tolerated.

Birds from the mountain area of the northwestern part of South Carolina are not typical of the Southern Robin, as they verge somewhat toward the Eastern Robin.

FOOD: The winter diet is composed largely of berries and wild fruit. Black gum, tupelo, wild orange, and chinaberry or Pride of India are favorites. Palmetto berries, cassina or yaupon, and dogwood also form a part of the diet. Twelve hundred stomachs showed nearly 58 per cent vegetable matter, representing some sixty-five kinds of wild fruit. Insects make up most of the 42 per cent animal diet, beetles, grasshoppers, and caterpillars predominating.

BLACK-BACKED ROBIN
289. *Turdus migratorius nigrideus* Aldrich (761d)

(Lat., *nigrideus*, blackish.)

DESCRIPTION: Similar to the Eastern Robin but upper parts darker, the black of the head extending in spots over the hind neck and even to the back.

RANGE: Breeds north to Newfoundland; ranges south in winter to Mississippi and southern South Carolina.

STATUS IN S. C.: Casual winter visitor in the southern part of the coast region.

HISTORY: Recently, E. von S. Dingle noted in his collection a dark-backed robin taken at Huger, Berkeley County, on March 4, 1942, and suspected that it might be referable to this race. Dr. John W. Aldrich of the U. S. Fish and Wildlife Service and Dr. Harry C. Oberholser have examined the specimen and confirmed the identification. Black-backed Robins are not readily distinguished from the typical form except in spring, when it may be noted that the black of the head extends well down the back. The Black-backed Robin breeds in Newfoundland, Labrador, and northern Quebec and winters southward into the Southeastern States. Further search will undoubtedly disclose that this form is a regular winter visitor to South Carolina. At present Dingle's bird is the only known specimen from the State and gives warrant for adding the race to the State List.

In habits and food the Black-backed Robin does not, so far as known, differ materially from the other races of the species.

290. WOOD THRUSH: *Hylocichla mustelina* (Gmelin) (755)

(Gr., *Hylocichla*, forest thrush; Lat., *mustelina*, weasel-colored.)

DESCRIPTION: Length 7.50 to 8.50 inches. Head tawny brown; back cinnamon brown; rump, upper tail coverts, and tail grayish olive; under parts white, the breast and sides with conspicuous brownish black spots.

RANGE: Breeds north to southeastern South Dakota and southern Maine; south to southeastern Texas and southern Florida. Winters north to northern Florida; south to Nicaragua and Panama.

STATUS IN S. C.: Common summer resident, March 7 to October 22. Observed north to Greenville, Chester, and Darlington counties; east to Horry County; south to Beaufort County; west to Greenwood and Oconee counties.

HISTORY: This thrush is easy to identify. In a family of confusing similarity, it stands out strongly. Though it dwells in woodlands and is at home in heavy forests and swamps, it is also common in residential sections of towns and cities, where it frequents the shade trees and shrubbery of gardens and lawns. It is the only thrush (other than the robins and the Bluebird) that summers in South Carolina, a fact which will automatically identify it at that season, and the breast is much more heavily spotted than that of any other thrush.

The Wood Thrush nests far more commonly in the Piedmont, or at least above the fall line, than on the ocean edge of the coastal plain. Even there, however, it is a regular breeder. Wayne said that "almost any large swamp will contain from two to five pairs." In places like Summerville, where the bird is increasing, it is becoming a garden species; on the coast it is usually a woodland bird.

Nesting varies with the season, but eggs may be found from late April to early June. A completed nest was found at Columbia on April 27 by B. F. Taylor, and fresh eggs were found in Charleston County on May 1 by Sprunt. The nest is made of leaves, moss, twigs, and paper; lined with rootlets; and placed at no great elevation (6 to 15 feet) in the crotch of a sapling. Sprunt once found a nest at Rock Hill, York County, which had much paper in it; on a flap dangling a little below the nest were the plainly legible words "Rooms for Rent." The eggs number three to five, and are plain, greenish blue, without markings. They average 26.6 x 18.3 millimeters. Incubation requires twelve to fourteen days. The interval between the two broods is very brief. One record, for example, makes note of young leaving a nest on June 6, while one parent was still feeding them, and of the other adult carrying nesting material two days later and settling into the completed second nest by June 11.

The song of the Wood Thrush is of very high quality. Typically thrush-like in its clear, liquid notes, it is regarded by many people as the finest of bird songs. Early morning and late afternoon are the best times for hearing it, though the bird sings at all times of the day and is audible for considerable distances. The flute-like tones are very musical, but the repetition may grow monotonous for there is not much variation.

FOOD: About 60 per cent of the total is composed of insects—beetles, ants, caterpillars, flies, bugs, and grasshoppers. The vegetable content is made up of wild fruits.

EASTERN HERMIT THRUSH
291. *Hylocichla guttata faxoni* Bangs and Penard (759b)

(Lat., *guttata*, spotted; *faxoni*, to Walter Faxon.)

DESCRIPTION: Length 6.50 to 7.50 inches. Head, back, and wings rufescent sepia brown; tail reddish brown; eye ring dull white; under parts white, the sides washed with buffy brown, the throat and breast tinged with pale buff, and marked with large blackish brown spots and streaks.

RANGE: Breeds north to southern Yukon and southern Labrador; south to central Alberta and western Maryland. Winters north to northwestern Arkansas and Maine (casually); south to southern Texas, southern Florida, and Cuba.

STATUS IN S. C.: Common winter resident, October 18 to May 3. Reported north to Spartanburg and Chester counties; east to Horry County; south to Beaufort County; west to Greenwood and Oconee counties.

HISTORY: The Hermit Thrush is the only brown thrush that is known to winter in South Carolina, therefore, any seen at that season is probably of this species. A marking easily seen and remembered is the distinctly reddish tail.

The Hermit Thrush arrives in South Carolina in late October but does not become really common until mid-November. From then, however, all through winter and early spring, it can be seen any day in suitable locations. It remains until late April, occasionally early May.

The Hermit is true to its name. It is nearly always to be seen by itself, though many may be seen in a day. It is the least shy of the woodland thrushes and allows approach to within a few feet, as it sits quietly looking at the observer. By remaining so still the bird blends into its surroundings wonderfully well.

There are people who regard the song of the Hermit Thrush as superior to that of every other North American bird. In winter, it is a generally silent bird except for the call note, which is a sort of "chuck," very distinctive when learned. It has another note, fairly rare and difficult to describe. It is rather harsh and in a sense not unlike the short, scolding voice of a squirrel.

Specimens of this race are necessary to distinguish it certainly from the Newfoundland Hermit Thrush. Many specimens from South Carolina are in the collections of the Charleston Museum, the United States National Museum, and the private collection of E. von S. Dingle.

All sight records of Hermit Thrushes from South Carolina not supported by specimens are included under the Eastern race, although some of these may belong to the Newfoundland subspecies.

FOOD: In winter, largely berries and wild fruits of some forty varieties. Among these are seeds of sumac, poison ivy, and oak; dogwood berries, privet berries, pokeberries, holly and service berries; and the fruit of greenbrier and Virginia creeper.

NEWFOUNDLAND HERMIT THRUSH
292. *Hylocichla guttata crymophila* Burleigh and Peters   (759g)

(Gr., *crymophila*, cold-loving.)

DESCRIPTION: Resembling the Eastern Hermit Thrush, but upper surface darker, less rufescent; and the flanks more grayish (less rufescent).

RANGE: Breeds in Newfoundland. Winters south to Louisiana and southern Georgia.

STATUS IN S. C.: Fairly common winter resident, November 9 to April 25, throughout the State. Recorded north to Greenville and Kershaw counties; east to Horry County; south to Beaufort; west to Caesar's Head.

PLATE XXIII: GROUP OF FAMILIAR BIRDS
Water Color by John Henry Dick

Upper left: Blue Jay. Center, left to right: Wood Thrush, Goldfinch (male, breeding plumage), and Goldfinch (adult, winter plumage). Bottom right: Brown Thrasher.

History: As far as actual specimens in collections are concerned, this recently discovered race seems to be fully half as numerous in South Carolina as is the Eastern Hermit Thrush. It was originally made known by T. D. Burleigh and H. S. Peters (*Proc. Biol. Soc. Wash., 61*: 1948, 117). During the breeding season it seems to be confined to Newfoundland.

Specimens from South Carolina identified by Dr. H. C. Oberholser are: Huger, Berkeley County, March 2 and 13, 1943, April 2, 1935, and April 13, 1943, collected by E. von S. Dingle; Kershaw County, January 7, February 1, 4, and 11, 1904, N. C. Brown; Lynchburg, November 9, 1940, Adrian, April 11, 1940 (two specimens), and Conway, April 16, 1940, W. M. Perrygo and J. S. Y. Hoyt; Christ Church Parish in Charleston County, April 25, 1911, J. H. Riley; Caesar's Head, February 2, 1934, T. D. Burleigh; and Beaufort, March 30, 1937, A. B. Fuller.

In habits and food this bird does not essentially differ from the Eastern Hermit Thrush.

RUSSET-BACKED THRUSH
293. *Hylocichla ustulata ustulata* (Nuttall) (758)

(Lat., *ustulata*, scorched.)

Description: Similar to the Eastern Olive-backed Thrush but upper parts, sides, and flanks much darker, more rufescent.

Range: Breeds coastwise north to southeastern Alaska; south to California. Winters north to Vera Cruz, Guatemala, and Costa Rica; south to Ecuador and British Guiana.

Status in S. C.: Accidental.

History: There is but one specimen of this bird now to be credited to South Carolina. It was taken by Wayne, at Mt. Pleasant, on October 22, 1901. It is now in the collection of the Charleston Museum and has been identified by Dr. H. C. Oberholser. The two other examples recorded by Wayne now prove to be Eastern Olive-backed Thrushes (*Auk, 37*: 1920, 465, and *38*: 1921, 123).

In habits and food this bird does not differ materially from the Eastern Olive-backed Thrush.

EASTERN OLIVE-BACKED THRUSH
294. *Hylocichla ustulata swainsoni* (Tschudi) (758a)

(Lat., *swainsoni*, to William Swainson.)

Description: Length 6.35 to 7.75 inches. Uniform greenish olive above, wings and tail the same; throat, breast, sides of head, and eye ring buff, with rounded blackish brown spots on the breast; flanks olive green.

Range: Breeds north to northern Michigan and New Brunswick; south to West Virginia, Pennsylvania, and Massachusetts. Winters north to southeastern Mexico and Venezuela; south to Bolivia and Argentina.

Status in S. C.: Fairly common transient, April 21 to May 21, and September 10 to October 27, over most of the State. Reported north to Greenville and Chester counties; east to Horry County; south to Charleston; west to Aiken and Oconee counties.

HISTORY: The thrushes are a puzzling group to beginners, and they sometimes present difficulties for even experienced observers. This is not strange, for all the thrushes are very much alike and the differences are likely to be discovered only by those who are patient enough to look for them carefully.

The Olive-back is a quiet, unobtrusive bird. It occurs in South Carolina as a transient. The best marks for recognizing it are the uniform grayish olive back and the buff eye ring and cheeks. It is found in low, damp woodlands, where one would expect the Hermit Thrush. It is usually very tame, and like the Hermit, sits quietly and allows close approach. It holds high rank as a songster in a family of beautiful singers, but the full volume of its song is not often heard as far south as South Carolina.

FOOD: Woodland berries of various kinds, and some insects.

WESTERN OLIVE-BACKED THRUSH
295. *Hylocichla ustulata almae* Oberholser (758b)

(Lat., *almae*, fair.)

DESCRIPTION: Similar to the Eastern Olive-backed Thrush in size, but in coloration differs by reason of its lighter, more grayish (less olivaceous) upper parts and flanks.

RANGE: Breeds north to Alaska and northern Manitoba; south to eastern California and Colorado. Winters north to Mexico; south to Argentina.

STATUS IN S. C.: Casual.

HISTORY: The only record for South Carolina is a single specimen collected at Chester on October 1, 1940, by W. M. Perrygo and J. S. Webb, and identified by Dr. H. C. Oberholser. This specimen is in the United States National Museum.

In habits and food this race does not materially differ from the Eastern Olive-backed Thrush.

GRAY-CHEEKED THRUSH
296. *Hylocichla minima minima* (Lafresnaye) (757)

(Lat., *minima*, smallest.)

DESCRIPTION: Length 7.00 to 8.00 inches. Upper surface including wings olive; no distinct eye ring; sides of head behind the eyes light grayish olive; undersurface white, the sides light grayish olive; breast white or faintly buff, moderately marked with triangular spots of grayish black.

RANGE: Breeds north to northeastern Siberia, northwestern Alaska, and northern Ungava; south to central southern Alaska and Newfoundland. Winters north to Colombia and Venezuela; south to Peru and British Guiana.

STATUS IN S. C.: Fairly common transient, April 13 to May 15, or near the end of the month, and September 17 to November 2. Reported north to Greenville and Chester counties; east to Horry County; south to Charleston County; west to Aiken and Oconee counties.

HISTORY: The Olive-backed and the Gray-cheeked Thrushes are so very much alike that field identification of the two is at times difficult.

The Gray-cheek is also a transient visitor to South Carolina. The dates of its stay cannot be very certainly defined, but they seem to be from about the second week of April to the end of May and from about the end of September to the end of October. Wayne says that "As common as this bird is during the migrations, it was unknown to both Bachman and Audubon, who undoubtedly overlooked or mistook it for some other species, probably Wilson's Thrush." This being so, modern observers might well take comfort in their difficulties with it.

Unlike others of its genus, it is shy and wild. While in South Carolina it prefers dark, swampy woods not easy to penetrate. The Hermit Thrush's habit of flitting its wings when perched, is characteristic of this bird also; and, if one can get a really good look, he may see the mark which gives the Gray-cheek its name. It is also (though not always) marked by an indistinct eye ring. The song is a fine one, consistent with that of other thrushes. The food is similar to that of others of the family, chiefly wild fruits and berries, with some insects.

BICKNELL'S THRUSH
297. *Hylocichla minima bicknelli* Ridgway (757a)

(Lat., *bicknelli*, to Eugene Pintard Bicknell, of New York.)

DESCRIPTION: Similar to the Gray-cheeked Thrush but decidedly smaller.

RANGE: Breeds north to northeastern New York and Nova Scotia; south to central eastern New York and western Massachusetts. Winters north to Haiti; and south to Venezuela.

STATUS IN S. C.: Rare transient, May 3 to 10, and in September, in the eastern and western sections. Identified north to Chester; east and south to Charleston County; west to Clemson College.

HISTORY: Bicknell's Thrush is a small race of the Gray-cheeked and so similar to it that separation in the field is practically impossible. Wayne wrote that he had secured but one specimen (May 10, 1900), and refrained from shooting others in migration because of the difficulty in telling it from the Gray-cheek, it being "needless," he said, to destroy it in order to ascertain its status as a migrant. L. M. Loomis secured two specimens at Chester, one on May 6, 1887 (*Auk, 4*: 1887, 261), the other September 17, 1887 (*Auk, 8*: 1891, 173). These two are now in the collection of the American Museum of Natural History. It remains in South Carolina, as far as we know, during May and September, and it is rare. It has been taken at Clemson by G. E. Hudson and F. Sherman, May 3, 1927, this being their only record for that area (*Auk, 53*: 1936, 313). Both this form and the Gray-cheek nest far to the northward of this latitude.

VEERY
298. *Hylocichla fuscescens fuscescens* (Stephens) (756)

(Lat., *fuscescens*, becoming dusky.)

LOCAL NAMES: Wilson's Thrush.

DESCRIPTION: Length 6.45 to 7.75 inches. Upper parts tawny to cinnamon brown, the tail duller; no distinct eye ring; upper breast pinkish buff mediumly marked with V-shaped spots of brown; belly white; sides pale brown.

RANGE: Breeds north to northern Michigan and southeastern Quebec; south to northern Indiana, southwestern North Carolina, and Rhode Island. Winters north to Colombia and British Guiana; south to south central Brazil.

STATUS IN S. C.: Fairly common transient, March 18 to May 24 and August 28 to November 21. Reported north to Greenville and Chester counties; east to Horry County; south to Beaufort County; west to Aiken and Oconee counties.

HISTORY: The Veery possesses one attribute which stands out above all others—its indescribably beautiful song. Perhaps it is not the song alone which is so exquisite, but the indefinable impression which it leaves upon the hearer. The prosaic "wheer, wheer" which is so often used to describe it is probably as close a description as inadequate words can give, but they convey no suggestion of the silvery, flute-like quality of the song.

Though the matchless voice of the Veery sets the bird apart from all other thrushes, it is much like the others in its habitat, behavior, and choice of food. It is a transient visitor to South Carolina, usually arriving the first week in April and remaining until late May. It returns in late August and may be found until mid-October. By that time the last one has departed for the tropics. All sight records of Veerys are included under this subspecies.

The Veery is a solitary bird. It keeps to heavy woods, preferably the darker swamps, slipping about like a brown ghost among the foliage. Though not excessively shy, it must be looked for, and its habitat is not conducive to casual observation. The song may be heard in South Carolina during the spring migration but it is on the nesting grounds that it is at its best, this being, at the nearest, the Blue Ridge Mountains of North Carolina.

The Veery is the least spotted of the thrushes. Its relatively clear breast and its uniform, tawny-brown back are good markings for the identification of the bird.

FOOD: The Veery eats insects in spring, vegetable foods in fall. Berries (often those of the dogwood) and some wild fruit compose the bulk of its food in South Carolina.

WILLOW THRUSH
299. *Hylocichla fuscescens salicicola* Ridgway   (756a)

(Lat., *salicicola*, a willow inhabitant.)

DESCRIPTION: Similar to the Veery but upper parts darker, duller, less rufescent; spots on breast larger.

RANGE: Breeds north to southern British Columbia and southern Manitoba; south to northern Nevada, northern New Mexico, and central Iowa. Winters north to Colombia and south to central western Brazil.

STATUS IN S. C.: Casual.

HISTORY: This western form of the Veery has been detected but once in South Carolina. A specimen was collected at Chester by Leverett M. Loomis on October 5, 1888 (*Auk, 6*: 1889, 194). This specimen has recently been examined by C. K. Nichols, and is in the collection of the American Museum of Natural History (No. 56121). The birds recorded by Wayne as having been obtained on October 7, 1921 (*Auk, 39*: 1922, 268), now prove to be the Newfoundland Veery.

The habits of the Willow Thrush are like those of the Veery.

NEWFOUNDLAND VEERY
300. *Hylocichla fuscescens fuliginosa* Howe (756b)

(Lat., *fuliginosa*, sooty.)

DESCRIPTION: Similar to the Willow Thrush but more rufescent and even darker.

RANGE: Breeds in Newfoundland. Migrates south to southern Mississippi and South Carolina. Winters probably in South America.

STATUS IN S. C.: Rare transient, September 29 to October 18, over practically the whole State. Recorded east to Mt. Pleasant; west to Clemson College.

HISTORY: There are four records of the Newfoundland Veery from South Carolina: three are based on specimens taken by Wayne at Mt. Pleasant on October 18, 1915, October 15, 1920, and October 7, 1921; the fourth on a bird collected by G. E. Hudson at Clemson College, September 29, 1927. These have been identified by Dr. H. C. Oberholser. The first three are in the collection of the Charleston Museum, the fourth at Clemson College.

In habits and food this thrush does not differ materially from the Veery.

EASTERN BLUEBIRD
301. *Sialia sialis sialis* (Linnaeus) (766)

(Gr., *Sialia*, name of some bird.)

DESCRIPTION: Length 6.30 to 7.70 inches. *Male*. Head and upper parts rich blue; throat, breast, and sides cinnamon rufous; belly white. *Female*. Head bluish gray, tinged with light blue; back grayish blue; rump and upper tail coverts blue; tail similar; breast and sides dull rufescent brown; abdomen white. *Immature*. Above brown or slate color, the back streaked with white; wings and tail blue; undersurface white heavily marked with brown.

RANGE: Breeds north to central Saskatchewan and Nova Scotia; south to central Texas and northern Florida. Winters north to central eastern Nebraska and central eastern Massachusetts; south to Texas and Florida.

STATUS IN S. C.: Common permanent resident in all the State. Observed north to Greenville, York, and Dillon counties; east to Horry County; south to Beaufort and Jasper counties; west to Greenwood and Oconee counties.

HISTORY: This beautiful species is a favorite with all who know it. It is a permanent resident of South Carolina and occurs in practically all counties. Though it is found in woodlands of oak and pine, it is also a door-yard bird in many places, and its confiding ways, melodious voice, and attractive plumage all make it an acceptable and desirable neighbor.

The nesting season usually begins in early March, though forward seasons may advance it to late February. It is a cavity nester in old woodpecker holes, fence posts, bird boxes, and hollows in stubs and trees. The elevation of the nest ranges usually from 5 to 20 feet, though it may be much higher. The bird carries weeds, grass, rootlets, leaves, and feathers into the hollow, and lays four to six eggs. These are pale blue, but may be white occasionally. Wayne took three sets of white eggs from a single pair of these birds in a single season. The dates were March 30, April 12, and May 6. A fourth set was laid in late May and was left unmolested. Egg dates range from March 26 to April 3 on the coast. A fall line date (at Columbia) for the nest of a first brood is March 8. The average egg measurement is 21.6 x 16.5 millimeters. Incubation requires about thirteen days, and three broods are sometimes raised.

Quite the most remarkable nesting site of which we are aware, was discovered at Clemson, Oconee County, in July, 1945, by Carl L. Epting. It was saddled on a limb of an oak tree. The late Prof. Franklin Sherman was notified of it and, on July 20 and 21, saw the female come to the nest and feed young birds.

Though well distributed during spring and summer, the Bluebird appears in greatest numbers in winter, not only because of the influx of migrants from the North but also because of the birds' winter habit of flocking. They may then often be seen in bands of from half a dozen to a score in open pine woods or along roadsides running through old fields. The Bluebird's plaintive, pleasing note is often heard in winter.

The Bluebird is sometimes seriously affected by severe cold waves. When food is not available in sufficient quantities, many of the birds die of exposure and starvation. The great freezes of 1895 and 1899 resulted, according to Wayne, in the destruction of great numbers. Murphey also comments on similar effects in the Aiken-Augusta region. These catastrophes so depleted the Bluebird population that the effects were noticeable for years afterward, but the reproductive capacities of the species are great, and the deficiencies were ultimately made up.

Food: The diet of this attractive bird has been carefully studied by Beal (1915). Examination of 855 stomachs showed that 68 per cent of the contents was animal and 32 per cent vegetable matter. Included among the insects were grasshoppers, crickets, katydids, 22 per cent; beetles, 20 per cent; caterpillars and moths, 10 per cent. The vegetable food was largely wild fruit, hackberry, wax myrtle, pokeberry, blueberry, elderberry, sumac, poison ivy, Virginia creeper, and dogwood.

Family Sylviidae: Gnatcatchers and Kinglets

BLUE-GRAY GNATCATCHER
302. *Polioptila caerulea caerulea* (Linnaeus)   (751)

(Gr., *Polioptila*, hoary-feathered; Lat., *caerulea*, blue.)

LOCAL NAMES: Chay-chay.

DESCRIPTION: Length 4.00 to 5.50 inches. Tail long. *Male*. Upper surface blue gray, the anterior forehead and stripe on each side of crown black; lower parts pale bluish gray; eye ring white; tail black, the outer feathers with much white. *Female*. Similar to the male but with no black on the head.

RANGE: Breeds north to eastern Nebraska, southwestern New York, and eastern New Jersey; south to southeastern Texas and central Florida. Winters north to Texas and Virginia; south to Guatemala, Cuba, and the Bahama Islands.

STATUS IN S. C.: Common permanent resident (much less numerous in winter) over the lower coastal plain; summer resident, March 21 to October 10, elsewhere in the State. As a permanent resident detected north to Horry County; south to Beaufort and Jasper counties; west to the Santee National Wildlife Refuge. As a summer resident reported north to Greenville and Cherokee counties; east to Florence County; south to Orangeburg County; west to Aiken, Greenwood, and Oconee counties.

HISTORY: To many people the Blue-gray Gnatcatcher seems like a "miniature Mockingbird." The trim shape, long tail, often cocked at a jaunty angle, and general coloration remind one strongly of a tiny Mockingbird. It is ordinarily a gentle, unsuspicious bird, and will readily come within a few feet of a motionless observer.

The Gnatcatcher's status in South Carolina is rather remarkable, in that it is a permanent resident on the coast but a summer resident only inland and in the Piedmont. At Columbia Mrs. G. E. Charles reports the bird from March 21 to September 20. At Clemson, Oconee County, G. E. Hudson noted spring arrival time as late March (27) to early April (6), but did not determine fall departure dates. In South Carolina the birds occur regularly in winter, in reduced numbers, in the swamps, drier woodlands, brushy field edges, and on the barrier islands south of the Santee River. North of that river they are uncommon or even lacking. R. G. Kuerzi, who worked in Horry County, says that it is "a common summer resident," his date limits being March 14 to December 18.

Wayne was under the impression that wintering birds on the coast were immatures, which is probably true as there is a marked increase in their numbers in spring, even on the lower coast, the result of an influx of birds from the south in early March. Mating takes place soon after arrival. The male bursts into melodies that are surprising in volume for so tiny a creature. He assists his mate in nest building, and their joint efforts result in one of the most beautiful examples of bird architecture. The nest is much like that of the hummingbird though larger; it is very deep and is covered externally with lichens. It is composed of grasses, plant down, and feathers, with cobwebs holding the lichens to the other material and to the branch, causing it to look like a knot on the limb to which it is attached. Incubating birds are concealed almost entirely, and one sees little more than the tail tip.

The eggs are laid about mid-April, sometimes not until early May, although E. J. DeCamps found a full set on April 10 in Beaufort County, and G. E. Hudson found a completed nest on April 9 at Clemson. There are four or five eggs, greenish blue, heavily speckled with brown. They average 14.5 x 11.2 millimeters. The incubation period is about thirteen days and both sexes may incubate. They may raise two broods. The live oak is a favorite nesting tree, but the loblolly pine, sweet gum, dogwood, and other trees occasionally contain their nests. Elevation of the nest varies from 4 or 5 feet to as much as 80.

Once learned, the call of this minute bird is instantly recognizable. It consists of a penetrating, insect-like "zee-ee-e," or perhaps "spee-e-e." Murphey remarks that in the Aiken-Augusta region this species is frequently referred to as "Chay-chay," because of this characteristic note. The call is given in winter as well as summer and often aids in locating the bird.

FOOD: The Gnatcatcher is almost wholly insectivorous and is a valuable control factor on such destructive forms as cotton-leaf worms, wood borers, weevils, flies, and gnats.

EASTERN GOLDEN-CROWNED KINGLET
303. *Regulus satrapa satrapa* Lichtenstein (748)

(Lat., *Regulus*, a little king; Gr., *satrapa*, a ruler.)

DESCRIPTION: Length 3.15 to 4.55 inches. *Male*. Upper parts greenish olive, the crown orange bordered on each side with a yellow stripe, then with a black stripe, then with a dull white stripe over the eye; two pale yellow or yellowish white wing bars, lower parts olive white to yellowish white. *Female*. Similar to the male, but orange of crown replaced by canary yellow.

RANGE: Breeds north to central Manitoba and central Labrador; south to northern Minnesota, southwestern North Carolina, and Massachusetts. Winters north to southern Minnesota and Nova Scotia; south to Mexico and north central Florida.

STATUS IN S. C.: Fairly common winter resident, October 10 to April 9, throughout the State. Observed north to Spartanburg, York, and Chesterfield counties; east to Horry County; south to Beaufort County; west to Aiken and Oconee counties.

HISTORY: With the Ruby-crowned Kinglet, the Golden-crown shares the distinction of being one of the smallest of the South Carolina birds. Perhaps because of its size, its habits, and the fact that it occurs only in winter, it is not well known and is often overlooked.

The Golden-crown is a high-ranging bird. It frequents the tops of forest trees and stretches of pineland, especially on the barrier islands. Sometimes during the coldest weather, however, it comes down into the smaller trees and bushes and allows close approach.

Kinglets go about in company with Titmice, Chickadees, and Nuthatches, and often will respond to "squeaking"; they can be lured sometimes almost to within

Male Red-winged Blackbird   S. A. GRIMES

Feeding Boat-tailed Grackle

ALLAN D. CRUICKSHANK
National Audubon Society

Swainson's Warbler on Nest

S. A. GRIMES

White-eyed Towhee at Home

arm's length. The beautiful crown patch, yellow in the female and orange in the male, is easily seen when the bird hangs upside down, seaching for insects on twig, branch, or cone.

With the exception of the note of the Brown Creeper, the note of this Kinglet is as thin and thread-like as any bird call known to the writers. But so closely does it resemble the Creeper's notes that one cannot always be sure which has been heard. The note carries well and is audible to good ears at some distance, a sure means of finding birds that otherwise would be easily passed by.

FOOD: Almost wholly small insects, particularly plant lice and aphids. It is a bird valuable to agriculture.

EASTERN RUBY-CROWNED KINGLET
304. *Regulus calendula calendula* (Linnaeus) (749)

(Italian, *calendula*, marigold, in allusion to the crest.)

DESCRIPTION: Length 3.75 to 4.60 inches. *Male.* Above grayish olive, with a large vermilion crown patch; broad eye ring white; lower parts pale grayish buff, more yellowish posteriorly. *Female.* Similar to the male but without the red crown patch.

RANGE: Breeds north to northwestern Alaska and central Labrador; south to Michigan (casually) and Maine. Winters north to southern British Columbia and Maine (casually); south to Guatemala and southern Florida.

STATUS IN S. C.: Common winter resident, September 22 to May 10, throughout the State. Reported north to Greenville, York, and Marlboro counties; east to Horry County; south to Jasper County; west to Aiken and Oconee counties.

HISTORY: The Ruby-crowned Kinglet is more common or at least more obvious and better known than its close relative the Golden-crown. Although it does not flock like the Golden-crown, it usually ranges and feeds at much lower levels and consequently is more often encountered. It winters throughout South Carolina. It cannot be called common, however, until late October. During cold weather it is one of our most abundant birds, coming into urban yards and gardens and into almost all wooded country areas.

The Ruby-crown's tiny size, conspicuous wing bars, and whitish eye ring, and its habit of almost constantly flitting its wings as it moves about the bushes, all constitute good field marks and make it easy to recognize. The concealed red patch on the crown of the male may be seen only when the crest is raised. Although not as readily seen as the Golden-crown's coronet, it is striking enough when glimpsed.

Any winter walk through woods, the edges of fields, myrtle thickets, or scrubby land will reveal these restless, active little birds. The alarm note is much like that of a wren, for which it can easily be mistaken. The song, delivered in April before the bird leaves for its breeding ground, is remarkably loud for so small a bird, rich in tone, and altogether pleasing.

FOOD: As much as 94 per cent animal matter, mainly insects. The 6 per cent vegetable content consists of weed seeds and small berries such as those of the wax myrtle. Wasps and ants make up 30 per cent of the animal food. The Ruby-crown also consumes numbers of beetles, flies, caterpillars, moths, and spiders.

Family *Motacillidae:* Wagtails and Pipits

American Pipit
305. *Anthus spinoletta rubescens* (Tunstall) (697)

(Gr., *Anthus*, a small bird; Italian, *spinoletta*, a pipit; Lat., *rubescens*, reddish.)

Local Names: Titlark.

Description: Length 6.00 to 7.00 inches. Bill slender. Above grayish olive or grayish brown, indistinctly streaked with dark brown; superciliary stripe and lower parts pinkish buff, the chest, sides, and flanks streaked with dark brown; outer feathers of tail with more or less white.

Range: Breeds north to northeastern Siberia and central western Greenland; south to central southern Mackenzie and Newfoundland. Winters north to southern British Columbia and southeastern Massachusetts; south to Guatemala and southern Florida.

Status in S. C.: Common winter resident, September 10 to April 22, in all the State. Observed north to Greenville and Florence counties; east to Horry County; south to Beaufort and Jasper counties; west to Aiken and Oconee counties.

History: The American Pipit, when spoken of at all in South Carolina, usually goes by the name "Titlark." Though it is common, it is for the most part overlooked as just another "sparrow." It deserves better acquaintance for it is a bird of value, especially to farmers.

The Pipit is a winter resident in South Carolina, and the colder the weather the better the bird seems to like it. It usually arrives after the middle of October, but in forward seasons, when the weather turns cool early, it comes sooner.

Pipits should be looked for only in perfectly open situations such as fields, airports, golf courses, and even the somewhat barren-looking areas of the sea islands, behind the dunes above high-water mark. Newly-ploughed or burned fields are favored habitats, for here the Pipits find insects recently turned up or killed by grass fires. The bird, though wary, will follow closely the operating plows and tractors, walking quickly, never hopping as do sparrows and other birds. When the Pipit is in flight its white outer tail feathers show conspicuously. Superficially Pipits resemble trim, streaked sparrows, but they may be recognized by their way of walking and their constant tail-wagging. In some regions this latter characteristic has earned them the name "Wag-tail." In habits and locality preferences Pipits resemble the Horned Larks. Their call notes, often uttered in flight, sound like "jee-eet," or as Peterson (1947) says "*pi-pit* by a stretch of imagination." Once learned, it is easy to recognize and remember, and one can hear it at times when the birds pass overhead, otherwise unnoticed.

Food: A most useful bird, because of its insect diet. Grasshoppers, beetles, crickets, and spiders form the bulk of the food. It also eats small mollusks, seeds, and small berries, including the seeds of the sea oats of the coastal islands. The Pipit is known to be a destroyer of the boll weevil; this trait alone should endear it to the cotton farmer.

306. SPRAGUE'S PIPIT: *Anthus spragueii* (Audubon) (700)

(Lat., *spragueii*, to Isaac Sprague.)

DESCRIPTION: Length 5.75 to 7.00 inches. Upper parts pale buffy grayish brown, broadly streaked, including the rump, with dark brown, these markings broadest on the back; superciliary stripe and lower parts dull buffy white, the chest narrowly streaked with grayish brown; outer tail feathers with much white.

RANGE: Breeds north to central Saskatchewan and southern Manitoba; south to western Montana and North Dakota. Winters north to Texas and South Carolina (accidentally); and south to Mexico.

STATUS IN S. C.: Accidental, November 1 to 24, in Charleston County.

HISTORY: That this western bird is included among the South Carolina species is due to the vigilance of Wayne, who added it to the State List on November 24, 1893, when he secured a specimen near Mt. Pleasant. On November 17, 1900, he shot another within a quarter mile of the place where the first was taken. He saw a third, and heard it sing, on November 1, 1904. All of these instances he recorded in the *Auk*, and in his book. There have been no further instances of its occurrence.

The 1893 specimen (now in the Charleston Museum), is the first eastern record for the bird and for nearly a decade remained the only one. Though he had never seen one previously, Wayne recognized the species by the fact that it did not wag its tail, as the American Pipit is in the habit of doing. Other than this, and the difference in the streaking of the back, the habits, appearance, and food of the Sprague's Pipit do not differ materially from those of the American Pipit.

Family Bombycillidae: Waxwings

307. CEDAR WAXWING: *Bombycilla cedrorum* Vieillot (619)

(Lat., *Bombycilla*, silky-tail; *cedrorum*, of the cedars.)

LOCAL NAMES: Cedar Bird.

DESCRIPTION: Length 6.50 to 8.00 inches. Head crested. Chin and a broad stripe through the eye black; rest of the head, neck, and chest pinkish wood brown; back similar but more grayish; wings slate gray, the secondaries tipped with red wax-like appendages; tail with a broad yellow tip; posterior lower parts yellow and white.

RANGE: Breeds north to central British Columbia and northern Nova Scotia; south to northwestern California and northern Georgia. Winters north to southern British Columbia and Nova Scotia (casually); south to Lower California, Panama, and Jamaica.

STATUS IN S. C.: Winter resident, common but irregular, August 28 to June 13, in all the State, more numerous during migrations. Occasional to June 26 in the mountains, where it possibly breeds. Observed north to Greenville and York counties; east to Horry County; south to Jasper County; west to Oconee County.

HISTORY: Though this gentle, attractive bird is abundant during migrations and winters here also, there are as yet no records of its nesting in the State, although it is known to nest in the higher North Carolina mountains and occasionally east to the south central parts of that state.

It is rarely seen singly, but travels in flocks and during migrations attracts a good deal of attention. The great numbers which appear during migrations dwindle sharply through the winter, but small flocks remain in open woodlands, in swampy areas, and even on the sea islands throughout the cold months.

The Cedar Waxwing derives its name from the bright red appendages on the secondary wing feathers, which look much like drops of sealing wax. At times, they appear also on the tail feathers. Few birds are so trim and sleek looking as the Cedar Waxwing. The prevailing brown color is attractive, and the crest aids in recognition. The bird's note is as distinctive as its plumage, and once learned is also an aid in identification. The note is a pecular, lisping sound, individually insignificant, but audible at a considerable distance when made by a flock. The birds give the call when feeding and in flight.

L. M. Loomis secured specimens on Mt. Pinnacle, Pickens County, on June 22, 1887, and June 26, 1889, and at Caesar's Head, Greenville County, on the same dates in 1891, but he made no mention of the birds' nesting (*Auk*, 7: 1890, 125; *8*: 1891, 329). More recently, Robert H. Coleman recorded the Waxwing at Table Rock State Park, Pickens County, June 2–9, 1947. It is in this part of the State that nesting might well occur.

FOOD: The food of the waxwing is 87 per cent vegetable. Wild fruits make up 74 per cent; cultivated varieties, 13 per cent. Although its fondness for cherries in many areas has given it a local name of "Cherry Bird," it seems equally fond of cedar berries. In South Carolina the main food consists of the fruit of such trees as the cherry laurel, black gum, and tupelo gum, and berries of smilax, palmetto, wax myrtle, and hackberry. E. Milby Burton has seen the Waxwing feeding on emerging larvae of May flies, taking them on the wing in the manner of a flycatcher.

Family Laniidae: Shrikes

LOGGERHEAD SHRIKE
308. *Lanius ludovicianus ludovicianus* Linnaeus (622)

(Lat., *Lanius*, a butcher; *ludovicianus*, of Louisiana.)

LOCAL NAMES: Butcher Bird; French Mockingbird.

DESCRIPTION: Length 8.50 to 9.50 inches. Bill conspicuously hooked at tip. Upper surface slate gray; forehead and broad stripe on side of head through the eye black; lower surface white; wings and tail black, the outer feathers of the latter with white tips; bill black.

RANGE: Resident and breeds north to northeastern Louisiana and central Virginia; south to southern Louisiana and southern Florida.

STATUS IN S. C.: Common permanent resident in all the State. Identified north to Greenville, York, and Marlboro counties; east to Horry County; south to Beaufort County; west to Aiken and Oconee counties.

HISTORY: The Loggerhead Shrike is the "French Mockingbird" and the "Butcher Bird" in the Low-country. It occurs as a permanent resident throughout South Carolina. The Loggerhead is a conspicuous bird and lives both in town and country. Like the flycatchers it perches on exposed places such as telephone wires, the top branches of trees, or isolated stubs, from which it makes sallies for insect prey. The Loggerhead Shrike's black, white, and gray plumage, its spectacular method of feeding, and its comparative fearlessness combine to render it easy to observe and study.

It mates in mid-February and usually begins to build the nest late in that month. Cold weather retards such activity in some years. Full sets of eggs are not common until the last of March. Wayne's earliest record was of five eggs on March 13 in which case the nest must have been started about March 1. In the previous year the same pair of birds had eggs on March 24. The earliest record for the coastal area, however, was made by F. M. Weston, who observed an adult feeding a full-grown young bird on March 30 at Otranto, Charleston County. The eggs must have been laid by March 1. Murphey gives a February 24 nesting date in the Aiken-Augusta region.

Sprunt's notes contain references to the mating of Loggerheads on February 10, near his former home in Charleston. They also read, "April 2nd, nest with four eggs, this pair of birds made nest for second brood in same tree within 5 feet of former nest, and had five eggs on June 22nd." A typical date for Beaufort County is April 12, five eggs (E. J. DeCamps). A late Sumter record is that of three young leaving the nest on June 23 (W. M. Levi).

The nest is bulky and well made of sticks, weeds, cotton, palm fibre, and feathers. It is placed in small, thick oaks, tall bushes, or even large trees, varying in elevation from 6 feet to as much as 50 or over. The majority are low. The Loggerhead raises three broods (Wayne) and the number of eggs usually drops one to a brood; that is, six for the first, then five, then four. They are greenish white with markings of brown and lavender, and they average 24.9 x 19.8 millimeters. Incubation requires thirteen days.

Though not a song bird, the Loggerhead performs surprisingly well at times, with mellow, liquid whistles, often a source of astonishment to those accustomed only to its rather harsh, unpleasing call note. The name "Butcher-Bird" comes from the bird's habit of impaling prey on thorns or barbed wire, presumably as a source of future food. In South Carolina the bird seldom if ever returns to the cache. One often finds mummified remains of insects or mice hanging on trees or fences. Chamberlain once saw a Loggerhead attack and finally kill a Hog-nose snake; the bird hovered over the reptile, diving down and pecking at it until it died.

The Loggerhead vividly illustrates the extraordinary eyesight possessed by birds. After sitting motionless on a wire, a bird will suddenly plunge downward, fly rapidly for some distance, drop into the grass or weeds, and emerge with an insect.

All sight records of shrikes are placed under this subspecies, though some may refer to the Migrant Shrike.

FOOD: A considerable amount of misunderstanding exists regarding this bird's food habits. Sentimentalists regard it with horror because it occasionally takes small birds. The impaling habit is also shocking. Actually, the small birds killed by the Loggerhead amount to only 8 per cent of the year's food and many of the birds thus destroyed are English Sparrows. Now and then the Loggerhead decapitates canaries when they stick their heads out between the bars of a cage. Animal matter is apparently the only food and is divided between vertebrates and invertebrates. The former compose 28 per cent, the latter 72 per cent. Small mammals, birds, lizards, frogs, and fish make up the vertebrates.

MIGRANT SHRIKE
309. *Lanius ludovicianus migrans* Palmer (622e)

(Lat., *migrans*, migrating.)

DESCRIPTION: Similar to the Loggerhead Shrike, but wings longer; tail shorter; bill shorter, more slender; and the upper parts paler.

RANGE: Breeds north to Manitoba and New Brunswick; south to Arkansas and Maryland. Winters north to northern limit of its breeding range; south to eastern Mexico and southeastern Georgia.

STATUS IN S. C.: Fairly common winter resident, August 18 to February 26, throughout the State. Recorded north to Greenville; east and south to Charleston County; west to Anderson and Clemson College.

HISTORY: The Migrant Shrike in the field is not distinguishable from the Loggerhead Shrike, and only specimens have been used to substantiate the records here given. The bird, however, is probably more numerous in South Carolina than these records indicate.

Specimens of this shrike have been taken at Clemson College, November 9, 1927, by G. E. Hudson; 8 miles southeast of Greenville, December 8, 1934, by G. R. Lunz, Jr.; Drayton Station in Charleston County, November 15, 1943, and John's Island, November 28, 1943, by H. S. Peters; Mt. Pleasant, February 26, 1912, by Wayne; James Island, November 13, 1943, by Chamberlain; Anderson, August 18, 1899, by H. T. Nowell. All of these have been identified by Dr. H. C. Oberholser.

Its habits and food are similar to those of the Loggerhead Shrike.

Family Sturnidae: Starlings

310. STARLING: *Sturnus vulgaris vulgaris* Linnaeus (493)

(Lat., *Sturnus*, a starling; *vulgaris*, common.)

DESCRIPTION: Length 7.50 to 8.50 inches. *Adult.* Head and neck iridescent purplish green, back dark glossy green, and all the upper parts heavily speckled with pale brownish buff; under parts iridescent purplish green, spotted with white; bill yellow in summer, dark brown in winter. *Immature.* Hair brown above; drab beneath with some white on throat and abdomen.

STARLINGS

RANGE: Breeds north to northern Norway and northern Russia; south to France and Italy. Winters south to northern Africa and Syria. Naturalized in North America north to Ontario and Nova Scotia; south to Texas and Florida, also in much of the western United States.

STATUS IN S. C.: Abundant permanent resident throughout the State. Reported north to Spartanburg, York, and Lancaster counties; east to Horry County; south to Jasper County; west to Barnwell and Oconee counties.

HISTORY: In March of 1890 an incident occurred which probably was of no interest to anyone except the perpetrator, but which grew into such proportions in subsequent years that it is now something of a national problem. This was the act of Eugene Scheiffer who, probably with good intentions, released forty pairs of a European bird in Central Park, New York. These birds were Starlings.

Much has been learned to our cost about the importation of exotic birds and animals since that time, and such a thing would not now be permitted without detailed and careful thought. Usually an exotic will either disappear quickly or become so numerous as to constitute a problem. The Starling did well, much too well, and its history closely parallels that of the English Sparrow. From that small start in 1890, the Starling has spread virtually over the United States east of the Rockies. South Florida is, as yet, uninvaded, but one would be hard put to it to find another place free of them.

This interesting, if objectionable, bird was first reported in South Carolina in the Spartanburg area by Gabriel Cannon in 1918. The second record was made by Emmett Blake at Greenwood, where he took one in late September, 1919. In the coastal section it was first seen at Dixie Plantation, St. Paul's Parish, Charleston County, February 22, 1920, by E. A. Williams. Four years later, the first coastal specimen was secured January 10, 1924, near Sewee Bay, Charleston County, by W. K. Moore, and presented to the Charleston Museum (No. 7679). As is usually the case, the first comers were very wild and shy, almost impossible to approach; their behavior was almost completely reversed when the bird became established.

The birds continued to increase rather slowly in the Piedmont, and appeared at Clemson for the first time, November 14, 1925, but they had become common by 1928. The first nesting below the fall line is a record for St. Matthews, Calhoun County, in July, 1922 (Lee Cain). There are also breeding records for Rock Hill and Chester in May, 1926 (P. M. Jenness).

The first record of coastal nesting was made on the plantation of William McLeod, James Island, Charleston County, in the spring of 1929, and for Charleston the first birds were noted on January 24, 1930, by E. Milby Burton and Sprunt. The comment by the writers in their *Supplement to the Birds of South Carolina* (1931) was as follows: "This species is well established in the upper portions of the state but continues to be rare and shy in the coast region." Needless to say, that is no longer true. The Starling is common the year round in cities, towns, and villages and in much of the surrounding area.

The first nesting record for the city of Charleston was established by E. A. Williams, April 20, 1932, when he found a pair building in a telephone pole on Church Street (*Auk, 49*: 1932, 354).

The principal charges against the bird are that it usurps nesting sites of native species, destroys their eggs and young, and constitutes a nuisance by roosting on buildings in cities which they befoul with their droppings. In appearance, at close range, it is a handsome bird, glossy black with golden flecks over the body. It often feeds on the ground. It is a good mimic and some of its notes are not unmusical. These birds gather in flocks in the fall and travel about like blackbirds and grackles, in whose company they may often be found.

Starlings nest in natural cavities or in bird boxes. They often take the boxes from Bluebirds and Martins. There are four to six pale blue eggs, unmarked and averaging 30.5 x 21.8 millimeters. Two or three broods are raised. Incubation requires eleven to fourteen days.

FOOD: It cannot be denied that in some degree the Starling is beneficial to agriculture. It consumes numerous insects, these amounting to as much as 41.5 per cent of the total annual food. Beetles, grasshoppers, crickets, caterpillars, and spiders constitute the usual diet. Wild fruits make up 24 per cent, among these being mulberries, blackberries, elderberries, bayberries, with Virginia creeper, poison ivy, and sumac. The balance of the food is made up of grains.

Family Vireonidae: Vireos

WHITE-EYED VIREO
311. *Vireo griseus griseus* (Boddaert) (631)

(Lat., *Vireo*, a kind of bird, possibly the Green Finch; *griseus*, gray.)

DESCRIPTION: Length 4.50 to 5.50 inches. Upper parts greenish olive, the head and neck washed with gray; undersurface white, the sides pale greenish yellow; wings fuscous, with two yellowish white bars; eye ring and stripe from eye to nostril yellow; iris white.

RANGE: Breeds north to central eastern Texas and northeastern North Carolina; south to southeastern Texas and northern Florida. Winters north to southern Louisiana and South Carolina; south to Mexico and southern Florida.

STATUS IN S. C.: Abundant summer resident, March 11 to November 12, throughout most of the State; a permanent resident, less common in winter, on the coast southward from Charleston County. Known north to Greenville, Cherokee, and Marlboro counties; east to Horry County; south to Beaufort and Jasper counties; west to Aiken, Greenwood, and Oconee counties.

PLATE XXIV: COTTON FIELD SCENE

Water Color by Edward von S. Dingle

Top birds, left to right: Loggerhead Shrike, Bluebird (female), and Bluebird (male). Bottom, left to right: Robin and Mockingbird.

VIREOS

HISTORY: Vireos are small, woodland birds that are apt to be overlooked unless one learns their songs, which are characteristic and frequently uttered. Most of the vireos possess some field mark which renders them identifiable on sight. The prominent wing-bars, yellowish sides, and greenish back of the White-eyed are good marks; a close view of the bird will reveal the white iris, and the slight hook at the tip of the bill characteristic of all the vireos may also be seen. The White-eyed is a dweller in thickets, tangles of vines, and shrubbery in both dry and wet woodlands. It is just as likely to be found in large swamps as on the edges of fields and clearings. It is an inquisitive little bird. It greets the observer with much scolding and dashing about in its leafy retreat, but comes readily to the "squeak" and may approach to within a few feet.

The White-eyed Vireo is the commonest of the family and occurs every month in the summer throughout South Carolina. It is a permanent resident on the coast, but as Wayne indicated, most of the winter birds there are possibly migrants from the north and not local breeders. Earliest migration dates in the spring include March 11 at Columbia, March 25 at Greenville, and March 29 at Gaffney and Clemson College. The main influx comes in late March and early April, and the birds soon become abundant. Latest date in the fall in the Piedmont is September 15 at Clemson. At Columbia, the White-eyed stays until October 9, occasionally to November 19.

Late April is nesting time, though Wayne found eggs as early as April 11. Vireos' nests are semi-pensile and are swung from the fork of a twig, often at the end of a drooping limb of a dogwood, sweet gum, or small oak. Because they are well made, they often survive winter storms into another season but are not used again. The White-eyed chooses low elevations, from about 2 to 10 feet, and the nest is woven of grasses, bark strippings, leaves, and weeds, bound with caterpillar silk, and frequently covered with lichens on the exterior walls. Eggs of the vireos are as distinctive as the nests, being pure white with a few fine brownish spots sprinkled about the large end. The eggs of the White-eyed average 19.0 x 14.0 millimeters and are three or four in number. Two, sometimes three, broods are raised and incubation requires about fourteen days.

The song of the White-eyed Vireo is one of the most frequently heard bird songs in spring and summer. It is very sharp and clipped, is repeated over and over, and has numerous "translations." Peterson (1947) gives it as "*chick-a-per-weeoo-chick*," but it sounds different to different ears. The sharp note which opens and closes the song is characteristic. It is easy to learn because of the insistence with which it is uttered.

FOOD: That this vireo is a valuable destroyer of insects is beyond doubt. Animal matter, mainly insects, comprises 88 per cent of the food. Moth and butterfly larvae and adults make up about one-third. Many stinkbugs and scale insects are included in the insect diet. Beetles make up 13 per cent, and wasps, bees, and flies, 12 per cent. The vegetable food is mainly the berries of sumac, dogwood, and wax myrtle.

NORTHERN WHITE-EYED VIREO
312. *Vireo griseus noveboracensis* (Gmelin) (631d)

(Lat., *noveboracensis*, of New York.)

DESCRIPTION: Similar to the White-eyed Vireo but upper surface more yellowish olive green (less grayish); sides and flanks more extensively golden yellow (less grayish).

RANGE: Breeds north to southeastern Nebraska and Massachusetts; south to Texas and southeastern Virginia. Winters north to southern Texas and South Carolina (probably); south to Guatemala (probably), Honduras, southern Louisiana, and southern Florida.

STATUS IN S. C.: Winter resident, probably not uncommon. Recorded from only the coast region.

HISTORY: Two specimens in the Charleston Museum, collected by Wayne and identified by Dr. H. C. Oberholser, are from Mt. Pleasant, September 28, 1906, and April 9, 1912.

In habits and food this bird is not essentially different from the southern White-eyed Vireo.

313. YELLOW-THROATED VIREO: *Vireo flavifrons* Vieillot (628)

(Lat., *flavifrons*, yellow-fronted.)

DESCRIPTION: Length 5.00 to 6.00 inches. Head, hind neck, and back yellowish olive; posterior upper parts slate gray; superciliary stripe and eye ring bright yellow; throat and breast bright yellow; belly and lower tail coverts white; wings dull black with two white bars.

RANGE: Breeds north to southern Saskatchewan and Maine; south to central Texas and southeastern Florida. Winters north to Yucatan and South Carolina (accidently); south to southern Mexico and Colombia.

STATUS IN S. C.: Fairly common summer resident, March 15 to September 21, throughout the State. Accidental in winter. Recorded north to Greenville and Chester counties; east to Horry County; south to Beaufort County; west to Greenwood and Clemson College.

HISTORY: The Yellow-throated is the handsomest of the vireos. It is not nearly as common as the others, and it must be searched for in rather heavy woods, where it keeps to the upper levels of the trees. Now and then, of course, it descends to low growth, particularly in cypress country, and in such situations can be easily seen and certainly easily recognized. It is a summer resident only, arriving in late March.

The song of the Yellow-throated is one of the best of the family, a rich, varied warble, something like that of the Red-eyed Vireo, but more deliberate and musical, though with a distinct vireo quality. Following the song is one's best chance of seeing the bird.

The nest is hard to find and harder to reach because of the elevation at which it is placed. It is usually built far out on a limb and may be as high as 90 feet from the ground. Most of the nests are from 40 to 60 feet above the ground. It is the most attractive of vireo nests, for it is adorned with lichens much like that of the Wood Pewee and hangs from a forked twig.

The Yellow-throated Vireo lays three or four white eggs with fine speckling about the large end. They average 20.3 x 15.2 millimeters. Two broods are raised. This vireo occasionally sings while on the nest. Incubation requires about twelve to fourteen days.

The earliest arrival date of the bird is March 15 on the coast and April 6 in the upper Piedmont (Clemson). Departure from the coast in fall is usually in late September, the latest date being October 20. No fall data are available from the Piedmont, but Mrs. G. E. Charles has noted the Yellow-throated on September 15 at Columbia. Southgate Y. Hoyt established the only winter record for the State on December 20, 1943, on Bull's Island.

FOOD: About 95 per cent insects, of which more than half are moths and butterflies in various stages of development, particularly caterpillars. For the rest, stinkbugs, beetles, and flies.

BLUE-HEADED VIREO
314.   *Vireo solitarius solitarius* (Wilson)   (629)

(Lat., *solitarius*, solitary.)

DESCRIPTION: Length 5.00 to 6.00 inches. Head and hind neck slate gray, with eye ring and stripe in front of eye white; remainder of upper surface yellowish olive; under parts white, the sides yellowish green; wings and tail slaty black, the former with two yellowish white bars.

RANGE: Breeds north to southern Mackenzie and northern Nova Scotia; south to central Alberta, southern Pennsylvania, and southern Connecticut. Winters north to Texas and South Carolina; south to Guatemala and southern Florida.

STATUS IN S. C.: Fairly common winter resident, in the lower part of the State, October 13 to April 27, transient throughout the State except in the mountains. Reported north to Chester and Florence counties; east to Horry County; south to the Edisto River; west to Aiken and Anderson counties.

HISTORY: The Blue-headed Vireo is one of the most attractive members of its family and one of the easiest to know. The slate-gray head, which seems rather large and overbalanced, and its conspicuous white eye ring and throat will identify it almost at a glance. Its scolding note suggests that of a wren, but its song is a fine melody, similar to the song of the Red-eyed Vireo but clearer and much less monotonous. The bird seems to be particularly fond of water and live oaks, and it likes to travel about with bands of Chickadees and Titmice. It can often be attracted by "squeaking."

Though it is primarily a woodland bird, it may be found in fairly open places such as roadsides, the edges of fields, and scattered timber. It occurs regularly on the barrier islands as well as on the mainland.

The Blue-headed is present throughout the winter in coastal South Carolina, to which it usually comes towards the end of October. It remains until late April.

There are few midwinter records of the Blue-headed from the interior of the State. J. D. Kuser observed one at Aiken on January 28, 1913; H. L. Harllee saw one at Florence on December 21, 1935; and a Christmas Bird Count group saw one in Clarendon County on December 29, 1944. It appears to be a transient visitor at the fall line; Columbia dates are March 26 to April 16, and October 22 to November 4. L. M. Loomis listed it as a transient in Chester County from April 4 to April 21, and from October 15 to the end of November.

FOOD: About 96 per cent animal matter, consisting of caterpillars, moths, beetles, grasshoppers, locusts, dragon flies, and crickets. Vegetable matter (wild grapes and the berries of the dogwood and wax myrtle) is the principal diet in winter.

MOUNTAIN VIREO
315. *Vireo solitarius alticola* Brewster (629c)

(Lat., *alticola*, an inhabitant of heights.)

DESCRIPTION: Length about 6.00 inches. Similar to the Blue-headed Vireo but larger, with a particularly larger bill; back more grayish, with less olive green tinge.

RANGE: Breeds in the mountains north to West Virginia; south to northwestern South Carolina. Winters north to South Carolina; south to central Florida.

STATUS IN S. C.: Fairly common summer resident, March 17 to October 29, in the mountains of the northwestern section. Uncommon winter resident, November 6 to March 30, in the coast region and probably also in the remaining portions of the State, excepting the mountains. In summer recorded from Greenville, Pickens, and Oconee counties. At other times of the year identified only north to Lynchburg (Lee County); south and east to Charleston County.

HISTORY: The Mountain Vireo is distinguished chiefly from the Blue-headed by a larger beak, a plumbeous rather than olive-green back, and a generally larger size. The Mountain Vireo is a permanent resident in South Carolina, for it nests in the upper counties and winters on the coast. It arrives in the coastal area in early November and remains until late March. It is not a common bird on the coast.

The nest is built in typical vireo fashion in deciduous trees, and the eggs are laid from early to late May. L. M. Loomis found the bird breeding about Mt. Pinnacle and Caesar's Head (*Auk*, 7: 1890, 126; *8*: 1891, 329). G. E. Hudson found it at Clemson from March 29 to October 29. John Kershaw took nests on Stumphouse Mountain, Oconee County, at 1500 feet elevation, June 17, 1910. The three or four eggs are like those of the Blue-headed, and average 20.3 x 13.5 millimeters. Incubation requires ten to twelve days.

Some of the specimens collected in South Carolina are as follows: Rocky Bottom in Pickens County, May 10, 1935, Chamberlain; Clemson College, October 29, 1927, G. E. Hudson; Lynchburg, Lee County, November 9, 1940, W. M. Perrygo and J. S. Webb; and Mt. Pleasant, December 29, 1896, January 11, 1912, November 6, 1914, and March 1 and 30, 1920, Wayne. All these have been identified by Dr. H. C. Oberholser.

The song is said to be an improvement on that of the Blue-headed, but the behavior and food of the two are alike.

316. RED-EYED VIREO: *Vireo olivaceus* (Linnaeus) (624)

(Lat., *olivaceus*, olivaceous.)

LOCAL NAMES: Magnolia Bird.

DESCRIPTION: Length 5.50 to 6.50 inches. Top of head mouse gray; remaining upper parts grayish olive green; lower surface white, the sides tinged with yellowish olive; wings and tail hair brown, edged exteriorly with yellowish olive; no light wing bars; a dark brown and a white stripe over eye; iris red.

RANGE: Breeds north to northern British Columbia, central southern Mackenzie, and southeastern Quebec; south to northern Mexico and central Florida. Winters north to Colombia and Venezuela; south to Bolivia and central Brazil.

STATUS IN S. C.: Common summer resident, March 15 to November 7, throughout the State. Reported north to Greenville and Marlboro counties; east to Horry County; south to Jasper County; west to Oconee County.

HISTORY: Though possibly not quite as abundant, and certainly not as obvious as the White-eyed, the Red-eyed Vireo is probably the next best known to most observers. Its outstanding characteristic is its persistent song which it pours forth almost constantly all day, to the point of monotony. If only one bird song is heard during the heat of a June day, it will be this one.

The Red-eyed is a common summer resident. It generally arrives in early April and leaves in mid-October. It usually leaves earlier and arrives later in the Piedmont than in the coastal area. G. E. Hudson gives extreme dates of April 6 and October 11 at Clemson College, but Gabriel Cannon reported it from Spartanburg on the unusually late date of November 7, 1915. It is a woodland dweller, usually in dry, high land, but it occurs in the river swamps also. It ranges rather high in the trees, and is therefore hard to see. It lacks the wing bars so characteristic of some of the other vireos, and the dark stripe over the eye is the best field mark, the red eye not being visible unless one is close.

Nesting takes place from early May to the end of that month, and apparently two broods are raised, for the young are to be seen in July. A typical nesting record is May 22, two eggs, Santee, Charleston County (Miss C. P. Rutledge). The nest is suspended by the rim between forks of twigs in forest trees in typical vireo fashion, and is made of bark strippings, bits of rotten wood, and grass, with a lining of pine needles or the inner fibre of moss. There are usually three or four eggs, white with a few fine dots. They average 21.6 x 14.0 millimeters and incubation requires twelve to fourteen days.

Wayne noted that the Red-eyed particularly likes seeds of the magnolia—so much so, he says, that the seeds are "The controlling influence upon the migration of this species in autumn. . . ." The oil in these bright red seeds makes the birds very fat. Wayne added that he had seen as many as fifty in a single magnolia, feeding on the seeds. Murphey made note of similar migrations in the Aiken-Augusta region.

FOOD: Examination of nearly six hundred stomachs of the Red-eyed Vireo has revealed some very interesting facts about its food preferences. Animal matter made up 85 per cent, nearly all of which was insects. Caterpillars composed 32 per cent; beetles, 10 per cent;

stinkbugs, 7 per cent; ants, bees, and wasps, 8 per cent; grasshoppers, 5 per cent. Vegetable content (15 per cent) was composed of mulberries, blackberries, elderberries, currants, blueberries, and grapes, with fruit of the spicebush, bay, Virginia creeper, and sassafras.

Family Parulidae: Wood Warblers

BLACK AND WHITE WARBLER
317. *Mniotilta varia* (Linnaeus) (636)

(Gr., *Mniotilta*, moss-plucking; Lat., *varia*, variegated.)

LOCAL NAMES: Black and White Creeper.

DESCRIPTION: Length 4.50 to 5.50 inches. *Male.* Upper parts black, streaked with white, the crown with a broad central white stripe; undersurface white, streaked with black, except in middle of belly. *Female.* Similar to the male but duller, the white more or less tinged with buff, the streaking of lower parts dull dark gray.

RANGE: Breeds north to southern Mackenzie and Newfoundland; south to central Texas and central South Carolina. Winters north to central California (casually) and South Carolina; south to Ecuador and Venezuela.

STATUS IN S. C.: Fairly common summer resident, March 19 to October 11, in the central and western portions of the State; rare winter resident, in the northwestern and eastern sections of the State. Reported in its summer range north to Caesar's Head and Spartanburg; east to Chester County and Columbia; south to Aiken; west to Oconee County. In winter, observed north to Spartanburg (casually): east to Georgetown County; south to Colleton County; west to Clemson College (casually).

HISTORY: Wayne considered the Black and White Warbler to be a transient visitor in the coastal area and wrote that it nested in the "mountains of South Carolina." The fact has now been definitely established that it breeds as far down as the fall line and that it is a winter visitor in the coastal sections. Therefore, it is a permanent resident of the State.

If all warblers were as easy to know as this interesting bird, there would be none of the confusion that actually exists in the identification of warblers. The Black and White Warbler reminds one strongly of a Nuthatch or a Creeper, and it is unmistakable in its combination of plumage and actions. Black and white it certainly is, for it is streaked above and below with these colors. It creeps about the limbs and trunks of trees exactly like a nuthatch, head up or down, on top of a limb or below it. It prefers to live in heavy swamp lands, but it also frequents dry woods and it sometimes is to be found in company with Chickadees, Titmice, and Kinglets. One reasonably good look at the bird is sufficient for its immediate identification.

The Black and White Warbler builds its nest on the ground, often at the base of a tree or against a log. The nest is composed of bark strippings, grasses, and leaves, and is lined with rootlets, sometimes with hair. It is often practically invisible from above, so well does it blend into its surroundings. There are four or five white eggs, with fine dots, sometimes wreaths of reddish brown. They average 16.8 x 13.7 millimeters. Only one brood is raised and incubation requires about thirteen days.

At or near the mountains the Black and White Warbler occurs from March 19 to October 11 (G. E. Hudson), and the eggs are usually laid in early May. Two breeding dates for Greenville County are April 30, five eggs; and May 7, four eggs (E. J. DeCamps). Nesting dates at the fall line are represented by four eggs at Columbia, April 27, and adult feeding young, May 6 (B. F. Taylor); and at Aiken by three young in nest, May 15, and adults feeding young, May 18 and 28 (Misses L. P. Ford and M. J. Pellew).

In the coast area the spring migration of the Black and White Warbler occurs from the latter part of March to mid-May. Unusually late (or early) was a female seen by E. Milby Burton on June 16, 1949, at Bivens Backwater, Dorchester County. The earliest fall date for the coastal region is July 2, 1909, when a specimen was taken at Summerton, Clarendon County, by E. von S. Dingle. Wayne recorded it in numbers on the coast on July 8, but the main fall migration takes place in late September and early October, with most of the birds continuing south.

The evidence that it winters in South Carolina is as follows: One seen December 1, 1906, in Charleston (H. R. Sass); one seen on January 17, 1907, at Summerville (M. T. Griswold); one taken on Edisto Island, February 10, 1932 (Sprunt); others seen since include birds at Ashepoo River, Colleton County, January 26, 1933; Yeaman's Hall, Charleston County, February 12, 1933; Hasty Point Plantation, Georgetown County, February 6, 1936 (Dr. R. C. Murphy, temperature at the time being 36° F. with sleet falling and swamps frozen); Bull's Island, December 15 and 19, 1942; Huger, Berkeley County, January 13, 1944; Christ Church Parish, Charleston County, December 26, 1946; and Oakland Plantation, Charleston County, February 4, 1948. In Spartanburg County it was recorded on November 25, and December 11 and 23, 1941, by Gabriel Cannon. At Clemson, C. M. Crawford and J. B. Shuler, Jr., found it on November 11 and in December, 1943.

FOOD: This warbler, like the nuthatches and woodpeckers, performs valuable service in consuming many wood-boring insects. It also consumes click and bark beetles, caterpillars, moths, and curculios.

PROTHONOTARY WARBLER
318. *Protonotaria citrea* (Boddaert) (637)

(Lat., *Protonotaria*, chief notary, referring to the yellow head, like a prothonotary's hood; *citrea*, lemon color.)

DESCRIPTION: Length 5.00 to 5.50 inches. *Male*. Head, neck, and anterior lower surface, excepting white lower tail coverts, bright orange yellow; back olive green; rump, wings, and tail slate gray, the last with white spots on outer feathers; bill black. *Female*. Similar, but yellow areas duller and top of the head similar to the back.

RANGE: Breeds north to eastern Nebraska and central Delaware, casually to northern New Jersey; south to eastern Texas and central Florida. Winters north to Yucatan, Nicaragua, and southern Florida; south to Ecuador and Venezuela.

STATUS IN S. C.: Fairly common summer resident, March 27 to September 8, in the eastern part of the State; casually in migration west to Greenwood and Oconee counties.

Recorded north to Chester County; east to Horry County; south to Jasper County; west to Edgefield and Oconee counties.

HISTORY: In attempting description of certain birds one is confronted by a sense of pronounced bafflement. Certainly, that is so in this case. Any adequate treatment of the Prothonotary Warbler in its environment is a difficult task. Dainty, fragile, ethereal, an animated sun ray amid the cool green gloom of watery woodlands, the Prothonotary Warbler seems the very genius of the cypress country. It belongs there; it is as much a part of the lagoons as the knees of the cypress itself or the glowing blossoms of the lotus and the graceful banners of the moss. Though it appears elsewhere, it never seems really at home away from the cypress trees.

It arrives in early April, as a rule, sometimes earlier in forward seasons. During the spring migration it may appear in towns in the tops of tall trees, a distinct departure from its habit of ranging low when it has settled for the season. It has been seen in early April in Charleston, feeding and singing in the tops of tall magnolias, where it looks very much out of place.

The Prothonotary is not common in the interior. G. E. Hudson and F. Sherman list but one record for Clemson, where two were seen on the campus of the College, May 2, 1931, by H. A. Rankin (*Auk*, *53*: 1936, 314). It has been recorded at West Columbia, Lexington County, on May 4 by Mrs. G. E. Charles and at Columbia on April 15 by B. F. Taylor. A. L. Pickens saw one near Troy, Greenwood County, in 1917, and P. M. Jenness saw one on the Catawba River, near Great Falls, Chester County, in May, 1926. W. B. Ward has recorded it near Florence from May to August 30, with one observation on July 18 in Darlington County.

Nesting takes place in late April and early May. The Prothonotary differs from other members of its family in placing its nest in natural cavities of stubs, trees, or wooden structures such as the timbers of old tram roads or trestles in swamps where logging has been carried on. These sites are almost invariably over water and at low elevations, normally 3 to 15 feet. The nest is made of small twigs, leaves, moss, and cypress foliage. There are four to seven eggs almost spherical, white, and heavily splashed with bright reddish brown. Average measurement is 17.5 x 19.2 millimeters. One or two broods are raised, and incubation requires ten to fourteen days.

Typical egg dates are May 2 and June 23 (second brood) and May 3, young just hatched, both Charleston County (E. von S. Dingle); May 21, four eggs, Colleton County (E. J. DeCamps). On May 10, 1926, Sprunt found five nests in a cypress backwater on the Charleston-Berkeley County line; four nests held four eggs; and the other, five. His dates for eggs, over a period of years, range from April 30 to May 15. R. G. Kuerzi found it nesting in Horry County on May 6. John Kershaw found a pair building a nest on April 19 near Graniteville, Aiken County. Misses Louise P. Ford and Marion J. Pellew also found it near Aiken. Kershaw took another nest in Clarendon County on May 4.

The Prothonotary presents no problems to the beginner in identification. Even outside its normal environment of swamp, watercourse, or willow thicket, its brilliant orange-yellow head, throat, and breast, soft gray wings and lower back, and jet-black bill are unlike the markings of any other bird. The song is hardly less distinctive. It usually consists of five notes, a beautiful, ringing whistle which sounds as much like "peet, tweet, tweet, tweet, tweet" as words can render it.

The Prothonotary begins to leave on the southward migration about mid-July. Birds which have nested north of South Carolina continue to appear, however, into early September.

FOOD: Little is definitely known about the diet of this warbler but it is very likely that it consists almost wholly of insects.

SWAINSON'S WARBLER
319. *Limnothlypis swainsonii* (Audubon) (638)

(Gr., *Limnothlypis*, a marsh finch; Lat., *swainsonii*, to William Swainson.)

DESCRIPTION: Length 5.15 to 6.50 inches. Crown olive brown; rump and rest of upper surface olive; a buffy white line over the eye; undersurface yellowish white with an olive gray tinge on the sides.

RANGE: Breeds north to northeastern Oklahoma and central West Virginia; south to southern Louisiana and northern Florida. Winters from Yucatan to Jamaica.

STATUS IN S. C.: Rare summer resident, April 1 to September 28, in all but the northwestern part of the State. Recorded north to Chester County; east to Horry County; south to Beaufort and Jasper counties; west to Aiken, Greenwood, and Oconee counties.

HISTORY: Swainson's Warbler is identified more with South Carolina than with any other State. The species was discovered by Dr. John Bachman in 1833 along the Edisto River of the Low-country, and was named by his famous colleague, Audubon, for William Swainson of England.

After Bachman took the first specimen it was practically a lost species for over half a century. On April 22, 1884, it was rediscovered in South Carolina by Wayne, who, between that date and September 25, 1884, secured forty-seven birds. An account of this remarkable piece of field work was published by William Brewster in the *Auk*, 2: 1885, 65. On June 6, 1885, Wayne found the first nest and eggs known to science, and on the thirtieth of that month obtained another. The first is preserved in the Smithsonian Institution at Washington (*Forest and Stream, 24*: 1885, and the *Auk*, 2: 1885, 346). Swainson's Warbler remains today one of the few land birds really difficult to find and study, being, as Howell (1932) puts it, "well known to only a few ornithologists."

Swainson's Warbler frequents "only deep, dark, and gloomy swamps where there are extensive tracts of cane and impenetrable thickets" (Wayne). While some of this kind of country still remains within the range of the species, it is far from common, and not every tract of even this sort will harbor the bird. Somewhat illustrative of its scarcity is the fact that Sprunt, though he searched for it on many trips with Wayne, and on many trips in the years since Wayne's death, has seen it only four times.

It is a summer resident of the lower half of South Carolina, arriving in early April and remaining until late September. Nesting begins in May and two broods are raised. Eggs of the first brood were found by Wayne on the following dates: May 6, Jasper County; May 15, Beaufort County; June 6 and 30, Charleston County. E. J. DeCamps found a nest with three eggs in Aiken County, June 8, and a second a few days later. A nest of four fresh eggs with a bird incubating was found near the Wando River on May 2 by F. M. Weston. E. von S. Dingle watched a pair about an empty nest near the Wando River, Berkeley County, June 8. R. G. Kuerzi reported a nest in Horry County, May 9. It has been found breeding at Graniteville, Aiken County, by Misses Louise P. Ford and Marion J. Pellew, who discovered a nest with three eggs on May 23, 1920, and one with three young on July 19, the same year.

There are two records from the upper Piedmont, both probably of migrants. One of these is a bird taken near Chester on August 30, 1887, by L. M. Loomis (*Auk*, 4: 1887, 347). The other record is that of a bird studied at close range by J. B. Shuler, Jr., on August 12, 1943, at Clemson. It was called a rare summer resident in Greenwood County by F. W. Hahn, who discovered a nest on July 3, 1924. Evidence that it may breed in the middle of the State was given by W. D. Quattlebaum, who saw and heard four birds in Lexington County on June 3, 1932.

The nest is made of dead leaves of the sweet gum, maple, and water oak, and it is lined with pine needles, cypress leaves, or the black, inner fibre of the Spanish moss. It is placed in low bushes, in clumps of vines, in the broad leaves of scrub palmetto, or in stands of swamp cane. Elevations vary from 1 or 2 feet to 10, and there may be water under the nest. There are usually three, sometimes four, eggs. They are white with a bluish tinge and are normally unmarked although spotted eggs are sometimes found. Measurements average 19.0 x 13.7 millimeters. There are no incubation data.

Swainson's Warbler is a plain bird, brownish above and yellowish white below. Though it is nondescript, the conspicuous white line over the eye is a distinct field aid. There are no wing bars. Because it is shy and retiring most of the time, dull colored, and living in remote, forbidding haunts, few people ever become acquainted with it. On migration it sometimes appears in open situations and seems to be less secretive.

The song is high in warbler performance. Wayne said that no warbler he knew sang "with such fervor as this one." The song period lasts during almost the whole period of the bird's stay in South Carolina, but there is apparently considerable variation in individual ability, for some birds perform more strikingly than others.

Food: What little is known of this warbler's diet indicates that the bird is wholly insectivorous.

WORM-EATING WARBLER

320. *Helmitheros vermivorus* (Gmelin) (639)

(Gr., *Helmitheros*, worm-hunting; Lat., *vermivorus*, worm-eating.)

DESCRIPTION: Length 5.00 to 5.75 inches. Center of crown with a broad stripe of olive buff, bordered on each side with a stripe of brownish black; a similar streak through the eye; remaining upper surface olive green; under parts dull buffy white.

RANGE: Breeds north to southern Iowa and southern Connecticut; south to Arkansas and northern South Carolina. Winters north to Mexico and northern Florida; south to Cuba and Panama.

STATUS IN S. C.: Rare summer resident, April 21 to September 21, in the mountains; a rare transient, April 7 to May 5, and July 3 to November 9, throughout the remainder of the State. In the mountains it has been recorded from Greenville, Pickens, and Oconee counties. In other parts of the State it has been observed north to Chester County; east and south to Charleston County; west to Aiken County.

HISTORY: Though not as uncommon as many of the warblers which visit only the upper portion of South Carolina, the Worm-eating Warbler is little known to most people. It is an unobtrusive bird, inconspicuously plumaged and living in rather heavy swamps not likely to be penetrated by anyone except nature students and hunters.

It is a summer resident in the upper portion of South Carolina and nests there, but it appears in the coastal plain only as a transient visitor. Indications are that it sometimes breeds in the Low-country. Audubon said that it did, on the strength of Dr. Bachman's statements to that effect. Wayne secured a bird, which must have "hatched not far from Charleston," on July 3, 1884, and another on August 1, 1902. L. M. Loomis found it nesting commonly at Caesar's Head and at Mt. Pinnacle in 1890-91, with young hardly able to fly on June 29. It has been noted at Clemson, Oconee County, from April 21 to September 21, by G. E. Hudson and probably nests in the vicinity during that period.

The nest is on the ground, usually in a slight depression; it is made of leaves, grasses, and rootlets and is lined with hair or fine grass. There are four to six white eggs, spotted and splashed in varying degrees with chestnut and lavender. They average 17.3 x 13.7 millimeters and incubation requires about thirteen days. One brood is raised.

The Worm-eating Warbler stays in the coastal section from early April to early May, and from early July to mid-October. There is one very late record near Charleston on November 9 (J. E. Mosimann and G. B. Rabb). L. M. Loomis recorded it as transient at Chester from April 19 to May 12, and from July 25 to October 6. It is more common in fall than spring, but as it is essentially a bird of remote situations, comparatively few are seen unless particularly looked for.

The Worm-eating Warbler lacks the brilliance of many of its colorful family. It is plain olive green above and whitish beneath, but the recognizable character is the head which is conspicuously striped. This is easily seen, for the bird is low ranging, often on the ground or in low bush growth.

Curiously enough, it does not hop like most of the other small birds, but walks. In this respect it reminds one of the Oven-bird and, at first glance, looks not unlike that warbler.

FOOD: Entirely insects—grasshoppers, beetles, caterpillars, saw-fly larvae, dragon flies, and bees.

GOLDEN-WINGED WARBLER
321. *Vermivora chrysoptera* (Linnaeus) (642)

(Lat., *Vermivora*, worm-eating; Gr., *chrysoptera*, golden-winged.)

DESCRIPTION: Length 4.50 to 5.30 inches. *Male.* Plain gray above, but the forehead, crown, and large wing patches yellow; throat and broad stripe from eye to behind the ear black; remaining lower parts white. *Female.* Similar, but pattern duller, the black of the male becoming gray.

RANGE: Breeds north to central Minnesota and southern New Hampshire; south to northern Missouri and northwestern South Carolina. Winters north to southern Mexico and Guatemala; south to Colombia and Venezuela.

STATUS IN S. C.: Rare summer resident, April 21 to September, in the mountains; rare transient elsewhere. Recorded in the mountains from Greenville, Pickens, and Oconee counties. As a transient elsewhere, reported from Chester, Aiken, and Dorchester counties.

HISTORY: The Golden-winged Warbler, distinctive and easily recognized, is unfortunately very uncommon in South Carolina. It occurs but rarely in the upper counties; there are only two records below the fall line, one established by Murphey with a specimen taken September 28, at Beech Island, Aiken County, a few miles south of Augusta, on the South Carolina side of the Savannah River; the other was a female taken on April 29, 1940, at St. George, Dorchester County, by W. M. Perrygo and J. S. Y. Hoyt. The latter specimen is in the United States National Museum.

Many years ago, L. M. Loomis found it nesting in the mountains of Pickens County and at Caesar's Head, Greenville County, thus establishing it as a summer resident there. He also secured specimens at Chester in late summer (August 20 to September 22) where he rated it as a rare migrant. The only records from Clemson are those of H. A. Rankin, two on April 25, ten on May 3, 1933; and one on April 21, 1935 (G. E. Hudson and F. Sherman). P. M. Jenness considered it an uncommon migrant at Greenville, where it has been recorded from April 28 to May 10. Such birds are probably en route to nearby nesting grounds at higher elevations.

The nest, made of bark strippings, grass, and plant fibres, is situated in weed clumps or briers close to the ground. The four or five eggs are white, lightly or heavily spotted and wreathed with gray and chestnut. Some markings are very small, others quite splashy. They average 15.7 x 12.7 millimeters. One brood is raised, and incubation requires about ten days.

The Golden-wing frequents open, brushy hillsides and pastures where low bushes and vines grow profusely. Its bright blacks and yellows, together with soft grays and white, make it a striking bird. As Peterson (1947) points out "No other Warbler has . . . *yellow wing-patch and black throat*." A line through the eye is also black.

The migration route of the Golden-wing is principally by way of the Gulf Coast, and the bird is rare anywhere in the South Atlantic area.

FOOD: Almost entirely insects.

322. BLUE-WINGED WARBLER: *Vermivora pinus* (Linnaeus) (641)

(Lat., *pinus*, a pine.)

DESCRIPTION: Length 4.50 to 5.00 inches. *Male*. Crown and entire undersurface bright yellow; a black line through the eye; back olive green; wings and tail gray, the former with two white bars, the tail with white spots on the four outer tail feathers. *Female*. Similar to the male but duller; yellow of crown and forehead obscured by olive green.

RANGE: Breeds north to eastern Nebraska and central eastern Massachusetts; south to Kansas and northern Georgia. Winters north to Mexico; south to Guatemala and Colombia.

STATUS IN S. C.: Rare transient, April 18 to 30, and August 21 to September 26, in the eastern half of the State. Reported north to Chester County; east to Horry County; south to Dewees Island and Summerville; west to Graniteville (Aiken County).

HISTORY: The Blue-winged Warbler is better known in South Carolina than the Golden-winged. It is not as striking a bird as the Golden-winged, the black about the head being confined to a thin line through the eye.

The Blue-wing does not nest in the State, being a transient visitor. It was first taken in the State near Chester by L. M. Loomis, April 30, 1887 (*Auk, 8*: 1891, 169). It was not until April 19, 1909, that another was recorded, a male seen by John Kershaw at Graniteville, Aiken County. It was first found on the coast by Wayne, who saw one on April 30, 1920. In the fall of that year he secured three, a male on September 4, and a male and female seven days later. It was again found in this region when E. von S. Dingle took one on September 10, 1928, and observed another on the twelfth of that month at Middleburg Plantation, Berkeley County. Since then there have been several observations: A male seen on Dewee's Island, Charleston County, on April 21, 1934, by C. A. Urner of New Jersey; a male seen May 5, 1940, by R. G. Kuerzi at Long Bay Plantation, Horry County; one observed at Columbia by Mrs. G. E. Charles on April 19, 1942; another seen in 1942 at Summerville, Dorchester County, by Mrs. M. J. Bischoff on April 18; one seen on August 21, 1943, by J. S. Y. Hoyt at Summerville; and most recently, a male recorded at Pawley's Island, Georgetown County, by C. S. Robbins on April 23, 1948.

BACHMAN'S WARBLER
323. *Vermivora bachmanii* (Audubon) (640)

(Lat., *bachmanii*, to Dr. John Bachman.)

DESCRIPTION: Length 4.25 to 4.50 inches. *Male*. Forehead, eye ring, chin, and abdomen yellow; anterior part of crown black edged with gray; hind head and hind neck gray; back olive green; chest with a black patch; wings and tail dull gray, edged with olive green, the latter with white markings near the tips of three to four outer feathers. *Female.* Similar to the male but without black on chest or head; breast shaded with gray.

RANGE: Breeds north to southeastern Missouri and Kentucky; south to central Alabama and southeastern South Carolina. Winters in Cuba.

STATUS IN S. C.: Rare summer resident from the first week in March to July 19, in the coast region. Reported from only Charleston County.

HISTORY: The history of this rare species parallels in many ways that of Swainson's Warbler. Both were discovered by Dr. John Bachman near Charleston in the 1830's; both were named by Audubon; both were lost to science for many years; and both were rediscovered in South Carolina by Wayne. The full history of the bird is too long for a detailed account, but it deserves at least to be outlined.

Wayne secured the second specimen for South Carolina on May 15, 1901, sixty-eight years after Bachman's record. His easily understood excitement over the discovery is reflected in his account in the *Auk, 18*: 1901, 274. The specimen was taken near Mt. Pleasant, Charleston County. On May 13, 1905, he took the first young birds known to science, one male and one female. These were recorded both by Wayne and by William Brewster, in the *Auk, 22*: 1905, 392, 399. These immature birds were secured in the same place (I'On Swamp) where Bachman probably took the type specimen in the 1830's, the area being on Fairlawn Plantation, Christ Church Parish, Charleston County.

On April 17, 1906, Wayne found two nests in this swamp, each with four eggs. One was in a scrub palmetto, the other in a clump of cane. The eggs were pure white, averaging 15.5 x 11.7 millimeters. Later in the same season, he found a nest holding one young bird (April 28), this being within "ten or twelve feet of the nest of a Swainson's Warbler, containing three eggs." A deserted nest was found May 9, holding three eggs, again very near the nest of a Swainson's Warbler. An empty nest was discovered on May 12. On June 2, the sixth nest was found, from which the young had flown. Curiously enough, the lining of the nests taken on April 17, a very lustrous black, thread-like fibre, was the same material found in the first nest known to science, discovered by Otto Widmann in southeastern Missouri, May 17, 1897.

The next season, 1907, Wayne found two more nests in I'On Swamp; one on March 27, which was left until the thirtieth when it held four eggs, and the other April 3, with five eggs, in an advanced state of incubation. He did not find another (the ninth) until April 20, 1916. The last nest he found was also in I'On Swamp. It was discovered on March 28, 1918, and recorded in the *Auk, 35*: 1918, 441. None has been found in South Carolina since 1918, a period of thirty-one years. These dates show that Bachman's Warbler breeds earlier than such resident species as the Yellow-throated and Pine Warblers, it being one of the very first spring migrants.

The last bird taken by Wayne was a young male on July 16, 1919, near his home, and from that time until very recently, the species disappeared again. Sprunt often accompanied Wayne on searches for it during the years from 1924 to 1930, the year of Wayne's death. They made trip after trip to I'On Swamp each season, not one of which was successful. The bird had simply vanished from this region, for, had it been there, they would certainly have found at least the male. Bachman's Warbler is primarily a bird of heavy swamp lands with much undergrowth of cane, scrub palmetto, thick bushes, and tangles of cat brier. It is difficult country to work in during spring, for the foliage is very dense, the mosquitoes and ticks are bad, and venomous snakes are not unknown.

As the years passed with no recurrence of the warbler, the few ornithological observers of the Low-country came to regard it as an almost legendary species. Curiously enough, it was a visiting ornithologist who found it again. In 1938, C. Chandler Ross, a member of the Delaware Valley Ornithological Club, Philadelphia, came to McClellanville, and spent some time in bird study there. On April 2, of that year, he saw a "full plumaged male" Bachman's Warbler. It being his first visit to South Carolina, he was unaware of the importance of his find, and did not communicate it until the summer of 1947, when he wrote to Sprunt about it. In his letter he says that the bird "was in a very dense tangle of bushes and vines. I squeaked him up to about eight feet from me, near enough to get a very good . . . look at him." This was the first specimen seen in twenty-one years, and might be termed a rediscovery of a rediscovery.

Another but shorter period of years intervened, and history repeated itself. Again the discoverer was a visitor. Henry Kennon, a former director of the Milwaukee Zoological Park, who was spending some time at McClellanville, saw, on July 19, 1946, a singing male Bachman's Warbler a few miles from that village. He recorded it again in the spring of 1947 near the same place. Like Ross, he did not make the observation known for some time.

On May 8, 1948, Thomas M. Uzzell, Jr.. and Thomas R. Rivers saw a warbler at Fairlawn Plantation which they felt sure was a male Bachman's. On May 11, J. E. Mosimann, G. B. Rabb, and N. H. Seebeck, Jr., were shown the bird and agreed to the identification. They communicated at once with Chamberlain, who with them and E. A. Williams, went to the swamp on the sixteenth and succeeded in finding the bird. On the twentieth, Chamberlain, Sprunt, and E. Milby Burton made a trip there, and though they several times heard the male singing, they could not locate it. Another attempt on the twenty-second proved successful for Sprunt, who at last saw the bird. This specimen was seen on the same plantation where most of Wayne's birds occurred and on which he found all of his nests. The female was never located, but that there was a nest nearby can scarcely be doubted.

During this same season (1948) the McClellanville area again produced Bachman's Warbler, for on May 30 a female was seen by Mrs. Robert D. Edwards, a short distance from the village. Not realizing its rarity, she said nothing of it for some time. On June 12, in the same place, she saw a male. These birds had no doubt completed nesting and were probably wandering.

In 1949, Bachman's Warbler was found once more at Fairlawn. Two males and a female were recorded during May by Seebeck, Uzzell, and Rabb and were shown to several visitors.

The above records constitute the history of this intensely interesting bird in South Carolina to date. It is one of the most elusive and unpredictable birds of the country, and the sight of it is the goal of every student, one which only a comparative few have attained.

Bachman's Warbler is, without any doubt, more difficult to locate in its environment than any other bird for which the writers have ever searched. Though it sings close at hand, its small size, the density of the undergrowth which it frequents, and its constant activity make it virtually impossible to see. The song is difficult to describe; it is high and thin, and Wayne likened it to the songs of the Worm-eating and Parula Warblers. It is much like the latter's without its characteristic ending. It has a certain ventriloquial quality which does not help in locating the singer.

FOOD: Virtually nothing is known about the food of Bachman's Warbler except that it consists of caterpillars and some ants. The kind of country frequented by the bird contains many insects, and other members of the genus are highly insectivorous. There is no reason to suppose that Bachman's Warbler differs from other warblers in its choice of food.

TENNESSEE WARBLER
324. *Vermivora peregrina* (Wilson) (647)

(Lat., *peregrina*, wandering.)

DESCRIPTION: Length 4.50 to 5.00 inches. *Male.* Upper parts olive green, the head and hind neck plain gray; a narrow white line over eye and a dark brown line through it; undersurface white. *Female.* Similar to the male but head tinged with green; lower parts yellowish white. *Immature.* Dull olive green above and mostly pale olive greenish yellow below.

RANGE: Breeds north to southern Yukon and southeastern Quebec; south to south central British Columbia and Maine. Winters north to Mexico; south to Colombia and Venezuela.

STATUS IN S. C.: Uncommon transient, September 8 to October 30, throughout the State, but most common in the northwestern portion. One spring record (May). Recorded north to Greenville and Chester counties; east and south to Charleston County; west to Oconee County.

HISTORY: The Tennessee Warbler, common enough in its range, is known in South Carolina as an uncommon migrant in the Piedmont. There are only two coastal records. L. M. Loomis, who was apparently the first to find it in the State, took a specimen on September 25, 1879, near Chester. He found it fairly regularly there during the years 1886 to 1888, and secured a total of twenty-three specimens, which

PLATE XXV: AVIAN MEDLEY
Water Color by John Henry Dick

Four birds at left, top to bottom: White-eyed Vireo, Yellow-throated Vireo, Blue-headed Vireo, and Blue-gray Gnatcatcher (male). Three birds at right, top to bottom: Cedar Waxwing, Carolina Chickadee, and Red-eyed Vireo.

he recorded in the *Auk, 8*: 1891, 170. The earliest of these was September 8 and the latest October 15. He never saw it in the spring.

J. R. Nowell told Wayne that he had frequently taken the Tennessee Warbler in Anderson County in the fall, and there are in the Charleston Museum two specimens which he secured at Anderson on October 16 and 17, 1896, which substantiate his statement. G. E. Hudson noted the bird at Clemson only from September 17 to 21, 1926, but C. M. Crawford and J. B. Shuler, Jr., saw at least five birds there from October 13 to 30, 1943. The only spring record is an observation at Aiken, where John Kershaw noted a male on May 11, 1909.

There are two instances of its occurrence on the coast, one a bird seen October 10, 1900, by Wayne, near Mt. Pleasant. He says it ". . . unfortunately was not secured." He stated that it was in a live oak hanging on the end of a leaf in a titmouse-like manner. Retreating to a "proper" distance, Wayne fired at it and missed, an extraordinary occurrence for him. The other coastal record was made by Allan R. Phillips, who secured a specimen on October 18, 1942, near Stark General Hospital, Charleston. The specimen is now in the Charleston Museum collection.

The Tennessee is a plain warbler, greenish above, white below, with a narrow white line over the eye and a dark one through it. It is well to remember that it ranges high, in the tops of tall trees, where it is difficult to see.

Food: Entirely composed of insects.

Orange-crowned Warbler
325. *Vermivora celata celata* (Say)   (646)

(Lat., *celata*, concealed, referring to crown patch.)

Description: Length 4.60 to 5.30 inches. Upper surface grayish olive green, with a tawny patch on the head, which is mostly concealed; undersurface pale yellow or yellowish white, but throat tinged with gray; wings and tail hair brown.

Range: Breeds north to northern Alaska and northern Mackenzie; south to central Alaska and northern Manitoba. Winters north to southern California and Massachusetts; south to Mexico and southern Florida.

Status in S. C.: Fairly common winter resident, September 20 to May 11, chiefly in the coast region. Observed north to Chester County; east to Horry County; south to Port Royal; west to Aiken and Oconee counties.

History: The Orange-crowned Warbler is a plain, unobtrusive, inconspicuous little warbler virtually unknown to most South Carolinians. To those who are not interested in birds, it is "just a little greenish bird," along with scores of other little greenish birds. As many students have often been told, its outstanding field mark is the fact that it does not possess any. Peterson (1947) terms it "The dingiest of all warblers." About all one can say of its appearance is that it is a grayish, olive-green bird, slightly paler beneath and having no wing bars.

Nevertheless it is an interesting little bird, not particularly hard to find in its some-what limited range in the State. It is a winter resident, occurring mainly below the fall line and at times being very common in the coastal counties. It has been recorded but once from Clemson. G. E. Hudson took one there on March 23, 1928. It has also been seen at Aiken, May 3, by John Kershaw. L. M. Loomis took one on October 21 and another on April 24 at Chester, indicating a scarce transient status there.

On the coast it arrives in late October and remains until the second week in April as a rule. In some years it is common in November, and the colder the weather, the more likely one is to find the bird. Wayne points out that "It is capable of enduring intense cold." He recalled seeing many birds years ago near Charleston, when the temperature ranged as low as 8° F. Such low temperatures are so rare in this latitude as to be phenomenal.

The Orange-crowned Warbler is not well named, for the orange-brown patch on the head is so well concealed, even in spring plumage, as to be hardly visible in the field even under the most advantageous conditions. In winter it is not present at all in many specimens. The bird is to be looked for in scrubby oak growth, the edges of woodlands, and thickets of myrtle, cassina, and similar vegetation, and in live oak avenues of the plantation country. It is common at times on the barrier islands, both in the jungle-like woods and in the clumps of myrtle between the forest and dunes of high-water mark.

FOOD: Chiefly insects—caterpillars, wasps, ants, flies, small beetles, and moths. In winter it eats a few seeds and berries.

ROCKY MOUNTAIN ORANGE-CROWNED WARBLER
326. *Vermivora celata orestera* Oberholser (646c)

(Gr., *orestera*, dwelling on the mountains.)

DESCRIPTION: Similar to the Orange-crowned Warbler, but larger, and more strongly suffused with yellow both above and below.

RANGE: Breeds north to British Columbia and Alberta; south to southeastern California and central New Mexico. Winters south to southern Lower California, Mexico, and South Carolina (accidentally).

STATUS IN S. C.: Accidental.

HISTORY: There is only one record of this race of the Orange-crowned Warbler from South Carolina, a specimen collected by Wayne at Mt. Pleasant, December 6, 1893, and identified by Dr. H. C. Oberholser. It is in the Charleston Museum collection.

In habits and food it does not differ from the Orange-crowned Warbler.

NASHVILLE WARBLER
327. *Vermivora ruficapilla ruficapilla* (Wilson) (645)

(Lat., *ruficapilla*, reddish-haired.)

DESCRIPTION: Length 4.50 to 5.00 inches. *Male*. Head and neck gray; crown bright chestnut; remainder of upper surface olive green; eye ring white; under parts yellow, posteriorly white. *Female*. Pattern of coloration similar to that of the male, but colors much duller and the crown patch smaller or absent.

RANGE: Breeds north to central Saskatchewan and northern Nova Scotia; south to Nebraska, New Jersey, and Connecticut. Winters north to southern Texas, southern Florida, and casually eastern Massachusetts; south to Mexico and Guatemala.

STATUS IN S. C.: Rare spring transient, April 19 to May 1, throughout the State. Identified north and east to Horry County; south to St. Helena Island; west to Aiken and Oconee counties.

HISTORY: Because it is a very rare visitor in South Carolina, the Nashville Warbler is practically unknown. For many years it was on the Hypothetical List, placed there by Wayne, who considered Coues' statement (1868) that it occurred in the State to be without sufficient justification. Wayne never saw it, nor did L. M. Loomis in the Piedmont. Indeed there are but two sight records and two specimens since the time Coues listed it.

The first specimen is a female taken on St. Helena Island, Beaufort County, on May 1, 1892, and now in the collection of the Chicago Natural History Museum. The collector is not designated on the label but was probably Walter J. Hoxie, who worked in the Beaufort region at that time. The next occurrence was at Aiken, where John Kershaw saw a male on April 19, 1909. Eighteen years elapsed before another was noted. This one was also a male, taken by G. E. Hudson on April 27, 1927, at Clemson College and recorded by him in the *Auk*, *45*: 1928, 103. The most recent record is of a singing male seen by R. G. Kuerzi at Long Bay Plantation, Horry County, on April 28, 1940.

The Nashville Warbler was discovered about 1811 at Nashville, Tennessee, by Alexander Wilson, who named the bird for that city. It breeds from the northern parts of the United States into Canada.

NORTHERN PARULA WARBLER
328. *Parula americana pusilla* (Wilson) (648a)

(Lat., *Parula*, a little titmouse; *americana*, of America; *pusilla*, very little.)

DESCRIPTION: Length 4.25 to 4.90 inches. Similar to the Southern Parula Warbler but larger, except the bill, which averages smaller; coloration darker above; and dark chest band wider.

RANGE: Breeds north to eastern Nebraska, northern Minnesota, and southeastern Quebec; south to Texas and Maryland. Winters north to Mexico and northern Florida; south to Nicaragua and the Barbados.

STATUS IN S. C.: Fairly common transient, March 18 to May 4, and in September, in the eastern and middle parts of the State, probably also in the western section. Reported north and west to York County; east to Horry County; south to Beaufort County.

HISTORY: The following specimens of the Northern Parula Warbler have been examined and identified by Dr. H. C. Oberholser: two, taken by Wayne at Mt. Pleasant on March 21, 1911, and March 18, 1921; one taken by E. von S. Dingle at Huger, Berkeley County, May 4, 1929; one taken at Gray's Hill, Beaufort County, by W. H. Corning, April 4, 1940; one taken at Conway, April 16, 1940, and another at Rock Hill, September 20, 1940, by W. M. Perrygo and J. S. Y. Hoyt. One was taken by Allan R. Phillips at Charleston on September 27, 1942, and identified by him as of this race.

The habits are approximately the same as those of the Southern Parula Warbler.

SOUTHERN PARULA WARBLER
329. *Parula americana americana* (Linnaeus) (648)

LOCAL NAMES: Blue Yellow-backed Warbler.

DESCRIPTION: Length 4.00 to 4.50 inches. *Male.* Sides and top of head, hind neck and sides of neck, bluish gray; back and rump similar but paler, the middle of back yellowish olive green; wings with two white bars; throat and chest lemon yellow, and a band of blackish brown across the latter, above an indistinct band of tawny; belly white; sides tinged with gray. *Female.* Similar but duller, usually without dark breast markings. *Immature.* Like the female but back washed with olive green.

RANGE: Breeds north to northern Alabama and the District of Columbia; south to southern Alabama and southern Florida. Winters north to northern Florida; and south to the Bahama Islands.

STATUS IN S. C.: Common summer resident, March 6 (casually February 20) to October 28, throughout the State. Recorded north to Greenville, Chester, and Marlboro counties; east to Horry County; south to Jasper County; west to Aiken and Oconee counties.

HISTORY: This dainty little bird has always seemed to us to be the most abundant of the summer warblers, certainly on the coast. It is among the earliest migrants, for it always appears in March, as Wayne says, "As soon as the sweet gum trees begin to bud. . . ." An unusually early occurrence of the Parula Warbler was recorded in February, 1927, when a dead bird was found on the twentieth of the month by P. G. Porcher, Jr., and taken to Wayne some days later. Wayne notes in his manuscript that it was the "first February record in all my experience in 43 years." It stays on the coast until late October, most birds having departed by the twenty-first. Spring dates for the Piedmont are later than for the coast, and the bird leaves the Piedmont earlier; G. E. Hudson noted it at Clemson from April 9 (earliest) to September 28 (latest).

It is in full song on arrival and sings indefatigably. In suburban and rural districts, there is an almost constant chorus all day long in spring and early summer. The song falls off sharply in July and is not heard late that month or until the birds leave, except very sporadically. It is difficult to describe, a very rapid little "zee-zee-zee" trill, rising abruptly at the end. Peterson (1939) describes it as "a buzzy trill which climbs the scale and tips over at the top."

Almost any woodland with Spanish moss will harbor the Parula. It particularly likes cypress swamps though it is not by any means confined to such areas. Outside the range of the moss, that is, outside of the Low-country, it resorts chiefly to deciduous growth.

Very small, intensely active, and fond of the thick foliage of live oaks, the Parula is sometimes hard to study, but it often feeds in low growth and is not at all shy; hence, one may occasionally watch it at very close range. At such time, the Audubonian name of Blue Yellow-backed Warbler seems very apt. The dark band across the chest is a good field mark.

Nesting starts soon after arrival, particularly in late March. Early April sees activity in selecting a site and building the nest, but this can happen throughout the month. Wayne took eggs on April 15, and B. F. Taylor noted nest building at Columbia April 14. Sprunt has yard dates of May 8, four eggs, and May 20, three eggs. In the coast country, the nest is always in Spanish moss, completely concealed in the swaying banners of this growth, and it is to be found only by watching the bird go to it. Elevation will vary from hardly more than 6 feet to over 100. The nest is composed of fine grass and strands of the moss, woven together and into the supporting festoon. It is a pretty structure. The eggs, usually four, may number from three to seven, and are white with flecks and larger markings of red brown and lilac. They average 16.8 x 11.9 millimeters. Two broods are often raised. Incubation requires about twelve days.

Food: Apparently limited to insects—ants, bees, wasps, beetles, weevils, scale insects, and fly larvae.

Eastern Yellow Warbler
330. *Dendroica petechia aestiva* (Gmelin) (652)

(Gr., *Dendroica*, tree-inhabiting; Lat., *petechia*, island-seeking; *aestiva*, pertaining to summer.)

Local Names: Summer Yellow-bird; Wild Canary.

Description: Length 4.50 to 5.25 inches. *Male*. Anterior part of top of head yellow, with a somewhat orange-tawny tinge; remainder of upper parts olive green; sides of head and under parts deep yellow, the latter streaked with chestnut; wings and tail edged with olive green, the latter with the inner webs yellow. *Female*. Similar to the male but duller, plain olive green above; and with lemon yellow under parts very faintly, sometimes not at all, streaked.

Range: Breeds north to Minnesota and Maine; south to southern Louisiana (casually) and northern South Carolina. Winters north to Mexico, Venezuela, and South Carolina (accidentally); south to central Peru and northern Brazil.

Status in S. C.: Common summer resident, April to July, in the northwestern section; common transient, April 1 to May 27, and July 4 to October 29, throughout the rest of the State. Accidental in winter in the coast region. Recorded in summer north to Greenville

County; east to Chester County; south to Anderson County; west to Oconee and Pickens counties.

HISTORY: This is one of the best known warblers of the east, and even beyond, for it has a tremendous range and breeds over much of North America. The Yellow Warbler is fond of willow thickets along streams and about ponds, though it also frequents brushy pasture lands, orchards, the grounds of farmhouses, and the edges of towns. It is known even to those who have little interest in birds, for it is an abundant, brightly colored species. It is often called "Wild Canary" and "Summer Yellow-bird." Certainly it is an easy warbler to recognize, for no other appears to be entirely yellow, as this bird does at a little distance. Actually, there are thin reddish streakings on the breast, but one must be near the bird to see them. The song of the Yellow Warbler is a bright little melody, frequently uttered, and likely to attract attention.

It arrives on the South Carolina coast in early April, and is to be seen there until about May 20 when it leaves for the interior, where it is a summer resident above the fall line. By early July it is back again on the coast. There it stays until the last of October. P. M. Jenness records its arrival date about Greenville as April 14 (earliest). L. M. Loomis found it nesting in the cultivated valleys of Pickens County in the 1880's. He also found it throughout the summer at Chester. A nest was taken by John Kershaw on the banks of the Chattooga River at Russell, Oconee County, on June 23, 1909. From the foothills southward toward the fall line, it is found all summer and no doubt breeds locally in that area.

There are three winter records for this species from the coastal area. Two of them were made by Dr. Eugene Swope at his Summerville feeding stations. He noted one there on January 21, 1940, and said he had also seen the species during the winter of 1939. The other record is an observation by James E. Mosimann and George B. Rabb of a male in bright plumage in Hampton Park, Charleston, on January 18, 1947.

The nest is a well made, symmetrical cup of vegetable fibres, grass, and plant down, lined with hair and placed in the crotch of a bush or tree. It is one of the most compact, neat, and finished structures of small birds. The eggs, generally four or five, are white, much speckled, splashed, and wreathed with shades of brown and lilac. They average 17.8 x 12.7 millimeters. The incubation period is about ten days.

FOOD: Almost entirely insects, among which are boring and bark beetles, weevils, caterpillars, cankerworms, and others.

ALASKA YELLOW WARBLER
331. *Dendroica petechia rubiginosa* (Pallas) (625b)

(Lat., *rubiginosa*, rusty.)

DESCRIPTION: Similar to the Eastern Yellow Warbler but upper parts darker; the head like the back; wings also duller.

RANGE: Breeds north to central southern Alaska; south to southeastern Alaska. Winters south to Mexico and Panama.

STATUS IN S. C.: Accidental.

HISTORY: The only record for South Carolina is a single immature individual which was picked up dead in the garden of the Heyward-Washington House in Charleston by Miss Emma B. Richardson on October 10, 1933, and taken to the Charleston Museum. It was subsequently identified by Dr. Alexander Wetmore as a specimen of the Alaska Yellow Warbler, which is of only accidental occurrence in the eastern United States.

In habits and food it differs little from the other yellow warblers.

NEWFOUNDLAND YELLOW WARBLER
332. *Dendroica petechia amnicola* Batchelder (652e)

(Lat., *amnicola*, a river dweller.)

DESCRIPTION: Similar to the Eastern Yellow Warbler but upper parts darker; the head more tinged with olive green. Similar to the Alaska Yellow Warbler but not so dark; the upper parts, and particularly the crown, more yellowish.

RANGE: Breeds north to northern Mackenzie, southern Ungava, and Newfoundland; south to central Alaska and Nova Scotia. Winters south to South America (probably).

STATUS IN S. C.: Rare transient.

HISTORY: There is only one South Carolina specimen of the Newfoundland Yellow Warbler. It is an immature bird taken by John F. Freeman at Mt. Pleasant on September 21, 1937, and identified by Dr. H. C. Oberholser. It is in the collection of the Charleston Museum. In all probability this race is, however, of more frequent occurrence than our present knowledge indicates.

In habits and food it is similar to the other yellow warblers.

MAGNOLIA WARBLER
333. *Dendroica magnolia* (Wilson) (657)

(Lat., *magnolia*, a genus of plants, dedicated to P. Magnol, a seventeenth century botanist.)

DESCRIPTION: Length 4.45 to 5.10 inches. *Male*. Crown slate color; post-ocular stripe white; a broad band through the eye, and hind neck, gray; back black, the feathers with olive edges; rump yellow; lower parts bright yellow with black streaks, but the under tail coverts white; wings and tail brownish black, each of the former with a white patch, the tail with a broad white band across the middle, excepting the central pair of feathers. *Female*. Similar to the male but colors much duller. *Immature*. Similar to the adult female, but head, back, and neck dull brownish olive; the white wing patches and the streaks on under parts much subdued.

RANGE: Breeds north to central Mackenzie (casually) and Newfoundland; south to central Alberta, southwestern North Carolina, and Massachusetts. Winters north to Mexico and northern Florida; south to Panama.

STATUS IN S. C.: Fairly common transient, April 17 to May 18, and September 3 to November 12, throughout the State, though more numerous in the northwestern section. Recorded north to Greenville, York, and Marlboro counties; east and south to Charleston and Colleton counties; west to Aiken, Anderson, and Oconee counties.

HISTORY: The Magnolia Warbler is one of the most striking of the wood warblers in appearance, a really beautiful species, whose former (Audubonian) name of Black and Yellow Warbler was rather more appropriate than its present one. It is highly variegated in plumage and the male is unmistakable. It has the Redstart habit of frequently spreading the tail, which appears at such times to be wholly white with a black terminal band.

Like many of its family it is more likely to be found in the Piedmont area of South Carolina than anywhere else in the State. It is a fairly common transient visitor there in autumn, but less so in spring. L. M. Loomis found it in Chester County during the first two weeks of May and from September 3 to mid-October. In Oconee County it has been noted from April 29 (Miss Elizabeth Ravenel) to May 18 (G. E. Hudson), and from September 18 (Hudson) to October 18 (C. M. Crawford and J. B. Shuler, Jr.). Other Piedmont records include a specimen taken at Anderson by H. T. Nowell on October 21, one seen by P. M. Jenness at Greenville on May 2, and one observed at Rock Hill, York County, on September 22 by J. E. Mosimann.

Mid-State records are few. Murphey found it rare in spring in the Aiken-Augusta region, but abundant in fall. In Clarendon County, John Kershaw observed a male on April 17. W. M. Perrygo and J. S. Webb secured an immature at Bennettsville on October 5, 1940.

On the coast it is so uncommon that all records are of interest. Wayne established the first one on September 29, 1912, when he took a male at Oakland Plantation, Charleston County (*Auk, 30*: 1913, 277). Two days later (October 1) F. M. Weston saw a female, and this was also noted in the *Auk, 30*: 1913, 114. Wayne took two other specimens, one on October 10, 1915, and the other on October 3, 1923. It was next found in the Low-country by Sprunt, who saw an immature bird on November 12, 1932, at Cherokee Plantation, Colleton County (*Auk, 50*: 1933, 117). On September 27, 1941, an immature was found in Charleston by E. A. Williams; the bird was later banded and released by Chamberlain. Since then, ob-

PLATE XXVI: WARBLERS

Water Color by Roger Tory Peterson

Three top birds, left to right: Redstart (female), Redstart (adult male), and Redstart (immature male). Right center, left to right: Yellow-throat (female), and Yellow-throat (male). Lower birds, left to right: Western Palm Warbler (fall plumage), Western Palm Warbler (spring plumage), Yellow Palm Warbler (spring plumage), and Black and White Warbler (male).

servations of this species have become more frequent. Allan R. Phillips secured one at Stark General Hospital, Charleston, on October 18, 1942. On October 11 and 12, 1943, three members of the Linnaean Society of New York, Eugene Eisenman, John Bull, Jr., and George Komorowski, saw a single bird on Bull's Island. J. E. Mosimann and G. B. Rabb saw several on October 18 and 19, 1946, near Charleston. The most recent record is of seven birds seen on the Charleston Museum grounds by Chamberlain, October 5, 1948.

The Magnolia is found in deciduous woodlands, shrubby openings and clearings, and damp thickets. It is an active, nervous species, being in this respect much like the other members of its family.

FOOD: The Magnolia Warbler is almost wholly insectivorous.

334. CAPE MAY WARBLER: *Dendroica tigrina* (Gmelin) (650)

(Lat., *tigrina*, striped like a tiger.)

DESCRIPTION: Length 4.70 to 5.65 inches. *Male.* Top of head black; remaining upper parts olive green spotted with black; rump olive yellow; sides of head rufous chestnut to auburn; lower parts and sides of neck yellow, heavily streaked on sides and breast with black; a prominent white patch on wing; outer tail feathers with white spots. *Female.* Head and back olive; no rufous chestnut cheek patches; not much white on wings; under parts dull pale yellow, streaked with brownish gray. *Immature.* Similar, but much duller than the adult female.

RANGE: Breeds north to southern Mackenzie and southeastern Quebec; south to northern Wisconsin and Nova Scotia. Winters north to southern Florida, the District of Columbia (casually), and the Bahama Islands; south to Tobago Island.

STATUS IN S. C.: Fairly common transient, April 15 to May 17, and September 4 to November 3, throughout the State, though more common in the northwestern section. Reported north to Greenville and York counties; east to Florence County; south to Charleston County; west to Aiken and Oconee counties.

HISTORY: It seems utterly incongruous to associate a small bird with a tiger but the scientific name of the Cape May Warbler does just that, for it is *tigrina*, that is, "striped like a tiger." It is bright yellow below, streaked with narrow lines of black; the cheeks are chestnut and the crown is black. Because it is so brilliant, it is likely at once to attract the attention of anyone fortunate enough to see it at close range.

The Cape May is a transient visitor, more likely to be encountered in the Piedmont than elsewhere in South Carolina. The first State record was apparently made by E. A. Smyth, who took a male near Summerton, Clarendon County, on September 20, 1885. It is more common in spring than in fall from mid-State to the mountains, with the reverse being true for the coastal plain. The range of dates in the Piedmont is April 15 to May 17 and October 1 to October 28. Murphey (1937) classed the Cape May in the Aiken-Augusta region as irregular, abundant in some years and rare in others. He noted a preference for the Piedmont plateau there.

Although it is fairly common in fall on the coast, there has been only one known spring occurrence there since Dr. Louis B. Bishop and Wayne took five birds at Mt.

Pleasant on April 23, 1912. The more recent record is of two males taken near Mt. Pleasant by E. A. Hyer on April 29, 1926. The earliest fall date for the coastal plain is September 4 (W. B. Ward at Florence), while the latest is November 3 (Wayne at Mt. Pleasant).

The Cape May (so named for Cape May, New Jersey) prefers the live oak avenues and groves of the coast area, and often appears subsequent to autumn storms. Small and active, it is typical of the family in its behavior and feeding habits.

Food: While insects form the great bulk of the diet, this warbler is one of the few of its family accused of depredations on man's agricultural interests. This because of its fondness for grapes. When such fruit is ripening the Cape May, in certain localities, causes considerable havoc by puncturing them.

BLACK-THROATED BLUE WARBLER
335. *Dendroica caerulescens caerulescens* (Gmelin) (654)

(Lat., *caerulescens*, becoming blue.)

DESCRIPTION: Length 4.70 to 5.50 inches. *Male*. Above dull grayish indigo blue; wings brownish black edged with the same blue; a conspicuous white patch at the base of the primaries; throat, sides of head and of body black; remainder of under parts white. *Female*. Upper surface olive; the wings with a white spot; below pale yellowish olive.

RANGE: Breeds north to northern Minnesota and central Quebec; south to central Minnesota and southwestern Pennsylvania. Winters north to southern Florida, southeastern South Carolina, and the Bahama Islands; south to Guatemala and Peru.

STATUS IN S. C.: Common transient, April 12 to May 22, and August 30 to November 4, in most of the State; accidental in winter in the coast region. Reported north to Greenville, Chester, and Chesterfield counties; east to Horry County; south to Beaufort and Jasper counties; west to Aiken and Anderson counties.

HISTORY: The Black-throated Blue Warbler is a handsome, clean-cut bird, one of the warblers easy to recognize. There is no blending of the color pattern; all areas are sharply defined, and even the obscure looking female may be identified at once by the white spot on the wings, which shows up plainly.

It is a common spring and fall visitor over most of South Carolina. It lives in deep, swampy woodlands, oak groves, and deciduous forests. Undergrowth attracts it, and it is often seen at low elevations. It is present in spring from mid-April to the third week in May, and in autumn from the end of August to early November. Wayne established the only winter record when he took an adult male near Pinopolis, Berkeley County, December 6, 1889 (*Auk*, 7: 1890, 410). All sight records not supported by specimens are included under this race—except those from the mountain counties.

Food: Mainly small insects, including beetles, ants, bugs, scale insects, and spiders.

CAIRNS'S WARBLER
336. *Dendroica caerulescens cairnsi* Coues (654a)

(Lat., *cairnsi*, to John S. Cairns.)

DESCRIPTION: Similar to the Black-throated Blue Warbler but blue of the upper surface darker and with often much more black on the back. Female darker than the female of the Black-throated Blue Warbler, also duller, more bluish (less olive) above and less yellowish below.

RANGE: Breeds north to northern Maryland and central southern Pennsylvania; south to northern Georgia and northwestern South Carolina. Winters in Cuba.

STATUS IN S. C.: Fairly common summer resident, April 15 to October 30, in the north-western section. A fairly common transient, April 21 to 28, and September 8 to October 12, in the remainder of the State. Breeds north to Caesar's Head, also Pickens County, and western Oconee County. Transient west to Clemson College and east to Charleston.

HISTORY: Cairns's Warbler was named by Elliott Coues for John S. Cairns, an observer who did much ornithological work in the mountains of North Carolina in the 1890's. It differs from the typical Black-throated Blue Warbler in two respects: the back is well spotted with black, and the bird's breeding range is in the mountains from Maryland to Georgia, well south of that of the Black-throated Blue.

In South Carolina, Cairns's Warbler is a summer resident of the mountain area and a transient visitor in the rest of the State. Evidence that it breeds in this State was established by G. E. Hudson and F. Sherman who, on June 26, 1934, collected an adult male and a young bird near the summit of Sassafras Mountain. Besides these, they saw three other males, one female, and another immature bird. They listed this as the first breeding record for South Carolina (*Auk, 53*: 1936, 314). However, Chamberlain and R. H. Coleman had taken immature males on Caesar's Head, Greenville County, on July 16 and 18, 1927. Chamberlain found it breeding in Pickens County in 1934 and 1935.

Wayne (1910) stated that, because of the similarity of this race to the Black-throated Blue, it was difficult to give dates of its arrival and departure on the coast. However, he secured a number of valid specimens. Though Cairns's Warbler is an excellent race, it is not with certainty distinguishable in the field from the Black-throated Blue Warbler, and for that reason only specimens taken in South Carolina are used to establish its range in the State.

The eggs, generally three to five in number, are grayish white, with olive-brown markings, chiefly about the larger end; they average 17.3 x 12.7 millimeters.

Its appearance, except for the spotted back, and its habits, food, and habitat are similar to those of the Black-throated Blue.

MYRTLE WARBLER
337. *Dendroica coronata coronata* (Linnaeus) (655)

(Lat., *coronata*, crowned.)

LOCAL NAMES: Yellow-rumped Warbler.

DESCRIPTION: Length 5.00 to 6.00 inches. *Spring.* Above bluish slate gray, streaked with black; wings dull black with two white wing bars; tail black with white spots on the outer feathers; lower parts white, more or less streaked with black, and with a black area on the chest, usually more or less invaded by white; a spot on the top of the head, one on each side of the chest, and on the rump bright yellow. *Winter.* Upper parts grayish brown, obscurely streaked with brownish black; sides of head brown; yellow crown patch concealed; yellow chest patches much duller as is often the case with the yellow rump; lower parts dull white or dull buffy brown with some obscure streaks.

RANGE: Breeds north to northern Manitoba and central Labrador; south to northern Minnesota and Massachusetts. Winters north to central Missouri and central Maine; south to Panama and Jamaica.

STATUS IN S. C.: Abundant winter resident, September 29 to May 14, accidentally July 16. Reported north to Greenville, York, and Chesterfield counties; east to Horry County; south to Beaufort and Jasper counties; west to Greenwood and Oconee counties.

HISTORY: For nearly half the year the Myrtle Warbler occurs in countless numbers in South Carolina, and from November through March is among the very commonest of wintering birds. From the Battery in Charleston to the border of the mountains, it covers practically every county in the State, and is just as likely to be a yard bird as a woodland dweller.

Yellow-rumped Warbler, Audubon called it, and rightly. The bright patch of yellow at the base of the tail is the Myrtle's hallmark, and when the bird is either at rest or in flight, the mark is conspicuous. "Rest" is an odd term to use for this feathered dynamo. It does not even perch for very long at a time. Active, alert, and thoroughly alive, it seems constantly on the go from sunrise to sunset, and the sharp, metallic "tchip" of the call note is as distinctive as the bird itself. The rather pleasing song is sometimes heard in spring before it departs.

The Myrtle Warbler arrives about mid-October and remains until early May. It is recorded, therefore, for parts of eight months, and there is one midsummer record, that of a male seen at Huger, Berkeley County, July 16, 1940, by E. von S. Dingle. In the upper Piedmont, it has been noted from October 3 at Greenville (P. M. Jenness) to May 10 at Clemson (G. E. Hudson).

The winter plumage is rather dull, plain brownish gray and white, with many dark streaks. The brightest mark is the yellow rump. Even the yellow shoulder patches, so bright in spring, are subdued in winter. Before this warbler starts north, however, it fairly blossoms, and then the yellow crown, wing patches, and rump gleam against the blue-gray back, the black of breast and sides, and the white of the under parts.

The name "Myrtle" is fitting, for the bird is fond of the thickets and clumps of the wax myrtle. It eats quantities of the berries of this shrub.

On two different occasions Sprunt has found Myrtle Warblers entrapped and dangling in tough spider-webs. One of the birds was dead; the other was still struggling though unable to free itself, and was liberated.

This species is often almost a nuisance to takers of the Christmas Bird Count; the birds are so numerous that it is difficult to estimate the numbers, and it is quite impossible to count them individually.

FOOD: Departing from warbler custom, the Myrtle Warbler adopts a vegetable diet in winter. It is particularly fond of berries of the wax myrtle, red cedar, cassina or yaupon, poison oak, and sumac. In fall and spring it eats beetles, plant lice, flies, and various kinds of insect larvae.

ALASKA MYRTLE WARBLER
338. *Dendroica coronata hooveri* McGregor (655a)

(Lat., *hooveri*, to Theodore J. Hoover.)

DESCRIPTION: Similar to the Myrtle Warbler of the east, but decidedly larger, the male with black of breast more extensive and often of a more solid color. Female, immature, and winter specimens have the upper parts more grayish (less rufescent).

RANGE: Breeds north to northwestern Alaska and northern Mackenzie; south to central British Columbia and central Alberta. Winters north to California, Louisiana, southern Mississippi, and southern South Carolina; south to Lower California and southern Vera Cruz.

STATUS IN S. C.: Common winter resident, November 2 to May 7, over probably all the State; actually recorded, however, only in the coastal area, north to Huger; south to Yemassee.

HISTORY: Judging from specimens examined, Alaska Myrtle Warblers may possibly be as numerous in South Carolina as is the eastern Myrtle Warbler. Birds have been taken at Charleston, March 12, 1929, by Sanford Olasov; at Huger, April 19, 1935, by E. von S. Dingle; at Charleston, November 2, 1923, by Sprunt; at Midland Park, February 22, 1924, by E. A. Hyer; at Yemassee, February 2, 1888, by Wayne; and at Mt. Pleasant, April 13 and 25, 1888, April 21, 1921, and May 7, 1920, by Wayne. All these have been identified by Dr. H. C. Oberholser.

Its habits and food are similar to those of the Myrtle Warbler.

BLACK-THROATED GRAY WARBLER
339. *Dendroica nigrescens* (Townsend) (665)

(Lat., *nigrescens*, becoming black.)

DESCRIPTION: Length 4.70 to 5.40 inches. Head, chin, and throat black; a yellow spot in front of the eye; a white stripe behind and a long white stripe below the cheeks; remainder of upper surface bluish gray, streaked with black; two broad white wing bars; outer tail feathers with much white; remainder of lower surface white.

RANGE: Breeds north to southern British Columbia and Wyoming; south to northern Lower California and southern New Mexico. Winters north to southern Lower California and Mexico, accidentally to Massachusetts and South Carolina; south to Mexico.

STATUS IN S. C.: Accidental.

HISTORY: The Black-throated Gray Warbler is a western bird. Its occurrence in South Carolina can be regarded only as abnormal. Its inclusion here is based on an observation made of a full-plumaged individual at close range on Bull's Island, December 13, 1941, by Sprunt and a group of Audubon Wildlife Tour members. The bird was seen in low bushes at the edge of a weedy garden and was in sight for several minutes in excellent light.

This constitutes the sole record for South Carolina (*Auk, 59*: 1942, 429). It was not possible to take the bird, but identification was certain.

In habits and food this warbler does not materially differ from other small related warblers.

BLACK-THROATED GREEN WARBLER
340. *Dendroica virens virens* (Gmelin) (667)

(Lat., *virens*, being green.)

DESCRIPTION: Length 4.35 to 5.30 inches. *Male.* Upper parts yellowish olive green, the back with faint darker streaks; wings blackish brown with two white bars; sides of head and of neck lemon yellow; throat and chest black; remainder of lower parts white or yellowish white, sides and flanks heavily streaked with black. *Female.* Pattern of coloration similar to that of the male but much subdued; chin and throat pale yellow. *Immature.* Similar to the adult female but upper surface more yellowish; lower parts white; sides of head and lower parts more strongly tinged with yellow.

RANGE: Breeds north to northeastern Alberta and Newfoundland; south to southern Minnesota, western Virginia, and Connecticut. Winters north to southern Texas and southern Florida; south to Guatemala and Panama.

STATUS IN S. C.: Uncommon transient, April 19 to May 10 (accidentally June 19) and October 5 to 10, in both eastern and western sections. Recorded north to Marlboro County; east and south to Horry County; west to Anderson and Oconee counties.

HISTORY: This attractive warbler is probably more common during migration than the specimens indicate. Until recently the Black-throated Green was thought to be the breeding bird in the mountains of the State, but study has shown that this is not true and that Wayne's Warbler is the breeding bird in that area as well as in the coastal region.

Specimens examined and identified by Dr. H. C. Oberholser are as follows: One taken by H. T. Nowell on October 10, 1896, at Anderson; one by Chamberlain on May 10, 1935, at Rocky Bottom, Pickens County; one on April 19, 1940, at Conway, Horry County, by W. M. Perrygo and J. S. Webb; one on June 19, 1940, at Walhalla, Oconee County, and one on October 5, 1940, at Bennettsville, Marlboro County, by the same collectors. Apparently there are no other records for South Carolina.

341. WAYNE'S WARBLER: *Dendroica virens waynei* Bangs (667a)

(Lat., *waynei*, to Arthur Trezevant Wayne.)

DESCRIPTION: Similar to the Black-throated Green Warbler, but bill decidedly smaller.

RANGE: Breeds north to southeastern Kentucky and southeastern Virginia; south to central Alabama, northwestern and southeastern South Carolina. Except for South Carolina, winter range unknown.

STATUS IN S. C.: Fairly common summer resident, March 20 to October 19, in the coastal region and in the mountains of the northwestern part of the State; accidental in winter in the coast region. Recorded in summer north to Greenville; south and west to Pickens and Oconee counties; and in the coast region breeds north to Cherry Grove Beach (Horry County); south to Yemassee and McPhersonville (Hampton County). In migration occurs also north to York and Chester counties; south to Greenwood.

HISTORY: That South Carolina has a very interesting ornithological history is beyond question, and not the least striking evidence of the fact is this dainty, fragile bird of the cypress lagoons and the mountain valleys. It properly bears the name of its discoverer.

For many years Wayne was puzzled by the fact that he saw and heard Black-throated Green Warblers on the coast from late March to June but could find no evidence of nesting. Then on April 11, 1917, he saw a female carrying nesting material. He made a determined effort to resolve the mystery and, in the spring of 1918, took specimens, compared them carefully, and found constant variation between these coastal birds and typical Black-throated Greens. The specimens were sent to Outram Bangs at the Museum of Comparative Zoölogy in Cambridge, Massachusetts. From them, Bangs described a new race, naming it *Dendroica virens waynei* (*Proc. New Eng. Zool. Club, 6*: 1918, 94). Thus Wayne's Warbler came into scientific being. The principal subspecific difference is the much smaller and more delicate bill, a character which is at once apparent in specimens in the hand.

Until recently it was thought that Wayne's Warbler was the breeding bird of the coast and that the Black-throated Green was the breeding race in the South Carolina mountain region. Further study, however, has shown that Wayne's Warbler is also the breeding bird of the mountains and that the Black-throated Green is only a migrant in the State. In this connection Dr. H. C. Oberholser has examined and identified, in addition to a number of coastal birds, the following specimens from the northwestern corner of the State as Wayne's Warblers: Anderson, October 5, 6, and 8, 1895, collected by H. T. Nowell; 11 miles northwest of Walhalla, Oconee County, June 18 and 21, 1940, by W. M. Perrygo and J. S. Y. Hoyt; and Saluda Gap, Greenville County, June 9, 1945, by T. D. Burleigh. All sight records have been placed under this race.

Wayne's Warbler arrives in late March and early April, a little later in the mountains than on the coast. It stays, in the Piedmont at least, until early October. The latest fall date is October 19, 1947, when North Carolina Bird Club members recorded it in York County. The only winter record for the State is that of a male seen on Bull's Island, January 8 and 9, 1940, by Allan D. Cruickshank. This was one of the coldest January's in many years, marked by a fall of snow, an extraordinary occurrence in the Low-country, and the bird would normally have been far south of Charleston County.

In the coast region, Wayne's Warbler is essentially a bird of the cypress country, though it feeds in fairly open mixed woodlands adjacent to the great reserves or backwaters where it nests. In the mountains it is very partial to wooded areas of conifers like hemlock, corresponding to the cypress habitat of the coast. It usually keeps well to the tops of tall trees. Wayne wrote that it "ranges higher than any eastern North American warbler with which I am acquainted." This is certainly generally true, though on several occasions it has been seen to good advantage feeding in saplings and second growth no more than 10 to 20 feet above the ground.

The females are extremely difficult to locate, and it is practically impossible to find the nest unless the birds are seen building or feeding their young. The males, however, are easy to locate because they sing frequently. The song is like that of the Black-throated Green and is one of the most readily recognizable of all warbler songs. It carries for considerable distances and consists of either five or seven notes (usually seven), a high, wiry "zee, zee, zee, zee, zee, zee, zeep," with the last note higher than the rest.

L. M. Loomis first found Wayne's Warbler breeding in the State in the mountains of Pickens County and at Caesar's Head when he worked there many years ago (*Auk*, *7:* 1890, 128; *8:* 1891, 331). Loomis recorded these as Black-throated Green Warblers, for at that time Wayne's Warbler had not yet been described. On April 18, 1919, the first nest and eggs in the Low-country were found by Wayne in a large swamp on Fairlawn Plantation, Charleston County.

The nest is saddled on the limb of a cypress, oak, magnolia, or hemlock, sometimes over water, and at elevations from 25 to 75 feet or more. It is made of bark strips, grass, leaves, and needles, (often with cypress twigs and moss in the coast region), and is a very neat cup. The three to four eggs are white, wreathed and speckled with brown and lilac; their average measurement is 16.5 x 11.7 millimeters. Egg dates on the coast range from mid-April to mid-May. Late May and early June is the nesting season in the mountains.

FOOD: Largely insects such as plant lice and leaf rollers. It also feeds upon berries and seeds, among them poison ivy and juniper.

PLATE XXVII: WARBLERS IN CYPRESS BACKWATER
Water Color by Edward von S. Dingle

Three birds at upper left, left to right: Yellow-throated Warbler (adult), Wayne's Warbler (male), and Wayne's Warbler (female). Two birds, upper right, top to bottom: Southern Parula Warbler (female), and Southern Parula Warbler (male). Four birds in lower foreground, left to right: Hooded Warbler (male), Hooded Warbler (female), Prothonotary Warbler (female), and Prothonotary Warbler (male).

WOOD WARBLERS

342. Cerulean Warbler: *Dendroica cerulea* (Wilson) (658)

(Lat., *cerulea*, blue.)

DESCRIPTION: Length 4.00 to 5.00 inches. *Male.* Greenish blue above with dull black streaks; wings and tail black with two white bars on the former, the latter with most of the feathers having white spots near the tips; undersurface white with a band of bluish black across the chest. *Female.* Duller and unstreaked, grayish olive green or light bluish gray above and yellowish white below; tail feathers with white spots near the tips.

RANGE: Breeds north to central western Nebraska and southeastern New York (casually); south to southeastern Louisiana and northern Georgia. Winters north to Panama and northern Venezuela; south to Bolivia.

STATUS IN S. C.: Rare transient, April 13 to May 1, and August 8 to October 24, in the western half of the State. Reported north to Greenville County; east to Chester County; south to Aiken; west to Clemson College.

HISTORY: Uncommon, if not rare, anywhere east of the mountains in the Southeast, the Cerulean Warbler is a rare transient visitor in the Piedmont of South Carolina and it is entirely unknown in the coastal plain.

L. M. Loomis found it rare, though regular, in Chester County from April 13 to 30 in spring, and from August 8 to October 22 in fall (*Auk, 8*: 1891, 170). F. Sherman, at Clemson, recorded it only once in spring, April 21, 1926, but H. A. Rankin has several previous records there—April 21, 1933, one; April 26, 1934, one; and in 1935, April 22, two; April 23, three; and April 25, one. P. M. Jenness recorded it up to May at Greenville, while F. W. Hahn noted it only once in Greenwood County, October 24, 1923. J. Kershaw found it at Aiken, April 20, 1909, this being the only instance at or near the fall line.

The bright blue male, streaked with black, is an active bird, like so many of the warblers, and often ranges well up in trees. It appears to be fond of river bottoms, where tall deciduous growth is the rule, swamps, uplands, mountain slopes, and even in more open situations. The song is not unlike that of the Parula Warbler.

343. Blackburnian Warbler: *Dendroica fusca* (Müller) (662)

(Lat., *fusca*, dusky.)

DESCRIPTION: Length 4.25 to 5.50 inches. *Male.* Upper parts generally black, but the crown patch, throat, chest, and line over eye bright orange, and the back streaked with white; belly and breast yellow; wings with a large white patch; lower tail coverts white; most of the tail feathers with white spots on their inner webs. *Female.* Similar to the male but duller; back greenish olive streaked with dull black and buffy gray; white in wings and tail less extensive. *Immature.* Colors still more obscure.

RANGE: Breeds north to south central Manitoba and northern Nova Scotia; south to central Minnesota, northern Georgia, and Connecticut. Winters north to Yucatan and southern Florida; south to central Peru and French Guiana.

STATUS IN S. C.: A fairly common transient, March 27 to May 11, and August 8 to October 22, throughout the State, although rare eastward. Occurs occasionally in summer in the mountains of Pickens and Oconee counties. Recorded north to Greenville and York

−459−

counties; east to Horry County; south to Charleston County; west to Greenwood and Clemson College.

HISTORY: In the opinion of many people, the Blackburnian is the most beautiful of the wood warblers. One glimpse of a Blackburnian is enough for identification, at least as far as the male is concerned. Peterson (1947) calls it "The fire-throat." The bird is predominantly black and white, but the flaming orange about the head and on the throat instantly arrests the eye, and there can be no mistake about what one is seeing. Even the more plainly attired female has enough of orange on the throat to identify herself. Summer residents of mountain resorts in the Blue Ridge of North Carolina have opportunities of seeing this brilliant warbler, for it nests there in the evergreens of the higher slopes, but in South Carolina it is no more than a brief visitor to limited portions of the State.

It is a transient bird in the Piedmont area, and very rare on the coast or, indeed, anywhere below the fall line. L. M. Loomis found it a regular migrant at Chester in both migrations, from late April through early May, and from August 8 to October 22, with the greatest concentration in late September and early October. G. E. Hudson and H. A. Rankin recorded it near Clemson from April 21 to May 11. J. E. Mosimann, G. B. Rabb, and T. M. Uzzell, Jr., found it a bit earlier (April 18) at Caesar's Head in 1949, despite frost.

Loomis secured three specimens in the mountains of Pickens County between June 18 and 24, 1889, two males and one female, at an elevation from 2500 to 3000 feet, but the testes of the males were not larger than pin heads. W. M. Perrygo took a male at Walhalla, Oconee County, on June 24, 1940.

The Blackburnian has been recorded in Aiken County on April 17 (Misses L. P. Ford and M. J. Pellew), and September 24 (Murphey). Farther north along the fall line, at Columbia, Edwin L. Green, Jr., recorded it from May 1 to 10, 1929.

Wayne in all his long experience on the coast, took but two birds, a male on September 4, 1901, and a female on September 29, 1902, both near Mt. Pleasant. There have been four observations of this bird along the coast since Wayne wrote. H. S. Peters reported a single bird about 17 miles west of the city on March 27, 1933. This is the earliest spring record. On April 12, 1936, Dunbar Robb noted a male near Hampton Plantation, in Georgetown County. Lester L. Walsh, of New York, saw one on April 6, 1948, on Bull's Island. Farther up the coast, R. G. Kuerzi saw a male on May 5, 1940, at Long Bay Plantation, Horry County.

Like all the warblers, the Blackburnian is almost wholly insectivorous.

YELLOW-THROATED WARBLER
344. *Dendroica dominica dominica* (Linnaeus) (663)

(Lat., *dominica*, of Santo Domingo.)

DESCRIPTION: Length 4.70 to 5.75 inches. *Male.* Forehead and sides of head black; a white line over the eye becoming yellow anteriorly; remaining upper surface slate gray; wings brownish black with two prominent white bars; tail with white markings on the outer feathers; throat and breast yellow; abdomen white, the sides streaked with black. *Female.* Similar to the male but with usually less black.

RANGE: Breeds north to Maryland and southern New Jersey; south to southern Alabama and central Florida. Winters north to South Carolina and the Bahama Islands; south to Jamaica and Puerto Rico.

STATUS IN S. C.: Common permanent resident throughout the State, possibly not wintering in the mountains. Recorded north to Greenville and York counties; east to Florence and Horry counties; south to Beaufort County; west to Aiken and Oconee counties.

HISTORY: This handsome and attractive warbler is among the finest of the warbler family. Long association with it can only intensify one's admiration for its appearance, song, and general behavior.

Though it occurs generally over South Carolina as a permanent resident, the coast dweller will always associate it with Spanish moss country. Bird and plant seem synonymous on the coast for where there is no moss one will not find the Yellow-throated Warbler. The generalization, however, cannot be pushed too far; even before the fall line is reached the moss disappears; yet the Yellow-throated Warbler goes straight on through the sandhills into the Piedmont and to the border of the mountains.

It is a woodland bird, abundant about cypress lagoons and heavy swamps. But it also occurs in settled districts and delights in the live oak avenues of the old plantations, and in the oak groves and tall pines which grow in many Low-country towns. Summerville, in Dorchester County, has a large population of these birds, and the residential districts of Charleston, Georgetown, and Beaufort ring with their melodies in spring.

The Yellow-throated Warbler does not appear to winter in the Piedmont. G. E. Hudson gives arrival dates for Clemson as April 6 to 15, but he gives no dates for its departure. It is not common in winter, even on the coast, though it may be seen every month if one looks for it. It is, of course, silent in winter, and Wayne was of the opinion that wintering birds are those which have bred north of South Carolina and migrated to the State. Such a view is certainly reasonable. Young raised on the coast leave early, some by the middle of June.

Nesting occurs early. Mating is complete in early March and building begins about a week later. Backward seasons delay it. In the Low-country, as already noted, the Yellow-throated is dependent on the Spanish moss and almost always chooses the moss as a nesting site. Wayne never saw more than two nests built elsewhere and they were both in short-leaf pines.

The nest is constructed by the female, and one must see her at work in order to locate the home, for it is always completely concealed in the clump selected. It is made by weaving the fibres together with cobwebs or caterpillar silk, and incorporating bits of bark, rotten wood, and fine grass in it. The finished nest is a beautiful structure. It may be anywhere from 8 to 10 feet above ground to well over 100. In the season of 1945 Sprunt found in his yard a nest which was 3 feet, 3 inches from the ground in a clump of moss in a cassina bush.

There are four or five white eggs, with spots and splashes of brown, gray, and lavender. They average 18.2 x 13.2 millimeters. The Yellow-throated raises two broods. Incubation requires twelve to fourteen days. Typical egg dates are April 10, 19, and 21, Beaufort (E. J. DeCamps); April 10, Charleston (Sprunt); March 31, Charleston (E. A. Cutts). A late date is May 28 (E. von S. Dingle).

The song of this warbler is uttered almost constantly in spring and rings out every hour of the day and many times an hour. The birds begin to sing in late February and increase their singing steadily until June when they become silent. The song is a series of somewhat slurred notes given in a descending scale.

The Yellow-throated is more deliberate in movement than most wood warblers, and it is not difficult to see. At first glance it seems to be a black and white bird with a bright yellow throat, but a closer look will reveal the gray back and the line over the eye.

Food: Apparently altogether insects. Beetles, flies, bugs, moths, grasshoppers, mouse crickets, scale insects, and a few spiders.

Of considerable interest is the food listed for an injured bird which was caught at Summerville on January 24, 1916, and cared for by M. P. Skinner. His note in the Charleston Museum files says, "During the time I had him he ate bread and milk, cracker and egg whites, and various flies, mosquitoes, moths, and crickets. One day I fed this bird fifty house flies one after the other as fast as I could catch them."

SYCAMORE WARBLER
345. *Dendroica dominica albilora* Ridgway (663a)

(Lat., *albilora*, white-lored.)

DESCRIPTION: Similar to the Yellow-throated Warbler but a white line anteriorly over the eye nearly always without yellow; the white areas on inner webs and tail feathers larger.

RANGE: Breeds north to southeastern Nebraska and West Virginia; south to eastern Texas and southeastern Mississippi. Winters north to central southern Texas; south to Mexico and Costa Rica.

STATUS IN S. C.: Casual transient in May, July, and September in the middle and eastern portions of the State. Recorded north to Chester; south and east to Mt. Pleasant.

HISTORY: This western form of the Yellow-throated Warbler was taken at Chester by L. M. Loomis on at least two occasions: May 7, 1885, and September 8, 1887, an adult male in the first instance, an immature male in the second. These specimens are now in the American Museum of Natural History, and Dr. John T. Zimmer has assured the writers that they are referable to the Sycamore. Loomis recorded the first one of these in the *Auk, 3*: 1886, 139. The following year he published a note on four specimens secured in September, 1886 (*Auk, 4*: 1887, 165). The character of some of these is intermediate, according to his description. Loomis says (*Auk, 8*: 1891, 171) that both *dominica* proper and *albilora* occur at Chester, being equally numerous and quite common, especially during the fall migration. His earliest date in spring (both forms) was March 22, while his latest in the fall was October 4.

In his account of the summer birds of Pickens County, Loomis tells of discovering a pair of Yellow-throated Warblers and their brood on a spur of Mt. Pinnacle on June 23, 1887 (*Auk, 7*: 1890, 127). He took the adults and one of the young. He describes the pair, and adds (page 128), "While not typical illustrations, I have placed these examples, without question, under *albilora*. . . ." Where these specimens are now, we do not know. Intermediates have been taken in the North Carolina mountains in recent years, but the status of the Yellow-throated Warbler in South Carolina mountains has not been further established since Loomis' time.

The only coastal record is by Wayne, who took a specimen near Mt. Pleasant on July 13, 1916, just before a storm (*Auk, 38*: 1921, 462). The specimen, now in the Charleston Museum, has been examined and referred to *albilora* by Dr. H. C. Oberholser.

The habits of the Sycamore Warbler are similar to those of the Yellow-throated.

CHESTNUT-SIDED WARBLER
346. *Dendroica pensylvanica* (Linnaeus) (659)

(Lat., *pensylvanica*, of Pennsylvania.)

DESCRIPTION: Length 4.60 to 5.25 inches. *Male*. Upper parts black, streaked with white or yellowish white, the crown olive yellow, bordered by black stripes from the bill through the eye; sides of head and lower surface white; a broad chestnut stripe on each side of the body; two broad wing bars yellow; three outer tail feathers with white terminal spots. *Female*. Similar to the male but much duller. *Immature*. Similar to the adult female but plain bright olive green above and white below, only now and then with a trace of chestnut on sides; wing bars yellow.

RANGE: Breeds north to south central Saskatchewan and Newfoundland; south to central eastern Nebraska, northwestern South Carolina, and New Jersey. Winters north to Guatemala; south to Panama.

STATUS IN S. C.: Fairly common summer resident in the mountains. Transient elsewhere in the State, April 24 to May 17, and August 16 to October 26. Breeds in the mountains of Greenville, Pickens, and probably Oconee counties. Recorded elsewhere north to Chester and Lancaster counties; east to Berkeley County; south to Aiken County; west to Clemson College.

HISTORY: This distinctive and abundant warbler should be well known to residents of the Piedmont region and to those coastal dwellers who themselves migrate to the mountains in summer. It is a common bird in its range and not at all shy. It frequents not only the woodlands and ravines of the high country but the open grounds of towns and cities as well.

It is a very active bird, as so many of its family are, and is fond of open, brushy pastures and hillsides, and deciduous woodlands. The male is easily recognized by the broad chestnut stripe on his sides, the yellow crown bordered with black, and the white under parts. No other warbler looks anything like it. The females and immature birds are much in evidence in the shrubbery of yards and gardens in middle and late summer; they are mainly greenish above and white below, with yellow wing patches. They are very tame.

The Chestnut-sided Warbler arrives in the Clemson area by April 25 and remains until May 17 (G. E. Hudson); then it moves on to the nearby mountains to nest.

L. M. Loomis noted similar dates at Chester, though his date for latest spring departure was somewhat earlier (May 15). He found the bird nesting infrequently at Mt. Pinnacle, but very often at Caesar's Head, the latter the lower elevation by a few hundred feet.

The nest is often no higher than 3 feet from the ground, or even lower, in bushes, tangles of vines, or thickets. Made of weeds, grasses, and leaves, it is lined with finer grass or hair. Eggs number four or five; they are white, speckled with dots and splashes of gray and brown. They average 17.5 x 12.7 millimeters. One, perhaps two, broods are raised. Incubation takes about ten days.

The fall migration is usually heavy, and the immatures are particularly numerous. About Chester migration occurs from August 16 to October 19. The latest Clemson record is October 26. W. M. Perrygo and J. S. Webb took a specimen at Lancaster on September 18, which is about the average arrival time at Clemson also. In the Aiken-Augusta region, Murphey (1937) calls the bird rare in spring, but abundant during the autumnal migration, giving a peak of September 27 to October 5. One spring date for Aiken is April 24 (J. Kershaw). Elliott Coues (*Proc. Bost. Soc. Nat. Hist.*, *12*: 1868, 110) lists the Chestnut-sided as common in migration at Columbia. On the coast it is practically unknown, there being but one record, April 24, 1929, when E. von S. Dingle secured a male at Middleburg Plantation, Berkeley County.

Food: Composed almost entirely of insects.

BAY-BREASTED WARBLER
347. *Dendroica castanea* (Wilson) (660)

(Lat., *castanea*, the chestnut.)

Description: Length 5.00 to 6.00 inches. *Male.* Forehead black; crown chestnut; sides of head black; back olive green streaked with black; wings with two white wing bars; sides of neck buff; chin, throat, and sides of body light chestnut; lower parts and belly pale buff or buffy white; two or three outer tail feathers with a white patch. *Female.* Nearly or quite lacks the chestnut on head and throat; the chestnut of under parts paler, duller, and less extensive; otherwise similar to the male. *Immature.* Upper surface pale yellowish olive green; under parts light buffy yellow, inclining to buff.

Range: Breeds north to northeastern Alberta and Newfoundland; south to southern Manitoba and central New Hampshire. Winters in Panama and Colombia.

Status in S. C.: Rare transient, April 11 to May 16, and October 10 to 24; very infrequent in the coast region. Casual in summer. Recorded north to Greenville and Chester counties; east and south to Charleston County; west to Aiken and Oconee counties.

History: The Bay-breast has only a brief history in South Carolina. It is hardly more than accidental in the coast area. As a matter of fact, it is fairly uncommon in the Southeast for its migratory route avoids the South Atlantic region and most of the birds enter the United States through the central and western Gulf States.

It is a rare transient in the Piedmont. L. M. Loomis took only two specimens at Chester, one on May 14, 1887, and the other on May 5, 1888. Gabriel Cannon noted it only four times at Spartanburg, during the decade from 1915 to 1925, each observation occurring between May 3 and May 7. G. E. Hudson recorded it at Clemson during 1926-28 from May 1 to 16, and R. B. Casey took one there on April 29, 1929. In the Charleston Museum there are six skins of birds taken by H. T. Nowell at Anderson, but only two are dated (October 10, 1896).

At Columbia, Elliott Coues listed the Bay-breast as common in migration, passing through, with several other warblers, chiefly in April and October (*Proc. Bost. Soc. Nat. Hist., 12*: 1868, 110). In the Aiken-Augusta region, Murphey (1937) called it a rare transient, less so in autumn than in spring. He gives the latest fall record there as October 24, 1908. Miss Marion J. Pellew found eight birds at Aiken on May 3, 1920. Farther upstate, F. W. Hahn saw ten birds near Greenwood on July 25, 1925, an unusual record.

There are only three known instances of the Bay-breasted Warbler's occurrence below the fall line. The first of these was an offshore record published by Gerald H. Thayer (*Auk, 16*: 1899, 275). He found a full-plumaged bird along with other species on the deck of the ship on which he was travelling, on April 19, 1898. The ship had been about 50 miles off the southern South Carolina coast and may have been above Charleston when the warbler came aboard. Wayne took a female near Mt. Pleasant on October 18, 1922, the only specimen from the coast (*Auk, 40*: 1923, 133). The third record from the coast is an observation of a male near the Edisto River, Charleston County, on April 11, 1948, by G. B. Rabb.

The spring-plumaged Bay-breast is characterized by its bright chestnut throat and sides, black forehead, and chestnut crown. In fall, however, it looks so much like a Black-poll Warbler that distinction between the two in the field is virtually impossible. Sight records of it at that season are therefore without value.

FOOD: The Bay-breast's food consists principally of insects.

BLACK-POLL WARBLER
348. *Dendroica striata* (Forster)   (661)

(Lat., *striata*, striped.)

DESCRIPTION: Length 5.00 to 5.75 inches. *Male.* Crown black; back and rump pale olive green streaked with black; under parts streaked on sides of neck and body with black; wings with two white wing bars; two or three outer tail feathers with white markings. *Female.* All upper parts olive green or gray, narrowly streaked with dull black; lower surface white to pale yellow, slightly streaked on the sides of breast and of body. *Immature.* Similar but with more yellow on the lower surface, though under tail coverts white or pale yellow.

RANGE: Breeds north to northwestern Alaska and Newfoundland; south to northern Michigan and New York. Winters north to Colombia and Venezuela; south to eastern Brazil and Chile.

STATUS IN S. C.: Common transient, April 1 to June 5, and September 2 to November 14, throughout the State. Reported north to Greenville and Chesterfield counties; east to Horry County; south to Beaufort County; west to Aiken and Oconee counties.

HISTORY: As puzzling as the females and immature warblers often are, the males are so distinctively marked that identification of them is usually simple. The male Black-poll is a case in point. It is gray above streaked with black, white beneath and wears a solid black cap. Females and young are by no means so easy to identify. They are so similar to the corresponding forms of the Bay-breasted Warbler in fall that field identification is highly problematical if not impossible.

The Black-poll is a common transient visitor to South Carolina, but, strangely enough, neither Audubon nor Bachman recorded it. Wayne says that they "evidently overlooked this bird." It usually arrives in spring in late April and remains until mid-May. It appears again in mid-September and is here until mid-November. A fast migrant in spring, its autumnal movement is correspondingly slow. The peak of abundance is from middle to late October.

G. E. Hudson recorded the Black-poll at Clemson from April 22 to May 24 in the spring migration. His May 24 date is the latest for the Piedmont, and E. von S. Dingle's date of June 5 the latest for the coast. On the coast, the Black-poll is often found on the barrier island beaches in clumps of wax myrtle and other shrubbery. On the mainland it likes deciduous woods, orchards, and the shade trees of towns and cities. It is not a shy bird and sings rather frequently. The black cap of the male is readily seen in spring.

The Black-poll as a species has an immense range; indeed, in a family famous for wide wanderings, it takes first place. It nests as far north as northwestern Alaska and it winters as far south as Chile, a truly impressive distance. How it manages to traverse such astonishing stretches of territory, mountains, forests, plains, and ocean is one of the fascinating mysteries of nature.

FOOD: Both animal and vegetable matter, but largely the former, chiefly insects. Aside from a modicum of berries and seeds, it devours huge numbers of such insects as plant lice, spanworms, cankerworms, beetles, ants, and gnats. It is an accomplished fly catcher and often takes prey on the wing.

NORTHERN PINE WARBLER
349. *Dendroica pinus pinus* (Wilson) (671)

(Lat., *pinus*, a pine.)

LOCAL NAMES: Pine-creeping Warbler.

DESCRIPTION: Length 4.95 to 5.75 inches. *Male.* Upper surface olive green; two grayish white or pale gray wing bars; two outer tail feathers with large white oblique patches; lower parts and line over eye yellow. *Female.* Similar but duller, more olive. *Immature.* Brown above, buffy white below.

RANGE: Breeds north to central Saskatchewan and New Brunswick; south to southeastern Texas and northern Florida. Winters north to southern Illinois, eastern Virginia, and Massachusetts (casually); south to Florida.

STATUS IN S. C.: Common permanent resident throughout the State. Observed north to Greenville, Lancaster, and Darlington counties; east to Horry County; south to Beaufort and Jasper counties; west to Aiken and Oconee counties.

HISTORY: Anyone interested in bird life may easily become acquainted with the Pine Warbler. It is one of the few warblers which is a permanent resident in South Carolina (the only warbler permanent in the Piedmont), and it is the only one that sings for most of the year; it occurs wherever the pine grows, and that means in most parts of the State. It lives in remote stretches of pine growth, but it lives also on the edges and interiors of towns, and is abundant, easily seen, and easily heard.

The song is not remarkable in quality, but is distinctive and easily learned—a simple little trill, all in the same key, uttered in every season. It is one of the most characteristic sounds of the pinelands, and often serves as a means of locating the bird. Though it usually ranges high and is therefore somewhat hard to see in tall pines, this warbler sometimes forages not only about the trunks and lower limbs but on the ground and in low undergrowth. Audubon called it the "Pine-creeping Warbler" because of its habit of working about the trunks of trees like a nuthatch or brown creeper. Its greenish back, yellow under parts, and conspicuous wing-bars are all good field characters.

Immature birds are nondescript and prove puzzling. They are obscurely plumaged in grayish brown, buff on the breast and dull white below. Peterson (1947) quotes James B. Young of Louisville, Kentucky, as saying that "a museum tray of Pine Warblers looks like a catch-all for the museum's ratty, discarded Warbler skins."

The breeding season of the Pine Warbler is a long one, beginning in March and running into June. During this period it may raise as many as three broods. The nest is invariably in a pine tree, saddled on a horizontal limb and frequently out toward the end of it. Sometimes it is almost totally concealed in a tuft of needles. Elevation is usually considerable, much oftener high than low. Wayne has found nests as much as 135 feet from the ground but he has found them also at 15 feet. Thirty to 50 feet appears to be the usual elevation. The nest is small, made of bark strippings, twigs, and grasses and is lined with pine needles, feathers, or hair and bound to the limb with cobwebs. Eggs are five in number (usually four in the second brood). Eggs are greenish white, with spots of brown and lavender. They average 17.8 x 13.2 millimeters. Incubation takes about twelve days.

First egg dates are normally from April 5 to 15, though there are seasonal variations. Wayne has taken them as early as March 28, and as late as April 24.

The Pine Warbler is often found in the company of Brown-headed Nuthatches and Red-cockaded Woodpeckers, which are also pineland birds.

FOOD: While an insectivorous bird for the most part, the Pine Warbler takes considerable vegetable matter in winter—berries of the dogwood and sumac and seeds of various pines. Grasshoppers, locusts, moths, beetles, flies, scale insects, and insect larvae compose the animal matter.

350. KIRTLAND'S WARBLER: *Dendroica kirtlandii* (Baird) (670)

(Lat., *kirtlandii*, to Jared Potter Kirtland.)

DESCRIPTION: Length 5.25 to 6.00 inches. *Male.* Above bluish to brownish gray; back broadly streaked with black; a narrow black band on forehead and lores; each eyelid with a white spot; under parts yellow, but under tail coverts white, the sides with black streaks; two outer tail feathers with white spots. *Female.* Pattern of coloration similar but colors duller.

RANGE: Breeds in central Michigan. Winters in the Bahama Islands.

STATUS IN S. C.: Rare transient, April 27 to May 5, and October 4 to 29, over most of the State. Recorded north to Cherokee and Chester counties; east to Charleston County; south to Beaufort County.

HISTORY: Wayne (1910) said of Kirtland's Warbler that "Until recently (1903), all ornithologists considered this species the rarest of the warblers." Although something has been learned of its habits, behavior, and food, it remains restricted in numbers, confined to a small part of one state as a breeder, and elsewhere occurs only sparingly as a migrant.

Its history in South Carolina is brief, though interesting. There are but five records. It was added to the State List on April 27, 1886, at St. Helena Island, Beaufort County, when a male was shot "by a native lad." This was recorded by Walter J. Hoxie, who also saw three a week later on the same island (*Auk, 3*: 1886, 412). A female was secured at Chester by L. M. Loomis, October 11, 1888 (*Auk, 6*: 1889, 74). A "superb" male was taken by Wayne, October 29, 1903, near Mt. Pleasant, Charleston County (*Auk, 21*: 1904, 83). Wayne saw another near his home on Oakland Plantation, October 4, 1910 (*Auk, 28*: 1911, 116). Fifteen years intervened before the fifth record, that of a bird seen by P. M. Jenness, May 5, 1925, in Gaffney, Cherokee County (*Bird-Lore, 27*: 1925, 252). From that time until the present (1949) there have been no records.

This remarkable warbler is known to breed in but one area in north central Michigan, in what is known as the "jack-pine country." There it is known as the Jack-pine Warbler. The area is about 100 miles long by 60 miles wide and lies in Oscoda, Crawford, and Roscommon counties.

Kirtland's Warbler is a bluish-gray bird, lemon yellow below, with black streaks on the back, a black mark on the face, and streaked sides. Sometimes, the breast is spotted. It has the habit of jerking its tail frequently, like the Palm Warbler, and it is a walker, not a hopper.

FOOD: Largely if not wholly, insects.

NORTHERN PRAIRIE WARBLER
351. *Dendroica discolor discolor* (Vieillot)   (673)

(Lat., *discolor*, of different colors.)

DESCRIPTION: Length 4.25 to 5.20 inches. *Male.* Upper parts yellowish olive green; back spotted with chestnut; line over eye and under parts lemon yellow; wings with two light yellow bars; sides of neck and of body with broad black streaks; tail with large white patches on the three outer feathers. *Female.* Similar but colors duller, and with no, or very obscure, chestnut spots on the back.

RANGE: Breeds north to eastern Nebraska and southern New Hampshire; south to southeastern Louisiana and southeastern Georgia. Winters north to central Florida, southeastern South Carolina, and the Bahama Islands; south to Jamaica and Martinique.

STATUS IN S. C.: Common permanent resident in the coast region, but rare in winter; common summer resident, March 31 to October 23, in the remainder of the State. Observed in its winter range, north to Bull's Island; south to Beaufort County. Breeds north to Greenville, York, and Marlboro counties; east to Horry County; south to Hampton County; west to Aiken and Oconee counties.

HISTORY: This brightly colored and attractive species is one of the most abundant summer residents of South Carolina. It occurs everywhere in suitable locations from one end of the State to the other. Its name is indicative of its haunts, for it lives in open country. Warm, sunny spots in scrubby, bush-grown pastures, old fields with thickets of briers and low bushes, and second-growth clearings form its home.

Its brilliant yellow is set off by the black streaks on the sides and the two stripes on the face. The bird is not at all shy and may be approached to within a few feet as it feeds busily in the bushes and low trees. The almost constantly uttered song is as characteristic as the plumage itself, a thin, high "zee-zee-zee-zee" sound of six or eight notes on a continually rising scale. Along highways in spring and early summer this song comes clearly to one's ears, and it may be heard dozens of times within a few miles. F. M. Weston once recorded a singing male on October 3.

Most of the Prairie Warblers arrive on the coast in late March and remain until October. In the Piedmont, it has been recorded from April 11 (G. E. Hudson) to September 25 (W. M. Perrygo and J. S. Webb). About the fall line, Columbia to Aiken, it appears in early April. Breeding is much commoner about this line than below it. L. M. Loomis found it common at Chester and "tolerably" common in upper Pickens County. On July 3, 1934, Hudson found what must have been a second brood of well-grown young at Jocassee. E. J. DeCamps found a fresh set of three eggs 15 miles north of Greenville on June 17, 1941. Wayne never found the Prairie Warbler nesting on the coast but others have been more successful. F. M. Weston saw an adult feeding young on June 18, 1909, at the Charleston Navy Yard, and on May 11, 1911, B. R. Chamberlain found a nest there, in which four eggs were laid by May 18. Adults were seen feeding young at Dixie Plantation, Charleston County, May 2, 1923 (E. A. Williams and Sprunt).

The nest is usually at low elevations in scrubby growth, 2 to 10 feet high. It is an attractive, well-made cup of weeds, grasses, and leaves, lined with hair or pine needles. There are four or five white eggs, speckled and wreathed with brown and lavender markings. They average 16.2 x 12.2 millimeters. One, possibly two, broods are raised. Incubation requires about fourteen days.

That the Prairie Warbler occurs at times in winter in South Carolina is now definitely established, though original reports of its presence in that season were not only questioned by Wayne but categorically denied. Walter J. Hoxie recorded it at Frogmore, Beaufort County, twice in early March, and once on February 19 (1888-1891) (*Dept. Agri. Bull. No. 18*, U. S. Biol. Surv.). Wayne was forced to revise his opinion when, on January 9, 1922, he saw a male Prairie Warbler in his yard at

Oakland Plantation, 75 miles north of Hoxie's location and nearly a month earlier than Hoxie's record. He attempted without success to secure the bird. On November 25, 1946, Sprunt saw three adult males in live oak trees on Bull's Island. December is the only month in which this warbler has not been recorded in South Carolina.

FOOD: Almost wholly insects. Moths and their larvae, beetles, bugs, flies, scale insects, grasshoppers, ants, and tree hoppers have been found in stomach examinations.

WESTERN PALM WARBLER
352. *Dendroica palmarum palmarum* (Gmelin) (672)

(Lat., *palmarum*, of palms.)

DESCRIPTION: Length 4.50 to 5.50 inches. Top of head chestnut; back greenish olive or light brown, indistinctly streaked with dark brown; two wing bars dull light brown; three outer tail feathers with white spots; line over eye, throat, chest, and lower tail coverts yellow; breast and belly dingy white; breast and sides with thin streaks of brown and chestnut.

RANGE: Breeds north to southern Mackenzie and northern Manitoba; south to northern Minnesota and central western Ontario. Winters north to southern Louisiana and Massachusetts; south to Yucatan, Jamaica, and Puerto Rico.

STATUS IN S. C.: Common winter resident, September 2 to April 27, casually June 8, throughout the State. Reported north to Greenville, York, and Marion counties; east to Horry County; south to Beaufort and Jasper counties; west to Aiken and Oconee counties.

HISTORY: This regular and often abundant warbler is a wintering species in South Carolina, a fact which has been frequently overlooked in books dealing with southern ornithology. Actually, in South Carolina it arrives in late September and remains until late April. Throughout the entire winter it may be seen on practically any trip afield, and in some years it is positively abundant. Although common throughout the State in migration, Palm Warblers are decidedly uncommon above the fall line in winter. L. M. Loomis found both races through the winter at Chester, but neither was very common. P. M. Jenness listed the Palm Warbler as an uncommon winter resident at Greenville. There are specimens of this race taken throughout the winter months near the coast in the Charleston Museum collection.

One summer record exists, that of two birds seen on Raccoon Key (Cape Romain Refuge) on June 8, 1927, by Chamberlain and Roger Tory Peterson.

Though plainly plumaged and therefore inconspicuous, the Western Palm Warbler is easy to recognize because of its almost incessant tail jerking. This habit (characteristic of some other birds, of course) is diagnostic for identification when coupled with the general appearance of this warbler and the habitat it frequents. It is often seen on the ground in open country such as field edges, hedgerows, the sandy wastes of the barrier islands, and yards and gardens. The presence of the bright patch of yellow under the base of the tail is an excellent field character.

It is usually more common in severe winters than in mild ones but sometimes dies in extremely cold winters, doubtless from a failure of its food supply rather than from the weather itself. It is a quiet bird, the note being a weak "chip," in sharp contrast to the frequently uttered note of the Myrtle Warbler with which it associates.

FOOD: The food is high in insect content. Weevils, other beetles, ants, bugs, caterpillars, cotton worms, flies, and cutworms all figure in the diet in varying degrees.

YELLOW PALM WARBLER
353. *Dendroica palmarum hypochrysea* Ridgway (672a)

(Gr., *hypochrysea*, gleaming with gold.)

DESCRIPTION: Similar to the Western Palm Warbler but larger; lower parts more deeply and extensively yellow and more conspicuously streaked with chestnut; upper surface more yellowish olive.

RANGE: Breeds north to southeastern Ontario and Newfoundland; south to southern Nova Scotia. Winters north to northeastern Louisiana and Massachusetts; south to southern Louisiana, southern Florida, and Jamaica (casually).

STATUS IN S. C.: Fairly common winter resident, August 18 to April 28, throughout the State, more numerous during migrations. Observed north to Chester and Chesterfield counties; east to Horry County; south to Charleston County; west to Aiken and Oconee counties.

HISTORY: This form of the Palm Warbler is apparently not as numerous in South Carolina as is the Western Palm Warbler, though most of the individuals in the field are relatively easy to identify. Specimens have been taken at Huger, Berkeley County, on November 28, 1928, by E. von S. Dingle; Charleston, November 27, 1908, by Chamberlain; Anderson, September 25, 1896, by H. T. Nowell. These have been identified by Dr. H. C. Oberholser.

In habits and food the Yellow Palm Warbler apparently does not differ from the Western Palm Warbler.

OVEN-BIRD
354. *Seiurus aurocapillus aurocapillus* (Linnaeus) (674)

(Gr., *Seiurus*, tail-waving; Lat., *aurocapillus*, golden-haired.)

LOCAL NAMES: Golden-crowned Thrush.

DESCRIPTION: Length 5.40 to 6.50 inches. Middle of crown ochraceous, bordered on each side with black; rest of upper parts plain greenish olive; lower surface white, the chest and sides streaked and spotted with brownish black.

RANGE: Breeds north to southeastern Mackenzie and southeastern Quebec; south to northern Louisiana and northwestern South Carolina. Winters north to Sinaloa and Nuevo Leon in Mexico, southern Louisiana, and southeastern South Carolina; south to Colombia, and St. Thomas Island in the West Indies.

STATUS IN S. C.: Fairly common summer resident, April 13 to October 17, in the mountains; rare winter resident, August 16 to May 15, in the southern part of the coast region, common, however, during migrations; a common transient, April 24 to May 18, and August 7 to October 29, in the middle portion of the State. Recorded in the northwestern area north to Greenville County; south to Greenwood; west to Oconee County. In its winter range in the State it has been observed north to Charleston County; south to Beaufort County. As a transient in the middle part of the State, it occurs north to Chester and Florence counties; east to Horry County; south and west to Aiken County.

HISTORY: Many people think of the Oven-bird as a thrush. It does look like one, but it is smaller and is actually one of the warblers, with habits which distinguish it sharply from the rest of the warbler family.

The Oven-bird summers in the upper Piedmont, is transient on the coast and in the middle of the State, and a few occasionally winter on the coast. Therefore, it is actually a permanent resident, since it occurs somewhere in South Carolina in every month of the year.

Late, in varying degrees, are Oven-birds recorded for October 29 at Chester (L. M. Loomis) and November 15 at Summerton (E. von S. Dingle). Extremely early is Dingle's record of a bird on July 7, 1914, at Summerton. On the coast there are few winter occurrences that have actually been recorded. Wayne took the bird near Mt. Pleasant, on November 24, 1900. E. B. and B. R. Chamberlain saw one bird near Charleston on December 23, 1911, and George B. Rabb observed another there on March 21, 1948. These are the only definite winter observations.

The Oven-bird was found breeding on Mt. Pinnacle, Pickens County, and at Caesar's Head, Greenville County, by Loomis in the 1890's. He noted the young awing by June 10. G. E. Hudson found a young bird on Mt. Pinnacle June 19, and a nest with four young on Sassafras Mountain, also Pickens County, June 26, 1934. F. Sherman discovered a nest and four eggs on Stumphouse Mountain, Oconee County, on May 15, 1932. F. W. Hahn, Jr., called the Oven-bird a rare summer resident at Greenwood but was not successful in finding a nest.

The Oven-bird derives its unusual name from the shape of its nest. Placed on the ground, the nest is completely arched over with grasses and leaves with the entrance on one side, the whole structure much resembling a Dutch oven. On a flat forest floor, one can sometimes find the nest by looking for a mound-like rise among the leaves. There are four or five eggs, white with markings of brownish and lilac, sometimes in a wreath about the large end. They average 20.3 x 15.2 millimeters. The Oven-bird may raise two broods in a season. The incubation period is twelve days.

The Oven-bird frequents heavy woods, often damp and dark. The rhododendron and laurel thickets of the mountain regions are its typical summer haunts. It is a low ranging bird and walks on the ground like a tiny chicken. The loud, penetrating song, given on a constantly ascending scale, with increasing volume on each note, is usually rendered as "teacher, teacher, teacher." It is heard during migration throughout the State.

The fact that the breast is heavily marked causes many people to identify the Oven-bird as a thrush, though these markings are streaks rather than spots. This character, together with the orange crown bordered with black, is the reason for the name "Golden-crowned Thrush." It is not a shy bird, and sometimes comes to houses in mountain resorts where food has been scattered for it.

FOOD: The food is varied, but it is composed chiefly of grasshoppers, crickets, ants, caterpillars, flies, moths, beetles, spiders, and small snails. The snails make up 30 per cent of the total, according to Henderson's *Practical Value of Birds*. The vegetable matter comprises about 38 per cent and consists of berries and seeds.

NEWFOUNDLAND OVEN-BIRD
355. *Seiurus aurocapillus furvior* Batchelder (647a)

(Lat., *furvior*, darker.)

DESCRIPTION: Similar to the Oven-bird, but upper parts, including the crown, darker.

RANGE: Breeds in Newfoundland. Winters south to Louisiana and South Carolina.

STATUS IN S. C.: Rare winter resident, September 30 to January 20, in the eastern and middle parts of the State.

HISTORY: At present there seem to be but two South Carolina records of the Newfoundland Oven-bird. These are a specimen collected by Wayne at Mt. Pleasant on January 20, 1904, and another taken by W. M. Perrygo and J. S. Webb at Rock Hill in York County, September 30, 1940. The first is in the Charleston Museum, the second in the United States National Museum. Both have been identified by Dr. H. C. Oberholser.

In habits and food there is little or no material difference between this race and the other forms of the species.

NORTHERN WATER-THRUSH
356. *Seiurus noveboracensis noveboracensis* (Gmelin) (675)

(Lat., *noveboracensis*, of New York.)

DESCRIPTION: Length 5.00 to 6.00 inches. Upper parts plain olive; stripe over eye buff; wings olive without markings; under parts pale yellow streaked and spotted with black.

RANGE: North to northern Ontario and northern Quebec; south to West Virginia and Pennsylvania. Winters north to the Valley of Mexico and South Carolina; south to Colombia and British Guiana.

STATUS IN S. C.: Common transient, March 24 to May 22, and July 27 to October 22, casually November, in most of the State. Recorded in migration north to Chester County; east to Charleston County; south to the Savannah River; west to Aiken and Oconee counties. In winter traced north to near Charleston.

HISTORY: Among the South Carolina specimens identified by Dr. H. C. Oberholser may be mentioned: those taken at Mt. Pleasant, May 13, 1901, May 6, 1915, July 29, 1912, August 16, 1918, September 7, 1922, and October 22, 1920, by Wayne; at Huger, May 8, 1929, by E. von S. Dingle; at Charleston, October 4, 1913, by E. A. Hyer; at Chester, May 8, 1891, by L. M. Loomis.

All sight records of birds of this species are included under the present race.

GRINNELL'S WATER-THRUSH

357. *Seiurus noveboracensis notabilis* Ridgway   (675a)

(Lat., *notabilis*, noteworthy.)

DESCRIPTION: Length 5.50 to 6.50 inches. Similar to the Northern Water-thrush but larger, especially the bill; upper parts darker, more sooty; lower parts and stripe over the eye less yellow, even nearly white.

RANGE: Breeds north to northwestern Alaska and northern Manitoba; south to Montana and western Pennsylvania. Winters north to Lower California, and the Bahama Islands, and (accidentally) South Carolina; south to northern South America.

STATUS IN S. C.: Uncommon transient, April 21 to May 22, and September 18 to 29, over much of the State; accidental in winter. Definitely recorded north to Chester County; east and south to Huger and Charleston; west to Oconee County. Accidental in winter.

HISTORY: Grinnell's Water-thrush is a transient visitor to South Carolina; it migrates through the Mississippi Valley and along the Atlantic Coastal Plain from North Carolina southward. It appears to be more common in the Piedmont than the Northern Water-thrush. The major difference between the two is that the eye stripe and under parts of Grinnell's are not so yellow. In habits and food the two subspecies are virtually alike.

Since Grinnell's Water-thrush usually cannot be distinguished in the field from the Northern Water-thrush, specimens furnish the only dependable records. The following specimens have been identified by Dr. Harry C. Oberholser: from Chester, April 28, 1888, September 18, 24, and 26, 1888, and May 7 and 9, 1889, collected by L. M. Loomis; from Huger, Berkeley County, September 29, 1930, by E. von S. Dingle; from Clemson College, May 3 and 22, 1926, and April 21, 1927, by G. E. Hudson; and from near Charleston, January 20, 1887, by Wayne. The last is an unusual record, as the bird was far north of its normal winter home. Wayne noted that the weather at the time resembled a blizzard.

PLATE XXVIII: WARBLER GROUP

Water Color by John Henry Dick

Four left birds, reading from top to bottom: Myrtle Warbler (male, breeding plumage), Myrtle Warbler (immature, fall plumage), Swainson's Warbler, and Worm-eating Warbler. Four right birds, top to bottom: Cairns's Warbler (male, breeding plumage), Cairns's Warbler (female), Magnolia Warbler (male, breeding plumage), and Magnolia Warbler (female, breeding plumage).

T.H.Dick
'48

LOUISIANA WATER-THRUSH
358. *Seiurus motacilla* (Vieillot) (676)

(Lat., *motacilla*, a wagtail.)

DESCRIPTION: Length 5.75 to 6.40 inches. Upper surface plain grayish olive; a white line over the eye; lower surface buffy white, the breast and sides streaked with grayish olive, the throat without such markings.

RANGE: Breeds north to central eastern Nebraska and Vermont; south to northeastern Texas and central South Carolina. Winters north to Mexico, northern Florida, and casually South Carolina; south to Colombia and the Island of Antigua.

STATUS IN S. C.: Fairly common summer resident, March 20 to October 19, in the northwestern two-thirds of the State. Uncommon transient, March 18 to April 26, and July 13 to September 11, in the eastern and southern sections of the State. Casual in winter in the coast region. Recorded in summer north to Greenville and Chester counties; east to Florence County; south to Richland and Aiken counties; west to Oconee and Pickens counties. As a transient observed north to Horry County; east and south to Charleston County; west to Clarendon County.

HISTORY: Though these birds bear the name "thrush," they should really be known as "water-warblers," since they are of the warbler, not the thrush, family. The Louisiana Water-thrush is not well known except to students, but it is a fairly common bird in South Carolina and not hard to find in suitable localities at the right season.

All of the water-thrushes are about sparrow-size, are brown-backed, and have a light line over the eye and heavily streaked under parts. They keep close to the ground and prefer to live near water, in low, damp situations such as swamps or along streams and about ponds. Their habitat and actions make one think of them as tiny woodland sandpipers rather than as warblers. All have the habit of bobbing up and down and tilting the body like the Spotted Sandpiper.

The Louisiana Water-thrush is a summer resident in South Carolina, though it was long thought to be only a transient visitor to the coastal plain. Recent observations have revealed that it nests below the fall line, though it is still far from numerous in summer in that area. The peaks of its migrations on the coast are in early April and in early August. There are two winter observations of the bird near the coast. Southgate Y. Hoyt saw one at Summerville on November 15, 1942, and J. B. Shuler, Jr., saw another at McClellanville, Charleston County, on December 29, 1947.

The nesting of this strange warbler was for many years thought to be confined to the upper Piedmont counties. L. M. Loomis found it breeding in the mountains of Greenville and Pickens counties from 1888 to 1890. Since that time breeding records from that area have been made at Clemson, Spartanburg, Rocky Bottom (Pickens County), and Greenwood. At and below the fall line, there are records from Graniteville (Aiken County), Columbia, Eastover (Richland County), Florence, and Summerton. It may nest closer to the coast than now supposed, as indicated by a bird seen near Kingstree on June 6, 1932, by A. H. Howell and T. D. Burleigh. An early nesting record is that of four young just hatched on May 2 at Greenwood (F. W. Hahn). Adults have been observed feeding young as late as June 24 (E. von S. Dingle).

The nest is built under roots, in cavities of banks or under the overhang, and on ledges over streams. It is composed of leaves, grasses, moss, and mud. The eggs number from four to six and are white with numerous markings of chestnut-brown and grayish shades. The average size is 18.0 x 15.2 millimeters. Incubation requires twelve or fourteen days.

Though it is not particularly shy during migration, the Louisiana Water-thrush is very shy during the nesting season. Wayne said that he knew of no bird of its size so difficult to approach. He added that he once "wore out an entire suit of clothes" trying for more than a week to follow one of these warblers in a dense swamp and yet never secured it.

The song of this water-thrush is among the finest of warbler songs. It is a wild, ringing melody, very musical and thrilling in the dark woods which are its home. The call-note is a distinct metallic "chink," recognizable at once.

FOOD: The Louisiana Water-thrush consumes mostly insects, dragon flies, crane-fly larvae, beetles, locusts, bugs, ants, caterpillars, and scale insects. It also eats small mollusks and fish, killifish having been found in some stomachs. Wayne took a bird that had eaten "a few small minnows."

359. KENTUCKY WARBLER: *Oporornis formosus* (Wilson) (677)

(Gr., *Oporornis*, autumn bird; Lat., *formosus*, comely.)

DESCRIPTION: Length 5.00 to 5.85 inches. Crown black, edged with gray; a partial eye ring and line over eye to bill yellow; a broad stripe under eye to neck black; remainder of upper parts olive green; undersurface clear lemon yellow.

RANGE: Breeds north to central eastern Nebraska and southern Connecticut; south to eastern Texas, northwestern Florida, and South Carolina. Winters north to Mexico; south to Colombia.

STATUS IN S. C.: Fairly common summer resident, April 7 to October 24, throughout the State. Found north to Greenville, Chester, and Florence counties; east to Horry County; south to Beaufort County; west to Aiken and Oconee counties.

HISTORY: Alexander Wilson named the Kentucky Warbler for the state in which he discovered it. But the bird is not confined to Kentucky; it includes half of the United States in its range.

The Kentucky is a bird dressed in olive and yellow. Its best field character is the broad black "whisker" line which runs from the bill down the sides of the neck. As bright as the bird is, its colors seem intensified by its chosen haunts, into which little sunlight penetrates. It likes to live in swamps, preferably dark and gloomy ones. Undergrowth and water are essential to its happiness. It searches for its food close to the ground, pausing now and then to give its ringing, melodious song, which is like that of the Carolina Wren.

Though long known as a summer resident above the fall line of South Carolina, it was generally until recently considered a transient visitor in the Low-country. Records of it in summer indicate that it occurs locally if sparingly in several parts of the coastal plain.

Wayne describes it as abundant in the autumn migration, August to mid-September, when it may be found along the edges of fields and in open pinelands. As he pointed out, the season of abundance is the hottest part of the summer.

The nest of this warbler is a bulky affair, by no means easy to find, built of leaves, grass, bark strips, and debris, usually on the ground at the base of a bush. There are four or five eggs, white, sprinkled with reddish and lilac spots and averaging 18.3 x 14.2 millimeters. Two broods are raised. There are no data on incubation.

Nests were found by L. M. Loomis in Pickens and Greenville counties in the 1880's (*Auk*, 7: 1890, 129; 8: 1891, 332). G. E. Hudson found a pair "showing concern" near Clemson, Oconee County, June 13, 1934. The breeding range was extended to the fall line in 1920 when Misses L. P. Ford and M. J. Pellew found adults feeding young at Aiken on June 6 and 7 (*Auk*, 37: 1920, 589). On June 6 of the following year (1921) these observers found a nest of four young. E. von S. Dingle had a similar experience at Summerton, Clarendon County, in June and July of 1920 and 1921, when he found young in a nest one year and on the wing the next (*Auk*, 38: 1921, 607). Murphey (1937) records a nest taken at Brook's Pond, Aiken County, on May 29. At Long Bay Plantation, Horry County, R. G. Kuerzi repeatedly found a singing male from May 10 to June 7, 1940. He did not find a nest but says (ms.) that it "probably bred." This is the closest approach to an actual nesting record on the coast.

FOOD: Little is known as to the exact nature of the Kentucky Warbler's food, but it is certainly composed largely of insects. Bugs, beetles, caterpillars, and ants have been found in the few stomach analyses made.

360. CONNECTICUT WARBLER: *Oporornis agilis* (Wilson) (678)

(Lat., *agilis*, agile.)

DESCRIPTION: Length 5.20 to 6.00 inches. *Male*. Head, chin, throat, and chest slate to slate gray; remainder of upper surface plain olive green; other lower parts yellow; eye ring white. *Female*. Similar to the male but all the upper parts olive green without gray; chin, throat, and breast brownish buff.

RANGE: Breeds north to central Alberta and southern Manitoba; south to central Minnesota and northern Michigan. Winters north to northern Colombia and Venezuela; south to Brazil.

STATUS IN S. C.: Rare transient, May 10 to 20, and in August, in the western half of the State. Recorded north to Spartanburg County; east to Chester County; south to Aiken; west to Greenwood and Clemson College.

HISTORY: The Connecticut Warbler and the Mourning Warbler are very much alike in appearance; both are gray headed, olive backed, and yellow underneath.

However, the Connecticut may usually be recognized by the presence of the distinct white eye ring which the Mourning lacks.

The Connecticut Warbler is rare in South Carolina. On May 10, 1889, L. M. Loomis took a male at Chester, thereby adding the species to the State List (*Auk, 8:* 1891, 172). Thirty-eight years later, G. E. Hudson secured a singing male at Clemson, Oconee County, May 20, 1927 (*Auk, 45:* 1928, 103). None has been taken since.

The following sight records complete the known occurrences in the State. An adult male Connecticut Warbler was seen by the Misses L. P. Ford and M. J. Pellew at Aiken on May 12, 1915, and was recorded by Wayne (*Auk, 35:* 1918, 442). On August 1, 1926, F. W. Hahn, Jr., observed one at Greenwood, the only fall record. Gabriel Cannon reported seeing one Connecticut, a male, at Spartanburg, on May 20, 1932.

During migrations it frequents low, wet lands where there are bushes and thickets. It stays close to the ground and walks like the Oven-bird.

FOOD: Chiefly insects.

MOURNING WARBLER
361.   *Oporornis philadelphia* (Wilson)   (679)

(Lat., *philadelphia*, to the city of Philadelphia [Pennsylvania].)

DESCRIPTION: Length 4.90 to 5.75 inches. *Adult male.* Head, neck, and chest dark gray; middle of throat and the chest much mixed, sometimes solidly black; rest of upper parts olive green; remaining lower parts yellow; no conspicuous white on eyelids. *Adult female.* Similar to the male, but chin and throat dull white or brownish white; chest dull gray; remainder of the head dull gray or olive. *Immature.* Similar to the adult female, but throat and chest more tinged with yellow.

RANGE: Breeds north to central Alberta and Newfoundland; south to southeastern Nebraska, central Minnesota, West Virginia, and Massachusetts. Winters north to Nicaragua and Costa Rica; south to Ecuador and Venezuela.

STATUS IN S. C.: Casual spring transient in the mountain region.

HISTORY: The Mourning Warbler has long been carried on the State List on the strength of Elliott Coues' statement that it is a "very rare migrant." Audubon, Bachman, Loomis, and Wayne all failed to note it in any part of the State, and only at a comparatively recent date has an observation been made which confirms Coues' statement. On May 24 and 25, 1940, Gabriel Cannon studied a male bird at close range and in good sunlight at Spartanburg (*Bird-Lore, 42:* 1940, 384). Although the species must be considered extremely rare in South Carolina, it should be pointed out that it has long been known as a fall migrant in the North Carolina mountains (Pearson and the Brimleys, *Birds of North Carolina,* 1942, 322).

The Mourning Warbler is closely related to the Connecticut Warbler and except for the fact that it is not quite so deliberate in its movements, it is very similar to that species in behavior and food habits.

WOOD WARBLERS

Northern Yellow-throat
362. *Geothlypis trichas brachidactyla* (Swainson)   (681d)

(Gr., *Geothlypis*, a ground finch; *trichas*, a thrush; *brachidactyla*, short digited.)

DESCRIPTION: Like the Maryland Yellow-throat, but wing and tail longer; male above more yellowish or brownish; light band on forehead lighter, more creamy (less grayish); yellow of throat more extended posteriorly; and flanks more brownish.

RANGE: Breeds north to Newfoundland and northern Pennsylvania; south to northern Georgia and northwestern South Carolina. Winters north to Louisiana and Massachusetts (accidentally); south to Guatemala and Jamaica.

STATUS IN S. C.: Common permanent resident in the northwestern part of the State. Recorded north to Greenville County; east and south to Newberry County; west to Anderson County. As a winter resident recorded east to Horry County; south to Beaufort County.

HISTORY: The various races of the Yellow-throats are practically impossible to distinguish in the field. Because of their similarity, only specimens collected and carefully identified have been used to delineate their ranges in South Carolina. Much work yet remains to be done on this group in the State. The specimens from which the identifications have been made are in the collections of the Charleston Museum, the United States National Museum, and the Cleveland Museum of Natural History, and in the private collection of E. von S. Dingle.

The Northern Yellow-throat is apparently the breeding form in the northwestern part of the State. Among the specimens that have been examined are: one taken on June 28, 1933, and one on June 1, 1934, at Anderson, by T. D. Burleigh; one taken on July 8, 1933, at Saluda Gap, Greenville County, by Burleigh; two taken on June 1 and 3, 1940, 5 miles southeast of Whitmire, Newberry County, by W. M. Perrygo and J. S. Y. Hoyt; one taken on July 19, 1940, 6 miles northwest of Marietta, Greenville County, by the same collectors; one taken on July 20, 1940, at Pumpkintown, Pickens County, by the same collectors. E. J. DeCamps found eggs on June 21, 1945, 15 miles north of Greenville.

In general habits and food the Northern Yellow-throat does not differ from the other races.

Maryland Yellow-throat
363. *Geothlypis trichas trichas* (Linnaeus)   (681)

DESCRIPTION: Length 4.40 to 5.65 inches. *Male.* Forehead and sides of head black; bordered behind by a band of pale gray forming a mask; remainder of upper surface plain olive green; throat and chest lemon yellow; under tail coverts paler; belly and the rest of the lower parts pale buff or buffy white, but the sides and flanks pale grayish brown. *Female.* Similar to the male but top of head of the same color as the back (olive green) with no black or gray markings; throat and breast pale yellow.

RANGE: Breeds north to southern Ohio and central northern Pennsylvania; south to eastern Texas and Virginia. Winters north to Louisiana and North Carolina; south to Nicaragua and the Bahama Islands.

STATUS IN S. C.: Uncommon winter resident, September 20 to May 1, probably over much of the State. Recorded, however, only from the eastern part, north to Marlboro County; south to Beaufort County.

HISTORY: The only specimens which are certainly referable to this race and which have been so far examined are as follows: Port Royal, January 26, 1891, taken by J. E. Benedict; Mt. Pleasant, May 1, 1898, taken by Wayne; John's Island, Charleston County, September 20, 1933, taken by Chamberlain and G. R. Lunz, Jr.; 14 miles northwest of Bennettsville, October 7, 1940, taken by W. M. Perrygo and J. S. Webb.

The Yellow-throat has figured in the occasional "rains" of small birds sometimes reported during the migratory seasons. An instance of such a "rain" occurred on the night of May 13, 1942, in several areas of northern South Carolina. Typical was the instance at Pageland, Chesterfield County, where from five hundred to one thousand small birds were found dead on the streets and in yards, on the morning of the fourteenth. Many of them, if not most, were Yellow-throats. Specimens were sent to the Bureau of Disease Investigation of the U. S. Fish and Wildlife Service at Washington. Dr. J. E. Shillinger reported that there was no sign of poisoning and that it was his opinion that since a "sudden drop in the temperature, with a change in the direction of wind frequently exposes the bodies of birds to severe chill because of air currents coming from the rear," it was probably such a condition that caused the mass losses.

FOOD: The food of these warblers is chiefly insects. They also take small mollusks and some seeds. Grasshoppers and crickets form the greatest number of insects, with ants, wasps, spiders, and bees next. Beetles, bugs, flies, and caterpillars also occur in the diet.

FLORIDA YELLOW-THROAT
364. *Geothlypis trichas ignota* Chapman   (681b)

(Lat., *ignota*, unknown.)

DESCRIPTION: Similar to the Athens Yellow-throat, but larger, particularly the bill; upper parts, sides, and flanks darker, more brownish; yellow of throat more orange-hued.

RANGE: Resident and breeds north to southeastern Louisiana and southeastern South Carolina; south to southern Florida. Winters also south to Costa Rica and Jamaica.

STATUS IN S. C.: Common permanent resident in the southeastern corner of the State. Recorded north to Huger, Berkeley County; east to Charleston County; south to Port Royal; limits of western distribution not determined.

HISTORY: The Yellow-throat, a little olive-green warbler with a black mask, is known to many people. It lives along field edges and ditches, on banks grown up in grass, in stubble and vines, cat-tail ponds, and fresh and salt marshes. The bright, rollicking song is usually rendered "witchity, witchity, witch." The alarm, or scolding note, is very wren-like in character and is often heard from the depths of a grassy bog or a thicket near the edges, while the bird remains unseen.

Yellow-throats begin to sing early in March and continue until mid-July. The males often sing while they are flying high in the air. Nesting occurs in late April. Wayne found fresh eggs on the twenty-fifth; Sprunt has records of four eggs on May 4 and young on May 14; and E. J. DeCamps has found eggs on April 17 at Brewton Plantation, Beaufort County.

The nest, which is usually well hidden, is placed in low bushes, grass clumps, or cane, not infrequently over water. On the coast and sometimes in the swampy districts of the interior, the nest is made altogether of cane leaves lined with grass. The eggs number three to five, and are white with markings of black and brown in endless variety; they average 17.8 x 12.7 millimeters. Two broods are raised, and eggs of the second are laid in early June. Incubation requires about twelve days.

Yellow-throats are more common in winter when their numbers are augmented by birds which have bred farther north. The migratory seasons, of course, show the greatest numbers.

The Florida Yellow-throat is the common breeding bird of Florida and is now known to be also a permanent resident of the southeastern corner of South Carolina. Specimens have been examined and identified by Dr. H. C. Oberholser from a series of study skins in the collection of the Charleston Museum and in the private collection of E. von S. Dingle.

There is little or no difference between the habits and food of the Florida Yellow-throat and those of the other Yellow-throats.

Athens Yellow-throat
365. *Geothlypis trichas typhicola* Burleigh (681j)

(Lat., *typhicola*, an inhabitant of cat-tails, genus *Typha*.)

DESCRIPTION: Similar to the Maryland Yellow-throat but larger; upper parts more brownish; yellow of lower surface more orange-hued; sides and flanks darker, more rufescent.

RANGE: Breeds north to central Alabama and southeastern Virginia; south to south central Alabama and central South Carolina. Winters north to southern Louisiana, central Alabama, and North Carolina (probably); south to Nicaragua and Jamaica.

STATUS IN S. C.: Common permanent resident except in the southeastern corner and the northwestern section of the State. Recorded to Cherokee, Lancaster, and Marlboro counties; east to Horry County; south to Beaufort County; west to Allendale County.

HISTORY: The Athens Yellow-throat is apparently the most numerous and generally distributed of all the races of the Yellow-throat occurring in South Carolina. Furthermore, it is probably the breeding bird over the greater portion of the State, excluding only the southeastern corner and the northwestern section. In order to determine definitely its time and place of occurrence within the range of the Florida Yellow-throat, only specimens can be used. A partial list of a number of specimens which have been identified by Dr. Harry C. Oberholser is added below: Port Royal, Beaufort County, January 18 and 26, 1891, taken by J. E. Benedict; Yemassee, January 28, 1888, taken by Wayne; Gray's Hill, Beaufort County, March 23 and 30, 1937, taken by A. B. Fuller; Mt. Pleasant, Charleston County, September 11, 1916, September 19, 1922, and November 29, 1920, taken by Wayne; Charleston, October 7, 1935, taken by Miss Day; same locality, October 22, 1932, taken by E. M. Burton; Huger, Berkeley County, October 2, 1930, and September 25, 1942, taken by E. von S. Dingle.

YELLOW-BREASTED CHAT
366. *Icteria virens virens* (Linnaeus) (683)

(Gr., *Icteria*, yellow; Lat., *virens*, being green.)

DESCRIPTION: Length 6.75 to 7.50 inches. Sides of head and upper parts plain grayish olive green; lores black; a white line to and over the eye; throat, breast, and upper abdomen bright yellow; lower abdomen white; bill black.

RANGE: Breeds north to southern Minnesota and northeastern Massachusetts; south to Texas and northern Florida. Winters north to Mexico, southern Florida (casually), and southeast central South Carolina (accidentally); south to Costa Rica.

STATUS IN S. C.: Common summer resident, March 25 to November 11, all over the State; accidental in winter. Observed as a summer bird north to Greenwood and Chester counties; east to Horry County; south to Jasper County; west to Edgefield and Oconee counties. Reported in winter from Clarendon County.

HISTORY: That the Yellow-breasted Chat is a warbler will come as a surprise to the beginner, for it is utterly unlike the rest of the family and, as a matter of fact, unlike any other bird. The Chat is an individualist of the first water and a clown among birds in its astonishing habits and behavior.

Few birds are noisier and few more shy and retiring. This may seem paradoxical, but much about the Chat is surprising. It is the largest of the warblers and it is easy to recognize in its olive-green and yellow plumage, but it is so secretive that good views of it are hard to obtain. It is a common summer resident of South Carolina and occurs generally from the mountains to the sea.

If when walking through a brushy field on a spring morning, one hears a sudden outbreak of clear whistles, deep clucks, gurgles, and other sounds coming from an undetermined point, he will have evidence that a Chat is nearby. The Chat is a ventriloquist of no mean ability; it seems first here, then there, and because it is always reluctant to show itself, one can never be quite certain just where the medley of sound is coming from. Now and then, patient watching will reveal the singer. The bird may rise into the air, fly upward for some distance, then with an amazing series of contortions, drop downward by jerky degrees into the thicket. With wings flopping as if they were about to come off, and with tail pumping and legs dangling, all to the accompaniment of weird whistles and clucks, the Chat reveals himself to be an acrobat as well as a ventriloquist. Added to these interesting accomplishments is the fact that the Chat often sings at night.

G. E. Hudson records the spring arrival of Yellow-breasted Chats at Clemson from April 18 to 24; on the coast they come about a week earlier. Most of them leave before the end of August. Though the birds breed abundantly, their nests are difficult to find because they are invariably built in dense thickets and tangles of briers and vines. Wayne during all his life on the coast found but two nests, explaining that the character of the sites are such that they absolutely preclude exploration. Wayne found the nests in May of 1879 and 1906, twenty-seven years apart. The first was in a Cherokee rose bush, the second "in an almost impenetrable thicket of sweet briars [sic]. . . . and blackberry brambles. . . ." The nest, which is always built near the ground, is composed of grasses and leaves and is lined with grass. There are three to five white eggs, marked with many spots or blotches of reddish brown and lilac. They average 22.9 x 16.8 millimeters. The Chat raises only one brood a season. A typical date for the Piedmont area is June 13, four eggs, Greenville County (E. J. DeCamps). John Kershaw, Jr., took a nest with only one egg on May 28 in Oconee County. Incubation is said to require fifteen days.

The Chat winters in Central America and is rarely to be seen in winter even in southern Florida. However, on January 11, 1947, a single Chat was seen and watched for some time by both authors and a small party in the Santee National Wildlife Refuge in Clarendon County. It is the only winter record for South Carolina (*Auk*, 64: 1947, 467).

FOOD: Mainly insects—weevils, beetles, bees, ants, tent caterpillars, moths, and May flies. The Chat sometimes also eats wild strawberries, wild grapes, raspberries, blackberries, and huckleberries.

367.   HOODED WARBLER: *Wilsonia citrina* (Boddaert)   (684)

(Lat., *Wilsonia*, to Alexander Wilson; *citrina*, lemon-colored.)

DESCRIPTION: Length 5.00 to 5.75 inches. *Male.* Forehead and sides of head lemon yellow; hood covering hinder part of crown and sides of neck black; remaining upper parts yellowish olive green; throat and chest black; rest of undersurface lemon yellow; three outer tail feathers with prominent white areas. *Female.* Similar but without black hood; upper parts yellowish olive green; below yellow.

RANGE: Breeds north to southeastern Nebraska and Massachusetts (probably); south to southeastern Texas and northern Florida. Winters north to Vera Cruz and Yucatan; south to Guatemala and Panama.

STATUS IN S. C.: Common summer resident, March 23 to October 15, casually November 11, over all the State. Reported north to Greenville, Chester, and Marlboro counties; east to Horry County; south to Beaufort County; west to Aiken, Greenwood, and Oconee counties.

HISTORY: In a generally beautiful family, the Hooded Warbler is particularly attractive. The dark haunts, resounding to the clear, far-carrying "wee-ta, wee-tée-o," seem the proper setting for its glowing brightness of plumage. Green and yellow, the black hood standing out in sharp contrast, it flits and sings through the cane clumps, cypress knees, and thickets like a feathered fairy.

The Hooded Warbler is a summer resident in South Carolina and occurs in most of the State. It arrives on the coastal plain in late March. G. E. Hudson has noted it at Clemson, in the Piedmont, as early as April 3. Throughout the State it remains into October. Like Swainson's Warbler it dwells in the undergrowth of swamps, but it is also to be found on open edges of swamp lands and along the roads that penetrate them. However, L. M. Loomis recorded it to a height of 2500 feet in the mountains of South Carolina.

Wayne (1910) termed it the "most abundant" of breeding warblers on the coast. While it is certainly very common, it has never seemed to the authors to equal in numbers either the Parula or Yellow-throated Warblers, both of which occur where the Hooded does and in many places where it does not. At any rate, the Hooded is never difficult to find in cypress country.

Nesting begins from the middle to the end of April, and two broods (perhaps three) are raised. The nest is rarely more than 6 feet from the ground, most of them are lower than that. Bushes, clumps of cane, scrub palmetto, and briery tangles are favorite sites. The nest is made of grass, leaves, and weed stalks and is lined with pine needles and the black inner fibre of the Spanish moss. The eggs, which number four or five as a rule, are white, variously dotted, splashed, or wreathed about the large end with lilac and reddish markings. They average 18.0 x 13.5 millimeters. Incubation takes about twelve days.

Wayne found full sets of eggs on April 25. Sprunt has dates of May 6, four eggs, and May 7, two young and one egg. Eggs of the second brood have been found June 26 (Wayne). A typical date for the upper Piedmont is June 11 at Clemson (G. E. Hudson). Two nests at Columbia held four eggs on May 3 (B. F. Taylor). John Kershaw, Jr., took a nest with only one egg on June 13 at Russell, Oconee County.

Migration is under way early in August, but birds continue to pass through the State until October, many of these having nested far to the northward of South Carolina. Abnormally late was a female or young male seen near Charleston on November 11, 1943, by E. A. Williams.

FOOD: The food is apparently made up wholly of insects—wasps, beetles, moths, flies, caddis-fly larvae, roundworms and their larvae.

WILSON'S WARBLER
368. *Wilsonia pusilla pusilla* (Wilson) (685)

(Lat., *pusilla*, very little.)

DESCRIPTION: Length 4.25 to 5.10 inches. *Male.* Crown black; remaining upper surface olive green, the forehead and region of the eye, together with under parts, bright yellow. *Female* and *immature*. Similar to the adult male but with black on crown much obscured or lacking.

RANGE: Breeds north to northwestern Mackenzie and southern Labrador; south to southeastern Alberta and Nova Scotia. Winters north to Mexico and southern Texas; south to Guatemala and Costa Rica.

STATUS IN S. C.: Rare transient, May 5 to 17, and in November, in both eastern and western portions of the State. Recorded north to Chester County; east and south to Charleston County; west to Clemson College.

HISTORY: This pretty little warbler, which is easy enough to recognize, occurs only as a brief transient in the upper counties, and there are but two records of it in the coastal area. It is almost entirely yellow, without streakings, but the small black cap of the male is at once diagnostic. The cap of the female is little more than a suggestion and is sometimes entirely wanting.

Wilson's Warbler is common nowhere in the South, but passes through in small numbers during migration. It was L. M. Loomis, that indefatigable worker in the Piedmont, who added it to the State List by taking one at Chester, May 10, 1887 (*Auk, 8*: 1891, 172). Wayne concluded that this species must be a regular migrant through the upper part of the State, but subsequent years have not borne out such a belief. G. E. Hudson secured two males at Clemson, one on May 14, 1926, and the other on May 17, 1927 (*Auk, 45*: 1928, 103). These and the Loomis bird are the only specimens ever secured in South Carolina.

The two records for the coastal area are sight observations by competent field men. One of these records is of an immature bird seen at Mt. Pleasant, Charleston County, November 8 and 9, 1932, by E. von S. Dingle; and the other, of an adult male seen on Bull's Island, May 5 to 7, 1948, by E. O. Mellinger.

Wilson's is a fly-catching warbler, often seizing its insect prey on the wing.

CANADA WARBLER
369. *Wilsonia canadensis* (Linnaeus)   (686)

(Lat., *canadensis*, of Canada.)

DESCRIPTION: Length 5.00 to 5.75 inches. *Male.* Upper surface gray, the forehead black edged with gray; stripe from bill to eye, eye ring, together with most of the lower parts, yellow; under tail coverts white; breast with necklace of black spots. *Female* and *immature.* Similar to the adult male but duller, almost or quite lacking the black spots on the breast.

RANGE: Breeds north to north central Alberta and southern Labrador; south to central Minnesota, northern Georgia, and Rhode Island. Winters north to Guatemala and Costa Rica; south to Ecuador and Peru.

STATUS IN S. C.: Rare transient, May 2 to 21, and in September to October 28. Observed north to Greenville and Chester counties; east to Horry County; south to Aiken County; west to Clemson College.

HISTORY: The Canada Warbler is an attractive member of the family, but it is uncommon and local in South Carolina. G. E. Hudson found it about Clemson from May 2 to 21, a brief stay but probably typical. L. M. Loomis never found it nesting at Caesar's Head or Mt. Pinnacle (3,218 and 3,416 feet respectively). (It has been known to nest in the North Carolina Blue Ridge at elevations of 3,000 feet.)

Loomis, who recorded it about Chester in September, said that it was rare or casual at that season but "not uncommon" in spring during the first two weeks of May. The only other fall record was made on October 28, 1943, at Clemson by C. M. Crawford. The only coastal record is that of a bird seen at Long Bay Plantation, Horry County, May 11, 1940, by R. G. Kuerzi.

The Canada is a handsome warbler, gray above and bright yellow beneath with a characteristic black necklace, which is much subdued in the female. It is a deep woodland bird, frequenting the rhododendron and laurel thickets of the high slopes as well as the heavy deciduous woods, where it feeds chiefly upon insects.

AMERICAN REDSTART
370.   *Setophaga ruticilla ruticilla* (Linnaeus)   (687)

(Gr., *Setophaga*, moth-eating; Lat., *ruticilla*, red-tailed.)

DESCRIPTION: Length 4.60 to 5.75 inches. *Male.* Head, neck, chest, and upper surface black; sides of breast and patches on wings and tail, orange; posterior lower parts white. *Female.* Head and hind neck gray, remaining upper surface olive; orange pattern of the male replaced by yellow.

RANGE: Breeds north to Illinois and Maine; south to Louisiana, central Georgia, and south central North Carolina. Winters north to Cuba; south to Ecuador and British Guiana.

STATUS IN S. C.: Fairly common summer resident, April 15 to October 1, in the mountains. Common transient, October 15 to May 27, and July 4 to November 4, in the remaining portion of the State. Recorded in summer north to Greenville County; south to Anderson County; west to Oconee County. In migrations recorded north to Cherokee and York counties; east to Horry County; south to Beaufort; west to Aiken and Richland counties.

HISTORY: The American Redstart is one of the easiest warblers to know, both because of its highly individual appearance and habits, and because of its abundance in much of South Carolina in the fall of the year. Even the most casual observer can hardly fail to note the bird's jet black, bright orange, and white plumage, together with its habit of almost constant wing flitting and tail spreading. Peterson (1947) refers to it as the most butterfly like of birds, and the comparison is very appropriate. Chapman (1932) says that most of our warblers are known in Cuba as "*Mariposas*" (butterflies) but the Redstart's brilliance has gained for it the name of "*Candelita*," or little torch.

Even the females and immatures, though much duller than the males in color, show the characteristic wing and tail pattern, yellow instead of orange, and their actions in exhibiting it are like those of the male.

The Redstart is a summer resident in the Piedmont, and on the coastal plain, as Wayne points out, it is absent in summer for only thirty-eight days. The full length of its stay in the mountain region of South Carolina is from April 11 to October 12 (G. E. Hudson) but, strangely enough, it has not yet been found nesting there. Wayne wrote that it "must breed within the state" and Hudson and F. Sherman (*Auk, 53*: 1936, 314) say that it undoubtedly does so in the mountains. Hudson found a singing male at Jocassee on July 3, and E. J. DeCamps recorded it singing in mid-May on the Tiger River, north of Greenville, and he believes that it breeds there. Nevertheless, no actual instance of its nesting has yet come to light.

As another race of the American Redstart has recently been separated, it is necessary to depend to a considerable extent on specimens in the delineation of the ranges of the two forms in South Carolina. Specimens of the present race have been identified by Dr. H. C. Oberholser as follows: Huger, Berkeley County, September 19, 1930, and May 10, 1929, E. von S. Dingle; Mt. Pleasant, September 18 and August 23, 1919, and Charleston, August 29, 1889, Wayne; Anderson, July 30, 1895, H. T. Nowell; and Beaufort, April 22 and May 1, 1941, T. H. Sandera.

This warbler is the best "flycatcher" of the family; it is highly proficient at seizing insects in mid-air. Its tameness is at times remarkable. Sprunt has on several occasions seen it come among a number of people seated on a porch, and catch flies with utter unconcern. Sometimes it actually alights on an outstretched foot or hand, or on the back of a chair.

The Redstart frequents both woodlands and open situations such as yards and brushy field edges; it also comes to barns and stables for flies. It appears to be fond of live oak avenues in the Low-country, and may be often found feeding about the abundant Pride of India or "umbrella" trees near Negro cabins and settlements.

FOOD: The variety of insects consumed by this warbler seems to exceed that of any other members of the family (Forbush, 1907). Even caterpillars, swinging by silken threads and out of reach of many birds, cannot escape the Redstart, as it hovers in the air and picks them off. Moths, gnats, flies in great numbers, beetles, and small grasshoppers are its prey, and the total insect destruction caused by this one species in a year must be beyond calculation.

NORTHERN REDSTART
371. *Setophaga ruticilla tricolora* (Müller) (687a)

(Lat., *tricolora*, three-colored.)

DESCRIPTION: Similar to the American Redstart but smaller; in the male, with orange wing spot smaller; in the female, with the yellow wing spot smaller and the upper parts more grayish or greenish olive, less brownish.

RANGE: Breeds north to northern British Columbia and Newfoundland; south to Oregon and northern Maine. Winters south to Ecuador and French Guiana.

STATUS IN S. C.: Fairly common transient, September 26 to October 16, over probably all the State; not yet recorded in spring. Identified north to Berkeley County; east and south to Charleston County; west to Anderson County (probably).

HISTORY: The Northern Redstart, which is a readily recognizable race, was recently separated by Dr. H. C. Oberholser (*Bird Life of Louisiana*, 1938, 572). It is the breeding bird of the northern part of the range of the species. It is probably more common in South Carolina than the few available specimens indicate. These specimens are: from Charleston, September 26, 1889, collected by Wayne; from Huger, Berkeley County, October 3, 1930, October 13 and 16, 1942, by E. von S. Dingle; and one, apparently from Anderson, collected by H. T. Nowell. All these have been identified by Dr. Oberholser.

Family Ploceidae: Weaver Finches

ENGLISH SPARROW
372. *Passer domesticus domesticus* (Linnaeus)   (688.2)

(Lat., *Passer*, a sparrow; *domesticus*, domestic.)

LOCAL NAMES: Sparrow; House Sparrow.

DESCRIPTION: Length 6.25 to 6.35 inches. *Male.* Crown gray; back streaked with chestnut and black; a stripe from the eye to nape, broader behind, chestnut; rump gray; middle of throat and chest black; belly dull white. *Female.* Head brown; back streaked with buff and black; rest of under parts buffy to grayish white, darker on sides, which are washed with pale brown.

RANGE: Resident and breeds north to Norway, northern Russia, and northern Siberia; south to Spain, Palestine, and Dauria. Naturalized in other parts of the world and particularly in North America, where it ranges north to British Columbia and Newfoundland; south to Lower California and Florida; also to Cuba and the Bahama Islands.

STATUS IN S. C.: Abundant permanent resident over the State. Reported north to Greenville, York, and Marlboro counties; east to Horry County; south to Jasper County; west to Aiken and Oconee counties.

HISTORY: For people whose knowledge of ornithology is limited to one bird, that bird is the English Sparrow. It is unattractive and generally despised, but its history is nevertheless of considerable interest.

The English Sparrow was brought to Brooklyn, New York, and liberated there in 1851; two years later it was reintroduced; and since that time it has spread to practically every part of the United States. According to Wayne it first appeared in Charleston in 1874 or 1875. He saw the first nests in St. Philip Street, near the Charleston Orphan House, but he was uncertain whether the birds had been brought to South Carolina or had entered by migration. L. M. Loomis (*Auk*, 2: 1885, 190) said that it was deliberately introduced at Chester. Six birds were brought there in 1873, and by the time Loomis wrote the aggressive little foreigners had become firmly established. Today, of course, the English Sparrow is a permanent resident throughout all of South Carolina.

The nesting season is a long one. It begins in March and ends late in September. During that period the birds raise three, four or even five broods. It is this remarkable reproductive ability which accounts in great part for the success which the Sparrows have had in spreading over the country. They build their trashy, untidy nests almost everywhere—in trees, natural cavities, church steeples, bird boxes, and behind shutters and under the eaves of buildings. There are from four to seven eggs, dull white speckled and spotted with purple and gray. The eggs average 21.8 x 15.6 millimeters. Incubation takes thirteen or fourteen days.

English Sparrows are noisy, quarrelsome, and aggressive. They force many native birds out of their natural haunts and appropriate feeding stations, bird baths, and nesting boxes to their own use. It must be admitted that for all their unpleasantness they have some qualities which are commendable. They destroy moths, cabbage worms, and other objectionable insects. Wayne says he has seen them eat the cotton caterpillar. City sparrows have learned that the radiator grills of motor cars often provide insects for the taking; the birds wait for the car to be parked, fly at once to the bumper, and examine the front end for insects caught there.

In recent years the English Sparrow population has diminished noticeably in many parts of the eastern United States. The reason is not yet understood.

By scientific classification the English Sparrow is one of the weaver finches. It is this species which is responsible for the opprobrium which has come to be attached to the term "sparrow," with consequent injustice to many native birds which properly bear the name.

Family Icteridae: Meadowlarks, Blackbirds, and Orioles

373. BOBOLINK: *Dolichonyx oryzivorus* (Linnaeus) (494)

(Gr., *Dolichonyx*, long-clawed; Lat., *oryzivorus*, rice-eating.)

LOCAL NAMES: Ricebird; Reedbird.

DESCRIPTION: Length 6.30 to 8.00 inches. Bill stout and conical. *Male in spring.* Head, neck, and lower parts black; hind neck buff; back black streaked with white; scapulars and rump dull white. *Male in autumn.* Similar to the female but larger. *Female.* Upper surface light buffy olive, streaked with dull olive and black; undersurface pale olive buff; throat and middle of abdomen yellowish white; sides streaked with dark brown. *Immature.* Similar to the adult female.

RANGE: Breeds north to southeastern British Columbia and northern Nova Scotia; south to northeastern California and New Jersey. Winters north to Peru and Paraguay; south to northern Argentina and southern Brazil.

STATUS IN S. C.: Abundant transient, April 10 to May 26, casually June 23, and July 11 to December 6, casually December 28, over all the State. Observed north to Greenville and Chester counties; east to Horry County; south to Jasper County; west to Aiken and Oconee counties.

HISTORY: The Bobolink is better known in South Carolina as the Ricebird. It is a great favorite of northern fields and meadows but it was received with anything but cordiality in the Carolina Low-country during the last century. It was, in fact, a very destructive form of avian life, one of the few birds which have merited such a characterization.

The all but universal disfavor in which it was held arose from the depredations of multitudes of Bobolinks on the rice crop at a time when rice was the major agricultural product of the Carolina coast country, the economic basis of plantation life in the era before 1860. The Ricebirds were responsible for the loss of millions of dollars. The term "bird-minders," which is even yet heard now and then, was applied to the plantation hands who, with torches, guns, and tin basins, were stationed about the fields in an effort to drive away the swarming hosts of birds, and reduce the losses to the crop. The specific name of this species, the Latin *oryzivorus*, means "rice-eating," and few birds have ever been better named.

The Bobolink, to give it its correct name, still comes to Carolina, but the rice is gone. Except in a few fields privately planted, worked, and harvested, rice is no longer grown. The association, therefore, between grain and bird is unfamiliar to most contemporary students of ornithology.

The Bobolink is a transient visitor, appearing in spring and fall. It arrives about April 10, and is common by the middle of that month. Considerable numbers pass through the State during the rest of April and until late May. A straggler may be seen in June, the latest record being June 23 (E. von S. Dingle). The Bobolink arrives in the Piedmont later than on the coast, G. E. Hudson noting the first birds at Clemson, Oconee County, on April 24 and 26, and May 16 in different years. The stay there is also shorter both in spring and in fall than on the coast. A belated migration of some two hundred was seen in Dillon County on December 6, 1943, by Mrs. Ruth Bryant Sneed. Stragglers at this season have been recorded on December 25 and 28 at Huger, Berkeley County, by Dingle. The fall migration peak is in September and early October.

On almost any September night one can hear the metallic "clink" of Bobolinks as they travel the dark skies, and at times, the sound is almost continuous. This "clink" note is unmistakable, and once learned it is infallible.

It is in spring that the bird shows to best advantage, for the male is then in his spectacular black, white, and buff dress. Open fields are the places to look for it, and since flocks keep up a chattering chorus while they feed, the bird is easy to find. It sometimes visits residential building lots; hence, even city dwellers can learn to know it. The female Bobolink bears very little resemblance to her mate except in the fall when the male has shed his brilliance. She looks very much like a sparrow.

Food: Nesting Bobolinks are almost entirely insectivorous. Of the total food for the year, some 58 per cent is animal matter, though the bird in some places is still detrimental to crops. It eats beggarweed seed in parts of the South. In South Carolina today definite data on the food of the Bobolink are hard to obtain, but the diet is known to be both animal and vegetable.

PLATE XXIX: PINEWOOD SCENE

Water Color by Edward von S. Dingle

Birds at left, reading from top to bottom: Red-cockaded Woodpecker (female), Red-cockaded Woodpecker (male), Red-cockaded Woodpecker (immature male), and Brown-headed Nuthatch (adult). Birds at right, top to bottom: Bachman's Sparrow (adult), Pine Warbler (male), Pine Warbler (female), Prairie Warbler (male), and Prairie Warbler (female).

EASTERN MEADOWLARK
374. *Sturnella magna magna* (Linnaeus) (501)

(Lat., *Sturnella*, a little starling; *magna*, large.)

LOCAL NAMES: Field Lark; Lark.

DESCRIPTION: Length 9.00 to 11.00 inches. Tail feathers narrow and pointed. Top of head streaked with buff and black; remaining upper parts dark brown, streaked and varied with black, buff, and white; eyebrow stripe yellow; lower surface mostly lemon yellow with a large black crescent on breast, the sides of body streaked and spotted with brown and black; outer tail feathers white.

RANGE: Breeds north to central eastern Minnesota and New Brunswick; south to Texas and Virginia. Winters north to southern Wisconsin and southern Maine; south to southeastern Texas and northern Florida.

STATUS IN S. C.: Abundant winter resident, October 23 to March 13, throughout the State but apparently more numerous in the coastal region. Identified north to Calhoun County; east to Charleston County; south to Beaufort County; west to Clemson College.

HISTORY: Most observers have probably noticed that more meadowlarks are to be seen in autumn and winter than in summer. The influx of birds to South Carolina from the north accounts for this difference but similarity between the incoming birds and those that breed in the State makes it difficult if not impossible to determine arrival and departure dates from field observations alone. These, as well as the range, have been determined from a large series of skins in the collection of the Charleston Museum.

In general habits and food the Eastern agrees with the Southern Meadowlark.

SOUTHERN MEADOWLARK
375. *Sturnella magna argutula* Bangs (501c)

(Lat., *argutula*, a little talkative.)

LOCAL NAMES: Field Lark; Lark.

DESCRIPTION: Length 8.50 to 10.00 inches. Similar to the Eastern Meadowlark but decidedly smaller, and averaging somewhat darker on the upper parts.

RANGE: Resident and breeds north to southern Illinois and North Carolina; south to southeastern Texas and southern Florida.

STATUS IN S. C.: Common permanent resident throughout the State. Reported north to Greenville and York counties; east to Horry County; south to Beaufort County; west to Aiken, Greenwood, and Oconee counties.

HISTORY: Practically everybody knows the Lark. From the coast to the mountains the farm boy, city man, bird student, hunter, and traveller know the brown bird which flushes from the grass and flies away with alternate flappings and sailings and a display of white outer tail feathers. This handsome bird, which is really not a lark at all, but a member of the blackbird-oriole family, is a permanent resident everywhere in South Carolina. It lives entirely in open country—fields, clearings, and sea islands—never in woodlands. Wonderfully colored on the back to match the grass and ground, the bird, seen from below with its bright yellow underparts and the black crescent of the breast, presents a totally different appearance.

The Meadowlark has been divided into races, of which this form, *argutula*, is the breeding bird of the State. Since the two races that occur here cannot be distinguished with certainty in the field, all the records of meadowlarks not supported by specimens are placed under the southern form, although in winter the northern subspecies is probably more numerous than the resident race.

As common a bird as the Lark is, few nests are ever found, for they are always well hidden in wide tracts of grass from a few inches to over a foot high. Looking for a nest is like looking for the needle in the haystack unless one uses systematic efforts. The nest is simply a depression in the ground, lined with, and often arched by grass. It is practically impossible to see a nest from above, and flushing the sitting bird with one's foot is about the best means of locating it. The three to six eggs are white, spotted with reddish brown and lilac, and average 27.9 x 20.3 millimeters. Incubation requires fifteen to seventeen days.

Wayne thought that the Meadowlark was a late nester, but subsequent work has shown that it breeds earlier (and later) than he supposed. He gave two dates—May 28, 1890, Beaufort County, fresh eggs; and June 10, 1903, Mt. Pleasant, slightly incubated eggs. Records since then include June 26, 1924, four eggs, Berkeley County (Chamberlain); July 30, 1933, four fresh eggs, Charleston Country Club (E. A. Simons); April 30, 1935, three eggs, Rantowles, Charleston County (Sprunt); May 16, 1935, two fresh eggs and female taken, Charleston County (E. M. Burton); April 26, 1947, four eggs, Ladies Island, Beaufort County (De-Camps). Murphey (1937) evidently found it a late nester in the Aiken-Augusta region for he says, "The young are fully fledged and taking care of themselves by the first week in July. . . ."

The Lark is a famous and persistent singer in early spring and summer. Even in winter it may sometimes be heard. The song is difficult to describe but Peterson (1947) renders it *"tee-yah, tee-yair."* It is a clear whistle with a very pleasing quality.

FOOD: About three-fourths of the total food is insects. Crickets and grasshoppers make up one-fourth, and in late summer, almost three-fourths. Beetles, boll weevils, caterpillars, and cutworms also appear in the diet. Of over fifteen hundred stomachs examined, at all seasons, 778 contained remains of grasshoppers, and one held thirty-seven of these insects.

YELLOW-HEADED BLACKBIRD
376. *Xanthocephalus xanthocephalus* (Bonaparte) (497)

(Gr., *Xanthocephalus*, yellow headed.)

DESCRIPTION: Length 8.70 to 11.00 inches. *Male.* Head, neck, and chest yellow, with black about the eye; remaining plumage black with a white patch on the wing. *Female.* Mostly dark brown, but a stripe above the eye, also the cheeks and throat dull yellow or dull white, and the chest dull yellow.

RANGE: Breeds north to south central British Columbia and central Manitoba; south to Lower California, the Toluca Valley in central Mexico, and Indiana. Winters north to southwestern California and southwestern Louisiana; south to Mexico.

STATUS IN S. C.: Accidental. Known only from Chester and Charleston counties.

HISTORY: This handsome dweller of the tule marshes of the West is a rarity in South Carolina. There are only two records of its occurrence. Leverett M. Loomis examined a specimen trapped in Chester on April 18, 1884 (*Auk, 1*: 1884, 293). He accounted for its presence in the State by the heavy southwest gales at that time. On April 21, 1926, Herbert K. Job saw a bright male from the Jacksonboro Bridge on U. S. Highway 17 crossing the Edisto River, the dividing line between Charleston and Colleton counties (*Auk, 44*: 1927, 114). Job was familiar with the species in the West, and his record may therefore be considered entirely valid.

Both sexes of the Yellow-headed Blackbird are unmistakable, but the male is much more brightly colored. It is a distinctly larger species than the resident Red-winged Blackbird.

EASTERN RED-WING
377. *Agelaius phoeniceus phoeniceus* (Linnaeus) (498)

(Gr., *Agelaius*, gregarious; *phoeniceus*, tyrian red.)

LOCAL NAMES: Red-winged Blackbird.

DESCRIPTION: *Male.* Length 8.50 to 10.00 inches. Body entirely black with the lesser wing coverts bright red, bordered by buff middle wing coverts. *Female.* Length 7.50 to 8.50 inches. Upper parts fuscous black streaked with grayish white or light buff; under parts grayish or buffy white streaked with brownish black; throat often buff or salmon pink.

RANGE: Breeds north to southern Ontario and Nova Scotia; south to east central Texas and central northern Florida. Winters north to Arkansas, Illinois, and New Hampshire; south to Texas and Florida.

STATUS IN S. C.: Permanent resident, common in summer, abundant in winter throughout the State, except in the extreme southern corner. In summer known north to Spartanburg and Lancaster counties; east to Horry County; south to Seabrook's Beach, Charleston County; west to Barnwell, Greenwood, and Oconee counties. Winters also in the southeastern corner, in Beaufort County.

HISTORY: The Eastern Red-wing hardly needs an introduction. It occurs as a permanent resident everywhere in South Carolina and is well known to every one. Wherever there are streams and ponds one will find this handsome, rollicking bird, its black coat vividly contrasting with the scarlet shoulders. Water is essential to it, for it is a marsh-swamp-pond dweller.

Red-wings are a gregarious species; they gather in great flocks in fall and winter and nest in colonies of varying size. They are more numerous in the winter because the population is augmented then by migrants from the north, but the resident population is always large. Female Red-wings, which are decidedly smaller than the males and completely unlike them in appearance, look like large, heavily streaked sparrows.

Nesting occurs in April, May, and June, when the back beaches of barrier islands, salt marshes, inland stream edges, and river and willow swamps all resound to the liquid "oak-a-lee" notes of the males. In the coastal area most of the eggs are laid in the first two weeks of May. The earliest record we have is that of a young bird on April 23, 1910, Charleston (E. A. Hyer). The eggs in this case were probably laid about April 10. Another early date is April 20, 1935, four eggs, Beaufort (E. J. DeCamps). The latest is June 25, 1946, three eggs in an advanced stage of incubation, Charleston (G. B. Rabb).

The nest is usually placed in low bushes or shrubby growth, from a foot above ground or water to a height of from 20 to 40 feet in trees. The wax myrtle and the "salt-water myrtle" or high tide bush often provide nesting sites on the coast. Wayne noted that he had seen nests in a water oak about 40 to 60 feet from the ground, but this is unusual. The nest is made of grasses, deeply cupped, strongly built, and securely attached to stems or supporting branches. The three to five eggs are pale bluish white, queerly scrawled and marbled with black, as if with pen and ink. They average 26.4 x 18.3 millimeters. Incubation takes about twelve to fourteen days.

The birds are very solicitous about the nest, hovering close overhead and setting up a vociferous outcry if disturbed. One brood is raised, but the birds will lay again if the eggs are destroyed. The sexes do not mix in fall and winter; flocks of each gather to themselves. Fields and marshes are the habitat in winter. Albinism sometimes occurs in this species, and the paradox of a white blackbird is the result.

Food: The diet of the Red-wing has been intensively studied by Prof. F. E. L. Beal, who examined more than a thousand stomachs. The animal content was found to be 26.6 per cent and the vegetable 73.4 per cent. Insects include beetles, grasshoppers, caterpillars, wasps, ants, flies, and dragon flies. Vegetable matter consists of grain and weed and grass seeds. The Red-wing is obviously very valuable to agriculture.

FLORIDA RED-WING
378. *Agelaius phoeniceus mearnsi* Howell and van Rossem   (498c)

(Lat., *mearnsi*, to Edgar Alexander Mearns, famous naturalist.)

DESCRIPTION: Similar to the Eastern Red-wing, but smaller; bill more slender; female lighter above and below.

RANGE: Resident and breeds north to southwestern Georgia and southeastern South Carolina; south to central Florida.

STATUS IN S. C.: Common permanent resident in the extreme southeastern corner of the State. Recorded from only Beaufort County.

HISTORY: The breeding Red-wings from Beaufort County are apparently Florida Red-wings. W. M. Perrygo and J. S. Y. Hoyt took two males and two females at Hilton Head Island on May 21, 1940, and another male at Bluffton on May 18, 1940. A. B. Fuller took a female at St. Phillips Island on March 26, 1937, and a male at Gray's Hill five days later (March 31). All these specimens have been identified by Dr. H. C. Oberholser. An analysis of all the characteristics distinguishing the Florida from the Eastern Red-wing indicates that the specimens from Beaufort County are intermediates but closer to the Florida race.

In habits and food there is no material difference between the Florida and the Eastern Red-wings.

THICK-BILLED RED-WING
379. *Agelaius phoeniceus fortis* Ridgway (498d)

(Lat., *fortis*, strong, *i. e.*, large.)

DESCRIPTION: Similar to the Eastern Red-wing, but larger; female lighter below and above.

RANGE: Breeds north to South Dakota; south to northern Texas. Winters south to Louisiana, Arkansas, and South Carolina (accidentally).

STATUS IN S. C.: Accidental winter visitor to the coast region.

HISTORY: The only record of the Thick-billed Red-wing for South Carolina is a single adult male obtained at McClellanville, Charleston County, on November 28, 1940, by W. M. Perrygo and J. S. Webb, and identified by Dr. H. C. Oberholser. The specimen is in the United States National Museum.

In habits and food this Red-wing is like the other races of the species.

380. ORCHARD ORIOLE: *Icterus spurius* (Linnaeus) (506)

(Gr., *Icterus*, yellow; Lat., *spurius*, false.)

LOCAL NAMES: Sanguillah; Fig-eater.

DESCRIPTION: Length 6.00 to 7.25 inches. *Male*. Head, neck, and anterior back dull black; rest of body chestnut; wings black, the lesser and middle wing coverts chestnut, the greater coverts and secondaries narrowly tipped with white. *Female*. Upper surface yellowish olive gray, darker and brown on the back; tail yellowish olive green; undersurface dull greenish yellow; two light bands on the wing. *Immature male*. Similar to the female but throat black.

RANGE: Breeds north to North Dakota and Maine; south to Mexico, southern Louisiana, and northern Florida. Winters north to southern Mexico; south to Colombia.

STATUS IN S. C.: Common summer resident, March 27 to September 14, throughout the State. Reported north to Greenville and Chester counties; east to Horry County; south to Beaufort County; west to Barnwell, Greenwood, and Oconee counties.

HISTORY: Many people probably know this attractive bird only by its pleasing song and have wondered what it is. There is a surprising lack of local names for it, considering the bird's abundance and its liking for human habitation. One name which is sometimes heard in the Low-country, though not often, is the Indian name "Sanguillah." In the Aiken-Augusta region it was at one time called "Fig-eater."

The name "oriole" almost invariably suggests the Baltimore Oriole, but the Orchard Oriole is much more common in the South. The male's chestnut and black plumage is as handsome as the gold and black of its relative. It is a common summer resident in South Carolina, to which it comes in early April and in which it remains until September, though most of them depart in mid-August. In the upper parts of the State it arrives a little later and leaves earlier than in the coast region.

As the name implies, it is a bird of fairly open woodlands. Field edges, shady streets of towns and cities, and groves of fruit trees are its habitat.

Nesting begins in early May and continues through that month into June. The earliest nesting record is an observation by Alexander Sprunt, IV, who saw a female on an apparently completed nest at Orangeburg, April 25, 1947. The latest was recorded by Mrs. G. E. Charles at West Columbia, Lexington County. She found a male building on June 20, 1941; by July 19 the nest had fledged a brood of three or four young. She was "quite sure" that the nest contained eggs as late as July 7.

The three to five eggs are bluish white, spotted and streaked with brown and lilac, and average 20.0 x 14.7 millimeters. Their incubation requires about fourteen days. Only one brood is raised.

The nest is built in the ends of drooping limbs of oaks, elms, walnut, sweet gum, and other trees. Sometimes it is placed in bushes, or, in the Low-country, in the pendant banners of Spanish moss. It is semi-pensile in form and excellently constructed of a bright green grass which bleaches to a yellowish color. It is often lined with plant down, cotton, or feathers. Elevation varies from only a few feet to as much as 70. A nest in Sprunt's yard in the season of 1947, was about 8 feet over salt marsh on the end of a drooping live oak limb. One of the most unusual nests we have ever heard of was reported by Mrs. Charles, who writes,

> On or about June 3 [1948] I found a brood of orchard orioles leaving a nest about 20 ft. up in the top of a long-leaf pine sapling. I had the pine top cut down, and the nest is woven into the needles, or rather, the needles are worked into the nest. . . . It is 25 inches from the top of the pine, and in a fork between two upright branches, one thumb-size, the other pencil-size. Nest rests against smaller branch, but does not quite touch the larger. It is held in place by the needles woven into it.

The female Orchard Oriole bears no resemblance to her handsome consort. Yellowish olive above, greenish yellow below, she is as inconspicuous as he is bright. This is as it should be, however, for in the light and shadow of the leafy greenery which she inhabits, she easily escapes observation. As if to complicate things further, one may now and then see an oriole similarly colored, but with a black patch on the throat, mated with a female. This black-throated bird is an immature male of the second year, a plumage in which it breeds. A remarkable combination of a black-throated *female* mated with an adult (chestnut and black) male, was noted at West Columbia, in the spring of 1944, by Mrs. Charles. The pair built a nest and raised a brood.

This oriole is an accomplished and persistent singer. Every spring day brings forth its clear, melodious whistles, a song quite impossible to translate into words.

FOOD: Because the Orchard Oriole lives almost entirely upon insects, it is a bird of great value to gardeners and farmers. It is particularly destructive to May flies, grasshoppers, beetles, boll weevils, cabbage and canker worms, and rosebugs. It has been seen to feed on drops of nectar of the coral honeysuckle (Mrs. F. Barrington).

381. BALTIMORE ORIOLE: *Icterus galbula* (Linnaeus) (507)

(Lat., *galbula*, ancient name of some bird.)

DESCRIPTION: Length 7.00 to 8.15 inches. *Male.* Head, hind neck, throat, and back black; rest of body above and below orange; tail orange yellow, black medially and basally; a prominent white wing bar. *Female.* Above saffron olive with dark brown spots on the back; belly dull saffron yellow; throat speckled with black.

RANGE: Breeds north to central Alberta and Nova Scotia; south to southern Texas and northwestern South Carolina. Winters north to southern Mexico, Vermont, and Massachusetts; south to Guatemala and Colombia.

STATUS IN S. C.: Uncommon and local permanent resident over the State. Rare in winter in the northwestern section. Only sporadically breeding in the eastern part of the State. Reported north to Greenville, Spartanburg, Chester, and Dillon counties; east to Charleston County; south to Beaufort County; west to Greenwood and Oconee counties.

HISTORY: The Baltimore Oriole has an unusual history in South Carolina, one which has changed considerably since the appearance of Wayne's book in 1910. At that time it was unknown in the coast region, and was regarded by Wayne as only "migratory in the upper counties." Wayne quotes Audubon and Elliott Coues on its summer status in the interior and expresses doubt about its breeding in the State, although Audubon said that it did and Coues implied it. However, L. M. Loomis did not include it in his accounts from upper South Carolina, and others searching in the same areas have also failed to find it.

By the time the authors of this volume had prepared the *Supplement to the Birds of South Carolina* (1931), much had been learned. The species had been definitely established as a breeder near the mountains in Oconee County. John Kershaw, Jr., found and took a nest in Walhalla, Oconee County, in June, 1909. This pair of birds returned in 1910 but he could not find the nest that year. Miss Elizabeth P. Ravenel (1912) found that it nested at Keowee, Oconee County, "nearly every year" in her yard. She saw at least two nests. Birds were observed in this locality in June and July, 1912, by Miss Laura M. Bragg. G. E. Hudson, on the other hand, noted the Baltimore at Clemson only between April 20 and May 9 during the years 1926-28.

The first observation of this brilliant bird in the coast region was of a pair seen by Kershaw on May 6, 1909, in Charleston. This was recorded in the *Supplement*, but still no specimen had been secured. Since then, records have accumulated, strangely enough, during a season when the bird might have been least expected. Though the Baltimore Oriole winters in the tropics, there are a few sporadic records for the eastern United States at that season, but in no state do so many records appear as in South Carolina. All of these but one are of recent date.

The first winter record goes back to December 26, 1911, when Kershaw secured a specimen at Summerton, Clarendon County. Nearly a quarter of a century later, Mrs. Abbott and Mrs. M. J. Bischoff watched a female for several days at Summerville, Dorchester County, in late January and early February, 1933. Their identification was corroborated by William P. Wharton, Vice-President of the Audubon Society, who was banding birds at that time in Summerville.

The following winter was severe, the coldest in several years. On February 12, 1934, an adult male was taken at the Oakland Club, Pineville, Berkeley County, by John B. Gadsden. The bird was first seen on January 30, and on the day it was taken, the temperature was 18° F. and there was snow on the ground. At the same time (February, 1934), Wharton reported a male at Summerville; a third specimen the same month was reported from St. Helena Island, Beaufort County, by Fred. R. Ford. Some two weeks previously he had seen another of "a different shade" from the other. Thus, during excessively severe weather, at least three birds in as many counties made their appearance in the coast region in early 1934. Wharton banded a specimen at Summerville the next winter, January, 1935, after seeing it since December, 1934.

After an inteval of several years, the bird again appeared in winter at Summerville. Again it was Wharton who observed it, this time on March 19, 1941. It was reported by his neighbors to have been on hand for some time. The next year, on February 2 and 19, Mrs. Bischoff saw a female at her bird bath in Summerville. Four years later, E. von S. Dingle saw a male at Mayesville, Lee County, on January 23, 1946.

In 1947 winter records came in from many places. A pair was seen at Honey Hill, Berkeley County, January 21, by Robert D. Edwards; an immature male was seen by Chamberlain near his home in St. Andrew's Parish, Charleston County, February 22; and one in winter plumage was collected at Sumter, March 16, by W. F. B. Haynsworth, who had seen it for ten days.

The following winter brought only one observation. This was made by Gabriel Cannon and others at Spartanburg on December 21, 1947. However, the next season brought more birds than ever. At Sumter, Haynsworth recorded at least four different birds from January 27 to February 16, 1949, collecting one on the last date. In Richland County, at Eastover, Mrs. W. H. Faver noted a female between January 30 and February 2. She had reports of a male at nearby Hopkins on February 16, and saw him on March 10.

The Baltimore Oriole continues to be a rare migrant along the coast; some recent records are an observation of an adult male on May 27, 1943 (Edward Manigault); one on April 24, 1944 (J. W. Cain, Jr.); an adult male on July 5, 1945 (A. J. C. Vaurie); and another adult male on April 30, 1949 (J. H. Dick). All of these were noted in Charleston County. A recent breeding record was made by Mrs. Ruth Bryant Sneed in May, 1943. It is of interest because it occurred at Lake View, Dillon County, only 55 miles from the coast.

The nest of the Baltimore Oriole is so distinctive as to be unmistakable even if the bird itself is not seen. It is a deep, purse-like bag of grasses, string, and yarn attached to terminal twigs of limbs, completely pensile and swaying to every breeze. Well made and strongly attached, it often withstands winter storms and is a conspicuous object in a leafless tree. This type of architecture is responsible for the local name of "hang-nest" in some localities.

The Baltimore Oriole lays four to six eggs, larger than those of the Orchard Oriole (23.9 x 16.0 millimeters) but similarly marked. Only one brood is raised. The incubation period is fourteen days.

The male Baltimore is one of the really brilliant birds of the country, giving a tropical look to the shade trees of the north. Black, white, and gold are always a compelling combination. The female is a dull looking bird by comparison; she is greenish yellow and olive and looks very much like the smaller female Orchard Oriole.

FOOD: In some places the Baltimore Oriole has been criticized for its liking for grapes. Its normal diet is composed of insects, the favorite item being caterpillars which form 34 per cent of the food.

RUSTY BLACKBIRD
382. *Euphagus carolinus carolinus* (Müller)   (509)

(Gr., *Euphagus*, eating well; Lat., *carolinus*, of Carolina.)

DESCRIPTION: Length 8.20 to 9.75 inches. *Male in summer.* Plumage black glossed with blue and green; iris yellow. *Female in summer.* Dull slate, darker above. *Winter plumage, male* and *female.* Similar to the corresponding summer plumage, but everywhere obscured by broad feather edgings of rufous, brown, or buff.

RANGE: Breeds north to northwestern Alaska, northern Ungava, and Labrador; south to central British Columbia and Nova Scotia. Winters north to Nebraska and southern Maine; south to eastern Texas and southern Florida.

STATUS IN S. C.: Common winter resident, October 19 to April 29. Observed north to Greenville and Chester counties; east to Horry County; south to Jasper County; west to Aiken and Oconee counties.

HISTORY: This all-black blackbird, much smaller than the grackles but larger than the Red-wing, is similar to Brewer's Blackbird but is much more of an eastern species. Field differences between the two are the purple reflections on the head of Brewer's as against the green of the Rusty; again, the eye of the female Brewer's is brown, that of the Rusty, whitish yellow.

The Rusty Blackbird arrives in South Carolina in the fall, remains during the winter, and goes north in spring. The extreme date limits of arrival and departure are October 19 (Clemson) and April 29 (Charleston County). The latter date is very late, most of the birds having left by late February or early March.

During its sojourn in the State, the Rusty Blackbird is a fresh-water swamp dweller. It is fond of heavy, wet woodlands, and can be found in flocks about the cypress lagoons, the borders of streams and ponds, and in adjacent fields. It associates with grackles, Cowbirds, and red-wings. The notes are remarkably creaky and nasal, sounding like the complaining hinges of dilapidated doors or gates. The female is a dark, slate gray which may be puzzling to beginners; it should be noted that in winter both adults and immatures show closely spaced barring beneath and are tinged with a rusty red.

FOOD: More than 50 per cent of the Rusty Blackbird's food is composed of insects—for the most part, beetles, grasshoppers, and caterpillars. The diet includes weed seeds and, in winter, grain (though whatever grain the Rusty picks up is waste).

NEWFOUNDLAND RUSTY BLACKBIRD
383. *Euphagus carolinus migrans* Burleigh and Peters

(Lat., *migrans*, migrating.)

DESCRIPTION: Similar to the common Rusty Blackbird, but male darker, brighter and with more metallic bluish rather than greenish colors. *Female*. Darker, more glossy above than the female of the other subspecies.

RANGE: Breeds north to Newfoundland; south to the Magdalen Islands and southeastern Quebec. Winters south at least to South Carolina.

STATUS IN S. C.: A winter resident, January 16 to February 26, probably fairly common. So far recorded from only the coast region, north to Huger; and south to Mt. Pleasant.

HISTORY: This well-marked race seems to be limited in its breeding range to the localities mentioned above. It was recently described by Thomas D. Burleigh and Harold S. Peters (*Proc. Biol. Soc. Wash., 61*: June 16, 1941, 121). It is believed to be a valid race, though its status is not yet fully established. As there are South Carolina specimens it is here included.

Up to the present time the only individuals actually taken in South Carolina are one at Mt. Pleasant, January 16, 1912, by Wayne; others at Huger, Berkeley County, February 13, 1929, and February 26, 1933, by E. von S. Dingle. The first was identified by Thomas D. Burleigh; the others by Dr. H. C. Oberholser.

BREWER'S BLACKBIRD
384. *Euphagus cyanocephalus* (Wagler) (510)

(Gr., *cyanocephalus*, blue-headed.)

DESCRIPTION: Length 8.75 to 10.25 inches. *Male*. Black, the head and neck with a violet metallic sheen, the rest of the plumage with bluish or greenish sheen. *Female*. Duller, uniform slate color, the head with dull violet reflections.

RANGE: Breeds north to central Alberta and central Manitoba; south to New Mexico and Texas (probably). Winters north to Kansas and Wisconsin; south to Guatemala and South Carolina.

STATUS IN S. C.: Casual winter resident, November 25 to April 17. Reported north to Chester; south and east to Beaufort; west to Clemson College.

HISTORY: This western blackbird has no normal place in South Carolina's avifauna, but like other western birds it has wandered to the east and has been recorded within the borders of the State. Its history as an accidental wanderer is therefore brief.

It was first taken in the State on December 9 and 10, 1886, at Chester, by L. M. Loomis, who secured three males and two females from a flock of over a dozen (*Auk, 4*: 1887, 76). Forty years passed with no further records. Then, on April

17, 1926, a Brewer's Blackbird was taken near Clemson, Oconee County, by the late Franklin Sherman. On December 18 of the same year, at the same place, two were taken from a flock of about twenty by George E. Hudson (*Auk, 44*: 1927, 567). All these occurrences were in the Piedmont, but on November 25, 1932, a specimen was taken at Dale, Beaufort County, by H. L. Harllee, and sent to Sprunt for verification. It is the first record for the coast.

The male is entirely black. There is not a feather of any other shade in the plumage. The plumage does, however, have a sheen of metallic green or blue. The female's plumage is a brownish gray. The male has a white iris, the female a dark one.

WESTON'S BOAT-TAILED GRACKLE
385. *Cassidix mexicanus westoni* Sprunt (513)

(Lat., *Cassidix*, a helmet; *mexicanus*, of Mexico; *westoni*, to Francis Marion Weston.)

LOCAL NAMES: Jackdaw.

DESCRIPTION: Tail long and strongly keeled. *Male.* Length 15.00 to 17.50 inches. Head and throat glossy dark violet; back and breast steel blue; wings and tail black; posterior lower parts dark bluish green. *Female.* Length 11.50 to 13.50 inches. Upper parts sepia brown anteriorly; darker and more sooty on the posterior portion; lower parts light brown; wings and tail fuscous.

RANGE: Resident and breeds north to South Carolina; south to southern Florida.

STATUS IN S. C.: Common permanent resident in the coastal region. Reported north to Horry County; and south to Beaufort and Jasper counties.

HISTORY: Apparently all the Boat-tailed Grackles of South Carolina belong to this race, which was originally described by Sprunt in the *Charleston Museum Leaflet, 6*: February 24, 1934. A good series of specimens in the Charleston Museum indicates clearly that the South Carolina bird is the same as the bird from Florida, on which Sprunt's name was originally based. Just how far this form extends, present material is inadequate to indicate. However, it is so much larger than the Boat-tailed Grackle of Louisiana (*C. m. major*) that its recognition as a separate subspecies is not doubtful. It differs also from the Boat-tailed Grackle of Louisiana chiefly in its greater wing length, which averages about 181.1 millimeters as against 171.4 millimeters and in its longer bill, which averages 42.4 millimeters, as compared to the 36.8 millimeters of the Louisiana bird. Its relationship to the subsequently described form, *torreyii*, from Virginia, is not determinable at the present moment.

In spite of its restricted range, Weston's Grackle is the best known of the grackles in South Carolina. Its local name of Jackdaw is far more common than "grackle," and practically everyone who lives along the coast is acquainted with the bird. In South Carolina it never occurs inland, but lives on the sea islands, barrier beaches, salt marshes, and edges of the mainland, where it is a common permanent resident.

There is much interest about this fine bird. Its great size, brilliant metallic plumage, remarkable keeled tail, and wide variety of notes combine to make it conspicuous at all times of year. In sea-coast cities and towns, it nests and feeds close to human habitation. People whom Weston's Grackle chooses for neighbors are never unaware of it. It is nothing if not noisy and makes itself known by means of as wide a medley of sounds as one can imagine. Unmusical as they are, the notes are not wholly objectionable. While there are striking differences between Weston's Grackle and its smaller relatives, perhaps the outstanding one is the utter dissimilarity between the sexes. Those unfamiliar with the bird would never suppose the female to be of the same species or even akin to the male. She is far smaller, has none of her mate's brilliance of plumage, and is plainly but pleasingly attired in sepia brown above and uniform buffy tan below.

Boat-tails nest in colonies and the males are polygamous (*Birds of North Carolina,* 1942, 337). On the islands, clumps of wax myrtles provide nesting sites. Weston found nests only 5 feet from the ground in myrtles and also found nests in palmetto leaves. Elsewhere, the birds like to build their nests in high live oaks or water oaks, 70 or 80 feet from the ground. Colonies of Boat-tails still nest in parts of Charleston, along the Ashley River and the grounds of the Citadel. Coastal towns such as Beaufort, McClellanville, and Georgetown also have their nesting birds. The nests are often infested with parasites, and are sometimes invaded by hordes of black ants, which destroy the young.

The nest is made of salt grass, deeply cupped, with a layer of mud in the walls which, when dry, makes the structure very substantial and rigid. It is strongly attached to supports, which may be anything from high grass and small bushes to low and tall trees. In it are laid three to five bluish-white eggs, curiously scrawled and splashed with dark brown and purple spots and lines, looking as if a child had practiced on them with ink. The eggs average 33.5 x 22.9 millimeters. Incubation takes fourteen to sixteen days. The nesting season, which is somewhat prolonged, occurs in late April, May, and June. One brood is raised, but if some accident occurs to the eggs, the bird will lay again.

A much-discussed characteristic of the Boat-tail is a peculiar sound which the male often produces. This has been variously described and accounted for. Some ornithologists believe that it is made by a movement of the wings; others, that it is vocal. The writings of Howell, Townsend, and Wayne contain references to it. Sprunt has devoted a good deal of study to it and is now convinced that the sound is vocal: the wings are often fluttered when it is made, but occasionally it may be heard when the wings are perfectly motionless. It has been noted that the sound is made when the bird is in flight as well as at rest and Sprunt believes it is produced by a rapid though sometimes hardly perceptible vibration of the mandibles.

The tremendous tail of the male frequently appears to be a handicap, particularly in windy weather. The Boat-tail's flight is labored, usually without undulation, the wings working very rapidly as if flying were hard work. The conspicuous yellow iris is plainly visible for some distance. The iris of the female is normally brown, though in some instances it too is yellow. The Boat-tail is an excellent fisherman, frequently wading belly deep in creeks or marshes in search of aquatic food.

FOOD: About 40 per cent animal and 60 per cent vegetable matter. This will vary seasonally. Wayne (1910) says that the Jackdaw takes little else than fiddler crabs, shrimp, and small fish in spring and early summer, and that they "commit great depredations" on corn as it begins to ripen. "Bird minders," he says, are necessary to keep it from oat fields planted in February. He also lists the eggs of the diamond-backed terrapin as being included in the Jackdaw's diet. Findings of the U. S. Fish and Wildlife Service analysts show that crustaceans (crayfish, crabs and shrimp) form about two-fifths of the animal food. Grasshoppers and beetles are eaten in July and August. Corn, they found, comprises nearly 47 per cent of the vegetable food.

PURPLE GRACKLE
386. *Quiscalus quiscula stonei* Chapman (511)

(Lat., *Quiscalus*, a quail; *quiscula*, a quail; *stonei*, to Witmer Stone.)

LOCAL NAMES: Crow Blackbird.

DESCRIPTION: Length 10.75 to 12.75 inches. Similar to the Florida Grackle, but larger, with a smaller bill; head bluish or greenish bronze; back purplish bronze, varied sometimes with blue or green.

RANGE: Breeds north to southeastern New York; south to Louisiana. Winters north to New Jersey; south to southern Louisiana and southern Georgia.

STATUS IN S. C.: Fairly common winter resident, November 10 to May 9. Occurs north to Spartanburg and Chester counties; east and south to Charleston County; west to Aiken and Oconee counties.

HISTORY: This large, handsome, black bird with gleaming plumage is a striking sight either singly or in flocks, into which the birds gather seasonally. The grackles are a puzzling group of birds to the systematist. Similar in size and, to a degree, in color except for varying shades of reflection, they require considerable study.

The Purple Grackle is not at all well known in the coastal plain, but it does occur in winter both on the coast and in the interior counties. G. E. Hudson has noted it at Clemson from early November to May, and F. Sherman included it there as a permanent resident. L. M. Loomis found it occasionally abundant at Chester. Apparently it does not breed in South Carolina.

The Crow Blackbird, as this grackle is often called, flocks in winter in large numbers. It frequents fields and open situations and often comes into towns. The birds sometimes establish great roosts, and, mingling with Cowbirds, Starlings, and other grackles, form flocks which run into thousands. Purple Grackles eat a great deal of grain, but much of it is secured in winter fields and is to be regarded economically as waste.

The following specimens of this race in the Charleston Museum's collection have recently been examined and identified by Dr. H. C. Oberholser: Pinopolis, Berkeley County, November 30, 1889, and Mt. Pleasant, March 1, 1917, Wayne; Charleston, March 23, 1931, William W. Humphreys; and April 3, 1937, Chamberlain.

Florida Grackle
387. *Quiscalus quiscula quiscula* (Linnaeus) (511a)

LOCAL NAMES: Crow Blackbird.

DESCRIPTION: Tail long and keeled. *Male.* Length 10.40 to 12.00 inches. Plumage purplish bronze to violet on head, neck, throat, and chest; back and lower parts dark metallic green; tail greenish or bluish black; wings black, the exposed surface metallic purple; iris light yellow. *Female.* Length 9.50 to 10.50 inches. Similar to the male but colors duller, with little metallic sheen.

RANGE: Resident and breeds north to northeastern North Carolina; south to Louisiana and southern Florida.

STATUS IN S. C.: Common permanent resident throughout the State. Reported north to Chester County; east to Horry County; south to Beaufort and Jasper counties; west to Barnwell, Greenwood, and Oconee counties.

HISTORY: The Florida Grackle is a permanent resident throughout much of South Carolina, and it is the breeding grackle of the interior. On the coast, it is common the year round, but unlike its larger relative, the Boat-tail, it is essentially a fresh-water bird. It is not usual to find it on the barrier islands, though in winter, flocks do occur there. It lives in the cypress swamps, rice fields, ponds, and river bottoms, and it often comes to the yards and streets of towns and cities where it walks about on lawns and open places. Its glossy, bottle-green plumage and light iris show to good advantage, for it is not at all shy.

The Florida Grackle nests in colonies near fresh water and builds its home of grasses, mud, and moss in small bushes, clumps of Spanish moss, or in the cavities of stubs standing in water. The three to seven greenish-white eggs are much blotched, scrawled, and marbled with dark brown and gray. They average 29.2 x 20.8 millimeters. Incubation takes from fourteen to fifteen days. Probably only a single brood is raised.

May is the nesting month, though Wayne has taken eggs as early as April 25. Sprunt's egg dates range from May 2 through May 10. The earliest nest in the Columbia area was found by Mrs. G. E. Charles on March 21, over a month earlier than Wayne's.

In winter, the Florida Grackle congregates and feeds with other blackbirds and occurs in great numbers in fields and open lands. In the past, it committed serious depredations on rice crops, but the virtual disappearance of this grain commercially has lessened much of the local criticism of the bird. It sometimes takes the eggs and young of other birds; Wayne says that it makes "a systematic search" for these, one of the sufferers being Swainson's Warbler. It sometimes robs the nests of herons in the cypress rookeries.

Like others of its family it is a noisy bird, with a long series of whistles, clacks, and wheezy sounds.

FOOD: One-third animal matter, two-thirds vegetable. Most of the animal food is composed of insects such as beetles, boll weevils, caterpillars, and grasshoppers. Grackles are good fishermen and may often be seen wading about in search of crayfish, mollusks, and minnows. They follow plows and tractors in the fields and secure the disturbed insects there. The vegetable food includes about 46 per cent grain, much of it taken in winter and therefore waste, but corn is attacked and eaten when in the ear, as well as when sprouting. Prof. F. E. L. Beal notes that the egg-eating tendencies of this grackle seem to be localized, and are "probably not of frequent occurrence."

BRONZED GRACKLE
388. *Quiscalus quiscula versicolor* Vieillot (511b)

(Lat., *versicolor*, of changeable color.)

DESCRIPTION: Length 11.00 to 13.50 inches. *Male.* Head, neck, and chest metallic purplish to steel blue; the remainder of upper and under parts uniform bronze, the line of demarcation being sharply drawn; tail purplish black; wings black, the exposed surfaces metallic violet. *Female.* Similar to the male but duller.

RANGE: Breeds north to Mackenzie and Newfoundland; south to Texas and Rhode Island. Winters north to Nebraska and Maine (casually); south to southern Texas and southeastern South Carolina.

STATUS IN S. C.: Fairly common winter resident, November 1 to March 14, over most of the State, but apparently less frequent in the eastern portion. Reported north to Chester County; east to Florence County; south to Charleston County; west to Aiken and Oconee counties.

HISTORY: The Bronzed Grackle is chiefly mid-western in its range, but it occurs often enough in the East to be noticeable in many localities. The back is distinctly bronze in color, almost in the form of a saddle which is sharply defined from the blue-green iridescence of the neck. It is practically identical in size with the Purple and Florida Grackles.

Hardly more than accidental in the coastal areas, the Bronzed Grackle is a winter visitor in the Piedmont, and G. E. Hudson found it at Clemson from late November to mid-March (*Auk, 47*: 1930, 399). L. M. Loomis found it regularly in Chester County and considered it most abundant in migration, though he noted that it winters from November 1 through March (*Auk, 8*: 1891, 167). H. L. Harllee has taken it in the Pee Dee River Swamp near Florence, and Wayne secured it near Mt. Pleasant on March 14, 1918.

Its general habits and food do not differ materially from those of other members of the genus *Quiscalus*, and it associates with them in flocks in fall and winter.

389. EASTERN COWBIRD: *Molothrus ater ater* (Boddaert) (495)

(Gr., *Molothrus*, vagabond; Lat., *ater*, black.)

DESCRIPTION: Length 7.00 to 8.25 inches. Bill stout and sparrowlike. *Male.* Head, neck, throat, and chest plain brown; remainder of body plumage greenish black. *Female.* Upper parts brownish gray; lower surface lighter brownish gray; throat paler, sometimes white.

RANGE: Breeds north to southern Ontario and Nova Scotia; south to Missouri and South Carolina. Winters north to southern Iowa and Maine (casually); south to Texas and southern Florida.

STATUS IN S. C.: Permanent resident; common winter resident, June 25 to March 19, throughout most of the State; rare in summer in the mountains (Oconee County) where it breeds sparingly. Reported in winter north to Greenville, Spartanburg, and Chester counties; east to Horry County; south to Beaufort County; west to Aiken County.

HISTORY: This species, unique in its nesting habits among North American birds, is likely to be overlooked by most people as "just another blackbird." This is not surprising for it is black for the most part and it associates with *bona fide* blackbirds. It is, however, quite distinct in behavior, if not in looks, for it is the one exclusively parasitic species of South Carolina.

The exact status of the Cowbird in South Carolina is something of a puzzle. It is present in the coast region from June 25 to March 19, but is common only in the winter months of January and February. At such times it congregates with grackles and blackbirds in mixed flocks. Murphey says that he has failed to observe it in December, January, or February in the Aiken-Augusta region. In the upper Piedmont (Clemson) it has been noted as arriving from late February to March 13.

Despite the fact that for years there was no nesting record, it was thought, in the light of some spring observations, that the bird nested in Oconee County. Miss Elizabeth P. Ravenel had observed it at Keowee, Oconee County, in May or June, 1910-11. G. E. Hudson saw a female on June 11, 1934, at Clemson College but could not secure it. Several years before this, Prof. F. Sherman observed some there in courtship antics (May, 1927). Then, on July 17, 1934, he and members of his bird class saw a fledgling Cowbird being fed by a foster-parent on the College campus. The adult bird was small and shy, and would not allow an approach close enough for identification, but it appeared to be a female warbler in worn plumage. This constitutes the first, and so far, the only breeding record for South Carolina (*Auk*, 53: 1936, 315).

The Cowbird builds no nest of its own, but lays its eggs in the nests of other birds, usually smaller than itself. Vireos and warblers are the birds most often victimized. The young Cowbird frequently crowds one or more of the rightful occupants out of the nest, but is assiduously attended by the foster parent. Many people associate this parasitic habit with the cuckoos, but it is the European Cuckoo rather than the American which is guilty of the practice.

Cowbirds stay close to the ground and often feed about barnyards with livestock, hence the name. They seem particularly susceptible to the "squeak" and will respond to it in numbers.

PLATE XXX: DARK-HUED BIRDS

Water Color by Roger Tory Peterson

Flying bird, Meadowlark. Perching birds, reading from bottom left to top right: Boat-tailed Grackle (female), Boat-tailed Grackle (male), Florida Grackle, Starling, Red-winged Blackbird (female), and Red-winged Blackbird (male).

Roger Tory Peterson

The male is easy to recognize because of the coffee-colored head and the entirely black body. No other blackbird has this combination. The female in her two shades of gray, is sometimes difficult to identify. The eggs of the Cowbird are white, covered with rather small markings of brown and yellowish brown; they average 21.8 x 16.5 millimeters. Incubation requires ten to fourteen days.

Food: Prof. F. E. L. Beal has worked out the Cowbird's food habits as follows: insects, 20 per cent, all of which are harmful or annoying; grain, 16 per cent, some of it waste but some representing crop damage; weed seeds, over 50 per cent, many of which are of noxious plants, the destruction of which is to be commended. The bird eats practically no fruit.

Family Thraupidae: Tanagers

390. SCARLET TANAGER: *Piranga olivacea* (Gmelin) (608)

(*Piranga*, name of some South American bird; Lat., *olivacea*, olivaceous.)

DESCRIPTION: Length 6.50 to 7.50 inches. *Male.* Body scarlet; wings and tail black. *Female.* Upper surface yellowish olive green; lower parts light yellow; olivaceous on sides; wings and tail brownish gray with olive green edgings.

RANGE: Breeds north to southeastern Saskatchewan and Nova Scotia; south to southeastern Oklahoma and northwestern South Carolina. Winters north to Colombia; south to Peru and Bolivia.

STATUS IN S. C.: Fairly common summer resident, April 17 to October 16, in the mountains of the northwestern section. Casual in summer in the coast region. Uncommon transient, April 6 to May 15, and September 23 to October 16, elsewhere in the State. In summer it breeds north to western Greenville County; south to Pickens and Oconee counties. As a transient it has been reported north to Greenville and Marion counties; east to Horry County; south to Beaufort County; west to Aiken and eastern Oconee County.

HISTORY: The Scarlet Tanager is one of America's most beautiful birds, but it is not common in South Carolina and comparatively few people see it or know it. Its range is rather sharply drawn between the mountains and the rest of the State; it is a fairly common summer resident in the former and an uncommon transient in the latter.

There are not many breeding data from the South Carolina mountains because of the lack of observers there. The first definite record was made by John Kershaw, Jr., who took a nest with two eggs on June 30, 1909, on Stumphouse Mountain, Oconee County; in July of the following two years, Miss Elizabeth P. Ravenel noted it breeding at Keowee, in the same county. Franklin Sherman saw a mated pair about Clemson in July, 1942. E. J. DeCamps told the writers that he found it nesting on the old Jones Gap Road, Caesar's Head, in Greenville County. Other observers have seen it in the mountainous sections of Pickens County. There is evidence that the Scarlet Tanager occasionally nests in the coastal region. Mrs. Ruth Bryant Sneed saw a pair apparently nesting in the top of an elm in Lake View, Dillon County, in the early 1930's. Dr. A. J. C. Vaurie and his wife, who are familiar with the bird in New York State, noted a male, female, and some young near McClellanville on July 10, 1945, and reasonably assumed that a nest was close at hand.

The nest is a frail structure, built of grasses and placed at elevations of 20 to 40 feet on the end of a horizontal tree limb. The eggs number three to five, are bluish green speckled with reddish brown, and average 22.3 x 17.3 millimeters. Incubation lasts thirteen days, and the tanager raises only one brood.

The Scarlet Tanager passes through South Carolina from early April to mid-May and again during September. There are only a few fall records. It has been noted on the coast only in spring.

The male Scarlet Tanager is one of the instantly recognizable birds of the country. The brilliance of its scarlet body is intensified by the jet black of the wings and tail, and the effect is striking in the extreme. The female is so utterly different as not to be associated with the male by those unfamiliar with the species. Plain olive green above and yellowish below, she is very inconspicuous in the light and shadow of the summer woodlands, a fact which is, of course, to her advantage.

The Scarlet Tanager frequents open forests and orchards; in some localities, it enters the limits of settled communities, and nests in shade trees.

FOOD: Though it occasionally eats fruit, the Scarlet Tanager is mainly insectivorous, with a marked fondness for caterpillars. It also likes gypsy moths, beetles, and weevils. Its value in an economic sense is beyond question.

391. SUMMER TANAGER: *Piranga rubra rubra* (Linnaeus) (610)

(Lat., *rubra*, red.)

LOCAL NAMES: Summer Redbird.

DESCRIPTION: Length 7.00 to 7.95 inches. *Male.* Body mainly dull red, with no black; wings and tail reddish brown, edged with dull red. *Female.* Upper parts yellowish olive green; lower surface dull yellow.

RANGE: Breeds north to southeastern Nebraska, Maryland, and New Jersey (formerly); south to eastern Texas and southern Florida. Winters north to Vera Cruz and Yucatan; south to Peru and British Guiana.

STATUS IN S. C.: Common summer resident, March 30 to October 14, over all the State. Recorded north to Greenville, Chester, Darlington, and Dillon counties; east to Horry County; south to Beaufort and Jasper counties; west to Barnwell, Greenwood, and Oconee counties.

HISTORY: A great many people know the Summer Tanager without being aware of the fact. The name "tanager" is entirely correct, but the bird is almost always called the "Summer Redbird." And the latter name certainly has the authority of antiquity behind it, for that was the name given it by Mark Catesby, who discovered the species in South Carolina and introduced it in 1731 to ornithology. Since the Cardinal is also known by the name "redbird," some distinction between the two was necessary, and the tanager, being a summer resident whereas the Cardinal occurs the year round, takes the name of the season. Though the Summer Tanager is red, the shade differs from that of the Cardinal, being a poppy red rather than vermilion.

Unlike the Cardinal, it has no black markings, and its bill is of an entirely different shape.

Because it is widely spread over the State, it is one of the most readily observed of our summer residents. It lives in open pinelands but it also comes into towns freely and nests there.

It breeds in May, from the tenth to the thirtieth, a period in which fresh eggs may be found. The nest is saddled on a horizontal limb of an oak or a pine and may be anywhere from 4 to 40 feet above the ground. Many occur in the 6 to 12 foot range. The nest is rather insecure, made of grasses and weed stalks and lined with a kind of grass which bleaches to a yellow color. The attachment to the limb is often so weak as to give way in a sudden squall of wind and cause the nest to fall.

There are normally three eggs, sometimes four. The eggs are bluish green, with spottings and splashes of brown and lavender. They average 24.4 x 17.3 millimeters. One brood is raised. Incubation requires about twelve days.

The call note of the Summer Tanager is a staccato *"pi-tuck* or *pik-i-tuck-i-tuck"* (Peterson), and its song is not to be confused with that of any other bird except the Scarlet Tanager. The female, though easily overlooked on account of her sober appearance, is a trim, pleasing bird in subdued olive and yellowish green. The patched looking red and green immature males breed their first spring and are good singers. Like other members of its family, the Summer Tanager is a proficient fly catcher.

FOOD: Though not yet critically studied, enough is known of the food preferences of the Summer Tanager to substantiate the many reports that it is fond of bees. This does not endear it to apiarists. Other insects in its diet are beetles, wasps, dragon flies, tomato worms, and spiders. It also eats such fruits as blackberries, figs, and mulberries.

Family Fringillidae: Grosbeaks, Finches, Sparrows, Buntings

EASTERN CARDINAL
392. *Richmondena cardinalis cardinalis* (Linnaeus) (593)

(Lat., *Richmondena,* to Charles Wallace Richmond; *cardinalis,* red, from color of a cardinal's hat.)

LOCAL NAMES: Redbird.

DESCRIPTION: Length 7.50 to 9.25 inches. Head prominently crested. *Male.* Head and lower surface deep vermilion; chin and area about base of bill black; back dull vermilion, the feathers edged with olive gray; tail and wings dull red. *Female.* Upper surface plain grayish olive; lower parts fulvous shading to buff on belly; tail and crest red; chin gray.

RANGE: Resident and breeds north to southeastern South Dakota and Massachusetts; south to eastern Kansas and Georgia.

STATUS IN S. C.: Common permanent resident throughout the State. Observed north to Greenville, York, and Dillon counties; east to Horry County; south to Jasper County; west to Barnwell, Greenwood and Oconee counties.

HISTORY: If a poll were taken on the best known bird of South Carolina, the result would probably be a close decision between the Cardinal and the Mockingbird.

Should a run-off be necessary, the final verdict might well be for the Cardinal. Such a choice would very likely be decided by color. Both birds are essentially Carolinian, both sing well, both live in every county and in the neighborhood of human beings, and both are present the year round; but the Cardinal has flashing color and the Mockingbird does not.

The Redbird is a universalist. At home in dense swamps, remote from anywhere, forests, roadsides, groves, thickets, orchards, and hedgerows, it is equally comfortable in city gardens and parks. Its song is one of its greatest attractions, a beautifully clear, melodious whistle, often the first bird song of the early summer morning, and it may even be heard in winter during mild weather. The female also sings, sometimes while she is on the nest. The song is remarkable in variation for, though it has an underlying quality which is unmistakable to those who know the bird well, many northerners confuse it with the Carolina Wren. Chamberlain has noted as many as sixteen distinct variations of the song.

Largely because of its vocal ability and, of course, its plumage, the Cardinal was a favorite cage bird years ago, and the market for it was brisk. The practice of caging it is now happily past.

The breeding season is about mid-April, varying with the weather. Eggs have been found from the first of that month. The nest may be almost anywhere but is always at low elevations (5 to 15 feet), in bushes, trees, vines, or thickets. It is often built very close to houses, perhaps at the end of a vine-clad porch or in ornamental shrubbery at the front steps. It is made of grasses, leaves, twigs, and moss, sometimes of grass only. The Cardinal lays two to four eggs, which have a light ground color, heavily spotted with reddish brown and lilac. The eggs average 25.4 x 17.8 millimeters. The incubation period is twelve days.

The Cardinal is a prolific bird; each season it raises three broods. Young birds have been known to leave the nest when nine days old (Mrs. G. E. Charles). Feeding by the parents, however, continues for some time afterwards. Chamberlain checked one youngster which, including the time spent in the nest, was fed for fifty-one days (August 6 to September 26).

Only the female labors at nest building and incubation. The male busies himself in staying nearby and warning away intruders of his kind by his territorial song. One-sided combats often take place between the males and their reflected images in cellar windows, lawn globes, or automobile hub-caps. The same bird will engage in such encounters day after day, in the most determined manner.

That the Cardinal is a migratory species is well known, though it is not generally considered a wide ranger in such journeys. Nevertheless, it sometimes makes extensive flights, an illustration of which is the record of a bird banded at Clemson by R. E. Ware and recovered in Arkansas. Not only is this distance remarkable, but the direction is no less so.

The Cardinal is one of the birds which has the curious habit of "anting," the queer practice of placing ants in the body plumage. The habit is not yet understood. E. B. Chamberlain, Jr., supplied the following observation:

When first noticed, the bird, an adult male, was hopping about on a wooden roof where a goodly number of large red ants were moving to and fro. After a moment, the bird began to catch ants, one at a time, with its beak, and to place them in the feathers under its wings, tail and on its back, fluffing out the feathers as it did so. These actions were continued for three or four minutes, during which time about forty ants were caught. It could not be determined whether the ants were simply killed, crushed, or alive when placed in the plumage.

This observation was made at the Bear's Bluff Marine Laboratories on Wadmalaw Island, Charleston County.

FOOD: The Cardinal has a stout, conical bill which equips it to be an eater of seeds like the other grosbeaks. A study of nearly five hundred stomachs (McAtee, 1908) proved that the food is 70 per cent vegetable and 30 per cent animal matter.

ROSE-BREASTED GROSBEAK
393. *Pheucticus ludovicianus* (Linnaeus) (595)

(Gr., *Pheucticus*, inclined to avoid, *i. e.*, retiring; Lat., *ludovicianus*, of Louisiana.)

DESCRIPTION: Length 7.00 to 8.50 inches. *Male.* Head, throat, and back black; wings black with large and small spots of white; outer tail feathers with white patches; rump and posterior under parts white; breast and wing linings rose-red. *Female.* Upper surface light buffy brown, heavily streaked with dark brown and white; belly light brown on breast and sides, thinly streaked with darker brown; wings lined with salmon yellow or saffron yellow.

RANGE: Breeds north to central southern Mackenzie and northern Nova Scotia; south to central eastern Kansas and northern Georgia. Winters north to Mexico and South Carolina (accidentally); south to Ecuador and Venezuela.

STATUS IN S. C.: Uncommon transient, April 19 to May 24, and October 1 to 15; less frequent in the coast region. Accidental in winter in the middle and eastern parts of the State. Reported as a transient north to Greenville and Chester counties; east to Sumter and Charleston counties; south to Yemassee; west to Oconee County. In winter reported east to Summerville; west to Aiken.

HISTORY: The Rose-breasted Grosbeak, which is a striking looking bird, is not common in South Carolina. It is possible, however, that it occurs in the State with more frequency than the records indicate. It is a shy bird and frequents thickets in which it can be seen only with difficulty.

There has never been any evidence that it nests in South Carolina. It has been recorded at Chester (L. M. Loomis), Clemson (G. E. Hudson), Greenville (P. M. Jenness), and in the Aiken-Augusta region (Murphey) as a fairly regular transient, apparently more common in spring than in fall. Occasional records in the spring from Greenwood, Columbia, and Sumter complete the picture in the upper part of the State.

The Rose-breasted is hardly more than accidental on the coast. The first record for the coast was a male, taken in the Salkehatchie Swamp near Yemassee, and brought to Wayne on May 9, 1890, by W. F. Colcock. Another was seen at the same place a few days later (*Auk*, 7: 1890, 410). More than fifty years passed before another coastal bird was noted, a female observed by Eugene Eisenmann and John Bull, Jr., on October 9, 1943, on Sewee Road, Charleston County. The only other coastal record is for a date abnormal anywhere in the southeast, for it concerns a winter appearance of the bird. On December 22, 1943, an immature male was found dead at Summerville by Mrs. M. J. Bischoff. It was brought to the Charleston Museum, and is the first winter specimen for South Carolina, although in 1908 a male and female were reported seen at Aiken on December 2 by John Kershaw, Jr.

The male, with his black and white plumage and rosy breast patch is not likely to be confused with any other bird, but the female looks much like a large, stout-billed sparrow.

FOOD: About equally divided between animal and vegetable matter. The Rose-breasted is one of the few birds that eats potato beetles. Its stay in South Carolina, however, is too brief to make much economic difference, one way or the other.

EASTERN BLUE GROSBEAK
394. *Guiraca caerulea caerulea* (Linnaeus) (597)

(*Guiraca*, Mexican or South American name of some bird; Lat., *caerulea*, blue.)
LOCAL NAMES: Big Indigo.

DESCRIPTION: Length 6.35 to 7.50 inches. *Male.* Body ultramarine blue; wings and tail fuscous black with bluish edgings, the former with two chestnut bars. *Female.* Upper surface olive brown, more or less shaded on rump with light blue; under parts brownish buff, darkest on breast; wings and tail fuscous, the former barred with cinnamon rufous or tawny.

RANGE: Breeds north to Iowa (casually) and New Jersey (casually); south to eastern Texas and central Florida. Winters north to Yucatan, Honduras, and northern South Carolina (accidentally); south to Guatemala and Costa Rica.

STATUS IN S. C.: Fairly common summer resident, April 6 to October 15, throughout the State, but most numerous in the middle portion; accidental in winter in the northern section of the State. In summer reported north to Greenville, Spartanburg, and Chester counties; east to Dillon County; south to Beaufort; west to Barnwell, Greenwood and Oconee counties.

HISTORY: The Blue Grosbeak, despite its rather bright plumage, is not generally well known, but it is far more common in South Carolina than its Rose-breasted relative. It is fairly well distributed in the interior of the State, but decidedly uncommon in the coastal area. It is a summer resident and nests regularly in suitable environment—open, scrubby tracts bordering woodlands and swamps. The bird also frequents vine-grown ditch banks and brier thickets, and from such retreats it voices a melodious song.

The Blue Grosbeak arrives in mid-April and remains until mid-October. When Wayne wrote in 1910, it was "a rare bird," but he said that "Fifteen years ago [1895] the Blue Grosbeak was comparatively abundant within a few miles of Charleston." He gave no reason for the change in status. It is certainly true today that the bird is rare on the coast. The authors have encountered it but two or three times in the Low-country, and only one nest ever came under Wayne's observation. As one proceeds inland, however, the bird begins to appear more frequently, and it may be seen along the roadside on telephone wires and in brushy pastures. At the fall line one meets it with more regularity than either in the Piedmont or on the coast, although even there it is locally distributed.

There is a single winter record for the State. This was a grosbeak observed at Jonesville, Union County, on February 10 and 11, 1948, by Mrs. Hayne Smith. There was heavy sleet and snow the day before the bird's appearance. Other information has accumulated since the publication of the authors' *Supplement to Birds of South Carolina* (1931). At that time, reports from Anderson, Clarendon, Marion, and Sumter counties, revealed that it occurred regularly in them, and that it bred fairly commonly in Clarendon and Sumter. Additional interior breeding localities and dates are: Spartanburg, eggs, May 31, and Clemson, small young, June 13 (G. E. Hudson); Clinton, four eggs, June 13 (J. Berly); Greenville, four eggs, June 18 (E. J. DeCamps); Newberry, young, about July 18 (R. H. Coleman); Sumter, young, also July 18 (Mrs. T. H. Siddall, Jr.)

The nest is built in bushes or low trees. It is composed of weeds, leaves, and grasses and is lined with rootlets. Almost always it contains a piece of cast snake skin. The eggs number three or four; they are clear, pale blue without markings, being in this respect unlike the eggs of other grosbeaks. They average 21.3 x 16.5 millimeters. Incubation takes from twelve to fourteen days and two broods are raised.

FOOD: Animal matter two-thirds, vegetable one-third. Weed seeds (the largest vegetable form) make up 18 per cent. Grain amounts to 14 per cent. Grasshoppers, weevils, cotton cutworms, crickets, snails, and spiders make up the animal diet.

395. INDIGO BUNTING: *Passerina cyanea* (Linnaeus) (598)

(Lat., *Passerina*, relating to a sparrow; *cyanea*, dark blue.)

LOCAL NAMES: Indigo-bird; Little Indigo.

DESCRIPTION: Length 4.75 to 5.75 inches. *Male.* Plain cerulean blue, head and foreneck somewhat purplish; wings and tail feathers with bluish edgings. *Female.* Above olive brown; lower surface brownish white, or pale brown, the belly dull white washed with olive buff; chest obscurely streaked with dark brown.

RANGE: Breeds north to central eastern North Dakota and southern New Brunswick; south to central Texas and northern Florida. Winters north to southern Louisiana and northern Florida; south to Mexico, Panama, and Cuba.

STATUS IN S. C.: Common summer resident, April 17 to November 10, in all the State. Observed north to Greenville and Chester counties; east to Horry County; south to Jasper County; west to Oconee and Pickens counties.

HISTORY: Although the Indigo Bunting is of high plumage, it is remarkably inconspicuous for so bright a bird. It really has more claim to the name "bluebird" than the species bearing that name, for it is blue all over, and the Bluebird is not. It can hardly be spoken of as well known, though it has a wider range in South Carolina than its more brilliant relative, the Painted Bunting. The distribution of the two buntings is almost reversed for the Indigo is more likely to be met with above the fall line than below, though it occurs as a fairly common migrant along the coast.

The Indigo Bunting is a summer resident in South Carolina. It arrives in mid-April and remains through October. It frequents brushy pasture lands, the edges of woodlands, and clearings adjacent to swamps. In the coastal area it is local, wide areas intervening between occupied territories, but such areas become smaller as one goes inland, and in many parts of the State it is a common bird. It sings persistently, which helps in locating the bird; bright as it is, it is sometimes difficult to see.

The nest is made of leaves and grasses and is placed in bushes or thickets at low elevations. The eggs are laid from mid-May to the last of that month and number three or four; they are pale bluish white, without markings, and average 18.5 x 14.5 millimeters. Incubation requires twelve or thirteen days. One or two broods are raised.

During the autumn large numbers of Indigo Buntings are seen on migration. By that time much of the brilliance of the spring plumage is lost, and the male looks a great deal like the immature bird. If the male is hard to locate in the breeding season, the female, as might be supposed, is even more difficult because of her sober attire.

FOOD: Seeds, for the most part; insects in appreciable numbers.

396. PAINTED BUNTING: *Passerina ciris ciris* (Linnaeus) (601)

(Gr., *ciris*, an ancient name for some bird.)

LOCAL NAMES: Nonpareil.

DESCRIPTION: Length 4.25 to 5.50 inches. *Male.* Head and sides of neck purplish blue; back yellowish green; rump purplish red; wings dark brown edged with dull purple and green; greater wing coverts parrot green; the middle wing coverts dull reddish purple; lower surface vermilion. *Female* and *immature male.* Upper parts oil green; lower surface olive yellow, shading to clear yellow on abdomen.

RANGE: Breeds north to southern Kansas and central eastern North Carolina; south to southeastern Texas and southern Florida. Winters north to southern Louisiana (casually), northern Florida, and central eastern South Carolina (accidentally); south to Yucatan and Panama.

STATUS IN S. C.: Common summer resident, March 21 to November 5, in the eastern and middle sections; less numerous in the latter. Accidental in winter in central eastern South Carolina. Reported in summer north to Columbia and Florence; east to Horry County; south to Beaufort and Jasper counties; west to Barnwell and Aiken counties. In winter recorded from Charleston County.

HISTORY: "Gorgeous" is the way Wayne (1910) describes the Nonpareil. And gorgeous the bird is. It is an affront to say of the Painted Bunting, as bird books often do, that it is gaudy. It is one of the most brilliantly plumaged North American birds, and those who live with it for a large part of the year and have it in their yards take delight in its beauty, song, and lively, attractive ways. Nonpareil, "without an equal," it is to those who know it.

The Nonpareil is a summer resident, arriving somewhat irregularly in April, usually about the fifteenth, and remaining into October. It belongs to the coastal plain and rarely penetrates into the interior beyond the fall line. Murphey found it sharply limited to the Savannah River Valley in the Aiken-Augusta region. There are a few records from Columbia, which is on the fall line. Specific dates there are April 21, 1912 (B. F. Taylor); May 21, 1933 (A. L. Pickens); and July 18, 1944 (Mrs. Edward Stull). It has been seen but once near Florence, on June 26, 1947 (H. L. Harllee). Although it usually follows the flood plains of rivers inland from the coast, as indicated by records from Columbia, Bamberg, and Barnwell, the Nonpareil has been found at substantial distances from them. Thomas D. Burleigh made note of this fact from observations along State Highway 28 from Yemassee to Allendale (*Auk*, 52: 1935, 95).

Winter occurrences of the Nonpareil were not known for South Carolina until this year. On January 19, 1949, Mrs. E. Milby Burton saw a male on John's Island, Charleston County. A few days later, on January 27, Mrs. Gertrude Miles and her husband observed two males near Mt. Pleasant. These birds may not actually have wintered in the State; the unseasonably warm weather at the time may have caused some of the population wintering in Florida to move up the coast in a premature migration.

The arrival of the first Nonpareil is a red-letter day for any observer, no matter how experienced he may be. The males always come first, followed in about a week by the females. Their arrival is announced by the song, a delightful melody which resembles that of the Indigo Bunting. Many bird books maintain that the bird, when singing, remains in the heart of a dense thicket, leafy tree, or some completely concealed position. No idea could be more mistaken. The Nonpareil sings from the most conspicuous perches, the tops of bushes and small trees, telephone wires and poles, and even from the roofs of houses. The bird sings with great regularity through April and May but becomes more quiet in June. The frequency and intensity of the song seem to increase again in July.

Mating starts as soon as the females arrive and the period of mating is tempestuous. The males have violent tempers and are as pugnacious as any bird could be. There is little of the bluff which characterizes many small birds in their conflicts. The battles are fought to an unquestioned conclusion and often terminate fatally. Few other birds fight so ferociously. The combatants can actually be picked up while fighting, so oblivious are they to everything but the encounter. One bird caught under such circumstances by Wayne had both eyes completely closed by injuries. Sprunt found one with the head practically denuded of feathers.

Nesting takes place in mid-May, and the season is a long one, for the Nonpareil raises three broods, sometimes possibly four. Wayne saw young birds as late as September 16. Eggs of the first brood are usually laid by May 15. Dates for succeeding broods are June 11 and July 15. The eggs number three or four and are white, spotted and splashed with brown markings; they average 19.8 x 14.2 millimeters. Incubation takes from ten to twelve days.

The nest is composed of grass, leaves, and weed stalks and is lined with hair or fine grass. Locations vary between bushes and trees but usually at elevations under 20 feet. Not infrequently, the nest is placed in a clump of Spanish moss. The bird often nests in yards and gardens in towns and cities, very near to dwellings, so it is known to urbanites as well as those living in the country.

The female is so utterly unlike the male that one unfamiliar with her would never suppose the two to be of the same species. Greenish above and yellowish below, the female is the only *green* member of the finch family. The plumages of the immature males are sometimes confusing, but the structure of the bird is diagnostic.

FOOD: Seventy-three per cent vegetable, consisting largely of seeds. Grasses compose much of the diet, foxtail grass being a favorite, with some pine seeds and the seeds of figs and sunflowers. Insects taken are beetles, grasshoppers, crickets, bugs, and flies. Because it consumes cotton worms and boll weevils, the Nonpareil has a definite economic value.

397. DICKCISSEL: *Spiza americana* (Gmelin)   (604)

(Gr., *Spiza*, a finch; Lat., *americana*, of America.)

LOCAL NAMES: Black-throated Bunting; Judas-bird.

DESCRIPTION: Length 5.75 to 7.00 inches. *Male.* Above gray, the back streaked with black; line above the eye pale yellow; lower cheeks and middle of lesser wing coverts cinnamon rufous; breast yellow; throat with a black patch; posterior lower parts yellowish white. *Female.* Similar to the male but duller and without a black throat patch.

RANGE: Breeds north to northeastern Wyoming, southeastern Ontario, and Massachusetts (formerly); south to southern Texas and South Carolina. Winters north to Guatemala, Costa Rica, and accidentally in southern Louisiana and southern South Carolina.

STATUS IN S. C.: Rare and erratic summer resident in the middle sections; only accidental on the coast; also accidental in winter in the southeastern portion of the State. Reported in summer from York, Chester, Fairfield, Richland, and Aiken counties. Recorded in spring from Charleston County. In winter reported only from Summerville.

HISTORY: This interesting bird is now mainly mid-western in range, though it occurred years ago on the Atlantic seaboard. Its history in South Carolina, though brief, warrants details.

At the time of the appearance of his book in 1910, Wayne had seen but two of these birds but he mentioned, on the evidence of other observers, that it had nested in Aiken and Fairfield counties. His own first observation was made in April, 1883, near Charleston. In the *Addenda* to his book he recorded a male which he took on May 13, 1910, in Christ Church Parish, Charleston County.

L. M. Loomis gives an indication of its irregularity in the *Auk*, *8*: 1891, 168. He found it commonly about Chester in 1883 and 1884 but made no further observations. He says, "It is remarkable that it should come so abruptly, be common for two seasons, and then utterly abandon the locality." Murphey (1937) attributes the diminution of the Dickcissel population in the Aiken-Augusta region to the destruction of its nesting habitat.

For eighteen years there were no further records. Then, on May 25, 1928, Thomas Smyth found a breeding colony of about fifty birds in a wheat field near Columbia. This colony was disturbed by harvesting and probably did not raise any young. Smyth saw a single bird on June 5, the same year, near the State line in York County. On May 18, 1929, B. H. Stevenson investigated the site of the colony found by Smyth the year before and found one bird. On June 1 of that year, E. L. Green, Jr., reported thirteen birds near Columbia.

A few years passed; then came the most extraordinary occurrence of all. A male Dickcissel was seen by William Gadsden in his yard at Summerville, Dorchester County, in late January, 1935. Chamberlain, W. W. Humphreys, and Dunbar Robb made a trip to Summerville and saw the bird on January 25. It remained in the Gadsden yard until April 10, then disappeared (*Auk, 52*: 1935, 459). This is the first published winter record for the species for the United States. Five years later this amazing occurrence was repeated at the same locality in the same month, when two birds were seen at a feeding station in Summerville on January 21, 1940, by Eugene Swope. They were watched for several days. The most recent record is of an observation by Sprunt of a Dickcissel near York on July 13, 1944.

The Dickcissel is about the size of the English Sparrow. It has a yellow breast and a black patch on the throat, suggestive, as Peterson points out, of a miniature Meadowlark. It inhabits open country, field edges, fences, roadside wires, small bushy growths, and grain fields. The song is usually of five or six notes, the first three being uttered more rapidly than the last ones. It is possible that it will again appear as a nesting bird, and watch should be kept for it in the central and northern portions of the State.

The Dickcissel lays four or five eggs in a bulky nest of coarse grasses and leaves lined with long hairs or fine grass. The nest is placed low on the ground, among weed stalks, or in a low bush. The pale blue eggs average 20.3 x 15.2 millimeters. Incubation requires ten to eleven days, and two broods are raised.

Food: Chiefly weed seeds.

EASTERN PURPLE FINCH
398. *Carpodacus purpureus purpureus* (Gmelin)   (517)

(Gr., *Carpodacus*, fruit biting; Lat., *purpureus*, purple.)

Description: Length 5.50 to 6.35 inches. *Male.* Head purplish red, brighter in summer; rump light red; back reddish brown, streaked with dark brown; anterior under parts pinkish purple, posteriorly dull white, the flanks streaked with dark brown; wings and tail brown edged with light brownish red. *Female.* Upper parts olive, streaked with dull black; under parts white, streaked or spotted with olive.

Range: Breeds north to central British Columbia and southeastern Quebec; south to southern Alberta, northern Maryland, and northern New Jersey. Winters north to Nebraska and Nova Scotia; south to Texas and north central Florida.

Status in S. C.: Fairly common winter resident, October 8 to April 27, in most of the State; reported north to Greenville, Spartanburg, Chester, and Florence counties; east to

Horry County; south to Charleston and Colleton counties; west to Aiken, Greenwood, and Oconee counties.

HISTORY: Although the Purple Finch is a winter visitor in South Carolina and breeds no nearer this State than the mountains of Maryland, the type locality for it is "Carolina." It was made known to science from Carolina by Mark Catesby in 1731, and it was described from Catesby's notes by Gmelin in his *Systema Natura* (1789).

The Purple Finches arrive by mid-November and remain in varying numbers until March when most of them depart, though a few may linger into April. Although fairly regular visitors, they come in varying numbers season by season. Some winters will see them in abundance, others will pass when it is hard to find even a few of the birds. The Purple Finch lives in deciduous forests, particularly in the great river swamps, but it sometimes comes into towns and cities. Flocks may be seen in the tops of tall trees, feeding on seeds. Now and then, the birds will invade city residential districts visiting feeding trays at window sills and bushes in gardens. At such times many are caught in banding traps. Banding the finches has helped greatly in tracing their migrations.

The song of the Purple Finch is a fine one, and may be heard locally on mild February days or even better in March, when the birds are about to leave.

FOOD: Buds, stamens, and the flowers of such trees as the maple, ash, sweet gum, sycamore, and cherry. The birds also like the dogwood berry, beechnuts, frost grapes, mulberries, and ragweed seed.

NORTHERN PINE SISKIN
399. *Spinus pinus pinus* (Wilson) (533)

(Gr., *Spinus*, name of some finch; Lat., *pinus*, a pine.)

LOCAL NAMES: Pine Linnet.

DESCRIPTION: Length 4.50 to 5.25 inches. Upper surface rather light brown streaked with dark brown; wings and tail fuscous, with patches of lemon yellow on the base of the secondaries and on the base of the tail feathers; under parts white streaked with dull brown.

RANGE: Breeds north to central Alaska and southern Labrador; south to southern California and western North Carolina. Winters north to British Columbia and southern Quebec; south to northern Mexico, Texas, and southern Florida.

STATUS IN S. C.: Fairly common winter resident, but erratic, occurring over most of the State, October 31 to April 21. Observed north to Spartanburg, Chester, and Lancaster counties; east to Horry County; south to Charleston County; west to Aiken and Greenville counties.

HISTORY: This unobtrusive little bird is known to few people not only because of its inconspicuous appearance, but also because of its very unpredictable occurrence. It comes to South Carolina only in winter, and even then irregularly. As a rule, severe winters bring the Siskin in greatest numbers, but this is not always true, and years may pass without the observation of a single bird.

At a glance Siskins may easily be mistaken for Goldfinches, in whose company they are sometimes found, for the size of the two birds is about the same. But a close look will reveal the Siskin's distinguishing streaks which appear above and below and the yellow spots on the wings and tail.

These birds travel in flocks of varying sizes, and are found in open woodlands, cypress swamps, and on the coast islands. They are very fond of seeds, particularly those of the sweet gum and pines. In the pine trees, they cling to the cones, sometimes upside down, as they extract the seeds. Their liking for sweet gum has been noted by both Audubon and Wayne.

The notes of the Pine Linnet, as these birds are sometimes called, are similar to those of the Goldfinch, but there is enough variation to distinguish the two songs at once, if one knows the Goldfinch well. The Siskins often sing in flight and the song is a means of locating the birds, both when they are flying overhead or when they alight in a distant tree.

The Siskin has been reported to nest in the high North Carolina mountains but there is no indication as yet of its ever having done so in the higher portions of South Carolina.

FOOD: Very largely the seeds of conifers—pines, fir, juniper, and spruce; the birds also eat the seeds of maple, sweet gum, birch, alder, thistles, dandelion, ragweed, and sunflower.

EASTERN GOLDFINCH
400. *Spinus tristis tristis* (Linnaeus) (529)

(Lat., *tristis*, sad, pertaining to the bird's call.)

LOCAL NAMES: Wild Canary.

DESCRIPTION: Length 4.45 to 6.00 inches. *Male in summer.* Body lemon yellow; crown black; wings black with a white bar; tail black with white terminal markings; upper tail coverts white. *Female in summer.* Above light brownish olive; below pale yellow or dull yellowish white; wings and tail brown, marked with white. *Male* and *female in winter.* Similar to the adult female in summer.

RANGE: Breeds north to central Manitoba and Newfoundland; south to Texas, southeastern Louisiana, and northwestern South Carolina. Winters north to Minnesota and Nova Scotia; south to Texas and southern Florida.

STATUS IN S. C.: Common permanent resident throughout the State, but rare in summer in the eastern portion. Occurs north to Greenville, York, and Chesterfield counties; east to Horry County; south to Jasper County; west to Aiken County, Greenwood, and Oconee County.

HISTORY: It has always seemed to the writers that "Sun-bird" should have been the name of the Goldfinch. Like a detached bit of sunshine it perches briefly on a weed stalk or goes bounding through the air in a golden streak, to an accompaniment of the clearly whistled notes, "per-chic-or-ree." But Goldfinch is perhaps an equally good name, for the bird is surely gold, and the combination of gold, black, and white in the plumage produces beauty in full measure. To call the Goldfinch by its popular name of "Wild Canary" robs the bird of all its proper association with sunshine and gold.

The Goldfinch is a permanent resident of South Carolina but it occurs in the lower portion of the State mainly in fall, winter, and spring, with a few summer records. In the coastal counties it appears by mid-October (sometimes as early as September 20) and remains until the middle of May. It then virtually disappears though it continues to be present above the fall line. It nests, uncommonly, in the upper counties. Nesting pairs have been noted at Sassafras Mountain, Pickens County, June 26; Caesar's Head, Greenville County, June 28; and Jocassee, Oconee County, July 3; all in 1934 (G. E. Hudson and Franklin Sherman). At Walhalla, Oconee County, John Kershaw, Jr., found four nests, some with eggs and others just hatched, on August 12, 1909. A late date is that of an adult feeding three young at Pageland, Chesterfield County, September 10, 1944 (Miss E. M. Charles.)

The nest is a pretty structure, placed in bushes or low trees, rarely more than 15 feet above the ground. It is made of plant fibres and thistledown, firmly woven and compact and saddled into an upright fork. The three to six eggs are plain bluish white, with no markings. They average 16.5 x 12.2 millimeters. Incubation requires twelve to fourteen days. Only one brood is raised. Wayne saw the Goldfinch in summer on the coast on a few occasions. One of the birds, seen on July 8, 1903, he believed to be "breeding in the near vicinity," judging from its actions. He saw another on July 1, 1907, and a third on July 10, 1917. The species was also reported from Charleston on August 12 and 14, 1948, by Peter Gething.

One accustomed to seeing males of the Goldfinch in summer plumage will be surprised at the transformation which winter brings. The brilliance disappears and the sexes look alike, buffy brown above and greenish yellow below. Goldfinches flock together in winter and feed at both high and low levels; they may often be seen in the tops of maples and sweet gums, picking away at the seeds. They keep up a fairly constant twittering, which is diagnostic. The call note, given frequently in flight, has a plaintive quality, as indicated in its scientific name which means "sad."

The flight of this bird is markedly undulatory; it appears as if the flier was riding waves of air, like a small boat at sea. Occurring frequently in towns and cities, it is as much at home in such situations as the open beaches of the islands, where it feeds on the seeds of sea oats.

FOOD: Largely seeds, including those of the sunflower, clematis, ragweed, thistles, sweet gum, alder, and birch. The Goldfinch is so fond of thistle seeds that one of its names in some parts of the country is "Thistle-bird." The insect food is composed of caterpillars, beetles, plant lice, and aphids. The Goldfinch renders highly valuable service to the farmer by the destruction of weed seeds.

RED CROSSBILL
401. *Loxia curvirostra minor* (Brehm) (521)

(Gr., *Loxia*, oblique; Lat., *curvirostra*, curve-billed; *minor*, smaller.)

DESCRIPTION: Length 5.50 to 6.40 inches. Mandibles crossed at their tips. *Male.* Body dark red, brighter on the rump; wings and tail dull brown edged with red. *Female.* Above dull grayish olive, washed with olive yellow, brighter on the rump; below olive yellow, sometimes olive gray.

RANGE: Breeds north to central Alaska and north central Ungava; south to Michigan, southwestern North Carolina, and northern Georgia (probably). Winters south to Kansas and northern Florida.

STATUS IN S. C.: Rare and irregular winter resident, November 20 to May 26. Reported north to Chester and Kershaw counties; east to Charleston County; south to Beaufort and Hampton counties; west to Aiken County.

HISTORY: The Red Crossbill is an erratic winter visitor to South Carolina. The first recorded instance of its occurrence in the State was the capture of a bird by Audubon's son, John Woodhouse Audubon, near Charleston in the 1830's. Wayne was the next to record it. He found it in Beaufort, Hampton, and Charleston counties during the winters from 1886 to 1900, and gives a detailed account both in his book and in the *Auk*, 4: 1887, 287, and 5: 1888, 115 and 208. A skin in the Charleston Museum collected by H. T. Nowell, was probably taken in one of these winters at Anderson. A male taken at Chester on February 17, 1887, by L. M. Loomis, is now in the American Museum of Natural History. Dr. Frank M. Chapman also recorded Crossbills in the State during this period. He saw one flock of about fifty birds near Aiken in the winter of 1888-89 (*Bird-Lore*, 2: 1900, 25).

The only other invasion of the State by Red Crossbills occurred during the winter of 1908-09. At that time, N. C. Brown found the Crossbill common up-state; he saw and heard it almost every day from mid-December to the first of January at Camden and found it occasionally in January at Aiken until the twenty-third of the month (*Auk*, 26: 1909, 432). On the coast, E. A. Hyer shot one in February, 1909, at Magnolia Cemetery, Charleston, and B. R. Chamberlain saw a male with some Goldfinches on March 6, 1909, in Charleston. The skull of a crossbill found at Summerville at this time was probably of this species.

There is usually little doubt about the identity of crossbills at any reasonable range, for the characteristic which names them is an outstanding feature. The strange beak is highly adapted to the extraction of seeds of coniferous trees, upon which the bird largely subsists. Wayne mentions that he has seen them eating the seeds of the long-leaf pine, short-leaf pine, and sweet gum.

SITKA CROSSBILL
402. *Loxia curvirostra sitkensis* Grinnell (521c)

(Lat., *sitkensis*, of Sitka [Alaska].)

DESCRIPTION: Like the Red Crossbill but smaller.

RANGE: Breeds north to southern Alaska; south to California. Winters southeast irregularly to New England and South Carolina (accidentally).

STATUS IN S. C.: Accidental.

HISTORY: The only record of the Sitka Crossbill in South Carolina is a single specimen shot by Wayne from a flock of other crossbills at Charleston on March 31, 1888 (Griscom, *Proc. Bost. Soc. Nat. Hist.*, 41: 1937, 168). It is now in the collection of the Museum of Comparative Zoölogy at Cambridge, Massachusetts.

In habits the Sitka is like the other crossbills.

GREEN-TAILED TOWHEE
403. *Chlorura chlorura* (Audubon) (592.1)

(Gr., *Chlorura*, green-tailed.)

DESCRIPTION: Length 7.00 to 7.85 inches. Crown rufous; upper parts grayish or yellowish olive green; throat white; cheek, chest, and sides of breast light gray; flanks buffy gray; abdomen white.

RANGE: Breeds north to Oregon and Montana; south to southern California and central western Texas. Winters north to southern California and western Texas; south to Mexico.

STATUS IN S. C.: Accidental.

HISTORY: A specimen of the Green-tailed Towhee, which is a far-western bird, was taken by Wayne on January 18, 1921, in his yard at Oakland Plantation, Christ Church Parish, Charleston County. Wayne recorded this extraordinary capture in the *Auk*, *38*: 1921, 278. The specimen is in the collection of the Charleston Museum (No. 30.147.1440). It is the sole record for the State, and there is but one other for the southeastern United States, a bird secured in Virginia in 1908.

RED-EYED TOWHEE
404. *Pipilo erythrophthalmus erythrophthalmus* (Linnaeus) (587)

(Lat., *Pipilo*, I peep or chirp; Gr., *erythrophthalmus*, red-eyed.)

LOCAL NAMES: Joree; Chewink; Bullfinch; Ground Robin.

DESCRIPTION: Length 7.50 to 8.75 inches. *Male.* Head, chest, upper parts, and tail black; wings fuscous with a white patch on primaries, and white edgings on inner secondaries; breast and belly white; sides cinnamon rufous; tail with large white patches on each of the outer feathers; iris red. *Female.* Upper parts, throat, and breast cinnamon brown; sides and remaining lower parts like those of the male.

RANGE: Breeds north to southeastern Saskatchewan and Maine; south to northeastern Oklahoma and northwestern North Carolina. Winters north to southeastern Nebraska, southern New Hampshire, and southeastern Massachusetts; south to Texas and southern Florida.

STATUS IN S. C.: Common winter resident, October 17 to May 1, occurring probably over most of the State. Recorded north and west to Clemson College; east to Georgetown County; south to Beaufort County.

HISTORY: The Red-eyed Towhee is one of the better known birds of South Carolina, though not by its book name. The country boy and city gardener call it the

---

PLATE XXXI: BIRDS IN MAGNOLIA

Water Color by Roger Tory Peterson

Top birds, left to right: Orchard Oriole (immature male), Orchard Oriole (adult male), and Orchard Oriole (female). Middle birds, left to right: Summer Tanager (male), and Summer Tanager (female). Lower birds, left to right: Cardinal (female), and Cardinal (male).

Roger Tory Peterson

"Joree" and certainly "Joree" is what the bird "says" in its often repeated, characteristic call note. "Chewink" is applied to it almost everywhere outside the Carolina Low-country. The call note, which is responsible for the names "Chewink," "Joree," and "Towhee," is a clear two-syllabled whistle, sounding more like "jo-ree" to the authors than either of the other two. The call makes the towhee a bird easy to know. The black head, throat, and back are in strong contrast to the white belly and chestnut sides; even the female in her browns and whites has the same pattern and can hardly be confused with any other bird.

The Towhee arrives in the coastal area in October and stays until late April. It is essentially a ground bird (hence the name "Ground Robin") living in brushy thickets, tangles of vines, ditch banks, hedgerows, dense swamps, and forests. It is not at all shy, comes without fear into the yards and gardens of cities and towns, and makes itself quite at home at feeding stations and bird baths. At times in the spring it will resort to tree tops in order to feed on the buds.

The song, which is heard briefly before the bird leaves the State, has been rather well described by the words "drink-your-tea-e-e." It differs from the song of the White-eyed Towhee, as anyone who has heard it on the nesting grounds will agree. The Towhee associates with White-throated and Fox Sparrows in surroundings which are attractive to all of them.

A bird banded at Demorest, New Jersey, on September 28, 1932, was recovered at Georgetown, on October 17 of the same year. The short interval of time may perhaps be taken as a general indication of the speed of their southern migration.

Food: The food preferences of the three towhees of South Carolina are probably similar, and are treated here together. Stomach analyses have shown that the animal content amounts to 32 per cent and the vegetable matter 68 per cent. Insects, spiders, and snails compose the former, with caterpillars, beetles, ants, bugs, flies, grasshoppers, locusts, and tree hoppers making up the bulk.

ALABAMA TOWHEE
405. *Pipilo erythrophthalmus canaster* Howell (578b)

(Lat., *canaster*, half gray.)

DESCRIPTION: Similar to the Red-eyed Towhee, but bill larger; the white wing spots and tail tips smaller; sides and flanks lighter. *Female.* Above duller, less rufescent than the female Red-eyed Towhee.

RANGE: Resident and breeds north to northeastern Louisiana, Tennessee, and southwestern North Carolina; south to southern Mississippi, northwestern Florida, and western South Carolina.

STATUS IN S. C.: Common permanent resident over most of the State, excepting the coast region. Winters also to a little southeast of its breeding range. Recorded as a breeding bird north to Greenville, Spartanburg, York, and Lancaster counties; east to Florence County (probably) and Sumter County; south to Bamberg and Barnwell counties (probably); west to Aiken, Greenwood, and Oconee counties. Winters also southeast to Berkeley, Dorchester, and Beaufort counties.

HISTORY: The Alabama Towhee is the breeding species everywhere in South Carolina except in the coastal area, which is occupied by the Southeastern White-eyed Towhee. Specimens of the Alabama Towhee, represented by skins in the collections of the Charleston Museum and the Cleveland Museum of Natural History, have been examined and identified by Dr. H. C. Oberholser.

In habits and food the Alabama Towhee does not differ from the Red-eyed Towhee.

SOUTHEASTERN WHITE-EYED TOWHEE
406. *Pipilo erythrophthalmus alleni* Coues (587a)

(Lat., *alleni*, to Joel A. Allen, of the Museum of Comparative Zoölogy.)

DESCRIPTION: Similar to the Red-eyed Towhee but smaller. Iris straw colored and the white tips of the outer tail feathers smaller.

RANGE: Resident and breeds in the Atlantic coast region north to northeastern North Carolina; south to southeastern Georgia.

STATUS IN S. C.: Common permanent resident in the coastal area. Occurs north to Horry County; south to Beaufort and Jasper counties; west (inland) to Berkeley and Dorchester counties.

HISTORY: The White-eyed Towhee differs from the Red-eye to a marked degree. The two can be distinguished without trouble in the field. There is much less white in the tail of the White-eyed Towhee, the iris is usually yellowish white, and the call note and song are individualistic. The call, instead of being distinctly two-syllabled, is slurred into one, a "t-wee" rather than "tow-hee." The White-eye is somewhat shyer than the Red-eye, but it often nests in yards close to houses.

The white or light iris, so often emphasized as a characteristic of this species, cannot always be depended upon in the identification of the bird, for the iris is not always white. A nest in Chamberlain's yard in the season of 1947, for example, was that of a pair of which the male was red-eyed and the female "pale-eyed." On the grounds of William Gadsden in Summerville, a white-eyed bird incubated and hatched eggs in a nest on June 5, 1944, on one side of the house, while a red-eyed bird repeatedly visited a feeding tray on the other side, and carried away peanuts to a low, tangled area some 200 yards away to feed young.

The White-eyed Towhee nests in May, the tenth to the fifteenth being normal for eggs of the first brood. Wayne has found fledged young as early as April 14 in a very early season. Two or three broods are raised. Sprunt has nest dates for May 5, three eggs; May 20, four eggs; May 28, two eggs; July 20, two eggs and one young. A Beaufort County date is May 24, three eggs (E. J. DeCamps).

The nest is made of grasses, leaves, moss, and weeds and is placed in low bushes, hardly ever more than 6 or 8 feet above ground and normally less than that. Sometimes it is actually on the ground. Clumps of yaupon or cassina and the tangles of cat brier and rose vines are favorite nesting sites. The eggs number four or five. They are white, thickly marked with reddish spots and average 22.9 x 17.8 millimeters. Incubation requires twelve to thirteen days.

FOOD: The food habits of this towhee do not differ from those of the other subspecies.

407. LARK BUNTING: *Calamospiza melanocorys* Stejneger (605)

(Gr., *Calamospiza*, a reed finch; *melanocorys*, a black lark.)

DESCRIPTION: Length 5.25 to 7.59 inches. *Male*. Black, each wing with a white patch. *Female*. Above grayish brown, streaked with dark brown; a white wing patch; lower surface white, the breast and sides streaked with dark brown.

RANGE: Breeds north to southern Alberta and southwestern Manitoba; south to southeastern New Mexico and northwestern Texas. Winters north to southern California and central Texas; south to Mexico.

STATUS IN S. C.: Accidental.

HISTORY: The Lark Bunting is a western species secured in South Carolina years ago by Wayne, whose record remains unique in South Carolina ornithological history. He secured an adult female on April 19, 1895, having wounded it eight days before, in Christ Church Parish, Charleston County (*Auk, 12*: 1895, 305). "It seems strange," he wrote, "that this bird was taken within 200 yards of the place where I shot the Missouri Skylark [Sprague's Pipit], and Little Brown Crane, recorded in recent numbers of 'The Auk.'" The specimen is now in the Charleston Museum (No. 30.147.1462).

408. IPSWICH SPARROW: *Passerculus princeps* Maynard (541)

(Lat., *Passerculus*, a little sparrow; *princeps*, chief.)

DESCRIPTION: Length 5.87 to 6.75 inches. Pale sand gray above, the head and neck with narrow streaks of brown; stripe over eye pale brownish buff or yellowish white; lower surface white, the sides and breast finely streaked with brown.

RANGE: Breeds on Sable Island, Nova Scotia. Winters north to Sable Island; south coastwise to southeastern Georgia.

STATUS IN S. C.: Uncommon winter resident, November 3 to April 8, along the coast. Known north to Horry County; south to Kiawah Island.

HISTORY: True sparrows are little known, and the Ipswich is probably the least familiar of the family. It occurs regularly enough in South Carolina and is not hard to find if one is determined to see it, but there are good reasons for its obscurity. The range and habitat are very limited, and the Ipswich looks a good bit like some of the other sparrows. The sand dunes above high-water mark constitute the home of the Ipswich Sparrow and it is useless to look for the bird anywhere else. It lives on the sea beaches of the barrier islands among the growths of sea oats and the stands of beach grass behind the front dunes, practically never out of sight or sound of the surf. During forty-six years in the field, Wayne found it on the mainland but three times. It bears a strong superficial resemblance to the Savannah Sparrows, with which it often associates; hence one must use care in making hasty identifications of the species.

The Ipswich, a winter visitor to South Carolina, arrives early in November and remains until April.

The Ipswich Sparrow was added to the State List by Daniel L. Taylor, who took three birds near Cape Romain on February 5, 1902, and sent them to Wayne (*Auk*, *19*: 1902, 203). Wayne was much interested in the species, and when the writers were in close association with him during the 1920's, they made many trips to the barrier islands opposite his home and plodded for many hours through the soft dunes in search of them. Illustrative of the labor required in the search of the Ipswich Sparrow is the fact that Sprunt walked a distance of 54 miles through soft sands, on sixteen trips, from November, 1930, to March, 1931, and in that time saw only thirteen specimens, some of which he secured. Difficult as the bird is to find, it still seems strange, as Wayne pointed out, that neither Bachman nor Audubon encountered it on the South Carolina coast.

The Ipswich Sparrow is a gray bird, as gray as the sands which it frequents. It is larger and much more pale than the Savannah Sparrow, which lives in the same locality, and a little practice will enable the observer to pick them out almost invariably. It runs about like a mouse, is adept at hiding in the grass, and makes short flights when flushed unless thoroughly alarmed.

The winter range covers much of the Atlantic Coast extending as far south as Cumberland Island, which is on the very edge of the Georgia-Florida state line.

FOOD: Little is definitely known of stomach contents, but it is fairly certain that seeds and a few insects compose the food. In this State it eats quantities of the seeds of sea oats, which Wayne said is the bird's mainstay.

EASTERN SAVANNAH SPARROW
409.   *Passerculus sandwichensis savanna* (Wilson)   (542a)

(Lat., *sandwichensis*, of Sandwich [Islands, Alaska]; *savanna*, named for Savannah, Georgia.)

LOCAL NAMES: Stink Bird.

DESCRIPTION: Length 4.85 to 5.50 inches. Upper parts grayish brown, streaked with brownish black and buffy white; line over eye pale yellow; undersurface white, streaked on breast and sides with fuscous.

RANGE: Breeds in Nova Scotia. Winters north to Massachusetts (probably); south to southeastern Georgia.

STATUS IN S. C.: Common winter resident, October 13 to May 10. Recorded north to Spartanburg and Lancaster counties; east to Horry County; south to Jasper County; west to Aiken, Greenwood, and Oconee counties.

HISTORY: Though it is certainly one of the most abundant wintering sparrows of South Carolina, the Savannah is known only to bird students. Named by Alexander Wilson for Savannah, Georgia, where he discovered it, the species is but a winter visitor in the South, and never nests farther south than New Jersey. It occurs over the whole State, but it is probably more common in the coastal plain than anywhere else. G. E. Hudson found its stay at Clemson to be from October 13 to April 29 (*Auk*, *48*: 1931, 399).

The Savannah Sparrow is found on the coastal islands in great numbers, in sand dunes, grassy flats, and any expanse that is not wooded. On the mainland, it occurs abundantly in cultivated and fallow fields, broom-grass areas, ditch banks, and roadsides. It spends much time on the ground, running about like a mouse, and flushing on short flights only, to drop quickly again into the grass. Frequently, it will run down a rut in front of a car or of a person walking, and it is unusual to see one alight even in a bush. Its characteristic call note is a thin "zee-e-e-p," often uttered. Its flight is rather jerky and erratic.

To see the bird's markings, one must stand patiently and try to get a field glass focused on it. A good view will reveal that there is a yellow line in front of the eye, the body is much streaked, and the legs and feet are pinkish. The tail is slightly notched. Like many of the other sparrows, it is sometimes albinistic, the sparrow family seeming particularly susceptible to such abnormality.

FOOD: Chiefly insects (46 per cent) and the seeds of various grasses (54 per cent). The cotton boll weevil and sea oats occur specifically in the diet.

LABRADOR SAVANNAH SPARROW
410. *Passerculus sandwichensis labradorius* Howe (542d)

(Lat., *labradorius*, of Labrador.)

DESCRIPTION: Similar to the Eastern Savannah Sparrow, but larger, darker, more rufescent, and more heavily streaked.

RANGE: Breeds north to northern Ungava; south to Labrador. Winters south to southeastern Georgia.

STATUS IN S. C.: Uncommon winter resident, November 1 to May 9. Known only in the eastern and central portions of the State. Recorded north to Lee County; east to Georgetown County; south to Beaufort County; west to Allendale County.

HISTORY: Some of the specimens examined and identified by Dr. H. C. Oberholser are: one taken on March 10, 1933, at Jones Island, at the Savannah River entrance, by Ivan R. Tomkins; one taken on January 29, 1935, at St. Matthews, Calhoun County, by Chamberlain; one taken on April 22, 1940, at Murrells Inlet, Georgetown County, by W. M. Perrygo and J. S. Y. Hoyt; one taken on November 1, 1940, 9 miles southwest of Allendale, by Perrygo and J. S. Webb; three taken on November 7, 8, and 16, 1940, at Lynchburg, Lee County, by the same collectors.

In habits and food the Labrador does not differ essentially from the Eastern Savannah Sparrow.

EASTERN GRASSHOPPER SPARROW
411. *Ammodramus savannarum pratensis* (Vieillot) (546)

(Gr., *Ammodramus*, sand-running; Lat., *savannarum*, of plains, from Spanish, *sabana*, a plain; *pratensis*, found in meadows.)

LOCAL NAMES: Stink Bird.

DESCRIPTION: Length 4.80 to 5.40 inches. Upper parts mixed chestnut, brownish black, and light buff; top of head dark brown with a median stripe of grayish buff; edge of wing yellow; lower parts plain light buff, the breast and sides darker, but the abdomen white.

RANGE: Breeds north to southern Michigan and southern Maine; south to southern Alabama and northern Florida. Winters north to southern Illinois and North Carolina; south to Guatemala and Cuba.

STATUS IN S. C.: Fairly common summer resident in the western half of the State, uncommon in winter. A fairly common winter resident, September 20 to May 8, in the eastern half. Resident and breeds north to Greenville County; east to Chester County; south to Aiken County; west to Oconee County. As a winter resident outside its permanent range reported north to Cat Island (Georgetown County); south to Charleston; west to Dorchester and Berkeley counties.

HISTORY: The little Grasshopper Sparrow, which is even harder to watch than the insect whose name it bears, is chiefly a summer resident in the Piedmont region of South Carolina, nests there, and winters mainly on the coast where it can be found in the same fields with Henslow's and LeConte's Sparrows. L. M. Loomis at Chester, G. E. Hudson and F. Sherman at Clemson, and Dr. E. E. Murphey in the Aiken-Augusta region found it a summer resident with some winter records.

The Grasshopper Sparrow is found in open, weed-grown fields where there is much grass, never in woodlands. It is a ground bird and seldom flushes when it can escape by running. One can all but step on it before it takes wing, and it flies only a short distance before dropping into the cover again. It rarely perches above ground and then in low bushes or on a fence post. A good look at it will reveal the yellow at the bend of the wing and the very flat appearance of the head. The tail is very short and the breast is unstreaked.

The term "grasshopper" really applies to the voice of the bird, which is very thin, high, and insect-like; Peterson (1947) calls the song a "long, sizzling insect-like tumble of notes." Once learned, it will always serve in locating the singer.

The nest is on the ground, often in a depression and near the foot of a bush, grass clump, or even a large clod. It is a rather frail structure made of grasses, frequently arched over. The three to five eggs are white with markings of reddish brown and average 18.5 x 13.7 millimeters, and the bird is a very close sitter. Hudson and Sherman found a colony of "several pairs" in a meadow on the Clemson College farm, in June, 1934, a nest with four young being examined on the twenty-second (*Auk*, *53*: 1936, 315). There are no data on the incubation period. Two broods may be raised.

FOOD: In some localities nearly 70 per cent animal matter—insects, spiders, grasshoppers, crickets, weevils, and beetles, as might be supposed from the type of habitat. Weed seeds make up most of the vegetable diet.

LeConte's Sparrow
412. *Passerherbulus caudacutus* (Latham) (548)

(Lat., *Passerherbulus*, an herb sparrow; *caudacutus*, sharp-tailed.)

DESCRIPTION: Length 4.40 to 5.50 inches. Tail feathers narrow and pointed; crown brownish black with a buff to white median stripe; line over eye cinnamon buff; nape chestnut edged with gray; remainder of upper parts brownish black varied with chestnut to light buff; breast anteriorly and laterally buff; belly white; sides somewhat streaked with brownish black.

RANGE: Breeds north to southern Mackenzie and southern Manitoba; south to North Dakota and southern Minnesota. Winters north to southern Kansas and South Carolina; south to Texas and southern Florida.

STATUS IN S. C.: Rare and erratic winter resident, October 25 to April 27. Reported north and west to Chester County; east to Georgetown County; south to Yemassee.

HISTORY: Some authorities consider this species the most elusive of the sparrows. It is certainly always a difficult bird to find and because it occurs rather sporadically and locally, few observers are familiar with it.

LeConte's Sparrow was added to the State List by L. M. Loomis who secured specimens in Chester County in November and December, 1881 (*Bull. Nutt. Orn. Club*, 7: 1882, 54). Loomis later published an extended account of their habits at Chester (*Auk*, 2: 1885, 191).

In January of 1886, Wayne took the first one in the coastal area, near Charleston, and William Brewster recorded it (*Auk*, 3: 1886, 410). Wayne, like Loomis, found it erratic in its appearance and numbers. For several years he saw none, but in one winter he secured forty specimens (*Auk*, 11: 1894, 256).

LeConte's Sparrow, which is a shy little bird, inhabits the heavy grass-grown fields of lowlands or old rice fields grown to broom grass. It has, however, been observed within the city limits of Charleston in the salt marshes bordering the Ashley River. Very difficult to flush, it flies only a few yards before dropping into the grass again.

Like other sparrows, LeConte's Sparrow has a late autumn moult, sometimes not completed until mid-January. The best field characters are not only the habitat and actions but the distinct buff color of the eye stripe, which extends to throat and breast, and the chestnut band on the neck. The sides are somewhat streaked and there is a light line through the crown.

FOOD: In South Carolina, probably weed seeds for the most part.

Eastern Henslow's Sparrow
413. *Passerherbulus henslowii susurrans* Brewster (547)

(Lat., *henslowii*, to J. S. Henslow, of England; *susurrans*, buzzing.)

DESCRIPTION: Similar to the Western Henslow's Sparrow but bill stouter; and chestnut area on the upper parts more extensive.

RANGE: Breeds north to New York and central New Hampshire; south to North Carolina. Winters north to central Alabama and South Carolina; south to southern Alabama and central Florida.

STATUS IN S. C.: Fairly common winter resident in the coast region, October 24 to April 13. Reported north to Horry County; south to Charleston County.

HISTORY: This race of Henslow's Sparrow seems to occur chiefly in the eastern part of South Carolina. A specimen taken in Horry County on April 13, 1940, by W. M. Perrygo and J. S. Y. Hoyt has been identified by Chamberlain. Other specimens in the collection of the Charleston Museum, recently identified by Dr. H. C. Oberholser, are from Mt. Pleasant, collected by Wayne on October 24, 1924, October 26, 1923, October 27, 1922, November 10, 1923, November 12, 1894, and November 12, 1910.

In habits and behavior the Eastern is indistinguishable from the Western Henslow's Sparrow. The food of the two is also probably the same.

WESTERN HENSLOW'S SPARROW
414. *Passerherbulus henslowii henslowii* (Audubon) (547a)

DESCRIPTION: Length 4.75 to 5.25 inches. Crown black streaked with white, the median line buffy brown; rest of head and neck buffy olive, streaked with black; back chestnut spotted with black and edged with buffy white; below buffy white, the breast and sides washed with buff and finely streaked with dark brown.

RANGE: Breeds north to South Dakota and Ontario; south to northern Texas and Ohio. Winters south to southern Texas and central Florida.

STATUS IN S. C.: Fairly common winter resident, October 21 to March 28, probably throughout most of the State. Recorded north to Chester County; east to Georgetown County; south to Beaufort County; west to Aiken County.

HISTORY: Henslow's Sparrow much resembles LeConte's in seasonal variation, habitat, and behavior; and the two birds are not unlike in appearance. It lives in low, wet situations, heavily grass-grown; and it is hard to flush. Broom-grass fields attract it, and it lives close to small settlements at times. If hunted persistently, it will sometimes alight in a bush or tree, but normally it is a ground bird and blends wonderfully well into its grassy haunts.

In some years it is very common; Wayne (1910) speaks of "enormous numbers" in certain seasons. L. M. Loomis found Henslow's only a "tolerably" common migrant in Chester County. However, it is an erratic bird for in some years it apparently does not come at all.

The olive buff of the neck and sides of the head is a good field character. The feathers of the back have a marbled appearance, due to the edging of color. It is a handsome sparrow but so difficult to see that few have become familiar with it.

The western race of the Henslow's Sparrow seems to be, so far as is possible to determine from specimens examined, about as numerous in South Carolina as the eastern race.

FOOD: Seeds and insects.

ACADIAN SPARROW
415. *Ammospiza caudacuta subvirgata* (Dwight) (549.1a)

(Gr., *Ammospiza*, a sand finch; Lat., *caudacuta*, sharp-tailed; *subvirgata*, somewhat striped.)

DESCRIPTION: Length 6.00 to 6.50 inches. Similar to the Sharp-tailed Sparrow, but bill smaller; upper parts lighter, more grayish, and more plainly colored, with few or no conspicuous light streaks; lower surface paler with streaks much less sharply defined.

RANGE: Breeds coastwise north to southeastern Quebec and Nova Scotia; south to southern Maine. Winters north to South Carolina; south to northeastern Florida.

STATUS IN S. C.: Common winter resident in the salt marshes of the coast, November 7 to May 29. Recorded north to Charleston County; south to Beaufort County.

HISTORY: This is a distinctly gray form of the Sharp-tailed Sparrow, but in the field it is difficult if not impossible to distinguish from the James Bay Sparrow. As Wayne (1910) pointed out, Audubon noted this grayness over a hundred years ago by saying that some specimens he shot near Charleston "were so pale as almost to tempt one to pronounce them of a different species." Wayne added, "A subspecies was unknown in those days!"

Thirteen South Carolina specimens of the Acadian Sparrow in the Charleston Museum have been identified by Dr. H. C. Oberholser.

In habits and food this race does not differ from the Sharp-tailed Sparrow.

SHARP-TAILED SPARROW
416. *Ammospiza caudacuta caudacuta* (Gmelin) (549)

DESCRIPTION: Length 4.80 to 5.85 inches. Tail graduated, the feathers narrow and pointed; crown brown with a median line of gray; cheeks deep gray; line over the eye and malar stripe deep buff; rest of upper parts dark grayish olive, the middle of back narrowly streaked with white; edge of wing pale yellow; undersurface white, the breast and sides tinged with buff and streaked with black.

RANGE: Breeds in the Atlantic coastal marshes north to southeastern New Hampshire; south to New Jersey. Winters north to southeastern Massachusetts (casually); south to central Florida.

STATUS IN S. C.: Common winter resident, September 21 to May 16, in the coast region. Identified north to Charleston County; south to Beaufort County.

HISTORY: The Sharp-tailed Sparrows are of a group of birds which inland observers never see. They are birds of the coast. They frequent the vast salt marshes which stretch from the Santee River to the Georgia line, and it is quite useless to expect them anywhere else. On the coast, however, there is little trouble in seeing them, for they are abundant and occur during a large part of the year.

Sharp-tails are winter residents. They are tidal to the extent that they live in the marsh until forced out by rising tides; then they congregate along the shoreline, on the back beaches of the islands, on the spoil banks of the Inland Waterway, or along the edges of the mainland. An observer, walking along the rim of such places at high water, will flush them by the score.

The Sharp-tail responds well to the "squeak." One may stop in a patch of marsh which is apparently quite birdless, make the squeak noise, and suddenly up will pop these inquisitive little birds, peering here and there and balancing and swaying on the marsh grass stems. By keeping still, one can easily pick out the bird's distinguishing characteristics.

Since all forms of the Sharp-tailed Sparrow are difficult to determine in the field, the main reliance for positive identification must rest on specimens. Examples of the present race which have been examined are specimens from Mt. Pleasant, May 1, 1916, December 9, 1919, January 28, 1913, and November 16, 1923, Wayne; Turtle Island in Beaufort County, January 27, 1935, I. R. Tomkins. These have all been identified recently by Dr. H. C. Oberholser.

FOOD: Mainly seeds of the salt marsh grass. Wayne (1910) says that "In spring . . . it feeds upon a species of maritime moth which frequents the salt marshes."

NELSON'S SPARROW
417. *Ammospiza caudacuta nelsoni* (Allen) (549.1)

(Lat., *nelsoni*, to Edward William Nelson, one time chief of the United States Biological Survey.)

DESCRIPTION: Length 5.15 to 5.50 inches. Similar to the Sharp-tailed Sparrow, but smaller and darker; the light streaks above more sharply defined; the lower parts and sides of head darker, more deeply buff or ochraceous, the streaks lighter and less sharply defined, often obscure on the chest.

RANGE: Breeds north to southern Mackenzie and central Alberta; south to northeastern South Dakota and northern Illinois. Winters north to North Carolina; south to southern Texas and central western Florida.

STATUS IN S. C.: Common winter resident, September 24 to May 17, in the marshes of the coast region. Recorded north to Charleston County; south to Beaufort County.

HISTORY: Though in its breeding range Nelson's Sparrow resorts to fresh-water marshes, it lives almost exclusively in salt marshes during its winter stay in South Carolina. Its buff-colored, unmarked anterior lower parts readily distinguish it even in the field from the common Sharp-tailed Sparrow, but it cannot be certainly distinguished from the James Bay Sparrow except by the examination of specimens. Thirteen study skins in the collection of the Charleston Museum have been determined by Dr. H. C. Oberholser to be of this race.

In habits and food this race is practically indistinguishable from the Sharp-tailed Sparrow.

SOUTHERN SHARP-TAILED SPARROW
418. *Ammospiza caudacuta diversa* (Bishop) (549a)

(Lat., *diversa*, different.)

DESCRIPTION: Length 5.57 to 5.94 inches. Similar to the Sharp-tailed Sparrow, but darker; colors above more contrasting, the markings buffy, not white; the stripe over the eye and the malar stripe brighter.

RANGE: Breeds in the coastal marshes north to southern Delaware; south to North Carolina. Winters north to central eastern North Carolina; south to southern Florida.

STATUS IN S. C.: Abundant winter resident, September 19 to May 20, in the coastal region. Determined north to Charleston County; south to Beaufort County.

HISTORY: The Southern Sharp-tailed Sparrow is difficult to distinguish from the other Sharp-tailed subspecies. Judging from the specimens collected, however, it is by far the most numerous of the Sharp-tailed Sparrows that winter in South Carolina. Thirteen specimens in the Charleston Museum have been identified recently by Dr. H. C. Oberholser.

There seems to be no difference in general behavior, habits, and food, between this Sharp-tailed Sparrow and those of the other races.

JAMES BAY SPARROW
419. *Ammospiza caudacuta altera* Todd (549b)

(Lat., *altera*, another, different.)

DESCRIPTION: Similar to Nelson's Sparrow, but general coloration lighter, and the white streaks on the back less conspicuous.

RANGE: Breeds in central western Quebec. Winters north to South Carolina; south to southern Louisiana and northern Florida.

STATUS IN S. C.: Common winter resident, September 24 to May 28, in the coastal region. Determined north to Charleston County; south to Beaufort County.

HISTORY: This race of the Sharp-tailed Sparrow was originally described by W. E. Clyde Todd from the region of James Bay, the southern extension of Hudson Bay in central western Quebec and northeastern Ontario. Like the other forms of the Sharp-tailed Sparrow, it is difficult to identify with certainty in the field and specimens are therefore the main basis for records of its occurrence and distribution. It seems to be common in winter on the coast of South Carolina, although it is not recorded inland. Sixteen specimens in the collection of the Charleston Museum have been determined by Dr. H. C. Oberholser to be of this race.

In habits and food this race is not distinguishable from the other subspecies of the Sharp-tailed Sparrow.

MACGILLIVRAY'S SEASIDE SPARROW
420. *Ammospiza maritima macgillivraii* (Audubon) (550d)

(Lat., *maritima*, maritime; *macgillivraii*, to William Macgillivray.)

DESCRIPTION: Length 5.75 to 6.25 inches. Upper surface dark olive gray, usually more or less streaked with black; line above eye yellow, but anteriorly white, posteriorly passing into gray above the ear coverts; lower parts mostly white, the chest tinged with buff, and broadly streaked with gray or dull black. It differs from the Northern Seaside Sparrow in its darker upper parts, these more broadly streaked with black, and in broader and darker stripes on the chest and sides.

RANGE: Coast from North Carolina to Georgia.

STATUS IN S. C.: Common permanent resident in the marshes of the coast region. Recorded north to Charleston County; south to Beaufort County.

HISTORY: Macgillivray's Seaside Sparrow is of particular interest in the history of South Carolina ornithology because it was discovered in South Carolina, near Charleston, by Dr. John Bachman and described by Audubon.

Macgillivray's is a permanent resident in the coastal area of South Carolina. The fact is now well established, though it was not when Wayne wrote in 1910. Wayne could not find the nest, but he strongly suspected that the bird bred in the State. Subsequent discoveries proved him correct. The reason Wayne did not find the nest was that he did not look for it in the right place. It was the good fortune of the authors to discover the nesting, more or less by accident.

In fall and winter Macgillivray's Sparrow inhabits the salt-water marshes together with Sharp-tails. Wayne secured them there and, in collecting for the Charleston Museum, so did the authors. This was, of course, the place where they all looked for the nest and Wayne wondered continually at his inability to find a nest when "the young in first plumage occur during the second week in July, and the adults in worn breeding plumage are to be seen during the third week in July."

On May 13, 1924, both the authors were on a collecting trip in the lower part of Charleston County. As they crossed a stretch of brackish marsh, some 13 miles from Charleston, on U. S. Highway 17 near Rantowles, they saw a Macgillivray's Sparrow on the side of the causeway and a few other flying about the marsh. They returned to the same spot on the sixteenth, and began to search for the nest. The birds were there in numbers, singing constantly. Walking about in the comparatively dry marsh and looking into clump after clump of bullrush, Sprunt found himself suddenly looking into a nest with three eggs, from which a sparrow had flushed. A few moments later, Chamberlain found another, holding four eggs. Before the search ended three more nests had been discovered. The breeding of this form in South Carolina had been established (*Auk*, *41*: 1924, 482).

The news was sent to Wayne, who, a few days later made a trip to the locality and found two nests. On May 22 a young bird was caught that could fly. Nests were found in this same marsh again during the seasons of 1925-26-27, and at Hanahan, Charleston County, on Goose Creek, a perfectly fresh-water situation miles away from Rantowles. Rantowles marsh has changed considerably in recent years; the isolated clumps of bullrush are now amalgamated and are spreading over an almost uniform area. Nevertheless E. J. DeCamps found the sparrows breeding there on May 9, 1947. He discovered one nest with one egg, two nests being built, and young out of the nest, flying.

Macgillivray's Sparrow, therefore, frequents brackish and fresh-water marshes in the nesting season, returning to salt marshes when the young are well on the wing. This of course accounts for the fact that Wayne could not find them near his home, which was situated directly on salt marsh.

The nest of Macgillivray's Sparrow is built only of dried grasses. It is placed close to the ground or even on it and is attached to the upright stems of marsh growth. The eggs, which number three or four, are white, thickly sprinkled with reddish-brown spots and average 20.3 x 16.0 millimeters. Incubation takes about twelve days and only one brood is raised.

The bird flies with a rapid fluttering of wings. Its song is of Seaside character and quite distinctive, Sprunt having described it in the foregoing *Auk* reference as "consisting of a sort of guttural roll, heard only when the observer is very near the bird, then a short trill, ending with a strange rasping buzz."

Food: More animal matter than vegetable. While seeds of the salt marsh and glasswort are eaten, the bulk seems to be insects and small marine life, such as marine worms, crabs, dragon flies, moths, bugs, beetles, and grasshoppers, as well as some spiders.

Eastern Vesper Sparrow
421. *Pooecetes gramineus gramineus* (Gmelin) (540)

(Gr., *Pooecetes*, a grass inhabitant; Lat., *gramineus*, pertaining to grass.)

Description: Length 5.50 to 6.70 inches. Upper parts light grayish brown, streaked with blackish brown; lesser wing coverts dull cinnamon; the breast and sides faintly washed with buff and streaked with dark brown; outer tail feathers white.

Range: Breeds north to southern Manitoba and Nova Scotia; south to eastern Kansas and northern North Carolina. Winters north to southern Indiana and southern Massachusetts; south to Mexico and southern Florida.

Status in S. C.: Common winter resident, September 22 to May 11, throughout the State. Reported north to Greenville, Cherokee, and Chester counties; east to Georgetown County; south to Beaufort and Jasper counties; west to Aiken and Oconee counties.

History: The sparrows, as a family, are notoriously difficult birds for the beginner. Even experienced observers find identification none too easy at times. Many of them are small, brown birds very much alike in appearance and living in open, grassy situations where they are hard to study because of their secretive habits. The flight is usually short and often erratic, and the bird drops quickly again into cover.

The name "sparrow" unfortunately carries with it undeserved opprobrium which has arisen solely from association with the House or English Sparrow which is not a native bird. The native American sparrows are certainly unlike this imported bird and are not to be confused with it. The true sparrows are valuable birds because of their tremendous destruction of weed seeds and insects.

The Vesper Sparrow is a typical native species and one of the "easy" birds of the family to know. Though somewhat nondescript in its brown, streaked plumage, its identifying mark is the white outer tail feathers which are so prominently seen in flight. As soon as the bird flushes the white tail feathers become visible and remain visible during the short, erratic flight; indeed, they can be seen even while the bird is on the ground. Other birds, of course, have this character but are otherwise so different in appearance as not to be confused. Examples are the junco (very dark on the head and breast) and the pipit (which has buff plumage and wags its tail constantly).

The Vesper is an open-country bird. Old fields, roadsides, grassy areas, and hedge-rows are its home. It is a winter visitor in South Carolina. Most of them arrive in this State in mid-October and remain until April. The males may be heard in song shortly before their departure.

Wayne said that he had never found many of these sparrows on the barrier islands, and the writers' experience confirms Wayne's. The Vesper is a bird of the mainland where, in suitable localities, it may be met with regularly and in numbers.

FOOD: Analysis of this sparrow's food reveals that insects make up 31 per cent, grain 11 per cent, grass seed 16 per cent, and weed seeds 42 per cent. The insect diet is composed largely of grasshoppers, beetles, and caterpillars.

EASTERN LARK SPARROW
422. *Chondestes grammacus grammacus* (Say) (552)

(Gr., *Chondestes*, a seed-eater; *grammacus*, lined, or striped.)

DESCRIPTION: Length 5.75 to 6.75 inches. Crown and ear coverts chestnut, with median and lateral stripes white; a black line through the eye; remaining upper parts grayish brown with fine black streaks; tail mostly black; the outer tail feathers white, the remainder broadly tipped, except on the middle pair, with the same color; lower parts white with a conspicuous spot in the middle of the breast.

RANGE: Breeds north to southern Manitoba and southeastern Ontario; south to southern Louisiana and central Alabama. Winters north to southern Mississippi and northern Florida; south to southern Florida.

STATUS IN S. C.: Accidental.

HISTORY: The Lark Sparrow is only accidental in South Carolina and until recently no record of it existed for the State. On October 12, 13, 14, and 15, 1943, Eugene Eisenmann, John Bull, Jr., and George Komorowski, of the Linnaean Society of New York, saw an immature of the species and studied it for some time on Bull's Island, Charleston County. They watched the bird on the ground, in a live oak, and in low bushes on a narrow check-bank traversing one of the ponds of the island. Because Bull's Island is a government refuge, the bird could not be taken. This species, however, was familiar to one of the observers from previous acquaintance and is relatively easy to identify. Therefore the record can be accepted as authentic. This observation provides the only existing record for the State.

The Lark Sparrow, which is one of the least common species of the eastern United States, is fairly common in some localities. Nowhere in the east does the species occur in numbers comparable to those in the western United States.

In habits and food the Eastern Lark Sparrow is not unlike the Vesper Sparrow, except that it is somewhat less terrestrial.

BACHMAN'S SPARROW
423. *Aimophila aestivalis bachmanii* (Audubon) (575a)

(Gr., *Aimophila*, thorn- or thicket-loving; Lat., *aestivalis*, of summer; *bachmanii*, to Dr. John Bachman.)

DESCRIPTION: Length 5.30 to 6.25 inches. Similar to the Pinewoods Sparrow but somewhat larger, lighter and more rufescent above, as well as more buffy (less grayish) above and below.

RANGE: Breeds north to West Virginia and the District of Columbia; south to southern Mississippi and South Carolina. Winters north to North Carolina; south to southeastern Louisiana and central western Florida.

STATUS IN S. C.: Fairly common permanent resident over most of the State, excepting the southeastern corner. Recorded north and west to York, Union, and Anderson counties; east to Horry County; south to Charleston, Dorchester, and Aiken counties. Winters also in the southeastern corner of the State.

HISTORY: This plain, nondescript little sparrow has much more character and attractiveness than mere appearance would indicate. Certainly there is little in its appearance to commend it, for its grays, browns, and whites are far from spectacular. Moreover, it is a shy bird and does not call much attention to itself. It is of particular interest to South Carolina, however, for it was discovered on the banks of the Edisto River in the Low-country by the famous naturalist whose name was bestowed upon it by his even more famous colleague, Audubon.

Bachman's Sparrow is a permanent resident, occurring everywhere except in the mountains and in the southeast corner of the State, where it is represented by its close relative, the Pine-woods Sparrow. Bachman's Finch, as the species is sometimes called, is more common below the fall line than above it, and in the once extensive pine barrens it was to be found with other characteristic dwellers such as the Red-cockaded Woodpecker and Brown-headed Nuthatch. Undergrowths of bushes and grass are essential to its needs, and it is largely a ground bird. When it sings, however, it will perch on a bush or stump.

The nesting season is variable; forward seasons advance it, backward ones will delay it. The nest is almost impossible to find for it is normally invisible from above. Composed of grass, it is nearly always arched over, with a kind of tunnel extending outward from it. Even if one marks the exact spot from which a bird flushes or into which it disappears, he will not necessarily have discovered the nest's location, though of course it will be somewhere near. It is often built at the base of a bush or grass clump, or an old stump. Watching the female is the best way of locating the nest, the male having nothing to do with the construction of the nest or with incubation.

There are four to five eggs which, unlike the eggs of most sparrows, are pure white. They average 18.8 x 15.2 millimeters. Variation of dates is illustrated by Wayne's having found eggs almost hatched as early as April 7, while in other seasons he found the birds building their first nest late in that month. An average time for eggs of the first brood would be between April 28 and May 4. Three broods are raised, with the last hatching in August. Two dates from near Beaufort are May 6, four eggs, and June 6, three eggs (E. J. DeCamps); these probably represented first and second broods. The incubation period is about twelve days.

Many bird-lovers find in the song of Bachman's Sparrow a musical richness, a variety of form and pitch unmatched in the songs of any other sparrows. The fact that the bird begins to sing very early in the year is illustrated by Wayne's striking comment, dated February 26, 1901: "Heard a Bachman's Finch sing beautifully at night. He sang as sweetly as if it were May, although the night was very cold and the ground partly covered with snow and ice." Bachman's Sparrow continues to sing into early September and has been heard in late December. However, it is usually a silent bird in winter except for the call note, which is not distinctive. During the winter it frequents large broom grass fields near pinelands, and is very hard to flush.

In addition to a number of specimens from the Low-country, specimens from the upper part of the State include the following: Anderson, July 13, 1894 (H. T. Nowell); 5 miles northeast of Rock Hill in York County, September 20, 1940, and 7 miles northwest of Lancaster, September 19, 1940 (W. M. Perrygo and J. S. Webb); 5 miles southeast of Whitmire in Newberry County, May 27, 1940 (Perrygo and J. S. Y. Hoyt). Specimens from outside its breeding range came from 9 miles southwest of Allendale, October 25, 26, and 31, 1940 (Perrygo and Webb); and Cumberland Island, Georgia, April 17, 1932 (Sprunt).

FOOD: More insectivorous than many other sparrows. It eats seeds, of course, but prefers insects. Grasshoppers, crickets, spiders, beetles, moths, caterpillars, and leaf hoppers have been found in analyses. Grass seeds and those of pines and various sedges make up the vegetable matter.

PINE-WOODS SPARROW
424. *Aimophila aestivalis aestivalis* (Lichtenstein) (575)

DESCRIPTION: Length 5.60 to 6.25 inches. Above gray, streaked with chestnut brown; the back spotted with brownish black; edge of wing light yellow; tail dark brown edged with gray; under parts dull light gray to grayish white, the breast and sides buffy gray.

RANGE: Resident and breeds north to southern Georgia and southeastern South Carolina; south to south central Florida.

STATUS IN S. C.: Fairly common permanent resident in the southeastern corner of the State. Identified northwest to Allendale County; southeast to Beaufort and Jasper counties.

HISTORY: The Pine-woods Sparrow is very similar to Bachman's Sparrow, which occupies a much wider area in the State. It was first reported from South Carolina by

---

PLATE XXXII: PAINTED BUNTINGS

Water Color by Edward von S. Dingle

Top, right: Painted Bunting (first year male, breeding plumage). Two birds, left center: Painted Buntings (adult males). Bottom three birds, left and right: Painted Buntings (males coming into adult plumage); center, Painted Bunting (adult female).

T. D. Burleigh (*Auk, 52*:1935, 194), who collected specimens at Allendale, July 25, 1934, and at Gillisonville in Jasper County, on the same day. Two other specimens have been identified by Dr. H. C. Oberholser as belonging to this race. One was collected by G. R. Rossignol at Purysburg, Jasper County, May 2, 1915; the other by W. M. Perrygo and J. S. Y. Hoyt, 3 miles northwest of Bluffton, May 9, 1940.

The specimen referred to this subspecies by Wayne in his *Birds of South Carolina* (1910), taken near Mt. Pleasant, April 1, 1895, is actually a Bachman's Sparrow.

The haunts, nesting, food, and other habits of the Pine-woods Sparrow are identical with those of Bachman's Sparrow.

ILLINOIS SPARROW
425. *Aimophila aestivalis illinoensis* (Ridgway) (575b)

(Lat., *illinoensis*, of Illinois.)

DESCRIPTION: Similar to the Bachman's Sparrow but upper parts brighter, lighter, and more uniformly rufous; the back with very small or no black markings.

RANGE: Breeds north to southeastern Iowa and southern Ohio; south to central Texas and southern Louisiana. Winters north to northern Louisiana and South Carolina (casually); south to southern Louisiana and Mississippi.

STATUS IN S. C.: Casual winter visitor. Recorded in only Charleston County.

HISTORY: This Mississippi Valley race of this species has only recently been recognized as distinct. It occasionally wanders southeastward from its breeding range in the Mississippi Valley. Its occurrence in South Carolina is based on two specimens taken by Wayne at Mt. Pleasant on January 24, 1911, and February 1, 1902, respectively. The specimens, now in the collection of the Charleston Museum, are perfectly typical individuals of the Illinois Sparrow and have been identified recently by Dr. H. C. Oberholser.

In habits and food this bird does not differ in any noteworthy way from Bachman's Sparrow.

SLATE-COLORED JUNCO
426. *Junco hyemalis hyemalis* (Linnaeus) (567)

(Lat., *Junco*, from *juncus*, a rush or reed; *hyemalis*, of winter.)

LOCAL NAMES: Snowbird.

DESCRIPTION: Length 5.75 to 6.50 inches. Head, neck, and upper surface slate-colored, the head darker; belly white; outer tail feathers white; bill pinkish or lilaceous white.

RANGE: Breeds north to northwestern Alaska and central Labrador; south to southern Yukon, southern Pennsylvania, and southern Connecticut. Winters north to western Washington and Nova Scotia; south to northern Lower California (casually) and northern Florida.

STATUS IN S. C.: Common winter resident, October 4 to May 2, throughout the State. Reported north to Greenville and Chester counties; east to Horry County; south to Beaufort County; west to Aiken and Oconee counties.

HISTORY: In practically all of its range the Slate-colored Junco is known by the name "Snowbird" rather than Junco. Even in the Low-country of South Carolina the name persists, in spite of the fact that snow is rare in that area. However, only those with a more than ordinary interest in birds know it by any name at all.

The Slate-colored Junco as a species is certainly one of the easiest of the sparrows in South Carolina to recognize, and presents no difficulty even to the most inexperienced beginner, for no other member of the family in any way resembles it. It is a two-colored bird, being a dark, slate gray above, with a perfectly white belly. The line between the lower breast and belly is sharply drawn, dark to light, and the outer tail feathers are white. These show plainly the instant the bird flies, but they can also be seen when it is on the ground. In addition to the distinctive plumage pattern, the conspicuous pinkish white bill is always an excellent mark.

Juncos are ground birds. They frequent roadside hedges, thickets, the borders of fields and woods, and at times even the interior of swamps and forests. They are often associated with White-throated and Fox Sparrows, towhees, and other thicket-dwelling species. Juncos occur in flocks, large or small, but are rarely, if ever, seen singly. They come readily about houses, visiting feeding stations and scratching about under bushes and shrubbery in yard or garden. Thus, they are easy for both the rural and urban observer to see and study.

The Slate-colored Junco is a winter visitor to South Carolina, but is more plentiful in some years than in others. It arrives in the Low-country in November and remains till late in March. Records kept by Richard H. Sullivan at Columbia from 1913 to 1941 show an average arrival date of November 7 (twenty-eight years) and an average departure date of April 23 (twenty-nine years). Clemson dates range from October 3 to April 21.

From the popular name Snowbird one might naturally conclude that the bird is associated with cold weather, and so it is. At the same time, it cannot, according to Wayne, survive in very low temperatures, at least when sudden drops occur. He wrote that in the great cold wave which the coast experienced in February, 1899, the weather "killed enormous numbers."

A banded Slate-colored Junco recovered in South Carolina apparently holds the longevity record for the species. The bird was banded at Lenox, Massachusetts, on April 7, 1931, and was shot, ten years later, on March 5, 1941, at Conway, Horry County, by R. D. Epps (*Bird-Banding, 14*: 1943, 46). For small birds age records above four or five years are uncommon.

FOOD: Almost exclusively the seeds of weeds and grasses. Analyses reveal ragweed, crab grass, pigweed, amaranth, broom sedge, pigeon grass, and thistles. Such a diet makes the bird a decided economic asset.

CAROLINA JUNCO
427. *Junco hyemalis carolinensis* Brewster (567e)

(Lat., *carolinensis*, of Carolina.)

DESCRIPTION: Similar to the Slate-colored Junco, but larger, especially the bill; upper parts more uniform, the head little if any darker than the back.

RANGE: Breeds north to Maryland; south to northwestern South Carolina. Winters north to Maryland; south to southern Georgia and southern South Carolina.

STATUS IN S. C.: Uncommon permanent resident in the high mountains of the western part of the State, chiefly in Pickens and Oconee counties. Rare winter resident, December 4 to February 4, in the coastal areas, reported there only from Charleston County.

HISTORY: This distinct race of the Slate-colored Junco nests in the higher mountains from Maryland into Georgia, and is a permanent resident of the mountain region of South Carolina. However, the South Carolina mountains are not as high as the birds actually prefer, and they are not common. The Carolina Junco was described in 1886 by William Brewster, who pointed out that it differs from the Slate-colored Junco in several noteworthy respects. It is larger; in color it is grayer, with no brown shades; it has a gray to horn-colored bill; and it breeds in a completely different range.

Though it is a mountain bird essentially, it occasionally wanders out of the mountains in winter as far down as the coast. The first record of its appearance there is a specimen taken by Wayne at Mt. Pleasant on February 4, 1922 (*Auk, 39*: 1922, 420). He recorded this as the first for the State, though the bird has always occurred in the mountains.

Thus far there has been no definite record of its nesting in South Carolina. On July 30, 1932, on Sassafras Mountain, at an altitude of 3200 feet, Franklin Sherman found a pair of Carolina Juncos whose actions gave every indication that they were nesting.

Unlike the Slate-colored Junco, the Carolina Junco is apparently not at all inconvenienced by severely cold weather. Burleigh (1941) says that he has seen Carolinas "at the top of Mt. Mitchell, with ground covered with snow, zero weather, and a blizzard blowing." This was on December 23, 1930, and the birds were "feeding contentedly in the shelter of fir thickets" at an altitude of 6684 feet.

EASTERN CHIPPING SPARROW
428. *Spizella passerina passerina* (Bechstein)   (560)

(Lat., *Spizella*, a little finch; *passerina*, relating to a sparrow.)

LOCAL NAMES: Chippy.

DESCRIPTION: Length 5.00 to 5.85 inches. *Adult.* Crown rufous chestnut; a white stripe over the eye; a black stripe through the eye; nape, sides of head, and rump gray; back light brown streaked with brownish black; a buff or white wing bar; lower surface white, but the chest and sides pale gray; bill black. *Immature.* Similar to the adult but head buffy brown, streaked with dark brown.

RANGE: Breeds north to northern Ontario and northern Nova Scotia; south to southern Texas, west central Georgia, and southeastern South Carolina. Winters north to Oklahoma and Massachusetts; south to southern Texas, southern Florida, and Cuba (casually).

STATUS IN S. C.: Common permanent resident throughout most of the State, abundant in winter eastward; absent in winter from the northwestern section (Oconee, Pickens, and Greenville counties); uncommon in the coast region in summer. Breeds north to Greenville, Spartanburg, and York counties; east to Horry County; south to Beaufort County; west to Aiken and Oconee counties.

HISTORY: Because the Chippy is a small, plain-looking bird, with nothing to make it outstanding, it is often overlooked. The best field characters are the reddish cap, the black line through the eye, bordered with white, and the clear, unstreaked breast. The song is a rather weak, thin trill all on one key, resembling that of some insects. It lives in brushy fields, roadside hedgerows, the edges of woods, and even in forested areas.

The Chipping Sparrow is a permanent resident of South Carolina. It does not, however, winter in the upper Piedmont. G. E. Hudson lists it as occurring about Clemson from March 13 to November 10.

It nests sparingly down to the coastline, but far more commonly in the interior. Wayne established it first as a coastal nester in 1886, when he took a female near Ridgeville, Dorchester County, on June 3, with an egg in the oviduct ready for laying. On May 29, 1896, he found a brood of young, just able to fly, in a large pine forest near Mt. Pleasant; and he adds that, as late as 1910, descendants of that pair were still nesting there, within a mile of the salt marshes. Another coastal record is a nest with four eggs found on May 3, 1937, near Beaufort by E. J. DeCamps. In Lexington County, Mrs. G. E. Charles found a Chippy feeding young as late as August 9, 1947. This nest was 30 feet from the ground in a pine. A Greenville County date for eggs is June 10 (DeCamps).

The nest is made of grasses, leaves, and weed stalks, and is often lined with horse-hair. It is placed in bushes, on the low horizontal limbs of trees, or in clumps of vines, sometimes near houses. The eggs are three to five, of a greenish-blue shade, with fine spots of black and purple about the large ends. They are among the most attractive looking sparrow eggs. They average 18.3 x 12.9 millimeters. The Chippy raises one or two broods and incubation requires twelve days.

Chipping Sparrows flock in fall and winter and mingle in those seasons with Field Sparrows, Myrtle Warblers, and other small, thicket-dwelling birds. They are often to be seen on the telephone wires along highways, where, as one passes in a car, they rise and scatter into the trees or fields.

FOOD: About 62 per cent vegetable matter. Grass seed makes up 48 per cent of this, weed seed 10 per cent, and grain 4 per cent. Caterpillars are favorite insect food. They also eat grasshoppers, weevils, beetles, ants, and wasps.

CLAY-COLORED SPARROW
429. *Spizella pallida* (Swainson) (561)

(Lat., *pallida*, pale.)

DESCRIPTION: Length 5.00 to 5.75 inches. Crown light brown, streaked with black, and with a pale median line; sides of head and hind neck gray; back grayish brown, broadly streaked with black; rump hair brown; lower parts dull white, tinged with buff on chest and sides.

RANGE: Breeds north to southern Mackenzie and northern Michigan; south to southeastern Colorado and northern Illinois. Winters north to southern New Mexico and southern Texas; south to southern Lower California and Chiapas.

STATUS IN S. C.: Accidental.

HISTORY: This pale edition of the Chipping Sparrow, a bird of the prairie regions of the west, has no normal place among South Carolina birds. Its inclusion rests on a single specimen, taken October 27, 1929, by E. von S. Dingle, who retains it in his private collection. He secured the bird on a rice-field bank at Middleburg Plantation, near Huger, Berkeley County. Not only is it the sole record for this State, but until that time there had been no record of its occurrence in the Atlantic States (*Auk*, 47: 1930, 257).

EASTERN FIELD SPARROW
430. *Spizella pusilla pusilla* (Wilson) (563)

(Lat., *pusilla*, very small.)

DESCRIPTION: Length 5.10 to 6.00 inches. Crown plain cinnamon rufous; back cinnamon rufous streaked with black and with buffy gray; two more or less buffy white wing bars; lower surface dull buffy white, the breast tinged with cinnamon; legs and feet flesh color or pale brown; bill pink.

RANGE: Breeds north to central Minnesota and Nova Scotia; south to central Texas and northern Florida. Winters north to central Missouri and Massachusetts; south to Mexico and central Florida.

STATUS IN S. C.: Common permanent resident throughout the State. Recorded north to Greenville, Spartanburg, York, and Lancaster counties; east to Horry County; south to Beaufort and Jasper counties; west to Barnwell and Oconee counties.

HISTORY: The unobtrusive and plain-looking little Field Sparrow is doubtless often dismissed as "just a little brown bird." It is a common species and occurs as a permanent resident over the whole of South Carolina. True to its name, it is fond of brushy fields and pastures in which there is much grass. It also frequents roadside hedges and it may often be seen perched on wires and fences. Its best characters are the generally reddish upper parts, rather long tail, and the pink bill. Except in young birds, the breast is without streaks.

The Field Sparrow nests throughout South Carolina and usually builds its home on the ground in a tuft of grass, beside a clod, or in low bushes. However, W. M. Levi has found nests at Sumter as high as 10 feet above the ground in the top tufts of young pines. The nest, which is made of grass, is rather frail as a rule. The eggs (two to five) are a pale bluish white speckled with purple and brown. They average 17.8 x 13.2 millimeters, and their incubation requires about thirteen days.

Curiously enough, Wayne never found the nest of the Field Sparrow, but from observing the young, he was sure that three broods are raised. This is often true. Dates for the first laying are April 23, two eggs; May 3, three eggs; May 7, three newly hatched young (all Charleston County, Sprunt); May 2, four eggs (Greenville County, E. J. DeCamps). A May 25 date, three eggs (Lexington County, Mrs. G. E. Charles) is more than likely a second laying. A probable third nesting date is June 28, three eggs (Sumter County, Levi). Wayne found young birds as late as August 16 in Beaufort County.

The Field Sparrow is one of the most persistent singers among our summer birds, reminding one of the indefatigable Red-eyed Vireo in this respect. No day seems too hot, and even at the hottest part of it, the simple, pleasing little trill can be heard, rising with the heat waves, from the brushy fields. The song period is a long one, running from early March into August.

This species, like all the sparrows, is subject to albinism and specimens showing this characteristic are not rare.

Food: About 60 per cent vegetable matter and 40 per cent animal matter. Field Sparrows consume great quantities of seeds, mainly of the grasses and sedges. They pick up small amounts of grain in stubble fields. Ants, flies, beetles, wasps, caterpillars, grasshoppers, and leaf hoppers are among the insects in the diet. The Field Sparrow is a decidedly valuable factor in weed and insect control.

WHITE-CROWNED SPARROW
431. *Zonotrichia leucophrys leucophrys* (Forster) (554)

(Gr., *Zonotrichia*, band-haired; *leucophrys*, white eye-browed.)

DESCRIPTION: Length 6.50 to 7.50 inches. *Adult.* Center of crown white, a broad black stripe on each side, touching the eye in front; neck and sides of head gray; back light brownish gray, streaked with chestnut brown; wings and tail brown, the wings with two white or whitish bars; under parts pale gray and brownish white. *Immature.* Similar to adult but head stripes brown, and lower and upper parts largely buffy brown.

RANGE: Breeds north to northeastern British Columbia and southern Greenland; south to Colorado and Newfoundland. Winters north to northern Lower California, southern Kansas, and Massachusetts; south to the Valley of Mexico, Louisiana, northern Florida, and Cuba (casually).

STATUS IN S. C.: Casual winter resident, October 9 to May 5. Reported north to Chester County; east to Berkeley County; south to Charleston County; west to Richland County.

HISTORY: This handsome species, often considered the aristocrat of its family, has every right to such a distinction. South Carolina is not its home; it is only a casual wanderer to the State. It belongs principally to the western states, where it is by no means rare.

In view of its rarity in South Carolina, all records are of interest. Audubon stated that in the winter of 1833 he took "at Charleston in South Carolina, one in its brown livery." On October 26, 1897, Wayne secured a young male near Mt. Pleasant. The specimen is now in the Charleston Museum. Wayne called this "the only valid record for the State," apparently disregarding Audubon's bird. There were no more records for many years. Then, on May 5, 1925, Herbert R. Sass saw one in his garden on Legare Street, in Charleston (*Auk, 42*: 1925, 590). This was followed the next year by Wayne's wounding another, near his Oakland Plantation home, March 4, 1926, but he did not secure it. He writes that "I was within a few inches of the bird several times . . . but it finally eluded me. . . ." On October 20, 1928, E. von S. Dingle saw one at Middleburg Plantation, Berkeley County, and on October 9, 1938, at the same place, secured a young male which is now in his collection. Mrs. G. E. Charles has recorded the White-crown but twice at Columbia; an adult on January 13 and 16, 1936, and an immature bird, January 24 and 28, 1946. The only other record from the Piedmont is an adult banded at Chester, March 28, 1937, by W. W. Neely, of the U. S. Soil Conservation Service. Such records serve to demonstrate how rare the White-crown is in the South Atlantic region.

The adult is easy to recognize because of the conspicuous black and white striping of the crown, but the immature must be studied carefully. The breast is clear gray, and there is no throat patch such as is carried by the White-throat.

GAMBEL'S SPARROW
432. *Zonotrichia leucophrys gambelii* (Nuttall) (554a)

(Lat., *gambelii*, to William Gambel.)

DESCRIPTION: Similar to the White-crowned Sparrow, but the black stripe on the side of the head not touching the eye, leaving the white superciliary stripe continuous, that is, not interrupted by black in front of the eye.

RANGE: Breeds north to northwestern Alaska and northern Mackenzie; south to southern Alaska, Montana, and northwestern Ontario. Winters north to northern California and Utah; south to Mexico, Texas, and southern South Carolina (accidentally).

STATUS IN S. C.: Accidental.

HISTORY: This is one of the far-western forms of the White-crowned Sparrow and is not to be expected in South Carolina at all. There is only one record of its occurrence. On October 23, 1925, Wayne secured a young male a short distance from his house (*Auk, 43*: 1926, 100). The specimen is now in the Charleston Museum and has been examined by Dr. H. C. Oberholser. This wanderer, to quote Wayne's manuscript notes, "makes the 47th species I have added to the avifauna of South Carolina." The pride which underlies this statement is readily understandable. That remarkable man added two more new birds to the State List than the number of years he was in the field, forty-seven birds in forty-five years.

White-crowned Sparrows are largely ground birds, scratching about in thickets and brushy cover for their food of seeds and insects.

WHITE-THROATED SPARROW
433. *Zonotrichia albicollis* (Gmelin) (558)

(Lat., *albicollis*, white-necked.)

DESCRIPTION: Length 6.30 to 7.65 inches. *Male.* Crown black mixed with brown posteriorly, and with a median white stripe; and another white stripe through the eye becoming yellow between the bill and eye; two white or buffy white wing bars; back reddish brown, broadly streaked with black; rump hair brown; tail dark brown; throat and belly white, the breast gray. *Female.* Similar to the male but with white of throat duller. *Immature.* Similar to the female but head mainly brown, with the median stripe on the crown buff rather than white; chest duller and somewhat streaked with dark brown.

RANGE: Breeds north to northwestern Mackenzie and southern Labrador; south to central Alberta, northern Pennsylvania, and Massachusetts. Winters north (casually) to central California and southern Maine; south to Guadalupe Island, Lower California (casually), Mexico, and southern Florida.

STATUS IN S. C.: Abundant winter resident, October 2 to May 17, throughout the State. Accidental in summer at Columbia. As a winter resident, recorded north to Greenville, York, and Lancaster counties; east to Horry County; south to Beaufort County; west to Aiken, Greenwood, and Oconee counties.

HISTORY: This attractive and gentle species is probably the best known of the wintering sparrows of South Carolina. Handsome, abundant, well distributed, and friendly, it can easily be known by anyone. Under woodland thickets or garden shrubbery it scratches away industriously among the dead leaves and often, even in midwinter, voices the sweet, plaintive little song which instantly identifies it. The White-throat is a woodland bird, frequenting thickets and brushy tangles, vine clad ditch banks, and the hedgerows of highways. It is not often found in open woodland which lacks undergrowth. It comes freely into towns, frequents gardens where there is a growth of shrubbery, and will remain in the same yard all winter unless greatly disturbed. It feeds on the ground, scratching with both feet simultaneously in the leaves and soil.

White-throats are winter visitors, coming in October and remaining until mid-May. Most of them arrive about the third week of October but there are several earlier records. They occur, as far as can be ascertained, in every county of South Carolina. A completely abnormal occurrence was recorded by Mrs. G. E. Charles in Lexington County, near Columbia, in the summer of 1943. A singing bird remained near her home from June 29 to July 18. It was apparently uninjured. This is probably the only midsummer record for the Southeastern States.

The White-throat is a favorite with bird banders as it can be easily trapped, and is common enough to increase one's banding record to imposing proportions. Some remarkable facts have been brought to light by the banding of White-throats. The bird breeds no nearer to South Carolina than Pennsylvania and New England, but individuals have been retaken in banding traps in the Low-country in the same part of the same yard where they were banded the year before. Extensive banding by William P. Wharton at Summerville has demonstrated this strong tendency to return to the same wintering grounds. Wharton trapped and banded 3,112 White-throats in twelve

PLATE XXXIII: BIRDS OF THE THICKET

Water Color by Roger Tory Peterson

Three top birds, left to right: White-throated Sparrow (male), White-throated Sparrow (female), and Song Sparrow. Right center: upper, Swamp Sparrow; lower, Red-eyed Towhee (male). Three lower birds, left to right: White-eyed Towhee (male), White-eyed Towhee (female), and Fox Sparrow.

Roger Tory Peterson

years and counted 570 returns to his station (counting a single bird each year it was retrapped). Three White-throats were retrapped six years after the original banding. The recovery of banded birds outside of Summerville was rare; only five were reported from elsewhere. Two of these were taken in Newfoundland, illustrating what is probably the chief migration route through the Atlantic States. Wharton's work was summarized in *Bird-Banding*, *12*: 1941, 137-147. Several other White-throats recovered in this State were originally banded in New England. One bird banded by R. E. Ware at Clemson was trapped and released at Oakes, North Dakota, in 1941, a year after it was banded.

The White-throat is well named, for the white mark on the throat is prominent and easily seen. The breast is without streakings, and the black and white stripes on the head, as well as the yellow in front of the eye, all make the bird unmistakable. It is a tame bird, and responds well to the "squeak." The rather tremulous whistled song is very characteristic and many know it, even if they do not recognize the singer. It has been interpreted as "Swee-e-t Canada, Canada," or sometimes "Pea-body-Pea-body." The call note too, is distinctive, a sharp "chink" together with a soft, lisping note. White-throats travel about in flocks, as well as singly. They are among the most attractive of winter birds.

FOOD: Largely seeds and wild fruits. Berries are a favorite, among which are those of the greenbrier, spice bush, blackberry, and dogwood. Ragweed and bindweed seeds amount to 25 per cent. Ragweed alone makes up 45 per cent of the total food in October. Insect diet includes beetles, ants, weevils, and wasps, with cottonboll weevils in high numbers.

EASTERN FOX SPARROW
434. *Passerella iliaca iliaca* (Merrem) (585)

(Lat., *Passerella*, a little sparrow; *iliaca*, pertaining to the flank.)

DESCRIPTION: Length 6.20 to 7.50 inches. Upper surface brownish gray, heavily streaked or otherwise marked with deep chestnut; exposed part of the tail chestnut; under parts white, heavily spotted with chestnut rufous on chest.

RANGE: Breeds north to northern Manitoba and northern Labrador; south to southern Massachusetts and Newfoundland. Winters north to eastern Nebraska and southern Maine (accidentally); south to Texas and northern Florida.

STATUS IN S. C.: Uncommon to abundant winter resident, November 1 to March 29, throughout the State. Reported north to Greenville, Chester, and Kershaw counties; east to Horry County; south to Jasper County; west to Aiken, Greenwood, and Oconee counties.

HISTORY: The Fox Sparrow is the most distinctive member of the entire family as far as identification goes; it is hardly to be confused with any other. It is one of the largest of the sparrows (about the size of the Hermit Thrush) and the name is indicative of the color, a rich, reddish brown.

It is a winter visitor to South Carolina and usually appears with rather severe weather; at least it is more numerous during cold waves. It ordinarily arrives in late November, but in some winters it is scarce and may not come until December. It usually remains until mid-March, although at Clemson G. E. Hudson noted it on March 29.

The Fox Sparrow is a woodland species, frequenting undergrowth and dense thickets. It stays close to the ground most of the time but ascends into trees and tangles of vines when disturbed. It is often found with White-throated Sparrows and Towhees, for it likes the same kind of cover which shelters them.

The Fox Sparrow is a handsome bird, bright rich brown, the neck gray, the sides and breast mottled with heavy streaks and spots, the tail a bright chestnut red. Though it is more shy and retiring than the White-throat, it is sometimes to be seen in great numbers in towns and cities during very cold weather. Many people will recall the "invasions" of these birds which parallel those of the Woodcock under similar conditions. Wayne vividly described one which took place in February, 1899, during one of the worst cold waves on record. He says that there was a tremendous migration of Fox Sparrows on the thirteenth and that "Thousands tarried in my yard all day long and swarmed in the piazza, fowl-yard, and every place that would afford protection. They would scratch away the snow in order to find a bare place, singing— that is the stronger birds—the whole time, while their companions were freezing by the hundreds." He found that when they were benumbed by the intense cold, Boat-tailed Grackles and Red-winged Blackbirds "would peck them at the base of the skull, killing them and eating them. The stronger Fox Sparrows would also eat their dead companions. It was a most pathetic sight."

There have been similar though smaller invasions of Charleston. A remarkable one occurred between January 13 and 18, 1912. Sprunt's notes for March, 1914, read: "Hundreds forced into the city by this cold wave. Scores seen along the Battery all day of the 14th." Astonished at the numbers of the birds, people attacked them with sticks and small boys had a field day. A smaller concentration was noted on January 25, 1922, during a sleet storm in Charleston.

FOOD: About 86 per cent vegetable matter—wild fruits (not cultivated ones), berries of the red cedar, holly, frost grapes, and pokeberries. About half the total is ragweed and bindweed seeds.

SWAMP SPARROW
435. *Melospiza georgiana georgiana* (Latham)   (584)

(Gr., *Melospiza*, a song finch; Lat., *georgiana*, of Georgia.)

DESCRIPTION: Length 4.80 to 6.00 inches. Crown chestnut, sometimes streaked with black, and with a gray median stripe; neck gray; back light brown, broadly streaked with dark brown, black, and white; rump olive brown; wings and tail dark brown; lower parts white, clouded with light gray on breast and with tawny brown on the flanks.

RANGE: Breeds north to Ontario and Newfoundland; south to southeastern Nebraska, central New Jersey, and Connecticut. Winters north to eastern Kansas and eastern Massachusetts; south to Texas and southern Florida.

STATUS IN S. C.: Common winter resident, September 28 to May 19, throughout most of the State. Reported north to Greenville, Spartanburg, and York counties; east to Horry County; south to Beaufort and Jasper counties; west to Aiken and Greenwood counties.

HISTORY: The Swamp Sparrow, one of the common sparrows that winter in South Carolina, is neither hard to find nor identify. It arrives in early October and remains until mid-May. Though common in migrations in the Piedmont, it is uncommon as a winter resident there, and it has not been recorded in the Clemson area.

The Swamp Sparrow is well named, for it frequents low, wet lands, but it is not necessarily found only in swamps. It is abundant in the rice fields, boggy meadows, cat-tail ponds, and willow thickets, and along the edges of streams. It comes readily to the "squeak," popping up from the grasses and reeds and swaying on the bending stems as it peers curiously at the intruder. The short call note is very easily learned and always serves to locate the bird. It sounds somewhat like that of the White-throat, but is markedly different from the Song Sparrow's.

It is a dark bird, rather stout-bodied with a clear, unstreaked breast and a heavily lined back. The adult has a chestnut crown in spring but this is not often apparent in winter. Color and habitat make the bird fairly easy to identify.

FOOD: About equally divided between animal and vegetable matter. It consumes grass seeds, and those of sedges and weeds, among which are ragweed and bindweed. The insect food includes caterpillars, grasshoppers, ants, and flies.

WESTERN SWAMP SPARROW
436. *Melospiza georgiana ericrypta* Oberholser (584a)

(Gr., *ericrypta*, much hidden.)

DESCRIPTION: Similar to the Swamp Sparrow but smaller, the upper parts lighter, brighter, less strongly rufescent (more grayish).

RANGE: Breeds north to central Alberta, central western Mackenzie, and northern Manitoba; south to North Dakota. Winters south to Mexico and Florida.

STATUS IN S. C.: Fairly common winter resident, October 28 to May 14, throughout the State. Recorded north and west to Anderson County; east to Horry and Charleston counties; south to Allendale County.

HISTORY: Judging from the specimens examined, the Western Swamp Sparrow, a recently described race, is not as numerous in South Carolina as is the more eastern form of the species. In the field it is not separable from the eastern race. Ten specimens identified by Dr. H. C. Oberholser are in the collections of the Charleston Museum, the United States National Museum, and in the private collection of E. von S. Dingle.

In habits and food this bird is not distinguishable from the Eastern Swamp Sparrow.

EASTERN SONG SPARROW
437. *Melospiza melodia melodia* (Wilson) (581)

(Lat., *melodia*, a melody.)

DESCRIPTION: Length 5.90 to 6.80 inches. Upper parts rufescent brown, the crown streaked with black, a narrow median stripe gray; back streaked with black and brownish gray; line over the eye olive gray; under parts white, heavily streaked on breast and sides with rufescent brown, tending to form a spot in the middle of the breast.

RANGE: Breeds north to southeastern Ontario and Newfoundland; south to Ohio and southern Virginia. Winters north to southeastern Ontario and southern Maine; south to Louisiana and southern Florida.

STATUS IN S. C.: Common winter resident, September 21 to April 23, throughout the State. Reported north to Greenville and York counties; east to Horry County; south to Beaufort and Jasper counties; west to Aiken, Anderson, and Oconee counties.

HISTORY: Winter is the season in which the Song Sparrow is common. It is abundant by early October and remains so until into March. It is particularly fond of low, wet lands where bushes grow in profusion, hedges, ditch banks, rice fields, cat-tail ponds, and the edges of woods. Often it is found with Swamp Sparrows and the two birds may respond to the "squeak" at the same time, from the same bush.

The thoroughly characteristic song is delivered throughout the winter except in very cold weather or on freezing days. The song is hard to translate; it starts with three clear notes, somewhat like "sweet-sweet-sweet," and ends in a series of bubbling whistles.

The Eastern Song Sparrow is easy to recognize. It is characterized by the distinctly reddish cast of the plumage, the heavily streaked breast where the markings merge into a large spot, and the fact that it pumps the rounded tail up and down as it flies. This is noticeable even when the bird travels only a few yards. The metallic call note is uttered frequently and has a harsh quality which is unmistakable when one learns it. There is no trouble in distinguishing this note from that of the Swamp Sparrow or the Yellow-throats with which the Song Sparrow associates. Even when it is unseen or impossible to flush from reeds and grasses, the "tchip" note will identify it. It comes to feeding stations readily.

On the basis of specimens examined, the Eastern Song Sparrow is found to be the most numerous of the races of the Song Sparrow in South Carolina. For this reason all the sight records of the species, except in the mountain area, are included under this race, notwithstanding the fact that some of them may belong to other subspecies. No one of the forms, however, is certainly distinguishable in the field.

FOOD: This sparrow's food has been critically studied in many parts of the country, with the result that vegetable matter has been found to compose 66 per cent and animal matter 34 per cent. The former is made up largely of seeds as follows; grass seed 24 per cent; bindweed 16 per cent; sunflower, clover, amaranth, dandelion, chickweed, and dock constitute the remainder. Insects are eaten such as grasshoppers, locusts, crickets, moths, ants, bees, bugs, and flies. It seems perfectly clear that the Song Sparrow is a valuable asset to agricultural interests.

ATLANTIC SONG SPARROW
438. *Melospiza melodia atlantica* Todd (581t)

(Lat., *atlantica*, of the Atlantic [Ocean].)

DESCRIPTION: Similar to the Eastern Song Sparrow but upper parts much more grayish; black spots above more distinct; the superciliary stripe more grayish (less buffy).

RANGE: Resident and breeds north to Rhode Island; south to North Carolina. South in winter to South Carolina.

STATUS IN S. C.: Uncommon winter resident, detected from January 25 to February 27, in the coastal region only. Traced north to Mt. Pleasant; south to Yemassee.

HISTORY: The Atlantic Song Sparrow may be of more frequent occurrence in South Carolina than is apparent, for in the field it is not with certainty to be distinguished from the other Song Sparrows. It is largely an inhabitant of salt and brackish marshes.

Specimens from South Carolina in the Charleston Museum, recently identified by Dr. H. C. Oberholser, are as follows: Mt. Pleasant, February 19, 21, 23, and 27, 1924, collected by Wayne; and Yemasee, January 25, 1936, by E. Milby Burton.

In general habits this bird does not materially differ from the Eastern Song Sparrow.

MISSISSIPPI SONG SPARROW
439. *Melospiza melodia euphonia* Wetmore (581u)

(Gr., *euphonia*, well-sounding.)

DESCRIPTION: Resembling the Eastern Song Sparrow, but upper surface darker, being grayer; the dark markings on the back more distinct.

RANGE: Breeds in the Allegheny Mountain region north to West Virginia; south to northern Georgia and northwestern South Carolina. Winters south to southern Georgia and Florida.

STATUS IN S. C.: Uncommon permanent resident of the mountain region of the northwestern part of the State, in Greenville, Pickens, and Oconee counties; and an uncommon winter resident, October 14 to February 25, in the remainder of the State. In its winter range recorded north to Kershaw and Marlboro counties; east to Mt. Pleasant; south to Seabrook's Beach, Charleston County.

HISTORY: The Mississippi is the only race of the Song Sparrow that breeds in South Carolina. It seems to be slightly increasing in numbers since it was first found breeding in 1931 by Thomas D. Burleigh. On May 25 of that year he saw a pair of adults feeding young just out of the nest at Saluda Gap, Greenville County, at an elevation of about 1800 feet, within a few miles of the North Carolina line (*Auk, 50*: 1933, 226).*

A. L. Pickens called it "common in summer in the lower mountains" (*Auk, 51*: 1934, 537)* but G. E. Hudson and Franklin Sherman in spite of a special search did not find it about Clemson as a breeder. Hudson saw a singing male on July 3, 1934, at Attakula Lodge, Jocassee, Oconee County, but this was the only bird found "during several weeks of intensive field work in the summer of 1934" (*Auk, 53*: 1936, 315).* Two were taken near Marietta, Greenville County, on July 19, 1940, by W. M. Perrygo and J. S. Y. Hoyt.

The nest is constructed of coarse grasses, leaves, and rootlets. There are four or five bluish white eggs, generously marked with rufous brown. They average 19.3 x

---

* Recorded as the Eastern Song Sparrow (*Melospiza m. melodia*).

15.2 millimeters, and incubation takes from ten to fourteen days. Three broods may be raised.

Specimens examined by Dr. H. C. Oberholser where taken 14 miles northwest of Bennettsville, October 14, 1940, by Perrygo and J. S. Webb; Kershaw County, January 8, 1904, by N. C. Brown; Seabrook's Beach, December 21, 1932, by Chamberlain; Mt. Pleasant, February 25, 1924, by Wayne; and Marietta, Greenville County, July 19, 1940, by Perrygo and Hoyt.

No difference in habits is evident between this race and the Eastern Song Sparrow.

LAPLAND LONGSPUR
440. *Calcarius lapponicus lapponicus* (Linnaeus) (536)

(Lat., *Calcarius*, spurred; *lapponicus*, of Lapland.)

DESCRIPTION: Length 5.50 to 7.00 inches. Claw of hind toe very long. *Male.* Head chestnut; hind neck deep chestnut; remainder of upper parts streaked with black and grayish brown; a stripe behind the eye to the side of the chest, white or buff; wings with two white wing bars; outer tail feathers mostly white; crown, lower throat, and patch on breast, black; rest of lower surface white, the sides streaked with black. *Female.* Similar to the male but duller; black only on crown; parts of sides of head, patch on throat, and chestnut of hind neck obscured.

RANGE: Breeds north to northern Mackenzie and central Greenland; south to central southern Mackenzie and northern Labrador. Winters north to South Dakota and southern Quebec; south to Texas, Louisiana, and South Carolina.

STATUS IN S. C.: Casual winter visitor in the eastern half of the State. Known north to Chester County; south to Jasper County.

HISTORY: The presence of the Lapland Longspur in South Carolina is accidental, and forms an illustration of sporadic, extralimital wandering. Even in winter, it very rarely appears anywhere in the southern United States. It was added to the State List on January 1, 1881, at Chester, by Leverett M. Loomis, who secured one specimen (*Auk*, 2: 1885, 190).

This was the sole record for forty-six years. Then, in the spring of 1935, a male was taken on April 20 by Ivan R. Tomkins, on Long Island Fill at the Savannah River entrance, Jasper County (*Auk*, 52: 1935, 315). The specimen is now in the Charleston Museum (No. 40.65.227). About a month before, Tomkins had taken one, and seen another of these birds on Oysterbed Island in the Savannah River on the Georgia side, very close to Long Island Fill.

Longspurs are small, sparrow-like birds with dark wings. They frequent open fields or beaches and like the Horned Lark with which they associate they walk rather than hop. The name arises from the presence of a very long spur on the hind toe. Only severe cold forces them south, and the presence in April of the specimen secured by Tomkins is remarkable.

441. SMITH'S LONGSPUR: *Calcarius pictus* (Swainson) (537)

(Lat., *pictus*, painted.)

DESCRIPTION: Length 5.50 to 6.50 inches. Claw of hind toe very long. *Male*. Top and sides of head black; a broad white stripe behind the eye; hind neck and lower parts ochraceous buff, the former streaked with dark brown; remainder of upper parts light brown streaked with dark brown; a white bar on the wing; and outer tail feathers largely white. *Female*. Similar to the male but without black areas, these replaced by brown streaked with buff; no pure white on wing coverts.

RANGE: Breeds north to northwestern Mackenzie; south to northern Manitoba. Winters north to Canada; south to Texas and South Carolina (accidentally).

STATUS IN S. C.: Accidental.

HISTORY: The history of Smith's Longspur in South Carolina closely parallels that of the Lapland Longspur. There are only two records of its occurrence and in both instances the bird was secured. It was Leverett M. Loomis who added the species to the State List, just as he did the Lapland Longspur. The first specimen he secured on December 1, 1880, at Chester (*Bull. Nutt. Orn. Club*, *6*: 1881, 115). The second was a female which he shot on February 9, 1889 (*Auk*, *8*: 1891, 167). The latter specimen is in the collection of the American Museum of Natural History (No. 56124).

Smith's Longspur is a buff-colored bird, the entire under parts being of this color. With others of its family it frequents open, wind-swept fields. It is likely to be found in company with Horned Larks and Snow Buntings in its winter range in the northern United States, though in the Central States it apparently penetrates more deeply southward than do the others.

EASTERN SNOW BUNTING
442. *Plectrophenax nivalis nivalis* (Linnaeus) (534)

(Gr., *Plectrophenax*, a spurred imposter; Lat., *nivalis*, snowy.)

DESCRIPTION: Length 6.00 to 7.25 inches. *Male in summer*. Chiefly pure white, but back, scapulars, most of wing feathers, and nearly all but two outer tail feathers on each side, black; bill and feet black. *Female in summer*. Crown brown edged with white or buff; back brownish black, margined with dull white; much of wing and tail black, as well as the under parts. *Male and female in winter*. Similar to birds in summer plumage, but the darker areas obscured by light buff; the light areas much clouded by the same.

RANGE: Breeds north to northern Alaska, northern Greenland, northern Norway, and the coast of northern Siberia; south to central western Alaska, northern Labrador, southern Sweden, and northern Siberia. Winters north to northern Alaska, northern Labrador, Norway, and northern Siberia; south to northern California, Florida, northern Africa, and the Mediterranean Sea.

STATUS IN S. C.: Casual winter visitor, November 4 to June 25, on the coast.

HISTORY: This far northern species is a casual wanderer to South Carolina. It was not until 1926 that it was added to the State List. Sprunt established the record. On

November 14 of that year, he saw one of these birds on the roadside about 15 miles north of Mt. Pleasant, Charleston County. He had no means of collecting it at the time, but he returned to the spot the following day (the fifteenth), accompanied by Mrs. Sprunt and Chamberlain, flushed the bird in exactly the same place, and secured it. It is now in the Charleston Museum collection (*Auk, 44*: 1927, 107).

Since that time there have been three additional records. On November 12, 1930, H. R. Sass saw three in Charleston. Eight more were seen on Morris Island, at the mouth of Charleston Harbor, on December 21, 1930, by A. B. Mikell and Edward Manigault; two of these were collected (*Auk, 48*: 1931, 275). On June 21, 1937, a most extraordinary date, E. von S. Dingle and his wife saw a male in summer plumage at the north end of Sullivan's Island, Charleston County. This bird was again seen and heard singing on June 25 by Dingle, G. Robert Lunz, Jr., Chamberlain, and E. B. Chamberlain, Jr. Recognizable photographs were secured by Lunz (*Auk, 55*: 1938, 547).

These records constitute the history of this boreal bird in South Carolina but it may, of course, occur in the future in severe winters and should be watched for. Its presence here in June is exceptional.

The food of the Snow Bunting consists almost entirely of seeds.

PLATE XXXIV: SPARROWS ON BEACH IN WINTER

Water Color by Edward von S. Dingle

Top, right: Macgillivray's Seaside Sparrow. Bottom, left to right: Ipswich Sparrow, Eastern Savannah Sparrow, Sharp-tailed Sparrow, and Macgillivray's Seaside Sparrow.

Hypothetical List

T HE remarkable increase in bird students all over the country, the high efficiency
attained in field identification by many, and the special aids now available that
were unknown a quarter century ago, have combined to make the "sight record"
far more valuable now than it was in the past. Nonetheless, it is inevitable that
there should be some records in the ornithological history of any state concerning
which there is an element of doubt, making desirable their inclusion in a hypothetical
list.

The following species have been recorded as birds of South Carolina. They fall
into three categories: (1) birds that for one reason or another are of doubtful occurrence in the State; (2) escaped cage birds; and (3) introduced birds which have
not yet become naturalized. In each case it has seemed desirable to explain their
exclusion from the main catalogue of birds of the State.

PACIFIC LOON: *Gavia arctica pacifica* (Lawrence)   (10)

Audubon has the following note on the Pacific Loon: "I well recollect that while I was
standing near the shore of a large inlet in South Carolina, one of these birds, being shot
while passing over my head at full speed, did not, on account of the impetus, reach the
ground until upwards of twenty yards beyond me" (*Birds of America*, 7: 1844, 296).

Wayne's comment is that "Audubon was unquestionably mistaken in the identification of
the bird shot . . . the bird he refers to was evidently a young Loon (*G. immer*), or a young
Red-throated Loon (*G. stellata*)." Wayne's statement is very positive, but it is probably
correct. The Black-throated Loon, as it was then called, is a bird of the Pacific Coast,
whereas the loons which occur in winter in South Carolina are the Common, Lesser, and
Red-throated Loons. Though accidental wanderers sometimes appear in strange places, the
casual appearances of the Pacific Loon in Eastern North America are limited to but two
instances, one in New Hampshire, the other on Long Island, N. Y.

Audubon's record, then, is very doubtful and the status of the Pacific Loon in South
Carolina is highly questionable. The bird has never been reported for South Carolina since
Audubon's day.

WHITE-FACED GLOSSY IBIS: *Plegadis mexicana* (Gmelin) (187)

In 1910 Wayne included the White-faced Glossy Ibis in his Hypothetical List because, he said, of the questionable record of Elliott Coues, who listed it as a summer resident (*Proc. Bost. Soc. Nat. Hist.*, *12*: 1868, 123). Wayne added that Coues had no definite reason for its inclusion. There has been no record of it since. The White-faced Glossy Ibis is western in distribution and normally comes no nearer to South Carolina than western Louisiana. However, Wayne apparently erred in assigning this record to this species because Coues listed it as "*Ibis Ordii*. Glossy Ibis" (= *Plegadis f. falcinellus*, the Eastern Glossy Ibis), which has been found in recent years along the coast of South Carolina.

TRUMPETER SWAN: *Cygnus buccinator* Richardson (181)

This swan was included as a bird of South Carolina by Lewis R. Gibbes in his *Catalogue of the Fauna of South Carolina* published as an appendix to Tuomey's *Report on the Geology of South Carolina*, 1848. Gibbes based his statement on a swan killed by Colonel Ferguson, probably on the Cooper River. There is, however, no certainty that this specimen was correctly identified.

Another specimen of a swan was recorded by Sprunt and Chamberlain (*Supplement to the Birds of South Carolina*, 1931) as a Trumpeter Swan, but further study has revealed it to be a Mute Swan. It is discussed under its proper heading in the present work.

WHITE-FRONTED GOOSE: *Anser albifrons albifrons* (Scopoli) (171)

Geese believed to be of this race were recorded for South Carolina in Sprunt and Chamberlain's *Supplement to the Birds of South Carolina* (1931). In the preparation of the present work there has been only one specimen from South Carolina of this species available for examination. It proved to belong to the newly described Greenland subspecies, *Anser albifrons flavirostris*. In consequence, all the South Carolina records have been entered under that race, although of course some of them may apply to the present form.

TULE GOOSE: *Anser albifrons gambelli* Hartlaub (171a)

What has been said concerning the White-fronted Goose (*Anser albifrons albifrons*) applies equally to the Tule Goose, except that the Tule Goose was first accredited to the State by Wayne, in his *Birds of South Carolina*, 1910, 205.

EASTERN GOSHAWK: *Accipiter gentilis atricapillus* (Wilson) (334)

Although Wayne did not include the Eastern Goshawk even in his Hypothetical List, it is inserted here because of his statement regarding it, contained in the account of Cooper's Hawk (*Accipiter cooperii*) in his *Birds of South Carolina*, 1910, 73. He says that Dr. Robert Wilson recorded a specimen of the Goshawk seen by him near Bull's Bay, November 3, 1905.

The specimen was not secured and it is obvious that Wayne considered it an instance of mistaken identity. Certainly Dr. Wilson's observation needs additional confirmation, for, as Wayne remarks, "large immature females [of the Cooper's Hawk] have been mistaken for the American Goshawk (*Astur atricapillus*) in its immature plumage." The Eastern Goshawk, which is a far northern bird of prey, has never been secured in either of the Carolinas and appears in Virginia only on very rare occasions during severe winter weather.

HYPOTHETICAL LIST

TEXAS BOBWHITE: *Colinus virginianus texanus* (Lawrence)   (289b)

A few years ago many Texas Bobwhite or "Mexican Quail" were imported by several plantation owners in the Low-country. "However, all evidence seems to indicate that it does not do well outside of its normal range and, although it may interbreed with the native bob-whites in the region where it is introduced, its characters are completely lost in a relatively few years" (Aldrich, *Auk, 63*: 1946, 505).

No evidence has been found of its having established itself in South Carolina.

RING-NECKED PHEASANT: *Phasianus colchicus torquatus* Gmelin   (309.1)

Although the Ring-necked Pheasant is not a native American bird, it is so well established in many parts of the United States that it has become commonplace, like the Starling, and can no longer properly be regarded as a foreigner. It has never flourished in the South, however, and probably never will, except possibly in the mountain regions. Too many things militate against it: the climate of the South is generally unsuitable, and predators to which it is unaccustomed destroy it more rapidly than it can breed. Thus far, every attempt to introduce it locally has failed.

The only reason for including the Ring-necked Pheasant among the birds of South Carolina is that attempts have been made to introduce it as a game bird. How unsuccessful these attempts have been is reflected in a statement from the State Game and Fish Department (1948): the introduction of the Ring-neck into the State has been "thoroughly tried out . . . they did not do well in any section . . . and seemed to disappear within three years." The statement is supported by the experience of plantation owners. Several years ago, for example, Coulter D. Huyler and Sumner Simpson liberated several birds on Dewees Island and Wadmalaw Island respectively, but all their birds vanished in a very short time.

It seems evident that South Carolina is not adapted to the living requirements of the Ring-necked Pheasant, though why the bird should not survive and increase in the northern counties of the State is not entirely clear. Since it has not become an integral part of South Carolina fauna, it is better placed on the Hypothetical List.

EUROPEAN TURNSTONE: *Arenaria interpres interpres* (Linnaeus)   (283)

Wayne recorded a bird taken on May 30, 1918, at Dewees Island, South Carolina, as the European Turnstone (*Auk, 35*: 1918, 439). Examination of this specimen by Dr. Alexander Wetmore and others proves it to be an example of the common Ruddy Turnstone of North America. Therefore the European Turnstone was removed from the State List by Chamberlain (*Auk, 53*: 1936, 441).

CURLEW SANDPIPER: *Erolia ferruginea* (Pontoppidan)   (244)

The Curlew Sandpiper, which is an Old World species, is accredited to South Carolina by Dr. Elliott Coues on the authority of Lewis R. Gibbes (*Proc. Bost. Soc. Nat. Hist., 12*: 1868, 122). Gibbes doubtless attributed the Curlew Sandpiper to the State on the strength of Audubon's statement that "my friend JOHN BACHMAN has one or two in his possession" (*Birds Amer., 5*: 1842, 269). Audubon does not say that the birds were taken in the State. That Dr. Bachman simply had the birds means little or nothing, and the chance that they were local specimens seems remote. The Curlew Sandpiper has never been taken anywhere in the southern part of the United States, though it has been found in other parts of North America.

ATLANTIC PUFFIN: *Fratercula arctica arctica* (Linnaeus)   (13)

The propriety of including the Atlantic Puffin on the South Carolina list is open to question. Audubon, in his *Birds of America* (7: 1844, 238) says; "The Sea Parrot, as this bird is usually called on the eastern coasts of the United States . . . sometimes proceeds as far south as the entrance of the river Savannah in Georgia, where I saw a good number in the winter of 1831-32."

Wayne (1910) in commenting on this statement says, "If the birds Audubon saw were really Puffins it is the most southern record for the species and the only one for either South Carolina or Georgia. . . . This record, however, is extremely doubtful and unsatisfactory, as the Puffin is rare in winter as far south as New Jersey."

No South Carolina record of the Atlantic Puffin has since been made.

LITTLE FLYCATCHER: *Empidonax traillii brewsteri* Oberholser   (466)

A specimen of this western race was recorded under the former name, *Empidonax trailli trailli*, by Wayne (*Auk, 30*: 1913, 274). He collected the specimen near Mt. Pleasant, Charleston County, on September 14, 1900. It now proves to be an example of the eastern form of the species, the Alder Flycatcher; therefore, the Little Flycatcher is no longer properly accredited to South Carolina.

COMMON ROCK WREN: *Salpinctes obsoletus obsoletus* (Say)   (715)

This western bird, which was credited to South Carolina by Audubon, has never been observed here since his day, if, indeed, it was then. Audubon did not see it himself, but says that "No other person has observed the Rocky Mountain Wren in any part of the country eastward of that great chain besides Dr. [John] BACHMAN, who shot one within a few miles of Charleston" (*Birds Amer., 2*: 1841, 70).

Wayne (1910) remarks that Dr. Bachman's account of the wrens he encountered in South Carolina is "considerably confused." He adds the reasonable conclusion that the identity of Bachman's specimen in this case "is open to question, as no second example has ever been taken in the State, and he doubtless confused it with the House Wren (*Troglodytes aëdon*)."

Though Wayne himself took specimens of western birds which have not since been seen in South Carolina, his statement concerning the Rock Wren is valid enough, not only because of the vast territory which lies between South Carolina and the normal range of the Rock Wren, but because of its similarity to the House Wren, which must have misled the usually accurate and astute Bachman. It is certainly safe to say that the status of the bird in this State is still "open to question."

EASTERN WARBLING VIREO: *Vireo gilvus gilvus* (Vieillot)   (627)

This is another of Dr. Elliott Coues' birds which no one else has ever seen or taken in South Carolina. Coues stated that the bird is not abundant and that it is migratory in April and October (*Proc. Bost. Soc. Nat. Hist., 12*: 1868, 111). Such an assertion certainly needs substantiation, for South Carolina seems to be out of the normal range of the species. However, it breeds in the mountains of North Carolina and has been observed as far east as Rocky Mount in that state (*Birds of North Carolina*, 1942, 292).

NORTHERN SEASIDE SPARROW: *Ammospiza maritima maritima* (Wilson)   (550)

This species, which is the northeastern form of the Seaside Sparrow, has been commonly attributed to South Carolina. However, it cannot be identified with certainty outside the limits of its breeding range. It seems better to treat it here as hypothetical until a banded specimen of unquestionable origin is collected in the State.

EASTERN TREE SPARROW: *Spizella arborea arborea* (Wilson) (559)

Dr. Elliott Coues was the observer responsible for the inclusion of the Eastern Tree Sparrow among the birds of South Carolina (*Proc. Bost. Soc. Nat. Hist.*, *12*: 1868, 115). Coues worked near Columbia as an army surgeon and at the time had had little experience with birds of the State. He simply says of it that it is not common and that it winters from November to March. Despite the very careful work of Leverett M. Loomis in northern South Carolina for fourteen years, and of Wayne on the coast, neither ever saw the bird in the State, and there are no definite contemporary records. The Tree Sparrow is rare in North Carolina, hardly more than an accidental visitor in the high Blue Ridge Mountains of that state in winter.

TROUPIAL: *Icterus icterus* (Linnaeus) (502)

The occurrence of this tropical species in North America is based on but two reported instances, one at Santa Barbara, California (*Condor*, *13*: 1911, 109), and the other at Charleston, the latter recorded by Audubon (*Birds of America*, 7: 1844, 357). Audubon wrote,

> This handsome bird was first observed at Charleston, South Carolina, by my son JOHN WOODHOUSE, who shot and figured a male the size of nature; the bird when first seen was perched on the point of a lightning-rod close by the house of my friend the Reverend JOHN BACHMAN, D.D. A few days afterwards others were seen, but although a female was shot, it fell in the river and was lost. I am informed that since that period, small groups of four or half a dozen make their appearance in the same city, and on the neighbouring islands.

Though there is no doubt concerning this actual record, the 1931 Edition of the A. O. U. Check-List places the Troupial on the North American Hypothetical List with the observation that both the California and South Carolina records were probably cage-birds; and the species is therefore here relegated to the South Carolina Hypothetical List.

There is no other instance of its occurrence either in the United States or in Mexico.

ADDENDA

The following observations and records, which were received too late for inclusion under their proper headings, are of sufficient importance to stand as addenda to the otherwise completed work:

EASTERN SOOTY TERN: *Sterna fuscata fuscata*

Following the tropical storm of August 26-28, 1949, a number of semi-tropical birds appeared near Charleston. Among them were a Sooty Tern seen by Mrs. Francis Barrington over the Stono River on August 28; two decomposed Sooties found on Folly Island by J. E. Mosimann, G. B. Rabb, T. M. Uzzell, Jr., and R. M. Barnett, Jr., on August 30; and another dead specimen picked up by E. von S. Dingle at Sullivan's Island on September 4. These records represent the ninth known occurrence of the Sooty in the State. Two Man-o'-war Birds were also seen during this period by Mrs. Barrington, Mosimann, Rabb, Uzzell, and Barnett.

NODDY TERN: *Anoüs stolidus stolidus*

The tropical storm of August 26-28, 1949, carried up at least one Noddy Tern from Florida to the Charleston region. One bird was seen at the Isle of Palms on August 28 by G. B. Rabb, J. E. Mosimann, and T. M. Uzzell, Jr. The winds at the time were at a velocity of about 40 miles an hour.

This is the fifth record of the species for South Carolina.

YELLOW-BILLED CUCKOO: *Coccyzus americanus americanus*

Wayne (1910) wrote that the Yellow-billed Cuckoo lays a set of eggs as late as August for the second incubation period of the season. The record of an even later date was established on September 5, 1949, at the site of the battle of Eutaw Springs, in Orangeburg County, when a number of observers from the Charleston Museum (G. B. Rabb, J. E. Mosimann, T. M. Uzzell, Jr., and E. M. Burton) saw a Yellow-billed Cuckoo fly to a nest, line it with a quantity of Spanish moss, and settle down, presumably to begin incubating. The nest was placed toward the end of a limb of a cedar tree and was about 35 feet from the ground. The bird remained on the nest during the half hour in which it was under observation.

EASTERN WHIP-POOR-WILL: *Caprimulgus vociferus vociferus*

Albert E. Hyder, Project Leader of the Francis Marion Turkey Project, and Frederick J. Ruff, Wildlife Biologist of the U. S. Forest Service, while making an inspection trip in the Francis Marion National Forest on September 2, 1949, heard a Whip-poor-will call several times. It is unusual to hear the call of the Whip-poor-will at any time in the Low-country. There is, however, no mistaking the Whip-poor-will's call for that of the Chuck-will's-widow. E. von S. Dingle heard it calling on August 27, 1945, at Middleburg, Berkeley County. The distance between the two places where the birds were heard is not great. It is quite possible that the birds were on their southern migration.

ADDENDA

KIRTLAND'S WARBLER: *Dendroica kirtlandii*

On October 14, 1949, Mrs. W. H. Faver saw a Kirtland's Warbler at her home near Eastover, Richland County. The bird was seen under excellent light conditions, with and without binoculars, and was observed at a distance of not over 40 feet. This constitutes the fourth fall record for the Kirtland's Warbler in South Carolina.

443. COMMON REDPOLL: *Acanthis flammea flammea* (Linnaeus) (528)

RANGE: Breeds north to northwestern Alaska and northern Quebec; south to northern Alberta and the Gulf of St. Lawrence. Winters irregularly south to northeastern California, Alabama, and South Carolina; also over the greater part of Europe and south to central Asia.

HISTORY: The Editor feels that the Common Redpoll should be included in the State List because of a record made by Walter J. Hoxie at Beaufort on February 23, 1901. He saw a single specimen near the gate of the Navy Yard at Beaufort on that date and again on the following day (*Wilson Bull., New Series, 8:* 1901, 36). Hoxie was familiar with the Redpoll in his youth in Massachusetts; moreover, he kept one in a cage for nearly a year and made extensive notes on its moults (Hoxie, ms. in the Charleston Museum). Hoxie attributed the bird's presence to cold weather during the previous week, when snow had fallen in Beaufort, a very rare occurrence there. There seems to have been no Weather Bureau in Beaufort at that time, but the records of the Charleston Weather Bureau show that 1-1/10 inches of snow fell on February 23, 1901, in Charleston.

The 1931 A. O. U. Check-List recognizes this record in delineating the winter range of the Common Redpoll.

LITERATURE CITED *

ALDRICH, JOHN WARREN
    1946. The United States Races of the Bob-white. Auk, 63: 493-508.
AMERICAN ORNITHOLOGISTS' UNION
    1931. Check-List of North American Birds, Fourth Edition. Lancaster, Pa.
ANONYMOUS
    1684. Carolina Described more fully than Heretofore. Dublin.
    1818. [Flamingo]. Charleston Courier, July 20.
    1822. [Roseate Spoonbill]. Charleston Courier, October 1.
    1824. [Man-o'-War Bird]. Charleston Courier, September 24.
ASHE, THOMAS
    1682. Carolina; or a Description of the Present State of that Country. London.
AUDUBON, JOHN JAMES
    1831. Ornithological Biography, 1. Philadelphia.
    1838. Ornithological Biography, 4. Edinburgh.
    1840-44. The Birds of America, 1-7. New York and Philadelphia.
BACHMAN, JOHN
    1834. An account of some experiments made on the habits of Vultures inhabiting Carolina, the Turkey Buzzard and the Carrion Crow. Charleston.
    1840. Unpublished letter in collection of the Charleston Museum. [White-tailed Kite]. March 9.
BALDWIN, WILLIAM PLEWS, JR.
    1946. Clam catches oyster-catcher. Auk, 63: 589.
BANGS, OUTRAM
    1918. A New Race of the Black-throated Green Wood Warbler. Proc. New Eng. Zoöl. Club, 6: 93-94.
BAYNARD, OSCAR EDWARD
    1912. Food of Herons and Ibises. Wilson Bull., 24: 167-169.
BEAL, FOSTER ELLENBOROUGH LASCELLES
    1911. Food of the Woodpeckers of the United States, U. S. Dept. Agri. Bull. 37.
    1915. Food of the Robins and Bluebirds of the United States. U. S. Dept. Agri. Bull. 171.
BENDIRE, CHARLES EMIL
    1895. Life Histories of North American Birds. U. S. Nat. Mus. Spec. Bull. 3. [Chuck-will's-widow].
BENT, ARTHUR CLEVELAND
    1922. Life Histories of North American Petrels and Pelicans and their Allies. U. S. Nat. Mus. Bull. 121.
    1927. Life Histories of North American Shore Birds. Part 1. U. S. Nat. Mus. Bull. 142.
    1929. Life Histories of North American Shore Birds. Part 2. U. S. Nat. Mus. Bull. 146.
    1937. Life Histories of North American Birds of Prey. Part 1. U. S. Nat. Mus. Bull. 167.
    1938. Life Histories of North American Birds of Prey. Part 2. U. S. Nat. Mus. Bull. 170.
    1940. Life Histories of North American Cuckoos, Goatsuckers, Hummingbirds and their Allies. U. S. Nat. Mus. Bull. 176.

---

* Only literature actually cited in the text is included in this listing. In each instance the form of the original, including italicization, is preserved.

1942. Life Histories of North American Flycatchers, Larks, Swallows, and their Allies. U. S. Nat. Mus. Bull. 179.

BOWDISH, BEECHER SCOVILLE, and PHILIPP, PHILIP BERNARD
1910. Bird Photographing in the Carolinas. With an Annotated List of the Birds Observed. Auk, 27: 305-322.

BOWLES, JOHN HOOPER
1911. The Troupial in California. Condor, 13: 109.

BREWSTER, WILLIAM
1883. The Common Cormorant on the Coast of South Carolina. Bull. Nutt. Orn. Club, 8: 186.
1885. Swainson's Warbler. Auk, 2: 65-80.
1885. Additional Notes on the Nest and Eggs of Swainson's Warbler (*Helinaia swainsoni*). Auk, 2: 346.
1885. The Nest and Eggs of Swainson's Warbler. Forest and Stream, 24: 468.
1886. The Bridled Tern (*Sterna anaethetus*) in South Carolina. Auk, 3: 131.
1886. Ammodramus lecontei near Charleston, South Carolina. Auk, 3: 410.
1905. Notes on the Breeding of Bachman's Warbler, *Helminthophila bachmanii* (Aud.), near Charleston, South Carolina, with a Description of the First Plumage of the Species. Auk, 22: 392-394.

BRIMLEY, HERBERT HUTCHINSON, PEARSON, T. G., and BRIMLEY, C. S. See Pearson, Brimley, C. S., and Brimley, H. H.

BRIMLEY, C. S. and GREY, J. H., JR. See Grey and Brimley, C. S.

BRIMLEY, CLEMENT SAMUEL, PEARSON, T. G., and BRIMLEY, H. H. See Pearson, Brimley, C. S., and Brimley, H. H.

BROLEY, CHARLES
1947. Migration and Nesting of Florida Bald Eagles. Wilson Bull., 59: 3-20.

BROUN, MAURICE
1943. A Longevity-Recovery Record of a Slate-colored Junco. Bird-Banding, 14: 46.

BROWN, JOHN WILCOX
1932. Lesser Snow Goose in South Carolina. Auk, 49: 343.
1932. The Snowy Owl in South Carolina. Auk, 49: 351.

BROWN, NATHAN CLIFFORD
1906. A Ruffed Grouse near Camden, South Carolina. Auk, 23: 336.
1909. Note on the Red Crossbill and the Pine Finch in South Carolina. Auk, 26: 432.

BULL, CHARLES LIVINGSTONE, and SASS, HERBERT RAVENEL
1926. Blue Goose (Chen caerulescens) in South Carolina. Auk, 43: 228.

BURLEIGH, THOMAS DEARBORN
1933. The Song Sparrow Now a Breeding Bird in South Carolina. Auk, 50: 226.
1935. The Pine-woods Sparrow a Breeding Bird in South Carolina. Auk, 52: 194.
1941. Bird Life on Mt. Mitchell. Auk, 58: 334-345.

BURLEIGH, T. D., and PETERS, H. S.
1948. Geographic Variation in Newfoundland Birds. Proc. Biol. Soc. Wash., 61: 111-126.

BURNETT, W. I.
1851. Notes on the Fauna of the Pine Barrens of upper South Carolina. Proc. Bost. Soc. Nat. Hist., 4: 115-118.

CAMAK, T. C. and WYLIE, H. S. See Wylie and Camak.

CANNON, GABRIEL. See Grey, J. H., Jr., and Brimley, C. S.

CATESBY, MARK
1731. The Natural History of Carolina, Florida and the Bahama Islands, 1. London.
1748. The Natural History of Carolina, Florida and the Bahama Islands, Appendix (in volume 2). London.

CHAMBERLAIN, BARNWELL RHETT
    1911. Breeding of the Barn Owl. Auk, 28: 112-113.

CHAMBERLAIN, EDWARD BURNHAM
    1911. Wilson's Phalarope, A New Species for South Carolina. Auk, 28: 109.
    1925. The Brant (Branta bernicla glaucogastra) at Charleston, S. C. Auk, 42: 265.
    1933. Bridled Tern in South Carolina. Auk, 50: 104-105.
    1936. Western Grebe in South Carolina. Auk, 53: 438.
    1936. European Turnstone, A Correction. Auk: 53: 441.

CHAMBERLAIN, E. B., and E. VON S. DINGLE. See Dingle and Chamberlain.

CHAMBERLAIN, E. B., and SPRUNT, A., JR. See Sprunt and Chamberlain.

CHAPMAN, FRANK MICHLER
    1895. Handbook of Birds of Eastern North America. 1st Ed. New York.
    1900. The Season's Flight of Crossbills. Bird-Lore, 2: 25-26.
    1932. Handbook of Birds of Eastern North America. 2nd Ed. New York.

CHISOLM, CASPAR S.
    1911. American Merganser in South Carolina. Auk, 28: 254.

COOKE, MAY THACHER
    1938. Returns of Banded Birds: Recoveries of Banded Marsh Birds. Bird-Banding, 9: 80-87.
    1941. Returns from Banded Birds: Recoveries of Some Banded Birds of Prey. Bird-Banding, 12: 151-160.
    1942. Returns from Banded Birds: Some Longevity Records of Wild Birds. Bird-Banding, 13: 34-37.

COOKE, WELLS WOODBRIDGE
    1904. Distribution and Migration of North American Warblers. U. S. Dept. Agri. Biol. Surv. Bull. No. 18 [W. J. Hoxie's Prairie Warbler records.]

COUES, ELLIOTT
    1868. Synopsis of the Birds of South Carolina. Proc. Bost. Soc. Nat. Hist., 12: 104-127.
    1874. Birds of the Northwest. U. S. Geol. Surv. Terr., Misc. Pub. No. 3.
    1897. Uria lomvia in South Carolina. Auk, 14: 203.
    1903. Key to North American Birds, 2 vols. Boston.

DALGETY, CHRISTOPHER T., and SCOTT, P. M.
    1948. A New Race of the Whitefronted Goose. Bull. Brit. Orn. Club, 68: 109-121.

DAVIS, HENRY EDWARDS
    1949. The American Wild Turkey. Georgetown, S. C.

DAWSON, CHARLES F.
    1941. Transmission of Hog Cholera by Buzzards. Florida State Board of Health, 26th Annual Report: 204-206.

DINGLE, EDWARD VON SIEBOLD
    1921. The Kentucky Warbler in Clarendon County, South Carolina. Auk, 38: 607-608.
    1922. Peculiar Note of Carolina Chickadee. Auk, 39: 572-573.
    1926. Red-cockaded Woodpeckers in Cornfields. Bird-Lore, 28: 124-125.
    1927. Sooty Tern (Sterna fuscata) and Bridled Tern (Sterna anaetheta) on the South Carolina coast. Auk, 44: 93-94.
    1928. Glossy Ibis (Plegadis falcinellus) in South Carolina. Auk, 45: 499.
    1930. Clay-colored Sparrow (Spizella pallida) in South Carolina. Auk, 47: 257.
    1938. Eastern Snow Bunting in South Carolina in summer. Auk, 55: 547.
    1948. Food of the Anhinga. Unpublished ms.
    1948. Chuck-will's-widow Calls. Unpublished ms.

DINGLE, E. VON S., and CHAMBERLAIN, E. B.
    1941. Cory's Shearwater in South Carolina. Auk, 58: 251.

DINGLE, E. VON S., and SPRUNT, A., JR.
    1932. A New Marsh Wren from North Carolina. Auk, 49: 454-455.

LITERATURE CITED

DRAYTON, JOHN
   1802. A View of South Carolina. Charleston, S. C.

DUMONT, PHILIP ATKINSON
   1929. Wilson's Phalarope and Baird's Sandpiper in South Carolina. Auk, 46: 539-540.

EIFRIG, CHARLES WILLIAM GUSTAVE
   1948. Wing-flashing of the Mockingbird Once More. Florida Naturalist, 21: 75-76.

ELLIOTT, WILLIAM
   1846. Carolina Sports by Land and Water. Columbia.

FARGO, WILLIAM GILBERT
   1934. Walter John Hoxie. Wilson Bull., 46: 169-196.

FORBUSH, EDWARD HOWE
   1907. Useful birds and their protection, 2nd Ed. Boston.

FORD, LOUISE PETTIGRU, and PELLEW, M. J. See Pellew and Ford.

GARVEY, FREDERICK KESLER
   1946. The Dovekie at Myrtle Beach, N. C. [sic, S. C.] Chat, 10: 38.

GEE, NATHANIEL GIST
   1936. South Carolina Vertebrate Fauna, Greenwood Birds. Printed sheets, pub. by Lander
      College, Greenwood, S. C.

GIBBES, LEWIS REEVE
   1848. Catalogue of the Fauna of South Carolina. (Appendix to Tuomey's Report on the
      Geology of South Carolina, 1848.)

GLEN, JAMES
   1761. A Description of South Carolina. London.

GMELIN, JOHANN FRIEDRICH
   1789. Caroli a Linné Systema Naturea, 2. Lipsiae.

GREENE, EARL ROSENBURY, GRIFFIN, W. W., ODUM, E. P., STODDARD, H. L., and TOMKINS, I. R.
   1945. Birds of Georgia. Georgia Orn. Soc. Occ. Pub. No. 2.

GREY, J. H. JR., and BRIMLEY, C. S.
   1940. Carolina Region [under The Season]. Bird-Lore, 42: 383-384 (contains Gabriel
      Cannon's record of Mourning Warbler).

GRIFFIN, WILLIAM, GREENE, E. R., and ODUM, E. P., STODDARD, H. L., and TOMKINS, I. R.
   See Greene, Griffin, Odum, Stoddard, and Tomkins.

GRISCOM, LUDLOW
   1927. The White-fronted Goose (Anser albifrons gambeli) in South Carolina. Auk, 44: 559.
   1937. A Monographic Study of the Red Crossbill. Proc. Bost. Soc. Nat. Hist. 41: 77-210.

HAHN, F. W. JR. [Greenwood Birds] See Gee, N. Gist

HARRIS, GEORGE E.
   1891. [Snowy Owl] Orn. and Ool., 16: 108.

HEISER, JOSEPH MATHEW, JR.
   1945. Eskimo Curlew in Texas. Auk, 62: 635.

HENDERSON, JUNIUS
   1933. The Practical Value of Birds. New York.

HENDRICKS, GEORGE BARTLETT
   1935. A Duck Hawk Attacks Four People. Auk, 52: 446.

HEWATT, ALEXANDER
   1779. Historical Account of the Rise and Progress of the Colonies of South Carolina and
      Georgia. 2 vols. London.

HILTON, WILLIAM
   1664. A Relation of a Discovery lately made on the Coast of Florida [actually S. C.].
      London.

HORNE, ROBERT
   1666. A Brief Description of the Province of Carolina. London.
HOWELL, ARTHUR HOLMES
   1924. Birds of Alabama. Montgomery, Ala.
   1932. Florida Bird Life. New York.
HOXIE, WALTER JOHN
   1868. Marginal notes in a personal copy of S. F. Baird's Birds, volume IX of the Pacific
      Railroad Report, ms. in Charleston Museum.
   1885. Notes on the Birds of the Sea Islands, Part II. Orn. and Ool., 10: 27-29.
   1886. Kirtland's Warbler on St. Helena Island, South Carolina. Auk, 3: 412.
   1901. The Redpoll Acanthis linaria in South Carolina. Wilson Bull., 8: 36-37.
HOXIE, W. J. See also Cooke, W. W.
HOYT, JOHN SOUTHGATE YEATON, and HOYT, S. F.
   1944. First record of Audubon's Caracara in South Carolina. Auk, 61: 145.
HOYT, SALLY F., and HOYT, J. S. Y. See Hoyt, J. S. Y. and Hoyt, S. F.
HUDSON, GEORGE ELFORD
   1927. Brewer's Blackbird (Euphagus cyanocephalus) in South Carolina. Auk, 44: 567.
   1928. The Nashville, Wilson's, and Connecticut Warblers in South Carolina. Auk, 45:
      103-104.
   1930. Two and a Half Years of Bird Migration at Clemson College, S. C. Auk, 47:
      397-402.
HUDSON, G. E. and SHERMAN, F.
   1936. Some Miscellaneous Notes on South Carolina Birds. Auk, 53: 311-315.
HUMPHREYS, WILLIAM WIRT
   1935. Dickcissel in South Carolina. Auk, 52: 459.
JENNESS, P. M.
   1925. Kirtland's Warbler in North Carolina [actually South Carolina]. Bird-Lore, 27:
      252-253.
JOB, HERBERT KEIGHTLEY
   1927. Notes from South Carolina. Auk, 44: 114-115.
JOPSON, HARRY G. M.
   1949. Dovekie Picked Up at Pawley's Island, S. C. Chat, 13: 17.
KORTRIGHT, FRANCIS H.
   1942. The Ducks, Geese and Swans of North America. Washington.
KUERZI, RICHARD GOTTRON
   1942. The Ecology of a Coastal Carolina Plantation. (Unpublished ms)
LAWSON, JOHN
   1718. History of Carolina. London.
LINCOLN, FREDERICK CHARLES
   1944. Chimney Swifts Winter Home Discovered. Auk, 61: 604-609.
LOGAN, JOHN HENRY
   1859. History of the Upper Country of South Carolina. Charleston, S. C.
LOOMIS, LEVERETT MILLS
   1879. A Partial List of the Birds of Chester County, South Carolina. Bull. Nutt. Orn.
      Club, 4: 209-218.
   1881. A New Bird (Plectrophanes pictus) for South Carolina. Bull. Nutt. Orn. Club,
      6: 115-116.
   1882. Occurrence of Coturniculus lecontei in Chester County, South Carolina. Bull. Nutt.
      Orn. Club, 7: 54-55.
   1883. Supplementary Notes on the Ornithology of Chester County, South Carolina. Auk,
      2: 188-193.
   1884. Xanthocephalus icterocephalus in Chester County, South Carolina. Auk, 1: 293.

LITERATURE CITED

1885. Supplementary Notes on the Ornithology of Chester County, South Carolina. Auk, 2: 188-193.

1886. On the Former Breeding of Psaltriparus minimus in South Carolina. Auk, 3: 137-138.

1886. Dendroica dominica albilora obtained in Chester County, South Carolina. Auk, 3: 139.

1887. On An Addition to the Ornithology of South Carolina. Auk, 4: 76.

1887. Remarks on Four Examples of the Yellow-throated Warbler from Chester County, S. C. Auk, 4: 165.

1887. Another Addition to the Avi-fauna of South Carolina. Auk, 4: 261.

1887. Helinaia swainsonii near Chester C. H., S. C. Auk, 4: 347-348.

1889. A Rare Bird in Chester Co., South Carolina. Auk, 6: 74.

1889. Another Western Bird in South Carolina. Auk, 6: 194.

1890. Observations on Some of the Summer Birds of the Mountain Portions of Pickens County, South Carolina. Auk, 7: 30-39 and 125-130.

1891. A Further Review of the Avian Fauna of Chester County, South Carolina. Auk, 8: 49-59, and 167-173.

1891. June Birds of Caesar's Head, South Carolina. Auk, 8: 323-333.

LYNCH, KENNETH M.
1913. Primary Cancer in the Lung of a Wild Double-crested Cormorant. Bull. Chas. Mus., 9: 70.

MCATEE, WALDO LEE
1908. Food Habits of the Grosbeaks. U. S. Dept. Agri. Biol. Survey Bull. 32.

MACKAY, GEORGE HENRY
1928. White-fronted Goose (Anser albifrons gambeli) in South Carolina. Auk, 45: 368.

MANIGAULT, EDWARD
1931. Second Occurrence of the Snow Bunting in South Carolina. Auk, 48: 275.

MAY, JOHN BICHARD
1935. The Hawks of North America. New York.

MERRIAM, CLINTON HART
1874. Ornithological Notes from the South. American Naturalist, 8: 6-9.

METCALF, JESSE
1929. Three Interesting Records from South Carolina. Auk, 46: 248.

MILLS, ROBERT
1826. Statistics of South Carolina. Charleston, S. C.

MURPHEY, EUGENE EDMUND
1937. Observations on the Bird Life of the Middle Savannah Valley 1890-1937. Contr. Chas. Mus. IX.

MURPHY, ROBERT CUSHMAN
1940. Purple Sandpiper in South Carolina. [Under Birds and the Winter of 1939-40.] Auk, 57: 401-402.

MURPHY, R. C., and VOGT, W.
1933. The Dovekie Influx of 1932. Auk, 50: 325-329.

NAIRNE, THOMAS
1732. A Letter from South Carolina, 2nd Ed. [actually 3rd Ed.]. London.

OBERHOLSER, HARRY CHURCH
1918. Notes on the Subspecies of Numenius americanus Bechstein. Auk, 35: 188-195.

1934. A Revision of the North American House Wrens. Ohio Journal of Science, 34: 86-96.

1938. The Bird Life of Louisiana. New Orleans.

ODUM, EUGENE P., GREENE, E. R., GRIFFIN, W. W., STODDARD, H. L., TOMKINS, I. R. See Greene, Griffin, Odum, Stoddard and Tomkins.

ORTON, JAMES
    1871. Notes on Some Birds in the Museum of Vassar College. American Naturalist, 4: 716.
PEARSON, THOMAS GILBERT
    1919. The Case of the Brown Pelican. Amer. Review of Reviews, 59: 509-511.
PEARSON, T. G., BRIMLEY, C. S. and BRIMLEY, H. H.
    1942. Birds of North Carolina. Raleigh.
PELLEW, MARION JAY, and FORD, L. P.
    1920. Notable Warblers Breeding Near Aiken, S. C. Auk, 37: 589-590.
    1930. Aiken, S. C. [under Bird-Lore's Thirtieth Christmas Census] Bird-Lore, 32: 40.
PETERS, HAROLD SEYMORE, and BURLEIGH, T. D. See Burleigh and Peters.
PETERS, JAMES LEE
    1924. A Second North American Record for Puffinus assimilis. Auk, 41: 337.
PETERSON, ROGER TORY
    1947. A Field Guide to the Birds. New York.
PHILIPP, PHILIP BERNARD, and BOWDISH, B. S. See Bowdish and Philipp.
PICKENS, ANDREW LEE
    1927. Supplementary Records for Upper South Carolina. Auk, 44: 428-429.
    1934. Intergradations of Life Zones and Sub-species in the Southern Piedmont. Auk, 51: 536-537.
RAMSAY, DAVID
    1809. History of South Carolina. Charleston, S. C.
REA, PAUL MARSHALL
    1905. Apropos of the Roseate Spoonbill. Bull. Chas. Mus., 1: 44.
    1910. White Pelican in South Carolina. Bull. Chas. Mus., 6: 57.
RIDGWAY, ROBERT
    1914. The Birds of North and Middle America, Part VI. U. S. Nat. Mus. Bull. 50.
ROSSIGNOL, GILBERT RICE, JR.
    1913. Another Bridled Tern for South Carolina. Auk, 30: 105.
SASS, HERBERT RAVENEL
    1908. The Snowy Heron in South Carolina. Auk, 25: 313-314.
    1908. The Return of the Snowy Heron. Bird-Lore, 10: 160.
    1925. White-crowned Sparrow at Charleston, S. C. Auk, 42: 590.
    1929. The Scissor-tailed Flycatcher (Muscivora forficata) in South Carolina. Auk, 46: 117.
SASS, H. R. and BULL, C. L. See Bull and Sass.
SCOTT, PETER M. and DALGETY, C. T. See Dalgety and Scott.
SHERMAN, FRANKLIN, and HUDSON, G. E. See Hudson and Sherman.
SHERMAN, FRANKLIN, and WAYNE, A. T. See Wayne and Sherman.
SIMMS, WILLIAM GILMORE
    1843. Geography of South Carolina. Charleston, S. C.
SPRUNT, ALEXANDER, JR.
    1924. Breeding of MacGillivray's Seaside Sparrow in South Carolina. Auk, 41: 482-484.
    1926. The Sooty Tern (Sterna fuscata) at Charleston, S. C. Auk, 43: 535.
    1927. The Snow Bunting (Plectrophenax n. nivalis) taken near Charleston, S. C. Auk, 44: 107-108.
    1929. The Rufus Hummingbird (Selasphorus rufus) in South Carolina. Auk, 46: 237-238.
    1930. Extension of the Winter Range of the Piping Plover (Charadrius melodus). Auk, 47: 250.
    1931. In Memoriam: Arthur Trezevant Wayne. Auk, 48: 1-16.
    1931. A Specimen of Baird's Sandpiper (Pisobia bairdi) from South Carolina. Auk, 48: 260-261.
    1931. Wilson's Phalarope (Steganopus tricolor) in South Carolina. Auk, 48: 597.

LITERATURE CITED

1932. Nesting of the Starling (Sternus vulgaris) in Charleston, S. C. Auk, 49: 354.

1933. The Magnolia Warbler (Dendroica magnolia) on the South Carolina Coast. Auk, 50: 117.

1933. The Cinnamon Teal: A New Bird for South Carolina. Auk, 50: 210.

1934. Notes from South Carolina. Auk, 51: 251-252.

1934. The Red Phalarope off South Carolina. Auk, 51: 374.

1934. A New Grackle from Florida. Chas. Mus. Leaflet No. 6.

1935. First Occurrence of the Reddish Egret (Dichromanassa r. rufescens) in South Carolina. Auk, 52: 77.

1935. The Noddy at Charleston, South Carolina. Auk, 52: 309.

1936. Swainson's Hawk in South Carolina. Auk, 53: 209.

1937. Mississippi Kite in South Carolina in Winter. Auk, 54: 384.

1939. Southern Robin breeding in coastal South Carolina. Auk, 56: 87.

1939. Predatory instincts in the American Egret. Auk, 56: 469.

1942. Black-throated Gray Warbler on the coast of South Carolina. Auk, 59: 429.

1943. The Dovekie in South Carolina. Auk, 60: 598-599.

1944. The Great White Heron, an addition to South Carolina avifauna. Auk, 61: 150.

1944. Two abnormal breeding records for South Carolina. Auk, 61: 306-307.

1947. First winter observance of the Yellow-breasted Chat in South Carolina. Auk, 64: 467-468.

SPRUNT, A., JR., and CHAMBERLAIN, E. B.
1931. Second Supplement to Arthur T. Wayne's Birds of South Carolina. Contr. Chas. Mus. VI.

SPRUNT, A., JR., and DINGLE, E. VON S. See Dingle and Sprunt.

STARRETT, W. C.
1947. Notes on the Pomarine Jaeger in the Atlantic and Caribbean. Auk, 64: 320.

STODDARD, HERBERT LEE
1931. The Bobwhite Quail; Its Habits, Preservation and Increase. New York.

STODDARD, H. L., GREENE, E. R., GRIFFIN, W. W., ODUM, E. P., and TOMKINS, I. R. See Greene, Griffin, Odum, Stoddard, and Tomkins.

STONE, WITMER
1934. European Teal in South Carolina. Auk, 51: 227.

TANNER, JAMES TAYLOR
1942. The Ivory-billed Woodpecker. Research Report No. 1 of the National Audubon Society.

THAYER, GERALD HANDERSON
1899. The Chuck-will's-Widow on Shipboard. Auk, 16: 273-276.
1902. The Red Phalarope in North Carolina. Auk, 19: 285-286.

TOMKINS, IVAN REXFORD
1930. Some Records from the Savannah River Entrance during 1929. Auk, 47: 577.
1931. A Snowy Owl from Coastal Georgia. Auk, 48: 268.
1931. Further Notes from the Savannah River Entrance. Auk, 48: 279.
1935. The Lapland Longspur (Calcarius l. lapponicus); A South Carolina Specimen, and a Georgia Sight Record. Auk, 52: 315.
1936. The White-rumped and Stilt Sandpipers in Southern South Carolina. Auk, 53: 80.
1936. Notes on the Winter Food of the Short-eared Owl. Wilson Bull., 48: 77-79.
1942. The range of the Little Sparrow Hawk in Georgia and South Carolina. Oriole, 7: 13-14.

TOMKINS, I. R., GREENE, E. R., GRIFFIN, W. W., ODUM, E. P., and STODDARD, H. L. See Greene, Griffin, Odum, Stoddard and Tomkins.

TRUE, FREDERICK WILLIAM
1883. A List of the Vertebrate Animals of South Carolina, pp. 209-264 in South Carolina, Resources and population, Institutions and industries. Charleston.

TUOMEY, MICHAEL
  1848. Report on the Geology of South Carolina. Columbia, S. C. (See also Lewis R. Gibbes.)
VOGT, WILLIAM and MURPHY, R. C. See Murphy and Vogt.
WATSON, JOHN BROADUS
  1908. Papers from the Tortugas Laboratory of the Carnegie Inst. Washington, 2, No. 103: 189-255.
WAYNE, ARTHUR TREZEVANT
  1887. The American Crossbill (*Loxia curvirostra minor*) in large Numbers near Charleston, S. C. Auk, 4: 287-289.
  1888. Loxia curvirostra minor again at Yemassee, S. C. Auk, 5: 115.
  1888. Loxia curvirostra minor taken again at Yemassee, S. C. Auk, 5: 208.
  1890. Two Notes from South Carolina. Auk, 7: 410.
  1891. The Sandhill Crane (*Grus mexicana*) in South Carolina. Auk, 8: 308.
  1894. Effect of the Great Cyclone of August 26-27 upon Certain Species of Birds. Auk, 11: 85.
  1894. Notes on the Capture of the Gray Kingbird (*Tyrannus dominicensis*) near Charleston, South Carolina. Auk, 11: 178-179.
  1894. Leconte's Sparrow (*Ammodramus leconteii*) in large numbers near Charleston, South Carolina. Auk, 11: 256.
  1894. The Sandhill Crane (*Grus mexicana*).—A Correction. Auk, 11: 324.
  1895. The Rough-winged Swallow (*Stelgidopteryx serripennis*) and Tree Swallows (*Tachycineta bicolor*) Wintering in South Carolina. Auk, 12: 184.
  1895. The Lark Bunting in South Carolina. Auk, 12: 305-306.
  1897. A Remarkable Nest of the Tufted Titmouse (*Parus bicolor*). Auk, 14: 98-99.
  1899. Destruction of Birds by the Great Cold Wave of February 13 and 14, 1899. Auk, 16: 197-198.
  1899. Notes on Marian's Marsh Wren, *Cistothorus marianae*, and Worthington's Marsh Wren, *Cistothorus palustris griseus*. Auk, 16: 361-362.
  1901. The Red Phalarope (*Crymophilus fulicarius*) on the Coast of South Carolina. Auk, 18: 271.
  1901. Bachman's Warbler (*Helminthophila bachmanii*) Rediscovered near Charleston, South Carolina. Auk, 18: 274.
  1902. The Ipswich Sparrow (*Ammodramus princeps*) on the Mainland of South Carolina. Auk, 19: 203.
  1903. Richardson's Merlin (*Falco columbarius richardsonii*) on the Coast of South Carolina. Auk, 20: 67.
  1904. Kirtland's Warbler (*Dendroica kirtlandi*) on the Coast of South Carolina. Auk, 21: 83-84.
  1905. Notes on South Carolina Birds [Bachman's Warbler]. Auk, 22: 399.
  1910. Birds of South Carolina. Contr. Chas. Mus. I.
  1910. The Snowy Owl (*Nyctea nyctea*) Taken in South Carolina. Auk, 27: 454-455.
  1911. A Fourth South Carolina Record for the Saw-Whet Owl (*Cryptoglaux acadica*). Auk, 28: 112.
  1911. A Third Autumnal Record of Kirtland's Warbler (*Dendroica kirtlandi*) for South Carolina. Auk, 28: 116.
  1911. The Black-billed Cuckoo (*Coccyzus erythrophthalmus*) Breeding on the Coast of South Carolina. Auk, 28: 485.
  1913. Two Flycatchers of the Genus Empidonax New to the Fauna of South Carolina. Auk, 30: 273-274.
  1913. The Magnolia Warbler (*Dendroica magnolia*): an Addition to the Fauna of the Coast Region of South Carolina. Auk, 30: 277.
  1918. Some Additions and Other Records New to the Ornithology of South Carolina. Auk, 35: 437-442.
  1920. The Russet-backed Thrush (*Hylocichla ustulata ustulata*) Taken near Charleston, S. C. Auk, 37: 465.

LITERATURE CITED

1921. Notes on Five Birds Taken Near Charleston, South Carolina. Auk, 38: 121-123.
1921. The Green-tailed Towhee (Oberholseria chlorura) on the coast of South Carolina. Auk, 38: 278.
1921. The Sycamore Warbler (Dendroica dominica albilora) on the Coast of South Carolina. Auk, 38: 462.
1922. The Willow Thrush (Hylocichla fuscescens salicicola) on the Coast of South Carolina. Auk, 39: 268.
1922. The Carolina Junco (Junco hyemalis carolinensis) on the Coast of South Carolina. Auk, 39: 420.
1923. A Third South Carolina Record for the Bay-breasted Warbler (Dendroica castanea) Auk, 40: 133.
1926. Gambel's Sparrow in South Carolina. Auk, 43: 100-101.
1926. The Sooty Tern and Audubon's Shearwater in South Carolina. Auk, 43: 534-535.
1927. The Rough-legged Hawk (*Archibuteo lagopus sancti-johannis*) at Capers' Island, S. C. Auk, 44: 249.

WAYNE, A. T. and SHERMAN, F.
1927. Two Birds New to the Fauna of South Carolina. Auk, 44: 94.

WESTON, FRANCIS MARION, JR.
1913. Magnolia Warbler in the Coast Region of South Carolina. Auk, 30: 114.

WETMORE, ALEXANDER
1924. Food and economic relations of North American grebes. U. S. Dept. Agri. Bull. 1196.
1925. Food of American phalaropes, avocets, and stilts. U. S. Dept. Agri. Bull. 1359.

WHARTON, WILLIAM PICKMAN
1941. Twelve Years of Banding at Summerville, S. C. Bird-Banding, 12: 137-147.

WICKERSHAM, CORNELIUS WENDELL
1902. Sickle-billed Curlew. Auk, 19: 353-356.

WIDMANN, OTTO
1884. How Young Birds Are Fed. Forest and Stream, 22: 484.

WILSON, ROBERT
1905. Some Ornithological Notes. Bull. Chas. Mus., 1: 31-32.

WILSON, SAMUEL
1682. An Acount of the Province of Carolina, in America. London.

WYLIE, HUGH S.
1943. [Letter on the Canada Goose] Winnsboro News and Herald, March 18.

WYLIE, H. S. and CAMAK, T. C.
1943. [Letters on the Passenger Pigeon] Winnsboro News and Herald, March 18 and 25.

Supplement

by E. Milby Burton

INTRODUCTION

In this Supplement I have endeavored to include all ornithological records of note that have occurred within the State since 1949—the date of publication of the original work—through 1968. Since the time of the earlier publication there has been a great increase shown in the interest in birds. Many observers have become highly qualified, and their reports can be relied upon implicitly. Many birds heretofore never reported from South Carolina have been added on the "State List"; ranges within the State have been expanded; migration dates have been changed; new nesting data have been added. However, for the description, life histories, and general ranges, *South Carolina Bird Life* must be consulted.

Most of this new information has appeared from time to time in various ornithological journals such as *The Auk, The Chat, The Wilson Bulletin, The Oriole, Audubon Field Notes*, and others. The *Lesser Squawk* is the mimeographed sheet of the Charleston Natural History Society telling of the activities of its members, and of their ornithological sightings. In addition, questionnaires were sent to many people, both within and without the State, with most gratifying results. I hope that little, if any, information of ornithological value has been overlooked.

The question of what constitutes a record, especially of a new species of bird, is a difficult one to answer. However, a committee appointed by the members of the Carolina Bird Club has come up with a very equitable solution between the "die-hards," who insist that a bird must be collected and examined carefully by competent ornithologists before becoming the basis of valid record, and the more modern school, who are of the opinion that a sight record is sufficient. These

SUPPLEMENT

rules and regulations governing such cases have been stated in detail in the March, 1968, issue of *The Chat*.

Basically these rules will be used in the compilation of this Supplement. The integrity of the person making a report is assumed without question. The following criteria have been employed in this work:

> (a) A bird that has been collected and is in some public institution where it can be examined, or, if in a private collection, is available to competent ornithologists for examination, unquestionably constitutes a record.
>
> (b) A clearly discernible photograph of a bird. With the telephoto lenses that are available such photographs are obtainable.
>
> (c) Multiple sight records consisting of at least three independent sightings by two or more competent observers seeing the same bird at the same time may be considered adequate evidence of the occurrence of certain species within the State.
>
> (d) In addition the bird in question must be taken or seen within the territorial (three mile) waters of the State. With more people doing offshore fishing, reports are coming in of shearwaters and other pelagic birds being observed. In rare instances exceptions may be made. If so, they will be clearly noted, and the reason for so doing given.

Migration arrival and departure dates, unless changed by a week's lapse of time, will remain the same. The extended range of a common bird will be based on the sight record of a competent observer. If a species has been collected previously within the State, the assumption can be made that it will probably be seen again; hence, a sight record is acceptable, based on the circumstances and the qualifications of the observer.

In 1963 the Charleston Museum published *Birds of the AEC Savannah River Plant Area*, by Robert A. Norris (*Museum Contribution No. XIV*). This 200,000 acre area is located in Aiken, Barnwell, and a small part of Allendale counties, and borders the Savannah River, lying on the south. Norris was a member of a group from the University of Georgia, headed by Dr. Eugene P. Odum, employed by the Atomic Energy Commission to carry out field studies of the area. For three years Norris was in the area and his ornithological findings were of such value that it was thought they warranted publication. Hereafter his work will be listed as (Norris, 1963) and the area referred to as "SRP area," Aiken.

South Carolina Birds of the Foothills, 1966, by Jay Shuler, will be referred to as (Shuler, 1966), and the *Check List of Birds of Richland and Lexington Counties, South Carolina 1936–1967*, will be listed as the (R–L list, 1968). The data for this list were compiled by the Columbia Bird Club, and the list was published in 1968 by the Columbia Science Museum.

The same order of species will be adhered to as they appear in *South Carolina Bird Life*. The American Ornithologists' Union's *Check-list of North American*

SUPPLEMENT

Birds, Fifth Edition (1957) will be followed in the use of scientific and common names. Some names in both categories have been changed since 1949.

Within the past two decades numbers of extremely high television towers have been erected throughout the State. During the fall, and under adverse weather conditions, literally thousands of migrating birds fly into the towers and their supporting wires and are killed or badly maimed. It is an appalling sight to see hundreds of dead birds at the base of the towers. In 1954 the dispatchers at the Charleston Airport reported that there were so many birds migrating during a heavy overcast that at times they dimmed the large beacons. When daylight arrived, thousands of birds were found to have died. Fortunately, these adverse weather conditions at the height of migration are infrequent; however, such tragedies have added greatly to our knowledge concerning the relative abundance of many species.

Seventy-seven birds have been made known to science for the first time from South Carolina. Since the publication of *South Carolina Bird Life* in 1949, the State has gained another type locality, but has also lost one, viz:

> Western Sandpiper *Ereunetes mauri Cabanis,* formerly thought to have been based on a specimen from Cuba but now considered to have been founded on one from South Carolina. *Journ. für Orn.,* 4, 1856 (1857) (South Carolina).

> Short-billed Marsh Wren, *Cistothorus platensis stellaris* (Naumann) regarded formerly as based on a specimen from South Carolina, but now considered to have been from "vicinity of Savannah," Georgia. (AOU Check-list, Fifth Ed. [1957], pp. 203 and 419).

In recent years the Hartwell Dam has been created near the headwaters of the Savannah River, impounding a tremendous amount of water and submerging an extensive area with a large part of it being in Anderson and Oconee counties. This has changed the ecology not only of that particular part of the State, but of migrating birds. In the early spring, quantities of various kinds of ducks are reported as being seen on the reservoir, some staying several days, presumably resting preparatory to the long overland journey to their nesting area. Terns, gulls, and herons, usually not expected so far inland, are reported being observed from time to time. Undoubtedly aquatic birds, as well as other water-loving birds, will become increasingly more common in the vicinity of this large body of water.

Hilton Head Island lies in a maritime environment, thereby making it several degrees warmer than the remainder of the coastal area of the State. This may have an effect on birds, either by delaying their migrations, or, in some cases, in a mild winter, by causing them to stay the entire year. Possibly this situation may have always been the case, but, with the development of the

SUPPLEMENT

island, large numbers of people are living on it the year around and consequently more ornithological reports from them are being received.

In order to facilitate the finding of any location, the name of the county is given, except where the city and/or town bear the same name. For instance, it would be redundant to say "seen near Spartanburg," then add Spartanburg County. In referring to an island this policy has not always been adhered to, for most of the islands are well known. Furthermore, anyone not being familiar with the State, on seeing the name "island" will first look for it on the coast.

The following birds have been added on the "State List" since the original publication of *South Carolina Bird Life* in 1949:

EARED GREBE	*Podiceps caspicus*
GREATER SHEARWATER	*Puffinus gravis*
BROWN BOOBY	*Sula leucogaster*
CATTLE EGRET	*Bubulcus ibis*
FULVOUS TREE DUCK	*Dendrocygna bicolor*
CINNAMON TEAL	*Anas cyanoptera*
COMMON EIDER	*Somateria mollissima*
ROUGH-LEGGED HAWK	*Buteo lagopus*
RUFF	*Philomachus pugnax*
POMERINE JAEGER	*Stercorarius pomarius*
ICELAND GULL	*Larus glaucoides*
FRANKLIN'S GULL	*Larus pipixcan*
WHITE-WINGED DOVE	*Zenaida asiatica*
VERMILION FLYCATCHER	*Pyrocephalus rubinus*
WESTERN MEADOWLARK	*Sturnella neglecta*
WESTERN TANAGER	*Piranga ludoviciana*
BLACK-HEADED GROSBEAK	*Pheucticus melanocephalus*
EVENING GROSBEAK	*Hesperiphona vespertima*
HOUSE FINCH	*Carpodacus mexicanus*
PINE GROSBEAK	*Pinicola enucleator*
COMMON REDPOLL	*Acanthis flammea*
LARK SPARROW	*Chondestes grammacus*
TREE SPARROW	*Spizella arborea*
HARRIS' SPARROW	*Zonotrichia querula*
LINCOLN'S SPARROW	*Melospiza lincolnii*

SUPPLEMENT

COMMON LOON: *Gavia immer*

The loon is a common winter visitor along the coast, but is reported as being "uncommon" in the Piedmont (Shuler, 1966: 6). One was seen at Eastover, Richland County, May 3, 1954, by Mrs. W. H. Faver (*Chat*, 18: 1954, 79), and another by Gabriel Cannon on June 1, 1957, near Spartanburg (*Chat*, 21: 1957, 71).

A close drifting flock of 18 was observed on the Stono River, Charleston County, May 2, 1957, by Mrs. Louise Barrington. They were seen in the late afternoon, and the birds were both in winter and summer plumage, apparently a flock on migration (*Lesser Squawk*, May, 1957). On April 10, 1968, a flock of between 90 and 100 birds was observed by Francis Barrington on the Stono River, apparently sitting out a heavy fog before continuing what must have been their northern migration (*Chat*, 32: 1968, 63).

A flightless loon, undoubtedly a cripple, was observed by Mrs. Ellison D. Smith at Murrell's Inlet, Georgetown County, August 2, 1966 (*Chat*, 30: 1966, 110). Inasmuch as this bird appeared crippled, the date cannot be regarded as either an early arrival or late departure one.

The Lesser Loon is now thought to be a small individual of the Common Loon; therefore it is no longer regarded as a subspecies and is not listed in the Fifth Edition of the AOU *Check-list of North American Birds* (1957).

RED-THROATED LOON: *Gavia stellata*

On March 10, 1962, over 1,000 Red-throated Loons were counted by J. Fred Denton feeding over the riffles at the mouth of the South Edisto River (*Chat*, 26: 1962, 49). This concentration of loons is by far the largest ever recorded in South Carolina.

RED-NECKED GREBE: *Podiceps grisegena*

Although a rare winter resident along the coast, the Red-necked Grebe is sometimes seen in the interior. Seven were observed at Hartwell Reservoir, Anderson County on the Christmas Bird Count held December 27, 1966. They were studied at a distance of 50 yards through a 50X scope by Adair and R. Conner Tedards (*AFN*, 21: 1967, 184).

HORNED GREBE: *Podiceps auritus*

Primarily an inhabitant of the coast during the winter months, and although reported "shunning fresh-water localities," it is sometimes observed in the interior of the State. Mrs. Ellison D. Smith saw one on Lake Katherine, Richland County, February 5, 1961, and another in 1963. One was captured at the same location, photographed, and released in March, 1964. There are two other records from Richland County.

SUPPLEMENT

On April 10, 1957, one was seen in the northwestern corner of the "SRP area," Aiken (Norris, 1963: 5). It is also reported as being an uncommon winter visitor in the Piedmont (Shuler, 1966: 6).

A Horned Grebe was seen in a small pond at Charleston Heights, October 10, 1955, by Joyce M. Moore (*Lesser Squawk*, November, 1955). Heretofore, the earliest date recorded is October 25. A pair in summer plumage was observed near the causeway leading to Sullivan's Island, Charleston County, in late May, 1957, by Mr. and Mrs. James O'Neill (*Lesser Squawk*, June, 1957), and Burton saw one in high plumage May 11, 1949, at Price's Inlet. It is most unusual to see the Horned Grebe in summer plumage in South Carolina.

EARED GREBE: *Podiceps caspicus*

Walter Dawn first observed this western species swimming with some Horned Grebes in the Old Yacht Basin in Charleston. He immediately notified E. Milby Burton, who collected the bird on January 14, 1959. The study skin is in the collection of the Charleston Museum No. 59.8. This record constitutes the first known occurrence of the specimen in the State (*Auk*, 76: 1959, 521).

WESTERN GREBE: *Aechmophorus occidentalis*

The first specimen of the Western Grebe taken in the State was on June 22, 1936, near McClellanville, Charleston County. One was seen by Norman Chamberlain November 23, 1966, at Fort Johnson, Charleston Harbor. It was 100 yards offshore with some Common Loons, and several Horned Grebes and was studied for about 20 minutes under excellent conditions with a 30X Balscope. The long neck and black-and-white color pattern were striking (*Chat*, 31: 1967, 24).

Two Western Grebes were studied offshore at Ocean Drive Beach, Horry County, early on April 14, 1957, by Robert Overing, William Hammett, B. Rhett Chamberlain and party (*AFN*, 11: 1957, 255).

SOOTY SHEARWATER: *Puffinus griseus*

While a Sooty Shearwater has been found in South Carolina and another observed (*S. C. Bird Life*, p. 60), it is doubtful if under normal conditions it comes close to shore. However, one was picked up dead 6 miles south of Windy Hill Beach, Horry County, by W. M. Craven on May 29, 1950, and is in the collection of the Charleston Museum No. 50.80 (alcohol).

AUDUBON'S SHEARWATER: *Puffinus lherminieri*

An Audubon's Shearwater was found by Jeff Belknap on the Isle of Palms, Charleston County, August 1, 1963. It had a broken wing and was taken to Anne Worsham Richardson. Not believing that it would live, she nevertheless

SUPPLEMENT

fed it shrimp and gave it care and, incredibly, it survived to April 11, 1964, a nine-month period. It became quite a pet and had its portrait painted several times. After its death it was made into a study skin and is preserved in the Charleston Museum No. 64.22.

GREATER SHEARWATER: *Puffinus gravis*

The Greater Shearwater is probably fairly common offshore during the summer months. However, when one is found on the beach, it is generally the victim of some meteorological disturbance. A decomposed body of one was picked up by Ivan R. Tomkins on Hilton Head Island, Beaufort County, June 19, 1958. Only the head could be saved, and in order to make positive identification it was sent to Dr. Herbert Friedmann, then Curator of Birds, United States National Museum, who pronounced it to be a Greater Shearwater, thus constituting the first record for the State (*Chat*, 23: 1959, 19).

Another was found dead on DeVeaux's Bank at the mouth of the North Edisto River by T. A. Beckett, III, July 10, 1966. It was made into a study skin and is in the Museum's collection No. 68.48.

WILSON'S PETREL: *Oceanites oceanicus*

On August 2, 1961, one was observed flying just outside the breakers at Litchfield Beach, Georgetown County, by Mrs. Ellison D. Smith (*Chat*, 25: 1961, 85). Another was seen near the beach at Hilton Head Island by Caroline Newhall on September 10, 1964. The probable cause of the latter bird being so close inshore was hurricane "Dora" that was passing off the coast (*Chat*, 28: 1964, 133). It is unusual at any time to see Wilson's Petrel from the beach.

WHITE-TAILED TROPICBIRD: *Phaëthon lepturus*

On October 16, 1954, the coast of South Carolina was visited by a devastating hurricane. Officially named "Hazel" by the U. S. Weather Bureau, it caused immense damage to the beaches between Georgetown, S. C., and Wilmington, N. C. The day after its passage, a White-tailed Tropicbird was found in a chicken pen at Dillon, S. C., a distance of approximately 60 miles from the coast. The bird lived only a short time, but there seems to have been no question as to its identification, even though it was not preserved (*Chat*, 23: 1959, 34). This record constitutes the second occurrence in the State; the first having been taken in Jocassee, Oconee County, at the foot of the Blue Ridge Mountains after a storm.

That the White-tailed Tropicbird comes relatively close to the coast under normal conditions is illustrated by an observation by Peter Manigault, 18 nautical miles SSE from Charleston, from the deck of the Minesweeper "U.S.S. Agile," on May, 1959 (*Chat*, 23: 1959, 62).

SUPPLEMENT

WHITE PELICAN: *Pelacanus erythrorhynchos*

The White Pelican is a casual visitor to the State, but during the winter of 1955–56 fifty or more wintered at the Cape Romain Refuge (*Chat*, 20: 1957, 42). A flock of 29 were seen in Charleston Harbor in late July, 1956. Most departed the following day, but three remained for a few days resting on the sand bank behind Fort Sumter (*News & Courier*, July 20, 1956).

BROWN PELICAN: *Pelecanus occidentalis*

In recent years there seems to have been a great decline in the number of Brown Pelicans. This statement is not based on surmise but on facts. During the past several years T. A. Beckett, III, has been banding a large number of pelicans and has noticed a steady decline in the number of young birds. It cannot be said with certainty, as yet, what is the cause, but all indications point to pollution, and more especially to pesticides. When a large fish kill occurred in the Ashley River a few years ago, hundreds of young pelicans were found dead on DeVeaux's Bank along with some adults, and many adults were observed nearby sitting on the sand banks, apparently ill and making no attempt at fishing. Undoubtedly the adult pelicans caught the dying fish and fed them to their young.

Five eggs were found in the nest of a year-old female. This number is an unusually large clutch of eggs, and it is surprising to know that some pelicans breed at one year of age. The female had been banded the previous year by Beckett.

BROWN BOOBY: *Sula leucogaster*

A Brown Booby was found sitting literally on the front doorsteps of Burton's residence at 25 East Battery, Charleston, January 4, 1968. On going out of his front door to get into his car he noted an unusual looking bird apparently asleep on the grass strip in front of the house. On being approached it awoke and appeared unafraid. Realizing that it was something with which he was not familiar, Burton placed it in the trunk of his car for identification. The reason for its lack of fear was soon learned, for it was found that it could inflict a painful cut with its powerful beak.

The specimen was identified as an immature Brown Booby, and the identification was confirmed by Mrs. Roxie Laybourne of the U. S. National Museum. This record constitutes the first for the State of this resident of the tropic seas. The study skin is in the collection of the Charleston Museum No. 68.30.

The only probable explanation of its unusual occurrence here is that there had been a great deal of fog along the coast during the previous four days, and, being an immature bird, it had become lost.

SUPPLEMENT

DOUBLE-CRESTED CORMORANT: *Phalacrocoray auritus*

This common winter resident along the coast occasionally wanders inland. Three were seen in the Hartwell Reservoir, Anderson County, by Gaston Gage; two on May 23, 1955; another on June 24, 1956 (*Chat*, 28: 1964, 125). It has also been observed in the "SRP area" in upper Barnwell County (Norris, 1963: 5).

In late winter a partial migration apparently begins, for on February 20, 1962, a great number of flocks, consisting of between 20 and 30 birds, were seen flying in a northeasterly direction over Charleston Harbor. None was in the customary "V" formation. Many of the birds that were feeding in the harbor left the water to join the flocks. An identical occurrence was noted on February 19 and 21, 1968 (Burton).

A tremendous flight of cormorants, estimated at 5,000 individuals, was seen moving north off Murrell's Inlet, Georgetown County, on March 22, 1964, by Mrs. Ellison D. Smith (*Chat*, 28: 1964, 143). They apparently were migrating.

MAGNIFICENT FRIGATEBIRD: *Fregata magnificens*

In the past whenever the Magnificent Frigatebird was seen over the coast it was thought to be associated with some meteorological disturbance, but this is apparently no longer the case, for several—not all—have been seen under normal conditions. Recent records are as follows: one off Charleston Jetties, June 10, 1951, by J. H. Dick; another in Charleston Harbor by Ellison A. Williams, June 26, 1953; one over Charleston, November 14, 1960, Francis Barrington; one over Edgewater Park near Charleston by Ernest Cutts, July 29, 1960; two seen at Garden City, Horry County, June 12, 1961, by Mr. and Mrs. William Cobey (*Chat*, 25: 1961, 68); another at Murrell's Inlet, Georgetown County, June 23, 1961, by Douglas Pratt; and one over the Wadmalaw River, Charleston County by Marvin D. Veronee, July 27, 1968. One heretofore unreported was observed by Burton in the late afternoon of July 21, 1931, between Cape Romain and McClellanville; the weather was normal at the time.

GREAT WHITE HERON: *Ardea occidentalis*

What is thought to have been a Great White Heron was sighted on Hilton Head Island, Beaufort County, September 19, 1961, by Mr. and Mrs. David McG. Harrall. The bird was observed at a distance of 60 feet through 7X glasses (*Chat*, 25: 1961, 88).

The only other record of the Great White Heron in South Carolina was one seen, but not collected, on May 24, 1943, by Sprunt and Chamberlain at Brewton Plantation near Yemassee (*S. C. Bird Life*, p. 78). Apparently this sight record of the latter has been accepted by the AOU *Check-list of North*

SUPPLEMENT

American Birds, Fifth Edition, 1957, in delineating the range of the species, which is an inhabitant of southern Florida and the Keys. Sprunt was not only familiar with the Great White Heron, but had earlier made an intensive study of it in the Florida Keys for the Audubon Society.

LITTLE BLUE HERON: *Florida caerulea*

Primarily an inhabitant of the coastal area, the Little Blue Heron has been found breeding far inland, for a nest was found 10 miles north of Aiken on the Edisto River in July, 1968, by William Post, Jr. An adult was seen April 16, 1966, by Adair Tedards at Hartwell Reservoir, Anderson County (*Chat,* 30: 1966, 90).

CATTLE EGRET: *Bubulcus ibis*

While the exact date when this species reached the United States is not known, it is certain that it was seen in Florida in 1942. What is thought to have been the first observance of the species in South Carolina was made by Mrs. Alva Hines of Hilton Head Island, who reported seeing several in the early summer of 1953 (*fide* Sprunt). On August 8, 1954, one was seen at Litchfield Plantation, Georgetown County, by Major Peter Gething and James F. Cooper (*Chat,* 18: 1954, 102), and during 1955 and 1956 several reports were received of individuals having been seen in various localities along the coast.

The first nesting record in South Carolina was established by Ellison A. Williams and H. Philip Staats when they saw two pair feeding young in the nests on July 8, 1956, on Drum Island, located in Charleston Harbor. Two years later six nests with eggs were found by Ernest Cutts at the same location.

In recent years the Cattle Egret has been extending its range inland, and has been seen in a pasture with a herd of cattle on Creech Farm in Northeast York County by Anne Wilcher, April 11, 1968 (*fide* Cobey). A breeding colony containing about 120 nests was located by William Post, Jr., June 8, 1968, three miles south of Springfield, Barnwell County. Now, the Cattle Egret can be looked for in any part of the State. On the basis of banding the fact has been established that some birds breed when they are a year old (*fide* Beckett).

Sprunt has made a definitive study of the Cattle Egret and has written an excellent article that appeared in *Audubon Magazine* (Vol. 58: 1956, 274–77).

SNOWY EGRET: *Leucophoyx thula*

This species has been reported as being rare in late summer in the Piedmont (Shuler, 1966: 10). Like so many members of this family there is a post-breeding wandering that occasionally takes Snowy Egrets far from their coastal nesting area.

SUPPLEMENT

LOUISIANA HERON: *Hydranassa tricolor*

This species is an inhabitant of the coastal area that occasionally straggles inland. It is reported as rare in late summer in the Piedmont (Shuler, 1966: 10) and a few have been seen throughout the year by Mrs. Ellison Smith in the Columbia area (*R–L list*, 1968).

YELLOW-CROWNED NIGHT HERON: *Nyctanassa violacea*

A sufficient number of winter records of the Yellow-crowned Night Heron have been reported to warrant its status being changed from "summer resident" to "permanent resident, rare in winter."

LEAST BITTERN: *Ixobrychus exilis*

Because of its having been seen so frequently during the winter months, the status of the Least Bittern can now be changed to "permanent resident, rare in winter." It is reported as being rare in the Piedmont (Shuler, 1966: 11).

AMERICAN BITTERN: *Botaurus lentiginosus*

Although long sought after, it was not until May 23, 1968, that the first nest and eggs were found in South Carolina. A nest containing three eggs was found on the border of a small pond at the Charleston Country Club by Ernest Cutts. Prior to that record preflight young had been seen at Magnolia Gardens, Charleston County, and two pairs were thought to have been breeding there, but all efforts to find the nests were unsuccessful.

GLOSSY IBIS: *Plegadis falcinellus*

Since the finding of the first nest in South Carolina in 1947, the Glossy Ibis has increased greatly in numbers. The rookery at Blake's Reserve at one time contained over 200 breeding pairs. It started breeding on Drum Island in Charleston Harbor in 1956 along with White Ibis and herons, and at one time its numbers reached several hundred pairs. It now nests in several localities on the coast.

From being reported as "rare" it now has become a "permanent resident, rare in winter."

WHITE IBIS: *Eudocimus albus*

In recent years the number of breeding pairs of White Ibises has increased greatly. At one time it was estimated that the rookery in Blake's Reserve, Santee River, contained over 5,000 pairs. After they left Blake's Reserve the vast majority of them moved to Drum Island, Charleston Harbor, and in 1959 it was estimated that between 6,000 to 8,000 birds were nesting there. There are rookeries in several other locations situated in the coastal area.

During the winter the majority go south, although a few remain throughout the year. At South Island, Georgetown County, Thomas A. Yawkey reported that about 150 adults and immature birds were seen the entire winter of 1954 with the temperature at one time reaching 15° Fahrenheit. The species can now be regarded as a "permanent resident, less abundant in winter."

In what is thought to have been an unusual nesting location, approximately 11,000 breeding pairs were seen at Pumpkin Seed Island on Hobcaw Plantation, Georgetown County (*fide* Beckett). The nests were located in spike-rush (*Spartina* sp.) a few inches from the ground to a height of two feet. Usually the White Ibis nests in low trees and bushes.

This species, too, has a tendency to wander inland after the breeding season. One was killed by a hunter in Calhoun County, November 21, 1962. The specimen was mounted and is now in the collection of the Columbia Science Museum. It is reported as being accidental in the Piedmont. One was seen at the Table Mountain State Park, Pickens County, located in the extreme northwestern part of the State in the mountains. T. M. Rial and John F. Twombly first saw it September 1, 1962, feeding along a small stream, but the Park Ranger stated that it had been there several months (*Chat*, 26: 1962, 96).

ROSEATE SPOONBILL: *Ajaia ajaja*

An immature bird was seen flying with about a dozen White Ibises on August 27, 1968, by John Henry Dick at Dixie Plantation, Charleston County. It was still present on September 17. Apparently a straggler, it had joined the large breeding colony of ibises located in Dungannon only a short distance from where it was first seen.

FLAMINGO: *Phoenicopterus ruber*

For about a month in the late winter of 1968 one was seen almost daily opposite the Port Commission Docks on the upper Cooper River above the Naval Base. Because of its extreme tameness it is thought to have been an escapee.

WHISTLING SWAN: *Olor columbianus*

The Whistling Swan is a rare winter resident seen mostly along the coast. However, two were observed just outside Columbia on January 3, 1965, and remained for several days (*Chat*, 29: 1965, 30). On December 19, 1964, two were seen and carefully studied by William Post, Jr., in a small pond located within the city limits of Barnwell, where they, too, remained for several days (*Chat*, 29: 1965, 52). Three were heard as well as seen near Anderson, December 26, 1967. When first observed they were flying less than 50 feet overhead (*Chat*, 32: 1968, 19). On other occasions they have been reported at Brookgreen

SUPPLEMENT

Gardens, and thirteen were seen on Bull's Island, January 20, 1968 (*Chat*, 32: 1968, 50).

CANADA GOOSE: *Branta canadensis*

Fifty years ago, the Canada Goose was extremely rare in South Carolina, but with the destruction of the eel grass in the North Carolina sounds, it has extended its winter range and can now be regarded as a fairly common winter resident in our State.

One of the earliest fall records was seven that were seen September 3, 1966, on the Waccamaw River, Georgetown County, by Mrs. Ellison D. Smith (*Chat*, 30: 1966, 110), and a flock of 60 were seen on Lake Issaquanna, near Clemson, by Douglas Wade, September 28, 1952 (*Chat*, 18: 1954, 25). A breeding pair and six young were observed by Gabriel Cannon on Zimmerman Lake near Spartanburg, May 8, 1952 (*Chat*, 18: 1954, 251 and 16: 1952, 98). Whether the breeding pair was wholly wild or partly domesticated is a matter of conjecture. During July and August of 1966–68 several were observed feeding around on Creech Pond, York County (*fide* Cobey).

A specimen of the small version of the Canada Goose was shot by John Henry Dick and G. A. Middleton on a plantation situated on the Combahee River, December 13, 1950. It is the first time it has been recorded from the State. The study skin is in the collection of the Charleston Museum No. 53.19. It was identified by Dr. Herbert Friedmann when he was Curator of Birds at the U. S. National Museum, as being a specimen of the race *hutchinsii*. Another was killed at Doar Point, Georgetown County, on January 9, 1968, out of a flock of five. These are the only two records for the State.

BRANT: *Branta bernicla*

A rare winter resident. Additional records for the State are: seven seen at Pawley's Island, Georgetown County during the 1955 Christmas Bird Count (*Chat*, 20: 1956, 4); one was shot by Dr. William Frampton in January, 1960, at the Santee Gun Club; two observed at Huntington State Park, Georgetown County by Mrs. N. Currie, Jr., November 2, 1966 (*Chat*, 31: 1967, 50); two seen by Ernest Cutts at Bull's Island on the Christmas Bird Count held December 31, 1966 (*AFN*, 21: 1967, 184).

WHITE-FRONTED GOOSE: *Anser albifrons*

One was captured at the Santee Wildlife Refuge on January 25, 1967, and five others seen February 9, by Thomas Martin, Refuge Manager (*Chat*, 31: 1967, 98). Eleven were observed in February, 1967, at Annandale Plantation, North Santee River, Georgetown County. They were seen feeding on one of the pastures of the Plantation (*Lesser Squawk*, March, 1967).

SUPPLEMENT

LESSER SNOW GOOSE: *Chen hyperborea*

This goose is still a fairly rare winter resident along the coast. It does, however, wander inland for two were seen in Ellenton Bay located in the "SRP area," Aiken, on November 8, 1960 (Norris, 1963: 9); two seen on February 14, 1954, by Robert L. Lemaire in the refuge portion of Lake Moultrie, Berkeley County (*Chat*, 18: 1954, 521); three observed by Mrs. Ellison Smith in a small pond within the city limits of Columbia from November 17, 1966, through January 3, 1967.

In recent years the Snow Goose is now reported as a regular winter resident in small numbers (*fide* Beckett).

The Blue Goose is now considered only a color phase of the Snow Goose. The first recorded Blue Goose for the Piedmont was a young bird seen by Gabriel Cannon on November 5, 1949, in Spartanburg County (*AFN*, 4: 1950, 100). An immature bird was seen at Clemson, October 19, 1953, by Professor and Mrs. Gaston Gage (*Chat*, 18: 1954, 25). Also one was reported from Eastover, Richland County, on the Christmas Bird Count held December 31, 1956 (*AFN*, 11: 1957, 128). Four immature birds were seen November 18, 1960, in Ellenton Bay, "SRP area," Aiken (Norris, 1963: 5).

The Blue Goose is increasing in numbers along the coast during the winter. Flocks of over 100 have been seen recently by Dick. Eight, arriving on October 25, 1966, spent six months with a captive group of geese at Dixie Plantation.

FULVOUS TREE DUCK: *Dendrocygna bicolor*

A native of the Gulf Coast, the Fulvous Tree Duck has been extending its range along the entire Atlantic Coast. The reason for this extension of range is still not clear. The first record of the appearance of the Fulvous Tree Duck in South Carolina occurred when one was taken out of a flock of four on December 16, 1955, by Gilliard Baldwin at Seabrook House Plantation, Edisto Island (*Chat*, 20: 1956, 17). On November 26, 1956, a flock of 24 was seen by E. O. Mellinger at the Savannah River Refuge, located in Jasper County (*Chat*, 21: 1957, 22). Since then the reports of the Tree Duck have been sporadic. In 1961, however, a great influx took place in South Carolina: thirty were seen on the Ashepoo River; at Fairlawn Plantation, Charleston County, twenty-five were reported; and another flock of ten was seen on the South Santee River. Several were killed by hunters and brought into the Charleston Museum for identification. A few specimens were retained and are now in the collections of the Charleston Museum.

The latest recorded date was when three were seen on April 28, 1962, at

Magnolia Gardens, Charleston County, but in 1963, T. A. Beckett, III, reported one or more remained during the entire summer (*Chat*, 27: 1963, 82).

Again in 1965, a great number was seen. William P. Baldwin reported that a flock of 45 were at Medway Plantation, Berkeley County, and in the spring of that year between 40 and 50 were seen on a pond at Point of Pines, Edisto Island, by J. G. Murray and others (*fide* May). Also, 32 were seen at Annandale Plantation, Georgetown County, by Dick in November.

MALLARD: *Anas platyrhynchos*

Apparently the Mallard has now become a breeding bird in South Carolina. In mid-April, 1959, a female was flushed from a nest that contained twelve eggs. The nest was located in the "SRP area" close to the Savannah River. Photographs of it were taken by John B. Hatcher. Later, returning to the site with Dr. Eugene P. Odum, he found the eggs in the process of hatching. (*Chat*, 23: 1959, 64).

A female with seven half-grown young was observed by Hatcher on May 2, 1961, two miles east of the Savannah River, Aiken County. The Mallard was again found nesting in the "SRP area" when a nest with eight eggs was found by Hatcher and William Post, Jr., on May 4, 1965, and on May 27 of the same year a female and three young were seen by Post in a "Carolina Bay" in Barnwell County (*Chat*, 29: 1965, 116). Beckett reports it as now breeding at Magnolia Gardens.

During recent years the U. S. Fish and Wildlife Service has been encouraging plantation owners to raise Mallards to augment the dwindling duck supply. In some places hundreds are raised successfully. Many of these birds revert to their wild state; others remain semi-domesticated. Doubtless some of these locally-raised ducks are now the breeding stock in the State.

GREEN-WINGED TEAL: *Anas carolinensis*

The Green-winged Teal usually arrives in South Carolina later in the fall than its near relative the Blue-wing. However, one was seen August 16, 1962, by John Henry Dick at Dixie Plantation, Charleston County (*Chat*, 26: 1962, 102). This constitutes the only summer record for the State.

BLUE-WINGED TEAL: *Anas discors*

On June 24, 1964, on Bull's Island, Hoyt Mills found two young Blue-winged Teals just beginning to fly. Further investigation established the presence of six pair of adults with a total count of 26 young on the island.

The records of E. Frank Johnson, Manager of the Cape Romain Refuge, show that the Blue-winged Teal has been breeding in small numbers on Cape

SUPPLEMENT

Island since 1960. In that year a nest with eggs was found, but was destroyed subsequently by raccoons. A few young were seen in 1961 and 1962. In 1963, a brood of two was hatched at Bull's Island (*Chat*, 29: 1965, 24).

CINNAMON TEAL: *Anas cyanoptera*

While there is a perfectly valid sight record for this western bird in South Carolina, it was not until December 31, 1961, that the first specimen was taken in the State. T. A. Beckett, III, shot a male while duck hunting at Magnolia Gardens, Charleston County. It was shown to Burton, who confirmed his identification. On January 15, 1962, Beckett was within 30 feet of another male in the same pond where he had killed his first bird. This bird was not shot.

A Cinnamon Teal was reported seen on Bull's Island April 21, 1961 (*AFN*, 15: 1961, 319).

EUROPEAN WIDGEON: *Mareca penelope*

The European Widgeon is rare any time in South Carolina and is usually seen along the coast. However, a male was seen on Furman Lake, near Greenville, by J. B. Shuler on March 23, 1957 (*Chat*, 21: 1957, 44). Another was shot at Lake Marion, Clarendon County, January 9, 1954, by Basil Richburg (*Chat*, 18: 1954, 52).

AMERICAN WIDGEON: *Mareca americana*

A few stragglers sometimes remain until the first week in June, but on June 18, 1958, a flock of about 50 widgeon were seen by Burton in a small pond between Columbia and Orangeburg. The flock was studied through 7X binoculars in order to be sure of the identification. Thomas S. Yawkey and Burton saw three males and three females, June 15, 1953, at South Island, Georgetown County. Presumably these birds were nonbreeders.

WOOD DUCK: *Aix sponsa*

Fifty years ago the Wood Duck, if not on the verge of extinction, was certainly at a very low ebb. At one time it was placed on the prohibit list for duck hunters; now some can be included in a day's bag. Because of these stringent laws it has made a remarkable comeback. At least 1,500 were seen in an evening flight by John Henry Dick and R. H. Pough, December 15, 1952, at Dixie Plantation, Charleston County. It is thought that this heavy concentration was attributable to an abundant Live Oak acorn crop.

A female and her half grown young were seen by Dudley Vaill at Darlington Plantation, Georgetown County, April 18, 1953. If the young were half grown at this date, the eggs must have been laid in March, which is an early date.

SUPPLEMENT

REDHEAD: *Aytha americana*

The Redhead has never been regarded as a common duck along the South Carolina coast. However, a flock of 500 was seen at Hartwell Reservoir, Anderson County, on March 11, 1962, by Mrs. R. C. Tedards. Ninety-eight were still present on March 17 (*Chat*, 26: 1962, 49). This unusually large concentration indicates that migrating birds were involved.

One was seen in a small pond in the northwest corner of York County by William and Flodie Cobey on November 11, and again on November 27, 1965 (*Chat*, 30: 1966, 31).

RING-NECKED DUCK: *Aytha collaris*

At an unusually late date, two male Ring-necks were seen by Gaston Gage and Sprunt, June 28, 1955, at Lake Issequenna near Clemson (*fide* Sprunt).

GREATER SCAUP: *Aytha marila*

This species has been reported as being rare in winter on the lakes and ponds in the Piedmont (Shuler, 1966: 14). Inasmuch as the Greater Scaup has a decided preference for salt water and is extremely difficult to tell apart in the field from the Lesser Scaup, a specimen should be secured for positive identification. It does occur, however, in the interior of the State, for two males were collected in the "SRP area," Aiken, the first in January, 1964, the other on June 6, 1965. The first specimen was identified by Ernest E. Provost, who has given the study skin to the University of Georgia; the other was identified by Joseph R. Fatoro (*Chat*, 29: 1965, 107).

LESSER SCAUP: *Aytha affinis*

A flock of 35 (actual count) was seen at South Island, Georgetown County, on June 22, 1949, and another flock of 12 were seen at the same locality on June 15, 1953, by Thomas A. Yawkey and Burton. Single individuals have been recorded until July, but it is unusual to see flocks at this late date as most have migrated by the end of April.

An incident occurred, witnessed by Andrew H. DuPre, formerly Manager of the Cape Romain Refuge, and Burton, that apparently has not appeared in the literature. In late October, on going into the Refuge one morning in the patrol boat, and upon rounding a curve near Raccoon Keys, the observers came upon a flock of 75 to 100 scaups. Instead of taking flight, as is customary upon hearing the sound of a motor, every duck dived. The motor was cut and the boat allowed to drift. Ducks kept popping up, some within a few feet of the boat. Many tried to fly, but were unsuccessful, and immediately dived again. DuPre had been that way the previous afternoon and stated the ducks had not been present at that time. There is no explanation for this remarkable behavior.

SUPPLEMENT

BUFFLEHEAD: *Bucephala albeola*

Preferring salt water, the Bufflehead is usually seen in winter along the coast. It is, however, reported as being uncommon in the Piedmont (Shuler, 1966: 15).

OLDSQUAW: *Clangula hyemalis*

This species is another winter resident of South Carolina that is usually associated with the coast. Occassionally it strays inland, for one was seen December 9, 1950, at the Union Bleachery Reservoir near Greenville, where it stayed ten days (*Chat*, 18: 1954, 97). Five were seen by J. Fred Denton in the Savannah River just above the Clark Hill Dam, December 10, 1960 (*Chat*, 25: 1961, 41). Another was observed at Pierces Pond near Spartanburg on the Christmas Bird Count held December 28, 1960 (*Chat*, 25: 1961, 6).

A flock of eleven was seen in the "SRP area" on Clearwater Pond, Aiken County, by William Post, Jr., on December 19, 1960 (Norris, 1963: 12). Such a large flock is unusual away from the coast.

COMMON EIDER: *Somateria mollissima*

While observing a large flock of scaup feeding near the dock of the Carolina Yacht Club in the Cooper River on January 29, 1962, Burton noted an unusual duck among them. Walking down on the dock, he observed it for several minutes through 7X binoculars. The duck was so close to the dock and so tame that the bill was easily seen; so it was realized that it was either a female or immature male Common Eider. Having no way of collecting it, Burton took a perfectly recognizable photograph of it. He alerted many of his friends who saw the bird at close range. At his request it was collected by Richard Hutson and the study skin is that of a young male and is in the collection of the Charleston Museum, No. 62.17.2. This record constitutes the first known occurrence of the Common Eider in the State.

Apparently this same bird, or possibly another, was seen by M. L. Cates, Jr., of Spartanburg while on a short visit to Charleston. On returning home he wrote to Ellison A. Williams telling him about seeing the bird, but by the time his letter arrived, the duck had been collected.

A Common Eider was studied for several moments at close range by Chamberlain and A. M. Wilcox on the Christmas Bird Count held December 30, 1967. The observation was made as it flew by their boat off Bull's Island (*AFN*, 22: 1968, 204).

WHITE-WINGED SCOTER: *Melanitta deglandi*

A rare winter visitor along the coast, this species has twice been recorded from the Piedmont (Shuler, 1966: 15). One of these records was of one that appeared

SUPPLEMENT

at the Union Bleachery Reservoir near Greenville on March 12, 1950, and remained twelve days (*Chat*, 18: 1954, 97).

SURF SCOTER: *Melanitta perspicillata*

The Surf Scoter is the rarest of the scoters that are seen off the coast of South Carolina during the winter. However, three were seen well within Dewees Inlet by Burton on December 12, 1968. They were immature birds; one was a male and two were females. Being extremely tame, they were studied from the beach at a distance of less than 40 yards.

COMMON SCOTER: *Oidema nigra*

On August 11, 1964, three male Common Scoters were seen just outside the surf off the beach at Hilton Head Island (*Chat*, 28: 1964, 135). On September 4, 1966, a small flock was seen by Mrs. Ellison Smith off Murrell's Inlet, Georgetown County (*Chat*, 30: 1966, 110). By mid-September, considerable numbers had arrived. This species is by far the earliest of the sea-ducks to arrive in numbers off the South Carolina coast (*fide* Dick).

RUDDY DUCK: *Oxyura jamaicensis*

The Ruddy Duck is now established as a nesting bird within the State. On June 27, 1959, Sidney Hill, Manager of the Bear's Island Game Management Area, Colleton County, reported seeing a pair of adult Ruddy Ducks with young in the area. Later, Hoyt Mills reported seeing a pair with five young in Jack Creek Pond, Bull's Island. Chamberlain and Robert H. Coleman went to Bull's Island to investigate and found not only one pair but two with five young each (*Chat*, 23: 1959, 87). After the expenditure of much effort, the nest of a Ruddy Duck, containing two eggs, was found May 8, 1963, at Magnolia Gardens, Charleston County, by Ernest Cutts and T. A. Beckett, IV (*Chat*, 27: 1963, 53).

HOODED MERGANSER: *Lophodytes cucullatus*

Heretofore the evidence of the Hooded Merganser breeding within the State has been based on very flimsy evidence. In 1839 Audubon on Bachman's statement reported it as breeding in South Carolina. On April 6, 1937, E. J. DeCamps secured a single egg from William W. Elliott of Beaufort, who had been given it by a workman, who, when felling a tree, found a duck that had been killed by the fall along with five broken eggs; the sixth was intact. Inasmuch as both the Wood Duck and the Hooded Merganser nest in trees, and the females of both have crests, and because the bird was not brought in for positive indentification, this left the evidence of the breeding of the Hooded Merganser still in doubt.

SUPPLEMENT

In May 1967, two young Hooded Mergansers were seen in the "back-water" at Magnolia Gardens, Charleston County. While fairly well feathered, they were unable to fly and one was secured by T. A. Beckett, III, and presented to the Charleston Museum. It was made into a study skin, No. 69.49. This constitutes the first positive evidence that the Hooded Merganser breeds in South Carolina.

This species is reported as being a common fall and spring visitor in the Piedmont, sometimes seen in winter (Shuler, 1966: 16).

COMMON MERGANSER: *Mergus merganser*

The Common Merganser has been usually regarded as a fairly rare winter resident, but it may be more prevalent than generally thought. Somewhat similar to its near relative the Red-breasted Merganser, it probably has been overlooked by many observers. Regarded primarily as a coastal visitor, it sometimes is seen further inland. A pair was observed by Robert H. Coleman and T. A. Beckett, III, at the Sandhill Wildlife Refuge at McBee, Kershaw County, January 1, 1958, and a remarkably large number were seen on the Hartwell Reservoir, Anderson County, by Mrs. R. C. Tedards, September 24, 1961. The flock consisted of 250 individuals (*Chat*, 25: 1961, 96). The only possible explanation is that they were early migrants that would break up into small groups upon reaching the coast.

Six were seen at Lake Murray, Lexington County, January 10, 1962, by Mrs. Ellison D. Smith (*fide* Sprunt).

RED-BREASTED MERGANSER: *Mergus serrator*

The Red-breasted Merganser has been gradually extending its breeding range to the south. On June 6, 1965, a female with two ducklings was seen sitting on a mudbank opposite Rockville, Charleston County, by T. A. Beckett, III. Upon being observed, they took to the water and swam into the nearby marsh. All further efforts to locate them failed. However, two years later, on June 28, 1967, a young bird with down feathers was seen at Wrightsville Beach, North Carolina (*Chat*, 32: 1968, 27).

This species is not usually observed inland. There are two records from the "SRP area," Aiken: one January 20, 1965, and the other during the month of April, 1965. The first was a juvenile male, the other an adult male (*Chat*, 29: 1965, 109). On the Christmas Bird Count held December 27, 1966, several females were seen at Hartwell Reservoir, Anderson County (*AFN*, 21: 1967, 184). It is reported as being an uncommon winter visitor in the Piedmont (Shuler, 1966: 16), and in the Columbia area (*R–L list*, 1968).

SUPPLEMENT

WHITE-TAILED KITE: *Elanus leucaurus*

This western bird is an extremely rare and sporadic visitor to South Carolina. In 1834, Audubon received a live specimen from Dr. Ravenel and others were shot and brought to him from "about 40 miles from Charleston." In recent years there has been only one sight record from within the State (*S. C. Bird Life*, p. 152). On June 6, 1952, about eleven miles from Clemson, a White-tailed Kite was seen by Douglas E. Wade and another was observed by him May 18, 1953, three miles north of Clemson. When first seen, both birds were extremely close, making it possible to view clearly their shape, size and color. (*Chat*, 17: 1953, 70 and *AFN*, 7: 1953, 267).

SWALLOW-TAILED KITE: *Elanoides forficatus*

In past years the Swallow-tailed Kite has become scarce, but ever since a nest was found in the Francis Marion National Forest in 1935, it has become more common in certain localities. In one season three nests were located. In the summer of 1967, Richard Stanland sighted nineteen swallow-tails flying over the rice fields on the North Santee River, but the distance from the nesting area to the rice fields is not great.

While the species may be looked for in any part of the State, though rarely seen, the residents of the city of Chester were very much excited when one was seen flying over the business district on August 1, 1967 (*Chat*, 31: 1967, 58). On August 2, 1968, another was observed in Richland County by Robert Desportes.

MISSISSIPPI KITE: *Ictinia misisippiensis*

While the Mississippi Kite is a fairly common summer resident, it is not generally seen by too many people. When at the Wateree Prison Farm, located in Sumter County, Dr. and Mrs. William G. Cobey saw 40 on May 24, 1961 (*Chat*, 25: 1961, 69). For one to see such a large concentration is unusual. Three were seen at the same location by Marcus B. Simpson, Jr., on June 24, 1967; In June and July of that year, Douglas Pratt found them common at the Prison Farm.

ROUGH-LEGGED HAWK: *Buteo lagopus*

Although a specimen of this boreal bird has never been collected in the State, multiple sightings by competent observers seem to justify its being added to the "State List." Beside the sight records that appear in *South Carolina Bird Life*, p. 170, others are: one seen by Peter Manigault at Fairlawn Plantation, Charleston County, on the Christmas Bird Count held December 23, 1957 (*AFN*, 12: 1958, 131); two observed by Adair Tedards, April 12, 1966, at Hartwell Reservoir, Anderson County. One was in the dark phases, the other in normal plumage. The former came within 30 or 40 yards of the observer and in so doing dropped its feet so that the feathered tarsi could be seen plainly (*Chat*, 30: 1966, 107). At the same location another was seen by Mr. and Mrs. Tedards on the Christmas Bird Count held December 27, 1966 (*AFN*, 21: 1967, 184). One was seen at Piedmont, Greenville County, on the Christmas Bird Count held December 29, 1967 (*AFN*, 22: 1968, 203). Another was observed at close range and studied carefully both when perched and in flight on January 1, 1968, near Anderson (*Chat*, 32: 1968, 19). From the aforementioned records, it appears that the Rough-legged Hawk is a rare visitor in the Piedmont and an accidental visitor in the coastal area.

GOLDEN EAGLE: *Aquila chrysaëtos*

Apparently the Golden Eagle is becoming more common throughout the State. Most of the South Carolina records are from birds wantonly shot by so-called sportsmen. A bird shot in the easternmost corner of Berkeley County, January 16, 1957, had a wing-spread of 6 feet, 8 inches, and weighed 9¼ pounds. The first summer record from the coastal area was one seen over Wappoo Creek, Charleston County, July 15, 1953, by E. Burnham Chamberlain.

Birds that have been shot have been reported from the Congaree Swamp, Richland County; near Russellville, Berkeley County; 10 miles southwest of Orangeburg. Records of birds observed are from Bull's Island, North Santee River, Ashley River, and many other localities.

A bird banded in the Pisgah National Forest, North Carolina, on March 9, 1937, was shot three weeks later at Tigerville, Greenville County, S. C. (*fide* Sprunt).

The status of the Golden Eagle in South Carolina can now be changed to a regular but rare winter visitor.

BALD EAGLE: *Haliaetus leulocephalus*

Due to pesticides, shooting, and other causes, the Bald Eagle is becoming scarce, not only in South Carolina, but throughout the nation. There are many who think that it will become extinct unless drastic actions are taken to save it. Several nests are known in the State: one is on Bull's Island, and during the nesting season people are not allowed to approach within half a mile of the nest to prevent disturbance of the birds; and another nest is at Middleburg Plantation, Berkeley County. One bird has been raised at the latter nest during each of the past several years.

Edward von S. Dingle reports that since the building of the Santee-Cooper Dam the eagles nesting at Middleburg Plantation seem to feed entirely on fish that have been killed by passing through the turbines.

SUPPLEMENT

On July 15, 1953, Miss Elizabeth Simons saw, out of her window in the Charleston Museum, five Bald Eagles in flight. The field marks were unmistakable; both the level position of the outstretched wings and the flash of white on heads and tails were clear. While fishing in the surf at Capers Island in late October many years ago, Burton counted 18 Bald Eagles drifting southward along the beach apparently migrating in a leisurely way. Such sightings will probably not be repeated unless some drastic laws are passed protecting the Bald Eagle.

PEREGRINE FALCON: *Falco peregrinus*

The Peregrine Falcon is now rarely seen in the State. The first record for Richland County is when one was found dead on a street in Columbia, January 2, 1954. It was a female with a wingspread of 46 inches and a weight of 2 pounds, 15 ounces (*Chat*, 18: 1954, 25).

EASTERN PIGEON HAWK: *Falco columbarius*

While regarded as a fairly common winter resident, the species is reported as being "rarely seen in the open fields in the Piedmont" (Shuler, 1966: 21) and rare in winter on Hilton Head Island (*fide* Newhall).

SANDHILL CRANE: *Grus canadensis*

The Sandhill Crane is such a large bird and flies so differently from the herons and egrets that it hardly can be mistaken for anything else. It occurs so rarely in South Carolina that any records of its sighting are noteworthy.

On July 23, 1963, at 6 P.M., eight Sandhill Cranes were observed by Burton flying across Charleston Harbor. While under observation they changed formation and flew "line abreast," with some starting to soar. Thinking they were heading for Drum Island in the center of the harbor, he called several "birders," but, unfortunately, none was at home. Two days later Mrs. C. B. Albrecht, who lives on the city end of Sullivan's Island, called to say she had seen "three very large grey birds" in the marsh back of the Island. She was sure they were Sandhill Cranes. On the same day a call was received from W. D. Magwood saying that "five large grey birds had flown right over him" when he was on his shrimp trawler at the mouth of Shem Creek, which is very near the place where the birds seen by Mrs. Albrecht were observed.

In December, 1964, first-hand reports were submitted to John Henry Dick that five Sandhill Cranes had been seen in the TI–TI, Colleton County, located between the Ashepoo and Edisto Rivers (*Chat*, 29: 1965, 26). On December 30, 1966, Dick had the thrill of seeing fourteen cranes in the marsh at Pon-Pon, just across the Edisto River from Willtown Bluff. There were eleven adults with three young. (*Chat*, 31: 1967, 24).

SUPPLEMENT

One was seen at Lavington Plantation, Colleton County, by Mr. and Mrs. David Maybank in late February or early March, 1966. The Maybanks were in an automobile and approached to within 60 feet of the bird before it flew. It was feeding in a recently burnt-over field.

Two sight records that have not been included in *South Carolina Bird Life* are: In July, 1924, one was seen by Burton near Cape Romain. It spent the greater part of the summer there; the other was one seen several times at Bull's Island by Spencer Meeks, December 26–28, 1941 (*fide* Sprunt).

LIMPKIN: *Aramus guarauna*

An inhabitant of certain fresh-water marshes of Florida and lower Georgia the Limpkin is so rare in South Carolina that only four records of its occurrence are known. However, on June 23, 1956, while driving in his car on the Bear Swamp Road, Charleston County, I. J. Metcalf saw a Limpkin crossing the road. He approached to within 25 feet of the bird before it flew, thereby giving him an excellent view of it (*News and Courier*, June 29, 1956).

KING RAIL: *Rallus elegans*

A late breeding record for this fresh-water rail occurred when a small downy black young was seen September 27, 1957, by L. L. Ferebee at Tillman, Jasper County (*fide* Sprunt).

WAYNE'S CLAPPER RAIL: *Rallus longirostris*

A late breeding record for the "marsh hen" is that of a downy young, estimated as being 10 days old, was seen following an adult near Rockville, Charleston County, by John Henry Dick, September 23, 1957.

SORA RAIL: *Porzana carolina*

The Sora Rail is regarded as a fairly common winter resident, but apparently some individuals remain during the summer. T. A. Beckett, III, has seen them at Magnolia Gardens, Charleston County, on the following dates: May 29, June 17, July 9, August 19 and 23.

BLACK RAIL: *Laterallus jamaicensis*

The smallest and most elusive of the rails, because of its small size, is rarely seen by ornithologists. One was noted by Robert H. Coleman, December 10, 1961, on the edge of Rantowles Pond, Charleston County. J. Fred Denton had the unique experience of having one fly into the screen surrounding the porch of his house at Edisto Beach on September 24, 1960. The bird was apparently blinded by nearby lights.

Two nests of the Black Rail were found at Cat Island, Georgetown County, by Ray H. Nicholson of Orlando, Florida. One was "new" the other "used." The date was June 26, 1947 (*Chat*, 15: 1951, 78).

PURPLE GALLINULE: *Porphyrula martinica*

If, throughout the State, a lookout is kept for ponds containing pickerel weed (*Pontederia cordata*), locally known as "wampee," there is a chance of seeing a Purple Gallinule, for they prefer this weed for their nests above all else. A specimen was collected at Lake Katherine, Richland County, April 17, 1961, and is now in the collection of the Columbia Science Museum. Another was seen in Kershaw County by Mrs. Ellison Smith, April 7, 1962.

Heretofore, the Purple Gallinule has been regarded as a summer resident, but one was seen on Bull's Island on the Christmas Bird Count held December 27, 1950. The temperature that day was 32° Fahrenheit (*AFN*, 5: 1951, 97). It can now be regarded as "casual" in winter.

COMMON GALLINULE: *Gallinula chloropus*

A late nesting record of the Common Gallinule is that of an adult with three downy young seen in a pond at Dixie Plantation, Charleston County, September 8, 1950, by John Henry Dick.

AMERICAN COOT: *Fulica americana*

Although this species was thought to nest in South Carolina, it was not until May 1, 1960, that a nest, with eight heavily incubated eggs, was found by T. A. Beckett, III, and Ernest Cutts in a small fresh-water pond at Magnolia Gardens, Charleston County. The previous year Beckett has found an eggshell that led him to suspect a coot was nesting there (*Chat*, 24: 1960, 75). It was also found nesting 3 miles southwest of Williston, Barnwell County, July 20, 1961, by William Post, Jr. The nest contained "two warm eggs." Altogether there were five adult coots in the area, and three days later one was seen with three chicks (*Chat*, 25: 1961, 88).

It now appears to have become a fairly common breeding bird in certain areas of the State, for 40 pairs were reported nesting on Bull's Island in 1964 (*fide* Cutts).

SEMIPALMATED PLOVER: *Charadrius semipalmatus*

Reported as being an uncommon migrant in the Piedmont (Shuler, 1966: 25).

WILSON'S PLOVER: *Charadruis wilsonia*

Wilson's Plover is predominantly an inhabitant of the beaches. Therefore, when Burton found one on May 10, 1952, feeding in a rice field at the Santee Gun Club, located several miles inland from the sea, the record was surprising.

SUPPLEMENT

KILLDEER: *Charadrius vociferus*

Although the Killdeer is known to breed in the State, additional nesting locations are as follows: Camp Barton, Lexington County (D. Monteith); near Spartanburg (Cannon); Silver Bluff, Aiken County (Norris); near St. George, Dorchester County (E. C. Clyde); near Pinopolis, Berkeley County (E. R. Cuthbert, Jr.).

Nests with eggs have been found as early as March 14 (Monteith) and as late as July 9 (J. D. Yount).

AMERICAN GOLDEN PLOVER: *Pluvialis dominica*

Inasmuch as the American Golden Plover is a rare transient in South Carolina and therefore seldom seen, the following sightings are worthy of note: one on Bull's Island, December 28, 1949, by Sprunt; another near McClellanville by Robert Edwards, May 8, 1951; one at Sol Legare Island by Ellison Williams and Arthur Wilcox, May 9, 1954; another within the city limits of Charleston by Mrs. J. C. Green and Robert H. Coleman, August 25, 1959; and one was observed at Jeremy Inlet, Edisto Island by Louise Button and E. R. Cuthbert, Jr., on December 19, 1967. All of the aforementioned places are located in Charleston County.

AMERICAN WOODCOCK: *Philohela minor*

Since the Woodcock is known to be a very early breeder, a nest that was found with eggs on February 2, 1951, near Beaufort, by J. K. Hollis elicited no great surprise (*fide* Sprunt).

UPLAND PLOVER: *Bartramia longicauda*

Inasmuch as the Upland Plover is a rare transient in the State, all sightings are considered noteworthy: two observed at Edisto Beach on May 14, 1962, by Mrs. P. L. Atwood and Mrs. B. H. Guy, Jr.; one at Secessionville, Charleston County, by Mr. and Mrs. R. H. Coleman, April 25, 1962; two seen at the Florence County Airport, July 26, 1963, and eleven observed at the Columbia Airport, Lexington County, July 18, 1966. Both of these observations were made by Mrs. Ellison Smith; a photograph of one was taken in late March, 1965, at Hilton Head Island by Mr. and Mrs. Aden Gokay.

SPOTTED SANDPIPER: *Actitus macularia*

South Carolina has long been thought to be in the breeding range of the Spotted Sandpiper, but this fact was not established until 1960. On a small island near Snelgroves Landing at Lake Murray, Lexington County, Mrs. Ellison Smith saw a young Spotted Sandpiper. Returning the next day, August 1, 1960, she flushed two young sandpipers that were just able to fly and she saw another not yet able to fly. A few days later the nest was discovered by Mrs. Smith. It held the "part-shell" of a hatched egg. The nest and egg fragments have been deposited in the Charleston Museum (*Chat*, 24: 1960, 100).

GREATER YELLOW-LEGS: *Totanus melanoleucus*

Winter records of the Greater Yellow-legs from the interior of the State are rare, but William Post, Jr., observed four at Reynolds Pond, 6 miles north of Aiken, December 31, 1961, and one was seen by him at the same location, December 22, 1962.

LESSER YELLOW-LEGS: *Totanus flavipes*

This species is reported as being an uncommon migrant in the Piedmont (Shuler, 1966: 26).

AMERICAN KNOT: *Calidris canutus*

The Knot is rarely seen inland, but one was observed by Annie R. Favor, Margaret H. King, and Kay Sisson on the Spring Bird Count held May 3, 1963, at Eastover, Richland County (*Chat*, 27: 1963, 45).

PURPLE SANDPIPER: *Erolia maritima*

If the jetties at Georgetown and Charleston were carefully watched during the winter months, in all probability numbers of Purple Sandpipers would be seen, and the species would be found to be a regular winter visitor. Ever since the first Purple Sandpiper was collected in the State by Burton and Dr. R. C. Murphy in 1939, it has been observed in increasing numbers. A flock of 50 Purple Sandpipers was seen on the rocks at Fort Sumter by John Henry Dick, February 19, 1953. A flock of 14 was seen at the same locality, February 20, 1954, by Rock Comstock, with some remaining as late as April 28 (*Lesser Squawk*, May, 1954).

On March 18, 1963, B. R. and Norman Chamberlain observed 26 on the South Jetty at Charleston (*Chat*, 27: 1963, 34). Several were observed on the North Jetty at the mouth of Charleston Harbor, March 24, 1967, by Julian Harrison and Norman Chamberlain.

WHITE-RUMPED SANDPIPER: *Erolia fuscicollis*

One was seen in the Columbia area in 1950 (*R–L list*, 1968). The latest spring record is that of 10 seen by Robert M. Coleman and Francis M. Weston on June 10, 1962, at Rantowles Pond, Charleston County (*Chat*, 26: 1962, 81).

BAIRD'S SANDPIPER: *Erolia bairdii*

There is only one record from the Piedmont, when one was seen near Greenville in April, 1955 (Shuler, 1966: 26).

SUPPLEMENT

DUNLIN: *Erolia alpina*

The Dunlin is another bird that is rarely seen inland. One was observed at Hartwell Reservoir, Anderson County, on the Christmas Bird Count held December 26, 1965. It had a broken leg, but was capable of flight (*Chat*, 30: 1966, 19). Another was observed May 6, 1967, in York County, by Mrs. W. G. Cobey (*Chat*, 31: 1967, 70).

STILT SANDPIPER: *Micropalma himantopus*

This species has been reported as an uncommon transient in the Piedmont (Shuler, 1966: 27). On July 15, 1954, two were observed in full plumage by Francis M. Weston on the mudflats on the western edge of Charleston. The date is by far the earliest recorded in the State for the fall migrations of this rare transient. (*Chat*, 19: 1955, 28). Two were observed by Ellison A. Williams and Arthur Wilcox, May 9, 1954, on Sol Legare Island, Charleston County.

SEMIPALMATED SANDPIPER: *Ereunetes pusillus*

The Semipalmated Sandpiper is an uncommon migrant in the Piedmont (Shuler, 1966: 27), and seen occasionally in the Columbia Area (*R–L list*, 1968).

BUFF-BREASTED SANDPIPER: *Tryngites subruficollis*

On September 7, 1957, a Buff-breasted Sandpiper was seen by Burton on the front beach of Sullivan's Island near Breach Inlet. It was with a group of Sanderlings and small sandpipers all in view at the same time through 7X binoculars, thereby giving an excellent comparison with regard to its size. The bird was extremely tame and was studied carefully for several minutes at a distance of 40 feet, as well as being examined from several angles. When it finally flushed, its flight was very fast and erratic (*Chat*, 21: 1957, 89). The only other occurrence of the Buff-breasted Sandpiper in South Carolina is one taken by Hoxie on St. Helena's Island in 1884 (*S. C. Bird Life*, p. 249).

Two Buff-breasted Sandpipers were seen at Ocracoke Island, North Carolina on September 17, 1957 (*Chat*, 21: 1957, 89), and a male was collected near Savannah, Georgia, by Ivan R. Tomkins, September 29, 1951 (Burleigh, *Georgia Birds*, p. 272), showing that this inland bird appears occasionally along the South Atlantic coast.

MARBLED GODWIT: *Limosa fedoa*

The only July record of the Marbled Godwit was one seen July 13–15, 1959 on the mudflats at the west end of Broad Street in Charleston, by Francis M. Weston.

SUPPLEMENT

RUFF: *Philomachus pugnax*

On January 22, 1961, a Ruff was seen at the Savannah National Wildlife Refuge, Jasper County, by J. Fred Denton and Winthrop Harrington. Realizing its importance, they notified E. O. Mellinger, Refuge Biologist, and Ivan R. Tomkins of Savannah, who both saw the bird. Because of the outstanding ability of those seeing this bird, plus the fact that several Ruffs have been reported from coastal North Carolina, an exception is being made and this species is being included on the "State List."

SANDERLING: *Crocethia alba*

Primarily a bird of the front beaches, a Sanderling was seen near the Hartwell Reservoir, Anderson County, September 18, 1962 (Shuler, 1966: 27).

AMERICAN AVOCET: *Recurvirostria americana*

In recent years the American Avocet has become increasingly common in South Carolina, especially during the winter months. On February 26, 1952, Thomas A. Yawkey reported that a flock of 50 had wintered at South Island, Georgetown County, and a flock of over 100 was reported as being in the Santee Delta on November 15, 1954 (*Chat*, 19: 1955, 46). Again, in 1956, Yawkey stated that between 100 and 200 were wintering on South Island.

A single bird was seen September 21, 1960, on Edisto Beach, Charleston County, by Harvey Lybrand and Mrs. Paul Atwood, and what is thought to have been the same bird was seen by Mr. and Mrs. A. S. Sprunt, Jr., and John Henry Dick (*Chat*, 24: 1960, 100). On December 18, 1965, six were observed by Arthur Wilcox and Burton feeding on the mudflats back of Sullivan's Island. One was observed at Huntington State Park, Georgetown County, by Superintendant Norman Cooler, October 18, 1968, and in February 1969, John Henry Dick and Robert V. Clem saw between 600 and 1,000 American Avocets on South Island, Georgetown County.

BLACK-NECKED STILT: *Himantopus mexicanus*

Since the finding of the first nest with eggs in the State by Ellison A. Williams in 1938, the Black-necked Stilt has become a fairly common summer resident in South Carolina during recent years. In June 1953, Thomas A. Yawkey reported seeing young at South Island and stated he had seen young the previous year.

About 50 stilts were seen at the Santee Gun Club, July 13, 1955, by Francis M. Weston, *et al.*, and the following year approximately the same number were observed by Burton, *et al.*, at the same location.

Nests have been found at Cape Romain, Drum Island, South Island, and at several plantations along the Santee River (*fide* Cutts).

SUPPLEMENT

RED PHALAROPE: *Phalaropus filicarus*

Any of the phalaropes are rare in South Carolina, but the Red Phalarope is the rarest of the three. One was seen at Cape Romain by Peter Manigault and William P. Baldwin, June 11, 1960 (*Chat*, 24: 1960, 76), and another was observed in a pond near Wallace River (Rantowles), Charleston County, September 15, 1963, by James B. Shuler and Lester L. Short, Jr. (*Chat*, 28: 1964, 30).

WILSON'S PHALAROPE: *Steganopus tricolor*

The Wilson's Phalarope differs from the other two phalaropes in being less pelagic and more terrestrial. It is seldom, if ever, seen on the ocean, being a bird of the inland marshes (Bent, 1927: 28). It is a rare transient in South Carolina.

Ellison A. Williams and Arthur Wilcox saw one on Sol Legare Island May 9, 1954. A pair was sighted by Drayton Hastie and T. A. Beckett, IV, at Magnolia Gardens, April 23, 1966. At Huntington State Park a female was studied at a distance of 150 feet through 20X binoculars on March 24, 1968, by Colonel and Mrs. Frederick M. Probst and Roger Parrott. The two former localities are in Charleston County, the latter in Georgetown.

NORTHERN PHALAROPE: *Lobipes lobatus*

The Northern Phalarope is not a bird that is seen commonly within the State, and it is usually looked for on the coast. However, a pair was seen in the "SRP area," Aiken, on May 2, 1956, by Hatcher, Van Denburg, and Norris. Another was seen in the Columbia Area on September 11, 1950 (*R–L list*, 1968).

A full-plumaged female was watched for several minutes, May 22, 1961, by Mr. and Mrs. Ellison D. Smith. It was swimming in its characteristically "spinning" motion on Lake Murray, Lexington County (*Chat*, 25: 1961, 68).

POMARINE JAEGER: *Stercorarius pomarius*

There are but two sight records of the Pomarine Jaeger for South Carolina. While on amphibious training exercises in 1943, Allan R. Phillips was in a "duck," (a small amphibious vehicle) close to shore off Bull's Island when two jaegers passed close by. "One bird showed no elongated feathers, doubtless an immature; but the other had the central tailfeathers elongated and with broadly rounded tips, clearly Pomarine." Another was seen off Stono Inlet, Charleston County, by Ludlow Griscom and John Henry Dick, May 5, 1950. It was chasing gulls and terns.

The only specimen that has been taken in South Carolina was procured in a most remarkable manner, and in a most unlooked-for place. Ben Scott Whaley, while fishing in Lake Moultrie, Berkeley County, October 28, 1950, secured a male Pomarine Jaeger. It was making an attack on a Laughing Gull and had

SUPPLEMENT

knocked the latter out of the air three times and was in the process of drowning it when Whaley came upon them in his boat. The jaeger was so intent upon drowning its victim that it did not notice his approach and Whaley killed it with his paddle. Lake Moultrie is 30 miles inland from the coast and hardly a place to look for a jaeger. Two others were seen and remained on the lake until November 25 (*Auk*, 68: 1951, 377). The specimen is in the collection of the Charleston Museum, No. 50.164.

PARASITIC JAEGER: *Stercorarius parasiticus*

The only specimen of this species taken in South Carolina was one collected by Burton in 1935 at the mouth of Charleston Harbor (*S. C. Bird Life*, p. 258). Being a pelagic species, the Parasitic Jaeger does not usually occur within territorial waters. B. Rhett Chamberlain, while crossing Charleston Harbor, February 27, 1955, saw a Parasitic Jaeger harrying a flock of gulls (*Chat*, 19: 1955, 47). Another was reported in Hog Island Channel, Charleston Harbor, on February 23, 1964, by Peter Manigault, who stated "it appeared to fly well enough, but on each occasion it was flushed, flew only a short distance." Obviously there must have been something wrong with the bird. What was probably the same bird was seen by Paul W. Sykes, Jr., March 7, 1964, and again by Manigault the next day (*Chat*, 28: 1964, 55). Two Parasitic Jaegers were seen from the beach at Bellefield Plantation, Georgetown County, by Edwin Blitch, III, and others, on November 17, 1968. During most of the day there was a heavy fog that was the probable cause of their coming so close to shore.

GLAUCOUS GULL: *Larus hyperboreus*

In the field the Glaucous Gull is extremely difficult to tell from the Iceland Gull. The first specimen for the State of the Glaucous Gull was collected by E. B. Chamberlain in 1947 (*S. C. Bird Life*, p. 260).

In March, 1959, Mr. and Mrs. Francis Barrington saw a large, very pale gull on the flats on the Ashley River side of Charleston. After careful study and after consulting Peterson's *Field Guide*, they were convinced it was a Glaucous Gull (*Lesser Squawk*, April, 1958).

Four large white gulls were seen February 22, 1966, by Edward A. Hyer, at the Ben Sawyer Bridge back of Sullivan's Island. They were of such large size that they were thought to be Glaucous and not Iceland Gulls.

ICELAND GULL: *Larus glaucoides*

One was seen by E. Burnham and Rhett Chamberlain near the Shen Creek Bridge, Charleston Harbor, on January 4, 1964. It was with a flock of Herring and Ring-billed Gulls and was studied for a period of two hours. Occasionally it would approach to within 30 or 40 feet of the observers and among the things noted was its bill, which was short and much more slender than the nearby Herring Gulls (*Chat*, 28: 1964, 49). Because of the outstanding ability of the observers and the conditions under which the gull was seen, an exception is being made and the Iceland Gull is being included on the "State List." One was taken by Tomkins at the mouth of the Savannah River (Burleigh, *Georgia Birds*, p. 280), which is the dividing line between South Carolina and Georgia.

GREAT BLACK-BACKED GULL: *Larus marinus*

In the original publication of *South Carolina Bird Life*, the authors predicted that this large gull "would be seen more frequently in the future." The prediction has come true, but the Black-backed Gull must still be considered a rare winter visitor. Sightings of it were made on the following dates: one seen in vicinity of Bull's Island on the Christmas Bird Count held December 29, 1954 (*Chat*, 20: 1956, 4); another seen sitting on a buoy in Charleston Harbor by Ellison A. Williams, December 20, 1955 (*Chat*, 20: 1956, 18); still another seen in the harbor by Arthur M. Wilcox on March 15, 1957 (*Chat*, 21: 1957, 45); one observed at the Citadel Yacht Club on the Ashley River by I. S. H. Metcalf on January 24, 1959; another reported from Hilton Head Island during December 1961 (*Chat*, 26: 1962, 6); one observed by John Henry Dick on Bull's Island, November 12, 1961; on December 30, 1962, two adults and an immature were at Murrell's Inlet and two more were seen at the same location by Mrs. Ellison D. Smith on March 22 (*Chat*, 28: 1964, 143); another was noted by Ernest Cutts in Price's Inlet on the Christmas Bird Count held December 31, 1966, and an immature was seen by Burton at the upper end of the Isle of Palms on December 12, 1968.

HERRING GULL: *Larus argentatus*

Reported as a regular winter resident in the Columbia Area (*R–L list*, 1968), the Herring Gull has also been found nesting on the North Carolina coast. Quite possibly nests will eventually be found, along with nests of other gulls in some of the colonies along the South Carolina coast. The Herring Gull is increasing in such numbers that it should be looked for at city dumps even in the interior of the State. Frequently, other, and sometimes rare gulls, are seen feeding with them at these locations.

RING-BILLED GULL: *Larus delawarensis*

This gull has been extending its range gradually into the interior of the State. It is now reported as a common winter resident along the Savannah River in the general area of the "SRP area" and the Clark Hill Dam (Norris, 1963: 23). It is also reported from the Piedmont (Shuler, 1966: 28) and in the Columbia Area (*R–L list*, 1968).

LAUGHING GULL: *Larus atricilla*

Ever since the finding of the first nest and eggs in 1933 (*S. C. Bird Life*, p. 263), the Laughing Gull has become an abundant breeding bird along the South Carolina coast. T. A. Beckett, III, estimated that 450 pair were nesting on DeVeaux's Bank, at the mouth of the North Edisto River in May, 1967 (*Chat*, 31: 1967, 80).

This species is a rare transient inland, two having been seen at Greenville on April 13, 1952 (Shuler, 1966: 28).

FRANKLIN'S GULL: *Larus pipixcan*

A goose hunter shot a young female Franklin's Gull on the Catawba River on October 13, 1952. It is now at the State Museum in Raleigh, N. C. The river is the dividing line between North and South Carolina. Therefore, I thought that this record could be regarded as a "first" for either State, but in a letter from Harry T. Davis, then director of the North Carolina State Museum, dated February 1, 1957, in answer to an inquiry as to the exact location where the bird was taken, Davis states: "From a map I would say that this bird certainly was in our geographical area." Thus, the gull, realizing that the river was the dividing line between the two states, made certain that it flew only within the boundary of North Carolina.

BONAPARTE'S GULL: *Larus philadelphia*

This gull is much more an inhabitant of the coastal area than either the Herring or Ring-billed, but nevertheless it does straggle inland. On the Christmas Bird Count held in 1948, ten were reported seen near Columbia (*AFN*, 3: 1949, 86); another seen by Denton, Norris, and Post, December 31, 1956, at Clearwater Pond, Aiken County, April 12, 1963 (*Chat*, 27: 1963, 58); and 16 were reported from the Clark Hill Dam, Anderson County, on November 23, 1962, by William Post, Jr.

GULL-BILLED TERN: *Gelochelidon nilotica*

In recent years the Gull-billed Tern has so increased its nesting along the South Carolina coast that in some localities it can be regarded as being fairly common. The Gull-billed Tern usually leaves the State by the end of September, but one was seen on the Christmas Bird Count held December 30, 1967, near Charleston, by Chamberlain and A. M. Wilcox (*AFN*, 22: 1968, 204).

FORSTER'S TERN: *Sterna forsteri*

This species has been reported twice from the interior of the State: one seen at

SUPPLEMENT

Hartwell Reservoir, Anderson County, in May, 1953 (Shuler, 1966: 29); another seen at the same location, May 2, 1964 (*Chat*, 28: 1964, 81).

COMMON TERN: *Sterna hirundo*

The Common Tern was found breeding for the first time in South Carolina, May 31, 1964, at DeVeaux's Bank, at the mouth of the North Edisto River, by Ernest Cutts and Roy Baker. Two nests were found; one contained three eggs and the other, two. The nests were less than two feet apart among a small colony of Gull-billed Terns (*Lesser Squawk*, September, 1964). Shortly afterwards, T. A. Beckett, III, reported finding six more nests with eggs.

Since the creation of the Hartwell Reservoir, in Anderson County, the Common Tern is seen during the spring and fall migrations in flocks of up to 50 birds (*Chat*, 29: 1965, 30). Records reported from Richland County are: September 13, 1965; August 6, 1967; and May 24–29, 1968, by Mrs. Ellison Smith.

ROSEATE TERN: *Sterna dougallii*

Wayne stated (1910) that a specimen of the Roseate Tern had been taken "near Charleston" by Ellison A. Smythe, Jr. No date or definite locality other than "near Charleston" is given. Smythe was collecting in the late 1880's and usually reported anything unusual in the *Auk* or in the *Proceedings of the Elliott Society*. In order to track down the basis of this record, for it is the only time that the species is reported as having been taken within the State, Burton contacted the son and daughter of Smythe. His son, Dr. Thomas Smythe, Professor of Biology at State Teacher's College in Pennsylvania, and his daughter Grace, living in their home in Salem, Virginia, after a diligent search through their father's collection, reported that they were unable to find the specimen. They did, however, find a study skin of the Roseate Tern that had been taken in Massachusetts in 1890. Smythe's log-book was consulted and it contained no reference to a Roseate Tern in South Carolina, though he speaks of shore birds including Forster Terns and Least Terns. In view of this evidence, Smythe's alleged specimen of the Roseate Tern from South Carolina should be expunged, and this leaves the inclusion of the species on the State List based solely on sight records.

Between April 17–21, 1966, H. Cook Anderson was "birding" on the Isle of Palms, Charleston County, when he saw three Roseate Terns. Cook was familiar with the bird, having seen it at various times in New Jersey and Delaware. Two were observed at DeVeaux's Bank, at the mouth of the North Edisto River, April 23, 1967, by Mr. and Mrs. Marvin Veronee (*fide* Beckett).

SUPPLEMENT

SOOTY TERN: *Sterna fuscata*

The Sooty Tern, if seen in South Carolina, is usually the victim of a tropical storm. This was literally true after hurricane "Cleo" skirted the coast in late August 1964. Birds were reported from the following places: one found alive but later died at Hilton Head Island; one noted flying over Edisto Beach; one found dead on Sullivan's Island and another on the Isle of Palms. The latter is in the Charleston Museum's Collection, No. 65.52.

Three were seen over the Ashley River at Charleston and were captured August 11, 1960, and taken to T. A. Beckett, III, who found them in poor physical condition. They were later released, apparently the victims of hurricane "Diane," which had just visited the coast. But on June 6, 1968, a sick or wounded Sooty Tern was found near Charleston in a rather congested subdivision. It died the following day. The weather was normal at the time (*Chat*, 32: 1968, 63). Another was picked up in an exhausted condition at Litchfield Beach, Georgetown County, by Mrs. Ellison D. Smith, October 20, 1968.

BRIDLED TERN: *Sterna anaethetus*

Like the Sooty, the Bridled Tern, if seen on our coast, is usually the victim of some meteorological disturbance. One was found on the front beach of Sullivan's Island, Charleston County, September 8, 1950, by John E. Gibbs (*Chat*, 19: 1955, 87), and the badly decomposed body of another was picked up on the Isle of Palms, August 31, 1952, by Sprunt (*Chat*, 16: 1952, 98), thus establishing the sixth and seventh records for the State.

LEAST TERN: *Sterna albifrons*

A small colony of Least Terns was found nesting on a small island near Snelgrove's Landing, Lake Murray, Lexington County, by Robert DesPortes, June 30, 1960. This record extends the breeding range in South Carolina about 110 miles from the coast (*Chat*, 24: 1960, 100). The terns returned to nest the next year at the same location. About 20 pair were found breeding at Lake Marion, Orangeburg County in June 1967, by William Post, Jr. (*Chat*, 31: 1967, 96). It is reported as being a rare summer visitor in the Piedmont (Shuler, 1966: 29).

Although a common summer resident, usually departing by the end of October, apparently a few remain during the winter months because they have been reported on the following dates: three seen at Hilton Head Island, December 30, 1966 (*AFN:* 21, 1967, 185); three reported from Bull's Island, December 30, 1967 (*AFN*, 22: 1968, 204); and several seen December 28, 1967, at Hilton Head Island (*Chat*, 30, 31, and 32: 1966–67–68).

SUPPLEMENT

SANDWICH TERN: *Thalasseus sandvicensis*

During recent years the breeding population of the Cabot's Tern has been showing a steady increase along the coast. At DeVeaux's Bank, North Edisto River, the population has now reached about 300 breeding pairs (*fide* Beckett).

CASPIAN TERN: *Hydroprogne caspia*

The Caspian Tern should be listed as a "permanent resident that does not breed." As far as known, no egg of this large tern has been collected in South Carolina. Burton has seen at least 100,000 nests of the Royal Tern and has banded over 10,000 of them, but in not a single instance was a Caspian Tern noted among them. Ernest Cutts and T. A. Beckett, III, probably have seen almost as many nests and studied many colonies of the Royal and they, too, report that they never have seen a Caspian flying around the area at any time nor found an egg.

The Caspian Tern is seldom seen inland. One was reported near Greenville, April 28, 1952, (Shuler, 1966: 29); another reported being at Par Pond, Barnwell County, April 29, 1964, by John Hutcher.

BLACK TERN: *Chlidonias niger*

While the Black Tern is an abundant, though not breeding, summer resident along the coast, it is unusual to see one in full plumage during the month of June. However, on June 5, 1949, four were seen at the grillage at Sullivan's Island by Burton; several were seen in full plumage at South Island, Georgetown County by Thomas A. Yawkey and Burton, June 15, 1953, and one was seen by Francis M. Weston, June 21, 1961, at Rantowles, Charleston County (*Chat*, 25: 1961, 96).

This species is occasionally reported from the Columbia Area (*R–L list*, 1968) and a very late record is one seen November 6, 1966, at Hartwell Reservoir, Anderson County, by Adair Tedards (*Chat*, 31: 1967, 28). An early inland record was one seen at the same location by the same observer on July 6, 1968 (*Chat*, 32: 1968, 80).

NODDY TERN: *Anous stolidus*

Three Noddy Terns were seen at close range from the beach at Pawley's Island, Georgetown County, August 9, 1948, by George W. Sciple (*Chat*, 15: 1951, 33). On September 8, 1950, an exhausted bird was picked up by Burton on the beach at the Isle of Palms. It made but little attempt to fly. It was frightfully thin, weighing only 3½ oz. Realizing that it could not survive, Burton collected it, and it is now in the collection of the Charleston Museum, No. 50.147.

SUPPLEMENT

RAZOR-BILLED AUK: *Alca torda*

While walking on the front beach of Sullivan's Island, Charleston County, Eugene J. DeVeaux found an oil-soaked Razor-billed Auk. Thinking that it might survive, he released it. The date was March 9, 1958 (*AFN*, 12: 1958, 270). On February 15, 1963, another was found in the same condition by Mary Enloe and Jesse Newsome at Bull's Island. After having some of the oil removed, it was fed fresh shrimp, but died the following day (*Chat*, 28: 1964, 51). The first record for the State was one found on Pawley's Island, Georgetown County, in a similar condition on January 12, 1948. It is in the collection of the Charleston Museum, No. 48.3 (*S. C. Bird Life*, p. 284).

That the Razor-billed Auk is off the coast of South Carolina is apparent, for one was seen March 12, 1964, approximately 30 nautical miles off Charleston by Paul W. Sykes, Jr. (*Chat*, 30: 1966, 26). A flock of 12 was observed for some time December 19, 1964, seven miles east of Tybee Island, located at the mouth of the Savannah River, Georgia. They were with a large concentration of seabirds (*Oriole*, 1, March, 1968). The only reason one of these birds ventures close to shore is if it is oil-soaked or ill.

DOVEKIE: *Plautus alle*

In December, 1950, a woman was washing clothes in her yard on American Street in Charleston when a strange bird flew in the side of the building just over her head. It was brought to the Museum for identification, and proved to be a Dovekie, which, though apparently unhurt, died the next day. A few days later another that had been found in St. Andrew's Parish near Charleston, was brought to the Museum by Chalmers McDermid. It, too, died shortly afterwards. Two more were brought in from nearby localities. When crossing Wallace Creek, Charleston County, on December 15, 1950, two were seen flying over the creek by John Henry Dick. The only inland record was one found in Florence County, December 10, 1950 (*fide* Sprunt).

WHITE-WINGED DOVE: *Zenaida asiatica*

While on a dove hunt on James Island, Charleston County, a White-winged Dove was shot by W. O. Bootle, December 6, 1965 (*Chat*, 30: 1966, 52). Not being sure to which race it belonged, it was sent to George Sanders, Research Biologist of the U. S. Fish and Wildlife Service, for positive identification. Sanders pronounced it belonging to the race *asiatica*. The bird was a male in good plumage, and is now in the collection of the Charleston Museum, No. 66.13. This is the first time that it has been recorded from the State. Another was shot on Wadmalaw Island in December, 1968.

SUPPLEMENT

YELLOW-BILLED CUCKOO: *Coccyzus americanus*

Wayne stated (1910) that the second set of eggs was laid in August. A nest with two eggs was found, September 18, 1963, by F. C. and E. C. Clyden in Florence County. The eggs hatched the following day (*Chat*, 28: 1964, 33). A bird was seen incubating on September 5, 1949, by Burton and others (*S. C. Bird Life*, p. 560). From the above facts, apparently two broods are sometimes raised by some birds.

One was seen at Hilton Head Island on the Christmas Bird Count held December 28, 1963 (*AFN*, 18: 1964, 166). As far as is known, this record provides the only winter occurrence of the species in South Carolina.

BLACK-BILLED CUCKOO: *Coccyzus erythropthalmus*

A late record of the Black-billed Cuckoo was one seen November 14, 1965, by Fred H. May at Edisto Beach (*Chat*, 30: 1966, 32).

SNOWY OWL: *Nyctea scandiaca*

The Snowy Owl is a sporadic visitor to South Carolina during the winter; therefore, any records of it should be noted. One was secured at Easley, Pickens County, December 19, 1949, by J. J. Cane (*Greenville Piedmont*, December 20, 1949); another at Traveler's Rest, Greenville County, in January 1952 (Shuler, 1966: 32); one seen several times at Hollywood, Charleston County, during February, 1956, by Henry W. H. Poole.

SHORT-EARED OWL: *Asio flammeus*

Usually seen in the coastal region, the Short-eared Owl had not been recorded in the northwestern section of the State until two were found at the backwater of Hartwell Reservoir, Anderson County, by Adair M. Tedards. Both had been shot by hunters: one on November 27, 1964; the other February 20, 1966. One recovered from its wounds and was released; the other did not survive.

SAW-WHET OWL: *Aegolius acadicus*

This diminutive owl is regarded as rare in South Carolina during the winter. The latest record is one that collided with an automobile driven by R. A. DesPortes about twenty miles south of Columbia, March 30, 1962 (*Chat*, 26: 1962, 41).

Other localities and dates are: Greenville, Shuler, November 12, 1952; Bull's Island, Kilham, February 25, 1953; Clyde, Florence County, Effingham, December 3, 1960. In December of 1963–64–65, one was caught and banded by Effingham in the same locality; McClellanville, Edwards, December 12, 1961; Clemson, Snyder, March 1, 1964; Magnolia Gardens, Beckett, January 31, 1965; near Kline, Barnwell County, Post, December 30, 1966.

SUPPLEMENT

From the aforementioned records, it is evident that this species is pretty well distributed over the State during the winter.

CHUCK-WILL'S-WIDOW: *Caprimulgus carolinensis*

The latest date when this species was heard calling was on the night of October 3, 1950, by John Henry Dick at Dixie Plantation, Charleston County.

WHIP-POOR-WILL: *Caprimulgus vociferus*

A Whip-poor-will was heard calling May 3, 1963, just before dawn by Martin H. Edwards. The location was on the Bull's Island Road, Christ Church Parish, Charleston County. This is the latest date recorded for the coast.

COMMON NIGHTHAWK: *Chordeiles minor*

A Common Nighthawk was seen at Magnolia Gardens, Charleston County, by T. A. Beckett, III, on March 8, 1953. This species was heretofore recorded as arriving March 20 (*Chat*, 17: 1953, 50).

RUBY-THROATED HUMMINGBIRD: *Archilochus colubris*

A hummingbird with red on its throat was seen by Mrs. W. H. Quattlebaum in her garden at North Charleston, January 28, 1956. The bird was feeding on her camellia bushes. The month of January, 1956, was unusually cold.

On January 6, 1959, another was seen by Mrs. John McCarthy at a distance of 20 feet, feeding on the camellia blooms in her garden in Charleston. The temperature 26 ° F, but no color was noticed on the throat. Still another was seen January 23, 1960, by Mrs. John Leland in her yard at Riverland Terrace near Charleston, and what is thought to have been the same bird had been observed by Mrs. Francis Barrington on January 14, 1960. The Barringtons and Lelands lived next door to each other at that time (*Lesser Squawk*, March, 1960). While photographing ducks from a blind at Dixie Plantation on January 28, 1958, Henry P. Staats saw a hummingbird that had a red throat.

Although none of these birds was collected, they were probably Ruby-throated Hummingbirds. The possibility exists however, that they were Rufus Hummingbirds (See *S. C. Bird Life*, p. 324). Under any circumstances, any hummingbird seen in winter should be collected for positive identification.

RED-COCKADED WOODPECKER: *Dendrocopus borealis*

The Red-cockaded is usually seen in the coastal area, but it is a well-established wintering and breeding species in the Carolina Sandhill National Wildlife Refuge located in Chesterfield County. The Refuge is located 125 miles from the coast. An extensive study of the area and the Red-cockaded was made by Lee Jones during 1962–63 (*Chat*, 27: 1963, 37).

SUPPLEMENT

IVORY-BILLED WOODPECKER: *Campephilus principalis*

This account is written for the record. *The Auk* is the official publication of the American Ornithologists' Union, and anything appearing in it is usually regarded as factual. The report of the Union's "Committee on Bird Protection, 1961" appears in *The Auk* (Vol. 79, 1962: 463–478). Under the Ivory-billed Woodpecker (p. 474), the report states: "No birds have been reported in Florida during the past year. A reliable observer was reported to have seen one bird in South Carolina during this period." No specific place in the State was named, because the Committee felt that under the circumstances this information should remain undisclosed. Inasmuch as this was a committee report, the editor of the journal had no alternative but to include it, especially as many other species were involved.

An investigation was initiated with the following results: The sight record of an Ivory-billed Woodpecker was made by the concessionaire of Bull's Island, which is part of the Cape Romain Refuge. Immediately upon hearing the report, the president of the National Audubon Society requested John Henry Dick to go to Bull's Island, at the Society's expense, to make a thorough investigation. As soon as he received the request, Dick went to the Island and spent seven days looking for the bird. He saw no sign of it, nor did he find any indication that one had been there. He did, however, see several Pileated Woodpeckers. Roughly, the Island is 6 miles in length and varies from ½ to 1½ miles wide, but the wooded area is somewhat less. During his stay there, Dick criss-crossed the Island many times with negative results.

A short time later the National Audubon Society instructed Alexander Sprunt, Jr., their Southern Regional Representative, to go to the Island to make another investigation. He spent two days there along with his son Alexander Sprunt, IV, and they, too, could find no trace of the bird. The person who made the report of the bird was working on some mechanical equipment at the garage at the time of the sighting. On the basis of these thorough investigations, there appears to be no ground for hope that Ivory-bills still exist in our area.

EASTERN KINGBIRD: *Tyrannus tyrannus*

The Eastern Kingbird, being a member of the flycatcher family, is thought to be wholly insectivorous; however, an instance of its deviation from its normal diet was witnessed by William K. Willard, on July 23, 1957. Willard watched a kingbird fly to the ground and pick up a small frog. After "working it over" it proceeded to eat it. This occurred in the "SRP area," Aiken, and was watched at a distance of 25 yards through binoculars (*Chat*, 21: 1957, 90).

This species is occasionally seen during the winter. One was noted at Bull's

SUPPLEMENT

Island, December 12, 1949, by Gumbart and Judd White on an Audubon tour (*fide* Sprunt); three seen at Hilton Head Island on the Christmas Bird Count held December 30, 1966 (*AFN*, 21: 1967, 186), and another seen at the same locality by Caroline Newhall. The latter bird remained until January 5, 1966 (*Chat*, 30: 1966; 22 and 55).

GRAY KINGBIRD: *Tyrannus dominicensis*

The Gray Kingbird is regarded as a rare summer visitor, but one was seen November 19, 1956, in the "SRP area," Aiken, by Eugene P. Odum (*Chat*, 21: 1957, 45). Other observations are: Edisto Beach, Mrs. Paul Atwood, May 13, 1961; Hunting Island, Mr. and Mrs. Tedards, May 24, 1962; three seen at the Golf Course, Parris Island, Attaway, May 24, 1962; Folly Island, Weston, June 15, 1962; Beaufort, Robert Russell, July 21, 1962; two at Hunting Island, Tedards, April 21, 1963; Edisto Beach, Atwood, May 1963, and April 9, 1964; Hilton Head Island, April 25, 1964, and April, 1966. There are also several other records of it having been observed. With the exception of the one seen by Odum, all of the others are from the coast region near the ocean.

WESTERN KINGBIRD: *Tyrannus verticalis*

While the Gray Kingbird is a rare summer resident, the Western Kingbird is a rare winter resident. At least ten have been recorded in recent years from the coastal area during the fall and winter months, the latest date being December 20–30, 1949, when one was seen by Sprunt on Bull's Island.

The only inland record is one observed by Hatcher and Van Denburg, November 11, 1956, in the "SRP area," Aiken (Norris, 1963: 30).

SCISSOR-TAILED FLYCATCHER: *Muscivora forficata*

There is no mistaking a Scissor-tailed Flycatcher. It is an accidental wanderer in South Carolina and is rarely seen. On July 7, 1952, one was observed by E. F. Holland, Refuge Manager at the Santee Wildlife Refuge near Summerton, Clarendon County; another was noted near the Sampit Bridge near Georgetown, June 16, 1952, by Mrs. Clyde Moses (*Chat*, 17: 1953, 73). One was seen between Clinton and Greenwood, June 28, 1953, by Miss Hallie Rogers (*fide* Sprunt).

EASTERN PHOEBE: *Sayornis phoebe*

This species was seen on August 17, 1968, at Bellefield Plantation, Georgetown County by T. A. Beckett, III, and John Dennis. The Eastern Phoebe is a common winter resident in the lower part of the State, usually arriving by early September.

SUPPLEMENT

EMPIDONAX FLYCATCHERS: *Empidona sp.*

Of the four confusing flycatchers of the genus *Empidonax*, the Acadian Flycatcher *E. virescens* is the common summer resident over most of the State. The others are extremely rare. In the field they can only be identified by their song, and even after a specimen has been collected, they are somewhat difficult to tell apart.

A female Traill's, *E. trailli*, was found dead at the base of the television tower at Aiken, October 5, 1957, by Norris. On the same date and at the same place, a female Least Flycatcher, *E. minimus*, was found. The latter specimen constitutes the third record for the State of the species. Both of these specimens have been examined by Allan R. Phillips and their identification confirmed. The skins are in his collection.

The fourth of these confusing flycatchers is the Yellow-bellied Flycatcher, *E. flaviventris*. Two specimens were taken by Wayne (*S. C. Bird Life*, p. 354), but later examination proved them to be immature specimens of the Acadian Flycatcher. Both the Yellow-bellied and Least Flycatchers are reported as having been seen several times in the Greenville area (Shuler, 1966: 38). However, until specimens are collected and identified by a competent ornithologist on this species, they will have to be regarded as being of hypothetical occurence.

EASTERN WOOD PEWEE: *Contopus virens*

The Eastern Wood Pewee is a common summer resident. One was seen March 20, 1957, at Quimby Bridge, Berkeley County, by E. B. Chamberlain. Heretofore, the earliest arrival date was April 14.

The first winter record was one seen on Bull's Island, December 31, 1949, by Alex Sprunt, IV (*fide* Sprunt); another seen at Hilton Head Island on the Christmas Bird Count, held December 29, 1965 (*Chat*, 30: 1966, 22), and another observed by Caroline Newhall at Hilton Head Island through the winter until January 5, 1966 (*Chat*, 30: 1966, 55).

VERMILION FLYCATCHER: *Pyrocephalus rubinus*

A male Vermilion Flycatcher was seen on the Christmas Bird Count, held December 29, 1954, by Arthur M. Wilcox and Julian Harrison at Mayrant's Reserve, Charleston County. It was collected a few days later and is now in the collection of the Charleston Museum, No. 56.2. This constitutes the first record for the State.

Another was seen by Ivan R. Tomkins at the Savannah River Refuge, Jasper County, January 10, 1959. It was also observed by E. O. Mellinger, Refuge Manager (*Chat*, 23: 1959, 37). On November 17, 1961, still another was seen at the Savannah River Refuge where it was observed by many people and re-

SUPPLEMENT

mained until January 28, 1962. At the boat landing at the Santee Gun Club, Charleston County, one was kept under observation for three quarters of an hour on January 5, 1962 (*Chat*, 26: 1962, 20). At the eastern edge of Columbia on the afternoon of April 14, 1963, a brilliant male Vermilion Flycatcher was seen by Mrs. B. W. Kendall (*Chat*, 27: 1963, 31).

HORNED LARK: *Eremophila alpestris*

The Horned Lark is a resident of the middle and upper part of the State; it is rare in the coastal area. A common permanent resident in the Piedmont, it has been reported nesting there since 1951 (Schuler, 1966: 41), and is fairly common in the Columbia Area (*R–L list*, 1968).

The first breeding record for the State was established by J. H. Fowles and Kay Sisson when an adult was seen feeding three young birds near Columbia in June 1950 (*Chat*, 14: 1950, 58). It was also found breeding at the old airport at Sumter during the first week in June 1957, by Mrs. C. Edmunds and William Haynesworth. In Greenville, Shuler found nest and eggs as early as March 16, 1954.

One was seen by Dr. Harry C. Oberholser, March 21, 1954, on Wadmalaw Island, Charleston County (*fide* Sprunt).

BANK SWALLOW: *Riparia riparia*

The earliest spring record for the Bank Swallow is one seen by Burton, April 20, 1958, at Dover Plantation, Georgetown County.

BARN SWALLOW: *Hurundo rustica*

Since Burton found the first nest of the Barn Swallow in the State in 1946 near McClellanville, it has been extending its breeding range along the coast during the subsequent years. However, the first nest of the Barn Swallow found in the upper part of the State was on July 19, 1961. Gaston Gage found one on the front porch of a house that had been vacated permanently prior to being flooded by the rising waters of Hartwell Reservoir. The location was at the Excelsior Mill Village near Clemson, Oconee County (*Chat*, 25: 1961, 89). With the inundation of the village, the swallows built their nests under the bridge at Hartwell Reservoir, 6 miles away, where they were found again by Gage (*Chat*, 26: 1962, 81). The species was also found nesting at Wateree Lake, Kershaw County, by Mrs. Ellison D. Smith in June 1967.

CLIFF SWALLOW: *Petrochelidon pyrrhonota*

At best, the Cliff Swallow is regarded as an uncommon transient throughout the State. However, on May 23, 1965, Caroline Watson was visiting Hartwell Reservoir Dam, Anderson County, when she noticed about 25 Cliff Swallows

SUPPLEMENT

flying directly over the river. She immediately notified Mrs. R. Connor Tedards, who, with her husband, visited the dam the next day, and was able to see
two nests. About 50 birds were in the vicinity, and from their activities they were
sure other nests were present, but were not visible because of the evening fog
rising from the river.

Two days later, the Tedards returned to the site accompanied by Jay Shuler,
who, in spite of adverse light conditions, took some perfectly recognizable
photographs of some of the nests. There were 13 complete nests, some being on
the Georgia side of the river. By July 16, some young birds were out of the nest
but perching in close proximity. Two days later some immatures were flying
with adults over the river below the dam, and by the middle of August all had
left (*Chat*, 29: 1965, 95). The following year they were again present, nesting
at the same location.

Nests were found under the Buster Boyd Bridge on Highway 49 that crosses
the river between York County, S. C., and Mecklenberg County, N. C., by Mr.
and Mrs. Joseph R. Norwood. Nests were found on both sides of the bridge.

Along the coast it is still regarded as a migrant. Two were observed July 13,
1955, at McClellanville, Charleston County, by Francis M. Weston and others.
Heretofore the earliest fall migration date was August 10.

PURPLE MARTIN: *Progne subis*

The Purple Martin was so abundant in Charleston in 1885 and had become
such a nuisance to the people promenading the Battery that the firemen were
called upon to play streams of water on them to try to get rid of them. It is not
reported how successful the firemen were (Jacob Schirmer Records in the S. C.
Historical Society). In recent years there has been a noticeable diminution in
their numbers in certain areas, probably because of pesticides.

COMMON RAVEN: *Corvus corax*

One was seen by Dr. James Martin, February 9, 1954, on Seabrook's Island,
Charleston County. The Common Raven was seen with several crows, presuma-
ble the Fish Crow, *C. ossifragus*. Dr. Martin was struck immediately by the
raven's large size, for it appeared at least twice the size of the crows.

This record is the second for the coastal area, one having been captured
November 21, 1943, by Noel B. Wright, in Beaufort County (*S. C. Bird Life*,
p. 370).

FISH CROW: *Corvus ossifragus*

While the Fish Crow is known as far inland as Aiken and Greenwood
counties, their abundance was not realized until William Post, Jr., found a roost
near Langley, Aiken County, seven miles east of Augusta, Georgia. On Septem-

SUPPLEMENT

ber 23, 1961, he counted nearly 3,000 birds as they approached the roost, which was located in about a six-acre section of damp woods on the site of a dried lake bed. During the day the crows foraged along the Savannah River, a distance of 12 miles from the roost (*Chat*, 25: 1961, 91).

In 1794, the Duc de Liancourt visited the United States, and while stopping at Runnymede, located on the Ashley River, commented on an enormous flight of crows. After 174 years this flight persists, although in somewhat diminished numbers. The question is whether or not crows have been using the same roost for countless generations.

RED-BREASTED NUTHATCH: *Sitta canadensis*

The Red-breasted Nuthatch is not often seen in South Carolina, for it is a sporadic winter visitor. A few have been observed in the vicinity of Aiken by William Post, Jr. Most are recorded during the month of December. Two were seen within the city limits of Charleston by Ellison A. Williams. From time to time they are observed in various parts of the State on Christmas Bird Counts.

BROWN-HEADED NUTHATCH: *Sitta pusilla*

Generally only one brood is raised by the Brown-headed Nuthatch, but T. A. Beckett, III, has found, through banding, that frequently two broods are raised.

HOUSE WREN: *Troglodytes aedon*

In the summer of 1950, a pair of House Wrens raised four young in the yard of Ruth Crick in Spartanburg (*Chat*, 14: 1950, 57). This is the first breeding record for the State. This species now appears to be a fairly common nesting bird in the vicinity of Rock Hill, York County (*Chat*, 28: 1964, 86).

LONG-BILLED MARSH WREN: *Telmatodytes palustris*

The Long-billed Marsh Wren is usually thought of as being an inhabitant of the marshes of the coastal area. However, several have been seen in the "SRP area," Aiken, and one was collected April 29, 1958. Another was found at the base of the television tower near Aiken, September 24, 1957 (Norris, 1963: 37). This species is probably more common inland than generally thought and should be looked for in winter in marshy areas.

SHORT-BILLED MARSH WREN: *Cisothorus platensis*

In the Savannah River Refuge, Jasper County, E. O. Mellinger, Refuge Manager, heard a number of males singing during August 1965–66–67. They were located on the border of a dried-up pool. These Short-billed Wrens were thought to be early migrants and not breeding birds, as none were heard singing during June and July.

SUPPLEMENT

AMERICAN ROBIN: *Turdus migratorius*

During recent years, the American Robin has been gradually extending its breeding range towards the coast. In July, 1957, a young bird was observed at Hampton Park located within the city of Charleston, by E. Burnham Chamberlain and Webber Mott (*News &Courier*, July 9, 1957). One was seen at Edisto Beach, June 3, 1956, by Mrs. Paul E. Atwood (*AFN*, 10: 1956, 378), but there was no evidence that this individual was a breeding bird.

Edward von S. Dingle states that, with experience, the Newfoundland subspecies, *T. m. nigridens*, is easily distinguished from the typical form. He writes that "the back of this subspecies is slate grey, with no indication of an olive tinge, as in the eastern bird; the under parts are very dark rusty red with no indication of orange brown." Dingle has several specimens in his collections that have been examined by Dr. John W. Aldrich of the U. S. Fish and Wildlife Service and Dr. Harry C. Oberholser, both of whom confirmed his identification.

WOOD THRUSH: *Hylocichla mustelina*

A common summer resident, one was seen near Charleston by T. A. Beckett, III, on the Christmas Bird Count held December 26, 1952 (*AFN*, 7: 1953, 101). On January 25, 1954, another was observed by J. S. Metcalf in St. Andrew's Parish, Charleston County, and on December 4, of that year still another was seen on John's Island, Charleston County, by Louise Holbrook (*fide* Sprunt).

EASTERN HERMIT THRUSH: *Hylocichla guttata*

One seen in the "SRP area," Aiken, on May 12, 1960 (Norris, 1963: 39). The latest date recorded is May 3.

Another was observed by Francis Barrington on James Island, Charleston County, September 13, 1968 (*Lesser Squawk*, October, 1968). Heretofore, the earliest arrival date noted was October 18.

SWAINSON'S THRUSH: *Hylocichla ustulata*

The one specimen of the western race, *H. u. ustulata*, in the collection of the Charleston Museum, was collected by A. T. Wayne on October 22, 1901, at Mt. Pleasant, Charleston County (*S. C. Bird Life*, p. 407). This specimen has been re-identified as the eastern race, *H. u. swainsoni* by Gorman H. Bond, author of the paper "Geographic Variations in the Thrush *Hylocichla ustulata*" (*Proceedings of the U. S. National Museum*, No. 3471, 1963: 114). The race *ustulata* is therefore removed from the State List.

OLIVE-BACKED THRUSH: *Hylocichla ustulata*

The Olive-backed Thrush is regarded as a fairly common transient in the spring and fall, but apparently a few remain later. One was seen on Bull's Island,

SUPPLEMENT

by Mrs. Francis Barrington and Mrs. Robert H. Colemen on the Christmas Bird Count held December 27, 1956. It was studied at a distance of 10 feet (*AFN*, 11: 1957, 128). This is the first mid-winter record, although it has been seen as late as November 10 in the Columbia Area (*R–L list*, 1968).

Another was seen near Charleston on the Christmas Bird Count held December 28, 1962 (*Chat*, 28: 1964, 22).

GRAY-CHEEKED THRUSH: *Hylocichla minima*

The Gray-cheeked Thrush is a fairly common transient, but a few remain into the winter. The following observations of it have been made, all being on the Christmas Bird Counts: Bull's Island, Cutts, December 31, 1960 (*Chat*, 25: 1961, 3); near Charleston, December 28, 1962, and near Aiken, January 3, 1963 (*Chat*, 28: 1964, 21 and 22); and another seen near Charleston, January 2, 1966 (*Chat*, 30: 1966, 20). One was studied at a distance of 30 feet with 7X glasses at the Santee Wildlife Refuge, January 1954 (*AFN*, 8: 1954, 118). Another was noted on Bull's Island on December 31, 1966 (*AFN*, 21: 1967, 185).

VEERY: *Hylocichla fuscensens*

The earliest fall migration date on which this species has been noted is August 21 (*R–L list*, 1968); heretofore, the earliest date was August 28.

EASTERN BLUEBIRD: *Sialia sialia*

The Eastern Bluebird usually nests in boxes or cavities in trees at least a few feet above the ground. E. R. Cuthbert, Jr., found a nest in May, 1967, that "was about 9 inches below the ground at the bottom of an earthen cavity in a pine savannah (*sic*) 1 mile east of Summerville," Dorchester County. As late as July 20, a female was seen by Dick feeding young at the nest.

BLUE-GRAY GNATCATCHER: *Polioptila caerulea*

While a permanent resident in the coastal area, the first winter record of this species above the fall line was one seen six miles north of Aiken by William Post, Jr., on December 30, 1957 (*AFN*, 12: 1958, 131).

GOLDEN-CROWNED KINGLET: *Regulus satrapa*

The Golden-crowned Kinglet is a fairly common winter resident. The earliest fall date is one that was seen by John Henry Dick and Mr. and Mrs. A. S. Sprunt, Jr., September 27, 1963, at Bay Point, Edisto Island.

RUBY-CROWNED KINGLET: *Regulus calendula*

This species has now been seen as late as June 7, in the Columbia Area (*R–L list*, 1968); heretofore, the latest date was May 10.

SUPPLEMENT

SPRAGUE'S PIPIT: *Anthus spragueii*

The Sprague's Pipit is so unusual in South Carolina that any occurrence of it should be noted. In November and December, 1956, several were seen and one was collected by Robert A. Norris in the "SRP area," Aiken. The following winter two more were seen and heard at the same location (Norris, 1963: 42). One was seen in the Columbia Area in 1950 (*R–L list*, 1968), and it is reported as being rare in the Piedmont (Shuler, 1966: 50).

The bird collected by Norris was the first taken in the State in 56 years, the last having been collected by Wayne in 1900 (*S. C. Bird Life*, p. 421).

WHITE-EYED VIREO: *Vireo griseus*

In the coastal area the White-eyed Vireo is a permanent resident, less common in winter; it is a summer resident in the interior of the State. However, one was seen in Aiken County on December 31, 1961 (*AFN*, 16: 1962, 155), and December 29, 1967, by William Post, Jr., in the same area. Another was seen in Richland County, December 10, 1967, by Bruce A. Mack (*Chat*, 32: 1968, 50).

YELLOW-THROATED VIREO: *Vireo flavirons*

The latest fall migration date of this species is one that was seen near Columbia on October 20 (*R–L list*, 1968); the latest date, heretofore, was September 21.

BLACK AND WHITE WARBLER: *Mniotilta varia*

The Black and White Warbler is a rare winter visitor in the central part of the State. One was seen near Columbia on the Christmas Bird Count held on December 29, 1956 (*AFN*, 11: 1957, 128). Two were observed near the Congaree River, Richland County, December 7, by Bruce A. Mack (*Chat*, 32: 1968, 51).

PROTHONOTARY WARBLER: *Protonotaria citrea*

Apparently, the Prothonotary Warbler is more common in the upper part of the State than generally thought, for Mr. and Mrs. R. C. Tedards have seen it frequently in the vicinity of Anderson and have found a nest with five eggs in a Red Maple stump 11½ feet from the ground near a small creek in Rocky River Swamp, Anderson County (*Chat*, 32: 1968, 77).

Ten singing males were heard along the Wateree River in Sumter County, and numbers were seen by Marcus B. Simpson, Jr., along the Wateree and Catawba Rivers in York and Kershaw counties.

An early spring arrival date is one seen March 11, 1967, at Magnolia Gardens, by T. A. Beckett, III (*Chat*, 31: 1967, 80).

SUPPLEMENT

SWAINSON'S WARBLER: *Limnothlypis swansonii*

The Swainson's Warbler has always been regarded as a rare summer resident, but Dr. Robert A. Norris found it fairly common in suitable localities in the Aiken area (Norris, 1963: 47), and James B. Shuler, Jr., has found it in the mountains of South Carolina in rhododendron-covered slopes of streams (*Chat*, 26: 1962, 75). Mark Simpson, Jr., saw and heard one singing, June 25, 1965, at Matthews Creek in northern Greenville County at an elevation of 3,000 feet; another was seen and heard by him in the gorge of the Horsepasture River, Pickens County, at an elevation of 1,200 feet.

Brooke M. Meanley, who has made a study of the Swainson's Warbler in the southeastern United States, says: "At the turn of this century Swainson's Warblers were apparently more numerous in the lower coastal plain than they are today." (*The Living Bird*, Vol. 5, October, 1966). This statement is apparently true of South Carolina, for more records are coming from the central part as well as the mountainous area of the State than from the low country. However, in recent years there are many more competent observers in this area of the State. Nonetheless, the Swainson's Warbler is now regarded as rare in the coastal area.

Two Swainson's Warblers were picked up by Burton at the foot of the television tower in Charleston on October 8, 1954. The latest fall date on which it had been previously noted was September 28.

WORM-EATING WARBLER: *Helmitheros vermivorus*

The Worm-eating Warbler is considered a rare transient along the coast, with the extreme dates given for the spring migrations as from April 7 to May 5. From birds captured in mist nets (for banding purposes) by T. A. Beckett, III, at Magnolia Gardens, it appears that the height of the migration covers a short period of time. Birds were first netted on April 12 and 15, and a great number were netted on April 18. Therefore, in the coastal area the species should be looked for in the second and third week of April (*Lesser Squawk*, June 1964).

This warbler is rarely found above the southern tip of Florida during the winter, but one was seen at Bull's Island by I. S. H. Metcalf, December 26, 1953, on the Christmas Bird Count. It was studied at a distance of 10 feet under good conditions (*Chat*, 18: 1954, 7 and *AFN*, 8: 1954, 116).

GOLDEN-WINGED WARBLER: *Vermivora chrysoptera*

A specimen of this species was found dead by Burton at the base of the television tower in Charleston, October 8, 1954. It was the only specimen found among the hundreds of dead birds. The latest date recorded previously was

SUPPLEMENT

September 28. The Golden-winged Warbler is rare anywhere in South Carolina, but is more so below the fall line.

BLUE-WINGED WARBLER: *Vermivora pinus*

This warbler is of sufficient rarity that any record of its occurrence within the State is worthy of note. An adult male was seen by Douglas Pratt and Dr. and Mrs. Vaud Travis, April 21, 1965, near the Congaree River, Richland County, and another was observed at Hilton Head Island, April 27, 1965, by Caroline Newhall. It is reported as being a rare transient in the Piedmont (Shuler, 1966: 57) and one was seen as early as April 4 in the Columbia area (*R–L list*, 1968).

BACHMAN'S WARBLER: *Vermivora bachmanii*

The Bachman's Warbler is one of the rarest warblers in the United States and possibly one of the most sought after, but it is rarely seen. During the past twenty years some singing males have been located in Charleston County and many "birders" have had the gratification of adding it to their "life list." However, for fear that some over-enthusiastic ornithologist will collect it, in spite of its rarity, the location is made known to only a few individuals. There is absolutely no need of collecting one, for there is already a sufficient number of study skins on deposit in museum collections for any study that need be made of them.

In the spring of 1950, a male was seen at Fairlawn Plantation in the early morning of April 22. There was frost still on the ground, but the cold in no way deterred the male from singing. It was watched for about 10 minutes by the several people who were present.

Another singing male was seen across the Ashley River near Charleston in the spring of 1958. It was also seen at exactly the same place in 1959 and is thought to have been the same bird. It was found in a most unlikely spot. The Bachman's Warbler is thought to be an inhabitant of swamp areas with dense undergrowth, but this one was in a cut over pine area near human habitation where it could be seen plainly.

A male was observed near Moore's Landing in the spring of 1960 (*Chat*, 24: 1960, 86), and two singing males were located by R. H. Coleman between March 19 and May 4, 1961. One was watched by scores of observers; the location of the second was withheld for its protection (*Chat*, 25: 1961, 96). On the Spring Count, May 5, 1962, one was seen about 15 miles from Charleston (*Chat*, 26: 1962, 62). A few more reports of birds having been seen have been received, but sometimes a year or more elapses between sightings. It is possible that the bird occurs sparsely in suitable areas along the coast—possibly further inland—but is never seen.

SUPPLEMENT

A female Bachman's Warbler has never been observed since the time Wayne collected one on April 18, 1912. All of the aforementioned sightings have been in Charleston County.

TENNESSEE WARBLER: *Vermivora peregrina*

Being such a plain bird, the Tennessee Warbler is probably overlooked during migration. The second spring record for the State was when one was seen by Annie F. Faver, May 4, 1953, near Columbia (*R–L list*, 1968); another was seen near Clemson on the Spring Bird Count, April 19, 1961; and one was observed on Bull's Island, May 6, 1961 (*Chat*, 25: 1961, 55–56).

On October 7, 1964, and again on October 10, 1965, two Tennessee Warblers were captured in a mist net by T. A. Beckett, III, at Magnolia Gardens, Charleston County. They were banded by him, but before being released they were examined by E. B. Chamberlain, who concurred with Beckett's identification. While it doubtlessly ranges high in the top of trees, these two birds were caught along a ditch bank at the edge of a field.

NASHVILLE WARBLER: *Vermivora ruficapilla*

Another of our rare transients, one was found at the base of the television tower near Aiken by Robert A. Norris, October 5, 1957, and now is in the collection of Allan R. Phillips (Norris, 1963: 49). One was seen by John B. Hatcher near Aiken, May 1, 1964, in his back yard. It was studied at a distance of 30 feet through 9X glasses (*Chat*, 28: 1964, 97). Another was observed near Anderson on the Spring Bird Count, May 2, 1965. It was seen in the yard of Adair Tedards and was studied by her and two other members of the party (*Chat*, 29: 1965, 74).

MAGNOLIA WARBLER: *Dendroica magnolia*

The Magnolia Warbler is a fairly common spring and fall transient in the Piedmont. On the coast it is uncommon. One was observed by Louise Barrington at her home on James Island, Charleston County, September 29, 1956; another on Bull's Island, May 2, 1959, by Robert Edwards and Dr. Cavanaugh (*Lesser Squawk*, October 1956, and June, 1959).

CAPE MAY WARBLER: *Dendroica tigrina*

This species is reported as arriving by April 8 in the Columbia Area (*R–L list*, 1968). It is usually not seen in the State until April 15.

MYRTLE WARBLER: *Dendroica coronata*

A Myrtle Warbler was picked up at the foot of the television tower in Kershaw County, September 7, 1962, by Mrs. Ellison D. Smith. The specimen

SUPPLEMENT

is in the Columbia Museum of Science, No. 62.2.60. Heretofore, the earliest fall migration date reported was September 29.

BLACK-THROATED GREEN WARBLER: *Dendroica virens*

A specimen was collected in the "SRP area," Aiken, October 19, 1955; heretofore, the latest fall migration date recorded was October 10 (Norris, 1963: 52).

CERULEAN WARBLER: *Dendroica cerulea*

This species is rare anywhere east of the mountains, and especially in the coastal area. The first record for the coast was one seen by John Henry Dick at the south end of Edisto Beach, September 23, 1954 (*News & Courier*, September 26, 1957). On September 6, 1961, a male was picked up at the foot of the television tower at Beach Island, Aiken County, by William Post, Jr. It is in his collection. Three more were picked up September 7, 1962, at the television tower of Aiken, by Post. They were given to the University of Georgia for fat analysis (*Chat*, 27, 1963: 23). On the same date another was found at the television tower near Columbia, by Mrs. Ellison Smith. The specimen is in the Columbia Museum of Science. Edwin Blitch, III, found an immature female at the base of the television tower, Mt. Pleasant, Charleston County, September 7, 1962. It is in the collection of the Charleston Museum, No. 62.78.2.

BLACKBURNIAN WARBLER: *Dendroica fusca*

This handsome warbler is rarely seen in migration along the coast. On May 3, 1960, a female was seen in I'on Swamp, Charleston County, by Phillips Street, R. H. Coleman and Burton. It was feeding in the top of a large tree. A young male was picked up by Burton at the foot of the television tower in Charleston, October 8, 1954. It is in the collection of the Charleston Museum, No. 62.79.8.

YELLOW-THROATED WARBLER: *Dendroica dominica*

Edward von S. Dingle, while examining some warbler skins in the collection of the Charleston Museum, was attracted by an unusually long and slender-billed Yellow-throated Warbler, No. 30.147.1085. This bird had been collected by Arthur T. Wayne near Mt. Pleasant, Charleston County, January 9, 1912. The skin was sent to George M. Sutton, who wrote to Dingle that it was unquestionably a specimen of *D. d. stoddardi*. A subspecies that he himself had described in 1951 from the northeastern Gulf coast. (*cf.* Dingle, *Auk*, 78: 1961, 640).

CHESTNUT-SIDED WARBLER: *Dendroica pensylvanica*

The second record of this species for the coastal area was one seen by Mrs. Francis Barrington, October 9, 1955, in her yard on James Island, Charleston

County. It was an immature bird (*Chat*, 20: 1956, 49). The first coastal record was a male secured by Edward von S. Dingle, April 24, 1929, at Middleburg, Charleston County (*S. C. Bird Life*, p. 464). Another was seen by Dick, September 12, 1968, at Dixie Plantation. During the fall migration the Chestnut-sided Warbler has been seen as late as November 10 in the vicinity of Columbia (*R–L list*, 1968).

KIRTLAND'S WARBLER: *Dendroica kirtlandii*

The Kirtland's, along with the Bachman's, is one of the rarest warblers in the United States. To Mrs. Annie R. Favor of Eastover, Richland County, goes the unique distinction of having seen several Kirtland's Warblers in her yard; the first October 14, 1949; the second, September 1, 1951; the third on September 22, 1967 (*Chat*, 15: 1951, 83 & 31; 1967, 98). One was seen at a distance of from 8 to 40 feet and kept under observation with 9X glasses for approximately half an hour by John B. Hatcher in the "SRP area," Aiken, October 5, 1960 (*Chat*, 24: 1960, 192).

OVENBIRD: *Seiurus aurocapillus*

An Ovenbird was seen at Dixie Plantation, Charleston County, by John Henry Dick and Devin Garrity on January 1, 1969. It is rarely observed in mid-winter in South Carolina.

NORTHERN WATERTHRUSH: *Seiurus noveboracensis*

This species was seen on Bull's Island on the Christmas Bird Count, December 31, 1960 (*AFN*, 15: 1961, 162). Previously it was thought to occur casually only to November.

KENTUCKY WARBLER: *Oporornis formosus*

The first record of the Kentucky Warbler breeding in the coastal area was made by Ernest Cutts, April 20, 1952. The nest with six eggs was located on the Bee's Ferry Road, Charleston County. Fifteen years later, May 6, 1967, at the same location, a nest with eggs was found by Edwin Blitch, III. An individual was seen near Hartsville, Darlington County, on December 2, 1967, by Mrs. Willie M. Morrison (*Chat*, 32: 1968, 51). Heretofore, the latest fall date was October 24.

CONNECTICUT WARBLER: *Oporornis agilis*

The Connecticut Warbler is a rare transient in the western half of the State; it was unknown in the coastal area until it was seen and studied carefully on September 22, 1967, by Mrs. Ellison Smith at Garden City, Horry County (*Chat*, 32: 1967, 31).

SUPPLEMENT

One was found at the television tower near Aiken, by Robert A. Norris, September 30, 1957. He made a study skin out of it. John B. Hatcher observed another bathing in a bird bath in his yard near Aiken, October 1, 1960 (Norris, 1963: 56).

YELLOW-BREASTED CHAT: *Icteria virens*

A common summer resident, the Chat heretofore has been regarded as only accidental if seen in winter. With more feeding trays and more qualified observers, however, the Chat is seen fairly regularly during the winter months. One was observed when the temperature had dropped to 11° Fahrenheit.

Arthur T. Wayne, during his lifetime, found only two nests of the Chat; one in 1879 and another in 1896. However, Ernest Cutts, along with his two companions, Roy Baker and Edwin Blitch, III, has found over 25 nests in the past dozen years, all in the month of May in the vicinity of Charleston. They have also found nests in Oconee and Greenville counties.

HOODED WARBLER: *Wilsonia citrina*

A delayed migrant was seen at Hilton Head Island on the Christmas Bird Count, December 29, 1965 (*Chat*, 30: 1966, 16). Heretofore, it has been reported "Casually November 11."

WILSON'S WARBLER: *Wilsonia pusilla*

This rare transient passes through the Columbia Area from August 21 to September 6, although it has been reported as late as November (*R–L list*, 1968). On the coast it is extremely rare. On September 25, 1966, a male was seen by John Henry Dick and Mr. and Mrs. A. S. Sprunt, Jr., on the south end of Edisto Beach, and T. A. Beckett, III, and Edwin Blitch, III, saw one on the early date of March 25, 1967, at Magnolia Gardens, Charleston County (*Chat*, 31: 1967, 80).

John B. Hatcher found one at the foot of the television tower near Aiken, October 17, 1959 (Norris, 1963: 58).

CANADA WARBLER: *Wilsonia canadensis*

The first Canada Warbler recorded below the fall line was an immature female that was picked up at the base of the television tower in Charleston, by Edwin Blitch, III, September 8, 1962. The specimen is now in the collection of the Charleston Museum, No. 62.78.1. An immature bird was seen by Dick on Edisto Island, September 24, 1966.

AMERICAN REDSTART: *Setophaga rusticilla*

Although this species was long thought to breed within the State, the first record of it doing so was made by James B. Shuler on July 21, 1956. On that

SUPPLEMENT

date he saw a female Redstart feeding an immature bird. The location was near Keowee River about a mile south of Jocasee, Oconee County (*Chat*, 20: 1956, 82). As yet no nest with eggs has been found in the State.

WESTERN MEADOWLARK: *Sturnella neglecta*

One was trapped in the "SRP area," Aiken, by Robert A. Norris, February 24, 1958. It was identified independently by Wesley Lanyon and Burt L. Monroe, Jr., both of whom stated it was a specimen of *neglecta* (Norris, 1963: 60). This is the first time it has been recorded in the State.

YELLOW-HEADED BLACKBIRD: *Xanthocephalus xanthocephalus*

A male Yellow-headed Blackbird in full plumage can hardly be mistaken for anything else. The first record for the State is one that was trapped in 1884 by Loomis at Chester. During the week of March 15, 1950, one was taken by Richard Stanland at Kinloch Plantation, North Santee River. This is the second record of one taken actually within the State. It is in the collection of the Charleston Museum, No. 50.28. A male in good plumage was watched in the yard of Dr. Kenneth Herbert in Charleston, March 31, 1961 (*Chat*, 25: 1961, 42).

John B. Hatcher kept a Yellow-headed Blackbird under observation for eleven days at his home near Aiken from March 11–22, 1965. It was feeding on horse feed along with Brown-headed Cowbirds and Common Grackles. No attempt was made to collect it, but two color slides showing the characteristic yellow head were sent to the Charleston Museum (*Chat*, 29: 1965, 2). Another was observed at Hilton Head Island by Dr. and Mrs. Maurice Chanock (*Chat*, 31: 1967, 99). A male was seen with a flock of Red-winged Blackbirds on Wadmalaw Island, by Mrs. R. H. Coleman, Mrs. Louis Miles, and E. R. Cuthbert, Jr., on January 11, 1969.

RED-WINGED BLACKBIRD: *Agelaius phoeniceus*

Three unusual nests of the Red-wing were found, May 24, 1950, by Edward von S. Dingle and Burton in the marsh by the John's Island Bridge near Rantowles, Charleston County. They were placed on small hummocks and were less than a foot off the ground by actual measurements.

ORCHARD ORIOLE: *Icterus spurius*

The Orchard Oriole is reported as being seen as late as September 23, during fall migration in the Columbia Area (*R–L list*, 1968). The latest date, heretofore, was September 14.

The only winter record is that of a female that was shot (by parties unknown) December 31, 1953, and brought to E. R. Cuthbert, Jr., of Summerville, Dorchester County.

BALTIMORE ORIOLE: *Icterus galbula*

So many records have been received in recent years that the Baltimore Oriole is now becoming a fairly common winter visitor. Mrs. A. E. Morrison of Hartsville, Darlington County, has had many individuals stay at her feeding tray throughout the winter. From January 10–13, 1968, with snow and ice on the ground, she counted as many as 36 feeding at one time. They arrived as early as September 14, but all had departed by April 24.

The Baltimore Oriole is a rare and sporadic breeder in the upper and central part of the State. J. Fred Denton observed a male feeding a young, that, apparently from its size, was just out of the nest, on June 8, 1961, at North Augusta, Aiken County (*Chat*, 25: 1961, 91).

BREWER'S BLACKBIRD: *Euphagus cyanocephalus*

The Brewer's looks so much like the Rusty Blackbird that it is probably overlooked by many. Undoubtedly it is much more common within the State than generally thought. On the morning of April 21, 1953, Gabriel Cannon and Ellison A. Williams saw some Brewer's Blackbirds near Landrum, Spartanburg County. They were observed at close range, and particularly noticeable were the dark eyes of the females (*Chat*, 17: 1953, 74). On the Christmas Bird Count, held December 27, 1956, at least 75 were seen on Bull's Island by Dr. Robert D. D. Edwards and son (*AFN*, 11: 1957, 128). Eight were seen on the Spring Bird Count, April 25, 1962, at Eastover, Richland County (*Chat*, 26: 1962, 63). Two were also observed at the feeding table of I. S. Metcalf, December 29, 1951, James Island, Charleston County (*Lesser Squawk*, January, 1957).

COMMON GRACKLE: *Quiscalus quiscula*

A pair of Grackle was banded at Clemson, April 24, 1956, by R. E. Ware. They nested and later were seen feeding their young (*fide* Sprunt).

BROWN-HEADED COWBIRD: *Molothrus ater*

The cowbird was long thought to have bred within the State, but what appears to be the first authentic record was established when Gaston Gage, Sr., noted at Clemson on May 25, 1957, a young Brown-headed Cowbird being fed by a Yellow-throated Vireo (*Chat*, 24: 1960, 90). As far as known, the first egg of the cowbird found in the State was located in the nest of a Wood Thrush at Clemson by Mr. and Mrs. Gaston Gage, May 19, 1964. The nest contained two thrush and a single cowbird egg. The thrush eggs hatched, but the cowbird egg was found to have a small hole in it and was addled. It is now in the collection

SUPPLEMENT

of Ernest Cutts (*Chat*, 28: 1964, 97). The first egg found in the Low Country was found near Hollywood, Charleston County, by Ernest Cutts, May 5, 1965. It was in the nest of a White-eyed Vireo.

At Magnolia Gardens in the spring of 1965, T. A. Beckett, III, saw a young cowbird being fed by a Cardinal. In late June, 1963, C. T. Downer found a cowbird egg pushed down in the lining of the nest of a Blue Grosbeak at Campobello, Spartanburg County (*fide* Cutts).

During the summer, the cowbird is seen sparingly over the State, but on July 13, 1955, a flock of about 50 were seen by Francis M. Weston and others at Mt. Pleasant, Charleston County. During recent years, the cowbird apparently has been increasing in the coastal area during the spring and early summer.

WESTERN TANAGER: *Piranga ludoviciana*

In view of the multiple sightings of the Western Tanager it is now included on the "State List." The first one reported was on Bull's Island, December 27, 1954, by G. L. Brody (*AFN*, 9: 1955, 129).

Other sightings are: a male seen at the Charleston Country Club, James Island, by Alice L. Lowndes, May 10, 1957 (*News & Courier*, May 14, 1957); on December 23–24, 1957, and again on January 17, 1958, a male was observed at the feed tray of Mr. and Mrs. Francis Barrington at their residence on James Island, Charleston County. It was seen twice on the latter date; another observed by Helen Kendall, December 30, 1960, on the Christmas Bird Count held in the Columbia Area (*Chat*, 25: 1961, 14); a female was observed eating suet at about a distance of 25 yards from the residence of Carl and Florence Bauer in Dillon on January 19, 1966 (*Chat*, 30: 1966, 52).

SCARLET TANAGER: *Piranger olivacea*

While it is known that the Scarlet Tanager breeds in the northwestern section of the State, the first record of its nesting in the central area was when a pair was seen at Cope, Orangeburg County, May 22, 1951, by Thomas T. Traywick (*fide* Sprunt).

SUMMER TANAGER: *Piranga rubra*

One of the few winter records of the Summer Tanager in the United States was on December 26, 1952, when one was seen on Bull's Island by John Henry Dick and Sprunt (*AFN*, 7: 1953, 101).

On migration it is recorded as being seen in the Columbia Area as late as October 30 (*R–L list*, 1968). Heretofore, the latest recorded date October 14.

ROSE-BREASTED GROSBEAK: *Pheucticus ludovicianus*

While a few Rose-breasted Grosbeaks remain throughout the entire winter,

SUPPLEMENT

spring migrants have been seen in the Columbia Area as early as March 27, and the fall migrants as late as December 30 (*R–L list*, 1968).

Along the coast it is hardly more than accidental, but because there are more observers it is being reported more frequently. The following sightings have been reported in Charleston County: Folly Island, April 25, 1962, two seen, Coleman; James Island, April 23, 1968, Susan Brown; a male and female seen on the Bee's Ferry Road, May 3, 1963, Edwards and String. One was seen at Summerville, Dorchester County on May 1, 1948, and April 29, 1953, by Edmund R. Cuthbert, Jr.

BLACK-HEADED GROSBEAK: *Pheucticus melanocephalus*

On February 26, 1957, an "unusual grosbeak" was killed by Jimmy Rogers at Kingstree, Williamsburg County. On bringing it to the Charleston Museum for identification, there was some question as to whether it was a female Rose-breasted or Black-headed Grosbeak. In order to settle the question, it was sent to Dr. Herbert Friedmann, then Curator of Birds, U. S. National Museum, who pronounced it to be a specimen of the Black-headed Grosbeak. The specimen was retained by Rogers. This constitutes the first record for the State (*Chat*, 21: 1957, 91).

A Black-headed Grosbeak was observed by T. A. Beckett, III, at Magnolia Gardens, April 20, 1962; another was seen at a feeding tray located on James Island, by John Henry Dick, February 11, 1963; one was also seen by Mrs. Robert H. Coleman, March 1963, on James Island. It was collected and is in the collection of the Charleston Museum. All of the sightings were in Charleston County.

EASTERN BLUE GROSBEAK: *Giuraca caerulea*

Heretofore, the Blue Grosbeak was thought not to nest in the coastal area, but that is no longer true, for nests have been found in the following places: at Aynor, Horry County, a nest containing three young was found in June, 1952, by Mrs. G. E. Charles; nests were found near Summerville in 1949–50–51 by E. R. Cuthbert, Jr.; a nest with four eggs was found at Ashley Hall Plantation, Charleston County, May 27, 1956, by Ernest Cutts, and still another was located by Edwin Blitch, III, at Porcher's Bluff, Charleston County. The latter place is practically on the edge of the salt-water marsh and only a few miles from the open ocean (*Chat*, Vols. 15, 16, and 21).

INDIGO BUNTING: *Passerina cyanae*

A moulting male individual of this common summer resident was seen from December 31, 1954, through January 6, 1955, at the feeding tray of Mrs. Paul

SUPPLEMENT

L. Atwood of Edisto Beach. This constitutes the first winter record for the State (*Chat*, 19: 1955, 71).

An unusually large concentration of Indigo Buntings was seen at Magnolia Gardens, Charleston County, by T. A. Beckett, III, between March 15, and the end of April. Heretofore, the earliest recorded date had been April 17 (*Chat*, 31: 1967, 81). However, one was seen at an even earlier date of March 6, 1964, by Mrs. Jack Button at Summerville, Dorchester County (*Lesser Squawk*, April 1964).

PAINTED BUNTING: *Passerina ciris*

This species is a common summer resident, but from the number of reports, apparently a few Painted Buntings remain in South Carolina during the winter. Usually a coastal breeder, a male was seen feeding two young near Acton, Richland County, by Kay Sisson and Annie R. Faver, July 18, 1953 (*Chat*, 16: 1952, 102). During the winter of 1968–69 a female was seen almost daily in North Augusta, S. C. at the feeding tray of Gerald E. Knighton (*fide* T. M. Rial).

DICKCISSEL: *Spiza americana*

On the basis of the many records the Dickcissel can now be regarded as a rare though sporadic visitor in the central and upper part of the State, having been seen mostly during the summer but occasionally in winter. In the coastal area it is much rarer. On February 5, 1961, a male was seen at the feeder of Mr. L. L. Harr at Myrtle Beach, Horry County (*Chat*, 25: 1961, 35), and another one was observed by Corinne N. Pettit on Wadmalaw Island, Charleston County, February 7, 1963 (*Chat*, 27: 1963, 32). There are a few more records from the coast.

EVENING GROSBEAK: *Hesperiphona vespertina*

The first record of the Evening Grosbeak in South Carolina was one seen by Mr. and Mrs. Sterling Smith at Paris Mountain, Greenville County, November 21, 1951. In the winter of 1954–55 there was a large influx of the Evening Grosbeak into the Carolinas; many were reported as having been seen at Greenville, and in Eastover, Richland County (*Chat*, 19: 1955, 29). The following winter, 1955–56, several flocks were reported from the coastal area (*Chat*, 20: 1956, 61). The latest spring record was one seen by Ann Worsham Richardson at Kershaw, May 11, 1966 (*Chat*, 30: 1966, 91). The earliest fall date is October 6, 1965, when a female was seen at the feeder of Mrs. Francis Barrington, James Island, Charleston County (*Chat*, 29: 1963, 117).

The Evening Grosbeak can be regarded as a sporadic winter visitor in South Carolina.

SUPPLEMENT

House Finch: *Carpodacus mexicanus*

The House Finch, an imported California species, has gradually been extending its range since 1941 when it was first reported from the New York area. Presumably, the birds were released by bird dealers when the Audubon Society looked into the legality of their having the birds in their possession.

The first sight record of the House Finch within the State was made on December 20, 1966, when one was seen at the feeder of Mrs. W. C. Grimm of Greenville. The bird was subsequently seen by Jay Shuler and others who confirmed her identification. Later, Shuler took an excellent photograph of the bird, documenting the first record (*Chat*, 31: 1967, 45). Another was trapped and banded at Hartsville, Darlington County, by Mrs. A. E. Morrison. While being photographed for positive identification, it escaped, but in doing so one of its tail feathers was pulled out. The feather was sent to Roxie C. Laybourne of the U. S. National Museum, who identified it as coming from a specimen of *mexicanus* (*Chat*, 31: 1967, 47).

One was seen at the feeder of T. A. Beckett, III, along with a flock of Purple Finches on March 30, 1962, at Magnolia Gardens. All attempts to collect it were unsuccessful. It was a male in full plumage, and it was seen by Beckett through the window at a distance of three feet.

Pine Grosbeak: *Pinicola enucleator*

What appears to be the first sight record of the Pine Grosbeak in South Carolina was that of eight seen by Mrs. Robert Edwards in early December, 1951, at her residence near McClellanville, Charleston County (*fide,* Sprunt). On January 24, 1964, Kay Sisson was sent for to corroborate a sighting of a male Pine Grosbeak that was at the feeder of Mr. and Mrs. Edwin McMaster of Winnsboro, Fairfield County. It was first seen at the feeder along with a Rose-breasted Grosbeak, several Evening Grosbeaks, and some Purple Finches. It was kept under observation for several hours.

Two Pine Grosbeaks, either females or immature males, were seen by six members of a party taking the Christmas Bird Count, January 2, 1965. The birds were studied for 15–20 minutes at a distance of 125 feet, not only with binoculars, but with a 30X telescope, as they were feeding on the buds of maples and oaks. They were observed in the upper reaches of the Wando River, Charleston County (*Chat*, 29: 1965, 17 and 28). T. A. Beckett, III, who was a member of the party, reported that an adult pair of Pine Grosbeaks were seen at his feeding station, at a distance of 20 feet, at Magnolia Gardens, March 12, 1963.

On March 17, 1968, Mrs. Alan M. Bills saw a male Pine Grosbeak in full plumage at her feeding tray at her home in Summerville, Dorchester County. It was with five Chipping Sparrows, so comparison was made as to size and to eliminate the possibility of its being a Purple Finch. Later in the day it was seen by Dr. Bills, and the following day it was seen by both of them.

In view of these multiple sightings, the Pine Grosbeak is being included on the "State list."

COMMON REDPOLL: *Acanthis flammea*

This boreal bird is only seen in South Carolina after a severe cold, usually accompanied by snow. The Common Redpoll was placed in the addenda of *South Carolina Bird Life*, p. 561, based on the sight record of one seen by Walter Hoxie at Beaufort, February 3, 1901, after a snow. Fifty-nine years later one was killed by a truck on Bull's Island, and fortunately the bird was preserved by Hoyt Mills. It is in the collection of the Charleston Museum, No. 60.16. It was found in March 1960.

On March 1, 1960, three were seen by John B. Hatcher near Aiken. There were two males and a female, accompanied by some White-throated and House Sparrows that were at his feeder (*Chat*, 24: 1960, 93). In February 1960, a cat belonging to Samuel P. Rodgers, Jr., of Kingstree, Williamsburg County, brought in a bird that was badly mauled. On being pieced together it was found to be a female Redpoll. A male, apparently exhausted, was picked up, examined, and released at McClellanville, February 9, 1963. A few days later eight or ten were seen feeding at the same place, recorded by Edgar Jaycocks, Manager of the Cape Romain Refuge (*Chat*, 27: 1963, 34). Another was observed at the feeder at the home of Campbell and Dorothy Freeman in Williston, Barnwell County. The red cap and black chin spot were clearly discernible. The observation was made on January 26, 1965. The day was sunny, but the week before had been cloudy and cold.

The Common Redpoll is a resident of the arctic and subarctic regions, irregularly seen even in the northern states. On March 11, 1960, the Low Country was covered with a heavy snow, the first since 1943. This may have been the reason for their coming so far south.

RED CROSSBILL: *Loxia curvirosta*

Four or five Red Crossbills were seen at Paris Mountain State Park, Greenville County, December 9, 1952 (Shuler, 1966: 68). This bird is a rare and irregular winter visitor in South Carolina.

RED-EYED TOWHEE: *Pipilo erythrophthalmus*

A new record for the State was established when Dr. John O. Watkins collected a specimen of the northwestern race of this species *P. e. arcticus,* at

SUPPLEMENT

Spartanburg, February 19, 1967. It was made into a study skin by E. Burnham Chamberlain, who identified it subspecifically as *arcticus*. Wishing to make sure of his identification, he sent it to Roxie C. Laybourne, Research Associate at the U. S. National Museum, who confirmed his findings. The study skin is in the collection of the Charleston Museum, No. 67.53.

LARK BUNTING: *Calamospiza melanocorys*

In 1895, Arthur T. Wayne collected a female Lark Bunting in Christ Church Parish, Charleston County. It was not until fifty-nine years later that one was seen on Bull's Island by Dr. Ralph Edwards on December 27, 1954 (*Chat*, 20: 1956, 62). A male was seen on James Island, Charleston County, February 9, 1956, by Isaac S. Metcalf. Three days later it came to his feeder, located seven feet from the living room window, giving an excellent opportunity for positive identification. A week later a female was seen sitting on a telephone wire over Wappoo Creek, not a great distance from where the male was sighted. A Lark Bunting was seen at the window feeder of Mr. and Mrs. John B. Hatcher of Aiken on the afternoon of February 24, 1969.

SAVANNAH SPARROW: *Passerculus sandwichensis*

The Savannah Sparrow is a common winter resident throughout the State. It is widely distributed over most of the United States and has been divided into many races, which are almost impossible to differentiate in the field. It is probably the most common of our sparrows during the winter, with some of the races arriving as early as September 27, and departing as late as May 16.

Intensive studies have been made of the Savannah Sparrow in the "SRP area," Aiken, by Odum, Johnson, Hight and Norris. They found five races present, which they divided into light and dark ones. The light races are *P. s. savanna*, *P. s. mediogriseus*, *P. s. nevadensis*; the dark ones: *P. s. labradorius*, and *P. s. oblitus*. Some 1,758 birds were banded with the following results:

P. s. mediogriseus	31%
P. s. savanna	29%
P. s. labradorius	21%
P. s. oblitus	15%
P. s. nevadensis	4%

There was no evidence of different habitat selection or of social segregation among the different races (Norris, 1963: 67). Among these races the far western birds are *nevadensis* and to a lesser extent *oblitus*. The former breeds as far away as British Columbia and Alberta, and the latter on the west side of Hudson Bay. The other three nest as far north as eastern Canada, some in

SUPPLEMENT

northern Ungava (Norris & Hight, *Condor*, 45: 1957; and *Auk*, 73: 1956, 454).

In fields that have an abundance of crabgrass, the density of the population varied from 5.5 birds up to 30 per acre. In the Aiken study "area" the favorite food of the Sparrow Hawk was found to be the Savannah Sparrow. Such is probably true elsewhere as well.

The subspecies that are new for the State list are the following: *mediogriseus*, *oblitus*, and *nevadensis*.

So far in the coastal area only two races are known: *savanna* and *labradorius*.

WESTERN GRASSHOPPER SPARROW: *Ammodramus savannarum*

A specimen of this species, identified as the race *perpallidus* was taken by Robert A. Norris in the "SRP area," Aiken, on March 19, 1957. It was obviously a straggler that had gotten mixed with a flock of the eastern race *savannarum* (*Chat*, 21: 1957, 91). It was made into a study skin that is in the collection of the University of Georgia. This specimen constitutes the first record of this race for South Carolina.

LECONTE'S SPARROW: *Passerherbulus caudacutus*

Regarded by many as the most elusive of sparrows, this species is a rare and erratic winter resident. While banding in the "SRP area" in the winter of 1954–55, several were taken. Despite intensive netting, the two following winters none was captured (Norris, 1963: 69).

HENSLOW'S SPARROW: *Passerherbulus henslowii*

The western race of this species, *P. h. henslowii* is reported as being a rare summer visitor in the Piedmont (Shuler, 1966: 68). The eastern race, *P. h. susurrans*, is thought to be more of an inhabitant of the coastal region, and is seen only during the winter.

SEASIDE SPARROW: *Ammospiza maritima*

The northern race of the Seaside Sparrow, *A. m. maritima*, was placed in the Hypothetical List of *South Carolina Bird Life*, p. 558, upon the advice of Dr. Alexander Wetmore. He stated that it was better to treat it as a "hypothetical" until a banded bird was secured. Since the publication of *South Carolina Bird Life*, the Fifth Edition of the *AOU Check-list of North American Birds* (1957) was published, and it gives the (p. 559) winter range as "Virginia south to northeastern Florida." Therefore both *maritima* and *macgillivraii* should be looked for in the coastal marshes during the winter months.

LARK SPARROW: *Chonestes grammacus*

The only previous record of the Lark Sparrow in the State was based on a

SUPPLEMENT

sight record, one having been seen on Bull's Island in October, 1943 (*S. C. Bird Life*, p. 536). The first specimen collected was first observed at the feeder of Mr. and Mrs. Paul Atwood at Edisto Beach, September 4, 1956. It was secured for positive identification, and is now in the collection of the Charleston Museum (*Chat*, 21: 1957, 47). It was identified as the race *grammacus* by Dr. Herbert Friedmann, then Curator of Birds, U. S. National Museum.

Several additional sightings of the Lark Sparrow have been made, one before the specimen was collected and several afterwards. On August 6, 1955, one was seen on a rice field bank near McClellanville, Charleston County, by Edwards and others (*Chat*, 19, 1955: 88); one on Folly Island, Charleston County, by Mr. and Mrs. Robert H. Coleman, September 30, 1956 (*Chat*, 21: 1957, 27); Annie R. Faver saw one in the Columbia Area, August 22, 1963; again another was kept under observation at Mrs. Atwood's feeder on Edisto Beach, October 7, 1960. Mr. and Mrs. Fred May and E. B. Chamberlain studied it carefully through a 19.5X telescope at a distance of 66 feet. The bird was in excellent plumage with the very distinct facial markings (*Chat*, 24: 1960, 103). There are many more records of its having been seen in the coastal area. One was collected by T. A. Beckett, III, at Magnolia Gardens, Charleston County, October 20, 1967. The specimen is in his collection and one was seen by Kay Sisson and Annie R. Faver in lower Richland County on September 23, 1968 (*Chat*, 32: 1968, 106).

TREE SPARROW: *Spizella arborea*

A specimen of the Tree Sparrow has never been collected in South Carolina. In 1868 Elliott Coues reported it as not being uncommon in the Columbia Area *S. C. Bird Life*, p. 559). On the afternoon of January 22, 1955, Douglas Wade and some members of the Columbia Bird Club saw one at the Santee National Wildlife Refuge near Summerton, Clarendon County. It was with a mixed flock of White-throated Sparrows and juncos (*Chat*, 19: 1955, 48).

While visiting Bull's Island, Charlotte Hilton Green and others observed a Tree Sparrow at close range in January, 1952 (*Chat*, 16: 1952, 48). Another was seen near Columbia on the Christmas Bird Count held December 29, 1953 (*Chat*, 18: 1954, 7). Eight were seen near Clemson on the Christmas Bird Count held in 1960. "The observers had previous experience with the species in eastern and western Virginia" (*AFN*, 15: 1961, 163). Arthur M. Wilcox saw one at his feeder at his residence in lower Charleston, March 27, 1968. And another was seen at South Island, Georgetown County by T. A. Beckett, III, on January 5, 1969.

SUPPLEMENT

In view of these multiple sightings by competent observers the Tree Sparrow is included on the State List.

CHIPPING SPARROW: *Spizella passerina*

During the winter, the Chipping Sparrow is usually absent in the extreme northwestern part of the State, but it was seen by Gaston Gage, Sr., at Clemson on February 10 and 23, 1961 (*fide* Sprunt).

CLAY-COLORED SPARROW: *Spizella pallida*

There is only one record for the State for this far western bird: one taken by Dingle on October 27, 1929 (*S. C. Bird Life*, p. 543). On April 20 and 21, 1968, one was seen, photographed, and its song recorded by Marcus B. Simpson, Jr., on the campus of the University of South Carolina in front of McKissick Library. The identification was confirmed by Vaud Travus who had known the bird in Oklahoma, and it was also seen by Kay Sisson and M. L. Hopkins (*Chat*, 32: 1968, 78).

HARRIS' SPARROW: *Zonotrichia querula*

A Harris' Sparrow appeared at the feeding station of Mrs. Edgar N. Woodfin at Gramling, Spartanburg County, on January 5, 1962. Struck by its unusual size, Mrs. Carol Davis was called in for confirmation. The bird stayed until January 22 and was seen by a great number of people, including Jay Shuler and Dr. John O. Watkins. Later Shuler was successful in photographing the bird. Because of these circumstances, including the length of time it was under observation and the number of qualified observers who saw it, this species is here included as a new species for the State List (*Chat*, 32: 1968, 78 and *AFN*, 16: 1962, 321).

WHITE-CROWNED SPARROW: *Zonotrichia leucophrys*

The White-crowned Sparrow has been recorded so many times and from so many different places that it can no longer be regarded as unusual in South Carolina.

Dr. John O. Watkins at his residence near Spartanburg banded 97 White-crowned Sparrows during January–March, 1964. He gives the date of the earliest arrival as October 14, and the latest as May 12 (*Chat*, 28: 1964, 98). Eight were seen near Charleston by Robert H. Coleman, December 21, 1955 (*Chat*, 20: 1956, 41).

A young male that was collected by Wayne, October 23, 1925, near his home at Mt. Pleasant, is the only record for the State for the race *gambelii*. For the past several years, Dr. John O. Watkins has been trapping and banding White-crowned Sparrows at his home near Spartanburg. On December 14, 1964, he noticed a bird in one of his traps that seemed slightly different from the other White-crowns. Careful examination, in addition to wing measurements, proved it to be an adult female *gambelii*. Comparison was easy because there were several examples of *leucophrys* in nearby traps. The bird was retrapped January 15, 1965 (*Chat*, 29: 1965, 56).

WHITE-THROATED SPARROW: *Zonotrichia albicollis*

This abundant winter resident usually leaves the State by the middle of May for its northern nesting range. However, one stayed in the yard of Anne Worsham Richardson, St. Andrew's Parish, Charleston County, from June 28 to July 10, 1956. It was in excellent plumage. An individual in juvenal plumage stayed the entire summer of 1966 in the garden at Middleburg Plantation, Berkeley County, where it was seen daily by Edward von S. Dingle. Also in 1966, one remained the entire year in the yard and adjacent area of E. C. Clyde at Effingham, Florence County.

The earliest fall migration date is that of an individual seen on September 1, 1951, by Robert Edwards near McClellanville, Charleston County.

LINCOLN'S SPARROW: *Melospiza lincolnii*

The first specimen of the Lincoln's Sparrow taken in South Carolina was attributed to two keen-eyed women, Mrs. R. C. Tedards and Mrs. Ellison D. Smith. On November 7, 1961, while visiting the television tower at Columbia, they noticed an unusual looking sparrow that had been killed the night before. Having the forethought to save it, they gave it to the Charleston Museum where it was made into a study skin, No. 62.31. For positive identification, it was sent to Dr. John T. Aldrich in Washington, who pronounced it as being an immature Lincoln's Sparrow of the eastern race, *lincolnii* (*Chat*, 26: 1962, 45). However, the first sight record for the State is one seen on Bull's Island, December 27, 1949, by Alex Sprunt, IV. On November 21, 1954, J. Fred Denton and members of the Augusta Bird Club saw one at the North Augusta pumping station located in Aiken County and on April 24, 1958, one was seen repeatedly in the "SRP area," Aiken (Norris, 1963: 73).

SONG SPARROW: *Melospiza melodia*

A nest containing five young Song Sparrows was found at Clemson, May 8, 1953, by Douglas Wade. This observation apparently is only the second time that a nest had been found in the State; the first was by Thomas D. Burleigh in 1931 at Saluda Gap, Greenville County (*Chat*, 17: 1953, 75).

SUPPLEMENT

EASTERN SNOW BUNTING: *Plectrophenax nivalis*

This far northern species is but rarely seen in South Carolina. A Snow Bunting remained on Fort Sumter from December 17, 1954, through January 15, 1955. It was first noted by Rock Comstock with a flight of Water Pipits. It was also observed by Ellison A. Williams, who studied it through a high-powered telescope (*Chat*, 19: 1955, 49). Another was seen on John's Island, Charleston County, by Robert H. Coleman, January 14, 1958. It was extremely tame and was studied through 20X glasses for half an hour (*Lesser Squawk*, February 1958).

Mrs. Jack Button saw one in Summerville, Dorchester County, November 24, 1966. It stayed in the neighborhood for at least ten days and was also seen by E. R. Cuthbert, Jr.

HYPOTHETICAL LIST

There is not sufficient evidence through sightings or other reasons to place the following records on anything other than a list of species of hypothetical occurrence.

REDDISH EGRET: *Dichromanassa refescens*

One was seen at Murrell's Inlet, Georgetown County by Priscilla H. Roth, July 17, 1959, and another was studied at close range by Caroline Newhall and Ellen Rogers at Hilton Head Island, Beaufort County, August, 1959. While these constitute three sightings (*S. C. Bird Life*, p. 84), only two were seen by a single individual. Therefore these sight records are automatically relegated to the hypothetical list.

RED-TAILED HAWK: *Buteo jamaicensis kriderii*

This light colored subspecies, *B. j. kriderii*, of the Red-tailed Hawk is a bird of the Great Northern Plains. What is thought to have been a representative of this race was seen at close range by John Henry Dick at Dixie Plantation, Charleston County. Apparently the same hawk returned to the same location for fourteen consecutive winters. On the possibility that it may have been a light colored Red-tailed Hawk, since as it was not collected for positive identification,

SUPPLEMENT

and Dick's outstanding reputation as an ornithologist notwithstanding, it is being placed on the hypothetical list.

One was reported seen on the Christmas Bird Count, December 27, 1962, at Hilton Head Island (*AFN*, 17: 1963, 151).

ESKIMO CURLEW: *Numenius borealis*

This small curlew was thought to be extinct and these sight records would not be included, even in a hypothetical list, were it not for the fact that one was not only seen by many competent observers but photographed at close range at Galveston Island, Texas, March 22, 1959 (*Auk*, 79: 1962, 474). Another was shot in Bermuda in 1965 and is in the collection of the Academy of Natural Sciences, Philadelphia.

In early June, 1946, a group of young "Nature Trailers" from the Charleston Museum was taken on a field trip to the Cape Romain Refuge. In order to get to the large colonies of terns at Cape Island, the trip had to be made by boat. On returning by way of Raccoon Key, upon hearing the sound of the motor, four curlews flushed about 100 yards in front of the boat from where they had been feeding on the mudflat. They flew from right to left, and the day being clear, gave an excellent opportunity for observation through binoculars. Three were unmistakably Whimbrels (formerly called Hudsonian Curlews), the other, the last bird, was noticeably smaller, but quite similar in appearance. It appeared to be having difficulty keeping up with the leading birds despite its faster wingbeat. Burton, as well as Dr. Julian Harrison, who is now professor of Biology at the College of Charleston, was able to keep them under observation for an appreciable time.

The other sight record was an Eskimo Curlew seen by the late Ellison A. Williams and Francis M. Weston, who observed it sitting on a sandspit about 100 yards distant at Folly Island, Charleston County, July 15, 1956. They watched it for approximately 30 minutes through a 40X telescope and reached the definite conclusion that it was an Eskimo Curlew. These two men are known for their careful and accurate observation.

HUDSONIAN GODWIT: *Limosa haemastica*

Forty-nine Hudsonian Godwits were seen at Hunting Island, Beaufort County, September 1, 1961, by Mr. and Mrs. R. Connor Tedards. They were with a concentration of shore birds that included several Marbled Godwits and permitted comparisons with that species. "Some of the birds had breasts so red that they looked bloody and the upper tail coverts were snow white." Also some were in "fall plumage, grayish-brown on the back and white underneath with no barring." (*Chat*, 26: 1962, 41). The only other sight record for the Hudsonian

SUPPLEMENT

Godwit in South Carolina was by Edward von S. Dingle in May, 1941 (*S. C. Bird Life*, p. 251).

During September and October, 1961, about 20 birds were observed in scattered locations in Delaware and Maryland. Hudsonian Godwits have also been seen at frequent intervals on the North Carolina coast.

LONG-TAILED JAEGER: *Stercorarius longicaudus*

One was seen off Pawley's Island, Georgetown County, July 13, 1958, by Kay Sisson. It came within 150 feet from the shore and was studied through 7X glasses where the black cap, hooked bill, as well as the white on the throat and neck, were clearly seen. Most importantly, the wedge-shaped tail with the long (8–10 inch) streamers could be clearly seen (*Chat*, 22: 1958, 83). The only other sight records of this pelagic bird were made by Wayne: one in 1896, the other in 1908 (*S. C. Bird Life*, p. 259).

BLACK GUILLEMOT: *Cepphus grylle*

An individual of this species was seen and actually touched by Alexander Mikell, September 21, 1958, as it was sitting on the jetty at Morris Island, situated at the mouth of Charleston Harbor. Not realizing its importance, no attempt was made to capture it, for obviously it was a sick bird. Mikell gave a complete description of it to Sprunt, who identified it as a Black Guillemot (*News & Courier*, September 24, 1958).

BURROWING OWL: *Speotyto cunicularia*

A Burrowing Owl was seen by Ivan R. Tomkins in Jasper County, November 3, 1959 (*Oriole*, 26: 1961, 2). The late Ivan R. Tomkins was a most careful observer, having added many new species of birds to the "Georgia List" (Burleigh, *Georgia Birds*, p. 14). He spent many years working at the mouth of the Savannah River for the U. S. Department of Engineers, and was afield almost daily.

He also saw another Burrowing Owl on December 7, 1943, in Beaufort County (*S. C. Bird Life*, p. 306). As neither bird was collected, they could be either the southern race *floridana* or the western race *hypugaea*. Consequently neither race is entitled to a place on the official State List.

SAY'S PHOEBE: *Sayornis saya*

The Say's Phoebe has never been seen in South Carolina, in fact it is only of accidental occurrence on the Atlantic seaboard. On January 18, 1969, one was seen and studied carefully by Annie R. Faver, and two of her friends near Eastover, Richland County. The three were on a "birding" expedition when they noticed a phoebe sitting on a fence post. "Then realizing that there was something decidedly different about this bird, we got out of the car and followed the bird, . . . thus getting to see it from every angle in the sunlight. The rusty underparts were clearly seen from the front, with the dark head and tail with lighter back visible from the rear view. Having with us the book, *Birds of North America* by Robbins, Bruun and Zim, we identified the bird as a Say's Phoebe."

PHILADELPHIA VIREO: *Vireo philadelphicus*

A few sight records have been reported from the Piedmont (Shuler, 1966: 53). Until a specimen is collected, the species will have to remain on the hypothetical list.

WARBLING VIREO: *Vireo gilvus*

A Warbling Vireo was observed July 21, 1956, by J. B. Shuler, Jr., near Jocassee, Oconee County. The bird was approached within six feet on several occasions and was watched for a period of at least five minutes (*Chat*, 20: 1956, 82). Two were seen September 1, 1958, by John B. Hatcher in his backyard in the "SRP area," Aiken. The two remained for a week and were studied at a distance of 25 feet with 8X glasses. While there, they associated with Black and White Warblers, Parula Warblers, and Tufted Titmice (*Chat*, 23: 1959, 38).

On the Spring Bird Count, held April 28, 1962, near Anderson, two were reported seen (*Chat*, 26: 1962, 59). This is a border-line case, but it is felt that, until a bird is collected, it should remain on the hypothetical list.

INDEX

(In cases where more than one reference to the common name of a species or race has been indexed, the principal reference is italicized.)

INDEX

Bittern, American, 95.
　Eastern Least, 96.
Blackbird, Brewer's, 500.
　Crow, 503, 504.
　Newfoundland Rusty, 500.
　Red-winged, 493.
　Rusty, 34, *499*.
　Yellow-headed, 492.
Black-breast, 217.
Blackhead, 131, 134, 135.
　Big, 134.
Blake, Emmet R., ix.
Blake's Reserve, 40.
Bluebill, 134, 135.
Bluebird, Eastern, 33, *411*.
Bluepeter, 203, 204, 206.
Bobolink, 34, 104, *489*.
Bobwhite, Eastern, 17, *186*, 187.
　Texas, 187, *557*.
Bombycilla cedrorum, 421.
Bonasa umbellus monticola, 185.
Booby, Atlantic Blue-faced, 14, *70*.
　White-bellied, 70.
Bo'sun-bird, 65.
Botaurus lentiginosus, 95.
Brant, American, 108.
Branta bernicla hrota, 108.
　canadensis canadensis, 107.
Braund, F. W., 23.
Brewer, Orlando S., ix.
Brewster, William, 8.
Broadbill, 134, 135.
Broley, Charles, 175.
Brown, Nathan Clifford, 389.
Bubo virginianus virginianus, 303.
Bucephala albeola, 137.
　clangula americana, 136.
Buffle-head, 137.
Bugbee Hunting Club, 121.
Bull-bat, 319.
Bullfinch, 522.
Bullhead, 131.
Bull, John, 17, 536.
Bull's Island, 2.
Bunting, Black-throated, 516.
　Eastern Snow, 14, *553*.
　Indigo, 35, *513*.
　Lark, 525.
　Painted, 35, *514*.
Burleigh, Thomas Dearborn, ix, 23, 162, 539.
Burnett, W. I., 6.
Burton, Edward Milby, *13*, 16, 140, 240, 258, 373.
Bush-tit, California, 377.
　Coast, 378.
Butcher Bird, 422.
Buteo harlani 161.
　jamaicensis borealis, 29, 159.
　jamaicensis kriderii, 161.
　jamaicensis umbrinus, 161.
　lagopus s. johannis, 170.

lineatus alleni, 162, 167.
lineatus lineatus, 162.
platypterus platyperus, 168.
swainsoni, 169.
Butorides virescens virescens, 28, 88.
Butterball, 137, 144.
Buzzard, 149, 150.
　Charleston, 150.
　Turkey, 149.

Calamospiza melanocorys, 525.
Calcarius lapponicus lapponicus, 552.
　pictus, 553.
Calico-back, 219.
Calidris canutus rufus, 239.
Campephilus principalis, 32, 340.
Canary, Wild, 447, 519.
Cannon, Gabriel, 15, 425.
Canvas-back, 119, 124, 131, *133*, 148.
Capella gallinago delicata, 222.
Caprimulgus carolinensis, 31, 315.
　vociferus vociferus, 317, 560.
Caracara, Audubon's, 18, *178*.
Cardinal, Eastern, 34, *509*.
Carnegie, Frank, 112.
Carpodacus purpureus purpureus, 35, 517.
Carroll, Mrs. J. J., x.
Casmerodius albus egretta, 81.
Cassidix mexicanus major, 501.
　mexicanus torreyii, 501.
　mexicanus westoni, 501.
Catbird, 399.
Catesby, Mark, 3, 43, 288, 291, 292, 333, 359, 508, 518.
Cathartes aura septentrionalis, 149.
Catoptrophorus semipalmatus inornatus, 232.
　semipalmatus semipalmatus, 231.
Cedar Bird, 421.
Centurus carolinus carolinus, 31, 332.
Certhia familiaris americana, 385.
　familiaris nigrescens, 386.
Chaetura pelagica, 31, 321.
Chamberlain, Edward Burnham, x, *14*, 49, 153, 219, 256, 294, 350.
Cham-chack, 332.
Chapman, Clarence E., 16, 84, 151, 204.
Chapman, Dr. Frank Michler, 16, 17, 45.
Charadrius hiaticula semipalmatus, 212.
　melodus circumcinctus, 212.
　melodus melodus, 211.
　vociferus vociferus, 29, 215.
　wilsonia wilsonia, 213.
Charles, Mrs. G. E., 15.
Charleston Museum,, x.
Chat, Yellow-breasted, 34, *482*.
Chay-chay, 413.
Chen caerulescens, 111.
　hyperborea atlantica, 111.
　hyperborea hyperborea, 110.
Cherry Bird, 422.
Cheweeka, 215.
Chewink, 522.

— 644 —

INDEX

INDEX

INDEX

INDEX

INDEX

INDEX